COPYRIGHT LAW
Fifth Edition

2002 CUMULATIVE SUPPLEMENT

Volume II

Part Two
International Materials

Part Three
Intellectual Property and the Networked Information Environment

Part Four
New Text and Case Law

Part Five
Cumulative Bibliography

By

Craig Joyce
Marshall Leaffer
Peter Jaszi

LexisNexis™
Matthew Bender®

Editorial Offices
744 Broad Street, Newark, NJ 07102 (973) 820-2000
201 Mission Street, San Francisco, CA 94105-1831 (415) 908-3200
701 East Water Street, Charlottesville, VA 22902-7587 (804) 972-7600
www.lexis.com

VOLUME II
TABLE OF CONTENTS

PART TWO:
INTERNATIONAL MATERIALS

...

PART THREE:

INTELLECTUAL PROPERTY AND THE NETWORKED INFORMATION ENVIRONMENT

PART FOUR:

NEW TEXT AND CASE LAW

PART FIVE
CUMULATIVE BIBLIOGRAPHY

PART TWO:

INTERNATIONAL MATERIALS

BERNE CONVENTION

The Berne Convention for the Protection of Literary and Artistic Works

Paris Text — July 24, 1971

TABLE OF CONTENTS[1]

---

[1] Prepared by World Intellectual Property Organization. Not part of original text.

APPENDIX
[Special Provisions Regarding Developing Countries]

———

Signed on September 9, 1886, completed at Paris on May 4, 1896, revised at Berlin on November 13, 1908, completed at Berne on March 20, 1914, and revised at Rome on June 2, 1928, at Brussels on June 26, 1948, at Stockholm on July 14, 1967, and at Paris on July 24, 1971.

The countries of the Union, being equally animated by the desire to protect, in as effective and uniform a manner as possible, the rights of authors in their literary and artistic works,

Recognizing the importance of the work of the Revision Conference held at Stockholm in 1967,

Have resolved to revise the Act adopted by the Stockholm Conference, while maintaining without change Articles 1 to 20 and 22 to 26 of that Act.

Consequently, the undersigned Plenipotentiaries, having presented their full power, recognized as in good and due form, have agreed as follows:

Article 1

The countries to which this Convention applies constitute a Union for the protection of the rights of authors in their literary and artistic works.

Article 2

(1) The expression "literary and artistic works" shall include every production in the literary, scientific and artistic domain, whatever may be the mode or form of its expression, such as books, pamphlets and other writings; lectures, addresses, sermons and other works of the same nature; dramatic or dramatico-musical works; choreographic works and entertainments in dumb show; musical compositions with or without words; cinematographic works to which are assimilated works expressed by a process analogous to cinematography; works of drawing, painting, architecture, sculpture, engraving and lithography; photographic works to which are assimilated works expressed by a process analogous to photography; works of applied art; illustrations, maps, plans, sketches and three-dimensional works relative to geography, topography, architecture or science.

(2) It shall, however, be a matter for legislation in the countries of the Union to prescribe that works in general or any specified categories of works shall not be protected unless they have been fixed in some material form.

(3) Translations, adaptations, arrangements of music and other alterations of a literary or artistic work shall be protected as original works without prejudice to the copyright in the original work.

(4) It shall be a matter for legislation in the countries of the Union to determine the protection to be granted to official texts of a legislative, administrative and legal nature, and to official translations of such texts.

(5) Collections of literary or artistic works such as encyclopedias and anthologies which, by reason of the selection and arrangement of their contents, constitute intellectual creations shall be protected as such, without prejudice to the copyright in each of the works forming part of such collections.

(6) The works mentioned in this Article shall enjoy protection in all countries of the Union. This protection shall operate for the benefit of the author and his successors in title.

(7) Subject to the provisions of Article 7(4) of this Convention, it shall be a matter for legislation in the countries of the Union to determine the extent of the application of their laws to works of applied art and industrial designs and models, as well as the conditions under which such works, designs and models shall be protected. Works protected in the country of origin solely as designs and models shall be entitled in another country of the Union only to such special protection as is granted in that country to designs and models; however, if no such special protection is granted in that country, such works shall be protected as artistic works.

(8) The protection of this Convention shall not apply to news of the day or to miscellaneous facts having the character of mere items of press information.

Article 2*bis*

(1) It shall be a matter for legislation in the countries of the Union to exclude, wholly or in part, from the protection provided by the preceding Article political speeches and speeches delivered in the course of legal proceedings.

(2) It shall also be a matter for legislation in the countries of the Union to determine the conditions under which lectures, addresses and other works of the same nature which are delivered in public may be reproduced by the press, broadcast, communicated to the public by wire and made the subject of public communication as envisaged in Article 11*bis* (1) of this Convention, when such use is justified by the informatory purpose.

(3) Nevertheless, the author shall enjoy the exclusive right of making a collection of his works mentioned in the preceding paragraphs.

Article 3

(1) The protection of this Convention shall apply to:

(a) authors who are nationals of one of the countries of the Union, for their works, whether published or not;

(b) authors who are not nationals of one of the countries of the Union, for their works first published in one of those countries, or simultaneously in a country outside the Union and in a country of the Union.

(2) Authors who are not nationals of one of the countries of the Union but who have their habitual residence in one of them shall, for the purpose of this Convention, be assimilated to nationals of that country.

(3) The expression "published works" means works published with the consent of their authors, whatever may be the means of manufacture of the copies, provided that the availability of such copies has been such as to satisfy the reasonable requirements of the public, having regard to the nature of the work. The performance of a dramatic, dramatico-musical, cinematographic or musical work, the public recitation of a literary work, the communication by wire or the broadcasting of literary or artistic works, the exhibition of a work of art and the construction of a work of architecture shall not constitute publication.

(4) A work shall be considered as having been published simultaneously in several countries if it has been published in two or more countries within thirty days of its first publication.

Article 4

The protection of this Convention shall apply, even if the conditions of Article 3 are not fulfilled, to:

(a) authors of cinematographic works the maker of which has his headquarters or habitual residence in one of the countries of the Union;

(b)   authors of works of architecture erected in a country of the Union or of other artistic works incorporated in a building or other structure located in a country of the Union.

Article 5

(1) Authors shall enjoy, in respect of works for which they are protected under this Convention, in countries of the Union other than the country of origin, the rights which their respective laws do now or may hereafter grant to their nationals, as well as the rights specially granted by this Convention.

(2) The enjoyment and the exercise of these rights shall not be subject to any formality; such enjoyment and such exercise shall be independent of the existence of protection in the country of origin of the work. Consequently, apart from the provisions of the Convention, the extent of protection, as well as the means of redress afforded to the author to protect his rights, shall be governed exclusively by the laws of the country where protection is claimed.

(3) Protection in the country of origin is governed by domestic law. However, when the author is not a national of the country of origin of the work for which he is protected under this Convention, he shall enjoy in that country the same rights as national authors.

(4) The country of origin shall be considered to be:

(a)   in the case of works first published in a country of the Union, that country; in the case of works published simultaneously in several countries of the Union which grant different terms of protection, the country whose legislation grants the shortest term of protection;

(b)   in the case of works published simultaneously in a country outside the Union and in a country of the Union, the latter country;

(c)   in the case of unpublished works or of works first published in a country outside the Union, without simultaneous publication in a country of the Union, the country of the Union of which the author is a national, provided that:

     (i)   when these are cinematographic works the maker of which has his headquarters or his habitual residence in a country of the Union, the country of origin shall be that country, and

     (ii)   when these are works of architecture erected in a country of the Union or other artistic works incorporated in a building or other structure located in a country of the Union, the country of origin shall be that country.

Article 6

(1) Where any country outside the Union Fails to protect in an adequate manner the works of authors who are nationals of one of the countries of the Union, the latter country may restrict the protection given to the works

of authors who are, at the date of the first publication thereof, nationals of the other country and are not habitually resident in one of the countries of the Union. If the country of first publication avails itself of this right, the other countries of the Union shall not be required to grant to works thus subjected to special treatment a wider protection than that granted to them in the country of first publication.

(2) No restrictions introduced by virtue of the preceding paragraph shall affect the rights which an author may have acquired in respect of a work published in a country of the Union before such restrictions were put into force.

(3) The countries of the Union which restrict the grant of copyright in accordance with this Article shall give notice thereof to the Director General of the World Intellectual Property Organization (hereinafter designated as "the Director General") by a written declaration specifying the countries in regard to which protection is restricted, and the restrictions to which rights of authors who are nationals of those countries are subjected. The Director General shall immediately communicate this declaration to all the countries of the Union.

Article 6bis

(1) Independently of the author's economic rights, and even after the transfer of the said rights, the author shall have the right to claim authorship of the work and to object to any distortion, mutilation, or other modification of, or other derogatory action in relation to, the said work, which would be prejudicial to his honor or reputation.

(2) The rights granted to the author in accordance with the preceding paragraph shall, after his death, be maintained, at least until the expiry of the economic rights, and shall be exercisable by the persons or institutions authorized by the legislation of the country where protection is claimed. However, those countries whose legislation, at the moment of their ratification of or accession to this Act, does not provide for the protection after the death of the author of all the rights set out in the preceding paragraph may provide that some of these rights may, after his death, cease to be maintained.

(3) The means of redress for safeguarding the rights granted by this Article shall be governed by the legislation of the country where protection is claimed.

Article 7

(1) The term of protection granted by this Convention shall be the life of the author and fifty years after his death.

(2) However, in the case of cinematographic works, the countries of the Union may provide that the term of protection shall expire fifty years after the work has been made available to the public with the consent of the author, or, failing such an event within fifty years from the making of such a work, fifty years after the making.

(3) In the case of anonymous or pseudonymous works, the term of protection granted by this Convention shall expire fifty years after the work has been lawfully made available to the public. However, when the pseudonym adopted by the author leaves no doubt as to his identity, the term of protection shall be that provided in paragraph (1). If the author of an anonymous or pseudonymous work discloses his identity during the above-mentioned period, the term of protection applicable shall be that provided in paragraph (1). The countries of the Union shall not be required to protect anonymous or pseudonymous works in respect of which it is reasonable to presume that their author has been dead for fifty years.

(4) It shall be a matter for legislation in the countries of the Union to determine the term of protection of photographic works and that of works of applied art in so far as they are protected as artistic works; however, this term shall last at least until the end of a period of twenty-five years from the making of such a work.

(5) The term of protection subsequent to the death of the author and the terms provided by paragraphs (2), (3) and (4) shall run from the date of death or of the event referred to in those paragraphs, but such terms shall always be deemed to begin on the first of January of the year following the death or such event.

(6) The countries of the Union may grant a term of protection in excess of those provided by the preceding paragraphs.

(7) Those countries of the Union bound by the Rome Act of this Convention which grant, in their national legislation in force at the time of signature of the present Act, shorter terms of protection than those provided for in the preceding paragraphs shall have the right to maintain such terms when ratifying or acceding to the present Act.

(8) In any case, the term shall be governed by the legislation of the country where protection is claimed; however, unless the legislation of that country otherwise provides, the term shall not exceed the term fixed in the country of origin of the work.

Article 7bis

The provisions of the preceding Article shall also apply in the case of a work of joint authorship, provided that the terms measured from the death of the author shall be calculated from the death of the last surviving author.

Article 8

Authors of literary and artistic works protected by this Convention shall enjoy the exclusive right of making and of authorizing the translation of their works throughout the term of protection of their rights in the original works.

Article 9

(1) Authors of literary and artistic works protected by this Convention shall have the exclusive right of authorizing the reproduction of these works, in any manner or form.

(2) It shall be a matter for legislation in the countries of the Union to permit the reproduction of such works in certain special cases, provided that such reproduction does not conflict with a normal exploitation of the work and does not unreasonably prejudice the legitimate interests of the author.

(3) Any sound or visual recording shall be considered as a reproduction for the purposes of this Convention.

Article 10

(1) It shall be permissible to make quotations from a work which has already been lawfully made available to the public, provided that their making is compatible with fair practice, and their extent does not exceed that justified by the purpose, including quotations from newspaper articles and periodicals in the form of press summaries.

(2) It shall be a matter for legislation in the countries of the Union, and for special agreements existing or to be concluded between them, to permit the utilization, to the extent justified by the purpose, of literary or artistic works by way of illustration in publications, broadcasts or sound or visual recordings for teaching, provided such utilization is compatible with fair practice.

(3) Where use is made of works in accordance with the preceding paragraphs of this Article, mention shall be made of the source, and of the name of the author if it appears thereon.

Article 10bis

(1) It shall be a matter for legislation in the countries of the Union to permit the reproduction by the press, the broadcasting or the communication to the public by wire of articles published in newspapers or periodicals on current economic, political or religious topics, and of broadcast works of the same character, in cases in which the reproduction, broadcasting or such communication thereof is not expressly reserved. Nevertheless, the source must always be clearly indicated; the legal consequences of a breach of this obligation shall be determined by the legislation of the country where protection is claimed.

(2) It shall also be a matter for legislation in the countries of the Union to determine the conditions under which, for the purpose of reporting current events by means of photography, cinematography, broadcasting or communication to the public by wire, literary or artistic works seen or heard in the course of the event may, to the extent justified by the informatory purpose, be reproduced and made available to the public.

Article 11

(1) Authors of dramatic, dramatico-musical and musical works shall enjoy the exclusive right of authorizing:

    (i)   the public performance of their works, including such public performance by any means or process;

(ii) any communication to the public of the performance of their works.

(2) Authors of dramatic or dramatico-musical works shall enjoy, during the full term of their rights in the original works, the same rights with respect to translations thereof.

Article 11*bis*

(1) Authors of literary and artistic works shall enjoy the exclusive right of authorizing:

(i) the broadcasting of their works or the communication thereof to the public by any other means of wireless diffusion of signs, sounds or images;

(ii) any communication to the public by wire or by rebroadcasting of the broadcast of the work, when this communication is made by an organization other than the original one;

(iii) the public communication by loudspeaker or any other analogous instrument transmitting, by signs, sounds or images, the broadcast of the work.

(2) It shall be a matter for legislation in the countries of the Union to determine the conditions under which the rights mentioned in the preceding paragraph may be exercised, but these conditions shall apply only in the countries where they have been prescribed. They shall not in any circumstances be prejudicial to the moral rights of the author, nor to his right to obtain equitable remuneration which, in the absence of agreement, shall be fixed by competent authority.

(3) In the absence of any contrary stipulation, permission granted in accordance with paragraph (1) of this Article shall not imply permission to record, by means of instruments recording sounds or images, the work broadcast. It shall, however, be a matter for legislation in the countries of the Union to determine the regulations for ephemeral recordings made by a broadcasting organization by means of its own facilities and used for its own broadcasts. The preservation of these recordings in official archives may, on the ground, of their exceptional documentary character, be authorized by such legislation.

Article 11*ter*

(1) Authors of literary works shall enjoy the exclusive right of authorizing:

(i) the public recitation of their works, including such public recitation by any means or process;

(ii) any communication to the public of the recitation of their works.

(2) Authors of literary works shall enjoy, during the full term of their rights in the original works, the same rights with respect to translations thereof.

Article 12

Authors of literary or artistic works shall enjoy the exclusive right of authorizing adaptations, arrangements and other alterations of their works.

Article 13

(1) Each country of the Union may impose for itself reservations and conditions on the exclusive right granted to the author of a musical work and to the author of any words, the recording of which together with the musical work has already been authorized by the latter, to authorize the sound recording of that musical work, together with such words, if any; but all such reservations and conditions shall apply only in the countries which have imposed them and shall not, in any circumstances, be prejudicial to the rights of these authors to obtain equitable remuneration which, in the absence of agreement, shall be fixed by competent authority.

(2) Recordings of musical works made in a country of the Union in accordance with Article 13(3) of the Conventions signed at Rome on June 2, 1928, and at Brussels on June 26, 1948, may be reproduced in that country without the permission of the author of the musical work until a date two years after that country becomes bound by this Act.

(3) Recordings made in accordance with paragraphs (1) and (2) of this Article and imported without permission from the parties concerned into a country where they are treated as infringing recordings shall be liable to seizure.

Article 14

(1) Authors of literary or artistic works shall have the exclusive right of authorizing:

(i)   the cinematographic adaptation and reproduction of these works, and the distribution of the works thus adapted or reproduced;

(ii) the public performance and communication to the public by wire of the works thus adapted or reproduced.

(2) The adaptation into any other artistic form of a cinematographic production derived from literary or artistic works shall, without prejudice to the authorization of the author of the cinematographic production, remain subject to the authorization of the authors of the original works.

(3) The provisions of Article 13(1) shall not apply.

Article 14bis

(1) Without prejudice to the copyright in any work which may have been adapted or reproduced, a cinematographic work shall be protected as an original work. The owner of copyright in a cinematographic work shall enjoy the same rights as the author of an original work, including the rights referred to in the preceding Article.

(2)*(a)* Ownership of copyright in a cinematographic work shall be a matter for legislation in the country where protection is claimed.

(b) However, in the countries of the Union which, by legislation, include among the owners of copyright in a cinematographic work authors who have brought contributions to the making of the work, such authors, if they have undertaken to bring such contributions, may not, in the absence of any contrary or special stipulation, object to the reproduction, distribution, public performance, communication to the public by wire, broadcasting or any other communication to the public, or to the subtitling or dubbing of texts, of the work.

(c) The question whether or not the form of the undertaking referred to above should, for the application of the preceding subparagraph *(b)*, be in a written agreement or a written act of the same effect shall be a matter for the legislation of the country where the maker of the cinematographic work has his headquarters or habitual residence. However, it shall be a matter for the legislation of the country of the Union where protection is claimed to provide that the said undertaking shall be in a written agreement or a written act of the same effect. The countries whose legislation so provides shall notify the Director General by means of a written declaration, which will be immediately communicated by him to all the other countries of the Union.

(d) By "contrary or special stipulation" is meant any restrictive condition which is relevant to the aforesaid undertaking.

(3) Unless the national legislation provides to the contrary, the provisions of paragraph (2)*(b)* above shall not be applicable to authors of scenarios, dialogues and musical works created for the making of the cinematographic work, or to the principal director thereof. However, those countries of the Union whose legislation does not contain rules providing for the application of the said paragraph (2)*(b)* to such director shall notify the Director General by means of a written declaration, which will be immediately communicated by him to all the other countries of the Union.

Article 14*ter*

(1) The author, or after his death the persons or institutions authorized by national legislation, shall, with respect to original works of art and original manuscripts of writers and composers, enjoy the inalienable right to an interest in any sale of the work subsequent to the first transfer by the author of the work.

(2) The protection provided by the preceding paragraph may be claimed in a country of the Union only if legislation in the country to which the author belongs so permits, and to the extent permitted by the country where this protection is claimed.

(3) The procedure for collection and the amounts shall be matters for determination by national legislation.

Article 15

(1) In order that the author of a literary or artistic work protected by this Convention shall, in the absence of proof to the contrary, be regarded as such, and consequently be entitled to institute infringement proceedings in the countries of the Union, it shall be sufficient for his name to appear on the work in the usual manner. This paragraph shall be applicable even if this name is a pseudonym, where the pseudonym adopted by the author leaves no doubt as to his identity.

(2) The person or body corporate whose name appears on a cinematographic work in the usual manner shall, in the absence of proof to the contrary, be presumed to be the maker of the said work.

(3) In the case of anonymous and pseudonymous works, other than those referred to in paragraph (1) above, the publisher whose name appears on the work shall, in the absence of proof to the contrary, be deemed to represent the author, and in this capacity he shall be entitled to protect and enforce the author's rights. The provisions of this paragraph shall cease to apply when the author reveals his identity and establishes his claim to authorship of the work.

(4)*(a)* In the case of unpublished works where the identity of the author is unknown, but where there is every ground to presume that he is a national of a country of the Union, it shall be a matter for legislation in that country to designate the competent authority which shall represent the author and shall be entitled to protect and enforce his rights in the countries of the Union.

(b) Countries of the Union which make such designation under the terms of this provision shall notify the Director General by means of a written declaration giving full information concerning the authority thus designated. The Director General shall at once communicate this declaration to all other countries of the Union.

Article 16

(1) Infringing copies of a work shall be liable to seizure in any country of the Union where the work enjoys legal protection.

(2) The provisions of the preceding paragraph shall also apply to reproductions coming from a country where the work is not protected, or has ceased to be protected.

(3) The seizure shall take place in accordance with the legislation of each country.

Article 17

The provisions of this Convention cannot in any way affect the right of the Government of each country of the Union to permit, to control, or to prohibit, by legislation or regulation, the circulation, presentation, or exhibition of any work or production in regard to which the competent authority may find it necessary to exercise that right.

Article 18

(1) This Convention shall apply to all works which, at the moment of its coming into force, have not yet fallen into the public domain in the country of origin through the expiry of the term of protection.

(2) If, however, through the expiry of the term of protection which was previously granted, a work has fallen into the public domain of the country where protection is claimed, that work shall not be protected anew.

(3) The application of this principle shall be subject to any provisions contained in special conventions to that effect existing or to be concluded between countries of the Union. In the absence of such provisions, the respective countries shall determine, each in so far as it is concerned, the conditions of application of this principle.

(4) The preceding provisions shall also apply in the case of new accessions to the Union and to cases in which protection is extended by the application of Article 7 or by the abandonment of reservations.

Article 19

The provisions of this Convention shall not preclude the making of a claim to the benefit of any greater protection which may be granted by legislation in a country of the Union.

Article 20

The Governments of the countries of the Union reserve the right to enter into special agreements among themselves, in so far as such agreements grant to authors more extensive rights than those granted by the Convention, or contain other provisions not contrary to this Convention. The provisions of existing agreements which satisfy these conditions shall remain applicable.

Article 21

(1) Special provisions regarding developing countries are included in the Appendix.

(2) Subject to the provisions of Article 28(1)(b), the Appendix forms an integral part of this Act.

Article 22

(1)(a) The Union shall have an Assembly consisting of those countries of the Union which are bound by Articles 22 to 26.

(b) The Government of each country shall be represented by one delegate, who may be assisted by alternate delegates, advisors, and experts.

(c) The expenses of each delegation shall be borne by the Government which has appointed it.

(2)(a) The Assembly shall:

(i) deal with all matters concerning the maintenance and development of the Union and the implementation of this Convention;

(ii) give directions concerning the preparation for conferences of revision to the International Bureau of Intellectual Property (hereinafter designated as "the International Bureau"8) referred to in the Convention Establishing the World Intellectual Property Organization (hereinafter designated as "the Organization"), due account being taken of any comments made by those countries of the Union which are not bound by Articles 22 to 26;

(iii) review and approve the reports and activities of the Director General of the Organization concerning the Union, and give him all necessary instructions concerning matters within the competence of the Union;

(iv) elect the members of the Executive Committee of the Assembly;

(v) review and approve the reports and activities of its Executive Committee, and give instructions to such Committee;

(vi) determine the program and adopt the triennial budget[2] of the Union, and approve its final accounts;

(vii) adopt the financial regulations of the Union;

(viii) establish such committees of experts and working groups as may be necessary for the work of the Union;

(ix) determine which countries not members of the Union and which intergovernmental and international nongovernmental organizations shall be admitted to its meetings as observers;

(xx) adopt amendments to Articles 22 to 26;

(xxi) take any other appropriate action designed to further the objectives of the Union;

(xxii) exercise such other functions as are appropriate under this Convention;

(xxiii) subject to its acceptance, exercise such rights as are given to it in the Convention establishing the Organization.

(b) With respect to matters which are of interest also to other Unions administered by the Organization, the Assembly shall make its decisions after having heard the advice of the Coordination Committee of the Organization.

(3)(a) Each country member of the Assembly shall have one vote.

(b) One-half of the countries members of the Assembly shall constitute a quorum.

(c) Notwithstanding the provisions of subparagraph (b), if, in any session, the number of countries represented is less than one-half but equal to or more than one-third of the countries members of the Assembly, the Assembly may make decisions but, with the exception of decisions concerning its own procedure, all such decisions shall take effect only if the following

---

2 By amendment adopted in 1979 (entered into force November 19, 1984), Art. 22(2)(a)(vi), "triennial" is replaced by "biennial".

conditions are fulfilled. The International Bureau shall communicate the said decisions to the countries members of the Assembly which were not represented and shall invite them to express in writing their vote or abstention within a period of three months from the date of the communication. If, at the expiration of this period, the number of countries having thus expressed their vote or abstention attains the number of countries which was lacking for attaining the quorum in the session itself, such decisions shall take effect provided that at the same time the required majority still obtains.

(d) Subject to the provisions of Article 26(2), the decisions of the Assembly shall require two-thirds of the votes cast.

(e) Abstentions shall not be considered as votes.

(f) A delegate may represent, and vote in the name of, one country only.

(g) Countries of the Union not members of the Assembly shall be admitted to its meetings as observers.

(4)(a) The Assembly shall meet once in every third calendar year[3] in ordinary session upon convocation by the Director General and, in the absence of exceptional circumstances, during the same period and at the same place as the General Assembly of the Organization.

(b) The Assembly shall meet in extraordinary session upon convocation by the Director General, at the request of the Executive Committee or at the request of one-fourth of the countries members of the Assembly.

(5) The Assembly shall adopt its own rules of procedure.

Article 23

(1) The Assembly shall have an Executive Committee.

(2)(a) The Executive Committee shall consist of countries elected by the Assembly from among countries members of the Assembly. Furthermore, the country on whose territory the Organization has its headquarters shall, subject to the provisions of Article 25(7)(b), have an *ex officio* seat on the Committee.

(b) The Government of each country member of the Executive Committee shall be represented by one delegate, who may be assisted by alternate delegates, advisors, and experts.

(c) The expenses of each delegation shall be borne by the Government which has appointed it.

(3) The number of countries members of the Executive Committee shall correspond to one-fourth of the number of countries members of the Assembly. In establishing the number of seats to be filled, remainders after division by four shall be disregarded.

---

[3] By amendment adopted in 1979 (entered into force November 19, 1984), Art. 22 (4)(a), "third" is replaced by "second".

(4) In electing the members of the Executive Committee, the Assembly shall have due regard to an equitable geographical distribution and to the need for countries party to the Special Agreements which might be established in relation with the Union to be among the countries constituting the Executive Committee.

(5)(a) Each member of the Executive Committee shall serve from the close of the session of the Assembly which elected it to the close of the next ordinary session of the Assembly.

(b) Members of the Executive Committee may be reelected, but not more than two-thirds of them.

(c) The Assembly shall establish the details of the rules governing the election and possible re-election of the members of the Executive Committee.

(6)(a) The Executive Committee shall:

    (i)   prepare the draft agenda of the Assembly;

    (ii) submit proposals to the Assembly respecting the draft program and triennial[4] budget of the Union prepared by the Director General;

    (iii) approve, within the limits of the program and the triennial[5] budget, the specific yearly budgets and programs prepared by the Director General;

    (iv) submit, with appropriate comments, to the Assembly the periodical reports of the Director General and the yearly audit reports on the accounts;

    (v) in accordance with the decisions of the Assembly and having regard to circumstances arising between two ordinary sessions of the Assembly, take all necessary measures to ensure the execution of the program of the Union by the Director General;

    (vi) perform such other functions as are allocated to it under this Convention.

(b) With respect to matters which are of interest also to other Unions administered by the Organization, the Executive Committee shall make its decisions after having heard the advice of the Coordination Committee of the Organization.

(7)(a) The Executive Committee shall meet once a year in ordinary session upon convocation by the Director General, preferably during the same period and at the same place as the Coordination Committee of the Organization.

---

[4] By amendments adopted in 1979 (entered into force November 19, 1984, Art. 23(6)(a)(ii), "triennial"is replaced by "biennial" and Art. 23(6)(a), item (iii) is deleted.

[5] By amendments adopted in 1979 (entered into force November 19, 1984, Art. 23(6)(a)(ii), "triennial"is replaced by "biennial" and Art. 23(6)(a), item (iii) is deleted.

(b) The Executive Committee shall meet in extraordinary session upon convocation by the Director General, either on his own initiative, or at the request of its Chairman or one-fourth of its members.

(8)*(a)* Each country member of the Executive Committee shall have one vote.

(b) One-half of the members of the Executive Committee shall constitute a quorum.

(c) Decisions shall be made by a simple majority of the votes cast.

(d) Abstentions shall not be considered as votes.

(e) A delegate may represent, and vote in the name of, one country only.

(9) Countries of the Union not members of the Executive Committee shall be admitted to its meetings as observers.

(10) The Executive Committee shall adopt its own rules of procedure.

Article 24

(1)*(a)* The administrative tasks with respect to the Union shall be performed by the International Bureau, which is a continuation of the Bureau of the Union united with the Bureau of the Union established by the International Convention for the Protection of Industrial Property.

(b) In particular, the International Bureau shall provide the secretariat of the various organs of the Union.

(c) The Director General of the Organization shall be the chief executive of the Union and shall represent the Union.

(2) The International Bureau shall assemble and publish information concerning the protection of copyright. Each country of the Union shall promptly communicate to the International Bureau all new laws and official texts concerning the protection of copyright.

(3) The International Bureau shall publish a monthly periodical.

(4) The International Bureau shall, on request, furnish information to any country of the Union on matters concerning the protection of copyright.

(5) The International Bureau shall conduct studies, and shall provide services, designed to facilitate the protection of copyright.

(6) The Director General and any staff member designated by him shall participate, without the right to vote, in all meetings of the Assembly, the Executive Committee and any other committee of experts or working group. The Director General, or a staff member designated by him, shall be *ex officio* secretary of these bodies.

(7)*(a)* The International Bureau shall, in accordance with the directions of the Assembly and in cooperation with the Executive Committee, make the preparations for the conferences of revision of the provisions of the Convention other than Articles 22 to 26.

(b) The International Bureau may consult with intergovernmental and international non-governmental organizations concerning preparations for conferences of revision.

(c) The Director General and persons designated by him shall take part, without the right to vote, in the discussions at these conferences.

(8) The International Bureau shall carry out any other tasks assigned to it.

Article 25

(1)*(a)* The Union shall have a budget.

(b) The budget of the Union shall include the income and expenses proper to the Union, its contribution to the budget of expenses common to the Unions, and, where applicable, the sum made available to the budget of the Conference of the Organization.

(c) Expenses not attributable exclusively to the Union but also to one or more other Unions administered by the Organization shall be considered as expenses common to the Unions. The share of the Union in such common expenses shall be in proportion to the interest the Union has in them.

(2) The budget of the Union shall be established with due regard to the requirements of coordination with the budgets of the other Unions administered by the Organization.

(3) The budget of the Union shall be financed from the following sources:

    (i)   contributions of the countries of the Union;

    (ii)   fees and charges due for services performed by the International Bureau in relation to the Union;

    (iii) sale of, or royalties on, the publications of the International Bureau concerning the Union;

    (iv) gifts, bequests, and subventions;

    (v)   rents, interests, and other miscellaneous income.

(4)*(a)* For the purpose of establishing its contribution towards the budget, each country of the Union shall belong to a class, and shall pay its annual contributions on the basis of a number of units fixed as follows:

Class I	25
Class II	20
Class III	15
Class IV	10
Class V	5
Class VI	3
Class VII	1

(b) Unless it has already done so, each country shall indicate, concurrently with depositing its instrument of ratification or accession, the class to which it wishes to belong. Any country may change class. If it chooses

a lower class, the country must announce it to the Assembly at one of its ordinary sessions. Any such change shall take effect at the beginning of the calendar year following the session.

(c) The annual contribution of each country shall be an amount in the same proportion to the total sum to be contributed to the annual budget of the Union by all countries as the number of its units is to the total of the units of all contributing countries.

(d) Contributions shall become due on the first of January of each year.

(e) A country which is in arrears in the payment of its contributions shall have no vote in any of the organs of the Union of which it is a member if the amount of its arrears equals or exceeds the amount of the contributions due from it for the preceding two full years. However, any organ of the Union may allow such a country to continue to exercise its vote in that organ if, and as long as, it is satisfied that the delay in payment is due to exceptional and unavoidable circumstances.

(f) If the budget is not adopted before the beginning of a new financial period, it shall be at the same level as the budget of the previous year, in accordance with the financial regulations.

(5) The amount of the fees and charges due for services rendered by the International Bureau in relation to the Union shall be established, and shall be reported to the Assembly and the Executive Committee, by the Director General.

(6)*(a)* The Union shall have a working capital fund which shall be constituted by a single payment made by each country of the Union. If the fund becomes insufficient, an increase shall be decided by the Assembly.

(b) The amount of the initial payment of each country to the said fund or of its participation in the increase thereof shall be a proportion of the contribution of that country for the year in which the fund is established or the increase decided.

(c) The proportion and the terms of payment shall be fixed by the Assembly on the proposal of the Director General and after it has heard the advice of the Coordination Committee of the Organization.

(7)*(a)* In the headquarters agreement concluded with the country on the territory of which the Organization has its headquarters, it shall be provided that, whenever the working capital fund is insufficient, such country shall grant advances. The amount of these advances and the conditions on which they are granted shall be the subject of separate agreements, in each case, between such country and the Organization. As long as it remains under the obligation to grant advances, such country shall have an *ex officio* seat on the Executive Committee.

(b) The country referred to in subparagraph *(a)* and the Organization shall each have the right to denounce the obligation to grant advances, by written notification. Denunciation shall take effect three years after the end of the year in which it has been notified.

(8) The auditing of the accounts shall be effected by one or more of the countries of the Union or by external auditors, as provided in the financial regulations. They shall be designated, with their agreement, by the Assembly.

Article 26

(1) Proposals for the amendment of Articles 22, 23, 24, 25, and the present Article, may be initiated by any country member of the Assembly, by the Executive Committee, or by the Director General. Such proposals shall be communicated by the Director General to the member countries of the Assembly at least six months in advance of their consideration by the Assembly.

(2) Amendments to the Articles referred to in paragraph (1) shall be adopted by the Assembly. Adoption shall require three-fourths of the votes cast, provided that any amendment of Article 22, and of the present paragraph, shall require four-fifths of the votes cast.

(3) Any amendment to the Articles referred to in paragraph (1) shall enter into force one month after written notifications of acceptance, effected in accordance with their respective constitutional processes, have been received by the Director General from three-fourths of the countries members of the Assembly at the time it adopted the amendment. Any amendment to the said Articles thus accepted shall bind all the countries which are members of the Assembly at the time the amendment enters into force, or which become members thereof at a subsequent date, provided that any amendment increasing the financial obligations of countries of the Union shall bind only those countries which have notified their acceptance of such amendment.

Article 27

(1) This Convention shall be submitted to revision with a view to the introduction of amendments designed to improve the system of the Union.

(2) For this purpose, conferences shall be held successively in one of the countries of the Union among the delegates of the said countries.

(3) Subject to the provisions of Article 26 which apply to the amendment of Articles 22 to 26, any revision of this Act, including the Appendix, shall require the unanimity of the votes cast.

Article 28

(1)(a) Any country of the Union which has signed this Act may ratify it, and, if it has not signed it, may accede to it. Instruments of ratification or accession shall be deposited with the Director General.

(b) Any country of the Union may declare in its instrument of ratification or accession that its ratification or accession shall not apply to Articles 1 to 21 and the Appendix, provided that, if such country has previously made a declaration under Article VI(1) of the Appendix, then it may declare in the said instrument only that its ratification or accession shall not apply to Articles 1 to 20.

(c) Any country of the Union which, in accordance with subparagraph *(b)*, has excluded provisions therein referred to from the effects of its ratification or accession may at any later time declare that it extends the effects of its ratification or accession to those provisions. Such declaration shall be deposited with the Director General.

(2)*(a)* Articles 1 to 21 and the Appendix shall enter into force three months after both of the following two conditions are fulfilled:

    (i)   at least five countries of the Union have ratified or acceded to this Act without making a declaration under paragraph (1)*(b)*,

    (ii)   France, Spain, the United Kingdom of Great Britain and Northern Ireland, and the United States of America, have become bound by the Universal Copyright Convention as revised at Paris on July 24, 1971.

(b) The entry into force referred to in subparagraph *(a)* shall apply to those countries of the Union which, at least three months before the said entry into force, have deposited instruments of ratification or accession not containing a declaration under paragraph (1)*(b)*.

(c) With respect to any country of the Union not covered by subparagraph *(b)* and which ratifies or accedes to this Act without making a declaration under paragraph (1)*(b)*, Articles 1 to 21 and the Appendix shall enter into force three months after the date on which the Director General has notified the deposit of the relevant instrument of ratification or accession, unless a subsequent date has been indicated in the instrument deposited. In the latter case, Articles 1 to 21 and the Appendix shall enter into force with respect to that country on the date thus indicated.

(d) The provisions of subparagraphs *(a)* to *(c)* do not affect the application of Article VI of the Appendix.

(3) With respect to any country of the Union which ratifies or accedes to this Act with or without a declaration made under paragraph (1)*(b)*, Articles 22 to 38 shall enter into force three months after the date on which the Director General has notified the deposit of the relevant instrument of ratification or accession, unless a subsequent date has been indicated in the instrument deposited. In the latter case, Articles 22 to 38 shall enter into force with respect to that country on the date thus indicated.

Article 29

(1) Any country outside the Union may accede to this Act and thereby become party to this Convention and a member of the Union. Instruments of accession shall be deposited with the Director General.

(2)*(a)* Subject to subparagraph *(b)*, this Convention shall enter into force with respect to any country outside the Union three months after the date on which the Director General has notified the deposit of its instrument of accession, unless a subsequent date has been indicated in the instrument deposited. In the latter case, this Convention shall enter into force with respect to that country on the date thus indicated.

(b) If the entry into force according to subparagraph *(a)* precedes the entry into force of Articles 1 to 21 and the Appendix according to Article 28(2)*(a)*, the said country shall, in the meantime, be bound, instead of by Articles 1 to 21 and the Appendix, by Articles 1 to 20 of the Brussels Act of this Convention.

Article 29*bis*

Ratification of or accession to this Act by any country not bound by Articles 22 to 38 of the Stockholm Act of this Convention shall, for the sole purposes of Article 14(2) of the Convention establishing the Organization, amount to ratification of or accession to the said Stockholm Act with the limitation set forth in Article 28(1)*(b)*(i) thereof.

Article 30

(1) Subject to the exceptions permitted by paragraph (2) of this Article, by Article 28(1)*(b)*, by Article 33(2), and by the Appendix, ratification or accession shall automatically entail acceptance of all the provisions and admission to all the advantages of this Convention.

(2)*(a)* Any country of the Union ratifying or acceding to this Act may, subject to Article V(2) of the Appendix, retain the benefit of the reservations it has previously formulated on condition that it makes a declaration to that effect at the time of the deposit of its instrument of ratification or accession.

(b) Any country outside the Union may declare, in acceding to this Convention and subject to Article V(2) of the Appendix, that it intends to substitute, temporarily at least, for Article 8 of this Act concerning the right of translation, the provisions of Article 5 of the Union Convention of 1886, as completed at Paris in 1896, on the clear understanding that the said provisions are applicable only to translations into a language in general use in the said country. Subject to Article I(6)*(b)* of the Appendix, any country has the right to apply, in relation to the right of translation of works whose country of origin is a country availing itself of such a reservation, a protection which is equivalent to the protection granted by the latter country.

(c) Any country may withdraw such reservations at any time by notification addressed to the Director General.

Article 31

(1) Any country may declare in its instrument of ratification or accession, or may inform the Director General by written notification at any time thereafter, that this Convention shall be applicable to all or part of those territories, designated in the declaration or notification, for the external relations of which it is responsible.

(2) Any country which has made such a declaration or given such a notification may, at any time, notify the Director General that this Convention shall cease to be applicable to all or part of such territories.

(3)(a) Any declaration made under paragraph (1) shall take effect on the same date as the ratification or accession in which it was included, and any notification given under that paragraph shall take effect three months after its notification by the Director General.

(b) Any notification given under paragraph (2) shall take effect twelve months after its receipt by the Director General.

(4) This Article shall in no way be understood as implying the recognition or tacit acceptance by a country of the Union of the factual situation concerning a territory to which this Convention is made applicable by another country of the Union by virtue of a declaration under paragraph (1).

Article 32

(1) This Act shall, as regards relations between the countries of the Union, and to the extent that it applies, replace the Berne Convention of September 9, 1886, and the subsequent Acts of revision. The Acts previously in force shall continue to be applicable, in their entirety or to the extent that this Act does not replace them by virtue of the preceding sentence, in relations with countries of the Union which do not ratify or accede to this Act.

(2) Countries outside the Union which become party to this Act shall, subject to paragraph (3), apply it with respect to any country of the Union not bound by this Act or which, although bound by this Act, has made a declaration pursuant to Article 28(1)(b). Such countries recognize that the said country of the Union, in its relations with them:

(i) may apply the provisions of the most recent Act by which it is bound, and

(ii) subject to Article I(6) of the Appendix, has the right to adapt the protection to the level provided for by this Act.

(3) Any country which has availed itself of any of the faculties provided for in the Appendix may apply the provisions of the Appendix relating to the faculty or faculties of which it has availed itself in its relations with any other country of the Union which is not bound by this Act, provided that the latter country has accepted the application of the said provisions.

Article 33

(1) Any dispute between two or more countries of the Union concerning the interpretation or application of this Convention, not settled by negotiation, may, by any one of the countries concerned, be brought before the International Court of Justice by application in conformity with the Statute of the Court, unless the countries concerned agree on some other method of settlement. The country bringing the dispute before the Court shall

inform the International Bureau; the International Bureau shall bring the matter to the attention of the other countries of the Union.

(2) Each country may, at the time it signs this Act or deposits its instrument of ratification or accession, declare that it does not consider itself bound by the provisions of paragraph (1). With regard to any dispute between such country and any other country of the Union, the provisions of paragraph (1) shall not apply.

(3) Any country having made a declaration in accordance with the provisions of paragraph (2) may, at any time, withdraw its declaration by notification addressed to the Director General.

Article 34

(1) Subject to Article 29bis, no country may ratify or accede to earlier Acts of this Convention once Articles 1 to 21 and the Appendix have entered into force.

(2) Once Articles 1 to 21 and the Appendix have entered into force, no country may make a declaration under Article 5 of the Protocol Regarding Developing Countries attached to the Stockholm Act.

Article 35

(1) This Convention shall remain in force without limitation as to time.

(2) Any country may denounce this Act by notification addressed to the Director General. Such denunciation shall constitute also denunciation of all earlier Acts and shall affect only the country making it, the Convention remaining in full force and effect as regards the other countries of the Union.

(3) Denunciation shall take effect one year after the day on which the Director General has received the notification.

(4) The right of denunciation provided by this Article shall not be exercised by any country before the expiration of five years from the date upon which it becomes a member of the Union.

Article 36

(1) Any country party to this Convention undertakes to adopt, in accordance with its constitution, the measures necessary to ensure the application of this Convention.

(2) It is understood that, at the time a country becomes bound by this Convention, it will be in a position under its domestic law to give effect to the provisions of this Convention.

Article 37

(1)(a) This Act shall be signed in a single copy in the French and English languages and, subject to paragraph (2), shall be deposited with the Director General.

(b) Official texts shall be established by the Director General, after consultation with the interested Governments, in the Arabic, German, Italian, Portuguese and Spanish languages, and such other languages as the Assembly may designate.

(c) In case of differences of opinion on the interpretation of the various texts, the French text shall prevail.

(2) This Act shall remain open for signature until January 31, 1972. Until that date, the copy referred to in paragraph (1)*(a)* shall be deposited with the Government of the French Republic.

(3) The Director General shall certify and transmit two copies of the signed text of this Act to the Governments of all countries of the Union and, on request, to the Government of any other country.

(4) The Director General shall register this Act with the Secretariat of the United Nations.

(5) The Director General shall notify the Governments of all countries of the Union of signatures, deposits of instruments of ratification or accession and any declarations included in such instruments or made pursuant to Articles 28(1)*(c)*, 30(2)*(a)* and *(b)*, and 33(2), entry into force of any provisions of this Act, notifications of denunciation, and notifications pursuant to Articles 30(2)*(c)*, 31(1) and (2), 33(3), and 38(1), as well as the Appendix.

Article 38

(1) Countries of the Union which have not ratified or acceded to this Act and which are not bound by Articles 22 to 26 of the Stockholm Act of this Convention may, until April 26, 1975, exercise, if they so desire, the rights provided under the said Articles as if they were bound by them. Any country desiring to exercise such rights shall give written notification to this effect to the Director General; this notification shall be effective on the date of its receipt. Such countries shall be deemed to be members of the Assembly until the said date.

(2) As long as all the countries of the Union have not become Members of the Organization, the International Bureau of the Organization shall also function as the Bureau of the Union, and the Director General as the Director of the said Bureau.

(3) Once all the countries of the Union have become Members of the Organization, the rights, obligations, and property, of the Bureau of the Union shall devolve on the International Bureau of the Organization.

APPENDIX

[Special Provisions Regarding Developing Countries]

Article I

(1) Any country regarded as a developing country in conformity with the established practice of the General Assembly of the United Nations which

ratifies or accedes to this Act, of which this Appendix forms an integral part, and which, having regard to its economic situation and its social or cultural needs, does not consider itself immediately in a position to make provision for the protection of all the rights as provided for in this Act, may, by a notification deposited with the Director General at the time of depositing its instrument of ratification or accession or, subject to Article V(1)*(c)*, at any time thereafter, declare that it will avail itself of the faculty provided for in Article II, or of the faculty provided for in Article III, or of both of those faculties. It may, instead of availing itself of the faculty provided for in Article II, make a declaration according to Article V(1)*(a)*.

(2)*(a)* Any declaration under paragraph (1) notified before the expiration of the period of ten years from the entry into force of Articles 1 to 21 and this Appendix according to Article 28(2) shall be effective until the expiration of the said period. Any such declaration may be renewed in whole or in part for periods of ten years each by a notification deposited with the Director General not more than fifteen months and not less than three months before the expiration of the ten-year period then running.

(b) Any declaration under paragraph (1) notified after the expiration of the period of ten years from the entry into force of Articles 1 to 21 and this Appendix according to Article 28(2) shall be effective until the expiration of the ten-year period then running. Any such declaration may be renewed as provided for in the second sentence of subparagraph *(a)*.

(3) Any country of the Union which has ceased to be regarded as a developing country as referred to in paragraph (1) shall no longer be entitled to renew its declaration as provided in paragraph (2), and, whether or not it formally withdraws its declaration, such country shall be precluded from availing itself of the faculties referred to in paragraph (1) from the expiration of the ten-year period then running or from the expiration of a period of three years after it has ceased to be regarded as a developing country, whichever period expires later.

(4) Where, at the time when the declaration made under paragraph (1) or (2) ceases to be effective, there are copies in stock which were made under a license granted by virtue of this Appendix, such copies may continue to be distributed until their stock is exhausted.

(5) Any country which is bound by the provisions of this Act and which has deposited a declaration or a notification in accordance with Article 31(1) with respect to the application of this Act to a particular territory, the situation of which can be regarded as analogous to that of the countries referred to in paragraph (1), may, in respect of such territory, make the declaration referred to in paragraph (1) and the notification of renewal referred to in paragraph (2). As long as such declaration or notification remains in effect, the provisions of this Appendix shall be applicable to the territory in respect of which it was made.

(6)*(a)* The fact that a country avails itself of any of the faculties referred to in paragraph (1) does not permit another country to give less protection to works of which the country of origin is the former country than it is obliged to grant under Articles 1 to 20.

(b) The right to apply reciprocal treatment provided for in Article 30(2)*(b)*, second sentence, shall not, until the date on which the period applicable under Article I(3) expires, be exercised in respect of works the country of origin of which is a country which has made a declaration according to Article V(1)*(a)*.

Article II

(1) Any country which has declared that it will avail itself of the faculty provided for in this Article shall be entitled, so far as works published in printed or analogous forms of reproduction are concerned, to substitute for the exclusive right of translation provided for in Article 8 a system of non-exclusive and non-transferable licenses, granted by the competent authority under the following conditions and subject to Article IV.

(2)*(a)* Subject to paragraph (3), if, after the expiration of a period of three years, or of any longer period determined by the national legislation of the said country, commencing on the date of the first publication of the work, a translation of such work has not been published in a language in general use in that country by the owner of the right of translation, or with his authorization, any national of such country may obtain a license to make a translation of the work in the said language and publish the translation in printed or analogous forms of reproduction.

(b) A license under the conditions provided for in this Article may also be granted if all the editions of the translation published in the language concerned are out of print.

(3)*(a)* In the case of translations into a language which is not in general use in one or more developed countries which are members of the Union, a period of one year shall be substituted for the period of three years referred to in paragraph (2)*(a)*.

(b) Any country referred to in paragraph (1) may, with the unanimous agreement of the developed countries which are members of the Union and in which the same language is in general use, substitute, in the case of translations into that language, for the period of three years referred to in paragraph (2)*(a)* a shorter period as determined by such agreement but not less than one year. However, the provisions of the foregoing sentence shall not apply where the language in question is English, French or Spanish. The Director General shall be notified of any such agreement by the Governments which have concluded it.

(4)*(a)* No license obtainable after three years shall be granted under this Article until a further period of six months has elapsed, and no license obtainable after one year shall be granted under this Article until a further period of nine months has elapsed

    (i)   from the date on which the applicant complies with the requirements mentioned in Article IV(1), or

(ii) where the identity or the address of the owner of the right of translation is unknown, from the date on which the applicant sends, as provided for in Article IV(2), copies of his application submitted to the authority competent to grant the license.

(b) If, during the said period of six or nine months, a translation in the language in respect of which the application was made is published by the owner of the right of translation or with his authorization, no license under this Article shall be granted.

(5) Any license under this Article shall be granted only for the purpose of teaching, scholarship or research.

(6) If a translation of a work is published by the owner of the right of translation or with his authorization at a price reasonably related to that normally charged in the country for comparable works, any license granted under this Article shall terminate if such translation is in the same language and with substantially the same content as the translation published under the license. Any copies already made before the license terminates may continue to be distributed until their stock is exhausted.

(7) For works which are composed mainly of illustrations, a license to make and publish a translation of the text and to reproduce and publish the illustrations may be granted only if the conditions of Article III are also fulfilled.

(8) No license shall be granted under this Article when the author has withdrawn from circulation all copies of his work.

(9)(a) A license to make a translation of a work which has been published in printed or analogous forms of reproduction may also be granted to any broadcasting organization having its headquarters in a country referred to in paragraph (1), upon an application made to the competent authority of that country by the said organization, provided that all of the following conditions are met:

(i) the translation is made from a copy made and acquired in accordance with the laws of the said country;

(ii) the translation is only for use in broadcasts intended exclusively for teaching or for the dissemination of the results of specialized technical or scientific research to experts in a particular profession;

(iii) the translation is used exclusively for the purposes referred to in condition (ii) through broadcasts made lawfully and intended for recipients on the territory of the said country, including broadcasts made through the medium of sound or visual recordings lawfully and exclusively made for the purpose of such broadcasts;

(iv) all uses made of the translation are without any commercial purpose.

(b) Sound or visual recordings of a translation which was made by a broadcasting organization under a license granted by virtue of this paragraph may, for the purposes subject to the conditions referred to in subparagraph *(a)* and with the agreement of that organization, also be used by any other broadcasting organization having its headquarters in the country whose competent authority granted the license in question.

(c) Provided that all of the criteria and conditions set out in subparagraph *(a)* are met, a license may also be granted to a broadcasting organization to translate any text incorporated in an audio-visual fixation where such fixation was itself prepared and published for the sole purpose of being used in connection with systematic instructional activities.

(d) Subject to subparagraphs *(a)* to *(c)*, the provisions of the preceding paragraphs shall apply to the grant and exercise of any license granted under this paragraph.

Article III

(1) Any country which has declared that it will avail itself of the faculty provided for in this Article shall be entitled to substitute for the exclusive right of reproduction provided for in Article 9 a system of non-exclusive and non-transferable licenses, granted by the competent authority under the following conditions and subject to Article IV.

(2)*(a)* If, in relation to a work to which this Article applies by virtue of paragraph (7), after the expiration of

    (i)   the relevant period specified in paragraph (3), commencing on the date of first publication of a particular edition of the work, or

    (ii) any longer period determined by national legislation of the country referred to in paragraph (1), commencing on the same date,

copies of such edition have not been distributed in that country to the general public or in connection with systematic instructional activities, by the owner of the right of reproduction or with his authorization, at a price reasonably related to that normally charged in the country for comparable works, any national of such country may obtain a license to reproduce and publish such edition at that or a lower price for use in connection with systematic instructional activities.

(b) A license to reproduce and publish an edition which has been distributed as described in subparagraph *(a)* may also be granted under the conditions provided for in this Article if, after the expiration of the applicable period, no authorized copies of that edition have been on sale for a period of six months in the country concerned to the general public or in connection with systematic instructional activities at a price reasonably related to that normally charged in the country for comparable works.

(3) The period referred to in paragraph (2)*(a)*(i) shall be five years, except that

    (i)   for works of the natural and physical sciences, including mathematics, and of technology, the period shall be three years;

    (ii) for works of fiction, poetry, drama and music, and for art books, the period shall be seven years.

(4)*(a)* No license obtainable after three years shall be granted under this Article until a period of six months has elapsed

(i) from the date on which the applicant complies with the requirements mentioned in Article IV(1), or

(ii) where the identity or the address of the owner of the right of reproduction is unknown, from the date on which the applicant sends, as provided for in Article IV(2), copies of his application submitted to the authority competent to grant the license.

(b) Where licenses are obtainable after other periods and Article IV(2) is applicable, no license shall be granted until a period of three months has elapsed from the date of the dispatch of the copies of the application.

(c) If, during the period of six or three months referred to in subparagraphs *(a)* and *(b)*, a distribution as described in paragraph (2)*(a)* has taken place, no license shall be granted under this Article.

(d) No license shall be granted if the author has withdrawn from circulation all copies of the edition for the reproduction and publication of which the license has been applied for.

(5) A license to reproduce and publish a translation of a work shall not be granted under this Article in the following cases:

(i) where the translation was not published by the owner of the right of translation or with his authorization, or

(ii) where the translation is not in a language in general use in the country in which the license is applied for.

(6) If copies of an edition of a work are distributed in the country referred to in paragraph (1) to the general public or in connection with systematic instructional activities, by the owner of the right of reproduction or with his authorization, at a price reasonably related to that normally charged in the country for comparable works, any license granted under this Article shall terminate if such edition is in the same language and with substantially the same content as the edition which was published under the said license. Any copies already made before the license terminates may continue to be distributed until their stock is exhausted.

(7)*(a)* Subject to subparagraph *(b)*, the works to which this Article applies shall be limited to works published in printed or analogous forms of reproduction.

(b) This Article shall also apply to the reproduction in audio-visual form of lawfully made audio-visual fixations including any protected works incorporated therein and to the translation of any incorporated text into a language in general use in the country in which the license is applied for, always provided that the audio-visual fixations in question were prepared and published for the sole purpose of being used in connection with systematic instructional activities.

Article IV

(1) A license under Article II or Article III may be granted only if the applicant, in accordance with the procedure of the country concerned, establishes either that he has requested, and has been denied, authorization by the owner of the right to make and publish the translation or to reproduce and publish the edition, as the case may be, or that, after due diligence on his part, he was unable to find the owner of the right. At the same time as making the request, the applicant shall inform any national or international information center referred to in paragraph (2).

(2) If the owner of the right cannot be found, the applicant for a license shall send, by registered airmail, copies of his application, submitted to the authority competent to grant the license, to the publisher whose name appears on the work and to any national or international information center which may have been designated, in a notification to that effect deposited with the Director General, by the Government of the country in which the publisher is believed to have his principal place of business.

(3) The name of the author shall be indicated on all copies of the translation or reproduction published under a license granted under Article II or Article III. The title of the work shall appear on all such copies. In the case of a translation, the original title of the work shall appear in any case on all the said copies.

(4)(a) No license granted under Article II or Article III shall extend to the export of copies, and any such license shall be valid only for publication of the translation or of the reproduction, as the case may be, in the territory of the country in which it has been applied for.

(b) For the purposes of subparagraph (a), the notion of export shall include the sending of copies from any territory to the country which, in respect of that territory, has made a declaration under Article I(5).

(c) Where a governmental or other public entity of a country which has granted a license to make a translation under Article II into a language other than English, French or Spanish sends copies of a translation published under such license to another country, such sending of copies shall not, for the purposes of subparagraph (a), be considered to constitute export if all of the following conditions are met:

    (i)   the recipients are individuals who are nationals of the country whose competent authority has granted the license, or organizations grouping such individuals;

    (ii)   the copies are to be used only for the purpose of teaching, scholarship or research;

    (iii) the sending of the copies and their subsequent distribution to recipients is without any commercial purpose; and

    (iv) the country to which the copies have been sent has agreed with the country whose competent authority has granted the license to allow the receipt, or distribution, or both, and the Director

General has been notified of the agreement by the Government of the country in which the license has been granted.

(5) All copies published under a license granted by virtue of Article II or Article III shall bear a notice in the appropriate language that the copies are available for distribution only in the country or territory to which the said license applies.

(6)(a) Due provision shall be made at the national level to ensure

    (i) that the license provides, in favour of the owner of the right of translation or of reproduction, as the case may be, for just compensation that is consistent with standards of royalties normally operating on licenses freely negotiated between persons in the two countries concerned, and

    (ii) payment and transmittal of the compensation: should national currency regulations intervene, the competent authority shall make all efforts, by the use of international machinery, to ensure transmittal in internationally convertible currency or its equivalent.

(b) Due provision shall be made by national legislation to ensure a correct translation of the work, or an accurate reproduction of the particular edition, as the case may be.

Article V

(1)(a) Any country entitled to make a declaration that it will avail itself of the faculty provided for in Article II may, instead, at the time of ratifying or acceding to this Act:

    (i) if it is a country to which Article 30(2)(a) applies, make a declaration under that provision as far as the right of translation is concerned;

    (ii) if it is a country to which Article 30(2)(a) does not apply, and even if it is not a country outside the Union, make a declaration as provided for in Article 30(2)(b), first sentence.

(b) In the case of a country which ceases to be regarded as a developing country as referred to in Article I(1), a declaration made according to this paragraph shall be effective until the date on which the period applicable under Article I(3) expires.

(c) Any country which has made a declaration according to this paragraph may not subsequently avail itself of the faculty provided for in Article I even if it withdraws the said declaration.

(2) Subject to paragraph (3), any country which has availed itself of the faculty provided for in Article II may not subsequently make a declaration according to paragraph (1).

(3) Any country which has ceased to be regarded as a developing country as referred to in Article I(1) may, not later than two years prior to the expiration of the period applicable under Article I(3), make a declaration

to the effect provided for in Article 30(2)*(b)*, first sentence, notwithstanding the fact that it is not a country outside the Union. Such declaration shall take effect at the date on which the period applicable under Article I(3) expires.

Article VI

(1) Any country of the Union may declare, as from the date of this Act, and at any time before becoming bound by Articles 1 to 21 and this Appendix:

(i)   if it is a country which, were it bound by Articles 1 to 21 and this Appendix, would be entitled to avail itself of the faculties referred to in Article I(1), that it will apply the provisions of Article II or of Article III or of both to works whose country of origin is a country which, pursuant to (ii) below, admits the application of those Articles to such works, or which is bound by Articles 1 to 21 and this Appendix; such declaration may, instead of referring to Article II, refer to Article V;

(ii)   that it admits the application of this Appendix to works of which it is the country of origin by countries which have made a declaration under (i) above or a notification under Article I.

(2) Any declaration made under paragraph (1) shall be in writing and shall be deposited with the Director General. The declaration shall become effective from the date of its deposit.

IN WITNESS WHEREOF, the undersigned, being duly authorized thereto, have signed this Act.[6]

DONE at Paris on July 24, 1971.

---

[6] On July 24, 1971, the Act was signed by the Plenipotentiaries of the 28 following countries; Brazil, Cameroon, Ceylon, Cyprus, Denmark, France, Germany (Federal Republic), Holy See, Hungary, India, Israel, Italy, Ivory Coast, Lebanon, Liechtenstein, Luxembourg, Mexico, Monaco, Morocco, Netherlands, People's Republic of the Congo, Senegal, Spain, Sweden, Switzerland, Tunisia, United Kingdom, Yugoslavia.

In accordance with Article 37, the Convention remained open for signature until January 31, 1972.

BERNE CONVENTION
IMPLEMENTATION ACT OF 1988

Summary Overview of the
Berne Convention Implementation Act of 1988

Effective March 1, 1989, the United States officially became the 80th adherent to the Berne Convention for the Protection of Literary and Artistic Works (the "Convention" or "Berne"). U.S. adherence was the product of two separate but coordinated acts: Senate ratification of the Convention (Oct. 20, 1988); and the signing by President Reagan of enabling legislation entitled the "Berne Convention Implementation Act of 1988" (Pub. L. 100–568, 102 Stat. 2853, Oct. 31, 1988) (the "Implementation Act" or "BCIA").

The Convention consists of the original treaty signed in Berne, Switzerland on September 9, 1886, and several revisions thereto (the most recent being the Paris Text of July 24, 1971, reproduced earlier). As between any two member nations, the latest version or "Text" of the Convention adopted by each controls within that country. In connection with U.S. adherence, Congress determined that the Paris Text should not be self–executing in this country. Rather, Congress decided that the United States would apply to so–called "Berne Convention works" its domestic law, the provisions of which, under the terms of the Convention, must in theory be compatible with the minimum standards of the Paris Text. Thus, to achieve minimal compatibility for U.S. adherence, Congress passed the Implementation Act, which is reproduced immediately following this overview.

Internationally, Berne Convention adherence provided several benefits to the United States. For one thing, the Convention is superior to existing multilateral means of protecting American creativity abroad, *e.g.,* the Universal Copyright Convention (the "U.C.C."). While both the Berne Convention and the U.C.C. require each member state to accord to nationals of other member states the same protection accorded to the member state's own nationals, Berne provides a higher, more detailed set of minimum standards and broader subject matter coverage. In addition to those advantages, Berne also provides a means of managing copyright relations with approximately two dozen countries with which the United States previously lacked even bilateral agreements. Taken together, these effects enhance this country's ability to combat international copyright piracy and protect its leading position in the world intellectual property marketplace. Finally, adherence to the Berne Convention transformed the United States from an observer into an active participant in the development of international copyright policy, as evidenced subsequently by GATT/TRIPs agreement in 1994 and the two new WIPO treaties in 1996.

Domestically, Berne Convention adherence effected significant changes in U.S. law. Precisely because the Convention is not self–executing, however, an understanding of those changes can be gleaned only from an examination of the amendments to existing copyright law mandated by the Berne Convention Implementation Act of 1988. Therefore, the remainder of this summary is devoted to a section–by–section overview of that legislation. To explore in more detail the effects of the Implementation Act on U.S. law, see the texts of the BCIA and the Convention, William F. Patry's COPYRIGHT LAW AND PRACTICE from BNA, and the latest edition of NIMMER ON COPYRIGHT from Matthew Bender & Co., Inc.

SECTION 1. SHORT TITLE

The Act may be cited as the "Berne Convention Implementation Act of 1988."

SECTION 2. DECLARATIONS

Paragraph 1 declares that the Berne Convention is not self–executing under the Constitution and laws of the United States.

Paragraph 2 states that the obligations of the United States under Berne may be performed only pursuant to appropriate domestic law.

Paragraph 3 declares that the amendments made by the Implementation Act to Title 17 of the U.S. Code (the Copyright Act) satisfy the United States' obligations in adhering to Berne, and that no further rights or interests shall be recognized or created for the purpose of adherence.

SECTION 3. CONSTRUCTION OF THE BERNE CONVENTION

By providing that the Convention's provisions are not enforceable under Berne itself, subsection 3(a) reinforces § 2. The subsection adds, however, that, besides Title 17, the Convention's provisions may be given effect under "any other relevant provision of Federal or State law, including common law." Subsection 3(b) makes explicit, however, that certain rights — specifically, the rights "to claim authorship of [a] work" or "to object to any distortion, mutilation, or other modification of, or other derogatory action in relation to, [a] work, that would prejudice the author's honor or reputation" — are not expanded or reduced by the Convention itself, by U. S. adherence thereto, or by satisfaction of U.S. obligations thereunder.

In other words, Congress in § 3 chose not to include within U.S. domestic law the *droit moral, i.e.,* noneconomic, moral rights, recognized by article 6bis of the Berne Convention, except insofar as rights consistent with the *droit moral* exist already under federal or state statutes, or common law. Whether in this respect the Implementation Act complies with article 5(1) of the Convention, requiring member states to provide to all authors coming within Berne's protection the rights "specially granted" by the Convention, seems debatable.

SECTION 4. SUBJECT MATTER AND SCOPE OF COPYRIGHTS

Subsection (a)(1)(A) amended the definition of "pictorial, graphic, and sculptural works" in § 101 of the Copyright Act to include architectural plans (but not architectural structures), thereby clarifying the application of American copyright law to such works, which are mentioned specifically in the Convention.

Subsection (a)(1)(B) further amended § 101 to identify works eligible for protection under the Implementation Act. In addition to defining "Berne Convention," the subsection particularized what constitutes a "Berne Convention work":

— The term comprehends an *unpublished* work if one or more of the authors is "a national of a nation adhering to the Berne Convention" (*i.e.,* is domiciled in or has his or her habitual residence in a nation adhering to the Convention). A *published* work is a "Berne Convention work" if one or more of the authors is such a national on the date of the first publication of the work.

— In order to qualify, the work must have been first published in a Berne Convention member state, or published in a member state and a nonadhering foreign country "simultaneously" (*i.e.,* the publications occurred within 30 days of one another).

— Also qualifying as a "Berne Convention work" are: audiovisual works, where one or more of a work's authors is a legal entity with its headquarters in a Berne member state or is an individual whose domicile or habitual residence is in such a state; and pictorial, graphic, or sculptural works, where the work is "incorporated in a building or other structure . . . located" in a member state.

Subsection 4(a)(1)(C) added to § 101 of the Copyright Act a definition of "country of origin" solely for purposes of § 411 (which, as revised by the Implementation Act, makes registration a prerequisite to infringement actions, except for Berne Convention works "whose country of origin is not the United States"):

— A work's "country of origin" *is* the United States, in the case of a published work, where the work is first published in the United States, or is first published "simultaneously" either in the U.S. and another Berne member state with the same or a longer term of protection, or in the U.S. and a non–Berne nation. The country of origin for a published work may be the United States even when the work is first published only in a non–Berne nation, provided that *all* of the authors are nationals, domiciliaries or habitual residents of, or, in the case of an audiovisual work, legal entities with their headquarters in, the United States.

— Likewise, in the case of an *un*published work, the United States is the country of origin where all of the authors are nationals, domiciliaries or habitual residents of, or, in the case of an audiovisual work, legal entities headquartered in, this country.

— In the case of a pictorial, graphic, or sculptural work incorporated in a building or structure, the United States is the country of origin if the building or structure is located here.

— In all other instances, the United States is *not* the "country of origin" for § 411 purposes.

Like §§ 2 and 3, § 4 contains a provision declaring that no rights or interests may be claimed under the Convention directly, but rather solely under Title 17, other federal or state statutes, or common law.

Finally, § 4 of the Implementation Act added to Title 17 a new § 116A, designed to encourage negotiated jukebox licenses for the performance of nondramatic musical works embodied in phonorecords. The provision was amended — and renumbered as § 116 — in 1993. New § 116 (replacing the compulsory licensing scheme under old § 116) permits owners of copyrights and operators of jukeboxes to negotiate voluntary licensing agreements (or have them arbitrated), thereby creating maximum flexibility as to terms and rates of royalty payments, etc. Negotiations that result in such voluntary agreements are to be given effect "in lieu of any otherwise applicable determination by a copyright arbitration royalty panel."

SECTION 5. RECORDATION

Section 205(d) of the Copyright Act, which prior to the effective date of the Implementation Act required recordation of the instrument of transfer as a prerequisite to the institution of an infringement action by a transferee, was stricken by § 5.

SECTION 6. PREEMPTION WITH RESPECT TO OTHER LAWS NOT AFFECTED

Section 301 of Title 17 was amended by adding a new subsection (e), providing that the scope of federal preemption "is not affected by the adherence of the United States to the Berne Convention or the satisfaction of the obligations of the United States thereunder."

SECTION 7. NOTICE OF COPYRIGHT

The mandatory notice requirements of former §§ 401 and 402 of the Copyright Act were made permissive for works publicly distributed by authority of the copyright owner on or after March 1, 1989. New subsections (d) were added to §§ 401 and 402, stating that, except as provided in the last sentence of 17 U.S.C. § 504(c)(2) (concerning certain nonprofit institutions), an innocent infringer defense asserted in mitigation of actual or statutory damages shall be given no weight where the defendant had access to a copy of a work bearing the specified notice. By amendment to § 403, however, the new subsections of §§ 401 and 402 are inapplicable to works consisting predominantly of one or more works of the United States Government unless "a statement identifying, either affirmatively or negatively, those portions" embodying protected material is included.

Section 404 (notice for contributions to collective works) also was tied to the revised innocent infringer provisions of new subsections 401(d) and 402(d).

The provisions in §§ 405 and 406 regarding curative steps for omission of notice, and for errors in name or date, were amended to apply solely to distributions before the effective date of the Act.

SECTION 8. DEPOSIT OF COPIES OR PHONORECORDS FOR LIBRARY OF CONGRESS

17 U.S.C. § 407(a), which formerly required deposit of copies of a work published in the United States "with notice of copyright," was amended by deleting the language just quoted. The effect was to expand the deposit requirement to apply to all published works, whether or not publication occurred with notice. Country of origin is irrelevant.

SECTION 9. COPYRIGHT REGISTRATION

Section 411, which as enacted in 1976 required registration (or a refusal of registration by the Copyright Office) before institution of an infringement actions, was substantially revised by establishing a two–tiered system. Under this system, a "Berne Convention work" whose "country of origin" is the United States still has to comply with the registration procedures. A Berne Convention work whose country of origin is not the United States is, however, exempt from the requirements of revised § 411. The incentives for registration found in § 412 (statutory damages and attorneys' fees) remain applicable to all works.

SECTION 10. COPYRIGHT INFRINGEMENT AND REMEDIES

In a measure logically unconnected with Berne Convention adherence, 17 U.S.C. § 504(c) was amended by doubling the minimum statutory damages from $250 to $500, the maximum nonwillful statutory damages from $10,000 to $20,000, the maximum willful statutory damages from $50,000 to $100,000, and the floor for innocent infringer remission from $100 to $200.

SECTION 11. COPYRIGHT ROYALTY TRIBUNAL

This section provided guidance for the Tribunal (now replaced by copyright arbitration royalty panels) in administering new § 116A (now amended and renumbered as § 116) (negotiated jukebox licenses).

SECTION 12. WORKS IN THE PUBLIC DOMAIN

This section, evidently the product of abundant caution on the part of Congress, made explicit that the Implementation Act "does not provide copyright protection for any work that is in the public domain in the United States" prior to the effective date of the Act.

SECTION 13. EFFECTIVE DATE; EFFECT ON PENDING CASES

Subsection (a) provided that the Implementation Act would take effect on the day on which the Berne Convention entered into force with respect to the United States (March 1, 1989). Subsection (b) provided that any action arising under Title 17 before the effective date of the legislation was to be governed by the provisions of Title 17 in effect when the cause of action arose.

BERNE CONVENTION IMPLEMENTATION ACT OF 1988

(Pub. L. 100-568, 102 Stat. 2853)

Sec. 1. Short Title and References to Title 17, United States Code

(a) Short title. This Act may be cited as the "Berne Convention Implementation Act of 1988."

(b) References to Title 17, United States Code. Whenever in this Act an amendment or repeal is expressed in terms of an amendment to or a repeal of a section or other provision, the reference shall be considered to be made to a section or other provision of title 17, United States Code.

Sec. 2. Declarations

The Congress makes the following declarations:

(1) The Convention for the Protection of Literary and Artistic Works, signed at Berne, Switzerland, on September 9, 1886, and all acts, protocols, and revisions thereto (hereafter in this Act referred to as the "Berne Convention") are not self–executing under the Constitution and laws of the United States.

(2) The obligations of the United States under the Berne Convention may be performed only pursuant to appropriate domestic law.

(3) The amendments made by this Act, together with the law as it exists on the date of the enactment of this Act, satisfy the obligations of the United States in adhering to the Berne Convention and no further rights or interests shall be recognized or created for that purpose.

Sec. 3. Construction of the Berne Convention

(a) Relationship with Domestic Law. The provisions of the Berne Convention—

(1) shall be given effect under title 17, as amended by this Act, and any other relevant provision of Federal or State law, including the common law; and

(2) shall not be enforceable in any action brought pursuant to the provisions of the Berne Convention itself.

(b) Certain Rights Not Affected. The provisions of the Berne Convention, the adherence of the United States thereto, and satisfaction of United States obligations thereunder, do not expand or reduce any right of an author of a work, whether claimed under Federal, State, or the common law —

(1) to claim authorship of the work; or

671

(2) to object to any distortion, mutilation, or other modification of, or other derogatory action in relation to, the work, that would prejudice the author's honor or reputation.

Sec. 4. Subject Matter and Scope of Copyrights

(a) Subject and Scope. Chapter 1 is amended —

(1) in section 101 —

(A) in the definition of "Pictorial, graphic, and sculptural works" by striking out in the first sentence "technical drawings, diagrams and models" and inserting in lieu thereof "diagrams, models, and technical drawings, including architectural plans";

(B) by inserting after the definition of "Audiovisual works", the following:

The "Berne Convention" is the Convention for the Protection of Literary and Artistic Works, signed at Berne, Switzerland, on September 9, 1886, and all acts protocols and revisions thereto.

A work is a "Berne Convention work" if —

(1) in the case of an unpublished work, one or more of the authors is a national of a nation adhering to the Berne Convention, or in the case of a published work, one or more of the authors is a national of a nation adhering to Berne Convention on the date of first publication;

(2) The work was first published in a nation adhering to the Berne Convention, or was simultaneously first published in a nation adhering to the Berne Convention and in a foreign nation that does not adhere to the Berne Convention;

(3) in the case of an audiovisual work —

(A) if one or more of the authors is a legal entity, that author has its headquarters in a nation adhering to the Berne Convention; or

(B) if one or more of the authors is an individual, that author is domiciled [in], or has his or her habitual residence in, a nation adhering to the Berne Convention; or

(4) in the case of a pictorial, graphic, or sculptural work that is incorporated in a building or other structure, the building or structure is located in a nation adhering to the Berne Convention.

For purposes of paragraph (1), an author who is domiciled in[,] or has his or her habitual residence in, a nation adhering to the Berne Convention is considered to be a national of that nation. For purposes of paragraph (2), a work is considered to have been simultaneously published in two or more nations if its dates of publication are within 30 days of one another"; and

(C) by inserting after the definition of "Copyright owner", the following:

The "country of origin" of a Berne Convention work, for purposes of section 411, is the United States if —

(1) in the case of a published work, the work is first published—

(A) in the United States;

(B) simultaneously in the United States and another nation or nations adhering to the Berne Convention, whose law grants a term of copyright protection that is the same as or longer than the term provided in the United States;

(C) simultaneously in the United States and a foreign nation that does not adhere to the Berne Convention; or

(D) in a foreign nation that does not adhere to the Berne Convention, and all of the authors of the work are nationals, domiciliaries, or habitual residents of, or in the case of an audiovisual work legal entities with headquarters in, the United States;

(2) in the case of an unpublished work, all the authors of the work are nationals, domiciliaries, or habitual residents of the United States, or, in the case of an unpublished audiovisual work, all the authors are legal entities with headquarters in the United States; or

(3) in the case of a pictorial, graphic, or sculptural work incorporated in a building or structure, the building or sculpture is located in the United States.

For the purposes of section 411, the "country of origin" of any other Berne Convention work is not in the United States;

(2) in section 104(b) —

(A) by redesignating paragraph (4) as paragraph (5); and

(B) by inserting after paragraph (3) the following new paragraph:

(4) the work is a Berne Convention work or;

(3) in section 104 by adding at the end thereof the following:

(c) Effect of Berne Convention. No right or interest in a work eligible for protection under this title may be claimed by virtue of, or in reliance upon, the provisions of the Berne Convention, or the adherence of the United States thereto. Any rights in a work eligible for protection under this title that derive from this title, other Federal or State statutes, or the common law, shall not be expanded or reduced by virtue of, or in reliance upon, the provisions of the Berne Convention, or the adherence of the United States thereto"; and

(4) by inserting after section 116 the following new section:

§ 116A. Negotiated licenses for public performances by means of coin–operated phonorecord players

(a) Applicability of Section. This section applies to any nondramatic musical work embodied in a phonorecord.

(b) Limitation on Exclusive Right if Licenses Not Negotiated

(1) Applicability. In the case of a work to which this section applies, the exclusive right under clause (4) of section 106 to perform the work publicly by means of a coin–operated phonorecord player is limited by section 116 to the extend provided in this section.

(2) Determination by Copyright Royalty Tribunal. The Copyright Royalty Tribunal, at the end of the 1–year period beginning on the effective date of the Berne Convention Implementation Act of 1988, and periodically thereafter to the extent necessary to carry out subsection (f), shall determine whether or not negotiated licenses authorized by subsection (c) are in effect so as to provide permission to use a quantity of musical works not substantially smaller than the quantity of such works performed on coin–operated phonorecord players during the 1–year period ending on the effective date of that Act. If the Copyright Royalty Tribunal determines that such negotiated licenses are not so in effect, the Tribunal shall, upon making the determination, publish the determination in the Federal Register. Upon such publication, section 116 shall apply with respect to musical works that are not the subject of such negotiated licenses.

(c) Negotiated Licenses

(1) Authority for Negotiations. Any owners of copyright in works to which this section applies and any operators of coin–operated phonorecord players may negotiate and agree upon the terms and rates of royalty payments for the performance of such works, and the proportionate division of fees paid among copyright owners, and may designate common agents to negotiate, agree to, pay, or receive such royalty payments.

(2) Arbitration. Parties to such a negotiation, within such time as may be specified by the Copyright Royalty Tribunal by regulation, may determine the result of the negotiation by arbitration. Such arbitration shall be governed by the provisions of title 9, to the extent such title is not inconsistent with this section. The parties shall give notice to the Copyright Royalty Tribunal of any determination reached by arbitration and any such determination shall, as between the parties to the arbitration, be dispositive of the issues to which it relates.

(d) License Agreements Superior to Copyright Royalty Tribunal Determinations. License agreements between one or more copyright owners and one or more operators of coin–operated phonorecord players, which are negotiated in accordance with subsection (c), shall be given effect in lieu of any otherwise applicable determination by the Copyright Royalty Tribunal.

(e) Negotiation Schedule. Not later than 60 days after the effective date of the Berne Convention Implementation Act of 1988, if the Chairman of the Copyright Royalty Tribunal has not received notice, from copyright owners and operators of coin–operated phonorecord players referred to in subsection (c)(1), of the date and location of the first meeting between such copyright owners and such operators to commence negotiations authorized by subsection (c), the Chairman shall announce the date and location of such meeting. Such meeting may not be held more than 90 days after the effective date of such Act.

(f) Copyright Royalty Tribunal to Suspend Various Activities. The Copyright Royalty Tribunal shall not conduct any ratemaking activity with respect to coin–operated phonorecord players unless, at any time more than one year after the effective date of the Berne Convention Implementation Act of 1988, the negotiated licenses adopted by the parties under this section do not provide permission to use a quantity of musical works not substantially smaller than the quantity of such works performed on coin–operated phonorecord players during the one–year period ending on the effective date of such Act.

(g) Transition Provisions; Retention of Copyright Royalty Tribunal Jurisdiction. Until such time as licensing provisions are determined by the parties under this section, the terms of the compulsory license under section 116, with respect to the public performance of nondramatic musical works by means of coin–operated phonorecord players, which is in effect on the day before the effective date of the Berne Convention Implementation Act of 1988, shall remain in force. If a negotiated license authorized by this section comes into force so as to supersede previous determinations of the Copyright Royalty Tribunal, as provided in subsection (d), but thereafter is terminated or expires and is not replaced by another licensing agreement, then section 116 shall be effective with respect to musical works that were the subject of such terminated or expired licenses.

(b) Technical Amendments —

(1) Section 116 is amended —

(A) by amending the section heading to read as follows:

§ 116. Scope of exclusive rights in nondramatic musical works: compulsory licenses for public performances by means of coin–operated phonorecord players;

(B) in subsection (a) in the matter preceding paragraph (1), by inserting after "in a phonorecord," the following: "the performance of which is subject to this section as provided in section 116A,"; and

(C) in subsection (e), by inserting "and section 116A" after "As used in this section".

(2) The table of section at the beginning of chapter 1 is amended by striking out the item relating to section 116, and inserting in lieu thereof the following:

§ 116. Scope of exclusive rights in nondramatic musical works: Compulsory licenses for public performances by means of coin–operated phonorecord players.

§ 116A. Negotiated licenses for public performances by means of coin–operated phonorecord players.

Sec. 5. Recordation

Section 205 is amended —

(1) by striking out subsection (d); and

(2) by redesignating subsections (e) and (f) as subsections (d) and (e), respectively.

Sec. 6. Preemption with Respect to Other Laws Not Affected

Section 301 is amended by adding at the end thereof the following:

(e) The scope of Federal preemption under this section is not affected by the adherence of the United States to the Berne Convention or the satisfaction of obligations of the United States thereunder.

Sec. 7. Notice of Copyright

(a) **Visually Perceptible Copies.** Section 401 is amended —

(1) in subsection (a), by amending the subsection heading to read as follows:

(a) General Provisions.;

(2) in subsection (a), by striking out "shall be placed on all" and inserting in lieu thereof "may be placed on";

(3) in subsection (b), by striking out "The notice appearing on the copies" and inserting in lieu thereof "If a notice appears on the copies, it"; and

(4) by adding at the end the following:

(d) Evidentiary Weight of Notice. If a notice of copyright in the form and position specified by this section appears on the published copy or copies to which a defendant in a copyright infringement suit had access, then no weight shall be given to such a defendant's interposition of a defense based on innocent infringement in mitigation of actual or statutory damages, except as provided in the last sentence of section 504(c)(2).

(b) Phonorecords of Sound Recordings. Section 402 is amended —

(1) in subsection (a), by amending the subsection heading to read as follows:

(a) General Provisions.;

(2) in subsection (a), by striking out "shall be placed on all" and inserting in lieu thereof "may be placed on";

(3) in subsection (b), by striking out "The notice appearing on the phonorecords" and inserting in lieu thereof "If a notice appears on the phonorecords, it"; and

(4) by adding at the end thereof the following new subsection:

(d) Evidentiary Weight of Notice. If a notice of copyright in the form and position specified by this section appears on the published phonorecord or phonorecords to which a defendant in a copyright infringement suit had access, then no weight shall be given to such a defendant's interposition of a defense based on innocent infringement in mitigation of actual or statutory damages, except as provided in the last sentence of section 504(c)(2).

(c) Publications Incorporating United States Government Works. Section 403 is amended to read as follows:

Sections 401(d) and 402(d) shall not apply to a work published in copies or phonorecords consisting predominantly of one or more works of the United States Government unless the notice of copyright appearing on the published copies or phonorecords to which a defendant in the copyright infringement suit had access includes a statement identifying, either affirmatively or negatively, those portions of the copies or phonorecords embodying any work or works protected under this title.

(d) Notice of Copyright: Contributions to Collective Works. Section 404 is amended —

(1) in subsection (a), by striking out "to satisfy the requirements of sections 401 through 403," and inserting in lieu thereof "to invoke the provisions of section 401(d) or 402(d), as applicable"; and

(2) in subsection (b), by striking out "Where" and inserting in lieu thereof "With respect to copies and phonorecords publicly distributed by authority of the copyright owner before the effective date of the Berne Convention Implementation Act of 1988, where".

(e) Omission of Notice. Section 405 is amended —

(1) in subsection (a), by striking out "The omission of the copyright notice prescribed by" and inserting in lieu thereof "With respect to copies and phonorecords publicly distributed by authority of the

copyright owner before the effective date of the Berne Convention Implementation Act of 1988, the omission of the copyright notice described in";

(2) in subsection (b), by striking out "omitted," in the first sentence and inserting in lieu thereof, "omitted and which was publicly distributed by authority of the copyright owner before the effective date of the Berne Convention Implementation Act of 1988,"; and

(3) by amending the section heading to read as follows:

§ 405. Notice of copyright: Omission of notice on certain copies and phonorecords

(f) Error in Name or Date. Section 406 is amended —

(1) in subsection (a) by striking out "Where" and inserting in lieu thereof "With respect to copies and phonorecords publicly distributed by authority of the copyright owner before the effective date of the Berne Convention Implementation Act of 1988, where";

(2) in subsection (b) by inserting "before the effective date of the Berne Convention Implementation Act of 1988" after "distribution";

(3) in subsection (c) —

(A) by inserting "before the effective date of the Berne Convention Implementation Act of 1988" after "publicly distributed"; and

(B) by inserting after "405" the following: "as in effect on the day before the effective date of the Berne Convention Implementation Act of 1988"; and

(4) by amending the section heading to read as follows:

Sec. 406. Notice of copyright: Error in name or date on certain copies and phonorecords.

(g) Clerical Amendment. The table of sections at the beginning of chapter 4 is amended by striking out the items relating to sections 405 and 406 and inserting in lieu thereof the following:

405. Notice of copyright: Omission of notice on certain copies and phonorecords.

406. Notice of copyright: Error in name or date on certain copies and phonorecords.

Sec. 8. Deposit of Copies or Phonorecords for Library of Congress

Section 407(a) is amended by striking out "with notice of copyright".

Sec. 9. Copyright Registration

(a) Registration in General. Section 408 is amended —

(1) in subsection (a), by striking out "Subject to the provisions of section 405(a), such" in the second sentence and inserting in lieu thereof "Such";

(2) in subsection (c)(2) —

(A) by striking out "all of the following conditions —" and inserting in lieu thereof "the following conditions";

(B) by striking out subparagraph (A); and

(C) by redesignating subparagraphs (B) and (C) as subparagraphs (A) and (B), respectively.

(b) Infringement Actions

(1) Registration as a Prerequisite. Section 411 is amended —

(A) by amending the section heading to read as follows:

§ 411. Registration and infringement actions;

(B) in subsection (a) by striking out "Subject" and inserting in lieu thereof "Except for actions for infringement of copyright in Berne Conventions works whose country of origin is not the United States, and subject"; and

(C) in subsection (b)(2) by inserting ", if required by subsection (a)," after "work".

(2) Table of Sections. The table of sections at the beginning of chapter 4 is amended by striking out the item relating to section 411 and inserting in lieu thereof the following:

§ 411. Registration and infringement actions

Sec. 10. Copyright Infringement and Remedies

(a) Infringement. Section 501(b) is amended by striking out "sections 205(d) and 411," and inserting in lieu thereof "section 411."

(b) Damages and Profits. Section 504(c) is amended —

(1) in paragraph (1) —

(A) by striking out "$250", and inserting in lieu thereof "$500"; and

(B) by striking out "$10,000", and inserting in lieu thereof "$20,000"; and

(2) in paragraph (2) —

(A) by striking out "$50,000.", and inserting in lieu thereof "100,000."; and

(B) by striking out "$100.", and inserting in lieu thereof "$200.".

Sec. 11. Copyright Royalty Tribunal

Chapter 8 is amended —

(1) in section 801, by adding at the end of subsection (b) the following:

In determining whether a return to a copyright owner under section 116 is fair, appropriate weight shall be given to —

(i) the rates previously determined by the Tribunal to provide a fair return to the copyright owner, and

(ii) the rates contained in any license negotiated pursuant to section 116A of this title; and

(2) by amending section 804(a)(2)(C) to read as follows:

(C)(i) In proceedings under section 801(b)(1) concerning the adjustment of royalty rates as provided in section 11[6], such petition may be filed in 1990 and in each subsequent tenth calendar year, and at any time within 1 year after negotiated licenses authorized by section 116A are terminated or expire and are not replaced by subsequent agreements.

(ii) If negotiated licenses authorized by section 116A come into force so as to supersede previous determinations of the Tribunal, as provided in section 116A(d), but thereafter are terminated or expire and are not replaced by subsequent agreements, the Tribunal shall, upon petition of any party to such terminated or expired negotiated license agreement, promptly establish an interim royalty rate or rates for the public performance by means of a coin–operated phonorecord player of nondramatic musical works embodied in phonorecords which had been subject to the terminated or expired negotiated license agreement. Such interim royalty rate or rates shall be the same as the last such rate or rates and shall remain in force until the conclusion of proceedings to adjust the royalty rates applicable to such works, or until superseded by a new negotiated license agreement, as provided in section 116A(d).

Sec. 12. Works in the Public Domain

Title 17, United States Code, as amended by this Act, does not provide copyright protection for any work that is in the public domain in the United States.

Sec. 13. Effective Date; Effect on Pending Cases

(a) Effective Date. This Act and the amendments made by this Act take effect on the date on which the Berne Convention (as defined in section 101 of title 17, United States Code) enters into force with respect to the United States.

(b) Effect on Pending Cases. Any cause of action arising under title 17, United States Code, before the effective date of this Act shall be governed by the provisions of such title as in effect when the cause of action arose.

GATT/TRIPs and NAFTA

Summary Overview of GATT/TRIPs and NAFTA[1]

INTRODUCTION

As copyright became a trade issue (first seen in the Caribbean Basin Economic Initiative of 1983 and the General System of Preferences renewal of 1984), the next logical step was to include intellectual property provisions in multilateral trade agreements.

NAFTA

The first trade agreement entered into by the United States to extend retroactive protection to foreign works was the North American Free Trade Agreement ("NAFTA") of January 1, 1994. This protection, limited to Canadian and Mexican motion pictures and works first published in motion pictures, was codified in § 104A of Title 17. Statements of intent to claim a restored copyright were required to be filed with the U.S. Copyright Office by December 31, 1995, else no protection could be claimed. Restored protection was granted for the term of protection the work would otherwise have been granted, but was limited to works that fell into the public domain for failure to comply with the 1976 Act's notice provisions.

The Copyright Office filed its list of those claiming protection under NAFTA § 104A on February 13, 1995. 60 Fed. Reg. 8252. The Office's final regulations establishing procedures for filing Statements of Intent for restoration were not published until November 15, 1994, 59 Fed. Reg. 1994, almost one year after NAFTA was signed, and only six weeks before the one-year window for filing such statements closed. Interim regulations were published on March 16, 1994. 59 Fed. Reg. 12162. Only four comments were received on the interim regulations, including one from the Mexican government, requesting that works published before January 1, 1978 without notice be included. The request was denied.

---

[1] Abbreviated, adapted and updated from an address by William F. Patry to the State Bar of Texas Section on Intellectual Property on June 3, 1995. For fuller discussion, see William F. Patry, COPYRIGHT AND THE GATT: AN INTERPRETATION AND LEGISLATIVE HISTORY OF THE URUGUAY ROUND AGREEMENTS ACT (BNA 1995).

GATT/TRIPs

The GATT Implementing Legislation

The biggest accomplishment of the 103d Congress in the field of copyright was, without question, passage of Public Law No. 103-465, legislation implementing the United States' obligations — and then some — under the Uruguay Round of the General Agreement on Tariffs and Trade ("GATT").

The United States' lack of success in solving serious disputes with the European Union over national treatment for audiovisual works and sound recordings, content quotas on broadcasts and television, and market access for audiovisual works threatened completion of the Uruguay Round. Nevertheless, the component of the Uruguay Round agreements concerning Trade–Related Aspects of Intellectual Property Rights ("TRIPs") contains a number of provisions that are beneficial for U.S. copyright owners, including (1) a requirement that GATT contracting parties comply with Articles 1 through 21 of the Berne Convention (with the important exception of Article 6 *bis*); (2) protection for computer programs as literary works under Berne; (3) protection for data bases; (4) a rental right for computer programs and phonorecords; (5) restrictions on countries' ability to provide extensive exceptions to protection; (6) protection for sound recordings; and (7) strong enforcement of rights requirements.

Two principles of the Uruguay Round Agreements must be mentioned. First, with respect to the United States at least, the Agreements are not self-executing. They must be implemented in our domestic laws. Second, the Agreements are not a treaty. The Senate did not give its advice and consent. The only action by the U.S. Congress was passage of the implementing legislation that became Public Law No. 103-465. Thus, as with the Berne Convention Implementation Act of 1988, the only law that matters is domestic U.S. law: actions cannot be brought in U.S. courts directly under the TRIPs Agreement, nor can that Agreement form the basis of U.S. law.

Enactment of the Uruguay Round Agreements Act

Shortly after the United States and its trading partners signed the Uruguay Round Agreements on April 15, 1994 in Marrakesh, informal discussions about the content of the implementing legislation began between the Clinton Administration, represented principally by the Office of the U.S. Trade Representative ("USTR"), and the Congressional copyright subcommittees. The USTR divided possible legislative initiatives into two categories: (1) necessary and (2) appropriate (or better, "discretionary"). According to the USTR, in the copyright field only, repeal of the October 1997 computer program rental sunset was necessary to satisfy the United States' TRIPs obligations. The Congressional copyright subcommittees expressed an interest, however, in including federal anti-bootlegging provisions and a provision to implement the retroactivity requirements of Article 18 of the Berne Convention.

On August 3, 1994, Rep. William J. Hughes, chair of the House Subcommittee on Intellectual Property and Judicial Administration, introduced for discussion purposes a bill containing a repeal of the computer program rental sunset, a civil federal anti-bootlegging statute, and retroactive protection for foreign works from Berne and WTO countries in the public domain in the United States. On August 5, 1994, Sen. Dennis DeConcini, chair of the Senate Subcommittee on Patents, Copyrights, and Trademarks, introduced, also for discussion purposes, the USTR's draft bill. The introduction of the bills was timed to coincide with a joint hearing held by the subcommittees on August 12, 1994. After the hearings, the subcommittees and the USTR jointly drafted compromise intellectual property provisions, which were included in the final text of the bill submitted by the Administration and introduced in both houses on September 27, 1994.

That bill, H.R. 5110, was passed by the House on November 29, 1994. The Senate debated H.R. 5110 on November 30 and December 1, 1994, passing it on December 1. On December 8, 1994, President Clinton signed the bill into law as the Uruguay Round Agreements Act ("URAA").

The Copyright Components of the URAA

Title V of the URAA contains a number of amendments to U.S. intellectual property laws. Subtitle A includes the provisions on copyright and related rights; Subtitle B, trademark; and Subtitle C, patents.

The copyright subtitle has four components:

1. Section 511 makes permanent the ban enacted by Congress in 1990, Act. of Dec. 1, 1990, Pub. L. No. 101-650, Title VIII, 101st Cong., 2d Sess., 104 Stat. 5089, 5134-37, on the rental of computer programs for purposes of direct or indirect commercial advantage. The legislation was scheduled to "sunset" on October 1, 1997. URAA § 511 strikes the sunset provision of the 1990 Act. No substantive amendment to the Copyright Act itself was required;

2. Section 512 adds to Title 17, United States Code, a new Chapter 11. Chapter 11 provides a new civil cause of action for performers to prevent the unauthorized fixation or communication to the public of the sound or sounds and images of their live musical performances, as well as the unauthorized reproduction, distribution, sale, rental, or "trafficking in" of copies or phonorecords made from such unauthorized fixations. New Chapter 11 — which contains a single section, § 1101 — is *not* a part of the Copyright Act;

3. Section 513 concerns the same activities as section 512 (*i.e.*, "bootlegs" of live musical performances). Section 513, however, provides new criminal penalties for such activities by adding to Title 18, United States Code, new § 2319A,

applicable where the bootlegging occurs "knowingly, and for purposes of commercial advantage or private financial gain"; and

4.   Section 514, the most far-reaching of the URAA provisions concerning copyright and related rights, provides retroactive protection for works whose source country is a member of the Berne Convention or the World Trade Organization or is the subject of a presidential proclamation, if the subject works are in the public domain in the United States through failure to comply with U.S. formalities, lack of national eligibility, or, in the case of pre-1972 sound recordings, lack of subject matter protection. URAA § 514 also amends the Copyright Act's § 109(a) first sale doctrine to provide that copies or phonorecords of *restored works* made or manufactured before the date of restoration — or, in the case of reliance parties, before notice — may be disposed of for "direct or indirect commercial advantage" *only* during the one-year sell-off period allowed for reliance parties.

Section 511[2] : Computer Program Rental

In 1990, Congress banned the rental of computer programs for purposes of direct or indirect commercial advantage. The legislation was scheduled to "sunset" (expire) on October 1, 1997. Section 511 of the URAA fulfills the United States' obligation under Article 11 of the TRIPs Agreement with respect to computer programs by striking the sunset provision in the 1990 Act, thereby making the rental ban permanent. No substantive changes were required or made to § 109 of the Copyright Act.

Sections 512 and 513: "Bootlegs" of Live Musical Performances

Section 512: Civil Cause of Action

1. The Right Granted

Section 512 of the URAA creates a new Chapter 11 in Title 17, United States Code. Chapter 11 contains one section, § 1101, the operative portion of which is subsection (a):

(a) Unauthorized acts. Anyone who, without the consent of the performer or performers involved—

(1) fixes the sounds or sounds and images of a live musical performance in a copy or phonorecord, or reproduces copies or phonorecords of such a performance from an unauthorized fixation,

---

[2] The section numbers in this and the following headings refer to the relevant section of the implementing legislation, not to a section of the Copyright Act.

(2) transmits or otherwise communicates to the public the sounds or sounds and images of a live musical performance, or

(3) distributes or offers to distribute, sells or offers to sell, rents or offers to rent, or traffics in any copy or phonorecord fixed as described in paragraph (1), regardless of whether the fixations occurred in the United States,

shall be subject to the remedies provided in §§ 502 through 505, to the same extent as an infringer of copyright.

2. Constitutional Basis of the Right

Although § 1101 is part of Title 17, it is not a copyright right, but instead an independent right based on the Commerce Clause, placed in Title 17 for purposes of administrative convenience, such as use of the definitions in § 101 (*e.g.*, "fixed," "copy," or "phonorecord").

3. Ownership of the Right

Section 1101(a) grants rights to the "performer or performers" of a "live musical performance." The term "performer" is not defined. In order to ensure that the § 1101(a) right can not be defeated by incidental or pick-up musicians, the term "or performers" was included so that the consent of *all* performers must be obtained. This rule of unanimity is absolute.

4. "Live Musical Performance"

Another important undefined term is "live musical performance." One interpretation of the term is to construe it in relation to its opposite: a prerecorded musical performance. Another interpretation of "live musical performance" would limit it to its colloquial meaning: performances in front of public audiences. This latter interpretation is, however, inconsistent another aspect of the § 1101 right that may easily be overlooked by copyright lawyers: the right is not limited to "public" live musical performances; *any* live musical performance is within the scope of the right.

5. National Eligibility Requirements

There is no national eligibility requirement in § 1101 since the section simply extends rights to a "performer or performers." Thus, all performers throughout the world are entitled to the rights granted in § 1101.

6. Remedies

Actions for violation of § 1101(a)(1) must be brought in federal district court by the performer or performers whose rights have been violated or by their heirs or assignees. Because there are no registration requirements or other formalities, actions are brought merely by filing a complaint, with the full remedies provided in §§ 502 through 505 of Title 17 being available, so long as the violation occurred within the three-year statute of limitations set forth in § 507(b).

7. Duration of the Right

There is no limitation on the duration of the § 1101 right, and the right is thus perpetual.

8. Protection of Preexisting Live Musical Performances

Section 1101 applies both to unauthorized fixations of live musical performances that occur on or after the date of enactment (December 8, 1994, which is also the effective date) and to unauthorized fixations and reproductions of such fixations that occurred before that date, although there is liability only for acts that occur after the date of enactment.

Section 513: Criminal Provisions for Bootlegs

Section 513 of the URAA makes it a criminal offense in new 18 U.S.C. § 2319A(a) to engage in the same activities covered by § 512 provided those activities are done "knowingly, and for purposes of commercial advantage or private financial gain." The quoted language is taken from the 1992 omnibus revision of the criminal copyright provisions, as are the penalties: five years and/or a fine for a first violation, and 10 years and/or a fine for a second or subsequent offense.

Section 514: Retroactivity

Article 9 of the TRIPs Agreement obligates WTO members to comply with Articles 1 through 21 of the 1971 text of the Berne Convention for the protection of Literary and Artistic Works, with the exception of Article 6*bis* (which provides for *droit moral*). Article 18 of the Berne Convention requires a country newly adhering to the Berne Union to provide protection to the preexisting works of already adhering members unless those works are in the public domain either in their country of origin or in the newly adhering country as a result of the expiration of their term of protection.

Article 18 of the Berne Convention has particular significance for the United States, because the U.S. is virtually the only country to have imposed formalities on the enjoyment and exercise of copyright, including at various times requirements of affixing a notice to copies of the work, filing a renewal application, mandatory deposit, and domestic manufacture.

Retroactivity Under the URAA

Nature of Protection and Effective Date

Retroactivity under NAFTA was conditioned on compliance with a formality (filing with the Copyright Office). By contrast, retroactivity as set forth in § 104A(a) as amended by the URAA is automatic: "Copyright subsists, in accordance with this section, and vests automatically on the date of restoration."

Effective Date

The date on which protection is granted for preexisting works under § 514 of the URAA is determined by reference to the "date of restoration." That term is defined in § 104A(h)(2) as the later of:

(A) the date on which the Agreement on Trade-Related Aspects of Intellectual Property referred to in § 101(d)(15) of the Uruguay Round Agreements Act enters into force with respect to the United States, if the source country of the restored work is a nation adhering to the Berne Convention or a WTO member country on such date; or

(B) the date of adherence or proclamation, in the case of any other source country of the restored work.

The Agreement on Trade-Related Aspects of Intellectual Property entered into force with respect to the United States according to § 101(b) of the URAA on the date the President determined that "a sufficient number of foreign countries are accepting the obligations of the Uruguay Round Agreements . . . to ensure the effective operation of, and adequate benefits for the United States" under, those agreements.

On December 23, 1994, by proclamation, President Clinton directed the United States Trade Representative to publish in the Federal Register a memorandum declaring, pursuant to § 101(b), that a sufficient number of countries had accepted the obligations of the Uruguay Round Agreements, and that the United States would, as of January 1, 1995, accept those agreements. The Agreement on the Trade-Related Aspects of Intellectual Property thus entered into force on January 1, 1995. From this, one might have concluded that, pursuant to § 104A(h)(2)(A), the "date of restoration" was January 1, 1995 for works whose source country was a nation that adhered either to the Berne Convention or was a WTO member as of that date.

Nevertheless, on March 23, 1995, President Clinton issued a second proclamation setting January 1, 1996 as the effective date for § 104A(h)(A). For elaboration, see 60 Fed. Reg. 15845 (Mar. 27, 1995).

In addition, the Copyright Office issued a policy decision specifying January 1, 1996 as the initial effective date, 60 Fed. Reg. 7793-95 (Feb. 9, 1995). And finally, in a technical corrections act, Pub. L. No. 105-80, 111 Stat. 1529, signed by President Clinton on November 5, 1997, Congress itself declared January 1, 1996 to have been the effective date of the restoration provisions. The matter, thus, appears to be settled.

Automatic Restoration

If the source country of the restored work was a Berne or WTO member, copyright in all preexisting original works of authorship from that country were automatically restored. No filing with the Copyright Office or other formality is required to obtain protection.

Ownership of the Restored Copyright: § 104A(b)

Section 104A(b) generally follows the principle of § 201(a): copyright in a restored work vests initially in the author of the work. Section 104A(b), however, adds to this basic principle the vesting of restored copyright in the "initial rightholder" to take into account the fact that in many countries sound recordings are protected under neighboring rights regimes, not under copyright. In such countries, there is no "author" of "copyright" in a sound recording; instead, there is an "initial rightholder." The term "initial rightholder" does *not* include other types of subject matter, such as motion pictures, nor more generally work-for-hire situations. "Initial rightholder" is strictly limited to sound recordings.

Transferees are *not* initial authors or rightholders. Instead, transferees of the initial author or rightholder are left to state court contract actions to secure whatever rights they have by virtue of their contract with the author or rightholder.

Under § 104A(b), the question of who is the initial author or rightholder is determined in federal court according to the law of the source country of the work. This statutory conflict of laws provision requires U.S. courts to decide the issue of initial ownership of the restored copyright not by looking at the U.S. Copyright Act, but by looking to the law of foreign source country, a task that may include examination not only of foreign statutes, but also foreign regulations and foreign case law.

Duration of Protection in Restored Works

Section 104A(1)(B) states that copyright in restored works will subsist "for the remainder of the term of copyright that the work would have otherwise been granted in the United States if the work never entered the public domain in the United States." Unlike ownership of restored works, which is determined by the law of the foreign source country, the term of protection is governed solely by U.S. law. That law will be either the 1909 or the 1976 Act, depending upon the date of first publication or creation of the work.

Remedies: § 104A(d)

For purposes of remedies only, the URAA distinguishes between two categories of persons: "reliance parties" and others (non-reliance parties). This distinction takes into account the interests of persons who before restoration (that is, while the work was in the public domain in the United States) either acquired copies or phonorecords of a restored work or created derivative works based on a restored work. Where a person is not a reliance party, all of the remedies granted in Chapter 5 of Title 17, United States Code, are available with respect to any act of infringement that commenced on or after the date of restoration (usually, January 1, 1995). All of the conditions applicable to the awarding of the Chapter 5 remedies also apply, such as registration with the Copyright Act before infringement in order to collect statutory damages and attorney's fees (§ 412), and in the case of works whose country of origin is not a member of the Berne Convention (or is the United States), registration before an infringement suit is instituted (§ 411(a)).

1. Remedies Against Reliance Parties: §§ 104A(d)(2)-(4)

"Reliance party" is defined in § 104A(h)(4) as any person who,

(A) with respect to a particular work, engages in acts, before the source country of that work becomes an eligible country, which would have violated section 106 if the restored work had been subject to copyright protection, and who, after the source country becomes an eligible country, continues to engage in such acts;

(B) before the source country of a particular work becomes an eligible country, makes or acquires one or more copies or phonorecords of that work; or

(C) as the result of the sale or other disposition of a derivative work covered under subsection(d)(3), or significant assets of a person described in subparagraph (A) or (B), is a successor, assignee, or licensee of that person.

Reliance status must be established for each individual work for which it is claimed: one does not gain such status for more than one work by establishing reliance party status for one work.

2. Notices of Intent and the Cut-Off of Reliance Party Immunity

Although the availability of reliance party status was generally cut off on January 1, 1996 (the general date of restoration), the remedies available against reliance parties are governed separately by § 104A(d)(2). Subparagraphs (A) and (B) of that section give the restored copyright owner two options for securing the maximum possible remedies. Under § 104A(d)(2)(A)(i), the restored copyright owner may, during the two-year period beginning on the date of restoration, file with the Copyright Office a notice of intent to enforce the restored copyright as provided by § 104A(e)(1). If such a notice is filed, it is effective, once published in the Federal Register, as to all reliance parties. Alternatively, at any time during the term of protection of the restored copyright, the restored copyright owner may serve directly on the reliance party a notice of intent to enforce the restored copyright as provided by § 104A(e)(2).

When a notice of intent to enforce a restored copyright has been filed either with the Copyright Office or directly on a reliance party, § 104A(d)(2)(A) & (B), with its backwards phrasing, creates the following results with respect to remedies: until the restored copyright owner either files a notice of intent to enforce its restored copyright with the Copyright Office (and that notice is published in the Federal Register) or serves actual notice on the reliance party, the reliance party may continue to exploit the work without liability even though such exploitation technically constitutes infringement. Once the notice has been published in the Federal Register or served on the reliance party, no further copies or phonorecords may be made; if they are made, full liability results. For conduct that would otherwise be infringing (except for reproduction), a reliance party may during the 12-month period after publication of the notice in the Federal Register or service of actual notice engage in that conduct (such as selling off existing stock). Full liability arises for infringing conduct that arises after the 12-month period expires.

The Copyright Office's Final Regulations

On September 29, 1995, the Copyright Office issued final regulations to implement the URAA, effective January 1, 1996. 60 Fed. Reg. 50414. With one exception,[3] the regulations are fairly unremarkable. The Office will permit an owner of multiple restored works to file a single notice of intent if each work is identified by title, has the same author, is owned by the same copyright owner, and the rights owned are the same. Acknowledgments of notices will be filed and records of notices filed will be stored in the Library of Congress's computer COPICS database and published in the Federal Register. Helpfully, the Office has created a suggested form for notices of intent, available also over the Internet.

For information concerning all of these matters, including forms for registering restored works (GATT, GATT/GRP, and GATT/CON) and current fees ($30 for a single work, effective through June 30, 2002), consult the Copyright Office website at www.loc.gov/copyright. Incidentally, in a "first" for the Office, credit cards are acceptable for filings but only under the URAA!

---

[3] Based on its belief that it "seems essential to retain the concept of claimant since the authors may no longer be alive," the Copyright Office will permit the "owner of an exclusive right" to file simultaneously for registration of a restored copyright (not to be confused with a notice of intent to enforce the restored copyright against reliance parties). The statute, however, in specifying who may file for simultaneous registration, refers in § 104A(e)(1)(D)(ii) to "owners of restored copyrights"; and § 104A(b) provides that ownership of a restored copyright "vests initially in the author or initial rightholder of the work as determined by the law of the source country of the work." Thus, the Office will accept multiple, and possibly adverse, registrations (and notices) for the same work. Congress appears to have distinguished, clearly and deliberately, between who may file a simultaneous registration for a restored work (the author) and who may file a notice of intent (the owner of the restored copyright *or* the owner of an exclusive right therein) — in short, to have limited the restoration right itself to the *author*, and not to assignees. By also permitting the *owner of an exclusive right* to file for registration, the regulations seem to defeat that Congressional purpose.

TRIPs AGREEMENT

AGREEMENT ON TRADE-RELATED ASPECTS OF INTELLECTUAL PROPERTY RIGHTS

Members,

Desiring to reduce distortions and impediments to international trade, and taking into account the need to promote effective and adequate protection of intellectual property rights, and to ensure that measures and procedures to enforce intellectual property rights do not themselves become barriers to legitimate trade;

Recognizing, to this end, the need for new rules and disciplines concerning:

(a) the applicability of the basic principles of GATT 1994 and of relevant international intellectual property agreements or conventions;

(b) the provision of adequate standards and principles concerning the availability, scope and use of trade-related intellectual property rights;

(c) the provision of effective and appropriate means for the enforcement of trade-related intellectual property rights, taking into account differences in national legal systems;

(d) the provision of effective and expeditious procedures for the multilateral prevention and settlement of disputes between governments; and

(e) transitional arrangements aiming at the fullest participation in the results of the negotiations;

Recognizing the need for a multilateral framework of principles, rules and disciplines dealing with international trade in counterfeit goods;

Recognizing that intellectual property rights are private rights;

Recognizing the underlying public policy objectives of national systems for the protection of intellectual property, including developmental and technological objectives;

Recognizing also the special needs of the least-developed country Members in respect of maximum flexibility in the domestic implementation of laws and regulations in order to enable them to create a sound and viable technological base;

Emphasizing the importance of reducing tensions by reaching strengthened commitments to resolve disputes on trade-related intellectual property issues through multilateral procedures;

Desiring to establish a mutually supportive relationship between the WTO and the World Intellectual Property Organization (referred to in this Agreement as "WIPO") as well as other relevant international organizations;

Hereby agree as follows:

PART I
GENERAL PROVISIONS AND BASIC PRINCIPLES

Article 1

1. Members shall give effect to the provisions of this Agreement. Members may, but shall not be obliged to, implement in their law more extensive protection than is required by this Agreement, provided that such protection does not contravene the provisions of this Agreement. Members shall be free to determine the appropriate method of implementing the provisions of this Agreement within their own legal system and practice.

2. For the purposes of this Agreement, the term "intellectual property" refers to all categories of intellectual property that are the subject of Sections 1 through 7 of Part II.

3. Members shall accord the treatment provided for in this Agreement to the nationals of other Members.[1] In respect of the relevant intellectual property right, the nationals of other Members shall be understood as those natural or legal persons that would meet the criteria for eligibility for

---

[1] When "nationals" are referred to in this Agreement, they shall be deemed, in the case of a separate customs territory Member of the WTO, to mean persons, natural or legal, who are domiciled or who have a real and effective industrial or commercial establishment in that customs territory.

protection provided for in the Paris Convention (1967), the Berne Convention (1971), the Rome Convention and the Treaty on Intellectual Property in Respect of Integrated Circuits, were all Members of the WTO members of those conventions.[2] Any Member availing itself of the possibilities provided in paragraph 3 of Article 5 or paragraph 2 of Article 6 of the Rome Convention shall make a notification as foreseen in those provisions to the Council for Trade-Related Aspects of Intellectual Property Rights (the "Council for TRIPS").

Article 2

1. In respect of Parts II, III and IV of this Agreement, Members shall comply with Articles 1 through 12, and Article 19, of the Paris Convention (1967).

2. Nothing in Parts I to IV of this Agreement shall derogate from existing obligations that Members may have to each other under the Paris Convention, the Berne Convention, the Rome Convention and the Treaty on Intellectual Property in Respect of Integrated Circuits.

Article 3

1. Each Member shall accord to the nationals of other Members treatment no less favourable than that it accords to its own nationals with regard to the protection[3] of intellectual property, subject to the exceptions already provided in, respectively, the Paris Convention (1967), the Berne Convention (1971), the Rome Convention or the Treaty on Intellectual Property in Respect of Integrated Circuits. In respect of performers, producers of phonograms and broadcasting organizations, this obligation only applies in respect of the rights provided under this Agreement. Any Member availing itself of the possibilities provided in Article 6 of the Berne Convention (1971) or paragraph 1(b) of Article 16 of the Rome Convention shall make a notification as foreseen in those provisions to the Council for TRIPS.

---

[2] In this Agreement, "Paris Convention" refers to the Paris Convention for the Protection of Industrial Property; "Paris Convention (1967)" refers to the Stockholm Act of this Convention of 14 July 1967. "Berne Convention" refers to the Berne Convention for the Protection of Literary and Artistic Works; "Berne Convention (1971)" refers to the Paris Act of this Convention of 24 July 1971. "Rome Convention" refers to the International Convention for the Protection of Performers, Producers of Phonograms and Broadcasting Organizations, adopted at Rome on 26 October 1961. "Treaty on Intellectual Property in Respect of Integrated Circuits" (IPIC Treaty) refers to the Treaty on Intellectual Property in Respect of Integrated Circuits, adopted at Washington on 26 May 1989. "WTO Agreement" refers to the Agreement Establishing the WTO.

[3] For the purposes of Articles 3 and 4, "protection" shall include matters affecting the availability, acquisition, scope, maintenance and enforcement of intellectual property rights as well as those matters affecting the use of intellectual property rights specifically addressed in this Agreement.

2. Members may avail themselves of the exceptions permitted under paragraph 1 in relation to judicial and administrative procedures, including the designation of an address for service or the appointment of an agent within the jurisdiction of a Member, only where such exceptions are necessary to secure compliance with laws and regulations which are not inconsistent with the provisions of this Agreement and where such practices are not applied in a manner which would constitute a disguised restriction on trade.

Article 4

With regard to the protection of intellectual property, any advantage, favour, privilege or immunity granted by a Member to the nationals of any other country shall be accorded immediately and unconditionally to the nationals of all other Members. Exempted from this obligation are any advantage, favour, privilege or immunity accorded by a Member:

(a) deriving from international agreements on judicial assistance or law enforcement of a general nature and not particularly confined to the protection of intellectual property;

(b) granted in accordance with the provisions of the Berne Convention (1971) or the Rome Convention authorizing that the treatment accorded be a function not of national treatment but of the treatment accorded in another country;

(c) in respect of the rights of performers, producers of phonograms and broadcasting organizations not provided under this Agreement;

(d) deriving from international agreements related to the protection of intellectual property which entered into force prior to the entry into force of the WTO Agreement, provided that such agreements are notified to the Council for TRIPS and do not constitute an arbitrary or unjustifiable discrimination against nationals of other Members.

Article 5

The obligations under Articles 3 and 4 do not apply to procedures provided in multilateral agreements concluded under the auspices of WIPO relating to the acquisition or maintenance of intellectual property rights.

Article 6

For the purposes of dispute settlement under this Agreement, subject to the provisions of Articles 3 and 4 nothing in this Agreement shall be used to address the issue of the exhaustion of intellectual property rights.

Article 7

The protection and enforcement of intellectual property rights should contribute to the promotion of technological innovation and to the transfer and dissemination of technology, to the mutual advantage of producers and users of technological knowledge and in a manner conducive to social and economic welfare, and to a balance of rights and obligations. *

Article 8

1. Members may, in formulating or amending their laws and regulations, adopt measures necessary to protect public health and nutrition, and to promote the public interest in sectors of vital importance to their socio-economic and technological development, provided that such measures are consistent with the provisions of this Agreement.

2. Appropriate measures, provided that they are consistent with the provisions of this Agreement, may be needed to prevent the abuse of intellectual property rights by right holders or the resort to practices which unreasonably restrain trade or adversely affect the international transfer of technology.

PART II
STANDARDS CONCERNING THE AVAILABILITY, SCOPE AND USE OF INTELLECTUAL PROPERTY RIGHTS

SECTION 1: COPYRIGHT AND RELATED RIGHTS

Article 9

1. Members shall comply with Articles 1 through 21 of the Berne Convention (1971) and the Appendix thereto. However, Members shall not have rights or obligations under this Agreement in respect of the rights conferred under Article 6*bis* of that Convention or of the rights derived therefrom.

2. Copyright protection shall extend to expressions and not to ideas, procedures, methods of operation or mathematical concepts as such.

Article 10

1. Computer programs, whether in source or object code, shall be protected as literary works under the Berne Convention (1971).

2. Compilations of data or other material, whether in machine readable or other form, which by reason of the selection or arrangement of their contents constitute intellectual creations shall be protected as such. Such protection, which shall not extend to the data or material itself, shall be without prejudice to any copyright subsisting in the data or material itself.

Article 11

In respect of at least computer programs and cinematographic works, a Member shall provide authors and their successors in title the right to authorize or to prohibit the commercial rental to the public of originals or copies of their copyright works. A Member shall be excepted from this obligation in respect of cinematographic works unless such rental has led to widespread copying of such works which is materially impairing the exclusive right of reproduction conferred in that Member on authors and their successors in title. In respect of computer programs, this obligation does not apply to rentals where the program itself is not the essential object of the rental.

Article 12

Whenever the term of protection of a work, other than a photographic work or a work of applied art, is calculated on a basis other than the life of a natural person, such term shall be no less than 50 years from the end of the calendar year of authorized publication, or, failing such authorized publication within 50 years from the making of the work, 50 years from the end of the calendar year of making.

Article 13

Members shall confine limitations or exceptions to exclusive rights to certain special cases which do not conflict with a normal exploitation of the work and do not unreasonably prejudice the legitimate interests of the right holder.

Article 14

1. In respect of a fixation of their performance on a phonogram, performers shall have the possibility of preventing the following acts when undertaken without their authorization: the fixation of their unfixed performance and the reproduction of such fixation. Performers shall also have the possibility of preventing the following acts when undertaken without their authorization: the broadcasting by wireless means and the communication to the public of their live performance.

2. Producers of phonograms shall enjoy the right to authorize or prohibit the direct or indirect reproduction of their phonograms.

3. Broadcasting organizations shall have the right to prohibit the following acts when undertaken without their authorization: the fixation, the reproduction of fixations, and the rebroadcasting by wireless means of broadcasts, as well as the communication to the public of television broadcasts of the same. Where Members do not grant such rights to broadcasting organizations, they shall provide owners of copyright in the subject matter of broadcasts with the possibility of preventing the above acts, subject to the provisions of the Berne Convention (1971).

4. The provisions of Article 11 in respect of computer programs shall apply *mutatis mutandis* to producers of phonograms and any other right holders in phonograms as determined in a Member's law. If on 15 April 1994 a Member has in force a system of equitable remuneration of right holders in respect of the rental of phonograms, it may maintain such system provided that the commercial rental of phonograms is not giving rise to the material impairment of the exclusive rights of reproduction of right holders.

5. The term of the protection available under this Agreement to performers and producers of phonograms shall last at least until the end of a period of 50 years computed from the end of the calendar year in which the fixation

was made or the performance took place. The term of protection granted pursuant to paragraph 3 shall last for at least 20 years from the end of the calendar year in which the broadcast took place.

6. Any Member may, in relation to the rights conferred under paragraphs 1, 2 and 3, provide for conditions, limitations, exceptions and reservations to the extent permitted by the Rome Convention. However, the provisions of Article 18 of the Berne Convention (1971) shall also apply, *mutatis mutandis,* to the rights of performers and producers of phonograms in phonograms.

SECTION 2: TRADEMARKS

Article 15

1. Any sign, or any combination of signs, capable of distinguishing the goods or services of one undertaking from those of other undertakings, shall be capable of constituting a trademark. Such signs, in particular words including personal names, letters, numerals, figurative elements and combinations of colours as well as any combination of such signs, shall be eligible for registration as trademarks. Where signs are not inherently capable of distinguishing the relevant goods or services, Members may make registrability depend on distinctiveness acquired through use. Members may require, as a condition of registration, that signs be visually perceptible.

2. Paragraph 1 shall not be understood to prevent a Member from denying registration of a trademark on other grounds, provided that they do not derogate from the provisions of the Paris Convention (1967).

3. Members may make registrability depend on use. However, actual use of a trademark shall not be a condition for filing an application for registration. An application shall not be refused solely on the ground that intended use has not taken place before the expiry of a period of three years from the date of application.

4. The nature of the goods or services to which a trademark is to be applied shall in no case form an obstacle to registration of the trademark.

5. Members shall publish each trademark either before it is registered or promptly after it is registered and shall afford a reasonable opportunity for petitions to cancel the registration. In addition, Members may afford an opportunity for the registration of a trademark to be opposed.

Article 16

1. The owner of a registered trademark shall have the exclusive right to prevent all third parties not having the owner's consent from using in the course of trade identical or similar signs for goods or services which are identical or similar to those in respect of which the trademark is registered where such use would result in a likelihood of confusion. In case

of the use of an identical sign for identical goods or services, a likelihood of confusion shall be presumed. The rights described above shall not prejudice any existing prior rights, nor shall they affect the possibility of Members making rights available on the basis of use.

2. Article 6 *bis* of the Paris Convention (1967) shall apply, *mutatis mutandis,* to services. In determining whether a trademark is well-known, Members shall take account of the knowledge of the trademark in the relevant sector of the public, including knowledge in the Member concerned which has been obtained as a result of the promotion of the trademark.

3. Article 6 *bis* of the Paris Convention (1967) shall apply, *mutatis mutandis,* to goods or services which are not similar to those in respect of which a trademark is registered, provided that use of that trademark in relation to those goods or services would indicate a connection between those goods or services and the owner of the registered trademark and provided that the interests of the owner of the registered trademark are likely to be damaged by such use.

Article 17

Members may provide limited exceptions to the rights conferred by a trademark, such as fair use of descriptive terms, provided that such exceptions take account of the legitimate interests of the owner of the trademark and of third parties.

Article 18

Initial registration, and each renewal of registration, of a trademark shall be for a term of no less than seven years. The registration of a trademark shall be renewable indefinitely.

Article 19

1. If use is required to maintain a registration, the registration may be cancelled only after an uninterrupted period of at least three years of non-use, unless valid reasons based on the existence of obstacles to such use are shown by the trademark owner. Circumstances arising independently of the will of the owner of the trademark which constitute an obstacle to the use of the trademark, such as import restrictions on or other government requirements for goods or services protected by the trademark, shall be recognized as valid reasons for non-use.

2. When subject to the control of its owner, use of a trademark by another person shall be recognized as use of the trademark for the purpose of maintaining the registration.

Article 20

The use of a trademark in the course of trade shall not be unjustifiably encumbered by special requirements, such as use with another trademark, use in a special form or use in a manner detrimental to its capability to distinguish the goods or services of one undertaking from those of other undertakings. This will not preclude a requirement prescribing the use of the trademark identifying the undertaking producing the goods or services along with, but without linking it to, the trademark distinguishing the specific goods or services in question of that undertaking.

Article 21

Members may determine conditions on the licensing and assignment of trademarks, it being understood that the compulsory licensing of trademarks shall not be permitted and that the owner of a registered trademark shall have the right to assign the trademark with or without the transfer of the business to which the trademark belongs.

SECTION 3: GEOGRAPHICAL INDICATIONS

Article 22

1. Geographical indications are, for the purposes of this Agreement, indications which identify a good as originating in the territory of a Member, or a region or locality in that territory, where a given quality, reputation or other characteristic of the good is essentially attributable to its geographical origin.

2. In respect of geographical indications, Members shall provide the legal means for interested parties to prevent:

(a) the use of any means in the designation or presentation of a good that indicates or suggests that the good in question originates in a geographical area other than the true place of origin in a manner which misleads the public as to the geographical origin of the good;

(b) any use which constitutes an act of unfair competition within the meaning of Article 10 *bis* of the Paris Convention (1967).

3. A Member shall, *ex officio* if its legislation so permits or at the request of an interested party, refuse or invalidate the registration of a trademark which contains or consists of a geographical indication with respect to goods not originating in the territory indicated, if use of the indication in the trademark for such goods in that Member is of such a nature as to mislead the public as to the true place of origin.

4. The protection under paragraphs 1, 2 and 3 shall be applicable against a geographical indication which, although literally true as to the territory, region or locality in which the goods originate, falsely represents to the public that the goods originate in another territory.

Article 23

1. Each Member shall provide the legal means for interested parties to prevent use of a geographical indication identifying wines for wines not originating in the place indicated by the geographical indication in question or identifying spirits for spirits not originating in the place indicated by

the geographical indication in question, even where the true origin of the goods is indicated or the geographical indication is used in translation or accompanied by expressions such as "kind", "type", "style", "imitation" or the like.[4]

2. The registration of a trademark for wines which contains or consists of a geographical indication identifying wines or for spirits which contains or consists of a geographical indication identifying spirits shall be refused or invalidated, *ex officio* if a Member's legislation so permits or at the request of an interested party, with respect to such wines or spirits not having this origin.

3. In the case of homonymous geographical indications for wines, protection shall be accorded to each indication, subject to the provisions of paragraph 4 of Article 22. Each Member shall determine the practical conditions under which the homonymous indications in question will be differentiated from each other, taking into account the need to ensure equitable treatment of the producers concerned and that consumers are not misled.

4. In order to facilitate the protection of geographical indications for wines, negotiations shall be undertaken in the Council for TRIPS concerning the establishment of a multilateral system of notification and registration of geographical indications for wines eligible for protection in those Members participating in the system.

Article 24

1. Members agree to enter into negotiations aimed at increasing the protection of individual geographical indications under Article 23. The provisions of paragraphs 4 through 8 below shall not be used by a Member to refuse to conduct negotiations or to conclude bilateral or multilateral agreements. In the context of such negotiations, Members shall be willing to consider the continued applicability of these provisions to individual geographical indications whose use was the subject of such negotiations.

2. The Council for TRIPS shall keep under review the application of the provisions of this Section; the first such review shall take place within two years of the entry into force of the WTO Agreement. Any matter affecting the compliance with the obligations under these provisions may be drawn to the attention of the Council, which, at the request of a Member, shall consult with any Member or Members in respect of such matter in respect of which it has not been possible to find a satisfactory solution through bilateral or plurilateral consultations between the Members concerned. The Council shall take such action as may be agreed to facilitate the operation and further the objectives of this Section.

3. In implementing this Section, a Member shall not diminish the protection of geographical indications that existed in that Member immediately prior to the date of entry into force of the WTO Agreement.

---

[4] Notwithstanding the first sentence of Article 42, Members may, with respect to these obligations, instead provide for enforcement by administrative action.

4. Nothing in this Section shall require a Member to prevent continued and similar use of a particular geographical indication of another Member identifying wines or spirits in connection with goods or services by any of its nationals or domiciliaries who have used that geographical indication in a continuous manner with regard to the same or related goods or services in the territory of that Member either (a) for at least 10 years preceding 15 April 1994 or (b) in good faith preceding that date.

5. Where a trademark has been applied for or registered in good faith, or where rights to a trademark have been acquired through use in good faith either:

(a) before the date of application of these provisions in that Member as defined in Part VI; or

(b) before the geographical indication is protected in its country of origin;measures adopted to implement this Section shall not prejudice eligibility for or the validity of the registration of a trademark, or the right to use a trademark, on the basis that such a trademark is identical with, or similar to, a geographical indication.

6. Nothing in this Section shall require a Member to apply its provisions in respect of a geographical indication of any other Member with respect to goods or services for which the relevant indication is identical with the term customary in common language as the common name for such goods or services in the territory of that Member. Nothing in this Section shall require a Member to apply its provisions in respect of a geographical indication of any other Member with respect to products of the vine for which the relevant indication is identical with the customary name of a grape variety existing in the territory of that Member as of the date of entry into force of the WTO Agreement.

7. A Member may provide that any request made under this Section in connection with the use or registration of a trademark must be presented within five years after the adverse use of the protected indication has become generally known in that Member or after the date of registration of the trademark in that Member provided that the trademark has been published by that date, if such date is earlier than the date on which the adverse use became generally known in that Member, provided that the geographical indication is not used or registered in bad faith.

8. The provisions of this Section shall in no way prejudice the right of any person to use, in the course of trade, that person's name or the name of that person's predecessor in business, except where such name is used in such a manner as to mislead the public.

9. There shall be no obligation under this Agreement to protect geographical indications which are not or cease to be protected in their country of origin, or which have fallen into disuse in that country.

SECTION 4: INDUSTRIAL DESIGNS

Article 25

1. Members shall provide for the protection of independently created industrial designs that are new or original. Members may provide that designs are not new or original if they do not significantly differ from known designs or combinations of known design features. Members may provide that such protection shall not extend to designs dictated essentially by technical or functional considerations.

2. Each Member shall ensure that requirements for securing protection for textile designs, in particular in regard to any cost, examination or publication, do not unreasonably impair the opportunity to seek and obtain such protection. Members shall be free to meet this obligation through industrial design law or through copyright law.

Article 26

1. The owner of a protected industrial design shall have the right to prevent third parties not having the owner's consent from making, selling or importing articles bearing or embodying a design which is a copy, or substantially a copy, of the protected design, when such acts are undertaken for commercial purposes.

2. Members may provide limited exceptions to the protection of industrial designs, provided that such exceptions do not unreasonably conflict with the normal exploitation of protected industrial designs and do not unreasonably prejudice the legitimate interests of the owner of the protected design, taking account of the legitimate interests of third parties.

3. The duration of protection available shall amount to at least 10 years.

SECTION 5: PATENTS

Article 27

1. Subject to the provisions of paragraphs 2 and 3, patents shall be available for any inventions, whether products or processes, in all fields of technology, provided that they are new, involve an inventive step and are capable of industrial application.[5] Subject to paragraph 4 of Article 65, paragraph 8 of Article 70 and paragraph 3 of this Article, patents shall be available and patent rights enjoyable without discrimination as to the place of invention, the field of technology and whether products are imported or locally produced.

2. Members may exclude from patentability inventions, the prevention within their territory of the commercial exploitation of which is necessary

---

[5] For the purposes of the Article, the terms "inventive step" and "capable of industrial application" may be deemed by a Member to be synonymous with the terms "non-obvious" and "useful" respectively.

to protect *ordre public* or morality, including to protect human, animal or plant life or health or to avoid serious prejudice to the environment, provided that such exclusion is not made merely because the exploitation is prohibited by their law.

3. Members may also exclude from patentability:

(a) diagnostic, therapeutic and surgical methods for the treatment of humans or animals;

(b) plants and animals other than micro-organisms, and essentially biological processes for the production of plants or animals other than non-biological and microbiological processes. However, Members shall provide for the protection of plant varieties either by patents or by an effective *sui generis* system or by any combination thereof. The provisions of this subparagraph shall be reviewed four years after the date of entry into force of the WTO Agreement.

Article 28

1. A patent shall confer on its owner the following exclusive rights:

(a) where the subject matter of a patent is a product, to prevent third parties not having the owner's consent from the acts of: making, using, offering for sale, selling, or importing[6] for these purposes that product;

(b) where the subject matter of a patent is a process, to prevent third parties not having the owner's consent from the act of using the process, and from the acts of: using, offering for sale, selling, or importing for these purposes at least the product obtained directly by that process.

2. Patent owners shall also have the right to assign, or transfer by succession, the patent and to conclude licensing contracts.

Article 29

1. Members shall require that an applicant for a patent shall disclose the invention in a manner sufficiently clear and complete for the invention to be carried out by a person skilled in the art and may require the applicant to indicate the best mode for carrying out the invention known to the inventor at the filing date or, where priority is claimed, at the priority date of the application.

2. Members may require an applicant for a patent to provide information concerning the applicant's corresponding foreign applications and grants.

Article 30

Members may provide limited exceptions to the exclusive rights conferred by a patent, provided that such exceptions do not unreasonably conflict with a normal exploitation of the patent and do not unreasonably prejudice the

---

[6] This right, like all other rights conferred under this Agreement in respect of the use, sale, importation or other distribution of goods, is subject to the provisions of Article 6.

legitimate interests of the patent owner, taking account of the legitimate interests of third parties.

Article 31

Where the law of a Member allows for other use[7] of the subject matter of a patent without the authorization of the right holder, including use by the government or third parties authorized by the government, the following provisions shall be respected:

(a) authorization of such use shall be considered on its individual merits;

(b) such use may only be permitted if, prior to such use, the proposed user has made efforts to obtain authorization from the right holder on reasonable commercial terms and conditions and that such efforts have not been successful within a reasonable period of time. This requirement may be waived by a Member in the case of a national emergency or other circumstances of extreme urgency or in cases of public non-commercial use. In situations of national emergency or other circumstances of extreme urgency, the right holder shall, nevertheless, be notified as soon as reasonably practicable. In the case of public non-commercial use, where the government or contractor, without making a patent search, knows or has demonstrable grounds to know that a valid patent is or will be used by or for the government, the right holder shall be informed promptly;

(c) the scope and duration of such use shall be limited to the purpose for which it was authorized, and in the case of semi-conductor technology shall only be for public non-commercial use or to remedy a practice determined after judicial or administrative process to be anti-competitive;

(d) such use shall be non-exclusive;

(e) such use shall be non-assignable, except with that part of the enterprise or goodwill which enjoys such use;

(f) any such use shall be authorized predominantly for the supply of the domestic market of the Member authorizing such use;

(g) authorization for such use shall be liable, subject to adequate protection of the legitimate interests of the persons so authorized, to be terminated if and when the circumstances which led to it cease to exist and are unlikely to recur. The competent authority shall have the authority to review, upon motivated request, the continued existence of these circumstances;

(h) the right holder shall be paid adequate remuneration in the circumstances of each case, taking into account the economic value of the authorization;

(i) the legal validity of any decision relating to the authorization of such use shall be subject to judicial review or other independent review by a distinct higher authority in that Member;

---

[7] "Other use" refers to use other than that allowed under Article 30.

(j) any decision relating to the remuneration provided in respect of such use shall be subject to judicial review or other independent review by a distinct higher authority in that Member;

(k) Members are not obliged to apply the conditions set forth in subparagraphs (b) and (f) where such use is permitted to remedy a practice determined after judicial or administrative process to be anti-competitive. The need to correct anti-competitive practices may be taken into account in determining the amount of remuneration in such cases. Competent authorities shall have the authority to refuse termination of authorization if and when the conditions which led to such authorization are likely to recur;

(l) where such use is authorized to permit the exploitation of a patent ("the second patent") which cannot be exploited without infringing another patent ("the first patent"), the following additional conditions shall apply:

(i) the invention claimed in the second patent shall involve an important technical advance of considerable economic significance in relation to the invention claimed in the first patent;

(ii) the owner of the first patent shall be entitled to a cross-licence on reasonable terms to use the invention claimed in the second patent; and

(iii) the use authorized in respect of the first patent shall be non-assignable except with the assignment of the second patent.

Article 32

An opportunity for judicial review of any decision to revoke or forfeit a patent shall be available.

Article 33

The term of protection available shall not end before the expiration of a period of twenty years counted from the filing date.[8]

Article 34

1. For the purposes of civil proceedings in respect of the infringement of the rights of the owner referred to in paragraph 1(b) of Article 28, if the subject matter of a patent is a process for obtaining a product, the judicial authorities shall have the authority to order the defendant to prove that the process to obtain an identical product is different from the patented process. Therefore, Members shall provide, in at least one of the following circumstances, that any identical product when produced without the consent of the patent owner shall, in the absence of proof to the contrary, be deemed to have been obtained by the patented process:

---

[8] It is understood that those Members which do not have a system of original grant may provide that the term of protection shall be computed from the filing date in the system of original grant.

(a) if the product obtained by the patented process is new;

(b) if there is a substantial likelihood that the identical product was made by the process and the owner of the patent has been unable through reasonable efforts to determine the process actually used.

2. Any Member shall be free to provide that the burden of proof indicated in paragraph 1 shall be on the alleged infringer only if the condition referred to in subparagraph (a) is fulfilled or only if the condition referred to in subparagraph (b) is fulfilled.

3. In the adduction of proof to the contrary, the legitimate interests of defendants in protecting their manufacturing and business secrets shall be taken into account.

SECTION 6: LAYOUT-DESIGNS (TOPOGRAPHIES) OF INTEGRATED CIRCUITS

Article 35

Members agree to provide protection to the layout-designs (topographies) of integrated circuits (referred to in this Agreement as "layout-designs") in accordance with Articles 2 through 7 (other than paragraph 3 of Article 6), Article 12 and paragraph 3 of Article 16 of the Treaty on Intellectual Property in Respect of Integrated Circuits and, in addition, to comply with the following provisions.

Article 36

Subject to the provisions of paragraph 1 of Article 37, Members shall consider unlawful the following acts if performed without the authorization of the right holder:[9] importing, selling, or otherwise distributing for commercial purposes a protected layout-design, an integrated circuit in which a protected layout-design is incorporated, or an article incorporating such an integrated circuit only in so far as it continues to contain an unlawfully reproduced layout-design.

Article 37

1. Notwithstanding Article 36, no Member shall consider unlawful the performance of any of the acts referred to in that Article in respect of an integrated circuit incorporating an unlawfully reproduced layout-design or any article incorporating such an integrated circuit where the person performing or ordering such acts did not know and had no reasonable ground to know, when acquiring the integrated circuit or article incorporating such an integrated circuit, that it incorporated an unlawfully reproduced layout-design. Members shall provide that, after the time that such person has received sufficient notice that the layout-design was unlawfully

---

[9] The term "right holder" in this Section shall be understood as having the same meaning as the term "holder of the right" in the IPIC Treaty.

reproduced, that person may perform any of the acts with respect to the stock on hand or ordered before such time, but shall be liable to pay to the right holder a sum equivalent to a reasonable royalty such as would be payable under a freely negotiated licence in respect of such a layout-design.

2. The conditions set out in subparagraphs (a) through (k) of Article 31 shall apply *mutatis mutandis* in the event of any non-voluntary licensing of a layout-design or of its use by or for the government without the authorization of the right holder.

Article 38

1. In Members requiring registration as a condition of protection, the term of protection of layout-designs shall not end before the expiration of a period of 10 years counted from the date of filing an application for registration or from the first commercial exploitation wherever in the world it occurs.

2. In Members not requiring registration as a condition for protection, layout-designs shall be protected for a term of no less than 10 years from the date of the first commercial exploitation wherever in the world it occurs.

3. Notwithstanding paragraphs 1 and 2, a Member may provide that protection shall lapse 15 years after the creation of the layout-design.

SECTION 7: PROTECTION OF UNDISCLOSED INFORMATION

Article 39

1. In the course of ensuring effective protection against unfair competition as provided in Article 10*bis* of the Paris Convention (1967), Members shall protect undisclosed information in accordance with paragraph 2 and data submitted to governments or governmental agencies in accordance with paragraph 3.

2. Natural and legal persons shall have the possibility of preventing information lawfully within their control from being disclosed to, acquired by, or used by others without their consent in a manner contrary to honest commercial practices[10] so long as such information:

(a) is secret in the sense that it is not, as a body or in the precise configuration and assembly of its components, generally known among or readily accessible to persons within the circles that normally deal with the kind of information in question;

(b) has commercial value because it is secret; and

---

[10] For the purpose of this provision, "a manner contrary to honest commercial practices" shall mean at least practices such as breach of contract, breach of confidence and inducement to breach, and includes the acquisition of undisclosed information by third parties who knew, or were grossly negligent in failing to know, that such practices were involved in the acquisition.

(c) has been subject to reasonable steps under the circumstances, by the person lawfully in control of the information, to keep it secret.

3. Members, when requiring, as a condition of approving the marketing of pharmaceutical or of agricultural chemical products which utilize new chemical entities, the submission of undisclosed test or other data, the origination of which involves a considerable effort, shall protect such data against unfair commercial use. In addition, Members shall protect such data against disclosure, except where necessary to protect the public, or unless steps are taken to ensure that the data are protected against unfair commercial use.

SECTION 8: CONTROL OF ANTI-COMPETITIVE PRACTICES IN CONTRACTUAL LICENCES

Article 40

1. Members agree that some licensing practices or conditions pertaining to intellectual property rights which restrain competition may have adverse effects on trade and may impede the transfer and dissemination of technology.

2. Nothing in this Agreement shall prevent Members from specifying in their legislation licensing practices or conditions that may in particular cases constitute an abuse of intellectual property rights having an adverse effect on competition in the relevant market. As provided above, a Member may adopt, consistently with the other provisions of this Agreement, appropriate measures to prevent or control such practices, which may include for example exclusive grantback conditions, conditions preventing challenges to validity and coercive package licensing, in the light of the relevant laws and regulations of that Member.

3. Each Member shall enter, upon request, into consultations with any other Member which has cause to believe that an intellectual property right owner that is a national or domiciliary of the Member to which the request for consultations has been addressed is undertaking practices in violation of the requesting Member's laws and regulations on the subject matter of this Section, and which wishes to secure compliance with such legislation, without prejudice to any action under the law and to the full freedom of an ultimate decision of either Member. The Member addressed shall accord full and sympathetic consideration to, and shall afford adequate opportunity for, consultations with the requesting Member, and shall cooperate through supply of publicly available non-confidential information of relevance to the matter in question and of other information available to the Member, subject to domestic law and to the conclusion of mutually satisfactory agreements concerning the safeguarding of its confidentiality by the requesting Member.

4. A Member whose nationals or domiciliaries are subject to proceedings in another Member concerning alleged violation of that other Member's

laws and regulations on the subject matter of this Section shall, upon request, be granted an opportunity for consultations by the other Member under the same conditions as those foreseen in paragraph 3.

PART III
ENFORCEMENT OF INTELLECTUAL PROPERTY RIGHTS

SECTION 1: GENERAL OBLIGATIONS

Article 41

1. Members shall ensure that enforcement procedures as specified in this Part are available under their law so as to permit effective action against any act of infringement of intellectual property rights covered by this Agreement, including expeditious remedies to prevent infringements and remedies which constitute a deterrent to further infringements. These procedures shall be applied in such a manner as to avoid the creation of barriers to legitimate trade and to provide for safeguards against their abuse.

2. Procedures concerning the enforcement of intellectual property rights shall be fair and equitable. They shall not be unnecessarily complicated or costly, or entail unreasonable time-limits or unwarranted delays.

3. Decisions on the merits of a case shall preferably be in writing and reasoned. They shall be made available at least to the parties to the proceeding without undue delay. Decisions on the merits of a case shall be based only on evidence in respect of which parties were offered the opportunity to be heard.

4. Parties to a proceeding shall have an opportunity for review by a judicial authority of final administrative decisions and, subject to jurisdictional provisions in a Member's law concerning the importance of a case, of at least the legal aspects of initial judicial decisions on the merits of a case. However, there shall be no obligation to provide an opportunity for review of acquittals in criminal cases.

5. It is understood that this Part does not create any obligation to put in place a judicial system for the enforcement of intellectual property rights distinct from that for the enforcement of law in general, nor does it affect the capacity of Members to enforce their law in general. Nothing in this Part creates any obligation with respect to the distribution of resources as between enforcement of intellectual property rights and the enforcement of law in general.

SECTION 2:   CIVIL AND ADMINISTRATIVE
PROCEDURES AND REMEDIES

Article 42

Members shall make available to right holders[11] civil judicial procedures concerning the enforcement of any intellectual property right covered by this Agreement. Defendants shall have the right to written notice which is timely and contains sufficient detail, including the basis of the claims. Parties shall be allowed to be represented by independent legal counsel, and procedures shall not impose overly burdensome requirements concerning mandatory personal appearances. All parties to such procedures shall be duly entitled to substantiate their claims and to present all relevant evidence. The procedure shall provide a means to identify and protect confidential information, unless this would be contrary to existing constitutional requirements.

Article 43

1. The judicial authorities shall have the authority, where a party has presented reasonably available evidence sufficient to support its claims and has specified evidence relevant to substantiation of its claims which lies in the control of the opposing party, to order that this evidence be produced by the opposing party, subject in appropriate cases to conditions which ensure the protection of confidential information.

2. In cases in which a party to a proceeding voluntarily and without good reason refuses access to, or otherwise does not provide necessary information within a reasonable period, or significantly impedes a procedure relating to an enforcement action, a Member may accord judicial authorities the authority to make preliminary and final determinations, affirmative or negative, on the basis of the information presented to them, including the complaint or the allegation presented by the party adversely affected by the denial of access to information, subject to providing the parties an opportunity to be heard on the allegations or evidence.

Article 44

1. The judicial authorities shall have the authority to order a party to desist from an infringement, *inter alia* to prevent the entry into the channels of commerce in their jurisdiction of imported goods that involve the infringement of an intellectual property right, immediately after customs clearance of such goods. Members are not obliged to accord such authority in respect of protected subject matter acquired or ordered by a person prior to knowing or having reasonable grounds to know that dealing in such subject matter would entail the infringement of an intellectual property right.

---

[11] For the purpose of this Part, the term "right holder" includes federations and associations having legal standing to assert such rights.

2. Notwithstanding the other provisions of this Part and provided that the provisions of Part II specifically addressing use by governments, or by third parties authorized by a government, without the authorization of the right holder are complied with, Members may limit the remedies available against such use to payment of remuneration in accordance with subparagraph (h) of Article 31. In other cases, the remedies under this Part shall apply or, where these remedies are inconsistent with a Member's law, declaratory judgments and adequate compensation shall be available.

Article 45

1. The judicial authorities shall have the authority to order the infringer to pay the right holder damages adequate to compensate for the injury the right holder has suffered because of an infringement of that person's intellectual property right by an infringer who knowingly, or with reasonable grounds to know, engaged in infringing activity.

2. The judicial authorities shall also have the authority to order the infringer to pay the right holder expenses, which may include appropriate attorney's fees. In appropriate cases, Members may authorize the judicial authorities to order recovery of profits and/or payment of pre-established damages even where the infringer did not knowingly, or with reasonable grounds to know, engage in infringing activity.

Article 46

In order to create an effective deterrent to infringement, the judicial authorities shall have the authority to order that goods that they have found to be infringing be, without compensation of any sort, disposed of outside the channels of commerce in such a manner as to avoid any harm caused to the right holder, or, unless this would be contrary to existing constitutional requirements, destroyed. The judicial authorities shall also have the authority to order that materials and implements the predominant use of which has been in the creation of the infringing goods be, without compensation of any sort, disposed of outside the channels of commerce in such a manner as to minimize the risks of further infringements. In considering such requests, the need for proportionality between the seriousness of the infringement and the remedies ordered as well as the interests of third parties shall be taken into account. In regard to counterfeit trademark goods, the simple removal of the trademark unlawfully affixed shall not be sufficient, other than in exceptional cases, to permit release of the goods into the channels of commerce.

Article 47

Members may provide that the judicial authorities shall have the authority, unless this would be out of proportion to the seriousness of the infringement, to order the infringer to inform the right holder of the identity of third persons involved in the production and distribution of the infringing goods or services and of their channels of distribution.

Article 48

1. The judicial authorities shall have the authority to order a party at whose request measures were taken and who has abused enforcement procedures to provide to a party wrongfully enjoined or restrained adequate compensation for the injury suffered because of such abuse. The judicial authorities shall also have the authority to order the applicant to pay the defendant expenses, which may include appropriate attorney's fees.

2. In respect of the administration of any law pertaining to the protection or enforcement of intellectual property rights, Members shall only exempt both public authorities and officials from liability to appropriate remedial measures where actions are taken or intended in good faith in the course of the administration of that law.

Article 49

To the extent that any civil remedy can be ordered as a result of administrative procedures on the merits of a case, such procedures shall conform to principles equivalent in substance to those set forth in this Section.

SECTION 3: PROVISIONAL MEASURES

Article 50

1. The judicial authorities shall have the authority to order prompt and effective provisional measures:

(a) to prevent an infringement of any intellectual property right from occurring, and in particular to prevent the entry into the channels of commerce in their jurisdiction of goods, including imported goods immediately after customs clearance;

(b) to preserve relevant evidence in regard to the alleged infringement.

2. The judicial authorities shall have the authority to adopt provisional measures *inaudita altera parte* where appropriate, in particular where any delay is likely to cause irreparable harm to the right holder, or where there is a demonstrable risk of evidence being destroyed.

3. The judicial authorities shall have the authority to require the applicant to provide any reasonably available evidence in order to satisfy themselves with a sufficient degree of certainty that the applicant is the right holder and that the applicant's right is being infringed or that such infringement is imminent, and to order the applicant to provide a security or equivalent assurance sufficient to protect the defendant and to prevent abuse.

4. Where provisional measures have been adopted *inaudita altera parte,* the parties affected shall be given notice, without delay after the execution of the measures at the latest. A review, including a right to be heard, shall take place upon request of the defendant with a view to deciding, within

a reasonable period after the notification of the measures, whether these measures shall be modified, revoked or confirmed.

5. The applicant may be required to supply other information necessary for the identification of the goods concerned by the authority that will execute the provisional measures.

6. Without prejudice to paragraph 4, provisional measures taken on the basis of paragraphs 1 and 2 shall, upon request by the defendant, be revoked or otherwise cease to have effect, if proceedings leading to a decision on the merits of the case are not initiated within a reasonable period, to be determined by the judicial authority ordering the measures where a Member's law so permits or, in the absence of such a determination, not to exceed 20 working days or 31 calendar days, whichever is the longer.

7. Where the provisional measures are revoked or where they lapse due to any act or omission by the applicant, or where it is subsequently found that there has been no infringement or threat of infringement of an intellectual property right, the judicial authorities shall have the authority to order the applicant, upon request of the defendant, to provide the defendant appropriate compensation for any injury caused by these measures.

8. To the extent that any provisional measure can be ordered as a result of administrative procedures, such procedures shall conform to principles equivalent in substance to those set forth in this Section.

SECTION 4: SPECIAL REQUIREMENTS RELATED TO BORDER MEASURES[12]

Article 51

Members shall, in conformity with the provisions set out below, adopt procedures[13] to enable a right holder, who has valid grounds for suspecting that the importation of counterfeit trademark or pirated copyright goods[14]

---

[12] Where a Member has dismantled substantially all controls over movement of goods across its border with another Member with which it forms part of a customs union, it shall not be required to apply the provisions of this Section at that border.

[13] It is understood that there shall be no obligation to apply such procedures to imports of goods put on the market in another country by or with the consent of the right holder, or to goods in transit.

[14] For the purposes of this Agreement:

(a) "counterfeit trademark goods" shall mean any goods, including packaging, bearing without authorization a trademark which is identical to the trademark validly registered in respect of such goods, or which cannot be distinguished in its essential aspects from such a trademark, and which thereby infringes the rights of the owner of the trademark in question under the law of the country of importation;

(b) "pirated copyright goods" shall mean any goods which are copies made

may take place, to lodge an application in writing with competent authorities, administrative or judicial, for the suspension by the customs authorities of the release into free circulation of such goods. Members may enable such an application to be made in respect of goods which involve other infringements of intellectual property rights, provided that the requirements of this Section are met. Members may also provide for corresponding procedures concerning the suspension by the customs authorities of the release of infringing goods destined for exportation from their territories.

Article 52

Any right holder initiating the procedures under Article 51 shall be required to provide adequate evidence to satisfy the competent authorities that, under the laws of the country of importation, there is *prima facie* an infringement of the right holder's intellectual property right and to supply a sufficiently detailed description of the goods to make them readily recognizable by the customs authorities. The competent authorities shall inform the applicant within a reasonable period whether they have accepted the application and, where determined by the competent authorities, the period for which the customs authorities will take action.

Article 53

1. The competent authorities shall have the authority to require an applicant to provide a security or equivalent assurance sufficient to protect the defendant and the competent authorities and to prevent abuse. Such security or equivalent assurance shall not unreasonably deter recourse to these procedures.

2. Where pursuant to an application under this Section the release of goods involving industrial designs, patents, layout-designs or undisclosed information into free circulation has been suspended by customs authorities on the basis of a decision other than by a judicial or other independent authority, and the period provided for in Article 55 has expired without the granting of provisional relief by the duly empowered authority, and provided that all other conditions for importation have been complied with, the owner, importer, or consignee of such goods shall be entitled to their release on the posting of a security in an amount sufficient to protect the right holder for any infringement. Payment of such security shall not prejudice any other remedy available to the right holder, it being understood that the security shall be released if the right holder fails to pursue the right of action within a reasonable period of time.

Article 54

The importer and the applicant shall be promptly notified of the suspension of the release of goods according to Article 51.

---

without the consent of the right holder or person duly authorized by the right holder in the country of production and which are made directly or indirectly from an article where the making of that copy would have constituted an infringement of a copyright or a related right under the law of the country of importation.

Article 55

If, within a period not exceeding 10 working days after the applicant has been served notice of the suspension, the customs authorities have not been informed that proceedings leading to a decision on the merits of the case have been initiated by a party other than the defendant, or that the duly empowered authority has taken provisional measures prolonging the suspension of the release of the goods, the goods shall be released, provided that all other conditions for importation or exportation have been complied with; in appropriate cases, this time-limit may be extended by another 10 working days. If proceedings leading to a decision on the merits of the case have been initiated, a review, including a right to be heard, shall take place upon request of the defendant with a view to deciding, within a reasonable period, whether these measures shall be modified, revoked or confirmed. Notwithstanding the above, where the suspension of the release of goods is carried out or continued in accordance with a provisional judicial measure, the provisions of paragraph 6 of Article 50 shall apply.

Article 56

Relevant authorities shall have the authority to order the applicant to pay the importer, the consignee and the owner of the goods appropriate compensation for any injury caused to them through the wrongful detention of goods or through the detention of goods released pursuant to Article 55.

Article 57

Without prejudice to the protection of confidential information, Members shall provide the competent authorities the authority to give the right holder sufficient opportunity to have any goods detained by the customs authorities inspected in order to substantiate the right holder's claims. The competent authorities shall also have authority to give the importer an equivalent opportunity to have any such goods inspected. Where a positive determination has been made on the merits of a case, Members may provide the competent authorities the authority to inform the right holder of the names and addresses of the consignor, the importer and the consignee and of the quantity of the goods in question.

Article 58

Where Members require competent authorities to act upon their own initiative and to suspend the release of goods in respect of which they have acquired *prima facie* evidence that an intellectual property right is being infringed:

(a) the competent authorities may at any time seek from the right holder any information that may assist them to exercise these powers;

(b) the importer and the right holder shall be promptly notified of the suspension. Where the importer has lodged an appeal against the suspension with the competent authorities, the suspension shall be subject to the conditions, *mutatis mutandis,* set out at Article 55;

(c) Members shall only exempt both public authorities and officials from liability to appropriate remedial measures where actions are taken or intended in good faith.

Article 59

Without prejudice to other rights of action open to the right holder and subject to the right of the defendant to seek review by a judicial authority, competent authorities shall have the authority to order the destruction or disposal of infringing goods in accordance with the principles set out in Article 46. In regard to counterfeit trademark goods, the authorities shall not allow the re-exportation of the infringing goods in an unaltered state or subject them to a different customs procedure, other than in exceptional circumstances.

Article 60

Members may exclude from the application of the above provisions small quantities of goods of a non-commercial nature contained in travellers' personal luggage or sent in small consignments.

SECTION 5: CRIMINAL PROCEDURES

Article 61

Members shall provide for criminal procedures and penalties to be applied at least in cases of wilful trademark counterfeiting or copyright piracy on a commercial scale. Remedies available shall include imprisonment and/or monetary fines sufficient to provide a deterrent, consistently with the level of penalties applied for crimes of a corresponding gravity. In appropriate cases, remedies available shall also include the seizure, forfeiture and destruction of the infringing goods and of any materials and implements the predominant use of which has been in the commission of the offence. Members may provide for criminal procedures and penalties to be applied in other cases of infringement of intellectual property rights, in particular where they are committed wilfully and on a commercial scale.

PART IV
ACQUISITION AND MAINTENANCE OF INTELLECTUAL PROPERTY RIGHTS AND RELATED INTER-PARTES PROCEDURES

Article 62

1. Members may require, as a condition of the acquisition or maintenance of the intellectual property rights provided for under Sections 2 through 6 of Part II, compliance with reasonable procedures and formalities. Such procedures and formalities shall be consistent with the provisions of this Agreement.

2. Where the acquisition of an intellectual property right is subject to the right being granted or registered, Members shall ensure that the procedures for grant or registration, subject to compliance with the substantive conditions for acquisition of the right, permit the granting or registration of the right within a reasonable period of time so as to avoid unwarranted curtailment of the period of protection.

3. Article 4 of the Paris Convention (1967) shall apply *mutatis mutandis* to service marks.

4. Procedures concerning the acquisition or maintenance of intellectual property rights and, where a Member's law provides for such procedures, administrative revocation and *inter partes* procedures such as opposition, revocation and cancellation, shall be governed by the general principles set out in paragraphs 2 and 3 of Article 41.

5. Final administrative decisions in any of the procedures referred to under paragraph 4 shall be subject to review by a judicial or quasi-judicial authority. However, there shall be no obligation to provide an opportunity for such review of decisions in cases of unsuccessful opposition or administrative revocation, provided that the grounds for such procedures can be the subject of invalidation procedures.

PART V
DISPUTE PREVENTION AND SETTLEMENT

Article 63

1. Laws and regulations, and final judicial decisions and administrative rulings of general application, made effective by a Member pertaining to the subject matter of this Agreement (the availability, scope, acquisition, enforcement and prevention of the abuse of intellectual property rights) shall be published, or where such publication is not practicable made publicly available, in a national language, in such a manner as to enable governments and right holders to become acquainted with them. Agreements concerning the subject matter of this Agreement which are in force between the government or a governmental agency of a Member and the government or a governmental agency of another Member shall also be published.

2. Members shall notify the laws and regulations referred to in paragraph 1 to the Council for TRIPS in order to assist that Council in its review of the operation of this Agreement. The Council shall attempt to minimize the burden on Members in carrying out this obligation and may decide to waive the obligation to notify such laws and regulations directly to the Council if consultations with WIPO on the establishment of a common register containing these laws and regulations are successful. The Council shall also consider in this connection any action required regarding notifications pursuant to the obligations under this Agreement stemming from the provisions of Article 6*ter* of the Paris Convention (1967).

3. Each Member shall be prepared to supply, in response to a written request from another Member, information of the sort referred to in paragraph 1. A Member, having reason to believe that a specific judicial decision or administrative ruling or bilateral agreement in the area of intellectual property rights affects its rights under this Agreement, may also request in writing to be given access to or be informed in sufficient detail of such specific judicial decisions or administrative rulings or bilateral agreements.

4. Nothing in paragraphs 1, 2 and 3 shall require Members to disclose confidential information which would impede law enforcement or otherwise be contrary to the public interest or would prejudice the legitimate commercial interests of particular enterprises, public or private.

Article 64

1. The provisions of Articles XXII and XXIII of GATT 1994 as elaborated and applied by the Dispute Settlement Understanding shall apply to consultations and the settlement of disputes under this Agreement except as otherwise specifically provided herein.

2. Subparagraphs 1(b) and 1(c) of Article XXIII of GATT 1994 shall not apply to the settlement of disputes under this Agreement for a period of five years from the date of entry into force of the WTO Agreement.

3. During the time period referred to in paragraph 2, the Council for TRIPS shall examine the scope and modalities for complaints of the type provided for under subparagraphs 1(b) and 1(c) of Article XXIII of GATT 1994 made pursuant to this Agreement, and submit its recommendations to the Ministerial Conference for approval. Any decision of the Ministerial Conference to approve such recommendations or to extend the period in paragraph 2 shall be made only by consensus, and approved recommendations shall be effective for all Members without further formal acceptance process.

PART VI
TRANSITIONAL ARRANGEMENTS

Article 65

1. Subject to the provisions of paragraphs 2, 3 and 4, no Member shall be obliged to apply the provisions of this Agreement before the expiry of a general period of one year following the date of entry into force of the WTO Agreement.

2. A developing country Member is entitled to delay for a further period of four years the date of application, as defined in paragraph 1, of the provisions of this Agreement other than Articles 3, 4 and 5.

3. Any other Member which is in the process of transformation from a centrally-planned into a market, free-enterprise economy and which is

undertaking structural reform of its intellectual property system and facing special problems in the preparation and implementation of intellectual property laws and regulations, may also benefit from a period of delay as foreseen in paragraph 2.

4. To the extent that a developing country Member is obliged by this Agreement to extend product patent protection to areas of technology not so protectable in its territory on the general date of application of this Agreement for that Member, as defined in paragraph 2, it may delay the application of the provisions on product patents of Section 5 of Part II to such areas of technology for an additional period of five years.

5. A Member availing itself of a transitional period under paragraphs 1, 2, 3 or 4 shall ensure that any changes in its laws, regulations and practice made during that period do not result in a lesser degree of consistency with the provisions of this Agreement.

Article 66

1. In view of the special needs and requirements of least-developed country Members, their economic, financial and administrative constraints, and their need for flexibility to create a viable technological base, such Members shall not be required to apply the provisions of this Agreement, other than Articles 3, 4 and 5, for a period of 10 years from the date of application as defined under paragraph 1 of Article 65. The Council for TRIPS shall, upon duly motivated request by a least-developed country Member, accord extensions of this period.

2. Developed country Members shall provide incentives to enterprises and institutions in their territories for the purpose of promoting and encouraging technology transfer to least-developed country Members in order to enable them to create a sound and viable technological base.

Article 67

In order to facilitate the implementation of this Agreement, developed country Members shall provide, on request and on mutually agreed terms and conditions, technical and financial cooperation in favour of developing and least-developed country Members. Such cooperation shall include assistance in the preparation of laws and regulations on the protection and enforcement of intellectual property rights as well as on the prevention of their abuse, and shall include support regarding the establishment or reinforcement of domestic offices and agencies relevant to these matters, including the training of personnel.

PART VII
INSTITUTIONAL ARRANGEMENTS; FINAL PROVISIONS

Article 68

The Council for TRIPS shall monitor the operation of this Agreement and, in particular, Members' compliance with their obligations hereunder, and shall afford Members the opportunity of consulting on matters relating to the trade-related aspects of intellectual property rights. It shall carry out such other responsibilities as assigned to it by the Members, and it shall, in particular, provide any assistance requested by them in the context of dispute settlement procedures. In carrying out its functions, the Council for TRIPS may consult with and seek information from any source it deems appropriate. In consultation with WIPO, the Council shall seek to establish, within one year of its first meeting, appropriate arrangements for cooperation with bodies of that Organization.

Article 69

Members agree to cooperate with each other with a view to eliminating international trade in goods infringing intellectual property rights. For this purpose, they shall establish and notify contact points in their administrations and be ready to exchange information on trade in infringing goods. They shall, in particular, promote the exchange of information and cooperation between customs authorities with regard to trade in counterfeit trademark goods and pirated copyright goods.

Article 70

1. This Agreement does not give rise to obligations in respect of acts which occurred before the date of application of the Agreement for the Member in question.

2. Except as otherwise provided for in this Agreement, this Agreement gives rise to obligations in respect of all subject matter existing at the date of application of this Agreement for the Member in question, and which is protected in that Member on the said date, or which meets or comes subsequently to meet the criteria for protection under the terms of this Agreement. In respect of this paragraph and paragraphs 3 and 4, copyright obligations with respect to existing works shall be solely determined under Article 18 of the Berne Convention (1971), and obligations with respect to the rights of producers of phonograms and performers in existing phonograms shall be determined solely under Article 18 of the Berne Convention (1971) as made applicable under paragraph 6 of Article 14 of this Agreement.

3. There shall be no obligation to restore protection to subject matter which on the date of application of this Agreement for the Member in question has fallen into the public domain.

4. In respect of any acts in respect of specific objects embodying protected subject matter which become infringing under the terms of legislation in conformity with this Agreement, and which were commenced, or in respect of which a significant investment was made, before the date of acceptance of the WTO Agreement by that Member, any Member may provide for a limitation of the remedies available to the right holder as to the continued performance of such acts after the date of application of this Agreement for that Member. In such cases the Member shall, however, at least provide for the payment of equitable remuneration.

5. A Member is not obliged to apply the provisions of Article 11 and of paragraph 4 of Article 14 with respect to originals or copies purchased prior to the date of application of this Agreement for that Member.

6. Members shall not be required to apply Article 31, or the requirement in paragraph 1 of Article 27 that patent rights shall be enjoyable without discrimination as to the field of technology, to use without the authorization of the right holder where authorization for such use was granted by the government before the date this Agreement became known.

7. In the case of intellectual property rights for which protection is conditional upon registration, applications for protection which are pending on the date of application of this Agreement for the Member in question shall be permitted to be amended to claim any enhanced protection provided under the provisions of this Agreement. Such amendments shall not include new matter.

8. Where a Member does not make available as of the date of entry into force of the WTO Agreement patent protection for pharmaceutical and agricultural chemical products commensurate with its obligations under Article 27, that Member shall:

(a) notwithstanding the provisions of Part VI, provide as from the date of entry into force of the WTO Agreement a means by which applications for patents for such inventions can be filed;

(b) apply to these applications, as of the date of application of this Agreement, the criteria for patentability as laid down in this Agreement as if those criteria were being applied on the date of filing in that Member or, where priority is available and claimed, the priority date of the application; and

(c) provide patent protection in accordance with this Agreement as from the grant of the patent and for the remainder of the patent term, counted from the filing date in accordance with Article 33 of this Agreement, for those of these applications that meet the criteria for protection referred to in subparagraph (b).

9. Where a product is the subject of a patent application in a Member in accordance with paragraph 8(a), exclusive marketing rights shall be granted, notwithstanding the provisions of Part VI, for a period of five years after obtaining marketing approval in that Member or until a product patent is granted or rejected in that Member, whichever period is shorter, provided that, subsequent to the entry into force of the WTO Agreement, a patent application has been filed and a patent granted for that product in another Member and marketing approval obtained in such other Member.

Article 71

1. The Council for TRIPS shall review the implementation of this Agreement after the expiration of the transitional period referred to in paragraph 2 of Article 65. The Council shall, having regard to the experience gained in its implementation, review it two years after that date, and

at identical intervals thereafter. The Council may also undertake reviews in the light of any relevant new developments which might warrant modification or amendment of this Agreement.

2. Amendments merely serving the purpose of adjusting to higher levels of protection of intellectual property rights achieved, and in force, in other multilateral agreements and accepted under those agreements by all Members of the WTO may be referred to the Ministerial Conference for action in accordance with paragraph 6 of Article X of the WTO Agreement on the basis of a consensus proposal from the Council for TRIPS.

Article 72

Reservations may not be entered in respect of any of the provisions of this Agreement without the consent of the other Members.

Article 73

Nothing in this Agreement shall be construed:

(a) to require a Member to furnish any information the disclosure of which it considers contrary to its essential security interests; or

(b) to prevent a Member from taking any action which it considers necessary for the protection of its essential security interests:

(i) relating to fissionable materials or the materials from which they are derived;

(ii) relating to the traffic in arms, ammunition and implements of war and to such traffic in other goods and materials as is carried on directly or indirectly for the purpose of supplying a military establishment;

(iii) taken in time of war or other emergency in international relations; or

(c) to prevent a Member from taking any action in pursuance of its obligations under the United Nations Charter for the maintenance of international peace and security.

THE 1996 W.I.P.O. TREATIES

Summary Overview of the 1996 Treaties[1]

As the casebook explains, from its inception in 1886 to the Paris Act of 1971, the Berne Convention for the Protection of Literary and Artistic Works was revised six times, with each revision the result of a consensus on new proposals arrived at in the course of an international diplomatic conference attended by all the member states of the Berne Union. By the early 1990s, however, it was clear that the stakes in international copyright had become so great, and the differences between Berne Union members on some issues so considerable, that another general revision of the treaty text was unlikely. At about the same time, however, the injection of copyright (and other intellectual property) issues into the agenda of the Uruguay Round of the General Agreement on Tariffs and Trade, which eventually would produce the GATT/TRIPs agreement, had begun to pose a challenge to position of Berne as the dominant international agreement relating to literary and artistic property — and, even, more specifically, to the position of W.I.P.O. as the preeminent international organization in the field.

W.I.P.O.'s response was to announce a program to update the Berne Convention by developing one or more new agreements, or "protocols," which would supplement but not displace the 1971 Act. Such agreements, and the enhanced international norms they would contain, would be binding only on those Berne Union countries which signed and ratified them. By the same token, however, they could be concluded by something less than the whole membership of the Union — thus offering a chance to avoid the likely stalemate which would result from any effort to achieve a general revision of the treaty itself.

In furtherance of this scheme, the International Bureau of W.I.P.O. convened a series of preparatory meetings, beginning in November, 1991, to discuss proposals to upgrade the kind and quality of protection available under Berne. Issues as to which there was a perceived lack of international uniformity, and which were discussed as possible topics of new treaty language at the early meetings of what was called the "Committee of Experts on a Possible Protocol to the Berne Convention," included: protection of computer programs; database protection; the position of artificial intelligence and computer-generated works; the scope of the right of reproduction (including personal and library photocopying); the future of compulsory licensing; the rights of distribution, display, rental, public lending, and importation; broadcasting rights; the term of protection for

---

[1] By Peter Jaszi. Copyright 1997. Used with permission.

photographic works; the proper application of the principle of national treatment; and copyright enforcement.

In addition, the delegations representing various governments at these meetings in Geneva agreed that protection for sound recordings was a likely topic for new treaty language, given the failures of the Rome Convention and the Geneva Phonogram Convention to attract sufficient numbers of adherents. But they also agreed that such language would be better contained in a new treaty separate from any "Berne Protocol," rather than as part of it. Thereafter, the "Committee of Experts" became the "Committees of Experts" — one to prepare for the "Protocol" and another for the so-called "New Instrument for the Protection of the Producers and Performers of Phonograms" — though their membership was substantially overlapping and their meetings generally occurred back-to-back.

As the deliberations of the Committees of Experts proceeded from year to year, many of these issues proved too controversial to be considered ripe for inclusion in a new treaty or treaties, and thus dropped out of the agenda. Moreover, since many of topics that remained were covered in the GATT/ TRIPs agreement concluded in April 1994, questions arose as to the continued relevance of the W.I.P.O. exercise. At the first post-TRIPs meeting of the Committees of Experts, in December 1994, the head of the U.S. delegation, Commissioner Bruce Lehman of the Patent and Trademark Office, offered an answer to those questions: The Committees of Experts, he urged, should shift their work program away from traditional copyright issues to those implicated by the emerging "global information infrastructure" — issues which, incidentally, had not been (at least for the most part) addressed in TRIPS!

On September 5, 1995, a government task force chaired by Commissioner Lehman released its "White Paper" on copyright and the networked digital environment simultaneously in Washington and at a meeting of the W.I.P.O. Committees of Experts in Geneva. The U.S. soon followed with proposals for specific language to implement what came to be called the "digital agenda" in the "Berne Protocol" and the "New Instrument" — language closely paralleling the "White Paper" 's draft for U.S. domestic legislation and variants on those proposals proffered by the European Union.

In February 1996, the dates of the Diplomatic Conference to consider the work product of the Committees of Experts were set for December of that year. In May, at the final meeting of the Committees of Experts, the U.S. and Europe rounded out the "digital agenda" by submitting competing versions of yet another new treaty, designed to require adhering countries to enact domestic legislation to provide sui generis protection for non-original databases (including but not limited to those in digital formats). Back in March, the European Parliament and the Council of the European Union had adopted a final "Directive on the Legal Protection of Databases" (96/9/EC), requiring countries of the Union to recognize a new right to protection to investment of time, money and effort by the maker of a database, irrespective of whether the database is in itself innovative, if there has been a "substantial investment," in qualitative or quantitative terms, in obtaining, verifying or presenting its contents. And legislation with the same general thrust, although proposing a 25-year term of protection rather than the 15 years provided for in the Directive, also had been introduced in the U.S. Congress. These initiatives provided the basis for the sui generis proposals in Geneva.

The "Basic Proposals" for three new intellectual property agreements were released in late August 1996 (and, like the other W.I.P.O. documents referred to in this note, can be found at http://www.wipo.org). These documents, synthesized by the chairperson of the Committees of Experts from the treaty language on various issues submitted by various government delegations and designed to be the basis for discussion at the December Diplomatic Conference, dealt with both traditional copyright issues and those which constituted the "digital agenda." They included: creation of a strong new "right of communication to the public" (the functional equivalent of the digital "transmission right" which had been proposed in the "White Paper"), extension (or, in the view of some, a clarification) of the reproduction right to cover all temporary and ephemeral digital reproductions (such as those in RAM and cache), restriction of the applicability of "limitations and exceptions" to copyright (such as "fair use") in cyberspace; prohibitions against the manufacture and sale of technologies (or the provision of services) which can be employed to circumvent technological protection measures employed to safeguard copyrighted works in the network environment; and further prohibitions against unauthorized tampering with digital records of so-called "copyright management information" — along with (in the third of the "Basic Proposals") a scheme of sui generis database protection.

At the Conference itself, these issues proved the most controversial. Some governments, particularly those of developing countries, already were skeptical about the merits of the "digital agenda" prior to arrival in Geneva. In addition, however, a wide range of groups and organizations (from telecommunications companies and electronics manufacturers to libraries and cultural associations) were on hand there to lobby the national delegations against adoption of these components of the "Basic Proposals" — and to demand that the Conference take up other related issues, such as the limitation of the liability of on-line Internet service providers (OSP/ISPs) for acts of infringement actually committed by the customers or subscribers to whom they provide network access. (An extremely useful summary of the events of the Diplomatic Conference, "Big Media Beaten Back" by Professor Pamela Samuelson can be found in the March 1997 issue of Wired magazine, at p. 61. In the same issue, there is a related article, "Africa 1, Hollywood 0," by John Browning.)

On December 20, 1996, when the Conference concluded, delegates had agreed on the texts of two new treaties: the "W.I.P.O. Copyright Treaty" (formerly known as the "Berne Protocol") and the "W.I.P.O. Performances and Phonograms Treaty" (the one-time "New Instrument"). No database treaty emerged from the Conference, at least in part because of the insistence of the delegates of developing countries that the development of international norms for the sui generis protection of non-original compilations should be closely linked to an issue that had not been on the agenda of the Conference — the development of a new international legal regime for the protection of folkloric works and other cultural property. In all likelihood, it will now be several years, at the very least, before W.I.P.O. puts forward a new proposal for a database treaty. Otherwise, the two treaties which did emerge were shorn of their most controversial provisions.

Where traditional copyright issues are concerned, the new Copyright Treaty provides for the protection of computer programs as literary works, and for copyright in original (as distinct from non-original) compilations of data. It obligates ratifying states to recognize a general right of distribution and a rental right limited to computer programs, movies and "works embodied in phonograms," and is itself subject to a number of significant exceptions. It also bars ratifying states from taking advantage of Berne Convention provisions which, standing alone, would permit them to allow lesser terms of protection to photographs than to other copyrighted works.

By contrast, the Performances and Phonograms Treaty breaks some significant new ground. Though to an extent it restates the obligations to provide significant protection for sound recordings, whether by means of copyright or by means of neighboring rights, already contained in the GATT/TRIPs agreement (which are derivative, in turn, of the Rome Convention), it goes further. In addition to a right to control reproduction and a limited commercial rental right, it provides record producers with a distribution right, and a right of remuneration in connection with broadcasting and communication to the public (the latter being qualified so as to permit countries such as the United States to continue to afford remuneration only in connection with digital broadcasts of sound recordings). Performers also fare better under the new treaty than under GATT/TRIPs: not only are they afforded more extensive economic rights, but (significantly) the text provides explicitly for the basic moral rights of the performer "as regards . . . live aural performances fixed in phonograms."

With respect to the digital agenda, the relevant provisions of the two treaties approved in December 1996 are substantially identical. Their preambles recognize explicitly the need to "maintain a balance between" the interests of right holders and "the larger public interest, particularly education, research, and access to information" — novel language that directly reflects the lobbying efforts of various "user" groups before and during the Diplomatic Conference. In their final forms, the treaty texts make no mention of the status of temporary and ephemeral reproduction. Among the obligations the final acts of the treaties do entail is a duty to recognize a right of "communication to the public," along with a limited mandate for the protection of "copyright management information" against tampering, and another relating to "anti-circumvention" technology. The last, however, is far less stringent than the version originally proposed. In effect, it requires ratifying signatories to do no more than adopt legislation specifically addressing the problem of "black boxes" — devices or systems specifically designed to break technological security systems — as such. And the clarifying "agreed statements" that accompany the text address some of the most difficult issues not resolved by the text, in terms that can only be called moderate and constructive. (These statements are important because, under Article 31 of the Vienna Convention on the Law of Treaties, such a consensus document has special status as a guide to interpretation of otherwise ambiguous treaty provisions.)

On the issue of the applicability of "fair use" and other limitations or exemptions to the digital networked environment, for example, the relevant "agreed statements" provide that:

It is understood that the provision of [these treaties] permit Contracting Parties to carry forward and appropriately extend into the digital environment limitations and exceptions in their national laws which have been considered acceptable under the Berne Convention. Similarly, these provisions should be understood to permit Contracting Parties to devise new exceptions and limitations that are appropriate in the digital network environment.

Likewise, the treaties also are accompanied by helpful "agreed statements" clarifying the applicability of the new "right of communication to the public" in connection with OSP/ISP liability:

It is understood that the mere provision of physical facilities for enabling or making a communication does not in itself amount to communication within the meaning of [these treaties] or the Berne Convention.

In addition, the Conference also produced an "agreed statement" relating to the issue of temporary and ephemeral reproduction, the significance of which is somewhat clouded by its particular history. In the final hours of the Conference, after debates during which a proposed sentence that would explicitly have identified temporary ephemeral reproductions as copyright-relevant "copies" was deleted, the following text emerged:

The reproduction right, as set out in . . . the Berne Convention, and the exceptions thereto, fully apply in the digital environment, in particular to the use of works in digital form. It is understood that the storage of a protected work in digital form in an electronic medium constitutes a reproduction within the meaning of the Berne Convention.

The first sentence represents an "agreed statement" in the classic sense in which that term is understood in international law, but (by contrast) the second was adopted only by a majority vote and over substantial objections. In light of this, efforts to portray it as a victory for the "digital agenda," snatched from the jaws of defeat, are open to question. Not only is the authority of the sentence doubtful in light of its procedural history, but there is a real question as to whether the reference to "storage" (a term with a specific, and limited, meaning in international copyright discourse) can fairly be understood to reach anything more than the making of permanent, stable, digital records.

In the United States, consideration of the treaties necessarily involved two formally independent (although functionally linked) Congressional processes: ratification by the Senate, and enactment of implementing legislation by the House and Senate together. These processes have been duly accomplished. See Title I of the Digital Millennium Copyright Act, Pub. L. No. 105-394, 112 Stat. 2860 (Oct. 28, 1998), for the final form of the implementing legislation signed into law by President Clinton.

Internationally, both the Copyright Treaty and the Performances and Phonograms Treaty entered into force in 2002 upon deposit with W.I.P.O.'s Director General of "instruments of ratification or accession" by 30 members states. For discussion of the issues posed by the treaties, see especially §§ 1.04, 7.07 and 9.06 in the casebook.

THE W.I.P.O. COPYRIGHT TREATY
(CRNR/DC/94)

Adopted by the Diplomatic Conference on December 20, 1996

Contents

Preamble

The Contracting Parties,

Desiring to develop and maintain the protection of the rights of authors in their literary and artistic works in a manner as effective and uniform as possible,

Recognizing the need to introduce new international rules and clarify the interpretation of certain existing rules in order to provide adequate solutions to the questions raised by new economic, social, cultural and technological developments,

Recognizing the profound impact of the development and convergence of information and communication technologies on the creation and use of literary and artistic works,

Emphasizing the outstanding significance of copyright protection as an incentive for literary and artistic creation,

Recognizing the need to maintain a balance between the rights of authors and the larger public interest, particularly education, research and access to information, as reflected in the Berne Convention,

Have agreed as follows:

Article 1
Relation to the Berne Convention

(1) This Treaty is a special agreement within the meaning of Article 20 of the Berne Convention for the Protection of Literary and Artistic Works, as regards Contracting Parties that are countries of the Union established by that Convention. This Treaty shall not have any connection with treaties other than the Berne Convention, nor shall it prejudice any rights and obligations under any other treaties.

(2) Nothing in this Treaty shall derogate from existing obligations that Contracting Parties have to each other under the Berne Convention for the Protection of Literary and Artistic Works.

(3) Hereinafter, "Berne Convention" shall refer to the Paris Act of July 24, 1971 of the Berne Convention for the Protection of Literary and Artistic Works.

(4) Contracting Parties shall comply with Articles 1 to 21 and the Appendix of the Berne Convention.

Article 2
Scope of Copyright Protection

Copyright protection extends to expressions and not to ideas, procedures, methods of operation or mathematical concepts as such.

Article 3
Application of Articles 2 to 6 of the Berne Convention

Contracting Parties shall apply mutatis mutandis the provisions of Articles 2 to 6 of the Berne Convention in respect of the protection provided for in this Treaty.

Article 4
Computer Programs

Computer programs are protected as literary works within the meaning of Article 2 of the Berne Convention. Such protection applies to computer programs, whatever may be the mode or form of their expression.

Article 5
Compilations of Data (Databases)

Compilations of data or other material, in any form, which by reason of the selection or arrangement of their contents constitute intellectual creations, are protected as such. This protection does not extend to the data or the material itself and is without prejudice to any copyright subsisting in the data or material contained in the compilation.

Article 6
Right of Distribution

(1) Authors of literary and artistic works shall enjoy the exclusive right of authorizing the making available to the public of the original and copies of their works through sale or other transfer of ownership.

(2) Nothing in this Treaty shall affect the freedom of Contracting Parties to determine the conditions, if any, under which the exhaustion of the right in paragraph (1) applies after the first sale or other transfer of ownership of the original or a copy of the work with the authorization of the author.

Article 7
Right of Rental

(1) Authors of:

(i) computer programs;

(ii) cinematographic works; and

(iii) works embodied in phonograms as determined in the national law of Contracting Parties, shall enjoy the exclusive right of authorizing commercial rental to the public of the originals or copies of their works.

(2) Paragraph (1) shall not apply:

(i) in the case of computer programs where the program itself is not the essential object of the rental; and

(ii) in the case of cinematographic works, unless such commercial rental has led to widespread copying of such works materially impairing the exclusive right of reproduction.

(3) Notwithstanding the provisions of paragraph (1), a Contracting Party that, on April 15, 1994, had and continues to have in force a system of equitable remuneration of authors for the rental of copies of their works embodied in phonograms may maintain that system provided that the

commercial rental of works embodied in phonograms is not giving rise to the material impairment of the exclusive rights of reproduction of authors.

Article 8
Right of Communication to the Public

Without prejudice to the provisions of Articles 11(1)(ii), 11bis(1)(i) and (ii), 11ter(1)(ii), 14(1)(ii) and 14bis(1) of the Berne Convention, authors of literary and artistic works shall enjoy the exclusive right of authorizing any communication to the public of their works, by wire or wireless means, including the making available to the public of their works in such a way that members of the public may access these works from a place and at a time individually chosen by them.

Article 9
Duration of the Protection of Photographic Works

In respect of photographic works, the Contracting Parties shall not apply the provisions of Article 7(4) of the Berne Convention.

Article 10
Limitations and Exceptions

(1) Contracting Parties may, in their national legislation, provide for limitations of or exceptions to the rights granted to authors of literary and artistic works under this Treaty in certain special cases that do not conflict with a normal exploitation of the work and do not unreasonably prejudice the legitimate interests of the author.

(2) Contracting Parties shall, when applying the Berne Convention, confine any limitations of or exceptions to rights provided for therein to certain special cases that do not conflict with a normal exploitation of the work and do not unreasonably prejudice the legitimate interests of the author.

Article 11
Obligations concerning Technological Measures

Contracting Parties shall provide adequate legal protection and effective legal remedies against the circumvention of effective technological measures that are used by authors in connection with the exercise of their rights under this Treaty or the Berne Convention and that restrict acts, in respect of their works, which are not authorized by the authors concerned or permitted by law.

Article 12
Obligations concerning Rights Management Information

(1) Contracting Parties shall provide adequate and effective legal remedies against any person knowingly performing any of the following acts knowing or, with respect to civil remedies having reasonable grounds to

know, that it will induce, enable, facilitate or conceal an infringement of any right covered by this Treaty or the Berne Convention:

(i) to remove or alter any electronic rights management information without authority;

(ii) to distribute, import for distribution, broadcast or communicate to the public, without authority, works or copies of works knowing that electronic rights management information has been removed or altered without authority.

(2) As used in this Article, "rights management information" means information which identifies the work, the author of the work, the owner of any right in the work, or information about the terms and conditions of use of the work, and any numbers or codes that represent such information, when any of these items of information is attached to a copy of a work or appears in connection with the communication of a work to the public.

Article 13
Application in Time

Contracting Parties shall apply the provisions of Article 18 of the Berne Convention to all protection provided for in this Treaty.

Article 14
Provisions on Enforcement of Rights

(1) Contracting Parties undertake to adopt, in accordance with their legal systems, the measures necessary to ensure the application of this Treaty.

(2) Contracting Parties shall ensure that enforcement procedures are available under their law so as to permit effective action against any act of infringement of rights covered by this Treaty, including expeditious remedies to prevent infringements and remedies which constitute a deterrent to further infringements.

Article 15
Assembly

(1)(a) The Contracting Parties shall have an Assembly.

(b) Each Contracting Party shall be represented by one delegate who may be assisted by alternate delegates, advisors and experts.

(c) The expenses of each delegation shall be borne by the Contracting Party that has appointed the delegation. The Assembly may ask the World Intellectual Property Organization (hereinafter referred to as "WIPO") to grant financial assistance to facilitate the participation of delegations of Contracting Parties that are regarded as developing countries in conformity with the established practice of the General Assembly of the United Nations or that are countries in transition to a market economy.

(2)(a) The Assembly shall deal with matters concerning the maintenance and development of this Treaty and the application and operation of this Treaty.

(b) The Assembly shall perform the function allocated to it under Article 17(2) in respect of the admission of certain intergovernmental organizations to become party to this Treaty.

(c) The Assembly shall decide the convocation of any diplomatic conference for the revision of this Treaty and give the necessary instructions to the Director General of WIPO for the preparation of such diplomatic conference.

(3)(a) Each Contracting Party that is a State shall have one vote and shall vote only in its own name.

(b) Any Contracting Party that is an intergovernmental organization may participate in the vote, in place of its Member States, with a number of votes equal to the number of its Member States which are party to this Treaty. No such intergovernmental organization shall participate in the vote if any one of its Member States exercises its right to vote and vice versa.

(4) The Assembly shall meet in ordinary session once every two years upon convocation by the Director General of WIPO.

(5) The Assembly shall establish its own rules of procedure, including the convocation of extraordinary sessions, the requirements of a quorum and, subject to the provisions of this Treaty, the required majority for various kinds of decisions.

Article 16
International Bureau

The International Bureau of WIPO shall perform the administrative tasks concerning the Treaty.

Article 17
Eligibility for Becoming Party to the Treaty

(1) Any Member State of WIPO may become party to this Treaty.

(2) The Assembly may decide to admit any intergovernmental organization to become party to this Treaty which declares that it is competent in respect of, and has its own legislation binding on all its Member States on, matters covered by this Treaty and that it has been duly authorized, in accordance with its internal procedures, to become party to this Treaty.

(3) The European Community, having made the declaration referred to in the preceding paragraph in the Diplomatic Conference that has adopted this Treaty, may become party to this Treaty.

Article 18
Rights and Obligations under the Treaty

Subject to any specific provisions to the contrary in this Treaty, each Contracting Party shall enjoy all of the rights and assume all of the obligations under this Treaty.

Article 19
Signature of the Treaty

This Treaty shall be open for signature until December 31, 1997, by any Member State of WIPO and by the European Community.

Article 20
Entry into Force of the Treaty

This Treaty shall enter into force three months after 30 instruments of ratification or accession by States have been deposited with the Director General of WIPO.

Article 21
Effective Date of Becoming Party to the Treaty

This Treaty shall bind

(i) the 30 States referred to in Article 20, from the date on which this Treaty has entered into force;

(ii) each other State from the expiration of three months from the date on which the State has deposited its instrument with the Director General of WIPO;

(iii) the European Community, from the expiration of three months after the deposit of its instrument of ratification or accession if such instrument has been deposited after the entry into force of this Treaty according to Article 20, or, three months after the entry into force of this Treaty if such instrument has been deposited before the entry into force of this Treaty;

(iv) any other intergovernmental organization that is admitted to become party to this Treaty, from the expiration of three months after the deposit of its instrument of accession.

Article 22
No Reservation to the Treaty

No reservation to this Treaty shall be admitted.

Article 23
Denunciation of the Treaty

This Treaty may be denounced by any Contracting Party by notification addressed to the Director General of WIPO. Any denunciation shall take effect one year from the date on which the Director General of WIPO received the notification.

Article 24
Languages of the Treaty

(1) This Treaty is signed in a single original in English, Arabic, Chinese, French, Russian and Spanish languages, the versions in all these languages being equally authentic.

(2) An official text in any language other than those referred to in paragraph (1) shall be established by the Director General of WIPO on the request of an interested party, after consultation with all the interested parties. For the purposes of this paragraph, "interested party" means any Member State of WIPO whose official language, or one of whose official languages, is involved and the European Community, and any other intergovernmental organization that may become party to this Treaty, if one of its official languages is involved.

Article 25
Depositary

The Director General of WIPO is the depositary of this Treaty.

THE W.I.P.O. PERFORMANCES AND PHONOGRAMS TREATY (CRNR/DC/95)

Adopted by the Diplomatic Conference on December 20, 1996

Contents

Preamble

The Contracting Parties,

Desiring to develop and maintain the protection of the rights of performers and producers of phonograms in a manner as effective and uniform as possible,

Recognizing the need to introduce new international rules in order to provide adequate solutions to the questions raised by economic, social, cultural and technological developments,

Recognizing the profound impact of the development and convergence of information and communication technologies on the production and use of performances and phonograms,

Recognizing the need to maintain a balance between the rights of the performers and producers of phonograms and the larger public interest, particularly education, research and access to information,

Have agreed as follows:

CHAPTER I

GENERAL PROVISIONS

Article 1
Relation to Other Conventions

(1) Nothing in this Treaty shall derogate from existing obligations that Contracting Parties have to each other under the International Convention for the Protection of Performers, Producers of Phonograms and Broadcasting Organizations done in Rome, October 26, 1961 (hereinafter the "Rome Convention").

(2) Protection granted under this Treaty shall leave intact and shall in no way affect the protection of copyright in literary and artistic works.

Consequently, no provision of this Treaty may be interpreted as prejudicing such protection.

(3) This Treaty shall not have any connection with, nor shall it prejudice any rights and obligations under, any other treaties.

Article 2
Definitions

For the purposes of this Treaty:

(a) "performers" are actors, singers, musicians, dancers, and other persons who act, sing, deliver, declaim, play in, interpret, or otherwise perform literary or artistic works or expressions of folklore;

(b) "phonogram" means the fixation of the sounds of a performance or of other sounds, or of a representation of sounds other than in the form of a fixation incorporated in a cinematographic or other audiovisual work;

(c) "fixation" means the embodiment of sounds, or of the representations thereof, from which they can be perceived, reproduced or communicated through a device;

(d) "producer of a phonogram" means the person, or the legal entity, who or which takes the initiative and has the responsibility for the first fixation of the sounds of a performance or other sounds, or the representations of sounds;

(e) "publication" of a fixed performance or a phonogram means the offering of copies of the fixed performance or the phonogram to the public, with the consent of the rightholder, and provided that copies are offered to the public in reasonable quantity;

(f) "broadcasting" means the transmission by wireless means for public reception of sounds or of images and sounds or of the representations thereof; such transmission by satellite is also "broadcasting"; transmission of encrypted signals is "broadcasting" where the means for decrypting are provided to the public by the broadcasting organization or with its consent;

(g) "communication to the public" of a performance or a phonogram means the transmission to the public by any medium, otherwise than by broadcasting, of sounds of a performance or the sounds or the representations of sounds fixed in a phonogram. For the purposes of Article 15, "communication to the public" includes making the sounds or representations of sounds fixed in a phonogram audible to the public.

Article 3
Beneficiaries of Protection under this Treaty

(1) Contracting Parties shall accord the protection provided under this Treaty to the performers and producers of phonograms who are nationals of other Contracting Parties.

(2) The nationals of other Contracting Parties shall be understood to be those performers or producers of phonograms who would meet the criteria for eligibility for protection provided under the Rome Convention, were all the Contracting Parties to this Treaty Contracting States of that Convention. In respect of these criteria of eligibility, Contracting Parties shall apply the relevant definitions in Article 2 of this Treaty.

(3) Any Contracting Party availing itself of the possibilities provided in Article 5(3) of the Rome Conventions or, for the purposes of Article 5 of the same Convention, Article 17 thereof shall make a notification as foreseen in those provisions to the Director General of the World Intellectual Property Organization (WIPO).

Article 4
National Treatment

(1) Each Contracting Party shall accord to nationals of other Contracting Parties, as defined in Article 3(2), the treatment it accords to its own nationals with regard to the exclusive rights specifically granted in this Treaty and to the right to equitable remuneration provided for in Article 15 of this Treaty.

(2) The obligation provided for in paragraph (1) does not apply to the extent that another Contracting Party makes use of the reservations permitted by Article 15(3) of this Treaty.

CHAPTER II

RIGHTS OF PERFORMERS

Article 5
Moral Rights of Performers

(1) Independently of a performer's economic rights, and even after the transfer of those rights, the performer shall, as regards his live aural performances or perfomances fixed in phonograms have the right to claim to be identified as the performer of his performances, except where omission is dictated by the manner of the use of the performance, and to object to any distortion, mutilation or other modification of his performances that would be prejudicial to his reputation.

(2) The rights granted to a performer in accordance with paragraph (1) shall, after his death, be maintained, at least until the expiry of the economic rights, and shall be exercisable by the persons or institutions authorized by the legislation of the Contracting Party where protection is claimed. However, those Contracting Parties whose legislation, at the moment of their ratification of or accession to this Treaty, does not provide for protection after the death of the performer of all rights set out in the preceding paragraph may provide that some of these rights will, after his death, cease to be maintained.

(3) The means of redress for safeguarding the rights granted under this Article shall be governed by the legislation of the Contracting Party where protection is claimed.

Article 6
Economic Rights of Performers in their Unfixed Performances

Performers shall enjoy the exclusive right of authorizing, as regards their performances:

(i) the broadcasting and communication to the public of their unfixed performances except where the performance is already a broadcast performance; and

(ii) the fixation of their unfixed performances.

Article 7
Right of Reproduction

Performers shall enjoy the exclusive right of authorizing the direct or indirect reproduction of their performances fixed in phonograms, in any manner or form.

Article 8
Right of Distribution

(1) Performers shall enjoy the exclusive right of authorizing the making available to the public of the original and copies of their performances fixed in phonograms through sale or other transfer of ownership.

(2) Nothing in this Treaty shall affect the freedom of Contracting Parties to determine the conditions, if any, under which the exhaustion of the right in paragraph (1) applies after the first sale or other transfer of ownership of the original or a copy of the fixed performance with the authorization of the performer.

Article 9
Right of Rental

(1) Performers shall enjoy the exclusive right of authorizing the commercial rental to the public of the original and copies of their performances fixed in phonograms as determined in the national law of Contracting Parties, even after distribution of them by, or pursuant to, authorization by the performer.

(2) Notwithstanding the provisions of paragraph (1), a Contracting Party that, on April 15, 1994, had and continues to have in force a system of equitable remuneration of performers for the rental of copies of their performances fixed in phonograms, may maintain that system provided that the commercial rental of phonograms is not giving rise to the material impairment of the exclusive rights of reproduction of performers.

Article 10
Right of Making Available of Fixed Performances

Performers shall enjoy the exclusive right of authorizing the making available to the public of their performances fixed in phonograms, by wire or wireless means, in such a way that members of the public may access them from a place and at a time individually chosen by them.

CHAPTER III

RIGHTS OF PRODUCERS OF PHONOGRAMS

Article 11
Right of Reproduction

Producers of phonograms shall enjoy the exclusive right of authorizing the direct or indirect reproduction of their phonograms, in any manner or form.

Article 12
Right of Distribution

(1) Producers of phonograms shall enjoy the exclusive right of authorizing the making available to the public of the original and copies of their phonograms through sale or other transfer of ownership.

(2) Nothing in this Treaty shall affect the freedom of Contracting Parties to determine the conditions, if any, under which the exhaustion of the right in paragraph (1) applies after the first sale or transfer of ownership of the original or a copy of the phonogram with the authorization of the producer of phonograms.

Article 13
Right of Rental

(1) Producers of phonograms shall enjoy the exclusive right of authorizing the commercial rental to the public of the original and copies of their phonograms, even after distribution of them by or pursuant to authorization by the producer.

(2) Notwithstanding the provisions of paragraph (1), a Contracting Party that, on April 15, 1994, had and continues to have in force a system of equitable remuneration of producers of phonograms for the rental of copies of their phonograms, may maintain that system provided that the commercial rental of phonograms is not giving rise to the material impairment of the exclusive rights of reproduction of producers of phonograms.

Article 14
Right of Making Available of Phonograms

Producers of phonograms shall enjoy the exclusive right of authorizing the making available to the public of their phonograms, by wire or wireless means, in such a way that members of the public may access them from a place and at a time individually chosen by them.

CHAPTER IV

COMMON PROVISIONS

Article 15
Right to Remuneration for Broadcasting and Communication to the Public

(1) Performers and producers of phonograms shall enjoy the right to a single equitable remuneration for the direct or indirect use of phonograms published for commercial purposes for broadcasting or for any communication to the public.

(2) Contracting Parties may establish in their national legislation that the single equitable remuneration shall be claimed from the user by the performer or by the producer of a phonogram or by both. Contracting Parties may enact national legislation that, in the absence of an agreement between the performer and the producer of a phonogram, sets the terms according to which performers and producers of phonograms shall share the single equitable remuneration.

(3) Any Contracting Party may in a notification deposited with the Director General of WIPO, declare that it will apply the provisions of paragraph (1) only in respect of certain uses, or that it will limit their application in some other way, or that it will not apply these provisions at all.

(4) For the purposes of this Article, phonograms made available to the to the public by wire or wireless means in such a way that members of the public may access them from a place and at a time individually chosen by them shall be considered as if they had been published for commercial purposes.

Article 16
Limitations and Exceptions

(1) Contracting Parties may, in their national legislation, provide for the same kinds of limitations or exceptions with regard to the protection of performers and producers of phonograms as they provide for, in their national legislation, in connection with the protection of copyright in literary and artistic works.

(2) Contracting Parties shall confine any limitations of or exceptions to rights provided for in this Treaty to certain special cases which do not conflict with a normal exploitation of the performance or phonogram and do not unreasonably prejudice the legitimate interests of the performer or of the producer of phonograms.

Article 17
Term of Protection

(1) The term of protection to be granted to performers under this Treaty shall last, at least, until the end of a period of 50 years computed from the end of the year in which the performance was fixed in a phonogram.

(2) The term of protection to be granted to producers of phonograms under this Treaty shall last, at least, until the end of a period of 50 years computed from the end of the year in which the phonogram was published, or failing such publication within 50 years from fixation of the phonogram, 50 years from the end of the year in which the fixation was made.

Article 18
Obligations concerning Technological Measures

Contracting Parties shall provide adequate legal protection and effective legal remedies against the circumvention of effective technological measures that are used by performers or producers of phonograms in connection with the exercise of their rights under this Treaty and that restrict acts, in respect of their performances or phonograms, which are not authorized by the performers or the producers of phonograms concerned or permitted by law.

Article 19
Obligations concerning Rights Management Information

(1) Contracting Parties shall provide adequate and effective legal remedies against any person knowingly performing any of the following acts knowing or, with respect to civil remedies, having reasonable grounds to know that it will induce, enable, facilitate or conceal an infringement of any right covered by this Treaty:

(i) to remove or alter any electronic rights management information without authority;

(ii) to distribute, import for distribution, broadcast, communicate or make available to the public, without authority, performances, copies of fixed performances or phonograms knowing that electronic rights management information has been removed or altered without authority.

(2) As used in this Article, "rights management information" means information which identifies the performer, the performance of the performer, the producer of the phonogram, the phonogram, the owner of any right in the performance or phonogram, or information about the terms and conditions of use of the performance or phonogram, and any numbers or codes that represent such information, when any of these items of information is attached to a copy of a fixed performance or a phonogram or appears in connection with the communication or making available of a fixed performance or a phonogram to the public.

Article 20
Formalities

The enjoyment and exercise of the rights provided for in this Treaty shall not be subject to any formality.

Article 21
Reservations

Subject to the provisions of Article 15(3), no reservations to this Treaty shall be permitted.

Article 22
Application in Time

(1) Contracting Parties shall apply the provisions of Article 18 of the Berne Convention, mutatis mutandis, to the rights of performers and producers of phonograms provided for in this Treaty.

(2) Notwithstanding paragraph (1), a Contracting Party may limit the application of Article 5 of this Treaty to performances which occurred after the entry into force of this Treaty for that Party.

Article 23
Provisions on Enforcement of Rights

(1) Contracting Parties undertake to adopt, in accordance with their legal systems, the measures necessary to ensure the application of this Treaty.

(2) Contracting Parties shall ensure that enforcement procedures are available under their law so as to permit effective action against any act of infringement of rights covered by this Treaty, including expeditious remedies to prevent infringements and remedies which constitute a deterrent to further infringements.

CHAPTER V

ADMINISTRATIVE AND FINAL CLAUSES

Article 24
Assembly

(1)(a) The Contracting Parties shall have an Assembly.

(b) Each Contracting Party shall be represented by one delegate who may be assisted by alternate delegates, advisors and experts.

(c) The expenses of each delegation shall be borne by the Contracting Party that has appointed the delegation. The Assembly may ask WIPO to grant financial assistance to facilitate the participation of delegations of Contracting Parties that are regarded as developing countries in conformity with the established practice of the General Assembly of the United Nations or that are countries in transition to a market economy.

(2)(a) The Assembly shall deal with matters concerning the maintenance and development of this Treaty and the application and operation of this Treaty.

(b) The Assembly shall perform the function allocated to it under Article 26(2) in respect of the admission of certain intergovernmental organizations to become party to this Treaty.

(c) The Assembly shall decide the convocation of any diplomatic conference for the revision of this Treaty and give the necessary instructions to the Director General of WIPO for the preparation of such diplomatic conference.

(3)(a) Each Contracting Party that is a State shall have one vote and shall vote only in its own name.

(b) Any Contracting Party that is an intergovernmental organization may participate in the vote, in place of its Member States, with a number of votes equal to the number of its Member States which are party to this Treaty. No such intergovernmental organization shall participate in the vote if any one of its Member States exercises its right to vote and vice versa.

(4) The Assembly shall meet in ordinary session once every two years upon convocation by the Director General of WIPO.

(5) The Assembly shall establish its own rules of procedure, including the convocation of extraordinary sessions, the requirements of a quorum and, subject to the provisions of this Treaty, the required majority for various kinds of decisions.

Article 25
International Bureau

The International Bureau of WIPO shall perform the administrative tasks concerning the Treaty.

Article 26
Eligibility for Becoming Party to the Treaty

(1) Any Member State of WIPO may become party to this Treaty.

(2) The Assembly may decide to admit any intergovernmental organization to become party to this Treaty which declares that it is competent in respect of, and has its own legislation binding on all its Member States on, matters covered by this Treaty and that it has been duly authorized, in accordance with its internal procedures, to become party to this Treaty.

(3) The European Community, having made the declaration referred to in the preceding paragraph in the Diplomatic Conference that has adopted this Treaty, may become party to this Treaty.

Article 27
Rights and Obligations under the Treaty

Subject to any specific provisions to the contrary in this Treaty, each Contracting Party shall enjoy all of the rights and assume all of the obligations under this Treaty.

Article 28
Signature of the Treaty

This Treaty shall be open for signature until December 31, 1997, by any Member State of WIPO and by the European Community.

Article 29
Entry into Force of the Treaty

This Treaty shall enter into force three months after 30 instruments of ratification or accession by States have been deposited with the Director General of WIPO.

Article 30
Effective Date of Becoming Party to the Treaty

This Treaty shall bind

(i) the 30 States referred to in Article 29, from the date on which this Treaty has entered into force;

(ii) each other State from the expiration of three months from the date on which the State has deposited its instrument with the Director General of WIPO;

(iii) the European Community, from the expiration of three months after the deposit of its instrument of ratification or accession if such instrument has been deposited after the entry into force of this Treaty according to Article 29, or, three months after the entry into force of this Treaty if such instrument has been deposited before the entry into force of this Treaty;

(iv) any other intergovernmental organization that is admitted to become party to this Treaty, from the expiration of three months after the deposit of its instrument of accession.

Article 31
Denunciation of the Treaty

This Treaty may be denounced by any Contracting Party by notification addressed to the Director General of WIPO. Any denunciation shall take effect one year from the date on which the Director General of WIPO received the notification.

Article 32
Languages of the Treaty

(1) This Treaty is signed in a single original in English, Arabic, Chinese, French, Russian and Spanish languages, the versions in all these languages being equally authentic.

(2) An official text in any language other than those referred to in paragraph (1) shall be established by the Director General of WIPO on the request of an interested party, after consultation with all the interested parties. For the purposes of this paragraph, "interested party" means any Member State of WIPO whose official language, or one of whose official languages, is involved and the European Community, and any other intergovernmental organization that may become party to this Treaty, if one of its official languages is involved.

Article 33
Depositary

The Director General of WIPO is the depositary of this Treaty.

EUROPEAN UNION INTERNET COPYRIGHT DIRECTIVE

Directive 2001/29/EC of the European Parliament and of the Council of 22 May 2001 on the harmonisation of certain aspects of copyright and related rights in the information society

THE EUROPEAN PARLIAMENT AND THE COUNCIL OF THE EUROPEAN UNION,

Having regard to the Treaty establishing the European Community, and in particular Articles 47(2), 55 and 95 thereof,

Having regard to the proposal from the Commission, [1]

Having regard to the Opinion of the Economic and Social Committee, [2]

Acting in accordance with the procedure laid down in Article 251 of the Treaty, [3]

Whereas:

(1) The Treaty provides for the establishment of an internal market and the institution of a system ensuring that competition in the internal market is not distorted. Harmonisation of the laws of the Member States on copyright and related rights contributes to the achievement of these objectives.

(2) The European Council, meeting at Corfu on 24 and 25 June 1994, stressed the need to create a general and flexible legal framework at Community level in order to foster the development of the information society in Europe. This requires, *inter alia*, the existence of an internal market for new products and services. Important Community legislation to ensure such a regulatory framework is already in place or its adoption is well under way. Copyright and related rights play an important role in this context as they protect and stimulate the development and marketing of new products and services and the creation and exploitation of their creative content.

(3) The proposed harmonisation will help to implement the four freedoms of the internal market and relates to compliance with the fundamental principles of law and especially of property, including intellectual property, and freedom of expression and the public interest.

---

[1] OJ C 108, 7.4.1998, p. 6 and OJ C 180, 25.6.1999, p. 6.

[2] OJ C 407, 28.12.1998, p. 30.

[3] Opinion of the European Parliament of 10 February 1999 (OJ C 150, 28.5.1999, p. 171), Council Common Position of 28 September 2000 (OJ C 344, 1.12.2000, p. 1) and Decision of the European Parliament of 14 February 2001 (not yet published in the Official Journal). Council Decision of 9 April 2001.

(4) A harmonised legal framework on copyright and related rights, through increased legal certainty and while providing for a high level of protection of intellectual property, will foster substantial investment in creativity and innovation, including network infrastructure, and lead in turn to growth and increased competitiveness of European industry, both in the area of content provision and information technology and more generally across a wide range of industrial and cultural sectors. This will safeguard employment and encourage new job creation.

(5) Technological development has multiplied and diversified the vectors for creation, production and exploitation. While no new concepts for the protection of intellectual property are needed, the current law on copyright and related rights should be adapted and supplemented to respond adequately to economic realities such as new forms of exploitation.

(6) Without harmonisation at Community level, legislative activities at national level which have already been initiated in a number of Member States in order to respond to the technological challenges might result in significant differences in protection and thereby in restrictions on the free movement of services and products incorporating, or based on, intellectual property, leading to a refragmentation of the internal market and legislative inconsistency. The impact of such legislative differences and uncertainties will become more significant with the further development of the information society, which has already greatly increased transborder exploitation of intellectual property. This development will and should further increase. Significant legal differences and uncertainties in protection may hinder economies of scale for new products and services containing copyright and related rights.

(7) The Community legal framework for the protection of copyright and related rights must, therefore, also be adapted and supplemented as far as is necessary for the smooth functioning of the internal market. To that end, those national provisions on copyright and related rights which vary considerably from one Member State to another or which cause legal uncertainties hindering the smooth functioning of the internal market and the proper development of the information society in Europe should be adjusted, and inconsistent national responses to the technological developments should be avoided, whilst differences not adversely affecting the functioning of the internal market need not be removed or prevented.

(8) The various social, societal and cultural implications of the information society require that account be taken of the specific features of the content of products and services.

(9) Any harmonisation of copyright and related rights must take as a basis a high level of protection, since such rights are crucial to intellectual creation. Their protection helps to ensure the maintenance and development of creativity in the interests of authors, performers, producers, consumers, culture, industry and the public at large. Intellectual property has therefore been recognised as an integral part of property.

(10) If authors or performers are to continue their creative and artistic work, they have to receive an appropriate reward for the use of their work, as must producers in order to be able to finance this work. The investment required to produce products such as phonograms, films or multimedia products, and services such as 'on-demand' services, is considerable. Adequate legal protection of intellectual property rights is necessary in order to guarantee the availability of such a reward and provide the opportunity for satisfactory returns on this investment.

(11) A rigorous, effective system for the protection of copyright and related rights is one of the main ways of ensuring that European cultural creativity and production receive the necessary resources and of safeguarding the independence and dignity of artistic creators and performers.

(12) Adequate protection of copyright works and subject-matter of related rights is also of great importance from a cultural standpoint. Article 151 of the Treaty requires the Community to take cultural aspects into account in its action.

(13) A common search for, and consistent application at European level of, technical measures to protect works and other subject-matter and to provide the necessary information on rights are essential insofar as the ultimate aim of these measures is to give effect to the principles and guarantees laid down in law.

(14) This Directive should seek to promote learning and culture by protecting works and other subject-matter while permitting exceptions or limitations in the public interest for the purpose of education and teaching.

(15) The Diplomatic Conference held under the auspices of the World Intellectual Property Organisation (WIPO) in December 1996 led to the adoption of two new Treaties, the 'WIPO Copyright Treaty' and the 'WIPO Performances and Phonograms Treaty', dealing respectively with the protection of authors and the protection of performers and phonogram producers. Those Treaties update the international protection for copyright and related rights significantly, not least with regard to the so-called 'digital agenda', and improve the means to fight piracy world-wide. The Community and a majority of Member States have already signed the Treaties and the process of making arrangements for the ratification of the Treaties by the Community and the Member States is under way. This Directive also serves to implement a number of the new international obligations.

(16) Liability for activities in the network environment concerns not only copyright and related rights but also other areas, such as defamation, misleading advertising, or infringement of trademarks, and is addressed horizontally in Directive 2000/31/EC of the European Parliament and of the Council of 8 June 2000 on certain legal aspects of information society services, in particular electronic commerce, in the internal market ('Directive on electronic commerce')[1] , which clarifies and harmonises various

[1] OJ L 178, 17.7.2000, p. 1.

legal issues relating to information society services including electronic commerce. This Directive should be implemented within a timescale similar to that for the implementation of the Directive on electronic commerce, since that Directive provides a harmonised framework of principles and provisions relevant *inter alia* to important parts of this Directive. This Directive is without prejudice to provisions relating to liability in that Directive.

(17) It is necessary, especially in the light of the requirements arising out of the digital environment, to ensure that collecting societies achieve a higher level of rationalisation and transparency with regard to compliance with competition rules.

(18) This Directive is without prejudice to the arrangements in the Member States concerning the management of rights such as extended collective licences.

(19) The moral rights of rightholders should be exercised according to the legislation of the Member States and the provisions of the Berne Convention for the Protection of Literary and Artistic Works, of the WIPO Copyright Treaty and of the WIPO Performances and Phonograms Treaty. Such moral rights remain outside the scope of this Directive.

(20) This Directive is based on principles and rules already laid down in the Directives currently in force in this area, in particular Directives 91/250/EEC,[2] 92/100/EEC,[3] 93/83/EEC,[4] 93/98/EEC[5] and 96/9/EC,[6] and it develops those principles and rules and places them in the context of the information society. The provisions of this Directive should be without prejudice to the provisions of those Directives, unless otherwise provided in this Directive.

(21) This Directive should define the scope of the acts covered by the reproduction right with regard to the different beneficiaries. This should be done in conformity with the acquis communautaire. A broad definition of these acts is needed to ensure legal certainty within the internal market.

(22) The objective of proper support for the dissemination of culture must not be achieved by sacrificing strict protection of rights or by tolerating illegal forms of distribution of counterfeited or pirated works.

---

[2] Council Directive 91/250/EEC of 14 May 1991 on the legal protection of computer programs (OJ L 122, 17.5.1991, p. 42). Directive as amended by Directive 93/98/EEC.

[3] Council Directive 92/100/EEC of 19 November 1992 on rental right and lending right and on certain rights related to copyright in the field of intellectual property (OJ L 346, 27.11.1992, p. 61). Directive as amended by Directive 93/98/EEC.

[4] Council Directive 93/83/EEC of 27 September 1993 on the coordination of certain rules concerning copyright and rights related to copyright applicable to satellite broadcasting and cable retransmission (OJ L 248, 6.10.1993, p. 15).

[5] Council Directive 93/98/EEC of 29 October 1993 harmonising the term of protection of copyright and certain related rights (OJ L 290, 24.11.1993, p. 9).

[6] Directive 96/9/EC of the European Parliament and of the Council of 11 March 1996 on the legal protection of databases (OJ L 77, 27.3.1996, p. 20).

(23) This Directive should harmonise further the author's right of communication to the public. This right should be understood in a broad sense covering all communication to the public not present at the place where the communication originates. This right should cover any such transmission or retransmission of a work to the public by wire or wireless means, including broadcasting. This right should not cover any other acts.

(24) The right to make available to the public subject-matter referred to in Article 3(2) should be understood as covering all acts of making available such subject-matter to members of the public not present at the place where the act of making available originates, and as not covering any other acts.

(25) The legal uncertainty regarding the nature and the level of protection of acts of on-demand transmission of copyright works and subject-matter protected by related rights over networks should be overcome by providing for harmonised protection at Community level. It should be made clear that all rightholders recognised by this Directive should have an exclusive right to make available to the public copyright works or any other subject-matter by way of interactive on-demand transmissions. Such interactive on-demand transmissions are characterised by the fact that members of the public may access them from a place and at a time individually chosen by them.

(26) With regard to the making available in on-demand services by broadcasters of their radio or television productions incorporating music from commercial phonograms as an integral part thereof, collective licensing arrangements are to be encouraged in order to facilitate the clearance of the rights concerned.

(27) The mere provision of physical facilities for enabling or making a communication does not in itself amount to communication within the meaning of this Directive.

(28) Copyright protection under this Directive includes the exclusive right to control distribution of the work incorporated in a tangible article. The first sale in the Community of the original of a work or copies thereof by the rightholder or with his consent exhausts the right to control resale of that object in the Community. This right should not be exhausted in respect of the original or of copies thereof sold by the rightholder or with his consent outside the Community. Rental and lending rights for authors have been established in Directive 92/100/EEC. The distribution right provided for in this Directive is without prejudice to the provisions relating to the rental and lending rights contained in Chapter I of that Directive.

(29) The question of exhaustion does not arise in the case of services and on-line services in particular. This also applies with regard to a material copy of a work or other subject-matter made by a user of such a service with the consent of the rightholder. Therefore, the same applies to rental and lending of the original and copies of works or other subject-matter which are services by nature. Unlike CD-ROM or CD-I, where the intellectual property is incorporated in a material medium, namely an item of

goods, every on-line service is in fact an act which should be subject to authorisation where the copyright or related right so provides.

(30) The rights referred to in this Directive may be transferred, assigned or subject to the granting of contractual licences, without prejudice to the relevant national legislation on copyright and related rights.

(31) A fair balance of rights and interests between the different categories of rightholders, as well as between the different categories of rightholders and users of protected subject-matter must be safeguarded. The existing exceptions and limitations to the rights as set out by the Member States have to be reassessed in the light of the new electronic environment. Existing differences in the exceptions and limitations to certain restricted acts have direct negative effects on the functioning of the internal market of copyright and related rights. Such differences could well become more pronounced in view of the further development of transborder exploitation of works and cross-border activities. In order to ensure the proper functioning of the internal market, such exceptions and limitations should be defined more harmoniously. The degree of their harmonisation should be based on their impact on the smooth functioning of the internal market.

(32) This Directive provides for an exhaustive enumeration of exceptions and limitations to the reproduction right and the right of communication to the public. Some exceptions or limitations only apply to the reproduction right, where appropriate. This list takes due account of the different legal traditions in Member States, while, at the same time, aiming to ensure a functioning internal market. Member States should arrive at a coherent application of these exceptions and limitations, which will be assessed when reviewing implementing legislation in the future.

(33) The exclusive right of reproduction should be subject to an exception to allow certain acts of temporary reproduction, which are transient or incidental reproductions, forming an integral and essential part of a technological process and carried out for the sole purpose of enabling either efficient transmission in a network between third parties by an intermediary, or a lawful use of a work or other subject-matter to be made. The acts of reproduction concerned should have no separate economic value on their own. To the extent that they meet these conditions, this exception should include acts which enable browsing as well as acts of caching to take place, including those which enable transmission systems to function efficiently, provided that the intermediary does not modify the information and does not interfere with the lawful use of technology, widely recognised and used by industry, to obtain data on the use of the information. A use should be considered lawful where it is authorised by the rightholder or not restricted by law.

(34) Member States should be given the option of providing for certain exceptions or limitations for cases such as educational and scientific purposes, for the benefit of public institutions such as libraries and archives, for purposes of news reporting, for quotations, for use by people

with disabilities, for public security uses and for uses in administrative and judicial proceedings.

(35) In certain cases of exceptions or limitations, rightholders should receive fair compensation to compensate them adequately for the use made of their protected works or other subject-matter. When determining the form, detailed arrangements and possible level of such fair compensation, account should be taken of the particular circumstances of each case. When evaluating these circumstances, a valuable criterion would be the possible harm to the rightholders resulting from the act in question. In cases where rightholders have already received payment in some other form, for instance as part of a licence fee, no specific or separate payment may be due. The level of fair compensation should take full account of the degree of use of technological protection measures referred to in this Directive. In certain situations where the prejudice to the rightholder would be minimal, no obligation for payment may arise.

(36) The Member States may provide for fair compensation for rightholders also when applying the optional provisions on exceptions or limitations which do not require such compensation.

(37) Existing national schemes on reprography, where they exist, do not create major barriers to the internal market. Member States should be allowed to provide for an exception or limitation in respect of reprography.

(38) Member States should be allowed to provide for an exception or limitation to the reproduction right for certain types of reproduction of audio, visual and audio-visual material for private use, accompanied by fair compensation. This may include the introduction or continuation of remuneration schemes to compensate for the prejudice to rightholders. Although differences between those remuneration schemes affect the functioning of the internal market, those differences, with respect to analogue private reproduction, should not have a significant impact on the development of the information society. Digital private copying is likely to be more widespread and have a greater economic impact. Due account should therefore be taken of the differences between digital and analogue private copying and a distinction should be made in certain respects between them.

(39) When applying the exception or limitation on private copying, Member States should take due account of technological and economic developments, in particular with respect to digital private copying and remuneration schemes, when effective technological protection measures are available. Such exceptions or limitations should not inhibit the use of technological measures or their enforcement against circumvention.

(40) Member States may provide for an exception or limitation for the benefit of certain non-profit making establishments, such as publicly accessible libraries and equivalent institutions, as well as archives. However, this should be limited to certain special cases covered by the reproduction right. Such an exception or limitation should not cover uses made in the context of on-line delivery of protected works or other subject-matter.

This Directive should be without prejudice to the Member States" option to derogate from the exclusive public lending right in accordance with Article 5 of Directive 92/100/EEC. Therefore, specific contracts or licences should be promoted which, without creating imbalances, favour such establishments and the disseminative purposes they serve.

(41) When applying the exception or limitation in respect of ephemeral recordings made by broadcasting organisations it is understood that a broadcaster"s own facilities include those of a person acting on behalf of and under the responsibility of the broadcasting organisation.

(42) When applying the exception or limitation for non-commercial educational and scientific research purposes, including distance learning, the non-commercial nature of the activity in question should be determined by that activity as such. The organisational structure and the means of funding of the establishment concerned are not the decisive factors in this respect.

(43) It is in any case important for the Member States to adopt all necessary measures to facilitate access to works by persons suffering from a disability which constitutes an obstacle to the use of the works themselves, and to pay particular attention to accessible formats.

(44) When applying the exceptions and limitations provided for in this Directive, they should be exercised in accordance with international obligations. Such exceptions and limitations may not be applied in a way which prejudices the legitimate interests of the rightholder or which conflicts with the normal exploitation of his work or other subject-matter. The provision of such exceptions or limitations by Member States should, in particular, duly reflect the increased economic impact that such exceptions or limitations may have in the context of the new electronic environment. Therefore, the scope of certain exceptions or limitations may have to be even more limited when it comes to certain new uses of copyright works and other subject-matter.

(45) The exceptions and limitations referred to in Article 5(2), (3) and (4) should not, however, prevent the definition of contractual relations designed to ensure fair compensation for the rightholders insofar as permitted by national law.

(46) Recourse to mediation could help users and rightholders to settle disputes. The Commission, in cooperation with the Member States within the Contact Committee, should undertake a study to consider new legal ways of settling disputes concerning copyright and related rights.

(47) Technological development will allow rightholders to make use of technological measures designed to prevent or restrict acts not authorised by the rightholders of any copyright, rights related to copyright or the *sui generis* right in databases. The danger, however, exists that illegal activities might be carried out in order to enable or facilitate the circumvention of the technical protection provided by these measures. In order to avoid fragmented legal approaches that could potentially hinder the functioning of

the internal market, there is a need to provide for harmonised legal protection against circumvention of effective technological measures and against provision of devices and products or services to this effect.

(48) Such legal protection should be provided in respect of technological measures that effectively restrict acts not authorised by the rightholders of any copyright, rights related to copyright or the *sui generis* right in databases without, however, preventing the normal operation of electronic equipment and its technological development. Such legal protection implies no obligation to design devices, products, components or services to correspond to technological measures, so long as such device, product, component or service does not otherwise fall under the prohibition of Article 6. Such legal protection should respect proportionality and should not prohibit those devices or activities which have a commercially significant purpose or use other than to circumvent the technical protection. In particular, this protection should not hinder research into cryptography.

(49) The legal protection of technological measures is without prejudice to the application of any national provisions which may prohibit the private possession of devices, products or components for the circumvention of technological measures.

(50) Such a harmonised legal protection does not affect the specific provisions on protection provided for by Directive 91/250/EEC. In particular, it should not apply to the protection of technological measures used in connection with computer programs, which is exclusively addressed in that Directive. It should neither inhibit nor prevent the development or use of any means of circumventing a technological measure that is necessary to enable acts to be undertaken in accordance with the terms of Article 5(3) or Article 6 of Directive 91/250/EEC. Articles 5 and 6 of that Directive exclusively determine exceptions to the exclusive rights applicable to computer programs.

(51) The legal protection of technological measures applies without prejudice to public policy, as reflected in Article 5, or public security. Member States should promote voluntary measures taken by rightholders, including the conclusion and implementation of agreements between rightholders and other parties concerned, to accommodate achieving the objectives of certain exceptions or limitations provided for in national law in accordance with this Directive. In the absence of such voluntary measures or agreements within a reasonable period of time, Member States should take appropriate measures to ensure that rightholders provide beneficiaries of such exceptions or limitations with appropriate means of benefiting from them, by modifying an implemented technological measure or by other means. However, in order to prevent abuse of such measures taken by rightholders, including within the framework of agreements, or taken by a Member State, any technological measures applied in implementation of such measures should enjoy legal protection.

(52) When implementing an exception or limitation for private copying in accordance with Article 5(2)(b), Member States should likewise promote

the use of voluntary measures to accommodate achieving the objectives of such exception or limitation. If, within a reasonable period of time, no such voluntary measures to make reproduction for private use possible have been taken, Member States may take measures to enable beneficiaries of the exception or limitation concerned to benefit from it. Voluntary measures taken by rightholders, including agreements between rightholders and other parties concerned, as well as measures taken by Member States, do not prevent rightholders from using technological measures which are consistent with the exceptions or limitations on private copying in national law in accordance with Article 5(2)(b), taking account of the condition of fair compensation under that provision and the possible differentiation between various conditions of use in accordance with Article 5(5), such as controlling the number of reproductions. In order to prevent abuse of such measures, any technological measures applied in their implementation should enjoy legal protection.

(53) The protection of technological measures should ensure a secure environment for the provision of interactive on-demand services, in such a way that members of the public may access works or other subject-matter from a place and at a time individually chosen by them. Where such services are governed by contractual arrangements, the first and second subparagraphs of Article 6(4) should not apply. Non-interactive forms of online use should remain subject to those provisions.

(54) Important progress has been made in the international standardisation of technical systems of identification of works and protected subject-matter in digital format. In an increasingly networked environment, differences between technological measures could lead to an incompatibility of systems within the Community. Compatibility and interoperability of the different systems should be encouraged. It would be highly desirable to encourage the development of global systems.

(55) Technological development will facilitate the distribution of works, notably on networks, and this will entail the need for rightholders to identify better the work or other subject-matter, the author or any other rightholder, and to provide information about the terms and conditions of use of the work or other subject-matter in order to render easier the management of rights attached to them. Rightholders should be encouraged to use markings indicating, in addition to the information referred to above, inter alia their authorisation when putting works or other subject-matter on networks.

(56) There is, however, the danger that illegal activities might be carried out in order to remove or alter the electronic copyright-management information attached to it, or otherwise to distribute, import for distribution, broadcast, communicate to the public or make available to the public works or other protected subject-matter from which such information has been removed without authority. In order to avoid fragmented legal approaches that could potentially hinder the functioning of the internal market, there is a need to provide for harmonised legal protection against any of these activities.

(57) Any such rights-management information systems referred to above may, depending on their design, at the same time process personal data about the consumption patterns of protected subject-matter by individuals and allow for tracing of on-line behaviour. These technical means, in their technical functions, should incorporate privacy safeguards in accordance with Directive 95/46/EC of the European Parliament and of the Council of 24 October 1995 on the protection of individuals with regard to the processing of personal data and the free movement of such data.[1]

(58) Member States should provide for effective sanctions and remedies for infringements of rights and obligations as set out in this Directive. They should take all the measures necessary to ensure that those sanctions and remedies are applied. The sanctions thus provided for should be effective, proportionate and dissuasive and should include the possibility of seeking damages and/or injunctive relief and, where appropriate, of applying for seizure of infringing material.

(59) In the digital environment, in particular, the services of intermediaries may increasingly be used by third parties for infringing activities. In many cases such intermediaries are best placed to bring such infringing activities to an end. Therefore, without prejudice to any other sanctions and remedies available, rightholders should have the possibility of applying for an injunction against an intermediary who carries a third party"s infringement of a protected work or other subject-matter in a network. This possibility should be available even where the acts carried out by the intermediary are exempted under Article 5. The conditions and modalities relating to such injunctions should be left to the national law of the Member States.

(60) The protection provided under this Directive should be without prejudice to national or Community legal provisions in other areas, such as industrial property, data protection, conditional access, access to public documents, and the rule of media exploitation chronology, which may affect the protection of copyright or related rights.

(61) In order to comply with the WIPO Performances and Phonograms Treaty, Directives 92/100/EEC and 93/98/EEC should be amended,

HAVE ADOPTED THIS DIRECTIVE:

CHAPTER I

OBJECTIVE AND SCOPE

Article 1

Scope

1. This Directive concerns the legal protection of copyright and related rights in the framework of the internal market, with particular emphasis on the information society.

---

[1] OJ L 281, 23.11.1995, p. 31.

2. Except in the cases referred to in Article 11, this Directive shall leave intact and shall in no way affect existing Community provisions relating to:

(a) the legal protection of computer programs;

(b) rental right, lending right and certain rights related to copyright in the field of intellectual property;

(c) copyright and related rights applicable to broadcasting of programmes by satellite and cable retransmission;

(d) the term of protection of copyright and certain related rights;

(e) the legal protection of databases.

CHAPTER II

RIGHTS AND EXCEPTIONS

Article 2

Reproduction right

Member States shall provide for the exclusive right to authorise or prohibit direct or indirect, temporary or permanent reproduction by any means and in any form, in whole or in part:

(a) for authors, of their works;

(b) for performers, of fixations of their performances;

(c) for phonogram producers, of their phonograms;

(d) for the producers of the first fixations of films, in respect of the original and copies of their films;

(e) for broadcasting organisations, of fixations of their broadcasts, whether those broadcasts are transmitted by wire or over the air, including by cable or satellite.

Article 3

Right of communication to the public of works and right of making available to the public other subject-matter

1. Member States shall provide authors with the exclusive right to authorise or prohibit any communication to the public of their works, by wire or wireless means, including the making available to the public of their works in such a way that members of the public may access them from a place and at a time individually chosen by them.

2. Member States shall provide for the exclusive right to authorise or prohibit the making available to the public, by wire or wireless means, in such a way that members of the public may access them from a place and at a time individually chosen by them:

(a) for performers, of fixations of their performances;

(b) for phonogram producers, of their phonograms;

(c) for the producers of the first fixations of films, of the original and copies of their films;

(d) for broadcasting organisations, of fixations of their broadcasts, whether these broadcasts are transmitted by wire or over the air, including by cable or satellite.

3. The rights referred to in paragraphs 1 and 2 shall not be exhausted by any act of communication to the public or making available to the public as set out in this Article.

Article 4

Distribution right

1. Member States shall provide for authors, in respect of the original of their works or of copies thereof, the exclusive right to authorise or prohibit any form of distribution to the public by sale or otherwise.

2. The distribution right shall not be exhausted within the Community in respect of the original or copies of the work, except where the first sale or other transfer of ownership in the Community of that object is made by the rightholder or with his consent.

Article 5

Exceptions and limitations

1. Temporary acts of reproduction referred to in Article 2, which are transient or incidental [and] an integral and essential part of a technological process and whose sole purpose is to enable:

(a) a transmission in a network between third parties by an intermediary, or

(b) a lawful use

of a work or other subject-matter to be made, and which have no independent economic significance, shall be exempted from the reproduction right provided for in Article 2.

2. Member States may provide for exceptions or limitations to the reproduction right provided for in Article 2 in the following cases:

(a) in respect of reproductions on paper or any similar medium, effected by the use of any kind of photographic technique or by some other process having similar effects, with the exception of sheet music, provided that the rightholders receive fair compensation;

(b) in respect of reproductions on any medium made by a natural person for private use and for ends that are neither directly nor indirectly commercial, on condition that the rightholders receive fair compensation which takes account of the application or non-application of technological measures referred to in Article 6 to the work or subject-matter concerned;

(c) in respect of specific acts of reproduction made by publicly accessible libraries, educational establishments or museums, or by archives, which are not for direct or indirect economic or commercial advantage;

(d) in respect of ephemeral recordings of works made by broadcasting organisations by means of their own facilities and for their own broadcasts; the preservation of these recordings in official archives may, on the ground of their exceptional documentary character, be permitted;

(e) in respect of reproductions of broadcasts made by social institutions pursuing non-commercial purposes, such as hospitals or prisons, on condition that the rightholders receive fair compensation.

3. Member States may provide for exceptions or limitations to the rights provided for in Articles 2 and 3 in the following cases:

(a) use for the sole purpose of illustration for teaching or scientific research, as long as the source, including the author's name, is indicated, unless this turns out to be impossible and to the extent justified by the non-commercial purpose to be achieved;

(b) uses, for the benefit of people with a disability, which are directly related to the disability and of a non-commercial nature, to the extent required by the specific disability;

(c) reproduction by the press, communication to the public or making available of published articles on current economic, political or religious topics or of broadcast works or other subject-matter of the same character, in cases where such use is not expressly reserved, and as long as the source, including the author's name, is indicated, or use of works or other subject-matter in connection with the reporting of current events, to the extent justified by the informatory purpose and as long as the source, including the author's name, is indicated, unless this turns out to be impossible;

(d) quotations for purposes such as criticism or review, provided that they relate to a work or other subject-matter which has already been lawfully made available to the public, that, unless this turns out to be impossible, the source, including the author's name, is indicated, and that their use is in accordance with fair practice, and to the extent required by the specific purpose;

(e) use for the purposes of public security or to ensure the proper performance or reporting of administrative, parliamentary or judicial proceedings;

(f) use of political speeches as well as extracts of public lectures or similar works or subject-matter to the extent justified by the informatory purpose and provided that the source, including the author's name, is indicated, except where this turns out to be impossible;

(g) use during religious celebrations or official celebrations organised by a public authority;

(h) use of works, such as works of architecture or sculpture, made to be located permanently in public places;

(i) incidental inclusion of a work or other subject-matter in other material;

(j) use for the purpose of advertising the public exhibition or sale of artistic works, to the extent necessary to promote the event, excluding any other commercial use;

(k) use for the purpose of caricature, parody or pastiche;

(l) use in connection with the demonstration or repair of equipment;

(m) use of an artistic work in the form of a building or a drawing or plan of a building for the purposes of reconstructing the building;

(n) use by communication or making available, for the purpose of research or private study, to individual members of the public by dedicated terminals on the premises of establishments referred to in paragraph 2(c) of works and other subject-matter not subject to purchase or licensing terms which are contained in their collections;

(o) use in certain other cases of minor importance where exceptions or limitations already exist under national law, provided that they only concern analogue uses and do not affect the free circulation of goods and services within the Community, without prejudice to the other exceptions and limitations contained in this Article.

4. Where the Member States may provide for an exception or limitation to the right of reproduction pursuant to paragraphs 2 and 3, they may provide similarly for an exception or limitation to the right of distribution as referred to in Article 4 to the extent justified by the purpose of the authorised act of reproduction.

5. The exceptions and limitations provided for in paragraphs 1, 2, 3 and 4 shall only be applied in certain special cases which do not conflict with a normal exploitation of the work or other subject-matter and do not unreasonably prejudice the legitimate interests of the rightholder.

CHAPTER III

PROTECTION OF TECHNOLOGICAL MEASURES AND RIGHTS-MANAGEMENT INFORMATION

Article 6

Obligations as to technological measures

1. Member States shall provide adequate legal protection against the circumvention of any effective technological measures, which the person concerned carries out in the knowledge, or with reasonable grounds to know, that he or she is pursuing that objective.

2. Member States shall provide adequate legal protection against the manufacture, import, distribution, sale, rental, advertisement for sale or rental, or possession for commercial purposes of devices, products or components or the provision of services which:

(a) are promoted, advertised or marketed for the purpose of circumvention of, or

(b) have only a limited commercially significant purpose or use other than to circumvent, or

(c) are primarily designed, produced, adapted or performed for the purpose of enabling or facilitating the circumvention of,

any effective technological measures.

3. For the purposes of this Directive, the expression 'technological measures' means any technology, device or component that, in the normal course of its operation, is designed to prevent or restrict acts, in respect of works or other subject-matter, which are not authorised by the rightholder of any copyright or any right related to copyright as provided for by law or the *sui generis* right provided for in Chapter III of Directive 96/9/EC. Technological measures shall be deemed 'effective' where the use of a protected work or other subject-matter is controlled by the rightholders through application of an access control or protection process, such as encryption, scrambling or other transformation of the work or other subject-matter or a copy control mechanism, which achieves the protection objective.

4. Notwithstanding the legal protection provided for in paragraph 1, in the absence of voluntary measures taken by rightholders, including agreements between rightholders and other parties concerned, Member States shall take appropriate measures to ensure that rightholders make available to the beneficiary of an exception or limitation provided for in national law in accordance with Article 5(2)(a), (2)(c), (2)(d), (2)(e), (3)(a), (3)(b) or (3)(e) the means of benefiting from that exception or limitation, to the extent necessary to benefit from that exception or limitation and where that beneficiary has legal access to the protected work or subject-matter concerned.

A Member State may also take such measures in respect of a beneficiary of an exception or limitation provided for in accordance with Article 5(2)(b), unless reproduction for private use has already been made possible by rightholders to the extent necessary to benefit from the exception or limitation concerned and in accordance with the provisions of Article 5(2)(b) and (5), without preventing rightholders from adopting adequate measures regarding the number of reproductions in accordance with these provisions.

The technological measures applied voluntarily by rightholders, including those applied in implementation of voluntary agreements, and technological measures applied in implementation of the measures taken by Member States, shall enjoy the legal protection provided for in paragraph 1.

The provisions of the first and second subparagraphs shall not apply to works or other subject-matter made available to the public on agreed contractual terms in such a way that members of the public may access them from a place and at a time individually chosen by them.

When this Article is applied in the context of Directives 92/100/EEC and 96/9/EC, this paragraph shall apply &it:mutatis mutandis.

Article 7

Obligations concerning rights-management information

1. Member States shall provide for adequate legal protection against any person knowingly performing without authority any of the following acts:

(a) the removal or alteration of any electronic rights-management information;

(b) the distribution, importation for distribution, broadcasting, communication or making available to the public of works or other subject-matter protected under this Directive or under Chapter III of Directive 96/9/EC from which electronic rights-management information has been removed or altered without authority,

if such person knows, or has reasonable grounds to know, that by so doing he is inducing, enabling, facilitating or concealing an infringement of any copyright or any rights related to copyright as provided by law, or of the *sui generis* right provided for in Chapter III of Directive 96/9/EC.

2. For the purposes of this Directive, the expression 'rights-management information' means any information provided by rightholders which identifies the work or other subject-matter referred to in this Directive or covered by the *sui generis* right provided for in Chapter III of Directive 96/9/EC, the author or any other rightholder, or information about the terms and conditions of use of the work or other subject-matter, and any numbers or codes that represent such information.

The first subparagraph shall apply when any of these items of information is associated with a copy of, or appears in connection with the communication to the public of, a work or other subject-matter referred to in this Directive or covered by the *sui generis* right provided for in Chapter III of Directive 96/9/EC.

CHAPTER IV

COMMON PROVISIONS

Article 8

Sanctions and remedies

1. Member States shall provide appropriate sanctions and remedies in respect of infringements of the rights and obligations set out in this

Directive and shall take all the measures necessary to ensure that those sanctions and remedies are applied. The sanctions thus provided for shall be effective, proportionate and dissuasive.

2. Each Member State shall take the measures necessary to ensure that rightholders whose interests are affected by an infringing activity carried out on its territory can bring an action for damages and/or apply for an injunction and, where appropriate, for the seizure of infringing material as well as of devices, products or components referred to in Article 6(2).

3. Member States shall ensure that rightholders are in a position to apply for an injunction against intermediaries whose services are used by a third party to infringe a copyright or related right.

Article 9

Continued application of other legal provisions

This Directive shall be without prejudice to provisions concerning in particular patent rights, trade marks, design rights, utility models, topographies of semi-conductor products, type faces, conditional access, access to cable of broadcasting services, protection of national treasures, legal deposit requirements, laws on restrictive practices and unfair competition, trade secrets, security, confidentiality, data protection and privacy, access to public documents, the law of contract.

Article 10

Application over time

1. The provisions of this Directive shall apply in respect of all works and other subject-matter referred to in this Directive which are, on 22 December 2002, protected by the Member States' legislation in the field of copyright and related rights, or which meet the criteria for protection under the provisions of this Directive or the provisions referred to in Article 1(2).

2. This Directive shall apply without prejudice to any acts concluded and rights acquired before 22 December 2002.

Article 11

Technical adaptations

1. Directive 92/100/EEC is hereby amended as follows:

(a) Article 7 shall be deleted;

(b) Article 10(3) shall be replaced by the following:

'3. The limitations shall only be applied in certain special cases which do not conflict with a normal exploitation of the subject-matter and do not unreasonably prejudice the legitimate interests of the rightholder.'

2. Article 3(2) of Directive 93/98/EEC shall be replaced by the following:

'2. The rights of producers of phonograms shall expire 50 years after the fixation is made. However, if the phonogram has been lawfully published within this period, the said rights shall expire 50 years from the date of the first lawful publication. If no lawful publication has taken place within the period mentioned in the first sentence, and if the phonogram has been lawfully communicated to the public within this period, the said rights shall expire 50 years from the date of the first lawful communication to the public.

However, where through the expiry of the term of protection granted pursuant to this paragraph in its version before amendment by Directive 2001/29/EC of the European Parliament and of the Council of 22 May 2001 on the harmonisation of certain aspects of copyright and related rights in the information society(*) the rights of producers of phonograms are no longer protected on 22 December 2002, this paragraph shall not have the effect of protecting those rights anew.'

Article 12

Final provisions

1. Not later than 22 December 2004 and every three years thereafter, the Commission shall submit to the European Parliament, the Council and the Economic and Social Committee a report on the application of this Directive, in which, *inter alia*, on the basis of specific information supplied by the Member States, it shall examine in particular the application of Articles 5, 6 and 8 in the light of the development of the digital market. In the case of Article 6, it shall examine in particular whether that Article confers a sufficient level of protection and whether acts which are permitted by law are being adversely affected by the use of effective technological measures. Where necessary, in particular to ensure the functioning of the internal market pursuant to Article 14 of the Treaty, it shall submit proposals for amendments to this Directive.

2. Protection of rights related to copyright under this Directive shall leave intact and shall in no way affect the protection of copyright.

3. A contact committee is hereby established. It shall be composed of representatives of the competent authorities of the Member States. It shall be chaired by a representative of the Commission and shall meet either on the initiative of the chairman or at the request of the delegation of a Member State.

4. The tasks of the committee shall be as follows:

(a) to examine the impact of this Directive on the functioning of the internal market, and to highlight any difficulties;

(*) OJ L 167, 22.6.2001, p. 10.

(b) to organise consultations on all questions deriving from the application of this Directive;

(c) to facilitate the exchange of information on relevant developments in legislation and case-law, as well as relevant economic, social, cultural and technological developments;

(d) to act as a forum for the assessment of the digital market in works and other items, including private copying and the use of technological measures.

Article 13

Implementation

1. Member States shall bring into force the laws, regulations and administrative provisions necessary to comply with this Directive before 22 December 2002. They shall forthwith inform the Commission thereof.

When Member States adopt these measures, they shall contain a reference to this Directive or shall be accompanied by such reference on the occasion of their official publication. The methods of making such reference shall be laid down by Member States.

2. Member States shall communicate to the Commission the text of the provisions of domestic law which they adopt in the field governed by this Directive.

Article 14

Entry into force

This Directive shall enter into force on the day of its publication in the *Official Journal of the European Communities.*

Article 15

Addressees

This Directive is addressed to the Member States.

Done at Brussels, 22 May 2001.

For the European Parliament

The President

N. FONTAINE

For the Council

The President

M. WINBERG

PART THREE:

INTELLECTUAL PROPERTY AND THE NETWORKED INFORMATION ENVIRONMENT

THE WHITE PAPER:
INTELLECTUAL PROPERTY AND THE
NATIONAL INFORMATION INFRASTRUCTURE *
(including H.R. 2441/S. 1284, 104th Cong., 2d Sess.)

THE REPORT OF THE WORKING GROUP ON
INTELLECTUAL PROPERTY RIGHTS

Bruce A. Lehman
Assistant Secretary of Commerce and
Commissioner of Patents and Trademarks
CHAIR

INFORMATION INFRASTRUCTURE TASK FORCE

Ronald H. Brown
Secretary of Commerce
CHAIR

SEPTEMBER 1995

INTRODUCTION

In February 1993, President Clinton formed the Information Infrastructure Task Force (IITF) to articulate and implement the Administration's vision for the National Information Infrastructure (NII). The IITF is chaired by Secretary of Commerce Ronald H. Brown and consists of high-level representatives of the Federal agencies that play a role in advancing the development and application of information technologies. Guided by the principles for government action described in *NII Agenda for Action*[1] and *GII Agenda for Cooperation*,[2] the participating agencies are working with the private sector, public interest groups, Congress, and State and local governments to develop comprehensive telecommunications and information policies and programs that will promote the development of the NII and best meet the country's needs.

To drive these efforts, the IITF is organized into three committees: the Telecommunications Policy Committee, which formulates Administration positions on relevant telecommunications issues; the Committee on Applications and Technology, which coordinates Administration efforts to develop, demonstrate and promote applications of information technologies in key

---

* Including selected footnotes only. — *Eds.*

[1] Information Infrastructure Task Force, *National Telecommunications and Information Administration, National Information Infrastructure: Agenda for Action* (Sept. 1993).

[2] Information Infrastructure Task Force, *Global Information Infrastructure: Agenda for Cooperation* (Feb. 1995).

areas; and the Information Policy Committee, which addresses critical information policy issues that must be dealt with if the NII is to be fully deployed and utilized. In addition, the IITF established a Security Issues Forum to assess the security needs and concerns of users, service providers, information providers, State and local governments and others. Finally, the U.S. Advisory Council on the National Information Infrastructure (NII Advisory Council) was established within the Department of Commerce to advise the Secretary of Commerce on a national strategy for promoting the development of the NII.

The Working Group on Intellectual Property Rights, which is chaired by Assistant Secretary of Commerce and Commissioner of Patents and Trademarks Bruce A. Lehman, was established within the Information Policy Committee to examine the intellectual property implications of the NII and make recommendations on any appropriate changes to U.S. intellectual property law and policy.

This Report represents the Working Group's examination and analysis of each of the major areas of intellectual property law, focusing primarily on copyright law and its application and effectiveness in the context of the NII.[5] The approach of this Report is to discuss the application of the existing copyright law and to recommend only those changes that are essential to adapt the law to the needs of the global information society. By providing a generalized legal framework, based on the extensive analysis and discussion of the way in which the law has been and should be interpreted, we can lay the groundwork for the rapid and efficient development of the NII.

To prepare this Report, the Working Group drew upon expertise within the participating departments and agencies of the Federal government. In addition, the Working Group received and considered views of the public, including those of the NII Advisory Council.

The Working Group held a public hearing in November 1993, at which 30 witnesses testified. The Working Group also solicited written comments and received some 70 statements during a public comment period which closed on December 10, 1993. Following its review of the public comments and analysis of the issues, the Working Group released a preliminary draft of its report ("Green Paper") on July 7, 1994.[10] The Working Group issued

---

[5] The "National Information Infrastructure," as it is discussed in this Report, encompasses digital, interactive services now available, such as the Internet, as well as those contemplated for the future. To make the analyses more concrete, however, the Working Group has, in many instances, evaluated the intellectual property implications of activity on the Internet, the superstructure whose protocols and rules effectively create (or permit the creation of) a "network of networks." This reflects neither an endorsement of the Internet nor a derogation of any other existing or proposed network or service that may be available via the NII, but, rather, an acknowledgment that a currently functioning structure lends itself more readily to legal analysis than a hypothetical construct based on future developments.

[10] *See* Information Infrastructure Task Force, Working Group on Intellectual Prop-

the report in preliminary draft form to ensure broad dissemination and ample opportunity for public comment prior to making final recommendations and issuing this Report. Thousands of copies of the Green Paper were distributed in paper form as well as electronically via the IITF Bulletin Board.[11]

Following the release of the Green Paper, the Working Group heard testimony from the public in four days of hearings in Chicago, Los Angeles and Washington, D.C., in September 1994. In addition, more than 1,500 pages of written comments on the Green Paper and reply comments were filed, in paper form and through the Internet, by more than 150 individuals and organizations — representing more than 425,000 members of the public — during the comment period, which extended over four months.

The Working Group convened a Conference on Fair Use (CONFU) to bring together copyright owner and user interests to discuss fair use issues and, if possible, to develop guidelines for uses of copyrighted works by librarians and educators. Some 60 interest groups are participants in the Conference and have been meeting regularly since September 1994 in sessions that are open to the public. The Working Group also kicked off a Copyright Awareness Campaign (CAC) in March 1995. Approximately 40 participating individuals and organizations are coordinating their educational efforts and joining with the Working Group and the Department of Education to raise public awareness of copyright. Meetings of the Campaign are also open to the public.

Interested parties had numerous opportunities to submit their views on the intellectual property implications of the development and use of the NII and on the Working Group's Green Paper, including its preliminary findings and recommendations. The open process instituted by the Working Group resulted in a well-developed, voluminous record indicating the views of a wide variety of interested parties, including various electronic industries, service providers, the academic, research, library and legal communities, and individual creators, copyright owners and users, as well as the computer software, motion picture, music, broadcasting, publishing and other information and entertainment industries.

The special intellectual property concerns and issues raised by the development and use of the NII are the subject of this Report.[14] It does

erty Rights, Intellectual Property and the National Information Infrastructure: A Preliminary Draft of the Report of the Working Group on Intellectual Property Rights (July 1994).

[11] The IITF Bulletin Board can be accessed through the Internet by pointing the Gopher Client to iitf.doc.gov or by telnet to iitf.doc.gov (log in as gopher). The Bulletin Board is also accessible at 202-501-1920 using a personal computer and a telephone modem.

[14] This Report does not attempt to address all existing intellectual property issues. For instance, current debates over protection of the design of useful articles and whether or to what extent certain aspects of computer programs are or should be protected under copyright law are not covered by this Report. Likewise, certain patent issues, such as pre-grant publication and reexamination, are not addressed.

not, however, provide all of the answers. It may not even present all of the questions. There is much that we do not — and cannot — now know about how the NII will develop. Technology is advancing at such an incredible pace that issues will certainly continue to arise in the future, perhaps demanding more comprehensive legislation. However, because there is much that we do know, the fact that future developments will raise additional issues not currently ripe should not deter us from addressing those that are.[15]

BACKGROUND

Intellectual property is a subtle and esoteric area of the law that evolves in response to technological change. Advances in technology particularly affect the operation and effectiveness of copyright law. Changes in technology generate new industries and new methods for reproduction and dissemination of works of authorship, which may present new opportunities for authors, but also create additional challenges. Copyright law has had to respond to those challenges, from Gutenberg's moveable type printing press to digital audio recorders and everything in between — photocopiers, radio, television, videocassette recorders, cable television and satellites.

Uses of computer technology — such as digitization — and communications technology — such as fiber optic cable — have had an enormous impact on the creation, reproduction and dissemination of copyrighted works. The merger of computer and communications technology into an integrated information technology has made possible the development of the National Information Infrastructure which will generate both unprecedented challenges and important opportunities for the copyright marketplace.

An information infrastructure already exists, but it is not integrated into a whole. Telephones, televisions, radios, computers and fax machines are used every day to receive, store, process, perform, display and transmit data, text, voice, sound and images in homes and businesses throughout the country. Fiber optics, wires, cables, switches, routers, microwave networks, satellites and other communications technologies currently connect telephones, computers and fax machines. The NII of tomorrow, however, will be much more than these separate communications networks; it will integrate them into an advanced high-speed, interactive, broadband,

---

[15] In the process of preparing this Report, the Working Group constantly received and evaluated information concerning a large variety of technological and other developments that bear on the NII and intellectual property rights in works distributed thereon. In April 1995, the Working Group was compelled to place the Report in concrete form, and, thus, to stop adjusting the text with respect to just-received news. As a result, the Working Group has elected to: (a) pose in some detail — but not try to definitively answer — certain questions, and (b) not discuss every possible technological development of which it recently became aware. We are confident that the legislative and political processes will offer the opportunity for additional comments from both the U.S. Government and interested parties.

digital communications system. Computers, telephones, televisions, radios, fax machines and more will be linked by the NII, and users will be able to communicate and interact with other computers, telephones, televisions, radios, fax machines and more — all in digital form.[18]

The NII has tremendous potential to improve and enhance our lives. It can increase access to a greater amount and variety of information and entertainment resources that can be delivered quickly and economically from and to virtually anywhere in the world in the blink of an eye. For instance, hundreds of channels of "television" programming, thousands of musical recordings, and literally millions of "magazines" and "books" can be made available to homes and businesses across the United States and around the world.[19]

The NII can provide access to rich cultural resources around the world, transforming and expanding the scope and reach of the arts and humanities. It will provide opportunities for the development of new markets for cultural products. It can broaden our cultural experiences through diversity of content, and increase our understanding of other societies.

The NII can support our education systems by, for example, linking students and educators in remote locations around the world. It can also improve the nation's health care systems by increasing public awareness of health issues, providing continuing education of health care professionals, and allowing patients to take a more active role in their own health care.

The NII can dramatically increase the opportunity for democratic participation in government. The Task Force has shown some of the potential in its work. For instance, the IITF Bulletin Board makes available copies of Task Force reports, testimony, speeches, meeting schedules and minutes, hearing notices, transcripts, and other documents related to the work of the Administration and opportunities for public participation. The Task Force has also accepted comments from the public through the Internet and has conducted an on-line public conference.

Individuals and entities that heretofore have been predominately consumers of works can now become authors and providers through the NII. It can put easier, more sophisticated communication and publishing tools in the hands of the public, increasing the ability to communicate with, and disseminate works of authorship to, others.

The NII can boost the ability of U.S. firms to compete and succeed in the global economy, thereby generating more jobs for Americans. It can spur

---

[18] These devices will be linked not only to each other (computer to computer, for example) but will also be cross-linked (computer to television set).

[19] The United States and other countries are working toward the development of an advanced Global Information Infrastructure (GII) that "will allow us to share information, to connect, and to communicate as a global community." And as that information moves through international channels, "[p]rotecting intellectual property is absolutely essential." *See* Remarks Prepared for Delivery by Vice President Al Gore at the International Telecommunications Union in Buenos Aires, Argentina (March 21, 1994).

economic growth. More than half of the U.S. work force is in information-based jobs, and the telecommunications and information sector is growing faster than any other sector of the U.S. economy. New job opportunities can be created in the processing, organizing, packaging and dissemination of the information and entertainment products flowing through the NII.

The NII can provide benefits to authors and consumers by reducing the time between creation and dissemination. It will open additional markets for authors. If authors choose to enter those new markets, it will provide a wider variety and greater number of choices for consumers, which should increase competition and reduce prices. The availability of these benefits is by no means assured, however. Authors are wary of entering this market because doing so exposes their works to a higher risk of piracy and other unauthorized uses than any of the traditional, current modes of dissemination. Therefore, authors may withhold their works from this environment. Further, even if authors choose not to expose their works to this more risky environment, the risk is not eliminated. Just one unauthorized uploading of a work onto a bulletin board, for instance — unlike, perhaps, most single reproductions and distributions in the analog or print environment — could have devastating effects on the market for the work.

Thus, the full potential of the NII will not be realized if the education, information and entertainment products protected by intellectual property laws are not protected effectively when disseminated via the NII. Creators and other owners of intellectual property rights will not be willing to put their interests at risk if appropriate systems — both in the U.S. and internationally — are not in place to permit them to set and enforce the terms and conditions under which their works are made available in the NII environment. Likewise, the public will not use the services available on the NII and generate the market necessary for its success unless a wide variety of works are available under equitable and reasonable terms and conditions, and the integrity of those works is assured. All the computers, telephones, fax machines, scanners, cameras, keyboards, televisions, monitors, printers, switches, routers, wires, cables, networks and satellites in the world will not create a successful NII, if there is no content. What will drive the NII is the content moving through it.

Ensuring consumer access to and enjoyment of both copyrighted works and new technologies is an attainable goal, and recent experience has confirmed this.[22] For example, the introduction of digital audio tape

---

[22] *See, e.g.*, Sony Corp. v. Universal City Studios, Inc., 464 U.S. 417, 430-31 nn.11-12 (1984) (hereinafter *Sony*) (discussing significance of changes in technology and their effect on copyright law); *Final Report of the National Commission on New Technological Uses of Copyrighted Works* (hereinafter *CONTU Final Report*) at 3 (reporting about the issues raised by photocopiers and computers back in 1978, in language that is equally applicable today) (citations omitted):

   The ownership and control of information and the means of disseminating it are emerging as national and international policy issues. Concerns about the impact on individual freedom posed by the control of the flow of information are at the forefront of public debate. The adequacy of the legal structure to cope with the pace and rate of technological change frequently has been called into question.

recorders recently posed significant problems for copyright owners. Congress responded to the increased threat of rampant unauthorized use with legislation that incorporated both technological and legal measures to protect the interests of both consumers and copyright owners.[23]

Advances in digital technology and the rapid development of electronic networks and other communications technologies raise the stakes considerably. Any two-dimensional work can readily be "digitized" — i.e., translated into a digital code (usually a series of zeros and ones). The work can then be stored and used in that digital form. This dramatically increases: the ease and speed with which a work can be reproduced; the quality of the copies (both the first and the hundredth "generation" are virtually identical); the ability to manipulate and change the work; and the speed with which copies (authorized and unauthorized) can be "delivered" to the public. Works also can be combined easily with other works into a single medium, such as a CD-ROM, which contributes to a blurring of the lines that typically divide types of works and the rights and limitations applicable thereto.

The establishment of high-speed, high-capacity electronic information systems makes it possible for one individual, with a few key strokes, to deliver perfect copies of digitized works to scores of other individuals — or to upload a copy to a bulletin board or other service where thousands of individuals can download it or print unlimited "hard" copies. The emergence of integrated information technology is dramatically changing, and will continue to change, how people and businesses deal in and with information and entertainment products and services, and how works are created, reproduced, distributed, adapted, displayed, performed, owned, licensed, managed, presented, organized, sold, accessed, used and stored. This leads, understandably, to a call for adaptation of — or change in — the law.

Thomas Jefferson stated:

I am not an advocate for frequent changes in laws and constitutions. But laws and institutions must go hand and hand with the progress of the human mind. As that becomes more developed, more enlightened, as new

---

[23] Congress enacted the Audio Home Recording Act of 1992, which combined legal and technological protection for sound recordings. *See* 17 U.S.C. 1001 et seq. (Supp. V 1993). The Audio Home Recording Act requires a serial copy management system in all digital audio recording devices and digital audio interface devices imported, manufactured or distributed in the United States. Such a system allows unlimited first generation digital copying of sound recordings, but prevents the making of digital copies from copies. The Act prohibits the importation, manufacture or distribution of any device, or the offering or performance of service, the primary purpose of which is to circumvent any program or circuit which implements a serial copy management system. The Act also establishes a royalty system through which importers and manufacturers of digital audio recording devices and digital audio recording media make royalty payments on each device or medium they distribute. Such payments are collected by the Copyright Office and distributed annually to record companies, performers, music publishers and songwriters.

discoveries are made, new truths discovered and manners and opinions change, with the change of circumstances, institutions must advance also to keep pace with the times. We might as well require a man to wear still the coat which fitted him when a boy . . . .[24] Our task is to determine whether the coat still fits in this new information age. An effective intellectual property regime must (1) ensure that users have access to the broadest feasible variety of works by (2) recognizing the legitimate rights and commercial expectations of persons and entities whose works are used in the NII environment.

For more than two centuries, copyright law, with periodic amendment, has provided protection for an increasing variety of works of authorship. The most recent complete revision of the law — The Copyright Act of 1976 — was enacted in response to "significant changes in technology [that had] affected the operation of the copyright law."[26] The legislative history of the 1976 Act notes that those changes had "generated new industries and new methods for the reproduction and dissemination of copyrighted works, and the business relations between authors and users [had] evolved new patterns."[27]

We are once again faced with significant changes in technology that upset the balance that currently exists under the Copyright Act. Our goal is to maintain the existing balance.

Some assert that copyright protection should be reduced in the NII environment. The public wants information to be free and unencumbered on the NII, it is argued, and the law should reflect the public interest. Without doubt, this is a valid concern. Information per se should not be protected by copyright law — nor is it. Facts and ideas from any work of authorship may be freely copied and distributed; the Copyright Act expressly excludes such information from the scope of the protection it accords. The copyright law should also serve the public interest — and it does. While, at first blush, it may appear to be in the public interest to reduce the protection granted works and to allow unfettered use by the public, such an analysis is incomplete. Protection of works of authorship provides the stimulus for creativity, thus leading to the availability of works of literature, culture, art and entertainment that the public desires and that form the backbone of our economy and political discourse. If these works are not protected, then the marketplace will not support their creation and dissemination, and the public will not receive the benefit of their existence or be able to have unrestricted use of the ideas and information they convey.

---

[24] See Inscription at the Jefferson Memorial, Washington, D.C. As Secretary of State, Thomas Jefferson was the first head of the U.S. Patent Office.

[26] See H.R. Rep. No. 1476, 94th Cong., 2d Sess. 47 (1976) (hereinafter House Report) ("During the past half century a wide range of new techniques for capturing and communicating printed matter, visual images, and recorded sounds have come into use, and the increasing use of information storage and retrieval devices, communications satellites, and laser technology promises even greater changes in the near future.").

[27] See House Report at 47.

Others assert that technological advances justify reduced protection. Since computer networks now make unauthorized reproduction, adaptation, distribution and other uses of protected works so incredibly easy, it is argued, the law should legitimize those uses or face widespread flouting. This argument is not valid. Technology makes many things possible. Computer networks can be and have been used to embezzle large sums of money and to commit other crimes. Yet, these acts are prohibited by law. Simply because a thing is possible does not mean that it should be condoned.

Finally, there are those who argue that intellectual property laws of any country are inapplicable to works on the NII or GII because all activity using these infrastructures takes place in "Cyberspace," a sovereignty unto itself that should be self-governed by its inhabitants, individuals who, it is suggested, will rely on their own ethics — or "netiquette" — to determine what uses of works, if any, are improper. First, this argument relies on the fantasy that users of the Internet, for instance, are somehow transported to "chat rooms" and other locations, such as virtual libraries. While such conceptualization helps to put in material terms what is considered rather abstract, activity on the Internet takes place neither in outer space nor in parallel, virtual locations. Satellite, broadcast, fax and telephone transmissions have not been thought to be outside the jurisdiction of the nations from which or to which they are sent. Computer network transmissions have no distinguishing characteristics warranting such other-world treatment. Further, such a legal free-for-all would transform the GII into a veritable copyright Dodge City. As enticing as this concept may seem to some users, it would hardly encourage creators to enter its confines.

Nonetheless, content providers are currently experimenting with a number of business models in the networked environment, and it is already clear that a wide variety of such models may coexist. Some content providers will choose not to enforce all — or any — of their rights; others may change their business practices. For instance, some newspaper publishers are selling individual articles using electronic payment mechanisms, in addition to selling subscriptions and individual issues. Some software companies are making their "client" software freely available for individual use in an effort to increase the market share of their "server" software. Some hypermedia magazine publishers on the World Wide Web are choosing to give away their product but charge sponsors for advertising space. A number of information service providers are charging for the use of the search engines that add value to freely available public domain content.

Some content providers will not be motivated by any commercial considerations. For instance, certain scientific communities are working together to create archives of freely available electronic pre-prints on the Internet. The copyright law allows copyright owners to exercise the rights granted to them, to license their rights to others, or to give them away. Those creators who wish to dedicate their works to the public domain may, of course, do so notwithstanding the availability of protection under the

Copyright Act. Nothing in the law prevents those who do not wish to claim copyright from waiving their rights and allowing unrestricted reproduction, distribution and other use of their works. Indeed, notices to that effect are not uncommon on the Internet.

The absence on the NII of copyrighted works for which authors do wish to exercise their rights — fully or to some limited extent — under the copyright law, of course, would not necessarily result in its demise. The Internet, for instance, could continue to serve as a communications tool and resource for Government, public domain and works of willing authors. However, unless the framework for legitimate commerce is preserved and adequate protection for copyrighted works is ensured, the vast communications network will not reach its full potential as a true, global marketplace. Copyright protection is not an obstacle in the way of the success of the NII; it is an essential component. Effective copyright protection is a fundamental way to promote the availability of works to the public.

Preserving the framework does not require, however, a dramatic increase in authors' rights, such as more limited or no further applicability of the fair use doctrine in the NII environment. Some have argued that because it may now be technically feasible to "meter" each use of a copyrighted work, and to charge a user a fee for the use, the concept of fair use has no place in the NII environment. They argue equally that other limitations on rights should be abolished or narrowed for similar reasons. The Working Group believes that weakening copyright owners' rights in the NII is not in the public interest; nor would a dramatic increase in their rights be justified.

With no more than minor clarification and limited amendment, the Copyright Act will provide the necessary balance of protection of rights — and limitations on those rights — to promote the progress of science and the useful arts.[29] Existing copyright law needs only the fine tuning that technological advances necessitate, in order to maintain the balance of the law in the face of onrushing technology. There must be, however, effort in three disciplines — law, technology and education — to successfully address the intellectual property issues raised by the development and use of the NII.

* * * * * *

IV. RECOMMENDATIONS

A. Copyright

It is difficult for intellectual property laws to keep pace with technology. When technological advances cause ambiguity in the law, courts look to the law's underlying purposes to resolve that ambiguity. However, when technology gets too far ahead of the law, and it becomes difficult and awkward to adapt the specific statutory provisions to comport with the law's

---

[29] The Working Group believes that no revision of the patent, trademark or trade secret law is warranted at this time . . . .

principles, it is time for reevaluation and change. "Even though the 1976 Copyright Act was carefully drafted to be flexible enough to be applied to future innovations, technology has a habit of outstripping even the most flexible statutes."[529]

From its beginning, the law of Copyright has developed in response to significant changes in technology. Indeed, it was the invention of a new form of copying equipment — the printing press — that gave rise to the original need for copyright protection. Repeatedly, as new developments have occurred in this country, it has been the Congress that has fashioned the new rules that new technology made necessary.[530]

The Working Group has examined the adequacy of the Copyright Act to cope with the pace of technological changes. In applying the law to new uses, media and technology, the issues presented vary. Certain issues merely require an explanation of the application of the current law, and clearly are appropriately covered. Others present rights or limitations that clearly fit within the spirit of the law but the letter of the law is in need of clarification to avoid uncertainty and unnecessary litigation. Still others need new solutions. Technology has altered the balance of the Copyright Act — in some instances, in favor of copyright owners and in others, in favor of users. The goal of these recommendations is to accommodate and adapt the law to technological change so that the intended balance is maintained and the Constitutional purpose is served.

While it is not advisable to propose amendment of the law with every technological step forward, neither is it appropriate to blindly cling to the status quo when the market has been altered.

Sound policy, as well as history, supports our consistent deference to Congress when major technological innovations alter the market for copyrighted materials. Congress has the constitutional authority and the institutional ability to accommodate fully the varied permutations of competing interests that are inevitably implicated by such new technology.[532]

Throughout more than 200 years of history, with periodic amendment, United States law has provided the necessary copyright protection for the betterment of our society. The Copyright Act is fundamentally adequate and effective. In a few areas, however, it needs to be amended to take proper account of the current technology. The coat is getting a little tight. There is no need for a new one, but the old one needs a few alterations.

---

[529] H.R. Rep. No. 101-735, 101st Cong., 2d Sess. 7 (1990) (report accompanying legislation granting copyright owners of computer software an exclusive rental right).

[530] *Sony*, [464 U.S. 417,] at 430-31 [(1984)].

[532] *Sony*, at 431.

1. The Transmission of Copies and Phonorecords

a. The Distribution Right

The Copyright Act gives a copyright owner the exclusive right "to distribute copies or phonorecords of the copyrighted work" to the public. It is not clear under the current law that a transmission can constitute a distribution of copies or phonorecords of a work. Yet, in the world of high-speed, communications systems, it is possible to transmit a copy of a work from one location to another. This may be the case, for instance, when a computer program is transmitted from one computer to ten other computers. When the transmission is complete, the original copy typically remains in the transmitting computer and a copy resides in the memory of, or in storage devices associated with, each of the other computers.[535] The transmission results essentially in the distribution of ten copies of the work. However, the extent of the distribution right under the present law may be somewhat uncertain and subject to challenge. Therefore, the Working Group recommends that the Copyright Act be amended to expressly recognize that copies or phonorecords of works can be distributed to the public by transmission, and that such transmissions fall within the exclusive distribution right of the copyright owner.

The proposed amendment does not create a new right. It is an express recognition that, as a result of technological developments, the distribution right can be exercised by means of transmission — just as the reproduction, public performance and public display rights may be.[536]

It is argued by some that the existing right of distribution encompasses transmissions of copies and that no amendment is necessary. Indeed, the distribution right, as set forth in Section 106(3) of the Copyright Act, can be — and, in at least one case, has been — interpreted to include transmissions which distribute copies of works to, for example, the memories of computers. Transmission, it is argued, is logically and legally a means of distribution. The Working Group has no argument with such an interpretation; it properly conforms to the intent of the distribution right and, we believe, is correct from both a practical and legal standpoint.

---

[535] In contrast, a "standard" distribution of a copy necessarily divests the distributor of his copy. In the case of a distribution by transmission, the distributor generally retains his copy of the work and a reproduction is distributed.

[536] It has been suggested that recognition of distribution by transmission may diminish the public performance right. However, if a work is publicly performed by transmission, then there has been a public performance — whether or not the distribution right is or is not also involved. The fact that some transmissions may constitute a reproduction and distribution of copies to the public does not mean that transmissions that constitute public performances are not public performances. The scope of the public performance right is not diminished by the recognition that a transmission may fall within the scope of the distribution right. If a copy of a motion picture is transmitted to a computer's memory, for instance, and in the process, the sounds are capable of being heard and the images viewed as they are received in memory, then the public performance right may well be implicated as well. *See* 17 U.S.C. § 101 (1988) (definition of "perform").

Others suggest that amendment of the law may not be necessary because even if the distribution right does not cover the distribution of reproductions by transmission, the reproduction right is clearly implicated and that will protect the copyright owner. However, the fact that more than one right may be involved in infringing activity does not, and should not, mean that only one right should apply. Each of the exclusive rights is distinct and separately alienable and different parties may be responsible for infringements or licensing of different rights — and different rights may be owned by different people. Because transmissions of copies may constitute both a reproduction and a distribution of a work, transmissions of copies should not constitute the exercise of just one of those rights. Indeed, those licensed only to reproduce a work should not be entitled to also distribute the work through transmission — thereby displacing the market for the copyright owner or his distribution licensee.

Infringement takes place when any one of the rights is violated: where, for example, a printer reproduces copies without selling them or a retailer sells copies without having anything to do with their reproduction.[539]

Clearly, not all transmissions of copies of copyrighted works will fall within the copyright owner's exclusive distribution right. Moreover, even if a transmission of a copy falls within the scope of the right, it is not necessarily unlawful. First, the distribution must be a distribution *to the public*. The case law interpreting "publication" provides guidance as to what constitutes distribution to the public.[540] If a distribution would not constitute a publication of the work, then it would likely be found to be outside the scope of the copyright owner's distribution right. Therefore, the transmission of a copyrighted work from one person to another in a private e-mail message would not constitute a distribution to the public.[541] Second, all of the limitations, exemptions and defenses that currently apply to the distribution right and allow users to distribute certain copies to the public or to distribute copies under certain circumstances will continue to apply. For example, any exercise of one of the exclusive rights may be fair use — including the reproduction and distribution of copies by transmission.

Some are of the view that the current language of the Act does not encompass distribution by transmission. They argue that the proposed amendment expands the copyright owner's rights without a concomitant expansion of the limitations on those rights. However, since transmissions of copies already clearly implicate the reproduction right, it is misleading to suggest that the proposed amendment of the distribution right would expand the copyright owner's rights into an arena previously unprotected.

---

[539] House Report at 61.

[540] . . . The term "public" as used in connection with the distribution right is not coincident with the meaning assigned to that term in connection with the public performance or public display right.

[541] If copies of works are offered to the public — even though they may be distributed one copy at a time — it would likely constitute distribution to the public. *See* 17 U.S.C. § 101 (1988) (definition of "publication") . . .

Further, even if the premise is correct (that the amendment expands the distribution right), the conclusion that the limitations of that right are not similarly expanded is invalid. The limitations on the right — which place certain distributions to the public outside the scope of the copyright owner's right — would necessarily expand to also place similar distributions by means of transmission outside the scope of the right.

Nevertheless, there is no reason to treat works that are distributed in copies to the public by means of transmission differently than works distributed in copies to the public by other, more conventional means.[542] Copies distributed via transmission are as tangible as any distributed over the counter or through the mail. Through each method of distribution, the consumer receives a tangible copy of the work.

When the public performance right was initially granted, it was thought to encompass only "live," in-person performances. When it became clear that copyrighted works could be publicly performed by other means — i.e., broadcast and, later, cable transmissions — the law was clarified. The same is true today with respect to the distribution right. Transmission is a means of distribution of copies, just as it can be a means of performance. However, the differences of opinion summarized above underscore the need for clarification and legal certainty. The costs and risks of litigation to define more clearly the right — and the time achieving such clarity would take — would discourage and delay use of the NII.

b. Related Definitional Amendments

The Working Group also recommends other related amendments to two definitions.

To "Transmit"

As explained above, under current technology, a copy of a work may be transmitted. However, the Copyright Act defines only what it is to transmit a performance or display of a work. Therefore, the Working Group recommends that the definition of "transmit" in Section 101 of the Copyright Act be amended to include a definition of a transmission of a reproduction.[543]

How to delineate between these types of transmissions is a difficult issue to resolve. The transmissions themselves hold no clues; one type often looks the same as the other during the transmission. If the transmitter intends to transmit a performance of the work, as well as to distribute a reproduction of it — or if the receiver is able to hear or see a performance of the work in the course of receiving a copy of it — what rights are exercised by the transmission? A transmission could be a transmission of a reproduction or a performance or both. The resolution of these issues should rest upon the specific facts of the case. Such issues will typically be clarified

---

[542] In the future, transmission may become the conventional means of distribution.

[543] Under the proposed definition, to transmit a reproduction is to distribute it by any device or process whereby a copy or phonorecord of the work is fixed beyond the place from which it was sent.

between rightsholders and users in appropriate license arrangements. If confusion or disagreement exists in a specific context, the courts — rather than Congress — are in the better position to determine which, if any, exclusive rights are involved in a particular transmission. Courts regularly make such determinations in other cases where rights overlap.[544]

"Publication"

The legislative history of the Copyright Act makes clear that "any form of dissemination in which a material object does not *change hands . . .* is not a publication no matter how many people are exposed to the work."[545] Thus, a work that is only displayed or performed via the NII would not be considered published, no matter how many people have access to the display or performance, because a material object — a copy of the work — does not change hands. However, in the case of transmissions of reproductions, the recipients of the transmissions receive copies of the work (*i.e.,* copies of the work have been distributed) — although they may not have "changed hands" in the literal sense.

Whether the transmission of copies of works is clearly within the scope of the distribution right is also a problem with respect to the act of publication by the transmission of copies. Indeed, the definition of "publication" incorporates the language used to describe the distribution right, which the Working Group's proposal amends.[547] Publication largely turns on whether the work has been distributed to the public. Thus, if copies of a work may be distributed to the public by transmission, then a work may be published by the transmission of copies to the public. Therefore, consistent with the proposed amendment of the distribution right, the Working Group recommends that the definition of "publication" in Section 101 of the Copyright Act be amended to recognize that a work may be published through the distribution of copies of the work to the public by transmission.[548]

---

[544] To delineate between those transmissions that are communications of performances or displays and those that are distributions of reproductions, one may look at both ends of the transmission. Did the transmitter intend to communicate a performance or display of the work or, rather, to distribute a reproduction of the work? Did the receiver simply hear or see the work or rather/also receive a copy of it? Did the receiver simply receive a copy or was it possible for her to hear or see it as well? License rates and terms will assist in determining the intent of the parties.

[545] *See* House Report at 138 (emphasis added).

[547] Under the current law, the distribution right is identified as the right "to distribute copies or phonorecords of the copyrighted work to the public by sale or other transfer of ownership, or by rental, lease, or lending." *See* 17 U.S.C. § 106(3) (1988). Publication is "the distribution of copies or phonorecords of the copyrighted work to the public by sale or other transfer of ownership, or by rental, lease, or lending." *See* 17 U.S.C. § 101 (1988) (part of definition of "publication").

[548] Under the law of the United Kingdom, making a work available to the public by means of an electronic retrieval system constitutes publication. *See* Copyright, Designs and Patents Act of 1988, § 175(1)(b).

The effects under the law of a work being considered published (rather than unpublished) generally are negative from the viewpoint of the copyright owner. Published works, for example: (1) must be deposited in the Library of Congress; (2) are subject to more limitations on the exclusive rights, including a broader application of fair use; (3) must meet certain author nationality or domicile requirements to be eligible for protection; and (4) must bear a copyright notice if published before March 1, 1989. However, the designation of works distributed to the public by transmission as published will be important in the case of works distributed first — or solely — on-line. The deposit requirement will aid in the preservation of those works, which otherwise might be updated or revised on-line, destroying — or at least obscuring — the original published versions. This may be particularly critical in preserving the scholarly and scientific record.[550]

Just as not all distributions of copies by transmission will constitute distributions to the public (and fall within the distribution right), not all transmissions of copies will constitute publication. Private e-mail messages would not be regarded as published. Neither would other restricted transmissions of copies, such as those in a typical corporate setting, where transmissions of copies within the company computer network are restricted as to further distribution. However, as in the print environment, the distribution of copies to a small group under circumstances where further distribution is authorized would publish the work.[553]

c. The Importation Provisions

The Working Group also recommends that the prohibitions on importation be amended to reflect the fact that, just as copies of copyrighted works can be distributed by transmission in the United States, they can also be imported into the U.S. by transmission. If an infringing literary work, for instance, were physically shipped into the U.S. in the form of a paper copy, a CD-ROM disk or even stored on a memory chip, then it would be an infringing importation if the statutory conditions existed.

Cross-border transmission of copies of copyrighted works should be subject to the same restrictions as shipping them by airmail. Just as the distribution of copies of a copyrighted work is no less a distribution than the distribution of copies by mail, the international transmission of copies of copyrighted works is no less an importation than the importation by airmail.

---

[550] In the print domain, prior published editions are more easily and generally available for reference, partially because of the deposit requirement, but primarily because subsequent versions do not override the originals — which is possible in the on-line environment.

[553] See White v. Kimmell, 193 F.2d 744 (9th Cir. 1952) (unrestricted circulation of 200 copies of a manuscript to friends and acquaintances published the work); Continental Casualty Co. v. Beardsley, 253 F.2d 702 (2d Cir. 1958) (distribution of approximately 100 sets of forms to corporate officers and surety companies for possible purchase of more constituted publication).

Although we recognize that the U.S. Customs Service cannot, for all practical purposes, enforce a prohibition on importation by transmission, given the global dimensions of the information infrastructure of the future, it is important that copyright owners have the other remedies for infringements of this type available to them. Therefore, the Working Group recommends that Section 602 of the Copyright Act be amended to include importation by carriage or shipping of copies as well as by transmission of them.

2. Public Performance Right for Sound Recordings

Transmissions of sound recordings will certainly supplement and may eventually replace the current forms of distribution of phonorecords. In the very near future, consumers will be able to receive digital transmissions of sound recordings on demand — for performance in the home or for downloading — from the so-called "celestial jukebox." The legal nature of such transmissions — whether they are performances or distributions — has been widely debated. As discussed above, the Working Group recommends that Section 106 of the Copyright Act be amended to make clear that copies or phonorecords can be distributed by transmission. However, many of these transmissions will clearly constitute exercise of the public performance right — a right which the Copyright Act fails to grant to copyright owners of sound recordings.[555]

The lack of a public performance right in sound recordings under U.S. law is an historical anomaly that does not have a strong policy justification — and certainly not a legal one. Sound recordings are the only copyrighted works that are capable of being performed that are not granted that right. Therefore, for example, to transmit a performance of a sound recording without infringement liability, an audio-on-demand service acting as a "celestial jukebox" must obtain a license from, and pay a royalty to, the copyright owner of the underlying musical work (*i.e.*, the person or entity who owns the rights in the notes and the lyrics), but it does not have to obtain permission from, or pay a license fee to, the copyright owner of the sound recording or the performer. The Working Group believes that this inequity should be rectified.

Public performance rights are granted in many foreign markets. Due to the lack of a performance right in the United States, U.S. performers and record companies are denied their fair share of foreign royalty pools for the public performance of U.S. sound recordings in some countries and are in danger of losing access to their share in others.

By granting performance rights in sound recordings, the United States will treat the creators of these culturally and economically important

---

[555] Some transmissions that clearly constitute public performances may, in effect, substitute for distributions in the future. If consumers are offered a service through which they can receive a performance of any sound recording at any time, they may stop buying phonorecords. The market for distributed phonorecords may shrink to include only the providers of that service to consumers.

copyrighted works the same as all other works capable of being publicly performed. This legislation will provide increased incentive for the creators of sound recordings to produce and disseminate more works, thereby expanding consumer choice. In addition, the enactment of these rights will strengthen the hand of Government negotiators and private advocates seeking a fair share of foreign royalty pools.

Some argue that copyright owners of sound recordings should not be granted a public performance right because they derive some indirect benefit from the public performance of their works. This argument is based on the theory that the public performance of a work increases the sales of reproductions of that work. Therefore, the copyright owner gets an indirect benefit (*i.e.*, increased sales of reproductions) from the so-called "free advertising" that public performances provide. This, in fact, may be true in some cases. However, it is not a valid policy argument against providing sound recording copyright owners with the full panoply of exclusive rights other copyright owners enjoy.

The exercise of one right often increases the value of the exercise of another right, but we do not restrict any other copyright owners from exercising *all* of his or her rights. For instance:

— The copyright owner of the musical composition embodied in a sound recording is paid both when recordings of the composition are sold and when the composition is publicly performed — even though the public performance might increase the number of records sold and thus benefit the copyright owner.

— Serial excerpts from a novel that are published in a magazine might increase sales of the book, but the magazine nonetheless must obtain permission from the author of the book.

— The copyright owner of that novel may also increase his book sales when a motion picture based on the novel is released. However, no one suggests that the motion picture company should not have to pay the copyright owner of the novel for the right to turn it into a movie, just because the movie might indirectly benefit the copyright owner.

The copyright owners of sound recordings should be able to decide for themselves, as do all other copyright owners, if "free advertising" is sufficient compensation for the use of their works. If the users' arguments regarding the benefit copyright owners derive from the public performance of their sound recordings are correct, the users should be able to negotiate a very low rate for a license to do so.

It also has been argued that the copyright owners of sound recordings should not be granted the "exclusive" right that all other copyright owners enjoy, but instead be subject to a compulsory license, so that they cannot act as a "gatekeeper" to the licensing of performances of the musical works embodied in sound recordings. It is asserted that while a copyright owner of a sound recording with an exclusive public performance right could block the performance of the musical work by denying a license to publicly perform the sound recording, the copyright owner of the musical work could not. This argument is based on the incorrect assumption that copyright owners of musical works are not granted exclusive public performance rights. Section 106(4) of the Copyright Act clearly grants exclusive rights to the copyright owners of musical works, and, while virtually all music performance licensing is handled for those copyright owners by performing rights societies on a nonexclusive basis, the copyright owners could license their performance rights on an exclusive basis if they chose to do so.[556]

Two bills introduced in the 104th Congress would grant a very limited performance right in sound recordings.[557] A *full* public performance right — *particularly* with respect to all *digital* transmissions — is warranted. There is no just reason to afford a lower level of protection to one class of creative artists. Further, *any* special limitations on this right weakens our position internationally. The digital communications revolution — the creation of advanced information infrastructures — is erasing the distinctions among different categories of protected works and the uses made of them.

3. Library Exemptions

The copyright law carefully balances the rights of copyright owners with the legitimate needs of users. Nowhere is this balancing more apparent than in the exemptions that are intended to permit libraries reasonable use of copyrighted works to serve the legitimate demands of their patrons.

Many have expressed concern that the special exemptions for libraries in Section 108 of the Copyright Act are no longer relevant in the digital era. Libraries, of course, may make fair use of any copyrighted works pursuant to the provisions of Section 107. Section 108, however, provides additional exemptions specifically for libraries and archives. On the one hand, there are those who believe that since licensing of transactions of works in digital form will be a feature of the digital distribution systems of the future, there is no need for library exceptions. Each copying transaction will be cheap and libraries can simply pay for all of the copying in which they engage. On the other hand, there are those who believe that unrestricted copying in libraries should be the rule, without the special conditions and limitations set forth in Section 108.

The Working Group agrees with neither those who would delete the exemptions for library copying nor those who would permit wholesale copying in libraries. It believes that there is an important public interest

---

[556] If the copyright owners of sound recordings abused the exclusivity that the law should provide, the solution would lie in the enforcement of the antitrust laws — where the music licensing problems have been addressed — not in the reduction of rights under the Copyright Act.

[557] *See* S. 227, 104th Cong., 1st Sess. (1995); H.R. 1506, 104th Cong., 1st Sess. (1995).

in exempting certain library uses of copyrighted works and that the public interest is no less important — and, indeed, may be more important — when such use involves digital technology. It also believes that there is an equally important interest in recognizing the legitimate interests of copyright owners in licensing uses of their works through voluntary systems.

Therefore, notwithstanding the legislative history of the 1976 Act which clearly intended that Section 108 did not permit digital reproduction,[559] the Working Group believes that it is important to expand the exemption so that digital copying by libraries and archives is permitted under certain circumstances. In supporting this departure from the generally accepted view of the scope and intention of Section 108, the Working Group believes that the law must preserve the role of libraries and archives in the digital era.

Libraries and archives are the trustees of our collective knowledge and must be able to make use of digital technology to preserve the Nation's heritage and scholarship. Therefore, the Working Group recommends that the library exemptions be amended: (1) to accommodate the reality of the computerized library by allowing the preparation of three copies of works in digital form, with no more than one copy in use at any time (while the others are archived); (2) to recognize that the use of a copyright notice on a published copy of a work is no longer mandatory; and (3) to authorize the making of digital copies for purposes of preservation.[560]

4. Reproduction for the Visually Impaired

The NII offers real opportunities to many visually impaired people to participate in learning, communication and discourse to a greater extent than when only conventional modes of communication are available. With the aid of software and computer equipment that is widely available, people now have the capacity to view text on CD-ROM on screen in a "large-type" format even if the publisher did not include such a feature, but the publication and distribution of large-type editions remains very important. To ensure fair access to all manner of printed materials, it is necessary to amend the copyright law.

The laws of many Berne Convention countries contain express exemptions from liability for the unauthorized manufacture and distribution of

---

[559] The legislative history makes it clear that digital uses are generally not encompassed by Section 108: "Under this exemption, for example, a repository could make photocopies of manuscripts by microfilm or electrostatic process, but *could not reproduce the work in 'machine-readable' language* for storage in an information system." House Report at 75; Senate Report at 67 (emphasis added). The Senate Report also speaks precisely of "the *photocopying* needs of . . . multi-county regional systems." *Id.* at 70 (emphasis added).

[560] The Working Group believes that replacement copies may be digital in nature, and may be made under this provision only when an unused replacement is not available in either digital or analog form.

Braille or other editions designed to assist the visually impaired.[561] The Working Group believes that similar provisions should be included in the Copyright Act, and has modeled its proposal on the Australian law, so as to maintain private rights while recognizing certain readers' special needs. The proposed amendment would provide an exemption for non-profit organizations to reproduce and distribute to the visually impaired — at cost — Braille, large type, audio or other editions of previously published literary works in forms intended to be perceived by the visually impaired, provided that the owner of the exclusive right to distribute the work in the United States has not entered the market for such editions during the first year following first publication of the work.[562]

5. Criminal Offenses

Although the Copyright Act provides criminal penalties when the infringement is willful and is for purposes of commercial advantage or private financial gain, the dismissal of the criminal charges in *United States v. LaMacchia* demonstrates a serious lacuna in the criminal copyright provisions: it does not now reach even the most wanton and malicious large-scale endeavors to copy and provide on the NII limitless numbers of unauthorized copies of valuable copyrighted works unless the copier seeks profits. Since there is virtually no cost to the infringer, certain individuals are willing to make such copies (or assist others in making them) for reasons other than monetary reward. For example, someone who believes that all works should be free in Cyberspace can easily make and distribute thousands of copies of a protected work and may have no desire for commercial advantage or private financial gain.

The Working Group agrees with the *LaMacchia* court:

> Criminal as well as civil penalties should probably attach to willful, multiple infringements of copyrighted software even absent a commercial motive on the part of the infringer. One could envision ways that the copyright law could be modified to permit such prosecution. But, "[i]t is the legislature, not the Court which is to define a crime, and ordain its punishment."

Therefore, the Working Group generally supports the amendments to the copyright law and the criminal law (which sets out sanctions for criminal

---

[561] *See, e.g.,* Section 53D of the Australian law (privilege conditioned on copyright owner's abstention from market for Braille edition); Section 18 of the Finnish law (Braille editions and talking books may be manufactured "for use by lending libraries for blind persons"); Section 80 of the Portuguese law (Braille editions may be manufactured if not for profit).

[562] The visually impaired were the only users with a disability who provided comments or testimony concerning a need for a narrow exemption to ensure the availability of literary works in a usable form. By its recommendation of such an exemption for the visually impaired, the Working Group does not intend to dismiss the possibility that other disabled users may have needs of which it has not been made aware and, therefore, has not considered.

copyright violations) set forth in S. 1122, introduced in the 104th Congress by Senators Leahy and Feingold following consultations with the Justice Department. The bill would make it a criminal offense to willfully infringe a copyright by reproducing or distributing copies with a retail value of $5,000 or more. By setting a monetary threshold and requiring willfulness, the bill ensures that merely casual or careless conduct resulting in distribution of only a few copies will not be subject to criminal prosecution and that criminal charges will not be brought unless there is a significant level of harm to the copyright owner's rights. [565]

6. Technological Protection

The ease of infringement and the difficulty of detection and enforcement will cause copyright owners to look to technology, as well as the law, for protection of their works. However, it is clear that technology can be used to defeat any protection that technology may provide. The Working Group finds that legal protection alone will not be adequate to provide incentive to authors to create and to disseminate works to the public. Similarly, technological protection likely will not be effective unless the law also provides some protection for the technological processes and systems used to prevent or restrict unauthorized uses of copyrighted works.

The Working Group finds that prohibition of devices, products, components and services that defeat technological methods of preventing unauthorized use is in the public interest and furthers the Constitutional purpose of copyright laws. Consumers of copyrighted works pay for the acts of infringers; copyright owners have suggested that the price of legitimate copies of copyrighted works may be higher due to infringement losses suffered by copyright owners. The public will also have access to more copyrighted works via the NII if they are not vulnerable to the defeat of protection systems.

Therefore, the Working Group recommends that the Copyright Act be amended to include a new Chapter 12, which would include a provision to prohibit the importation, manufacture or distribution of any device, product or component incorporated into a device or product, or the provision of any service, the primary purpose or effect of which is to avoid, bypass, remove, deactivate, or otherwise circumvent, without authority of the copyright owner or the law, any process, treatment, mechanism or system which prevents or inhibits the violation of any of the exclusive rights under Section 106. The provision will not eliminate the risk that protection systems will be defeated, but it will reduce it.

---

[565] . . . [T]he idea/expression dichotomy and the limitations on the exclusive rights, including fair use, address First Amendment concerns . . . . *See also* Harper & Row, Publishers, Inc. v. Nation Enterprises, 471 U.S. 539, 560 (1985) ("First Amendment protections [are] embodied in the [Copyright] Act's distinction between copyrightable expression and uncopyrightable facts and ideas, and the latitude for scholarship and comment traditionally afforded by fair use").

The proposed prohibition is intended to assist copyright owners in the protection of their works.[566] The Working Group recognizes, however, that copyright owners may wish to use such systems to prevent the unauthorized reproduction, for instance, of their works, but may also wish to allow some users to deactivate the systems. Furthermore, certain uses of copyrighted works are not unlawful under the Copyright Act. Therefore, the proposed legislation prohibits only those devices or products, the primary purpose or effect of which is to circumvent such systems *without authority*. That authority may be granted by the copyright owner or by limitations on the copyright owner's rights under the Copyright Act.

It has been suggested that the prohibition is incompatible with fair use. First, the fair use doctrine does not require a copyright owner to allow or to facilitate unauthorized access or use of a work. Otherwise, copyright owners could not withhold works from publication; movie theatres could not charge admission or prevent audio or video recording; museums could not require entry fees or prohibit the taking of photographs. Indeed, if the provision of access and the ability to make fair use of copyrighted works were required of copyright owners — or an affirmative right of the public — even passwords for access to computer databases would be considered illegal. Second, if the circumvention device is primarily intended and used for legal purposes, such as fair use, the device would not violate the provision, because a device with such purposes and effects would fall under the "authorized by law" exemption.

Concern has also been expressed with regard to the ability to defeat technological protection for copies of works not protected by copyright law, such as those whose term of protection has expired or those in the public domain for other reasons (such as ineligibility for protection). However, devices whose primary purpose and effect is to defeat the protection for such works would not violate the provision. The proposed provision exempts all devices, products and services primarily intended and used for legal purposes, which would include the reproduction and distribution of copies of works in the public domain. Further, a protection system on copies of works in the public domain would not qualify with respect to such copies as a system which "prevents or inhibits the violation of any of the exclusive rights of the copyright owner under Section 106." Works in the public domain are not protected by copyright, and thus have no copyright owner or exclusive rights applicable to them. Finally, while technological protection may be applied to copies of works in the public domain, such protection attaches only to those particular copies — not to the underlying work itself.[567]

---

[566] Legislation of a similar type has been introduced with respect to technological protection of audiovisual works. *See, e.g.,* S. 1096, 102d Cong., 1st Sess., 137 Cong. Rec. S. 6034 (1991); H.R. 3568, 101st Cong., 1st Sess., 135 Cong. Rec. H. 7924 (1989).

[567] Copies of the work in the marketplace free from copyright protection could be freely reproduced (and, in fact, the lower distribution costs of the NII may encourage increased availability of public domain works). Further, technological protection that restricts the ability to reproduce the work by technical means does not prevent reproduction by other means (such as quoting, manually copying, etc.).

It has also been suggested that the provision places an unwarranted burden on manufacturers. The proposed amendment would impose no requirement on manufacturers to accommodate any protection systems, such as those required in Chapter 10 of manufacturers of digital audio recording devices.[568] The provision would only prohibit the manufacture of circumvention devices.[569]

Neither does the proposed amendment require copyright owners to use technological protection, or, if they do, to employ any particular type. Copyright owners should be free to determine what level or type of protection (if any) is appropriate for their works, taking into consideration cost and security needs, and different consumer and market preferences. Moreover, there is no evidence that one technological protection system could — or should — take care of all types of works.

Legislation of this type is not unprecedented. The Copyright Act already protects sound recordings and musical works by prohibiting the circumvention of any program or circuit that implements a serial copy management system or similar system included in digital audio recording devices and digital audio interface devices. Section 1002 provides:

> No person shall import, manufacture, or distribute any device, or offer or perform any service, the primary purpose or effect of which is to avoid, bypass, remove, deactivate, or otherwise circumvent any program or circuit which implements, in whole or in part, a [serial copy management system or similar system].[570]

---

[568] However, the Working Group does encourage the equipment manufacturing and copyright industries to work together on bilateral solutions for other types of recording devices and categories of works. In response to a request from Congressional leaders, representatives of the motion picture industry and the consumer electronics industry are presently drafting a joint legislative proposal addressing legal and technical measures pertaining to consumer recording of motion pictures. This proposal would set forth a technical means to be applied that would respect the legitimate commercial expectations of copyright owners and the reasonable and customary copying practices of consumers.

[569] Some have suggested that while manufacturers will surely know the primary purpose of the devices they produce, they may inadvertently find themselves liable for devices which they intended for legal purposes, but which have the incidental effect of circumventing copyright protection systems. For a manufacturer to find himself in this situation, the device would have to fail to be used primarily for the purpose for which it was sold, and be primarily used, to the surprise of its manufacturer, for defeating protection systems. It is likely that such a situation would occur rarely, if ever. (It would be self-defeating for copyright owners to begin using a protection system that an existing device could defeat.) However, the chapter contains an "innocent violation" provision for just such a case. A court would have the ability to reduce or eliminate altogether any damages for which the manufacturer would otherwise be liable, to avoid an unfair result but still protect the copyright owner.

[570] 17 U.S.C. § 1002(c) (Supp. V 1993).

The Communications Act includes a similar provision:

Any person who manufactures, assembles, modifies, imports, exports, sells, or distributes any electronic, mechanical, or other device or equipment, knowing or having reason to know that the device or equipment is primarily of assistance in the unauthorized decryption of satellite cable programming, or is intended for any other activity prohibited by [Section 605(a)] shall be fined not more than $500,000 for each violation, or imprisoned for not more than 5 years for each violation, or both. For purposes of all penalties and remedies established for violations of this paragraph, the prohibited activity established herein as it applies to each such device shall be deemed a separate violation.[571]

Precedent for this type of legislation is also found in the international arena. The NAFTA requires each party to make it a criminal offense to "manufacture, import, sell, lease or otherwise make available a device or system that is primarily of assistance in decoding an encrypted program-carrying satellite signal without the authorization of the lawful distributor of such signal . . . ."[572] In 1988, the United Kingdom enacted legislation prohibiting the manufacture, distribution or sale of a device designed or adapted to circumvent copy-protection systems.[573]

7. Copyright Management Information

In the future, the copyright management information associated with a work — such as the name of the copyright owner and the terms and conditions for uses of the work — may be critical to the efficient operation and success of the NII. Copyright management information will serve as a kind of license plate for a work on the information superhighway, from which a user may obtain important information about the work. The accuracy of such information will be crucial to the ability of consumers to find and make authorized uses of copyrighted works on the NII. Reliable information will also facilitate efficient licensing and reduce transaction costs for licensable uses of copyrighted works (both fee-based and royalty-free).

The public should be protected from false information about who created the work, who owns rights in it, and what uses may be authorized by the copyright owner. Therefore, the Working Group recommends that the Copyright Act be amended to prohibit the provision, distribution or importation for distribution of copyright management information known to be false and the unauthorized removal or alteration of copyright management information. Under the proposed amendment, copyright management information

---

[571] 47 U.S.C. § 605(e)(4) (1988).

[572] *See* NAFTA, at art. 1707(a). The NAFTA also requires parties to make it a civil offense to "receive, in connection with commercial activities, or further distribute, an encrypted program-carrying satellite signal that has been decoded without the authorization of the lawful distributor of the signal or to engage in any activity prohibited under [the criminal provisions]." *See* NAFTA, at art. 1707(b).

[573] *See* Copyright, Designs and Patents Act of 1988, Part VII, § 296.

is defined as the name and other identifying information of the author of a work, the name and other identifying information of the copyright owner, terms and conditions for uses of the work, and such other information as the Register of Copyrights may prescribe by regulation — to provide adequate flexibility in the future.[574]

While the proposed amendment does not require copyright owners to provide copyright management information, it does require that when such information is included, it be accurate. However, the Working Group encourages copyright owners to include the information to enable consumers to more easily find and make authorized uses of copyrighted works. Nor does it specify standardized formats or content, although private sector initiatives in this area are underway and are also encouraged by the Working Group. Finally, it does not require transmitting entities to include the copyright information as part of their transmission of a work where such information has been included in the work.[575] However, such a proposal deserves further consideration.

The proposal prohibits the falsification, alteration or removal of any copyright management information — not just that which is included in or digitally linked to the copyrighted work. Many users will obtain such information from public registers, where the integrity of such information will be no less important. The proposal also contains a knowledge requirement; therefore, inadvertent falsification, alteration or removal would not be a violation.[576]

B. PATENT

The present law governing the eligibility of inventions for patent protection and the enforcement of patent rights appears adequate to address the needs of inventors and the public with regard to technology used on the NII. The NII will increase the accessibility and content of the body of prior art, which in turn will affect patentability determinations. The law governing information that properly is considered part of the prior art appears to be adequate to address new forms of "printed" publications; however, some issues related to the authenticity, including the date of origination, the contents as originally disclosed, and the extent of dissemination of electronically disseminated publications, deserve further study.

The Working Group recommends that the Patent and Trademark Office obtain public input related to measures that can be adopted to ensure the

---

[574] Other information that may become important to the efficient operation of the NII includes the country of origin of the work, the year of creation or first publication, a description of the work, the name and other identifying information of licensees and standardized codes.

[575] While a transmitting entity may not remove the copyright management information, if such information is not included in the normal course of the transmission (such as when a work in digital form is broadcast through analog transmission), no violation would occur.

[576] For criminal liability, both knowledge and the intent to defraud are required.

authenticity of electronically-disseminated publications, particularly with respect to verifying the contents and date of first public dissemination of the publication, and evaluating the substantive value of the information contained in the publication as to its role in patentability determinations.

The Working Group also recommends that the PTO explore the feasibility of establishing requirements or standards that would govern authentication of the date and contents of electronically-disseminated information for purposes of establishing their use as prior art. Such standards would assist in patentability determinations, whether they occur before the PTO or before a court. To develop such standards, the PTO should invite public comment and work with other interested Federal agencies working on authentication standards outside the direct sphere of the patent system.

C. TRADEMARK

The Nice Agreement Concerning the International Classification of Goods and Services for the Purposes of the Registration of Marks must be sufficiently flexible to accommodate the changing goods and services available in connection with the NII and the GII. Such flexibility is essential to the owners of marks identifying goods and services connected with the NII and the GII, as well as to the continued viability of the International Classification system in the electronic information age. Therefore, the Working Group recommends that the Patent and Trademark Office, in the context of WIPO experts meetings on the International Classification system, propose changes to the International Classification system to ensure that the system reflects the goods and services of modern information technology. Additionally, the Working Group recommends that the Patent and Trademark Office regularly update its Manual for the Identification of Goods and Services to reflect new goods and services used on or in connection with the NII and GII.

Appendix 1

Proposed Legislation

NII Copyright Protection Act of 1995

104th Congress, 1st Session
[S. 1284/H.R. 2441]

A BILL

To amend title 17 to adapt the copyright law to the digital, networked environment of the National Information Infrastructure, and for other purposes.

Be it enacted by the Senate and House of Representatives of the United States of America in Congress assembled,

SEC. 1. SHORT TITLE.

This Act may be cited as the "NII Copyright Protection Act of 1995".

SEC. 2. TRANSMISSION OF COPIES.

(a) DISTRIBUTION.—Section 106(3) of title 17, United States Code, is amended by striking "or by rental, lease, or lending" and inserting "by rental, lease, or lending, or by transmission".

(b) DEFINITIONS.—Section 101 of title 17, United States Code, is amended—

(1) in the definition of "publication" by striking "or by rental, lease, or lending" in the first sentence and insert "by rental, lease, or lending, or by transmission"; and

(2) in the definition of "transmit" by inserting at the end thereof the following: "To 'transmit' a reproduction is to distribute it by any device or process whereby a copy or phonorecord of the work is fixed beyond the place from which it was sent."

(c) IMPORTATION.—Section 602 of title 17, United States Code, is amended by inserting "whether by carriage of tangible goods or by transmission," after "Importation into the United States,".

SEC. 3. EXEMPTIONS FOR LIBRARIES AND THE VISU-ALLY IMPAIRED.

(a) LIBRARIES.—Section 108 of title 17, United States Code, is amended—

(1) in subsection (a) by deleting "one copy or phonorecord" and inserting in lieu thereof "three copies or phonorecords";

(2) in subsection (a) by deleting "such copy or phonorecord" and inserting in lieu thereof "no more than one of such copies or phonorecords";

(3) by inserting at the end of subsection (a)(3) "if such notice appears on the copy or phonorecord that is reproduced under the provisions of this section";

(4) in subsection (b) by inserting "or digital" after "facsimile" and by inserting "in facsimile form" before "for deposit for research use"; and

(5) in subsection (c) by inserting "or digital" after "facsimile".

(b) Visually Impaired.—Title 17, United States Code, is amended by adding the following new section:

§ 108A. Limitations on exclusive rights: Reproduction for the Visually Impaired

Notwithstanding the provision of section 106, it is not an infringement of copyright for a non-profit organization to reproduce and distribute to the visually impaired, at cost, a Braille, large type, audio or other edition of a previously published literary work in a form intended to be perceived by the visually impaired, provided that, during a period of at least one year after the first publication of a standard edition of such work in the United States, the owner of the exclusive right to distribute such work in the United States has not entered the market for editions intended to be perceived by the visually impaired.

SEC. 4. COPYRIGHT PROTECTION SYSTEMS AND COPYRIGHT MANAGEMENT INFORMATION.

Title 17, United States Code, is amended by adding the following new chapter:

Chapter 12.—COPYRIGHT PROTECTION AND MANAGEMENT SYSTEMS

Sec.

1201. Circumvention of Copyright Protection Systems

1202. Integrity of Copyright Management Information

1203. Civil Remedies

1204. Criminal Offenses and Penalties

1201. Circumvention of Copyright Protection Systems

No person shall import, manufacture or distribute any device, product, or component incorporated into a device or product, or offer or perform any service, the primary purpose or effect of which is to avoid, bypass, remove, deactivate, or otherwise circumvent, without the authority of the copyright owner or the law, any process, treatment, mechanism or system which prevents or inhibits the violation of any of the exclusive rights of the copyright owner under section 106.

1201. Integrity of Copyright Management Information

(a) FALSE COPYRIGHT MANAGEMENT INFORMATION.—No person shall knowingly provide copyright management information that is false, or knowingly publicly distribute or import for public distribution copyright management information that is false.

(b) REMOVAL OR ALTERATION OF COPYRIGHT MANAGEMENT INFORMATION.—No person shall, without authority of the copyright owner or the law, (i) knowingly remove or alter any copyright management information, (ii) knowingly distribute or import for distribution copyright management information that has been altered without authority of the copyright owner or the law, or (iii) knowingly distribute or import for distribution copies or phonorecords from which copyright management information has been removed without authority of the copyright owner or the law.

(c) DEFINITION.—As used in this chapter, "copyright management information" means the name and other identifying information of the author of a work, the name and other identifying information of the copyright owner, terms and conditions for uses of the work, and such other information as the Register of Copyrights may prescribe by regulation.

1203. Civil Remedies

(a) CIVIL ACTIONS.—Any person injured by a violation of Sec. 1201 or 1202 may bring a civil action in an appropriate United States district court for such violation.

(b) POWERS OF THE COURT.—In an action brought under subsection (a), the court—

(1) may grant temporary and permanent injunctions on such terms as it deems reasonable to prevent or restrain a violation;

(2) at any time while an action is pending, may order the impounding, on such terms as it deems reasonable, of any device or product that is in the custody or control of the alleged violator and that the court has reasonable cause to believe was involved in a violation;

(3) may award damages under subsection (c);

(4) in its discretion may allow the recovery of costs by or against any party other than the United States or an officer thereof;

(5) in its discretion may award reasonable attorney's fees to the prevailing party; and

(6) may, as part of a final judgment or decree finding a violation, order the remedial modification or the destruction of any device or product involved in the violation that is in the custody or control of the violator or has been impounded under subsection (2).

(c) AWARD OF DAMAGES.—

(1) IN GENERAL.—Except as otherwise provided in this chapter, a violator is liable for either (i) the actual damages and any additional profits of the violator, as provided by subsection (2) or (ii) statutory damages, as provided by subsection (3).

(2) ACTUAL DAMAGES.—The court shall award to the complaining party the actual damages suffered by him or her as a result of the violation, and any profits of the violator that are attributable to the violation and are not taken into account in computing the actual damages, if the complaining party elects such damages at any time before final judgment is entered.

(3) STATUTORY DAMAGES.—

(A) At any time before final judgment is entered, a complaining party may elect to recover an award of statutory damages for each violation of section 1201 in the sum of not less than $200 or more than $2,500 per device, product, offer or performance of service, as the court considers just.

(B) At any time before final judgment is entered, a complaining party may elect to recover an award of statutory damages for each violation of section 1202 in the sum of not less than $2,500 or more than $25,000.

(4) REPEATED VIOLATIONS.—In any case in which the injured party sustains the burden of proving, and the court finds, that a person has violated section 1201 or 1202 within three years after a final judgment was entered against that person for another such violation, the court may increase the award of damages up to triple the amount that would otherwise be awarded, as the court considers just.

(5) INNOCENT VIOLATIONS.—The court in its discretion may reduce or remit altogether the total award of damages in any case in which the violator sustains the burden of proving, and the court finds, that the violator was not aware and had no reason to believe that its acts constituted a violation.

1204. Criminal Offenses and Penalties

Any person who violates section 1202 with intent to defraud shall be fined not more than $500,000 or imprisoned for not more than 5 years, or both.

SEC. 5. CONFORMING AMENDMENTS.

(a) TABLE OF SECTIONS.—The table of sections for chapter 1 of title 17, United States Code, is amended by inserting after the item relating to section 108 the following:

108A.   Limitations on exclusive rights: Reproduction for the Visually Impaired.

(b) Table of Chapters.—The table of chapters for title 17, United States Code, is amended by adding at the end the following:

12.   COPYRIGHT PROTECTION AND MANAGEMENT SYSTEMS. . . . 1201.

SEC. 6. EFFECTIVE DATE.

This Act, and the amendments made by this Act, shall take effect on the date of the enactment of this Act.

DIGITAL FUTURE COALITION TESTIMONY ON THE "NII COPYRIGHT PROTECTION ACT OF 1995"

Digital Future Coalition Testimony

United States Senate
Committee on the Judiciary
Presented by Prof. Robert L. Oakley
May 7, 1996

Good morning, Mr. Chairman, Sen. Biden, and Members of the Committee. My name is Robert Oakley. I am a Professor of Law at the Georgetown University Law Center and Director of the Law Center's Library. I also serve as Washington Affairs Representative for the American Association of Law Libraries, a member of the Digital Future Coalition.

I am honored and pleased to appear before the Committee today on behalf of the Digital Future Coalition to share with you not only our large and diverse group's broad views on copyright and the National Information Infrastructure ("NII"), but to offer for the record a specific, seven-point package of amendments to S. 1284. The DFC respectfully requests that its proposals be considered and incorporated into S. 1284 before that legislation is reported out of this Committee.

Introduction

Before detailing the DFC's legislative package, Mr. Chairman, it is important that the Committee know who and what the Digital Future Coalition is, and what we stand for. If I may say, our very existence and the diversity of our membership are testimony themselves to the importance, breadth and complexity of the issues raised by S. 1284.

The Digital Future Coalition includes many public and private organizations that have been instrumental in building, and that will continue to expand, the Internet and broader NII now emerging.

We are, most simply, over two dozen distinct organizations with a cumulative membership of well over 2 million Americans.

We are also, through our organizational members: major technology and telecommunications corporations; educators; the nation's school boards and libraries; nationally recognized consumer advocates; scholars and teachers of many disciplines, including intellectual property; and leading experts on privacy, the First Amendment and on information technology's pitfalls and potential.

We are — to a member — corporations and organizations with a bedrock commitment to intelligent and balanced copyright law made after substantial scrutiny by Congress. That means on the one hand, Mr. Chairman, that we respect and support strong copyright protection and, on the other hand, that we are committed to equally strong statutory respect for the Constitutional objective that undergirds all of copyright law: "the Progress of Science and useful Arts," and to the principle of Fair Use.

We agree that copyright is at root about promoting creativity. As creators ourselves, however, we understand that creativity results not just from the financial incentive for authors and inventors codified in Title 17 of the U.S. Code, but from that same statute's guarantee of access to copyrighted information. The truest and best measure of our copyright law's success is whether it succeeds in fairly balancing those equal priorities in the service of the Framer's commitment to the broad dissemination of knowledge and information in a Democracy.

Overview of Proposals

The Digital Future Coalition understands, Mr. Chairman, that you, Sen. Leahy and this Committee are eager to get down to the "brass tacks" of assuring that the development and marketplace deployment of 21st century information technology is not hindered by a 20th century statute. The DFC wishes to be absolutely clear that it shares that goal.

Our Coalition is also convinced, however, that — in pursuit of that end — Congress now has an opportunity (and a responsibility) to bring ALL of the critical precepts at the core of copyright law into the digital future together and in balance. In practical terms:

That means that, if the nature and scope of the monopoly rights granted to copyright holders is to be "clarified" by changing the U.S. Code, then the nature and scope of a key counterbalance to those rights — the Fair Use Doctrine — must be made equally clear in the law;

It means that, even as the Fair Use Doctrine is philosophically reaffirmed, Congress must practically assure that the continued ability of Americans in business, academia and the public at large to rely on and use copyrighted information — and to develop new business models for its distribution — are not precluded by overbroad restrictions on the manufacture of devices and systems needed to make fair use rights real.

It also means, Mr. Chairman, that Congress must deal directly in S. 1284 with the issue of who should be liable, when, and to what extent if a commercial, academic or library computer network carries copyrighted information without the author's permission.

Without increased certainty in this critical area of the law, however, both commercial and non-commercial use of the NII and GII will be dramatically chilled by the potential for crippling litigation and liability.

Precluding Premature International Action
on a "Digital Agenda"

The Digital Future Coalition is also critically concerned, Mr. Chairman, that — unless checked — activities by the Executive Branch in the international arena could moot the Legislative Branch's policy making prerogatives in this critical area of the law. Proposals virtually identical to those now before this Committee have already been presented by the U.S. delegation to the World Intellectual Property Organization by the United States' delegation, which confirmed just days ago that it intends to continue to call for a diplomatic conference to draft treaty language prior to the end of this year which would, in effect, codify the pending legislation in international law.

That call will next be heard from the U.S. delegation in Rome starting tomorrow as the "Stockholm Group" of industrialized nations meets for three days to consider and potentially endorse the U.S. agenda for a December 1996 diplomatic conference to be held in Geneva. The Governing Body of WIPO itself will meet in Geneva on May 20, less than two weeks from now, to cast plans for the conference in concrete. The DFC believes that the Framers would take a dim view of such de facto preemption of Congress' sole authority to make copyright policy. That possibility, however, now looms large on the international horizon.

Accordingly, Mr. Chairman, we urge you, the Committee and the Senate to immediately send a strong message to the Executive Branch that: (1) the Administration's "Digital Agenda" is premature for consideration by WIPO pending the formation of a domestic consensus and the conclusion of Congressional action on the legislation before us; and (2) the United States' delegation to WIPO should work affirmatively to assure that any such "Digital Agenda" is not placed before a 1996 or early 1997 diplomatic conference intended to amend the Berne Convention for the first time in 25 years.

Legislative Proposals

Turning now to the DFC's specific legislative proposals, I would like to request, Mr. Chairman, that they be incorporated in the record of these hearings at the conclusion of my remarks, together with relevant explanatory materials. These proposals, for the record, have been expressly endorsed by the undersigned members of the Digital Future Coalition.

In sum, the DFC proposes:

— that new provisions concerning the Fair Use and First Sale Doctrines, distance education and ephemeral digital reproductions of copyrighted works be added to S. 1284;

— that Section 1201, regarding "Circumvention of Copyright Protection Systems," simply be stricken from the bill in favor of technology-specific solutions based on negotiated solutions among those most concerned; and

— that proposed changes in two of the remaining provisions of the legislation be modified to better assure that the critical "balance" in copyright law just described is maintained. (Those provisions concern preservation activities addressed in Section 108, and "copyright management information" systems covered by new Section 1202.)

In addition, the undersigned DFC members urge the Committee not to approve S. 1284 unless and until it is amended to clarify and define the scope of network service providers' liability under the Copyright Act in a manner that does not require or encourage such providers to compromise the privacy rights of their users.

For the Committee's convenience, I will address the undersigned DFC members' proposed amendments in the order of the statutory sections to which they relate, beginning with Section 106 of the Copyright Act.

Section 106: Ephemeral Digital Reproductions

As introduced, S. 1284 would amend Section 106 of the Copyright Act to provide for a "transmission" right as an aspect of the "distribution" right already identified in subsection (3). If such a right is made explicit in the Act, however, further clarification of the statute is needed to assure that the mere act of reading a digital document will not constitute copyright infringement.

Such liability could well be imposed if the new transmission right is interpreted by courts to support a finding that every temporary reproduction of a work in a computer's random access memory (RAM) or "cache" storage (incidental to its use on a computer system) is a technical "copy" for all purposes under the Copyright Act. Under this construction of the law, activities that can now be undertaken without risk of liability in the analog environment would become a potential source of liability in the digital one.

While a few courts have considered "RAM" reproduction to be "copying" under the Copyright Act (see particularly Ninth Circuit decisions, such as *MAI v. Peak*, 991 F.2d 511 [1993]), this interpretation has been substantively addressed only in a few jurisdictions and has not been reviewed by the Supreme Court. It is, therefore, far from being settled law. It is, however, one of the central tenets of the White Paper on "Intellectual Property and the National Information Infrastructure" and thus clouds all discussions of rights and wrongs in cyberspace.

The "NII Copyright Protection Act" offers the Congress an opportunity to definitively clarify that the mere fact that a work in digital form is loaded into the random access or cache memory of a computer — creating temporary electronic versions of the work destined for automatic erasure — does not constitute the sort of "copying" with which the law of copyright is now or need be concerned. Accordingly, the DFC proposes that — in addition to modifying Section 106(3) — S. 1284 be broadened to amend the description of the "reproduction right" in Section 106(1) of the Copyright Act as follows:

> For the purposes of this subsection, the ephemeral reproduction of a work in temporary computer memory or digital storage, which is incidental to the otherwise lawful use of that work, and which does not lead to the making of a permanent reproduction, is not a copy. This language is intended to apply only to necessary and incidental reproduction of digital works in connection with their use on computer systems. It will have no application to situations in which permanent electronic copies, such as those made on a computer's disks (or other permanent or semi-permanent storage media) are made.

Section 107: Fair Use

As noted earlier in these remarks, it is critical that the copyright law strike an appropriate balance between protecting the rights of copyright owners and otherwise promoting "Progress in Science and the useful Arts." In the scheme of American copyright, "fair use" safeguards our collective interest in the flow of information — which is, in turn, a source of economically valuable knowledge.

Fair use, in addition to reflecting in copyright law First Amendment-based principles of free speech, provides the basis for many of our most important day-to-day activities in scholarship and education. Moreover, it is no less vital to American industries, which lead the world in technological innovation. It is also of tremendous value to the Judiciary in dealing with the challenge of precisely such innovation, and repeatedly has been recognized by the Supreme Court as essential to the work of writers and others who creatively transmogrify the earlier works of others in the alchemy that we call "Art."

The maintenance of a robust Fair Use Doctrine in the new legal environment of cyberspace thus remains a high priority of the Digital Future Coalition and, we respectfully submit, should rank among Congress' highest priorities, as well.

S. 1284 proposes to "clarify" that transmission is a form of distribution under the Copyright Act, one of the "bundle of rights" granted to copyright holders by Section 106 of the Act. Many also consider the proposed language an expansion of those rights. Under either interpretation, the Digital Future Coalition believes that a comparable change is necessary and appropriate in the "Fair Use" portion of the statute (Section 107) in order to assure that the scope of fair use parallels the scope of the rights to which it relates. Including such language in the pending legislation and the Act also will reaffirm Congress' commitment to the vibrancy of the Fair Use Doctrine in the digital future.

To those ends, the DFC proposes that the introductory [sentence] of Section 107 be amended to read as follows (with proposed new language indicated by italics):

Notwithstanding the provisions of Sections 106 and 106A, the fair use of a copyrighted work, including such use by reproduction in copies or phonorecords, *by transmission,* or by any other means specified by that section, for purposes such as criticism, comment, news reporting, teaching (including multiple copies for classroom use), scholarship, or research is not an infringement of copyright.

Section 108: Library Exemptions

The transformation of the information environment gives rise to both challenges and opportunities for many important social institutions, including libraries. The undersigned members of the Digital Future Coalition agree with you and Sen. Leahy, Mr. Chairman, that a "digital update" to Section 108 of the Copyright Act is required if the needs of libraries and researchers are to be met. Moreover, such an update is vital to libraries' ongoing and uphill efforts to solve a preservation problem which now ranks as nothing short of a national intellectual and historical crisis.

The Digital Future Coalition supports technical revisions to S. 1284 advanced by several of its member organizations (the American Association of Law Libraries, the American Library Association, the Association of Research Libraries, the Medical Library Association, and the Special Libraries Association) and supported by the Register of Copyrights. These revisions would make Sec. 108 "technology-neutral" throughout, thus allowing libraries to use the best and newest technology platform to carry out the activities authorized by Section 108.

Our proposal would also add an important new subsection designed to help the library community meet the special preservation challenges posed by digital works in obsolete formats (i.e., works which can no longer be accessed by the technologies that produced them because such technologies are no longer reasonably available).

Specifically, the DFC proposes that Section 108 be revised in a manner largely consistent with S. 1284 to read as follows (proposed new language in italics; deletions in square brackets):

(a) *Except as otherwise provided,* notwithstanding the provisions of Section 106, it is not an infringement of copyright for a library or archives, or any of its employees acting within the scope of their employment, to reproduce no more than one copy or phonorecord of a work, *or to distribute such copy or phonorecord,* under the conditions specified by this section, if—

(Subsections 1 and 2 remain unchanged);

(3) the reproduction or distribution of the work includes a notice of copyright *if such notice appears on the copy or phonorecord that is reproduced under the provisions of this section.*

(b) The rights of reproduction and distribution under this section apply to [a copy or phonorecord] *three copies or phonorecords* of an unpublished work duplicated [in facsimile form] solely for purposes of preservation and security or for deposit for research use in another library or archives of the type described by clause (2) of subsection (a), if the copy or phonorecord reproduced is currently in the collections of the library or archives.

(c) The right of reproduction under this section applies to [a copy or phonorecord] *three copies or phonorecords* of a published work duplicated [in facsimile form] solely for the purpose of replacement of a copy or phonorecord that is damaged, deteriorating, lost, or stolen, *or if the existing format in which the work is stored has become obsolete,* if the library or archives has, after a reasonable effort, determined that an unused replacement cannot be obtained at a fair price.

Section 109: The First Sale Doctrine

It has long been recognized in American law that someone who legally obtains a book or video cassette, for example, may — without the permission of the owner or fear of liability — give, sell or otherwise transfer possession of that work to someone else. Library lending, for example, is a direct outgrowth of this "First Sale Doctrine" now codified at Section 109(a) of the Copyright Act.

The Digital Future Coalition rejects the suggestion, made in the report on "Intellectual Property and the National Information Infrastructure" (produced by the Working Group on Intellectual Property Rights of the President's Information and Infrastructure Task Force) and elsewhere, that the First Sale Doctrine applies only to the physical transfer of an actual object and does not apply to the electronic transmission of a work under any circumstances. Such analysis, in any event, misses the critical point that Congress now has the opportunity to determine whether some digital equivalent to the traditional "first sale" doctrine, as it exists in the analog information environment, should apply in cyberspace. We believe that it should.

Historically, the ability to pass on lawfully obtained copies of works has been important to libraries, scholars, and ordinary information consumers. It has also be a crucial factor in the emergence of new business models. Just as "first sale" in the past has given us everything from lending libraries to video rental outlets, we believe that the digital equivalent of "first sale" could be the basis for important new cultural and economic developments in cyberspace. One means to that end would be to add to Section 109 of the Copyright Act the following new subsection:

(f) The privilege set forth in subsection (a) extends to any transmission of a single copy or phonorecord so long as the transmitter erases or destroys his or her copy or phonorecord at substantially the same time. The reproduction of a work, to the extent required to exercise this privilege, is not an infringement.

If adopted, this proposal would codify a standard with which responsible users of the NII may reasonably be expected to comply, and one which would be no more difficult to enforce than a flat prohibition on all retransmissions of lawfully acquired digital copies of copyrighted works. Indeed, content providers could take advantage of increasingly sophisticated technological means to make it difficult, if not practically impossible, to forward such copies without simultaneously deleting them.

Sections 110 and 112: Distance Education

"Distance Education" is one of the most exciting and potentially productivity-enhancing trends in American education today. Using television and other technologies, educators are increasingly able to deliver non-profit educational services critical to success in the global economy to students in rural communities, disabled individuals, adults enrolled in continuing education programs, and many other special communities of learners. Literally millions of Americans benefit from these efforts. The Digital Future Coalition is concerned, however, that if the current law and pending legislation are not modified, the tremendous educational and social benefits of distance learning will be lost to millions of children and adults across the nation.

Students today enjoy the benefits of distance education in large part because of provisions contained in Sec. 110(2) of the Copyright Act of 1976, which allow for the "performance or display" of certain works delivered by means of "transmission" in non-profit educational settings.

Today, that typically means television. Increasingly, however, distance educators will want and need to make use of digital transmissions over local networks and the Internet in order to maximize the reach and effectiveness of their services.

Under S. 1284, however, Sec. 106(3) of the Copyright Act would be amended to define transmissions of copyrighted works by means of digital networks as "distributions" of copies. The existing exemptions for education in Sec. 110, however, do not apply to the "distribution right." S. 1284, as written, thus promises to clarify and expand the rights of copyright proprietors while narrowing the continued ability of distance educators (in both government and non-profit institutions) to use the latest and best technology to carry on their crucial work.

Furthermore, unlike the broadcast technologies of the mid-1970s, digital networks make it possible to deliver distance non-profit educational services to students individually and outside traditional classroom settings through individual computer terminals. At present, however, the locations to which educators may deliver "distance ed" programming are limited under Sec. 110(2) of the Copyright Act. Moreover, the limitations of the Sec. 110(2) exemptions to certain classes of copyrighted works are increasingly outdated in an era of digital "convergence" and "multimedia" presentations.

Ideally, the best way to assure that the technologies of learning continue to flourish in the digital age would be to engage in a comprehensive rethinking of the relationship between educational practice and copyright, starting from first premises. Such an effort, however, would take time. If there is to be legislation in the near term to adapt copyright to the networked information environment, the undersigned DFC members believe it is essential that any such legislation include language that addresses these important distance education issues.

Specifically, the DFC proposes amending Sec. 110(2) — and its companion Sec. 112(b) — to bring distance education into the digital age by adding "distribution" to the list of conditionally exempt educational uses. Sec. 110 should be further updated by eliminating current restrictions on the kinds of places in which exempt transmissions may legally be received, and on the kinds of works subject to the exemption. Finally, to help assure that these provisions are not abused, the DFC also proposes new restrictive language which would limit the scope of Sections 110 and 112 to transmissions primarily intended for the use of "officially enrolled" students. As modified according to our suggestions, Secs. 110(2) and 112(b) would read as follows:

Section 110(2):

(2) performance, display or distribution of a work by or in the course of transmission if —

(A) the performance, display or distribution is a regular part of the systematic instructional activities of a governmental body or a nonprofit educational institution, and

(B) the performance, display or distribution is directly related and of material assistance to the teaching content of the transmission, and

(C) the transmission is made primarily for reception by students officially enrolled in the course in connection with which it is offered, or

(D) the transmission is made primarily for reception by officers or employees of governmental bodies as a part of their official duties or employment;

Section 112(b):

Notwithstanding the provisions of section 106, it is not an infringement of copyright for a governmental body or other nonprofit organization entitled to perform, display or distribute a work by or in the course of a transmission, under section 110(2) or under the limitations on exclusive rights in sound recordings specified by section 114(a) to make no more than thirty copies or phonorecords of a particular transmission program embodying the performance, display or distribution, if —

(. . . the balance of the statute as in the original . . .)

Proposed Section 1201: Circumvention of Copyright Protection Systems

The Digital Future Coalition does not take lightly, and does not believe frivolous, the concern of many in the entertainment and information industries that digital technology creates new dilemmas. The DFC does, however, take strong issue with the suggestion that proposed Section 1201 is an appropriately measured and balanced response to this concern.

As representatives of entertainment industries now readily admit, similar concerns over technological innovation have proven unfounded in the past. Originally viewed as a deadly threat to the motion picture industry, for example, the VCR actually spawned a new and previously unenvisioned market for that industry which now accounts for the majority of its domestic revenues.

Despite that experience (and positive experience in the past with narrow device-specific "black box" prohibition laws aimed at satellite signal piracy) the NII Working Group has offered Congress a vague and sweeping provision — one which would, in effect, overturn the Supreme Court's decision that made the VCR industry viable and established the public's fair use right to "time shift" programs by recording them for private use.

In the Betamax decision, the Supreme Court held that because the Betamax is "capable of substantial noninfringing uses, . . . Sony's sale of such equipment to the general public does not constitute contributory infringement of respondents' copyrights." Since Section 1201, as drafted, could outlaw devices that have substantial noninfringing uses if they do not also respond to all anticopying technology, we believe it reverses the Supreme Court's decision.

Moreover, because Section 1201 covers components as well as devices, it could be used by courts to outlaw entirely the sale of a variety of products including recording devices with substantial noninfringing uses. Such products should not be expected to comply with anti-copying encoding that would prevent fair use copying, would distort regular TV pictures, would require expensive licenses, or otherwise would frustrate consumers.

Members of the DFC do not advocate allowing consumers to circumvent properly protected copyright works through such systems as "black boxes" that have no commercially significant use other than to circumvent copy protection. But our members do support the right of consumers to continue to make legal, fair use reproductions of copyrighted works. We therefore recommend that Congress not adopt Section 1201. Rather, we urge Congress, working with concerned industries, to address copying issues on a more specific basis in terms of devices and technologies.

Technically expert DFC member organizations look forward to sharing with the Committee additional information regarding the viability of relying on technology to guard against the unauthorized use of copyrighted digital works in a manner consistent with the Fair Use Doctrine.

Section 1202: Copyright Management Information

The Digital Future Coalition is similarly concerned that proposed Section 1202, as incorporated in S. 1284, goes too far in attempting to further the laudable purpose of counteracting piracy by forbidding the misrepresentation of "copyright management information." Clearly, the development of systems and programs intended to provide consumers and other information users with information about who holds the rights to a copyrighted work, how to contact the rights holder, and (if permission to use the work is legally required) under what terms it may be obtained are not inherently objectionable. Penalizing individuals who remove or alter such information in order to further actual copyright infringement also seems appropriate.

As drafted, however, proposed Section 1202(a) also would penalize a potentially wide range of non-infringing activities. For example, a legitimate wholesaler which acquired several thousand copies of a copyrighted book or videotape each of which included accurate "copyright management information" (CMI) at the time of the acquisition might subsequently learn through the trade press that the rights to those works had been transferred as part of a major corporate acquisition. Under Section 1202(a), because the wholesaler knew that the CMI imbedded in each copy in his inventory had now been rendered "false" by market events outside its control, he or she would risk liability for redistributing them in the normal course of otherwise lawful business activities. Similar liability would be faced by libraries and educators.

This certainly unintended result would obtain because the only requirement for liability under Section 1202(a) is mere knowledge that false CMI has been distributed. Nonsensically, the distributor's intent and the reason that the information is or became inaccurate are irrelevant.

Section 1202(b), by contrast, speaks to the true heart of the problem — the wrongful alteration or removal of such information. By incorporating a similar concept in Section 1202(a) the inadvertent sweep of the provision will be appropriately narrowed. Specifically, we propose that liability for transmitting false copyright management information be imposed only on those who do so in furtherance of actual copyright infringement. So modified, Sec. 1202(a) would read as follows:

False Copyright Management Information.— No person shall knowingly provide copyright management information that is false, or knowingly publicly distribute or import for public distribution copyright management information that is false, in furtherance of infringement.

The DFC also is concerned that, by making the definition of "copyright management information" ("CMI") open-ended, S. 1284 effectively delegates to the Copyright Office the authority to define what will and will not be a criminal offense. Such determinations, the Coalition believes should continue to be made by Congress itself. In addition, if broadly defined, it is clear that CMI systems will be capable not only of providing information users with information about copyright proprietors, but will furnish such proprietors with data about the information user (*see Chronicle of Higher Education*, March 22, 1996, p. A23). Absent effective privacy safeguards (such as the development of anonymous payment mechanisms), serious privacy problems will result.

For both of these reasons, the DFC strongly urges that detailed hearings be conducted on the appropriate scope of the definition of CMI for purposes of the pending legislation. Not incidentally, such hearings also will afford authors an opportunity to be heard as to how CMI technology may best advance their significant interests in the digital information marketplace.

On-Line Service Provider Liability

Finally, the DFC wishes to highlight for the Committee an additional issue of very substantial concern to its members. While we are not presently proposing a legislative solution in deference to ongoing multi-party negotiations, the Digital Future Coalition believes that S. 1284 should not be reported out of the Judiciary Committee (or, certainly, approved by the Senate) unless it is explicitly amended to define the circumstances under (and the extent to) which Internet access providers, bulletin board operators, libraries, educational institutions, and other system operators will be held liable for violations of the new "transmission" right for copyright infringement by subscribers and other end-users. Such legislation is needed for many reasons, including the protection of privacy. Given the uncertain and fluid state of case law in this area, absent clear lines of liability service providers may have no practical defense to crippling damages but the invasive monitoring and supervision of their subscribers' private communications.

Conclusion

Like most participants in the networked information environment, the members of the Digital Future Coalition are creators of copyrighted works, as well as consumers of information. As such, we believe strongly in the importance of providing appropriate copyright protection in cyberspace for large content providers and individual authors alike. The new "transmission" right included in S. 1284 may be an appropriate means to this end. As we have indicated, however, the DFC is gravely concerned that the codification of that right — without other compensating adjustments to the Copyright Act — may miscalibrate the traditional balance of interests reflected in the Copyright Act today.

Such imbalance not only threatens to injure consumer interests and to inhibit or preclude the emergence of new business models in cyberspace, but also promises to retard the very "Progress in Science and the useful Arts" that led the Framers of the Constitution to grant Congress the power to award copyrights over two centuries ago.

The undersigned members of the Digital Future Coalition appreciate this opportunity to present our views on S. 1284. We look forward to working with the Committee and its staff to craft legislation which honors the Constitution by reaffirming and guarding the balance at copyright's core.

Thank you again, Mr. Chairman.

Alliance for Public Technology

American Association of Law Libraries

American Committee for Interoperable Systems

American Council of Learned Societies

American Historical Association

American Library Association

Art Libraries Society of North America

Association of American Geographers

Association of Research Libraries

Committee of Concerned Intellectual Property Educators

Computer & Communications Industry Association

Conference on College Composition and Communication

Consortium of Social Science Associations

Consumer Federation of America

Consumer Project on Technology

Electronic Frontier Foundation

Electronic Privacy Information Center

Home Recording Rights Coalition

Medical Library Association

National Council of Teachers of English

National Education Association

National Humanities Alliance

National School Boards Association

People for the American Way Action Fund

Special Libraries Association

DIGITAL MILLENNIUM COPYRIGHT ACT

For the legislation ultimately enacted by Congress in response to the White Paper and the two W.I.P.O. treaties agreed on in December 1996 (as detailed in Part Two above), see the "Digital Millennium Copyright Act," Pub. L. No. 105-304, 112 Stat. 2860 (Oct. 28, 1998), reproduced in Part One of this Supplement.

RELEVANT PENDING LEGISLATION

For relevant legislation pending before the 107th Congress, Second Session, see Part One of this Supplement. And see the websites for Congress and the Copyright Office, *http://thomas.loc.gov/* and *http://lcweb.loc.gov/copyright/*, respectively for important legislative developments expected, but not yet in the hopper, as the Supplement goes to press.

COPYRIGHT OFFICE REPORT ON COPYRIGHT AND DIGITAL DISTANCE EDUCATION: EXECUTIVE SUMMARY

May 1999

EXECUTIVE SUMMARY

INTRODUCTION

Over the past five years, the application of copyright law to distance education using digital technologies has become the subject of public debate and attention in the United States. In the Digital Millennium Copyright Act of 1998 (DMCA), Congress charged the Copyright Office with responsibility to study the issue and report back with recommendations within six months. After an intensive process of identifying stakeholders, holding public hearings, soliciting comments, conducting research, and consulting with experts in various fields, the Office has issued this Report.

Part I of the Report gives an overview of the nature of distance education today. Part II describes current licensing practices in digital distance education, including problems and future trends. Part III describes the status of technologies relating to the delivery and protection of distance education materials. Part IV analyzes the application of current copyright law to digital distance education activities. Part V discusses prior initiatives addressing copyright and digital distance education. Part VI examines the question of whether the law should be changed, first summarizing the views of interested parties and then providing the Copyright Office's analysis and recommendations.

I. THE NATURE OF DISTANCE EDUCATION TODAY

Distance education in the United States today is a vibrant and burgeoning field. Although it is far from new, digital technologies have fostered a rapid expansion in recent years, as well as change in profile. The technologies used in distance education, the populations served, the institutions offering such programs, and the partnerships that have emerged differ in nature and scale from earlier models.

The most fundamental definition of distance education is a form of education in which students are separated from their instructors by time and/or space. Distance education is utilized in some form at every level of the educational spectrum, with the most extensive use in higher education. An individual course may contain both classroom and distance education components. Digital technology is used extensively for varied purposes and in varied ways, depending on the intended audience for the course, and the availability and cost of the technology. The capabilities of the new technologies have made possible a more interactive experience that more closely parallels face-to-face teaching effect creating a virtual classroom. They have also made distance education courses more convenient and better suited to the needs of different students, including by providing the benefits of both synchronous and asynchronous methods.

Distance education is reaching wider audiences, covering all segments of the population. The college audience is increasing particularly rapidly, in part due to responsiveness to the needs of an older, non-traditional student population, as well as students in other countries. Students also include professionals engaging in professional development or training, and retirees. The expansion of the field has led to changes among providers, with courses offered by both nonprofit and for-profit entities, on both a nonprofit and for-profit basis, and through varieties of partnerships among educational institutions and corporations. The federal government has been active in promoting the benefits of distance education, with recent legislation providing funding and recognition in various forms.

Educational institutions offering distance education draw on library resources in several ways, including to provide support for online courses and to provide access to supplemental materials in digital form. Institutions are engaged in adopting copyright policies, training faculty and staff, and educating students about copyright law. They are increasingly seeking and obtaining formal accreditation.

II. LICENSING OF COPYRIGHTED WORKS

Although substantial licensing activities are taking place today in connection with the provision of materials to distance education students, so far relatively few licenses are requested or granted for digital uses. Most licensing relates to supplemental materials in analog form, or, increasingly, in digital form; the least common type of licensing is for digital uses of copyrighted works incorporated into the class itself. Most of the works licensed for digital use are textual materials; licenses for other types of content are much less frequent. As an alternative to seeking a license, an educational institution may avoid the use of preexisting copyrighted works in distance education courses, or may rely on exemptions in the copyright law. There is wide diversity in licensing procedures among educational institutions and copyright owners. In general, the more resources devoted to licensing, and the more centralized the responsibility, the more efficient and successful the process.

Many educational institutions describe having experienced recurrent problems with licensing for digital distance education, primarily involving difficulty locating the copyright owner inability to obtain a timely response, or unreasonable prices or other terms. The problems are reported to be most serious with respect to journal articles and audiovisual works. They appear to be exacerbated in the digital context, which may be explained in part by the perception of copyright owners that the risks of unauthorized dissemination are greater, and in part by the elements of novelty and unfamiliarity.

A number of trends may facilitate the development of more effective digital licensing in the near future, including advances in technology used to protect works, the use of electronic copyright management information, and online licensing systems. New collective initiatives should also ease the licensing process for many types of uses. As digital uses become more common and familiar, copyright owners are becoming more flexible. It is difficult to predict the extent to which licensing problems will subside or how long the improvement will take, but given the current state of development of these trends, a more definitive evaluation will be possible in the next few years.

III. TECHNOLOGIES INVOLVED IN DIGITAL DISTANCE EDUCATION

Technology that facilitates licensing includes the ability to attach information to a work in digital format, and online rights and permissions services supporting a range of license and delivery functions. A number of different delivery technologies are used in distance education today, including traditional media used to carry digital information, such as digital television broadcasts or video conferencing. These may be used in combination with digital network technology, such as computer connections between students and instructors.

The computer is the most versatile of distance education instruments, since it can perform the same function as a television or telephone, but also provide more interactivity, deliver more content, and support more comprehensive services. Computers can be used to transmit texts and graphics, connect users in a variety of real-time and asynchronous dialogues, deliver messages between users, and receive both audio and video transmissions.

There is no "typical" digital distance education course. Instructors sometimes build courses from scratch, and sometimes customize templates provided by commercial software. They may combine any or all of the technological tools available today, including e-mail, threaded discussions, chat rooms, whiteboard programs, shared applications, streaming video or audio, video or audio files, course management infrastructure, links to websites, and interactive CD-ROMs and DVD-ROMs. In addition, programs for self-paced independent learning may be obtained from commercial vendors or through an educational institution.

The need to provide technological security for copyrighted works in the digital environment has been recognized in all sectors, not just for distance education. Technology companies and content providers are working to develop commercially viable protection technologies, and industries are collaborating to develop standards. Some technologies limit access to works;

others prevent or detect uses of works after access. Each method varies in its cost and degree of security; although many are highly effective, none provides absolute certainty. The goal is to provide a high enough level of protection that the cost of circumvention outweighs the value of access to the material protected.

Educational organizations can, and commonly do, limit access to students enrolled in a particular class or institution through several different methods used separately or in combination: password protection, firewalls, screening for IP addresses or domain names, hardware connections, encryption, or using CD-ROMs as a delivery mechanism.

After access has been gained, however, material is available to students for further use, including downloading or electronic distribution. Technologies that address such downstream uses do exist today, with several on the market, others expected to be released very soon, and others projected for release in the next year. Most, but not all, are designed to handle a single type of content. The most effective are secure container/proprietary viewer technologies, which allow copyright owners to set rules for the use of their works, which are then attached to all digital copies, and prevent anyone from making a use that is not in accordance with the rules. For example, students could be allowed to view the work or print a single copy, but not to save it to disk or distribute it to others electronically. Streaming formats, which do not facilitate the making of copies, and the use of low resolution digital copies, also offer some degree of protection against redistribution.

Technologies for embedding information in digital works to identify and track usage are also in development and use, with the practice of digital watermarking the most effective. Using commercially available software or services, these identifiers can be used as a search object to find unauthorized copies of some types of works on the World Wide Web.

Significant developments are occurring in all of these areas, and a few generalizations can be made. More efficient licensing mechanisms will become more widespread, and delivery systems will become more efficient, sophisticated and interoperable. Developments in protecting content are harder to predict. In the near future it will be technically possible to protect works against both unauthorized access and dissemination with a high degree of effectiveness. Because it remains to be seen whether technologies to prevent downstream uses will gain widespread market acceptance, the extent to which they will be available in practical form for use in digital distance education at any given point in time is unclear.

IV. APPLICATION OF COPYRIGHT LAW TO DISTANCE EDUCATION

Different copyright rights are implicated by different educational activities, depending in part on the technologies used. When a performance or display of a work is accomplished by means of a digital network transmission, temporary RAM copies are made in the computers through which the material passes, by virtue of the technological process. As a result, not only the rights of public performance or display are implicated, but also the rights of reproduction and/or distribution. This does not mean that the use is necessarily an infringement. Permission to use the work could be granted by the copyright owner, either through an express license or implied from the circumstances. If not, the use may fall within one of the various exemptions in the Copyright Act.

Three exemptions together largely define the scope of permitted uses for digital distance education: two specific instructional exemptions in section 110, and the fair use doctrine of section 107. Sections 110(1) and (2) together were intended to cover all of the methods by which performances or displays in the course of systematic instruction take place. Section 110(1)exempts the performance or display of any work in the course of face-to-face teaching activities. Section 110(2) covers the forms of distance education existing when the statute was enacted in 1976, exempting certain performances or displays in the course of instructional broadcasting. Both subsections contain a number of limitations and restrictions. In particular, the section 110(2) exemption from the performance right applies only to nondramatic literary and musical works (although the display right exemption applies to all categories of works). Section 110(2) also contains limitations on the nature and content of the transmission, and the identity and location of the recipients. The performance or display must be made as a regular part of systematic instructional activity by a nonprofit educational institution or governmental body; it must be directly related and of material assistance to the teaching content; and it must be made primarily for reception in classrooms or places of instruction, or to persons whose disabilities or other special circumstances prevent their attendance in classrooms, or to government employees.

As written, section 110(2) has only limited application to courses offered over a digital network. Because it exempts only acts of performance or display, it would not authorize the reproduction or distribution involved in this type of digital transmission. In addition, students who choose to take a distance course without special circumstances that prevent their attendance in classrooms may not qualify as eligible recipients.

Fair use is the broadest and most general limitation on the exclusive rights of copyright owners, and can exempt distance education uses not covered by the specific instructional exemptions. It is flexible and technology-neutral, and continues to be a critical exemption for educational users in the digital world. It requires courts to examine all the facts and circumstances, weighing four nonexclusive statutory factors. While there are not yet any cases addressing the application of fair use to digital distance education, a court's analysis will depend on elements such as the subject matter of the course, the nature of the educational institution, the ways in which the instructor uses the material, and the kinds and amounts of materials used. Guidelines have in the past been negotiated among interested parties to provide greater certainty as to how fair use applies to education; such guidelines for certain analog uses were included in legislative history around the time of enactment of the Copyright Act.

Other exemptions in the Copyright Act may exempt some distance education uses in limited circumstances, but do not significantly expand the scope of permitted instructional uses in a digital environment. These include the ephemeral recordings exemption in section 112, the limitations on exclusive rights in sound recordings in section 114, and the exemption for certain secondary transmissions in section 111. Compulsory licenses could permit distance educators to use some works in limited ways, but are not likely to be much used.

Two titles of the DMCA are also relevant, one providing limitations on the liability of online service providers and the other establishing new technological adjuncts to copyright protection. While these provisions do not affect the scope of permitted digital distance education uses, they add a degree of security for both educational institutions and copyright owners disseminating and licensing material in the digital environment. New section 512 of the Copyright Act provides greater certainty that educational institutions providing network access for faculty, staff, and students will not, merely by doing so, become liable for infringing material transmitted over the network. New Chapter 12 contains a prohibition against various forms of circumvention of technological measures used by copyright owners to protect their works, and a provision protecting the integrity of copyright management information.

The international context raises two separate issues: treaty obligations and the impact of any amendments abroad. The major treaties that impose obligations on the United States with respect to copyright are the Berne Convention and the TRIPs Agreement. Both contain rules governing the permissibility of exceptions to copyright owners' rights. Any new or amended exemption for distance education should be drafted to be compatible with these standards. In addition, the enactment of any new exemption will have an impact abroad, primarily due to doctrines of choice of law. When an educational institution in the United States transmits courses to students in other countries, it is unclear whether U.S. law will apply to such transmissions, or the law of the country where the transmission is received, making it difficult for educators to determine what uses of works are permissible. Other countries are also making or considering amendments to their copyright laws to address digital distance education.

V. PRIOR INITIATIVES ADDRESSING COPYRIGHT AND DIGITAL DISTANCE EDUCATION

Two different initiatives begun in 1994 sought to develop guidelines interpreting the application of fair use to educational uses through digital technology. One group, initiated by the Consortium of College and University Media Centers (CCUMC) and the Agency for Instructional Technology, issued a set of guidelines in 1996 addressing the use of portions of copyrighted works in educational multimedia projects created by educators or students as part of systematic learning activity at nonprofit educational institutions. The other group, established by the Conference on Fair Use (CONFU) convened by the Administration's Information Infrastructure Task Force, prepared draft guidelines relating to the performance and display of copyrighted works in distance learning classes of nonprofit educational institutions, not including asynchronous delivery over computer networks. CONFU considered both sets of guidelines as proposals, but did not formally adopt either of them. A number of organizations and companies, however, have endorsed one or both sets of guidelines, or use them as a reference.

In 1997, the issue of copyright and digital distance education was raised in Congress by the introduction of bills in the House and Senate proposing an amendment to section 110(2). The amendment would have clarified that the exemption covered digital transmissions, and would have broadened its scope, removing the limitation on categories of works covered, adding the right of distribution, and removing the requirement that the transmission be made primarily for reception in classrooms and by people unable to attend classrooms. No floor action was taken on these bills, but they became the subject of discussion in the Senate during consideration of the WIPO Copyright and Performances and Phonograms Treaty Implementation Act. After intensive discussions among interested parties, it became clear that many complex and interrelated issues were involved that could not be given adequate consideration in the time available. Congress therefore provided for a longer-term study in section 403 of the DMCA.

VI. SHOULD CURRENT LAW BE CHANGED?

A. The Views of the Parties

The educational community (including both educators and academic libraries) believes that a change in the law is required to optimize the quality and availability of forms of distance education that take full advantage of today's technological capabilities. Members of this community argue that fair use is uncertain in its application to the digital environment, and that the exemptions in section 110 are outmoded and do not extend to the fall range of activities involved in digital distance education. They report that licensing for such uses is not working well, and therefore does not offer a satisfactory alternative. Some educators also note that distance education is already an expensive proposition, involving substantial start-up and maintenance costs, and warn that adding the cost of licensing fees for copyrighted materials could make it prohibitive.

Copyright owners, on the other hand, do not believe statutory amendment is necessary or advisable, pointing out that digital distance education is flourishing under current law. They see the fair use doctrine as strong and healthy, and are concerned that expanding the section 110 exemptions would harm both their primary and secondary markets. They assert that more efficient licensing systems are developing, and that the reported difficulties in obtaining permissions will ease with time and experience. Finally, they argue that educators who wish to use preexisting copyrighted content in their courses should regard licensing fees as one of the costs of distance education, comparable to the purchase of the necessary hardware and software.

There is virtual unanimity that the doctrine of fair use is fully applicable to uses of copyrighted works in the digital environment, including in distance education. (This does not mean that all agree as to which digital distance education activities would qualify as fair.) As the role of guidelines, the messages were mixed. Many copyright owners recommend pursuing the development of guidelines regarding the fair use of copyrighted materials in digital distance education, and suggest that further discussion could be productive in achieving greater mutual understanding and certainty. Educational and library groups were less positive, expressing varying views. Some educators see guidelines as valuable guides to decision-making; other participants are critical of the concept or doubtful about the efficacy of any results.

As to the specific instructional exemptions, copyright owners argue that section 110(2)should not be changed. They are concerned that a broadening of the exemption would result in the loss of opportunities to license works for use in digital distance education a new, growing, and potentially lucrative market. They urge that Congress not foreclose the potential market by legislating prematurely or overbroadly.

The other major concern of copyright owners is the increased risk of unauthorized downstream uses of their works posed by digital technology. When works are distributed in digital form, once a student obtains access, it is easy to further distribute multiple copies to acquaintances around the world. Depending on the type of work involved and the amount used, the result could be a significant impact on the market for sales of copies.

Most educational and library groups, in contrast, support a broadening of section 110(2). They view fair use alone as either not clear enough or not extensive enough in its application. Their primary goals are to avoid discrimination against remote site students in their educational experience vis-a-vis on-site students; to avoid discrimination against new technologies vis-a-vis old ones; and to avoid the difficulties in licensing that many describe having experienced. In general, the educational community seeks the following changes: (1) elimination of the concept of the physical classroom as a limitation on the availability of the exemption; (2) coverage of rights in addition to performance and display, at least to the extent necessary to permit digital transmissions; and (3) expansion of the categories of works covered, by broadening the performance right exemption to apply to works other than nondramatic literary and musical works. Some would go further, advocating an exemption that allows educators to do anything by means of digital transmission that they can do in the classroom under section 110(1). Libraries in particular also seek exemptions for additional activities, stressing the importance of being able to give access to electronic reserves and other resource materials in order to provide a high-quality educational experience for students at remote sites.

As to the risks involved, educational institutions are willing to take steps to safeguard the security of the materials they disseminate. In fact, they point out that they already make such efforts; the use of password protection and other access controls is widespread. Many also require compliance with copyright policies and inform students, faculty and staff about the law. Finally, educators believe that licensing should continue to play some role in distance education.

B. Analysis and Recommendations

The analysis of whether the law should be changed is complicated by the context: a time of rapid development in both technologies and markets. While such rapid development is a hallmark of the digital age, in the area of distance education we are at a particularly crucial point in time. Sophisticated technologies capable of protecting content against unauthorized post-access use are just now in development or coming to market, although it is not clear when they will be widely available in a convenient and affordable form that can protect all varieties of works. Meanwhile, licensing systems for digital distance education are evolving, including online and collective licensing mechanisms, and initial fears are beginning to ebb.

Many of the concerns on all sides stem from the inability to depend on the effective functioning of technological protections and licensing mechanisms. If technology were further along, broadened exemptions could be less dangerous to copyright owners; if licensing were further evolved, broadened exemptions could be less important for educators. The technical tools for both exist today; it will be clearer within the next few years how successfully they can be integrated into the real world of distance education. Given the timetable of the legislative process, the question is what steps Congress can and should take in the interim.

Over the course of this study, numerous issues have been raised and discussed. Given the limited time allotted, the specific mandate for the Register to consider primarily "the need for an exemption from exclusive rights of copyright owners for distance education through digital networks," and the origin of that mandate in proposed amendments to section 110(2), our analysis focuses on the appropriate treatment under copyright law of materials delivered to students through digital technology in the course of mediated instruction. We do not address other uses of copyrighted works in the course of digital distance education, including student use of supplemental or research materials in digital form; the creation of multimedia works by teachers or students; and the downloading and retention of materials by students. Such activities, although an important part of digital distance education, do not involve uses analogous to the performances and displays addressed in section 110(2).

As a fundamental premise, the Copyright Office believes that emerging markets should be permitted to develop with minimal government regulation. When changes in technology lead to the development of new markets for copyrighted works, copyright owners and users should have the opportunity to establish mutually satisfactory relationships. A certain degree of growing pains may have to be tolerated in order to give market mechanisms the chance to evolve in an acceptable direction. At some point, however, existing but dysfunctional markets may require adjustments in the law. Timing is therefore key.

The desire to let markets evolve does not mean that the law must remain frozen. Where a statutory provision intended to implement a particular policy is written in such a way that it becomes obsolete due to changes in technology, the provision may require updating if that policy is to continue. Doing so may be seen not as preempting a new market, but as accommodating existing markets that are being tapped by new methods. In the view of the Copyright Office, section 110(2) represents an example of this phenomenon.

The exemptions in sections 110(1) and (2) embody a policy determination that performances or displays of copyrighted works in the course of systematic instruction should be permitted without the need to obtain a license or rely on fair use. The technological characteristics of digital transmissions have rendered the language of section 110(2) inapplicable to the most advanced delivery method for systematic instruction. Without an amendment to accommodate these new technologies, the policy behind the law will be increasingly diminished.

At the same time, it must be borne in mind that existing law was crafted to embody a balance of interests between copyright owners and users of works. In order to maintain a comparable balance, the coverage of an exemption cannot be expanded without considering the impact of the expansion on markets for copyrighted works. If the law is updated to address new technology, the risks posed by that technology must be adequately taken into account.

Updating section 110(2) to allow the same activities to take place using digital delivery mechanisms, while controlling the risks involved, would continue the basic policy balance struck in 1976. In our view, such action is advisable.

Other amendments have been suggested that would go further, and entail varying degrees of change in legislative policy. These include expanding the exemption to cover more categories of works or additional exclusive rights beyond those necessary for digital delivery, and otherwise resolving problems experienced in the licensing process. Here, the elements of timing and burden of proof are critical. From a pedagogical perspective, these suggested expansions are desirable. From a copyright owner's perspective, they endanger primary or secondary markets for valuable works. The question should not be whether users have established a need to expand the exemption, any more than whether copyright owners have established a need to retain its limits, but rather whether given current conditions, the policy balance struck in 1976 should be recalibrated in certain respects.

We conclude that some policy recalibration may be appropriate at this point, relating primarily to categories of works covered. In other areas, we believe that existing restrictions should be retained and markets permitted to evolve, subject to further review. Critical to this conclusion is the continued availability of the fair use doctrine as a safety valve.

1. Recommendations as to Statutory Language.

In order to accomplish the goal of updating the language and the policy balance of section 110(2), the Copyright Office offers the following recommendations:

(a) *Clarify meaning of "transmission."* It should be clarified through legislative history that the term "transmission" in section 110(2) covers transmissions by digital means as well as analog.

(b) *Expand coverage of rights to extent technologically necessary.* Because the exemption in its current form permits only acts of performance and display, digital transmissions over computer networks would not be excused. We therefore recommend expanding the scope of the rights covered, in order to add those needed to accomplish this type of transmission. The rights of reproduction and/or distribution should not be added in their entirety, but only to the extent technologically required in order to transmit the performance or display authorized by the exemption.

(c) *Emphasize concept of mediated instruction.* An exemption that includes elements of the reproduction right so as to allow a student to access individual works asynchronously raises an unintended problem. If an entire work can be viewed on a computer screen, repeatedly, whenever a student chooses and for an indefinite duration, the performance or display could conceivably function as a substitute for the purchase of a copy. In updating section 110(2), it is therefore critical to ensure that the performance or display is analogous to the type of performance or display that would take place in a live classroom setting. This might be accomplished by amending paragraph (A) of section 110(2), which requires the performance or display to be "a regular part of . . . systematic instructional activities," to focus on the concept of mediated instruction. Additional language could specify that the performance or display must be made by or at the direction of an instructor to illustrate a point in, or as an integral part of, the equivalent of a class session in a particular course.

(d) *Eliminate requirement of physical classroom. In its current form, section 110(2) requires transmissions to be sent to a classroom or similar place normally devoted to instruction, or to persons who cannot attend a classroom. The nature of digital distance education, where the goal is to permit instruction to take place anywhere, makes this limitation conceptually and practically obsolete. Eliminating the physical classroom limitation would better reflect today's realities.*

At the same time, it is important to retain meaningful limitations on the eligible recipients; the performances or displays should not be made available to the general public. We recommend permitting transmissions to be made to students officially enrolled in the course, regardless of their physical location. Since today's digital and scrambling technologies allow transmissions to be targeted more precisely, the requirement should be added that the transmission must be made solely, to the extent technologically feasible, for reception by the defined class of eligible recipients.

(e) *Add new safeguards to counteract new risks.* Because the transmission of works to students in digital form poses greater risks of uncontrolled copying and distribution, a broadened exemption could cause harm to markets beyond the primary educational market. It is therefore critical, if section 110(2) is expanded to cover digital transmissions, that safeguards be incorporated into the statute to minimize these risks. We recommend including a number of safeguards as conditions on the applicability of the exemption: First, any transient copies permitted under the exemption should be retained for no longer than reasonably necessary to complete the transmission. Second, those seeking to invoke the exemption should be required to institute policies regarding copyright; to provide informational materials to faculty, students, and relevant staff members that accurately describe and promote compliance with copyright law; and to provide notice to students that materials may be subject to copyright protection.

Third, when works are transmitted in digital form, technological measures should be in place to control unauthorized uses. In order to effectively limit the risks to copyright owners' markets, these measures should protect against both unauthorized access and unauthorized dissemination after access has been obtained. The exemption should require the transmitting institution to apply such measures, described in simple and technology-neutral language. Because no technology is one hundred percent effective, only measures that "reasonably" prevent these acts should be required. In addition, the law should impose an obligation not to intentionally interfere with protections applied by the copyright owners themselves. If copyrighted works are to be placed on networks, and exposed to the resulting risks, it is appropriate to condition the availability of the exemption on the application of adequate technological protections.

(f) *Maintain existing standards of eligibility.* An educational institution must be "nonprofit" to be eligible for the exemption in section 110(2). There was extensive debate over the appropriateness of retaining the "nonprofit" requirement, and/or adding a requirement of accreditation. In the area of digital distance education, the lines between for-profit and nonprofit have blurred, and the issue has arisen as to how to guarantee the bona fides of an entity that is entitled to the exemption at a time when anyone can transmit educational material over the Internet. The Copyright Office is not convinced at this point that a change in the law is desirable, given the policy implications of permitting commercial entities to profit from activities using copyrighted works without compensating the owners of those works; the potential inconsistency with other provisions of the Act, including section 110(1), that refer to "nonprofit educational institutions"; and the DMCA mandate to consult specifically with nonprofit educational institutions and nonprofit libraries and archives. This is nevertheless an important and evolving issue that deserves further attention.

(g) *Expand categories of works covered.* One of the most difficult issues to resolve is whether to expand the categories of works exempted from the performance right beyond the current coverage of nondramatic literary and musical works. On the one hand, pedagogical considerations militate against continuing to limit the types of works covered. On the other hand, the existing distinctions have been embedded in the law for more than twenty years, based on the potentially greater market harm to works such as dramatic works or audiovisual works. The question is why this policy judgment should be altered now.

The main categories of works that could be affected by an expansion are audiovisual works, sound recordings, and dramatic literary and musical works. In terms of primary markets, educational licensing may represent a major source of revenue only for educational videos. The potential effect on secondary markets, however, remains a serious concern for all such works. This concern has been exacerbated beyond the threats perceived in 1976 by the capacities of digital technology. For entertainment products like motion pictures, transmission could well substitute for students paying to view them elsewhere, and if digital copies can be made or disseminated, could affect the broader public market.

The considerations are different for sound recordings than for other categories. Because there was no public performance right for sound recordings when section 110(2) was enacted in 1976, educators were free to transmit performances of sound recordings to students (assuming the use of any other work embodied in the sound recording was authorized by statute or license). When owners of sound recordings were granted a limited public performance right in 1996, there was no discussion of whether sound recordings should be added to the coverage of section 110(2). This issue thus represents a new policy question that has not yet been considered, rather than a potential change in a judgment already made.

It is the exclusion of audiovisual works, however, about which educators express the strongest concern, in part due to difficulties in obtaining licenses for digital uses from motion picture producers. Moreover, as digital distance education uses more multimedia works, which incorporate audiovisual works and may be considered audiovisual works themselves, the failure to cover this category may have an increasing impact.

On balance we suggest a compromise. If audiovisual and other works are added, it should be done in a limited way, with greater restrictions than section 110(2) currently imposes. Thus, section 110(2) could be amended to allow performances of categories in addition to nondramatic literary and musical works, but not of entire works. An expanded exemption should cover only the performance of reasonable and limited portions of these additional works.

It is important to note that under the current language of section 110(2), the portion performed would have to be the subject of study in the course, rather than mere entertainment for the students, or unrelated background or transitional material. This requirement, combined with the limitation on the amount of the work that could be used, should further serve to limit any impact on primary or secondary markets.

It nevertheless may be advisable to exclude those works that are produced primarily for instructional use. For such works, unlike entertainment products or materials of a general educational nature, the exemption could significantly cut into primary markets, impairing incentives to create.

(h) *Require use of lawful copies.* If the categories of works covered by section 110(2) are expanded, we recommend an additional safeguard: requiring the performance or display to be made from a lawful copy. Such a requirement is already contained in section 110(1) for the performance or display of an audiovisual work in the classroom.

(i) *Add new ephemeral recording exemption.* Finally, in order to allow the digital distance education that would be permitted under section 110(2) to take place asynchronously, we recommend adding a new subsection to section 112, the ephemeral recordings exemption. The new subsection would permit an educator to upload a copyrighted work onto a server, to be subsequently transmitted under the conditions set out in section 110(2) to students enrolled in her course. The benefit of the new subsection should be limited to an entity entitled to transmit a performance or display of a work in digital form under section 110(2). Various limits should be imposed similar to those set out in other subsections of section 112, including the requirements that any such copy be retained and used solely by the entity that made it; that no further copies be reproduced from it (except the transient technologically necessary copies that would be permitted by section 110(2)); that the copy be used solely for transmissions authorized under section 110(2); and that retention of the copy be limited in time, remaining on the server in a form accessible to students only for the duration of the course. In addition, the reproduction should have to be made from a lawful copy. Finally, the entity making the reproduction should not be permitted to remove technological protections applied by the copyright owner to prevent subsequent unlawful copying.

2. Clarification of Fair Use.

Because there is confusion and misunderstanding about the fair use doctrine, including the function of guidelines, we believe it is important for Congress to provide some clarification. The statutory language of section 107 is technology-neutral, and does not require amendment. But if any legislative action is taken with regard to distance education, we recommend that report language explicitly address certain fair use principles.

First, the legislative history should confirm that the fair use doctrine is technology-neutral and applies to activities in the digital environment. It might be useful to provide some examples of digital uses that are likely to qualify as fair. It should be explained that the lack of established guidelines for any particular type of use does not mean that fair use is inapplicable. Finally, the relationship of guidelines to fair use and other statutory defenses should be clarified. The public should understand that guidelines are intended as a safe harbor, rather than a ceiling on what is permitted.

Although flexibility is a major benefit of the fair use doctrine, the corollary is a degree of uncertainty. This drawback is exacerbated by the context of new technologies, where little case law is available. In the analog world, efforts such as the photocopying and off-air taping guidelines have proved helpful in giving practical guidance for day-to-day decision-making by educators. The Copyright Office believes that additional discussion among the interested parties of fair use as applied to digital distance education could be productive in achieving a greater degree of consensus. In the past, efforts to develop guidelines have been successful where a consistent group of participants worked within a structure established under the auspices of a government agency, with some direction provided by Congress.

3. Licensing Issues.

The fact that digital technologies impose new costs on delivering distance education does not itself justify abandoning or regulating the long-standing licensing system. Digital distance education entails the use of computer hardware and software, and the employment of trained support staff, all of which cost money. Digital distance education may also entail the use of preexisting copyrighted works. This content is at least as valuable as the infrastructure to deliver it, and represents another cost to be calculated in the equation.

The critical question here is whether the markets in which distance educators participate are dysfunctional, and if so, to a degree that calls for a legislative remedy. While the problems experienced in licensing are not unique to digital distance education, they are heightened in the digital context due to factors such as fear about increased risks; lack of certainty as to the scope of pre-digital transfers of rights; and general unfamiliarity with new uses. Many of these factors should diminish with time and experience, and there are some indications that this is already happening. In addition, online and collective licensing for digital uses will increasingly facilitate transactions. Nevertheless, problems will persist for the foreseeable future, as long as risks are perceived as high or benefits low.

One of the problems identified by educators has special characteristics that can block the functioning of the marketplace. Where the owner of the work simply cannot be located, there is no opportunity to negotiate. Particularly because the problem of such "orphan works" may become more acute due to longer copyright terms and the expanded audience for older works made possible by digital technology, we believe that the time may be ripe for Congressional attention to this issue generally.

We have not otherwise seen sufficient evidence of a need for a legislative solution moving away from the general free market approach of current law. Given the state of flux of online licensing systems and technological measures, and the waning influence of the elements of fear and unfamiliarity, problems of delay and cost may subside to an acceptable level. At this point in time we recommend giving the market for licensing of nonexempted uses leeway to evolve and mature. Because the field of digital distance education is growing so quickly, and effective licensing and technologies may be on the horizon, we suggest revisiting the issue in a relatively short period of time.

4. International Considerations.

In making these recommendations, the Copyright Office is mindful of the constraints of U.S. treaty obligations. In our view, the relevant criteria of the Berne Convention and the TRIPs Agreement are fundamentally in harmony with domestic policy considerations. We believe that our recommendations are fully consistent with these criteria, and would not alter the fundamental balance of either section 110(2) or 112, which have been part of U.S. law for more than twenty years.

The balance struck in U.S. law will have an importance beyond our borders, both through its potential application abroad and as a model for other countries examining the issue. Whether a distance education transmission initiated in one country and sent to a student in another country constitutes an infringement, falls within a collective or compulsory licensing scheme, or is exempted, will depend on which country's law a court applies. This means both that the scope of the exemptions in the U.S. Copyright Act may have an impact on foreign markets for U.S. works, and that U.S. copyright owners and users have an interest in the scope of exemptions or statutory licensing rules adopted in foreign laws.

JOINT STUDY REQUIRED BY
DMCA SECTION 104: EXECUTIVE SUMMARY

When Congress enacted the Digital Millennium Copyright Act, Pub. L. No. 105-304, 112 Stat. 2860, on October 28, 1998, Congress directed the Copyright Office and the Commerce Department to prepare a joint study concerning the impact of the DMCA on existing and emerging technology and the operation of certain sections of Title 17. Section 104 of the DMCA provided:

SEC. 104. EVALUATION OF IMPACT OF COPYRIGHT LAW AND AMENDMENTS ON ELECTRONIC COMMERCE AND TECHNOLOGICAL DEVELOPMENT.

(a) EVALUATION BY THE REGISTER OF COPYRIGHTS AND THE ASSISTANT SECRETARY FOR COMMUNICATIONS AND INFORMATION—The Register of Copyrights and the Assistant Secretary for Communications and Information of the Department of Commerce shall jointly evaluate—

(1) the effects of the amendments made by this title and the development of electronic commerce and associated technology on the operation of sections 109 and 117 of title 17, United States Code; and

(2) the relationship between existing and emergent technology and the operation of sections 109 and 117 of title 17, United States Code.

(b) REPORT TO CONGRESS—The Register of Copyrights and the Assistant Secretary for Communications and Information of the Department of Commerce shall, not later than 24 months after the date of the enactment of this Act, submit to the Congress a joint report on the evaluation conducted under subsection (a), including any legislative recommendations the Register and the Assistant Secretary may have.

The report was submitted to Congress in August 2001 in three volumes. The report's Executive Summary follows:

EXECUTIVE SUMMARY
DIGITAL MILLENNIUM COPYRIGHT ACT
SECTION 104 REPORT

INTRODUCTION

The Digital Millennium Copyright Act of 1998 (DMCA) was the foundation of an effort by Congress to implement United States treaty obligations and to move the nation's copyright law into the digital age. But as Congress recognized, the only thing that remains constant is change. The enactment of the DMCA was only the beginning of an ongoing evaluation by Congress on the relationship between technological change and U.S. copyright law.

This Report of the Register of Copyrights was mandated in the DMCA to assist Congress in that continuing process.

Our mandate was to evaluate "the effects of the amendments made by [title I of the DMCA] and the development of electronic commerce and associated technology on the operation of sections 109 and 117 of title17, United States Code; and the relationship between existing and emergent technology and the operation of sections 109 and 117 . . . ." Specifically, this Report focuses on three proposals that were put forward during our consultations with the public: creation of a "digital first sale doctrine;" creation of an exemption for the making of certain temporary incidental copies; and the expansion of the archival copying exemption for computer programs in section 117 of the Act.

Part I of this Report describes the circumstances leading up to the enactment of the DMCA and the genesis of this study. Part I also examines the historical basis of sections 109 and 117 of the Act. Part II discusses the wide range of views expressed in the public comments and testimony. This input from the public, academia, libraries, copyright organizations and copyright owners formed the core information considered by the Office in its evaluation and recommendations. Part III evaluates the effect of title I of the DMCA and the development of electronic commerce and associated technology on the operations of sections 109 and 117 in light of the information received and states our conclusions and recommendations regarding the advisability of statutory change.

I. BACKGROUND

A. THE DIGITAL MILLENNIUM COPYRIGHT ACT

The World Intellectual Property Organization (WIPO) treaties were the impetus for the U.S. legislation. In order to facilitate the development of electronic commerce in the digital age, Congress implemented the WIPO treaties by enacting legislation to address those treaty obligations that were not adequately addressed under existing U.S. law. Legal prohibitions against circumvention of technological protection measures employed by copyright owners to protect their works, and against the removal or alteration of copyright management information, were required in order to implement U.S. treaty obligations.

The congressional determination to promote electronic commerce and the distribution of digital works by providing copyright owners with legal tools to prevent widespread piracy was tempered with concern for maintaining the integrity of the statutory limitations on the exclusive rights of copyright owners. In addition to the provisions adopted by Congress in 1998, there were other proposals — including amendments to sections 109 and 117, that were not adopted, but were the subjects of a number of studies mandated by the DMCA. Section 104 of the DMCA requires the Register of Copyrights and the Assistant Secretary for Communications and Information to report on the effects of the DMCA on the operation of sections 109 and 117 and the relationship between existing and emergent technology on the operation of sections 109 and 117 of title 17 of the United States Code.

The inclusion of section 109 in the study has a clear relationship to the digital first sale proposal contained in a bill introduced in 1997 by Congressmen Rick Boucher and Tom Campbell. The reasons for including section 117 in the study are less obvious. While there is no legislative history explaining why section 117 is included in the study, it appears that the reference was intended to include within the scope of the study a proposed exemption for incidental copies found in the Boucher-Campbell bill, which would have been codified in section 117 of the Copyright Act.

B. SECTION 109(a) AND THE FIRST SALE DOCTRINE

The common-law roots of the first sale doctrine allowed the owner of a particular copy of a work to dispose of that copy. This judicial doctrine was grounded in the common-law principle that restraints on the alienation of tangible property are to be avoided in the absence of clear congressional intent to abrogate this principle. This doctrine appears in section 109 of the Copyright Act of 1976. Section 109(a) specified that this notwithstanding a copyright owner's exclusive distribution right under section 106 the owner of a particular copy or phonorecord that was lawfully made under title 17 is entitled to sell or further dispose of the possession of that copy or phonorecord.

C. SECTION 117 COMPUTER PROGRAM EXEMPTIONS

Section 117 of the Copyright Act of 1976 was enacted in the Computer Software Copyright Amendments of 1980 in response to the recommendations of the National Commission on New Technological Uses of Copyrighted Works' (CONTU). Section 117 permits the owner of a copy of a computer program to make an additional copy of the program for purely archival purposes if all archival copies are destroyed in the event that continued possession of the computer program should cease to be rightful, or where the making of such a copy is an essential step in the utilization of the computer program in conjunction with a machine and that it is used in no other manner.

II. VIEWS OF THE PUBLIC

Section II of the report summarizes the views received from the public through comments, reply comments and hearing testimony. The summaries are grouped into three categories: views concerning section 109, views concerning section 117, and views on other miscellaneous issues.

A. VIEWS CONCERNING SECTION 109

Most of the comments dealt with section 109 whether of not they addressed section 117. While there was a broad range of views on the effect of the DMCA on the first sale doctrine, most of the commenters believed that the anticircumvention provisions of 17 U.S.C. section 1201 allowed copyright owners to restrict the operation of section 109. Of particular concern to many commenters was the Content Scrambling System (CSS) and the "region coding" used to protect motion pictures on Digital Versatile Disks (DVDs). They argued that use of CSS forces a consumer to make two purchases in order to view a motion picture on DVD: the DVD and the authorized decryption device. In the view of these commenters, this system reduces or eliminates the value of and market for DVDs by interfering with their free alienability on the market. A similar argument was advanced for the region coding on DVDs in that the geographic market for resale is restricted by this technological protection measure.

Another concern expressed by a number of commenters was the growing use of nonnegotiable licenses accompanying copyrighted works that are written to restrict or eliminate statutorily permitted uses, including uses permitted under section 109. In some cases, these license restrictions are enforced through technological measures. It was argued that these licensing practices and the prohibition on circumvention frustrate the goals of the first sale doctrine by allowing copyright owners to maintain control on works beyond the first sale of a particular copy. These commenters stated that this interference with the operation of the first sale doctrine has the capacity to inhibit the function of traditional library operations, such as interlibrary loan, preservation, and use of donated copies of works.

Other commenters rebutted these claims, arguing that over-restrictive technological protection measures or licenses would not survive in the marketplace, since competition would be a limiting principle. It was also argued that the effect of licensing terms on the first sale doctrine is beyond the scope of this study.

Commenters generally viewed section 1202 of the DMCA, which prohibits the alteration or removal of copyright management information, as having no impact of the operation of the first sale doctrine.

The greatest area of contention in the comments was the question of whether to expand the first sale doctrine to permit digital transmission of lawfully made copies of works. Although some proponents argued that such transmissions are already permitted by the current language of section 109, most thought that clarification of this conclusion by Congress would be advisable since the absence of express statutory language could lead to uncertainty.

The proponents of revising section 109 argued that the transmission of a work that was subsequently deleted from the sender's computer is the digital equivalent of giving, lending, or selling a book. Allowing consumers to transfer the copy of the work efficiently by means of online transmission would foster the principles of the first sale doctrine. These principles have promoted economic growth and creativity in the analog world and should be extended to the digital environment. Proponents of this argument sought amendment to section 109 to allow a person to forward a work over the Internet and then delete that work from his computer.

Others opposed such an amendment for a number of reasons. Opponents pointed out that the first sale doctrine is a limitation on the distribution right of copyright owners and has never implicated the reproduction right which is, in their view, a "cornerstone" of copyright protection. In addition, the impact of the doctrine on copyright owners was also limited in the off-line world by a number of factors, including geography and the gradual degradation of books and analog works. The absence of such limitations would have an adverse effect on the market for digital works. Opponents also believed that proposals that depend on the user deleting his copy would be unverifiable, leading to virtually undetectable cheating. Given the expanding market for digital works without a digital first sale doctrine, opponents questioned the consumer demand for such a change in the law.

B. VIEWS CONCERNING SECTION 117

The comments related to section 117 fell into two main categories: those addressing the status of temporary copies in RAM and those concerning the scope of the archival exemption.

Many commenters advocated a blanket exemption for temporary copies that are incidental to the operation of a device in the course of use of a work when that use is lawful under title 17. Such an exemption was originally proposed in the Boucher-Campbell bill as an amendment to section 117.

Other commenters vigorously opposed any exemption for incidental copies at this time. They argued that such an exemption would dramatically expand the scope of section 117 in contrast to the carefully calibrated adjustment made to section 117 in the DMCA to address the problems experienced by independent computer service organizations at issue in *MAI Systems Corp. v. Peak Computer, Inc.* These commenters stated that Congress' narrow adjustment to section 117 in the DMCA reaffirmed the conclusion that temporary copies in random access memory (RAM) are copies that are subject to the copyright owner's exclusive reproduction right. Further change would undercut the reproduction right in all works and endanger international treaty obligations.

There was disagreement on the economic value of temporary copies. Proponents of an amendment argued that temporary buffer copies are necessary to carry out streaming of performances of works on the Internet and have no value apart from that performance. They argued that the limitations under other sections of the Copyright Act, including sections 107 and 512, were insufficient to sustain the operation of businesses that stream audio performances to the public.

Opponents, on the other hand, argued that these copies are within the scope of the copyright owner's exclusive rights and do possess value. Particular emphasis was placed on the value of temporary copies of computer programs. It was also argued that as streaming performances become more common, these temporary copies will increase in value because of the adverse effect of the performances on the market for purchases of copies of these works. Opponents believed it would be premature to change the law because of the absence of specific evidence of harm and the high potential for adverse unintended consequences. It was noted that when Congress was presented with concrete evidence of harm to independent service organizations after the *MAI v. Peak* decision, Congress took steps to remedy the situation. Similarly, section 512 of the DMCA created limitations on the remedies available against Internet service providers for incidental copying that is essential to the operation of the Internet.

The other major concern involving section 117 concerned the scope of the archival exemption. Proponents of amending section 117 raised two primary points. First, they argued that the policy behind the archival exemption needs to be updated to encompass all digital works rather than just computer programs. Since computers are vulnerable to crashes, viruses, and other failures, downloaded music, electronic books and other works face the same risks that precipitated the exemption for computer programs. Some argued that all digital media is susceptible to accidental deletion or corruption. Consumers should be permitted to protect their investments in works.

Proponents of expansion of the archival exemption offered another argument — section 117 does not comport with reality. Systematic backup practices do not fit the structure of section 117, which is limited to making a copy of an individual program at the time the consumer obtains it. It was argued that such a discrepancy between the law and commonly accepted practices undermines the integrity of the law. Such a fundamental mismatch creates the perception that the law need not be literally followed, thereby creating a slippery slope.

Opponents of an expansion of the archival exemption countered that the justification behind section 117 no longer exists. Most software is distributed on CD-ROM, which is far more robust than floppy disks. Consumers need merely retain the original CD as a backup, since it is a simple operation to reinstall software that is compromised. In addition, these opponents argued that there is currently an inaccurate public perception of the scope of the backup copy exception. These commenters argue that many invoke the archival exception as a shield to commercial piracy.

Opponents of an amendment to section 117 asserted that even if there is a mismatch between actual backup practices and the current exception, no one has been harmed by it. Commenters noted that no one has been sued as a result of backing up material outside the scope of section 117, and no one has stopped performing backups. It was also argued that if a particular activity does not fall within the terms of section 117, it may nevertheless be privileged under the fair use doctrine.

C. VIEWS CONCERNING OTHER MISCELLANEOUS ISSUES

There were assorted other comments and testimony on a range of issues. There were concerns raised about the potential adverse effects of sections

1201 and 1202 on the traditional concepts of first sale, fair use, and the archival and preservation exemptions. It was argued that these prohibitions are likely to diminish, if not eliminate, otherwise lawful uses. It was asserted that copyright management information may also have the capacity to reveal user information in a manner that would chill legitimate uses of copyrighted works.

Another prevalent concern was that licenses are being used increasingly by copyright owners to undermine the first sale doctrine and restrict other user privileges under the copyright law. These commenters argue that this trend is displacing the uniformity of federal copyright law with a wide variation of contract terms that must be evaluated and interpreted. This poses a particular challenge to large institutions, such as universities and libraries, in determining legal and acceptable use in any given work. A number of commenters argued that federal copyright law should preempt such license terms.

Other commenters argued that Congress did not intend copyright law broadly to preempt contract provisions. They argue that the freedom to contract serves the interests on both copyright owners and the public by allowing greater flexibility in determining pricing, terms and conditions of use, and other options.

III. EVALUATION AND RECOMMENDATIONS

We are not persuaded that title I of the DMCA has had a significant effect on the operation of sections 109 and 117 of title 17. The adverse effects that section 1201, for example, is alleged to have had on these sections cannot accurately be ascribed to section 1201. The causal relationship between the problems identified and section 1201 are currently either minimal or easily attributable to other factors such as the increasing use of license terms. Accordingly, none of our legislative recommendations are based on the effects of section 1201 on the operation of sections 109 and 117.

A. THE EFFECT OF TITLE I OF THE DMCA ON THE OPERATION OF SECTIONS 109 AND 117

The arguments raised concerning the adverse effects of the CSS technological protection measure on the operation of section 109 are flawed. The first sale doctrine is primarily a limitation on copyright owner's distribution right. Section 109 does not guarantee the existence of secondary markets for works. There are many factors which could affect the resale market for works, none of which could be said to interfere with the operation of section 109. The need for a particular device on which to view the work is not a novel concept and does not constitute an effect on section 109. VHS videocassettes for example, must be played on VHS VCRs.

A plausible argument can be made that section 1201 may have a negative effect on the operation of the first sale doctrine in the context of works tethered to a particular device. In the case of tethered works, even if the work is on removable media, the content cannot be accessed on any device other than the one on which it was originally made. This process effectively prevents disposition of the work. However, the practice of tethering a copy of a work to a particular hardware device does not appear to be widespread at this time, at least outside the context of electronic books. Given the relative infancy of digital rights management, it is premature to consider any legislative change at this time. Should this practice become widespread, it could have serious consequences for the operation of the first sale doctrine, although the ultimate effect on consumers is unclear.

We also find that the use of technological measures that prevent the copying of a work potentially could have a negative effect on the operation of section 117. To the extent that a technological measure prohibits access to a copyrighted work, the prohibition on the circumvention of measures that protect access in section 1201(a)(1) may have an adverse impact on the operation of the archival exception in section 117. Again, however, the current impact of such a concern appears to be minimal, since licenses generally define the scope of permissible archiving of software, and the use of CD-ROM reduces the need to make backup copies.

Given the minimal adverse impact at the present time, we conclude that no legislative change is warranted to mitigate any effect of section 1201 on section 117.

B. THE EFFECT OF ELECTRONIC COMMERCE AND TECHNO-LOGICAL CHANGE ON SECTIONS 109 AND 117

There is no dispute that section 109 applies to works in digital form. Physical copies of works in a digital format, such as CDs or DVDs, are subject to section 109 in the same way as physical copies in analog form. Similarly, a lawfully made tangible copy of a digitally downloaded work, such as a work downloaded to a floppy disk, Zip disk, or CD-RW, is clearly subject to section 109. The question we address here is whether the transmission of a work to another person falls within — or should fall within — the scope of section 109.

1. *The First Sale Doctrine in the Digital World*

a. *Evaluation of Arguments Concerning First Sale*

The first sale doctrine is primarily a limitation on the copyright owner's exclusive right of distribution. It does not limit the exclusive right of reproduction. While disposition of a work downloaded to a floppy disk would only implicate the distribution right, the transmission of a work from one person to another over the Internet results in a reproduction on the recipient's computer, even if the sender subsequently deletes the original copy of the work. This activity therefore entails an exercise of an exclusive right that is not covered by section 109.

Proponents of expansion of the scope of section 109 to include the transmission and deletion of a digital file argue that this activity is essentially identical to the transfer of a physical copy and that the similarities outweigh the differences. While it is true that there are similarities, we find the analogy to the physical world to be flawed and unconvincing.

Physical copies degrade with time and use; digital information does not. Works in digital format can be reproduced flawlessly, and disseminated to nearly any point on the globe instantly and at negligible cost. Digital transmissions can adversely effect the market for the original to a much greater degree than transfers of physical copies. Additionally, unless a "forward-and delete" technology is employed to automatically delete the sender's copy, the deletion of a work requires an additional affirmative act on the part of the sender subsequent to the transmission. This act is difficult to prove or disprove, as is a person's claim to have transmitted only a single copy, thereby raising complex evidentiary concerns. There were conflicting views on whether effective forward and delete technologies exist today. Even if they do, it is not clear that the market will bear the cost of an expensive technological measure.

The underlying policy of the first sale doctrine as adopted by the courts was to give effect to the common law rule against restraints on the alienation of tangible property. The tangible nature of a copy is a defining element of the first sale doctrine and critical to its rationale. The digital transmission of a work does not implicate the alienability of a physical artifact. When a work is transmitted, the sender is exercising control over the intangible work through its reproduction rather than common law dominion over an item of tangible personal property. Unlike the physical distribution of digital works on a tangible medium, such as a floppy disk, the transmission of works interferes with the copyright owner's control over the intangible work and the exclusive right of reproduction. The benefits to further expansion simply do not outweigh the likelihood of increased harm.

Digital communications technology enables authors and publishers to develop new business models, with a more flexible array of products that can be tailored and priced to meet the needs of different consumers. We are concerned that these proposals for a digital first sale doctrine endeavor to fit the exploitation of works online into a distribution model — the sale of copies — that was developed within the confines of pre-digital technology. If the sale model is to continue as the dominant method of distribution, it should be the choice of the market, not due to legislative fiat.

We also examined how other countries are addressing the applicability of the first sale — or exhaustion — doctrine to digital transmissions. We found that other countries are addressing digital transmissions under the communication to the public right and are not applying the principle of exhaustion, or any other analog thereof, to digital transmissions.

b. Recommendation Concerning the Digital First Sale Doctrine

We recommend no change to section 109 at this time. Although speculative concerns have been raised, there was no convincing evidence of present-day problems. In order to recommend a change in the law, there should be a demonstrated need for the change that outweighs the negative aspects of the proposal. The Copyright Office does not believe that this is the case with the proposal to expand the scope of section 109 to include digital transmissions. The time may come when Congress may wish to address these concerns should they materialize.

The fact that we do not recommend adopting a "digital first sale" provision at this time does not mean that the issues raised by libraries are not potentially valid concerns. Similarly, our conclusion that certain issues are beyond the scope of the present study does not reflect our judgment on the merits of those issues.

The library community has raised concerns about how the current marketing of works in digital form affects libraries with regard to five specifically enumerated categories: interlibrary loans, off-site accessibility, archiving/preservation, availability of works, and use of donated copies. Most of these issues arise from terms and conditions of use, and costs of license agreements. One arises because, when the library has only online access to the work, it lacks a physical copy of the copyrighted work that can be transferred. These issues arise from existing business models and are therefore subject to market forces. We are in the early stages of electronic commerce. We hope and expect that the marketplace will respond to the various concerns of customers in the library community. However, these issues may require further consideration at some point in the future. Libraries serve a vital function in society, and we will continue to work with the library and publishing communities on ways to ensure the continuation of library functions that are critical to our national interest.

2. The Legal Status of Temporary Copies

a. RAM Reproductions as "Copies" under the Copyright Act

All of the familiar activities that one performs on a computer, from the execution of a computer program to browsing the World Wide Web, necessarily involve copies stored in integrated circuits known as RAM. This information can remain in memory until the power is switched off or the information is overwritten. These reproductions generally persist only for as long as the particular activity takes place.

The legal status of RAM reproductions has arisen in this study almost exclusively in the context of streaming audio delivery, including webcasting. In order to render the packets of audio information in an audio "stream" smoothly, in spite of inconsistencies in the rate of delivery, packets of audio information are saved in a portion of RAM called a buffer until they are ready to be rendered.

Based on an the text of the Copyright Act — including the definition of "copies" in section 101 — and its legislative history, we conclude that the making of temporary copies of a work in RAM implicates the reproduction right so long as the reproduction persists long enough to be perceived, copied, or communicated.

Every court that has addressed the issue of reproductions in RAM has expressly or impliedly found such reproductions to be copies within the scope of the reproduction right. The seminal case on this subject, *MAI[] Sys. Corp. v. Peak Computer, Inc.,* found that the loading of copyrighted software into RAM creates a "copy" of that software. At least nine other courts have followed *MAI v. Peak* in holding RAM reproductions to be "copies" and several other cases have held that loading a computer program into a computer entails making a copy, without mentioning RAM specifically.

b. Evaluation of Arguments Concerning Temporary Incidental Copy Exceptions

In the course of this study, arguments were advanced in support of a blanket exemption for incidental copies similar to that proposed in the Boucher-Campbell bill. Most of the arguments advanced on such a proposal focused exclusively on the specific issue of buffer copies made in the course of audio streaming, rather than the broader issue of incidental copying generally. This focus suggests that legislation tailored to address the specific problems raised in the context of audio streaming should be examined. This focus is particularly appropriate since there was no compelling evidence presented in support of a blanket exemption for incidental copies and there was evidence that such an exemption could lead to unintended adverse consequences for copyright owners.

There was compelling evidence presented, however, on the uncertainty surrounding temporary buffer copies made in RAM in the course of rendering a digital musical stream. Specifically, webcasters asserted that the unknown legal status of buffer copies exposes webcasters to demands for additional royalty payments from the owner of the sound recording, as well as potential infringement liability.

The buffer copies identified by the webcasting industry exist for only a short period of time and consist of small portions of the work. Webcasters argue that these reproductions are incidental to the licensed performance of the work and should not be subject to an additional license for a reproduction that is only a means to an authorized end. Buffer copies implicate the reproduction right, thus potentially resulting in liability. There is, therefore, a legitimate concern on the part of webcasters and other streaming music services as to their potential liability.

We believe that there is a strong case that the making of a buffer copy in the course of streaming is a fair use. Fair use is a defense that may limit any of the copyright owner's exclusive rights, including the reproduction right implicated in temporary copies. In order to assess whether a particular use of the works at issue is a fair use, section 107 requires the consideration and balancing of four mandatory, but nonexclusive, factors on a case-by-case basis.

In examining the first factor — the purpose and character of the use — it appears that the making of buffer copies is commercial and not transformative. However, the use does not supersede or supplant the market for the original works. Buffer copies are a means to a noninfringing and socially beneficial end — the licensed performance of these works. There is no commercial exploitation intended or made of the buffer copy in itself. The first factor weighs in favor of fair use.

The second factor — the nature of the copyrighted work — weighs against a finding of fair use because musical works are generally creative. The third factor — the amount and substantiality of the portion used in relation to the copyrighted work as a whole — would also be likely to weigh against fair use since, in aggregate, an entire musical work is copied in the RAM buffer. Since this is necessary in order to carry out a licensed performance of the work, however, the factor should be of little weight.

In analyzing the fourth factor — the effect of the use on the actual or potential market for the work — the effect appears to be minimal or nonexistent. This factor strongly weighs in favor of fair use.

Two of the four statutory factors weigh in favor of fair use, but fair use is also an "equitable rule of reason." In the case of temporary buffer copies, we believe that the equities unquestionably favor the user. The sole purpose for making the buffer copies is to permit an activity that is licensed by the copyright owner and for which the copyright owner receives a performance royalty. In essence, copyright owners appear to be seeking to be paid twice for the same activity. Additionally, it is technologically necessary to make buffer copies in order to carry out a digital performance of music over the Internet. Finally, the buffer copies exist for too short a period of time to be exploited in any way other than as a narrowly tailored means to enable the authorized performance of the work. On balance, therefore, the equities weigh heavily in favor of fair use.

c. Recommendation Concerning Temporary Incidental Copies

Representatives of the webcasting industry expressed concern that the case-by-case fair use defense is too uncertain a basis for making rational business decisions. We agree. While we recommend against the adoption of a general exemption from the reproduction right to render noninfringing all temporary copies that are incidental to lawful uses, a more carefully tailored approach is desirable.

We recommend that Congress enact legislation amending the Copyright Act to preclude any liability arising from the assertion of a copyright owner's reproduction right with respect to temporary buffer copies that are incidental to a licensed digital transmission of a public performance of a sound recording and any underlying musical work.

The economic value of licensed streaming is in the public performances of the musical work and the sound recording, both of which are paid for. The buffer copies have no independent economic significance. They are made solely to enable the performance of these works. The uncertainty of the present law potentially allows those who administer the reproduction right in musical works to prevent webcasting from taking place — to the detriment of other copyright owners, webcasters and consumers alike — or to extract an additional payment that is not justified by the economic value of the copies at issue. Congressional action is desirable to remove the uncertainty and to allow the activity that Congress sought to encourage through the adoption of the section 114 webcasting compulsory license to take place.

Although we believe that the fair use defense probably does apply to temporary buffer copies, this approach is fraught with uncertain application in the courts. This uncertainty, coupled with the apparent willingness of some copyright owners to assert claims based on the making of buffer copies, argues for statutory change. We believe that the narrowly tailored scope of our recommendation will minimize, if not eliminate, concerns expressed by copyright owners about potential unanticipated consequences.

Given our recommendations concerning temporary copies that are incidental to digital performances of sound recordings and musical works, fairness requires that we acknowledge the symmetrical difficulty that is faced in the online music industry: digital performances that are incidental to digital music downloads. Just as webcasters appear to be facing demands for royalty payments for incidental exercise of the reproduction right in the course of licensed public performances, it appears that companies that sell licensed digital downloads of music are facing demands for public performance royalties for a technical "performance" of the underlying musical work that allegedly occurs in the course of transmitting it from the vendor's server to the consumer's computer.

Although we recognize that it is an unsettled point of law that is subject to debate, we do not endorse the proposition that a digital download constitutes a public performance even when no contemporaneous performance takes place. If a court were to find that such a download can be considered a public performance within the language of the Copyright Act, we believe the that arguments concerning fair use and the making of buffer copies are applicable to this performance issue as well. It is our view that no liability should result from a technical "performance" that takes place in the course of a download.

3. Archival Exemption

a. Evaluation of Arguments Concerning the Scope of Section 117(a)(2)

Currently the archival exemption under section 117(a)(2) is limited to computer programs. This section allows the owner of a copy of a computer program to make or authorize the making of an additional copy of the program "for archival purposes," provided that "all archival copies are destroyed in the event that continued possession of the computer program should cease to be rightful." A number of arguments were advanced in the course of this study for an expansion of this archival exemption in order to cover the kind of routine backups that are performed on computers and to allow consumers to archive material in digital format other than computer programs.

Commenters asserted that consumers need to backup works in digital form because they are vulnerable. That was CONTU's rationale for recommending that Congress create an exemption to permit archival copies of computer programs. In both cases, the vulnerability stems from the digital nature of the works. It would be perfectly consistent with the rationale of CONTU's recommendations and Congress' enactment of section 117 to extend the archival exemption to protect against the vulnerabilities that may afflict all works in digital format.

Evidence was presented to us noting that the archival exemption under section 117 does not permit the prevailing practices and procedures most people and businesses follow for backing up data on a computer hard drive. There is a fundamental mismatch between accepted, prudent practices among most system administrators and other users, on the one hand, and section 117 on the other. As a consequence, few adhere to the law.

While there is no question that this mismatch exists, nobody was able to identify any actual harm to consumers as a result of the limited scope of the archival exemption. Additionally, it was argued that the need to make archival copies of computer programs has diminished, because almost all software sold in the United States is distributed on CD-ROM, which itself serves as an archival copy in the event of hard drive problems or upgrades.

b. Recommendations Concerning the Archival Exemption

Although there has been a complete absence of any demonstrated harm to the prospective beneficiaries of an expanded archival exemption, and although we believe that a strong case could be made that most common archival activities by computer users would qualify as fair use, we have identified a potential concern — the interplay between sections 107 and 109. It appears that the language of the Copyright Act could lead a court to conclude that copies lawfully made under the fair use doctrine may be freely distributed under section 109.

Section 109 permits "the owner of a particular copy or phonorecord lawfully made" under title 17 to distribute that copy without the copyright owner's permission. To the extent that section 107 permits a user to make a backup copy of a work stored on a hard drive, that copy is lawfully made and the user owns it. Section 109, on its face, appears to permit the user to sell or otherwise dispose of the possession of that backup copy. The legislative history can be read to support either view.

We conclude that a statutory change is desirable, and recommend that Congress amend the copyright law in one of two ways.

Given the uncertain state of authority on the issue, we cannot conclude with a satisfactory level of certainty that a court will not, in the future, find a backup copy made by virtue of section 107 to be eligible for distribution under section 109. We believe that such a result is contrary to the intent of Congress and would have the capacity to do serious damage to the copyright owner's market. We therefore recommend that Congress either (1) amend section 109 to ensure that fair use copies are not subject to the first sale doctrine or (2) create a new archival exemption that provides expressly that backup copies may not be distributed. We express no preference as between the two options, and note that they are not mutually exclusive.

The first option would entail amending section 109(a) to state that only copies lawfully made *and lawfully distributed* are subject to the first sale doctrine. This proposed change would not preclude the distribution of copies made pursuant to the fair use doctrine since the exclusive right of distribution is equally subject to the fair use doctrine. It would, however, require that a separate fair use analysis be applied to the distribution of that copy.

The second option entails creating a new exemption for making backups of lawful copies of material in digital form, and amending section 117 to delete references to archival copies. The new exemption should follow the general contours of section 117(a)(2) and (b), and include the following elements: it should permit the making of one or more backup copies of a work. The copy from which the backup copies are made must be in digital form on a medium that is subject to accidental erasure, damage, or destruction in the ordinary course of its use. It should stipulate that the copies may be made and used solely for archival purposes or for use in lieu of the original copy. It should also specify that, notwithstanding the provisions of section 109, the archival copy may not be transferred except as part of a lawful transfer of all rights in the work. Finally, it should specify that the archival copies may not be used in any manner in the event that continued possession of the work ceases to be rightful.

4. *Contract Preemption*

The question of contract preemption was raised by a number commenters who argued that the Copyright Act should be amended to insure that contract provisions that override consumer privileges in the copyright law, or are otherwise unreasonable, are not enforceable. Although the general issue of contract preemption is outside the scope of this Report, we do note that this issue is complex and of increasing practical importance, and thus legislative action appears to be premature. On the one hand, copyright law has long coexisted with contract law. On the other hand, the movement at the state level toward resolving questions as to the enforceability of nonnegotiated contracts coupled with legally-protected technological measures that give right holders the technological capability of imposing contractual provisions unilaterally, increases the possibility that right holders, rather than Congress, will determine the landscape of consumer privileges in the future. Although market forces may well prevent right holders from unreasonably limiting consumer privileges, it is possible that at some point in the future a case could be made for statutory change.

PART FOUR:

NEW TEXT AND CASE LAW·

*****Updating Note re 2001 Reprint:** The casebook, published in Spring 2000, entered its third printing in Summer 2001 due to unprecedented demand. Subsequent to the original printing, the co-authors, with the aid of eagle-eyed adoptors, identified a number of what Leo Raskind generously describes as "printer's gremlins": *i.e.,* misprints in need of correction. The 2001 reprint of the casebook, and subsequent printings, accomplish that task. The most important of the corrections are "flagged" by asterisked notes in the following chapters of Part Four.

Chapter 1

THE LANDSCAPE OF COPYRIGHT

§ 1.02 Copyright and Related Bodies of Law[*]

COMPARISON:
COPYRIGHT, PATENT AND TRADEMARK

	COPYRIGHT	PATENT[*]	TRADEMARK
SUBJECT MATTER	Literary, dramatic, and musical works; pantomimes and choreography; pictorial, graphic, and sculptural works; audiovisual works; sound recordings; architectural works	Utility patent: Functional features of products and processes Design patent: Ornamental designs for manufactured goods	Words, names, symbols, or devices
STANDARDS FOR VALIDITY	Originality and fixation in a tangible medium of expression	Utility patent: Novelty, nonobviousness, and utility Design patent: What is obvious to ordinary designer	Use of mark to distinguish one's goods or services
WHEN PROTECTION BEGINS	Upon fixation of original expression	When granted by U.S. Patent and Trademark Office	Upon use of mark
DURATION OF PROTECTION	Life of the author (or longest-lived joint author), plus 70 years; or 95 years from publication or 120 years from creation, whichever expires first	Utility patent: Until 20 years from date filed Design patent: 14 years from date issued	So long as properly used as trademark
STANDARDS FOR INFRINGEMENT	Copying and improper appropriation	Utility patent: Mainly by making, using, or selling something covered by the claim language Design patent: Similarity of the designs to the ordinary observer	Likelihood of confusion

[*] Summary omits patents for distinct and new plant varieties asexually reproduced (*i.e.*, without using seeds) (same term of protection as utility patents). *See* 35 U.S.C. §§ 161-164.

---

[*] **Updating Note re 2001 Reprint.** The initial printing of the casebook, on page 5 thereof, erroneously carried over the chart prepared for the Fourth Edition, prior to the 20 years added to copyright duration by the Copyright Term Extension Act of 1998. The chart above reflects the post-CTEA terms of copyright protection.

§ 1.03   History of Anglo-American Copyright Law

[D]   The Copyright Act of 1976

USAGE: At page 27, ADD the following text after the last paragraph in § 1.04[D][2]:

Legislative Developments Since the Fifth Edition

For the text of the "Work Made for Hire and Copyright Corrections Act of 2000," see Part One of this Supplement. The statutory revisions made by Pub. L. No. 106-379 are discussed as appropriate hereinafter.

For legislation pending as these materials went to press, including the "Technology, Education and Copyright Harmonization Act of 2001" (S. 487), the "Intellectual Property and High Technology Technical Amendments Act of 2001" (S. 1320) and the "Copyright Technical Corrections Act of 2001" (H.R. 614), also see Part One of this Supplement.

§ 1.04   Copyright in a Changing World

[C]   U.S. Entry Into Berne

USAGE: At the bottom of page 38, SUBSTITUTE the following text for footnote 53:

U.S. adherence seems to have set off a kind of chain reaction: China eventually joined in 1992, and Russia in 1995. As of April 15, 2002, the total number of Berne members stood at 149, up about 50% since U.S. adherence.

[E]   Intellectual Property and International Trade

USAGE: On page 48, SUBSTITUTE the following text for the last paragraph of § 1.04[E][4]:

The two new treaties are now being considered at the domestic level around the world. In the United States, the Senate gave its advice and consent to the treaties on October 21, 1998. Implementing legislation, including provisions on "anti-circumvention" and "copyright management information" (but not moral rights of performers), was signed into law as the Digital Millennium Copyright Act ("DMCA") on October 28, 1998. The WIPO Copyright Treaty entered into force on March 6, 2000, three months after Gabon became the 30th country to join. As of mid-April, 2002, WIPO counted a total of 35 adherents. Honduras put the WIPO Performances and Phonogram Treaty over the top, so that it could enter into force on May 20, 2002. The mid-May, 2002 total for this agreement was 33 states.

The list of adhering states does not, as yet, include any of the countries of the European Union, which is still working through its process. Recently,

EU official Jorg Reinbothe left no doubt that the EU eventually would adhere, but explained that treaty obligations must be implemented not only by the EU but also by each of its 15 separate countries. Currently, the new EU "Directive on the harmonisation of certain aspects of copyright and related rights in the Information Society" (2001/29/EC) is being considered by the member states, who are working toward a December deadline. It remains to be seen whether they will make it, but according to Reinbothe: "Believe me, we are working on it." *PTO Head Concerned Over Review of Copyright Term Extension Law,* Washington Internet Daily, April 26, 2002, at 4. The Directive is reproduced in Part Two of this Supplement. As you will see, it takes an approach that differs in some notable ways from that of the U.S. DMCA legislation — as is suggested in the Notes and Questions following *Universal City Studios, Inc. v. Corley* in § 7.02 of this Part.

USAGE: At pages 48-49, SUBSTITUTE the following text for the first two paragraphs of § 1.04[E][5]:

Events and developments described in this chapter, of which the new WIPO treaties are only the most recent, suggest that the character of the international copyright regime continues to undergo significant change. A system which traditionally has emphasized national treatment, supplemented by a relatively few and easily satisfied treaty minima, is moving closer to one with an emphasis on true harmonization of national laws.

Moreover, thanks to TRIPs and its dispute-resolution procedures, there now exists a procedure which will yield authoritative interpretations of international norms and conclusive adjudications of the compliance of particular countries with those norms. Although the United States itself was the first to initiate such a procedure with the WTO,[76] it soon found itself on the receiving end of a challenge brought by European countries against § 110(5) of the Title 17 (arguably, one of the more peculiar features of U.S. copyright law), about which we will have more to say in § 9.06. Future challenges may address other aspects of U.S. law, such as our broadly conceived and generously applied doctrine of "fair use" (treated in detail in Chapter 9).

§ 1.05 Copyright and the Digital Challenge

[E] Digital Copyright at Home and Abroad

USAGE: On page 56, SUBSTITUTE the following text for the final paragraph of § 1.05[E]:

Notwithstanding the controversy, however, the WIPO treaties implementing legislation, as amended, did ultimately pass Congress. On October 28, 1998, President Clinton signed into law the Digital Millennium Copyright Act ("DMCA"). The DMCA differed in a number of significant respects

---

[76] *See Record Firms See More Gold in Oldies in Wake of U.S.-Japan Copyright Pact,* J. of Com., Jan. 28, 1997, at 3A.

from the earlier Administration proposals. As will emerge from the discussion of some of the provisions of the DMCA in following chapters, the final bill represented an attempt to compromise some of the issues which had divided the different interest groups in the "copyright wars" triggered by the release of the White Paper more than three years before.

Thus, for example, the DMCA incorporated a number of provisions designed to safeguard "fair use" and privacy, and it included detailed provisions limiting the liability of service providers in connection with infringing activities on the Internet. It also left a number of issues to be resolved, mandating several follow-up studies on the effects of the new legislation on network-based culture and commerce, with a possible eye toward future legislation, and relegating other issues to administrative rule-making. See Part Three of this Supplement for further information.

There are persistent suggestions that legislation to revisit some of the issues seemingly settled in the DMCA, and — specifically — to make more allowances for consumer access to protected works, soon will be introduced — see, for example, the remarks of Cong. Rick Boucher, D-Va., at the March 2001 "Digital Download" Conference sponsored by the Consumer Electronics Association, available at *http://www.techlawjournal.com/intelpro/ 20010306boucher.asp* — and *House Judiciary Likely to Offer Digital Copyright Bill*, Washington Internet Daily, May 13, 2002, at p. 1. No bill had been offered, however, when this Supplement went to press. In any event, it seems fair to say that the end of the debate over copyright in the network environment is nowhere in sight.

Meanwhile, members of Congress who support even stricter enforcement of technological controls on works in digital formats have been active. On March 21, 2002, Senator Ernest Hollings, D-S.C., and five colleagues introduced S. 2048, the "Consumer Broadband and Digital Television Promotion Act," designed to promote and, if necessary, mandate industry-wide adoption of security system standards for digital media devices. Despite the anodyne title, this bill has provoked a small firestorm of adverse reactions from consumers and technologists. More information follows in § 7.02 below.

[F]   The Issues in Context

USAGE: On page 57, SUBSTITUTE the following text for the second paragraph of § 1.05[F]:

The state of the law on the enforceability of such terms is still unsettled, both as a matter of contract doctrine and with respect to the law of copyright preemption (discussed below in Chapter 10). The recent effort to adopt a new Article 2B of the Uniform Commercial Code to deal with information commerce in the digital environment — now transformed into the Uniform Computer Information Transactions Act promulgated by the National Conference of Commissioners on Uniform State Laws in 1999 — seemed to bolster the momentum favoring enforceability of these restrictions and

conditions, although UCITA may now be running into some resistance in
the state legislatures. This topic is treated in more depth in § 3.03.

[G] Looking Forward

USAGE: On page 58, ADD the following new subsection after subsection
1.06[G]:

[H] A Case in Point

Perhaps the future is now. As many of you no doubt already know, the
Ninth Circuit Court of Appeals recently decided the first phase of an
important case involving the application of copyright law principles to the
new information environment. The *Napster* decision will be a point of
reference in many later chapters. Without further comment, we present an
edited version of that opinion. Adoptors and students might consider giving
it a quick once-over now in preparation for returning to it repeatedly during
the course — or you may wish to defer consideration now and refer back
to this excerpt when students have greater knowledge of the substantive
doctrines at issue. Our point here is simply to alert you to the existence
of this latest (and fascinating) iteration of the "digital challenge" to
traditional copyright law.

A&M RECORDS, INC. v. NAPSTER, INC.

United States Court of Appeals, Ninth Circuit
239 F.3d 1004 (2001)

BEEZER, CIRCUIT JUDGE:

Plaintiffs are engaged in the commercial recording, distribution and sale
of copyrighted musical compositions and sound recordings. The complaint
alleges that Napster, Inc. ("Napster") is a contributory and vicarious
copyright infringer. On July 26, 2000, the district court granted plaintiffs'
motion for a preliminary injunction. The injunction was slightly modified
by written opinion on August 10, 2000. *A&M Records, Inc. v. Napster, Inc.,*
114 F. Supp. 2d 896 (N.D. Cal. 2000). The district court preliminarily enjoined Napster "from engaging in, or facilitating others in copying, downloading, uploading, transmitting, or distributing plaintiffs' copyrighted
musical compositions and sound recordings, protected by either federal or
state law, without express permission of the rights owner." . . .

We entered a temporary stay of the preliminary injunction pending
resolution of this appeal. We have jurisdiction pursuant to 28 U.S.C.
§ 1292(a)(1). We affirm in part, reverse in part and remand.

I

We have examined the papers submitted in support of and in response
to the injunction application and it appears that Napster has designed and

operates a system which permits the transmission and retention of sound recordings employing digital technology.

In 1987, the Moving Picture Experts Group set a standard file format for the storage of audio recordings in a digital format called MPEG-3, abbreviated as "MP3." Digital MP3 files are created through a process colloquially called "ripping." Ripping software allows a computer owner to copy an audio compact disk ("audio CD") directly onto a computer's hard drive by compressing the audio information on the CD into the MP3 format. The MP3's compressed format allows for rapid transmission of digital audio files from one computer to another by electronic mail or any other file transfer protocol.

Napster facilitates the transmission of MP3 files between and among its users. Through a process commonly called "peer-to-peer" file sharing, Napster allows its users to: (1) make MP3 music files stored on individual computer hard drives available for copying by other Napster users; (2) search for MP3 music files stored on other users' computers; and (3) transfer exact copies of the contents of other users' MP3 files from one computer to another via the Internet. These functions are made possible by Napster's MusicShare software, available free of charge from Napster's Internet site, and Napster's network servers and server-side software. Napster provides technical support for the indexing and searching of MP3 files, as well as for its other functions, including a "chat room," where users can meet to discuss music, and a directory where participating artists can provide information about their music.

A. Accessing the System

In order to copy MP3 files through the Napster system, a user must first access Napster's Internet site and download the MusicShare software to his individual computer. *See http://www.Napster.com.* Once the software is installed, the user can access the Napster system. A first-time user is required to register with the Napster system by creating a "user name" and password.

B. Listing Available Files

If a registered user wants to list available files stored in his computer's hard drive on Napster for others to access, he must first create a "user library" directory on his computer's hard drive. The user then saves his MP3 files in the library directory, using self-designated file names. He next must log into the Napster system using his user name and password. His MusicShare software then searches his user library and verifies that the available files are properly formatted. If in the correct MP3 format, the names of the MP3 files will be uploaded from the user's computer to the Napster servers. The content of the MP3 files remains stored in the user's computer.

Once uploaded to the Napster servers, the user's MP3 file names are stored in a server-side "library" under the user's name and become part of a "collective directory" of files available for transfer during the time the user is logged onto the Napster system. The collective directory is fluid; it tracks users who are connected in real time, displaying only file names that are immediately accessible.

C. Searching For Available Files

Napster allows a user to locate other users' MP3 files in two ways: through Napster's search function and through its "hotlist" function.

Software located on the Napster servers maintains a "search index" of Napster's collective directory. To search the files available from Napster users currently connected to the net-work servers, the individual user accesses a form in the MusicShare software stored in his computer and enters either the name of a song or an artist as the object of the search. The form is then transmitted to a Napster server and automatically compared to the MP3 file names listed in the server's search index. Napster's server compiles a list of all MP3 file names pulled from the search index which include the same search terms entered on the search form and transmits the list to the searching user. The Napster server does not search the contents of any MP3 file; rather, the search is limited to "a text search of the file names indexed in a particular cluster. Those file names may contain typographical errors or otherwise inaccurate descriptions of the content of the files since they are designated by other users." *Napster*, 114 F. Supp. 2d at 906.

To use the "hotlist" function, the Napster user creates a list of other users' names from whom he has obtained MP3 files in the past. When logged onto Napster's servers, the system alerts the user if any user on his list (a "hotlisted user") is also logged onto the system. If so, the user can access an index of all MP3 file names in a particular hotlisted user's library and request a file in the library by selecting the file name. The contents of the hotlisted user's MP3 file are not stored on the Napster system.

D. Transferring Copies of an MP3 file

To transfer a copy of the contents of a requested MP3 file, the Napster server software obtains the Internet address of the requesting user and the Internet address of the "host user" (the user with the available files). *See generally Brookfield Communications, Inc. v. West Coast Entm't Corp.*, 174 F.3d 1036, 1044 (9th Cir. 1999) (describing, in detail, the structure of the Internet). The Napster servers then communicate the host user's Internet address to the requesting user. The requesting user's computer uses this information to establish a connection with the host user and downloads a copy of the contents of the MP3 file from one computer to the other over the Internet, "peer-to-peer." A downloaded MP3 file can be played directly from the user's hard drive using Napster's Music-Share program or other software. The file may also be transferred back onto an audio CD if the user has access to equipment designed for that purpose. In both cases, the quality of the original sound recording is slightly diminished by transfer to the MP3 format.

This architecture is described in some detail to promote an understanding of transmission mechanics as opposed to the content of the transmissions. The content is the subject of our copyright infringement analysis.

II

We review a grant or denial of a preliminary injunction for abuse of discretion. . . .

On review, we are required to determine "whether the court employed the appropriate legal standards governing the issuance of a preliminary injunction and whether the district court correctly apprehended the law with respect to the underlying issues in the case." . . .

Preliminary injunctive relief is available to a party who demonstrates either: (1) a combination of probable success on the merits and the possibility of irreparable harm; or (2) that serious questions are raised and the balance of hardships tips in its favor. *Prudential Real Estate Affiliates, Inc. v. PPR Realty, Inc.*, 204 F.3d 867, 874 (9th Cir. 2000). These two formulations represent two points on a sliding scale in which the required degree of irreparable harm increases as the probability of success decreases. Id.

III

Plaintiffs claim Napster users are engaged in the wholesale reproduction and distribution of copyrighted works, all constituting direct infringement.[2] The district court agreed. We note that the district court's conclusion that plaintiffs have presented a prima facie case of direct infringement by Napster users is not presently appealed by Napster. We only need briefly address the threshold requirements.

A. Infringement

Plaintiffs must satisfy two requirements to present a prima facie case of direct infringement: (1) they must show ownership of the allegedly infringed material and (2) they must demonstrate that the alleged infringers violate at least one exclusive right granted to copyright holders under 17 U.S.C. § 106 . . . . Plaintiffs have sufficiently demonstrated ownership. The record supports the district court's determination that "as much as eighty-seven percent of the files available on Napster may be copyrighted and more than seventy percent may be owned or administered by plaintiffs." *Napster*, 114 F. Supp. 2d at 911.

---

[2] Secondary liability for copyright infringement does not exist in the absence of direct infringement by a third party. *Religious Tech. Ctr. v. Netcom On-Line Communication Servs., Inc.*, 907 F. Supp. 1361, 1371 (N.D. Cal. 1995) ("There can be no contributory infringement by a defendant without direct infringement by another."). It follows that Napster does not facilitate infringement of the copyright laws in the absence of direct infringement by its users.

The district court further determined that plaintiffs' exclusive rights under § 106 were violated: "here the evidence establishes that a majority of Napster users use the service to download and upload copyrighted music . . . . We agree that plaintiffs have shown that Napster users infringe at least two of the copyright holders' exclusive rights: the rights of reproduction, § 106(1); and distribution, § 106(3). Napster users who upload file names to the search index for others to copy violate plaintiffs' distribution rights. Napster users who download files containing copyrighted music violate plaintiffs' reproduction rights.

Napster asserts an affirmative defense to the charge that its users directly infringe plaintiffs' copyrighted musical compositions and sound recordings.

B. Fair Use

Napster contends that its users do not directly infringe plaintiffs' copyrights because the users are engaged in fair use of the material. *See* 17 U.S.C. § 107 ("The fair use of a copyrighted work . . . is not an infringement of copyright."). Napster identifies three specific alleged fair uses: sampling, where users make temporary copies of a work before purchasing; space-shifting, where users access a sound recording through the Napster system that they already own in audio CD format; and permissive distribution of recordings by both new and established artists.

The district court considered factors listed in 17 U.S.C. § 107, which guide a court's fair use determination. These factors are: (1) the purpose and character of the use; (2) the nature of the copyrighted work; (3) the "amount and substantiality of the portion used" in relation to the work as a whole; and (4) the effect of the use upon the potential market for the work or the value of the work. *See* 17 U.S.C. § 107. The district court first conducted a general analysis of Napster system uses under § 107, and then applied its reasoning to the alleged fair uses identified by Napster. The district court concluded that Napster users are not fair users . . . .

[NOTE: More extensive excerpts from the court's opinion on "fair use" appear in § 9.04 of this Supplement. — *Eds.*]

4. Effect of Use on Market

"Fair use, when properly applied, is limited to copying by others which does not materially impair the marketability of the work which is copied." *Harper & Row Publishers, Inc. v. Nation Enters.*, 471 U.S. 539, 566-67 (1985). "The importance of this [fourth] factor will vary, not only with the amount of harm, but also with the relative strength of the showing on the other factors." *Campbell*, 510 U.S. at 591 n.21. The proof required to demonstrate present or future market harm varies with the purpose and character of the use:

A challenge to a noncommercial use of a copyrighted work requires proof either that the particular use is harmful, or that if it should become wide-spread, it would adversely affect the potential market for the copyrighted work. . . . *If the intended use is for commercial gain, that likelihood [of market harm] may be presumed. But if it is for a noncommercial purpose, the likelihood must be demonstrated. Sony*, 464 U.S. at 451 (emphases added).

Addressing this factor, the district court concluded that Napster harms the market in "at least" two ways: it reduces audio CD sales among college students and it "raises barriers to plaintiffs' entry into the market for the digital downloading of music." *Napster*, 114 F. Supp. 2d at 913. The district court relied on evidence plaintiffs submitted to show that Napster use harms the market for their copyrighted musical compositions and sound recordings. In a separate memorandum and order regarding the parties' objections to the expert reports, the district court examined each report, finding some more appropriate and probative than others. *A&M Records, Inc. v. Napster, Inc.*, 114 F. Supp. 2d 896 (N.D. Cal. 2000). Notably, plaintiffs' expert, Dr. E. Deborah Jay, conducted a survey (the "Jay Report") using a random sample of college and university students to track their reasons for using Napster and the impact Napster had on their music purchases. . . .

We, therefore, conclude that the district court made sound findings related to Napster's deleterious effect on the present and future digital download market. Moreover, lack of harm to an established market cannot deprive the copyright holder of the right to develop alternative markets for the works. *See L.A. Times v. Free Republic*, 2000 U.S. Dist. LEXIS 5669 (C.D. Cal. 2000)(stating that online market for plaintiff newspapers' articles was harmed because plaintiffs demonstrated that "[defendants] are attempting to exploit the market for viewing their articles online"); *see also UMG Recordings*, 92 F. Supp. 2d at 352 ("Any allegedly positive impact of defendant's activities on plaintiffs' prior market in no way frees defendant to usurp a further market that directly derives from reproduction of the plaintiffs' copyrighted works."). Here, similar to *L.A. Times* and *UMG Recordings*, the record supports the district court's finding that the "record company plaintiffs have already expended considerable funds and effort to commence Internet sales and licensing for digital downloads." 114 F. Supp. 2d at 915. Having digital downloads available for free on the Napster system necessarily harms the copyright holders' attempts to charge for the same downloads . . . .

5. Identified Uses

Napster maintains that its identified uses of sampling and space-shifting were wrongly excluded as fair uses by the district court.

a. Sampling

Napster contends that its users download MP3 files to "sample" the music in order to decide whether to purchase the recording. Napster argues that the district court: (1) erred in concluding that sampling is a commercial use because it conflated a noncommercial use with a personal use; (2) erred in determining that sampling adversely affects the market for plaintiffs' copyrighted music, a requirement if the use is non-commercial; and (3) erroneously concluded that sampling is not a fair use because it determined that samplers may also engage in other infringing activity.

The district court determined that sampling remains a commercial use even if some users eventually purchase the music. We find no error in the district court's determination. Plaintiffs have established that they are likely to succeed in proving that even authorized temporary downloading of individual songs for sampling purposes is commercial in nature . . . .

Napster further argues that the district court erred in rejecting its evidence that the users' downloading of "samples" increases or tends to increase audio CD sales. The district court, however, correctly noted that "any potential enhancement of plaintiffs' sales . . . would not tip the fair use analysis conclusively in favor of defendant." *Id.* at 914. We agree that increased sales of copyrighted material attributable to unauthorized use should not deprive the copyright holder of the right to license the material. *See Campbell*, 510 U.S. at 591 n.21 ("Even favorable evidence, without more, is no guarantee of fairness. Judge Leval gives the example of the film producer's appropriation of a composer's previously unknown song that turns the song into a commercial success; the boon to the song does not make the film's simple copying fair."); *see also L.A. Times*, 54 U.S.P.Q.2D (BNA) at 1471-72. Nor does positive impact in one market, here the audio CD market, deprive the copyright holder of the right to develop identified alternative markets, here the digital download market. *See* 114 F. Supp. 2d at 1469-71.

We find no error in the district court's factual findings or abuse of discretion in the court's conclusion that plaintiffs will likely prevail in establishing that sampling does not constitute a fair use.

b. Space-Shifting

Napster also maintains that space-shifting is a fair use. Space-shifting occurs when a Napster user downloads MP3 music files in order to listen to music he already owns on audio CD. *See id.* at 915-16. Napster asserts that we have already held that space-shifting of musical compositions and sound recordings is a fair use. *See Recording Indus. Ass'n of Am. v. Diamond Multimedia Sys., Inc.*, 180 F.3d 1072, 1079 (9th Cir. 1999)("Rio [a portable MP3 player] merely makes copies in order to render portable, or 'space-shift', those files that already reside on a user's hard drive. . . . Such copying is a paradigmatic noncommercial personal use."). *See also generally Sony*, 464 U.S. at 423 (holding that "time-shifting," where a video tape recorder owner records a television show for later viewing, is a fair use).

We conclude that the district court did not err when it refused to apply the "shifting" analyses of *Sony* and *Diamond*. Both *Diamond* and *Sony* are inapposite because the methods of shifting in these cases did not also simultaneously involve distribution of the copyrighted material to the general public; the time or space-shifting of copyrighted material exposed the material only to the original user . . . .

c. Other Uses

Permissive reproduction by either independent or established artists is the final fair use claim made by Napster. The district court noted that plaintiffs did not seek to enjoin this and any other noninfringing use of the Napster system, including: chat rooms, message boards and Napster's New Artist Program. *Napster*, 114 F. Supp. 2d at 917. Plaintiffs do not challenge these uses on appeal.

We find no error in the district court's determination that plaintiffs will likely succeed in establishing that Napster users do not have a fair use defense. Accordingly, we next address whether Napster is secondarily liable for the direct infringement under two doctrines of copyright law: contributory copyright infringement and vicarious copyright infringement.

IV

We first address plaintiffs' claim that Napster is liable for contributory copyright infringement. Traditionally, "one who, with knowledge of the infringing activity, induces, causes or materially contributes to the infringing conduct of another, may be held liable as a 'contributory' infringer." *Gershwin Publ'g Corp. v. Columbia Artists Mgmt., Inc.*, 443 F.2d 1159, 1162 (2d Cir. 1971) . . . differently, liability exists if the defendant engages in "personal conduct that encourages or assists the infringement." *Matthew Bender & Co. v. West Publ'g Co.*, 158 F.3d 693, 706 (2d Cir. 1998).

The district court determined that plaintiffs in all likelihood would establish Napster's liability as a contributory infringer. The district court did not err; Napster, by its conduct, knowingly encourages and assists the infringement of plaintiffs' copyrights.

A. Knowledge

Contributory liability requires that the secondary infringer "know or have reason to know" of direct infringement. *Cable / Home Communication Corp. Network Prods., Inc.*, 902 F.2d 829, 845 & 846 n. 29 (11th Cir. 1990) . . . The district court found that Napster had both actual and constructive knowledge that its users exchanged copyrighted music. The district court also concluded that the law does not require knowledge of "specific acts of infringement" and rejected Napster's contention that because the company cannot distinguish infringing from noninfringing files, it does not "know" of the direct infringement. 114 F. Supp. 2d at 917.

It is apparent from the record that Napster has knowledge, both actual and constructive,[5] of direct infringement. Napster claims that it is nevertheless protected from contributory liability by the teaching of *Sony Corp. v. Universal City Studios, Inc.*, 464 U.S. 417 (1984). We disagree. We observe that Napster's actual, specific knowledge of direct infringement renders Sony's holding of limited assistance to Napster. We are compelled to make a clear distinction between the architecture of the Napster system and Napster's conduct in relation to the operational capacity of the system.

The *Sony* Court refused to hold the manufacturer and retailers of video tape recorders liable for contributory infringement despite evidence that such machines could be and were used to infringe plaintiffs' copyrighted television shows. *Sony* stated that if liability "is to be imposed on petitioners in this case, it must rest on the fact that *they have sold equipment with constructive knowledge of the fact that their customers may use that equipment to make unauthorized copies of* copy-righted material." *Id.* at 439 (emphasis added). The *Sony* Court declined to impute the requisite level of knowledge where the defendants made and sold equipment capable of both infringing and "substantial noninfringing uses." *Id.* at 442 . . .

We are bound to follow *Sony*, and will not impute the requisite level of knowledge to Napster merely because peer-to-peer file sharing technology may be used to infringe plaintiffs' copyrights. . . . We depart from the reasoning of the district court that Napster failed to demonstrate that its system is capable of commercially significant noninfringing uses. *See Napster*, 114 F. Supp. 2d at 916, 917-18. The district court improperly confined the use analysis to current uses, ignoring the system's capabilities . . . . Consequently, the district court placed undue weight on the proportion of current infringing use as compared to current and future noninfringing use. *See generally Vault Corp. v. Quaid Software Ltd.*, 847 F.2d 255, 264-67 (5th Cir. 1997) (single noninfringing use implicated *Sony*). . . . [However, r]egardless of the number of Napster's infringing versus noninfringing uses, the evidentiary record here supported the district court's finding that plaintiffs would likely prevail in establishing that Napster knew or had reason to know of its users' infringement of plaintiffs' copyrights.

This analysis is similar to that of *Religious Technology Center v. Netcom On-Line Communication Services, Inc.*, which suggests that in an online

---

[5] The district court found actual knowledge because: (1) a document authored by Napster co-founder Sean Parker mentioned "the need to remain ignorant of users' real names and IP addresses 'since they are exchanging pirated music' "; and (2) the Recording Industry Association of America ("RIAA") informed Napster of more than 12,000 infringing files, some of which are still available. 114 F. Supp. 2d at 918. The district court found constructive knowledge because: (a) Napster executives have recording industry experience; (b) they have enforced intellectual property rights in other instances; (c) Napster executives have downloaded copy-righted songs from the system; and (d) they have promoted the site with "screen shots listing infringing files." *Id.* at 919.

context, evidence of actual knowledge of specific acts of infringement is required to hold a computer system operator liable for contributory copyright infringement. 907 F. Supp. at 1371. . . .

The court determined that for the operator to have sufficient knowledge, the copyright holder must "provide the necessary documentation to show there is likely infringement." 907 F. Supp. at 1374; *cf. Cubby, Inc. v. Compuserve, Inc.*, 776 F. Supp. 135, 141 (S.D.N.Y. 1991) (recognizing that online service provider does not and cannot examine every hyperlink for potentially defamatory material). If such documentation was provided, the court reasoned that Netcom would be liable for contributory infringement because its failure to remove the material "and thereby stop an infringing copy from being distributed worldwide constitutes substantial participation" in distribution of copyrighted material. *Id.*

We agree that if a computer system operator learns of specific infringing material available on his system and fails to purge such material from the system, the operator knows of and contributes to direct infringement. . . . [But t]o enjoin simply because a computer network allows for infringing use would, in our opinion, violate *Sony* and potentially restrict activity unrelated to infringing use.

We nevertheless conclude that sufficient knowledge exists to impose contributory liability when linked to demonstrated infringing use of the Napster system. *See Napster*, 114 F. Supp. 2d at 919 (*"Religious Technology Center* would not mandate a determination that Napster, Inc. lacks the knowledge requisite to contributory infringement."). The record supports the district court's finding that Napster has *actual* knowledge that *specific* infringing material is available using its system, that it could block access to the system by suppliers of the infringing material, and that it failed to remove the material. *See Napster*, 114 F. Supp. 2d at 918, 920-21.[6]

B. Material Contribution

Under the facts as found by the district court, Napster materially contributes to the infringing activity. Relying on *Fonovisa [v. Cherry Auction, Inc.*, 76 F.3d 259 (9th Cir. 1996)], the district court concluded that "[w]ithout the support services defendant provides, Napster users could not find and download the music they want with the ease of which defendant boasts." *Napster*, 114 F. Supp. 2d at 919-20 ("Napster is an integrated service designed to enable users to locate and download MP3 music files."). We agree that Napster provides "the site and facilities" for direct infringement . . . .

---

[6] As stated by the district court:

Plaintiffs . . . demonstrate that defendant had actual notice of direct infringement because the RIAA informed it of more than 12,000 infringing files. Although Napster, Inc. purportedly terminated the users offering these files, the songs are still available using the Napster service, as are the copyrighted works which the record company plaintiffs identified in Schedules A and B of their complaint . . . .

114 F. Supp. 2d at 918.

We affirm the district court's conclusion that plaintiffs have demonstrated a likelihood of success on the merits of the contributory copyright infringement claim. We will address the scope of the injunction in part VIII of this opinion.

V

We turn to the question whether Napster engages in vicarious copyright infringement. Vicarious copyright liability is an "outgrowth" of respondeat superior. *Fonovisa*, 76 F.3d at 262. In the context of copyright law, vicarious liability extends beyond an employer/employee relationship to cases in which a defendant "has the right and ability to supervise the infringing activity and also has a direct financial interest in such activities." *Id.* . . .

Before moving into this discussion, we note that *Sony*'s "staple article of commerce" analysis has no application to Napster's potential liability for vicarious copyright infringement. *See Sony*, 464 U.S. at 434-435; *see generally* 3 Melville B. Nimmer & David Nimmer, Nimmer On Copyright §§ 12.04[A][2] & [A][2][b] (2000) (confining *Sony* to contributory infringement analysis: "Contributory infringement itself is of two types — personal conduct that forms part of or furthers the infringement and contribution of machinery or goods that provide the means to infringe"). . . . The issues of Sony's liability under the "doctrines of 'direct infringement' and 'vicarious liability' "were not before the Supreme Court, although the Court recognized that the "lines between direct infringement, contributory infringement, and vicarious liability are not clearly drawn." *Id.* at 435 n. 17. Consequently, when the *Sony* Court used the term "vicarious liability," it did so broadly and outside of a technical analysis of the doctrine of vicarious copyright infringement. *Id.* at 435. . . .

A. Financial Benefit

The district court determined that plaintiffs had demonstrated they would likely succeed in establishing that Napster has a direct financial interest in the infringing activity. *Napster*, 114 F. Supp. 2d at 921-22. We agree. Financial benefit exists where the availability of infringing material "acts as a 'draw' for customers." *Fonovisa*, 76 F.3d at 263-64 (stating that financial benefit may be shown "where infringing performances enhance the attractiveness of a venue"). Ample evidence supports the district court's finding that Napster's future revenue is directly dependent upon "increases in user-base." More users register with the Napster system as the "quality and quantity of available music increases." 114 F. Supp. 2d at 902. We conclude that the district court did not err in determining that Napster financially benefits from the availability of protected works on its system.

B. Supervision

The district court determined that Napster has the right and ability to supervise its users' conduct. *Napster*, 114 F. Supp. 2d at 920-21 (finding that Napster's representations to the court regarding "its improved methods of blocking users about whom rights holders complain . . . is tantamount to an admission that defendant can, and sometimes does, police its service"). We agree in part.

The ability to block infringers' access to a particular environment for any reason whatsoever is evidence of the right and ability to supervise. . . . Here, plaintiffs have demonstrated that Napster retains the right to control access to its system. Napster has an express reservation of rights policy, stating on its website that it expressly reserves the "right to refuse service and terminate accounts in [its] discretion, including, but not limited to, if Napster believes that user conduct violates applicable law . . . or for any reason in Napster's sole discretion, with or without cause."

To escape imposition of vicarious liability, the reserved right to police must be exercised to its fullest extent. Turning a blind eye to detectable acts of infringement for the sake of profit gives rise to liability. *See, e.g.,* *Fonovisa*, 76 F.3d at 261 ("There is no dispute for the purposes of this appeal that Cherry Auction and its operators were aware that vendors in their swap meets were selling counterfeit recordings.") . . . .

The district court correctly determined that Napster had the right and ability to police its system and failed to exercise that right to prevent the exchange of copyrighted material. The district court, however, failed to recognize that the boundaries of the premises that Napster "controls and patrols" are limited. *See, e.g., Fonovisa*, 76 F.3d at 262-63 (in addition to having the right to exclude vendors, defendant "controlled and patrolled" the premises); *see also Polygram*, 855 F. Supp. at 1328-29 (in addition to having the contractual right to remove exhibitors, trade show operator reserved the right to police during the show and had its "employees walk the aisles to ensure 'rules compliance' "). Put differently, Napster's reserved "right and ability" to police is cabined by the system's current architecture. As shown by the record, the Napster system does not "read" the content of indexed files, other than to check that they are in the proper MP3 format.

Napster, however, has the ability to locate infringing material listed on its search indices, and the right to terminate users' access to the system. The file name indices, therefore, are within the "premises" that Napster has the ability to police. We recognize that the files are user-named and may not match copyrighted material exactly (for example, the artist or song could be spelled wrong). For Napster to function effectively, however, file names must reasonably or roughly correspond to the material contained in the files, otherwise no user could ever locate any desired music. As a practical matter, Napster, its users and the record company plaintiffs have equal access to infringing material by employing Napster's "search function."

Our review of the record requires us to accept the district court's conclusion that plaintiffs have demonstrated a likelihood of success on the merits of the vicarious copyright infringement claim. Napster's failure to police the system's "premises," combined with a showing that Napster financially benefits from the continuing availability of infringing files on its system, leads to the imposition of vicarious liability. We address the scope of the injunction in part VIII of this opinion.

VI

We next address whether Napster has asserted defenses which would preclude the entry of a preliminary injunction.

[NOTE: Portions of the opinion dealing with Napster's defenses under the Audio Home Recording Act of 1992 and the Digital Millennium Copyright Act of 1998 are reproduced in §§ 7.07 and 7.02[C], respectively, of this Part. — Eds.]

The district court considered ample evidence to support its determination that the balance of hardships tips in plaintiffs' favor:

Any destruction of Napster, Inc. by a preliminary injunction is speculative compared to the statistical evidence of massive, unauthorized downloading and uploading of plaintiffs' copyrighted works—as many as 10,000 files per second by defendant's own admission. The court has every reason to believe that, without a preliminary injunction, these numbers will mushroom as Napster users, and newcomers attracted by the publicity, scramble to obtain as much free music as possible before trial. 114 F. Supp. 2d at 926.

VII

Napster contends that even if the district court's preliminary determinations that it is liable for facilitating copyright infringement are correct, the district court improperly rejected valid affirmative defenses of waiver, implied license and copyright misuse. We address the defenses in turn.

A. Waiver

Waiver is the intentional relinquishment of a known right with knowledge of its existence and the intent to relinquish it." *United States v. King Features Entm't, Inc.*, 843 F.2d 394, 399 (9th Cir. 1988). In copyright, waiver or abandonment of copyright "occurs only if there is an intent by the copyright proprietor to surrender rights in his work." 4 Melville B. Nimmer & David Nimmer, Nimmer On Copyright § 13.06 (2000) . . . Napster argues that the district court erred in not finding that plaintiffs knowingly provided consumers with technology designed to copy and distribute MP3 files over the Internet and, thus, waived any legal authority to exercise exclusive control over creation and distribution of MP3 files. The district court, however, was not convinced "that the record companies created the monster that is now devouring their intellectual property rights." . . .

B. Implied License

Napster also argues that plaintiffs granted the company an implied license by encouraging MP3 file exchange over the Internet. Courts have found implied licenses only in "narrow" circumstances where one party "created a work at [the other's] request and handed it over, intending that [the other] copy and distribute it." *SmithKline Beecham Consumer Health-care, L.P. v. Watson Pharms., Inc.*, 211 F.3d 21, 25 (2d Cir. 2000) (quoting *Effects Assocs., Inc. v. Cohen*, 908 F.2d 555, 558 (9th Cir. 1990)), *cert. denied*, 121 S. Ct. 173 (2000). The district court observed that no evidence exists to support this defense: "indeed, the RIAA gave defendant express notice that it objected to the availability of its members' copy-righted music on Napster." *Napster*, 114 F. Supp. 2d at 924-25. The record supports this conclusion.

C. Misuse

The defense of copyright misuse forbids a copyright holder from "securing an exclusive right or limited monopoly not granted by the Copyright Office." *Lasercomb Am., Inc. v. Reynolds*, 911 F.2d 970, 977-79 (4th Cir. 1990), *quoted* in *Practice Mgmt. Info. Corp. v. American Med. Ass'n*, 121 F.3d 516, 520 (9th Cir.), *amended by* 133 F.3d 1140 (9th Cir. 1997). Napster alleges that online distribution is not within the copyright monopoly. According to Napster, plaintiffs have colluded to "use their copyrights to extend their control to online distributions."

We find no error in the district court's preliminary rejection of this affirmative defense. . . . [8] There is no evidence here that plaintiffs seek to control areas outside of their grant of monopoly. Rather, plaintiffs seek to control reproduction and distribution of their copyrighted works, exclusive rights of copyright holders. 17 U.S.C. § 106. . . .

VIII

The district court correctly recognized that a preliminary injunction against Napster's participation in copyright infringement is not only warranted but required. We believe, however, that the scope of the injunction needs modification in light of our opinion. Specifically, we reiterate that contributory liability may potentially be imposed only to the extent that Napster: (1) receives reasonable knowledge of specific infringing files with copyrighted musical compositions and sound recordings; (2) knows or should know that such files are available on the Napster system; and (3) fails to act to prevent viral distribution of the works . . . . The mere

---

[8] The district court correctly stated that "most of the cases" that recognize the affirmative defense of copyright misuse involve unduly restrictive licensing schemes. *See Napster*, 114 F. Supp. 2d at 923; *see also Lasercomb*, 911 F.2d at 973 (stating that "a misuse of copyright defense is inherent in the law of copyright"). We have also suggested, however, that a unilateral refusal to license a copyright may constitute wrongful exclusionary conduct giving rise to a claim of misuse, but assume that the "desire to exclude others . . . is a presumptively valid business justification for any immediate harm to consumers." *See Image Tech. Servs. v. Eastman Kodak Co.*, 125 F.3d 1195, 1218 (9th Cir. 1997) . . . .

existence of the Napster system, absent actual notice and Napster's demonstrated failure to remove the offending material, is insufficient to impose contributory liability . . . .

Conversely, Napster may be vicariously liable when it fails to affirmatively use its ability to patrol its system and preclude access to potentially infringing files listed in its search index. Napster has both the ability to use its search function to identify infringing musical recordings and the right to bar participation of users who engage in the transmission of infringing files.

The preliminary injunction which we stayed is overbroad because it places on Napster the entire burden of ensuring that no "copying, downloading, uploading, transmitting, or distributing" of plaintiffs' works occur on the system. As stated, we place the burden on plaintiffs to provide notice to Napster of copyrighted works and files containing such works available on the Napster system before Napster has the duty to disable access to the offending content. Napster, however, also bears the burden of policing the system within the limits of the system. Here, we recognize that this is not an exact science in that the files are user named. In crafting the injunction on remand, the district court should recognize that Napster's system does not currently appear to allow Napster access to users' MP3 files.

Based on our decision to remand, Napster's additional arguments on appeal going to the scope of the injunction need not be addressed. We, however, briefly address Napster's First Amendment argument so that it is not reasserted on remand. Napster contends that the present injunction violates the First Amendment because it is broader than necessary. The company asserts two distinct free speech rights: (1) its right to publish a "directory" (here, the search index) and (2) its users' right to exchange information. We note that First Amendment concerns in copyright are allayed by the presence of the fair use doctrine . . . . There was a preliminary determination here that Napster users are not fair users. Uses of copyrighted material that are not fair uses are rightfully enjoined . . . .

[NOTE: Additional discussion of the remedies in the *Napster* case, including the preliminary injunction imposed by the District Court upon remand, can be found in § 10.01[B][1] of this Part. — *Eds.*]

IX

We address Napster's remaining arguments: (1) that the court erred in setting a $5 million bond, and (2) that the district court should have imposed a constructive royalty payment structure in lieu of an injunction.

A. Bond

Napster argues that the $5 million bond is insufficient because the company's value is between $1.5 and $2 billion. We review objections to the amount of a bond for abuse of discretion. *Walczak v. EPL Prolong, Inc.*, 198 F.3d 725 (9th Cir. 1999).

. . . We cannot say that Judge Patel abused her discretion when she fixed the penal sum required for the bond.

B. Royalties

Napster contends that the district court should have imposed a monetary penalty by way of a compulsory royalty in place of an injunction. We are asked to do what the district court refused.

Napster tells us that "where great public injury would be worked by an injunction, the courts might . . . award damages or a continuing royalty instead of an injunction in such special circumstances." *Abend v. MCA, Inc.,* 863 F.2d 1465, 1479 (9th Cir. 1988). . . We are at a total loss to find any "special circumstances" simply because this case requires us to apply well-established doctrines of copyright law to a new technology. Neither do we agree with Napster that an injunction would cause "great public injury." Further, we narrowly construe any suggestion that compulsory royalties are appropriate in this context because Congress has arguably limited the application of compulsory royalties to specific circumstances, none of which are present here. *See* 17 U.S.C. § 115. . . .

Imposing a compulsory royalty payment schedule would give Napster an "easy out" of this case. If such royalties were imposed, Napster would avoid penalties for any future violation of an injunction, statutory copyright damages and any possible criminal penalties for continuing infringement. The royalty structure would also grant Napster the luxury of either choosing to continue and pay royalties or shut down. On the other hand, the wronged parties would be forced to do business with a company that profits from the wrongful use of intellectual properties. Plaintiffs would lose the power to control their intellectual property: they could not make a business decision not to license their property to Napster, and, in the event they planned to do business with Napster, compulsory royalties would take away the copyright holders' ability to negotiate the terms of any contractual arrangement.

X

We affirm in part, reverse in part and remand.

We direct that the preliminary injunction fashioned by the district court prior to this appeal shall remain stayed until it is modified by the district court to conform to the requirements of this opinion. We order a partial remand of this case on the date of the filing of this opinion for the limited purpose of permitting the district court to proceed with the settlement and entry of the modified preliminary injunction.

Even though the preliminary injunction requires modification, appellees have substantially and primarily prevailed on appeal. Appellees shall recover their statutory costs on appeal. *See* Fed. R. App. P. 39(a)(4) ("[i]f a judgment is affirmed in part, reversed in part, modified, or vacated, costs are taxed only as the court orders.").

Affirmed in Part, Reversed in Part and Remanded.

A NOTE ON THE AFTERMATH TO THE *NAPSTER* DECISION

In the months since the Ninth Circuit's decision, there have been further developments in both the case itself and the larger story of which it is an embedded part. At least for now, legal wrangling continues in the District Court, where it took almost a year to work out the final terms of the preliminary injunction, reported at 2001 U.S. Dist. LEXIS 2186. In the meantime, the defendants had scored a significant procedural victory when they persuaded Judge Patel to hold off her consideration of summary judgment until more discovery had been had on two issues: the plaintiffs' ownership of the musical works at issue (raised by a challenge to the recording industry's practice, see § 4.01 of Part Four below, of registering sound recordings as work-made-for-hire), and the defendants' affirmative defense of copyright misuse (based on assertions, see *In Re Napster, Inc., Copyright Litigation,* 2002 U.S. Dist. LEXIS 2963 (2002), at 57, that "the plaintiffs' entry into the digital distribution market is rife with actual anti-competitive effects and potential antitrust concerns").

The music industry, of course, has not been sleeping. A new group of plaintiffs, including the Academy of Motion Picture Arts and Sciences (!) has filed against Napster, see *Fonovisa, Inc. v. Napster, Inc.,* 2002 U.S. Dist. LEXIS 4270 (C.D. Cal. 2002) (denying a motion to dismiss), and various post-Napster peer-to-peer file sharing services (Music City/Morpheus, Grokster, and Kazaa, all of which are applications of the so-called Fast-Track software architecture) were named in an October 2001 lawsuit in Los Angeles Federal District Court. The defendants argue that their services are (and have been marketed as) general-purpose utilities, with more obvious non-infringing uses than Napster itself, and have pointed out that they differ from Napster in another important respect as well: rather than utilizing a single central index server, the listing of available files in a FastTrack network is done by specially designated "supernodes" within the peer-to-peer network — creating what amounts to a shifting series of small central servers. *See* Russell Garrity, *Victory Eludes Legal Fight over File Swapping, Billboard,* April 13, 2002, at p. 11. It remains to be seen, however, whether any court will actually rule on these issues, given that the defendants seem to be dropping right and left, unable to keep up with the pace (and expense) of litigation. *See* Steven Bonisteel, *Kazaa Creators*

Say Lawsuits Too Costly to Continue — Update, Washington Post News-bytes, May 23, 2002, at *www.newsbytes.com/news/02/176729.html.* Of course, others may rise to take their place, in the market and in court.

Meanwhile, the on-again, off-again story of Napster's courtship by elements of the music industry has taken yet another turn, with German media conglomerate Bertlesmann announcing that it would acquire the near-bankrupt company. *See* D.C. Denison, *Bertlesmann Deal Rescues Napster; Top Executives Return as Media Giant Puts Up $8M, Plans to Pay Debt,* Boston Globe, May 18, 2002, p. D1, col. 3. As it turned out, however, the move was too little, too late. *See* Jim Hu, *Napster: Gimme shelter in Chapter 11,* CNet News.com, June 3, 2002, at *http://news.com.com/2100-1023-930467.html.* And, off to one side, a procedurally complex battle continues over the so-called Aimster file-sharing service, which permits users of various instant messaging utilties (such as America Online's Instant Messenger) to exchange various kinds of digital files, and encrypts all traffic between users. This design raises some unique issues of copyright and privacy law, and the case is of additional interest because of Aimster's attempt to claim the initiative by filing first, for a declaratory judgment, in Federal District Court in Albany, New York. Late in 2001, this action and eight others subsequently filed by music industry companies against Aimster's parent firm were consolidated in the Northern District of Illinois, *In Re Aimster Copyright Ligitation,* 177 F. Supp. 2d 1380 (Judical Panel on Multidistrict Ligitation).

Chapter 2

PREREQUISITES FOR COPYRIGHT PROTECTION

§ 2.02 Originality

For an exhaustive (and often exhilarating) exploration of a host of originality issues, including the interesting question of whether originality requires an *intent* to originate, see the series of *Houston Law Review* articles keynoted by David Nimmer, *Copyright in the Dead Sea Scrolls: Authorship and Originality,* 38 Hous. L. Rev. 1 (2001), cited in the bibliography in Part Five of this Supplement.

USAGE: On page 136, ADD the following text after note (10):

(11) Issues involving rights in recipes long have tried our understanding of the idea/expression distinction. How many different ways are there in which to describe usefully the preparation of a particular dish? The question resurfaces in an amusing decision (beginning "This case involves a rustled cowboy cookbook"), *Barbour v. Head,* 178 F. Supp. 2d 758 (S.D. Tex. 2001— evidently one of our harder-working federal courts, as the decision is dated December 26, 2001!). The case also illustrates the dangers of relying too heavily on the Internet, which apparently is where the defendants had found the plaintiffs' uncredited recipes.

§ 2.03 OTHER PRELIMINARY CONSIDERATIONS

USAGE: On page 137, SUBSTITUTE the following text for the third paragraph of § 2.03[A]:

You should review § 104 and the related definitions in § 101 (especially those involving works by "treaty part[ies]") to learn more of the technical details about how the "national origin" of a work may affect the availability to U.S. copyright protection.*

USAGE: On page 139, CONSIDER the following recent development in connection with the cases cited in the third paragraph of § 2.03[B]:

Privately drafted model codes enacted into law. A recurring question: When privately enacted model building codes are adopted by local governments, do they lose copyright protection? In *Veeck v. Southern Building Code Congress International Inc.*, 241 F.3d 398 (5th Cir. 2001),

---

* **Updating Note re 2001 Reprint:** Throughout the casebook, § 101 references to "Berne Convention work[s]" have been superseded in the 2001 Reprint by references to works by "treaty parties" under the various "international agreements" now more broadly defined by the statute.

the court held that copyright protection for privately codes does not "evanesce" when the codes are adopted by local governments. In affirming a summary judgment of copyright infringement against a web site operator, the court rejected the contention that the public's due process interest in free access to the codes extinguished the codes' copyrights and plunged them into the public domain once they became law. The court also rejected free speech, merger, misuse, waiver and fair use defenses.

Chapter 3
WORKS OF AUTHORSHIP

§ 3.02 Original Works of Authorship Under § 102

[A] Literary Works, Including Computer Software

USAGE: On page 153, ADD the following text after note (5):

(5A) *Copyright in works derived from traditional knowledge.* There is a growing debate about to what extent, and in what way, intellectual property law should provide protection for songs, stories, designs and other items of cultural heritage that are transmitted from generation to generation within indigenous communities. *See, e.g,* Peter Seitel (ed.), Safeguarding Traditional Cultures: A Global Assessment (Smithsonian Center for Folklife and Cultural Heritage, 2001) and WIPO, *Intellectual Property Needs and Expectations of Traditional Knowledge Holders* (1999). But while this discussion continues, how should old-fashioned copyright law deal with new works that borrow or steal from traditional sources? *See Bell v. Davis International, Inc.,* 2002 U.S. Dist. LEXIS 5969 (W.D.N.C. 2002) (denying protection for plaintiff's miniature "War Bonnet" handicraft designs).

USAGE: On page 173, SUBSTITUTE the following text for the second paragraph of "Reverse Engineering":

In both *Sega Enterprises Ltd. v. Accolade, Inc.*, 977 F.2d 1510 (9th Cir. 1993) (reproduced and discussed below in Chapter 9), and *Atari Games, Inc. v. Nintendo of America, Inc.*, 975 F.2d 832 (Fed. Cir. 1992), federal appellate courts offered useful guidance to the software industry, carving out a substantial "fair use" exception for "reverse engineering." These decisions now have been joined by an important new decision, *Sony Computer Entertainment, Inc. v. Connectix Corp.*, 203 F.3d 596 (9th Cir. 2000), discussed at great length in the notes accompanying *Sega* in Chapter 9. *Connectix* represents the most liberal application to date of the "fair use" principle in the context of software design. Although these decisions may not be the last word on the subject, they seem generally consistent in approach with the emerging judicial approaches to other "second generation" issues.

USAGE: On pages 176-177, SUBSTITUTE the following text for the second and third paragraphs of "Miscellaneous Protections":

A decade ago, various forms of "copy protection" were frequently applied to consumer software products in an effort to frustrate their casual reproduction. This approach, however, met with considerable resistance on the part of customers, and as a result it has been largely abandoned in favor of other alternatives. A notable example of this practice is the use of so-called "shrink-wrap" licenses, *i.e.*, form agreements packaged with consumer software products, the restrictive terms of which the consumer is said to "accept" by virtue of his or her decision to open the package and to remove (and utilize) its contents. Under the terms of a typical "shrink-wrap" license, various otherwise permissible or "fair" uses of the purchased program are contractually prohibited. Although questions linger about the enforceability of such agreements, recent case law — like the decision in *ProCD v. Zeidenberg*, 86 F.3d 1447 (7th Cir. 1996) (reproduced in Chapter 10 of this book) — suggests that they may indeed have the legal effect which software manufacturers have claimed for them.

Moreover, the July 1999 decision of the National Conference of Commissioners on Uniform State Laws (NCCUSL) to adopt the Uniform Computer Information Transactions Act (formerly proposed as new Article 2B of the Uniform Commercial Code), dealing specifically with the sale and licensing of information products in digital formats, signaled the beginning of a campaign to validate the use of "shrink-wraps" under state law. As of May 2002, UCITA (as the proposed legislation is generally known) has been adopted in two states: Maryland and Virginia. In a number of other jurisdictions, it has met with strong and effective local opposition. To make matters still more complicated, NCCUSL's Standing Committee on UCITA has twice in the last six months recommended changes in the model law itself — some of them relevant to the issue of its potential interaction with copyright. More information on UCITA and its provisions is included in § 10.02 of this Part in the notes accompanying the *ProCD* case.

A close cousin to the "shrink-wrap" license, the "click-on" license (the terms of which the consumer typically acknowledges by clicking a computer mouse on a virtual "button" marked "OK" or "Accept") is now becoming more familiar as various kinds of information products, including software, are sold on-line or by way of the World Wide Web. This trend, too, is likely to be reinforced by the adoption of UCITA in the states. Meanwhile, electronic information vendors making use of digital networks also are employing various "technological safeguards," such as encryption and scrambling, to assure that only those consumers who have agreed to specified conditions of use can gain access to their products, and to exercise control over the uses which can be made of those products once access has been established.

[F] Architectural Works

USAGE: On page 224, CONSIDER the following recent development in connection with note (7):

Pictorial representation of architectural works. For an application of § 120(a), see *Leicester v. Warner Brothers*, 232 F.3d 1212 (9th Cir. 2000) (holding that the pictorial representations of an architectural work displayed in comic books, promotional materials and the motion picture *Batman Forever* were allowed under the exception).

§ 3.03   Derivative Works and Compilations Under § 103

USAGE: On pages 254-255, CONSIDER the following recent development in connection with note (8):

"Soft" and "hard" facts. *Maclean Hunter* was applied in *CDN Inc. v. Kapes,* 197 F.3d 1256 (9th Cir. 1999) (holding that the wholesale prices for collectible U.S. coins are copyrightable compilations as the product of the author's creative process of considering relevant price information).

USAGE: On page 270, SUBSTITUTE the following text for the last two paragraphs on the page:

The latter approach previewed by Senator Hatch was represented by draft legislation included in his statement (the so-called "Database Fair Competition and Research Promotion Act of 1999") and by the legislation actually introduced in the House by Rep. Tom Bliley on May 20, 1999 as H.R. 1858 (the "Consumer and Investor Access to Information Act of 1999"). Because the basic thrust of H.R. 1858 was to provide remedies for predatory competitive practices in the database marketplace, that legislation was a good deal simpler in structure and detail than H.R. 354. Ultimately, the standoff between the dramatically different approaches of these two powerful and important committees resulted in there being no database legislation enacted in the 106th Congress.

On March 29, 2001, the new chairs of the House Judiciary and Commerce Committees, Reps. James Sensenbrenner (R-Wis.) and W.J. "Billy" Tauzin (R-La.), announced that the committees intended to work together to draft consensus legislation on database protection, after extensive staff discussions with so-called "stakeholders" (*i.e.,* proponents and opponents of protection). An interesting story detailing the intended collaborative project appears at *www.newsbytes.com/news/01/163856.html.* In it, writers David MaGuire and Robert MacMillan make the point that new "players" now have emerged in the database game: operators of Internet portal sites (like Yahoo), for example, are skeptical about the impact of enhanced database protection on their operations, while the National Association of Realtors (concerned about protecting its "Multiple Listing Service" from poaching) has emerged as an important backer of strong new laws. As of this writing, the meetings of committee staff and stakeholders are continuing. Ah, politics!

Chapter 4

OWNERSHIP AND TRANSFERS

§ 4.01 Initial Ownership

[B] Works Made for Hire *

USAGE: On page 290, CONSIDER the following recent development in connection with note (9):

Sound recordings as works made for hire: Returning to the status quo ante. On October 27, 2000, President Clinton signed into law new legislation, Pub.L.No. 106-379, to undo a controversial Copyright Act amendment enacted on November 29, 1999, which had added sound recordings to the list of works that may be treated as works made for hire. Under the 1999 amendment, authorship and copyright ownership in a qualified sound recording were to be vested in the commissioning party — typically, a record company. At the time of its enactment, proponents called the amendment "clarifying and technical," arguing that it was already generally accepted that sound recordings are works for hire. Critics condemned the hasty manner in which the amendment was added and the effect of the amendment on the rights of recording artists. With sound recordings explicitly designated as works made for hire under the statute, recording artists would be unable to undo unfavorable contracts with record companies by exercising the termination rights otherwise available under § 203 of the Copyright Act. In the end, critics won the day and were able to restore the *status quo ante.* Thus, while § 2(a)(1) of the 2000 legislation strikes the term "sound recording" from § 101(2) of Title 17, § 2(a)(2) explicitly provides that "neither the amendment contained in section 1011(d) of the [1999 Act] nor the deletion of the words added by that amendment— (A) shall be considered or otherwise given any legal significance, or (B) shall be interpreted to indicate congressional approval or disapproval of, or acquiescence in, any judicial determination, by the courts or the Copyright Office."

USAGE: On page 293, ADD the following text after note (15):

(16) The application of the *CCNV* standard to the business of website design is explored in *Holtzbrinck Publishing Holdings, L.P. v. Vyne Communications, Inc.,* 2000 U.S. Dist. LEXIS 5444 (S.D.N.Y. 2000), as is an alternative analysis based on the concept of "joint works."

---

* **Updating Note re 2001 Reprint:** On page 292, in the carryover paragraph at the top of the page, the text introducing *Dolman v. Agee* has been corrected to read: "For an example of a work that *escaped* the 1909 Act's work-for-hire presumption, . . . "

[C] Joint Works

USAGE: On pages 303-304, CONSIDER the following recent development in connection with notes (3)-(5):

Who is a "joint author" in highly collaborative works? In *Childress*, the joint work issue arose in a dispute between two parties. The issue of determining who is a joint author is much more complicated in situations involving highly collaborative works like motion pictures.

In *Aalmuhammed v. Lee*, 202 F.3d 1227 (9th Cir 2000), the Ninth Circuit had to grapple with this problem in a case involving an individual who added significant material in the production of a major film. Plaintiff Aalmuhammed was hired to work on the Spike Lee's movie *Malcolm X.* While on the set, Aalmuhammed created at least two entire scenes with new characters, translated Arabic into English for subtitles, and supplied his own voice for voice-overs. He also selected the proper prayers and religious practices for the characters and edited parts of the movie during post-production. Aalmuhammed received compensation for his work but never had a written contract with either Lee or Warner Brothers. He sued Lee and others for a declaratory judgment of his joint ownership.

The Court of Appeals affirmed a grant of summary judgment to the defendants. The court held that authorship is not the same thing as making a valuable and copyrightable contribution. The court recognized that a contributor of expression may be deemed to be the author of that expression to determine whether it is independently copyrightable. The definition of a "joint work" under § 101 requires two or more authors, but the term "author" becomes harder to apply as the number of contributors grows. Although the *Feist* standard for a copyrightable work is some minimal level of creativity or originality, such a standard would be too broad and indeterminate to decide authorship of a movie.

Absent a contract, who should be the author of a movie?

[D] Collective Works

USAGE: On page 310, ADD the following text at the end of § 4.01[D]:

The story is, however, far from ended. Tasini's petition for *certiorari* was granted by the Supreme Court of the United States. 121 S.Ct. 425 (2000).

Shortly prior to argument in *Tasini*, the Eleventh Circuit weighed in with its own views, in *Greenberg v. National Geographic Society*, 244 F.3d 1267 (2001). There, in an action brought by a long-time *National Geographic* photographer, it was determined that a CD-ROM "library" consisting of exact, page-by-page digital reproductions of all the contents (including text, images, and advertisement) of a complete run of the magazine, along with a computer program enabling users to "navigate" their contents and a computer animated introductory sequence of "morphing" cover designs, constituted a new "collective work" rather than a "revision" within the meaning of § 201(c): "By creating a work," the court stated, "the Society forfeited any privilege it might have enjoyed with respect to only one component thereof," *i.e.,* the digitized collection of back issues. 244 F.3d at 1274.

On June 25, 2001, the Supreme Court handed down its own authoritative word. As you will see, at least some of the majority's language — in particular, the distinction it recognizes between electronic archives and microform publications — seems to cast doubt on the continued viability of the *Greenberg* decision. Nevertheless, a petition for *certiorari* in that case was denied at 122 S. Ct. 347 (2001). For an early reflection on the implications of *Tasini* (and its relationship to *Greenberg*), see Peter Jaszi, *Tasini and Beyond,* 23 Eur. Intell. Prop. L. Rev. 595 (2001).

NEW YORK TIMES COMPANY, INC. v. TASINI

Supreme Court of the United States
2001 U.S. LEXIS 4667
March 28, 2001, Argued
June 25, 2001, Decided

JUSTICE GINSBURG delivered the opinion of the Court.

This copyright case concerns the rights of freelance authors and a presumptive privilege of their publishers. The litigation was initiated by six freelance authors and relates to articles they contributed to three print periodicals (two newspapers and one magazine). Under agreements with the periodicals' publishers, but without the freelancers' consent, two computer database companies placed copies of the freelancers' articles — along with all other articles from the periodicals in which the freelancers' work appeared — into three databases. Whether written by a freelancer or staff member, each article is presented to, and retrievable by, the user in isolation, clear of the context the original print publication presented.

The freelance authors' complaint alleged that their copyrights had been infringed by the inclusion of their articles in the databases. The publishers, in response, relied on the privilege of reproduction and distribution accorded them by § 201(c) of the Copyright Act, which provides:

> "Copyright in each separate contribution to a collective work is distinct from copyright in the collective work as a whole, and vests initially in the author of the contribution. In the absence of an express transfer of the copyright or of any rights under it, the owner of copyright in the collective work is presumed to have acquired only the privilege of reproducing and distributing the contribution as part of that particular collective work, any revision of that collective work, and any later collective work in the same series." 17 U.S.C. § 201(c).

Specifically, the publishers maintained that, as copyright owners of collective works, *i.e.,* the original print publications, they had merely exercised "the privilege" § 201(c) accords them to "reproduc[e] and distribut[e]" the author's discretely copyrighted contribution.

In agreement with the Second Circuit, we hold that § 201(c) does not authorize the copying at issue here. The publishers are not sheltered by § 201(c), we conclude, because the databases reproduce and distribute articles standing alone and not in context, not "as part of that particular collective work" to which the author contributed, "as part of . . . any revision" thereof, or "as part of . . . any later collective work in the same series." Both the print publishers and the electronic publishers, we rule, have infringed the copyrights of the freelance authors.

I

A

Respondents Jonathan Tasini, Mary Kay Blakely, Barbara Garson, Margot Mifflin, Sonia Jaffe Robbins, and David S. Whitford are authors (Authors). Between 1990 and 1993, they wrote the 21 articles (Articles) on which this dispute centers. Tasini, Mifflin, and Blakely contributed 12 Articles to The New York Times, the daily newspaper published by petitioner The New York Times Company (Times). Tasini, Garson, Robbins, and Whitford wrote eight Articles for Newsday, another New York daily paper, published by petitioner Newsday, Inc. (Newsday). Whitford also contributed one Article to Sports Illustrated, a weekly magazine published by petitioner Time, Inc. (Time). The Authors registered copyrights in each of the Articles. The Times, Newsday, and Time (Print Publishers) registered collective work copyrights in each periodical edition in which an Article originally appeared. The Print Publishers engaged the Authors as independent contractors (freelancers) under contracts that in no instance secured consent from an Author to placement of an Article in an electronic database.[1]

At the time the Articles were published, all three Print Publishers had agreements with petitioner LEXIS/NEXIS (formerly Mead Data Central Corp.), owner and operator of NEXIS, a computerized database that stores information in a text-only format. NEXIS contains articles from hundreds of journals (newspapers and periodicals) spanning many years. The Print Publishers have licensed to LEXIS/NEXIS the text of articles appearing in the three periodicals. The licenses authorize LEXIS/NEXIS to copy and sell any portion of those texts.

Pursuant to the licensing agreements, the Print Publishers regularly provide LEXIS/NEXIS with a batch of all the articles published in each periodical edition. The Print Publisher codes each article to facilitate computerized retrieval, then transmits it in a separate file. After further coding, LEXIS/NEXIS places the article in the central discs of its database.

---

[1] In the District Court, Newsday and Time contended that the freelancers who wrote for their publications had entered into agreements authorizing reproduction of the Articles in the databases. The Court of Appeals ruled that Newsday's defense was waived, and rejected Time's argument on the merits. Neither petitioner presses the contention here.

Subscribers to NEXIS, accessing the system through a computer, may search for articles by author, subject, date, publication, headline, key term, words in text, or other criteria. Responding to a search command, NEXIS scans the database and informs the user of the number of articles meeting the user's search criteria. The user then may view, print, or download each of the articles yielded by the search. The display of each article includes the print publication (*e.g.*, The New York Times), date (September 23, 1990), section (Magazine), initial page number (26), headline or title ("Remembering Jane"), and author (Mary Kay Blakely). Each article appears as a separate, isolated "story" — without any visible link to the other stories originally published in the same newspaper or magazine edition. NEXIS does not contain pictures or advertisements, and it does not reproduce the original print publication's formatting features such as headline size, page placement (e.g., above or below the fold for newspapers), or location of continuation pages.

The Times (but not Newsday or Time) also has licensing agreements with petitioner University Microfilms International (UMI). The agreements authorize reproduction of Times materials on two CD-ROM products, the New York Times OnDisc (NYTO) and General Periodicals OnDisc (GPO).

Like NEXIS, NYTO is a text-only system. Unlike NEXIS, NYTO, as its name suggests, contains only the Times. Pursuant to a three-way agreement, LEXIS/NEXIS provides UMI with computer files containing each article as transmitted by the Times to LEXIS/NEXIS. Like LEXIS/NEXIS, UMI marks each article with special codes. UMI also provides an index of all the articles in NYTO. Articles appear in NYTO in essentially the same way they appear in NEXIS, *i.e.*, with identifying information (author, title, etc.), but without original formatting or accompanying images.

GPO contains articles from approximately 200 publications or sections of publications. Unlike NEXIS and NYTO, GPO is an image-based, rather than a text-based, system. The Times has licensed GPO to provide a facsimile of the Times' Sunday Book Review and Magazine. UMI "burns" images of each page of these sections onto CD-ROMs. The CD-ROMs show each article exactly as it appeared on printed pages, complete with photographs, captions, advertisements, and other surrounding materials. UMI provides an index and abstracts of all the articles in GPO.

Articles are accessed through NYTO and GPO much as they are accessed through NEXIS. The user enters a search query using similar criteria (*e.g.*, author, headline, date). The computer program searches available indexes and abstracts, and retrieves a list of results matching the query. The user then may view each article within the search result, and may print the article or download it to a disc. The display of each article provides no links to articles appearing on other pages of the original print publications.[2]

---

[2] For example, the GPO user who retrieves Blakely's "Remembering Jane" article will see the entirety of Magazine page 26, where the article begins, and Magazine page 78, where the article continues and ends. The NYTO user who retrieves Blakely's article will see only the text of the article and its identifying information

B

On December 16, 1993, the Authors filed this civil action in the United States District Court for the Southern District of New York. The Authors alleged that their copyrights were infringed when, as permitted and facilitated by the Print Publishers, LEXIS/NEXIS and UMI (Electronic Publishers) placed the Articles in the NEXIS, NYTO, and GPO databases (Databases). The Authors sought declaratory and injunctive relief, and damages. In response to the Authors' complaint, the Print and Electronic Publishers raised the reproduction and distribution privilege accorded collective work copyright owners by 17 U.S.C. § 201(c). After discovery, both sides moved for summary judgment.

The District Court granted summary judgment for the Publishers, holding that § 201(c) shielded the Database reproductions. 972 F. Supp. 804, 806 (1997). The privilege conferred by § 201(c) is transferable, the court first concluded, and therefore could be conveyed from the original Print Publishers to the Electronic Publishers. *Id.* at 816. Next, the court determined, the Databases reproduced and distributed the Authors' works, in § 201(c)'s words, "as part of . . . [a] revision of that collective work" to which the Authors had first contributed. To qualify as "revisions," according to the court, works need only "preserve some significant original aspect of [collective works] — whether an original selection or an original arrangement." *Id.* at 821. This criterion was met, in the District Court's view, because the Databases preserved the Print Publishers' "selection of articles" by copying all of the articles originally assembled in the periodicals' daily or weekly issues. *Id.* at 823. The Databases "highlighted" the connection between the articles and the print periodicals, the court observed, by showing for each article not only the author and periodical, but also the print publication's particular issue and page numbers. *Id.* at 824 ("[T]he electronic technologies not only copy the publisher defendants' complete original 'selection' of articles, they tag those articles in such a way that the publisher defendants' original selection remains evident online.").

The Authors appealed, and the Second Circuit reversed. 206 F.3d 161 (1999). The Court of Appeals granted summary judgment for the Authors on the ground that the Databases were not among the collective works covered by § 201(c), and specifically, were not "revisions" of the periodicals in which the Articles first appeared. *Id.* at 167-170. Just as § 201(c) does not "permit a Publisher to sell a hard copy of an Author's article directly to the public even if the Publisher also offered for individual sale all of the other articles from the particular edition," the court reasoned, so § 201(c) does not allow a Publisher to "achieve the same goal indirectly" through computer databases. *Id.* at 168. In the Second Circuit's view, the Databases effectively achieved this result by providing multitudes of "individually

---

(author, headline, publication, page number, etc.). Neither the GPO retrieval nor the NYTO retrieval produces any text on page 27, page 79, or any other page. The user who wishes to see other pages may not simply "flip" to them. She must conduct a new search.

retrievable" articles. *Ibid.* As stated by the Court of Appeals, the Databases might fairly be described as containing "new anthologies of innumerable" editions or publications, but they do not qualify as "revisions" of particular editions of periodicals in the Databases. *Id.* at 169. Having concluded that § 201(c) "does not permit the Publishers," acting without the author's consent, "to license individually copyrighted works for inclusion in the electronic databases," the court did not reach the question whether the § 201(c) privilege is transferable. *Id.* at 165, and n. 2.

We granted certiorari to determine whether the copying of the Authors' Articles in the Databases is privileged by 17 U.S.C. § 201(c). 531 U.S. 978 (2000). Like the Court of Appeals, we conclude that the § 201(c) privilege does not override the Authors' copyrights, for the Databases do not reproduce and distribute the Articles as part of a collective work privileged by § 201(c). Accordingly, and again like the Court of Appeals, we find it unnecessary to determine whether the privilege is transferable.

II

Under the Copyright Act, as amended in 1976, "copyright protection subsists . . . in original works of authorship fixed in any tangible medium of expression . . . from which they can be perceived, reproduced, or otherwise communicated." 17 U.S.C. § 102(a). When, as in this case, a freelance author has contributed an article to a "collective work" such as a newspaper or magazine, see § 101 (defining "collective work"), the statute recognizes two distinct copyrighted works: "Copyright in *each separate contribution to a collective work is distinct from copyright in the collective work as a whole. . . .*" § 201(c) (emphasis added). Copyright in the separate contribution "vests initially in the author of the contribution" (here, the freelancer). *Ibid.* Copyright in the collective work vests in the collective author (here, the newspaper or magazine publisher) and extends only to the creative material contributed by that author, not to "the preexisting material employed in the work," § 103(b). See also *Feist Publications, Inc. v. Rural Telephone Service Co.*, 499 U.S. 340, 358 (1991)(copyright in "compilation" — a term that includes "collective works," 17 U.S.C. § 101 — is limited to the compiler's original "selection, coordination, and arrangement").

Prior to the 1976 revision, as the courts below recognized, see 206 F.3d at 168; 972 F. Supp. at 815, authors risked losing their rights when they placed an article in a collective work. Pre-1976 copyright law recognized a freelance author's copyright in a published article only when the article was printed with a copyright notice in the author's name. See Copyright Act of 1909, § 18, 35 Stat. 1079. When publishers, exercising their superior bargaining power over authors, declined to print notices in each contributor's name, the author's copyright was put in jeopardy. See A. Kaminstein, Divisibility of Copyrights, Study No. 11, in Copyright Law Revision Studies Nos. 11-13, prepared for the Senate Committee on the Judiciary, 86th Cong., 2d Sess., p. 18 (1960). The author did not have the option to assign only the right of publication in the periodical; such a partial assignment was blocked by the doctrine of copyright "indivisibility." See *id.* at 11. Thus, when a copyright notice appeared only in the publisher's name, the author's work would fall into the public domain, unless the author's copyright, in its entirety, had passed to the publisher. See *id.* at 18. Such complete transfer might be accomplished by a contract, perhaps one with a provision, not easily enforced, for later retransfer of rights back to the author. See *id.* at 20-22. Or, absent a specific contract, a court might find that an author had tacitly transferred the entire copyright to a publisher, in turn deemed to hold the copyright in "trust" for the author's benefit. See *id.* at 18-19; see generally 3 M. Nimmer, Copyright § 10.01[C][2], pp. 10-12 to 10-14 (2000).

In the 1976 revision, Congress acted to "clarify and improve [this] confused and frequently unfair legal situation with respect to rights in contributions." H. R. Rep. No. 94-1476, p. 122 (1976) (hereinafter H. R. Rep.).[3] The 1976 Act rejected the doctrine of indivisibility, recasting the copyright as a bundle of discrete "exclusive rights," 17 U.S.C. § 106 (1994 ed. and Supp. V),[4] each of which "may be transferred . . . and owned

---

[3] Two Registers of Copyrights have observed that the 1976 revision of the Copyright Act represented "a break with the two-hundred-year-old tradition that has identified copyright more closely with the publisher than with the author." Letter from M. Peters to Rep. McGovern, reprinted in 147 Cong. Rec. E182 (Feb. 14, 2001) (hereinafter Peters Letter) (quoting Ringer, First Thoughts on the Copyright Act of 1976, 22 N. Y. L. S. L. Rev. 477, 490 (1977)). The intent to enhance the author's position vis-a-vis the patron is also evident in the 1976 Act's work-for-hire provisions. See *Community for Creative Non-Violence v. Reid*, 490 U.S. 730, 742-750 (1989); see also 17 U.S.C. § 203(a)(5) (inalienable authorial right to revoke a copyright transfer). Congress' adjustment of the author/publisher balance is a permissible expression of the "economic philosophy behind the [Copyright Clause]," *i.e.*, "the conviction that encouragement of individual effort [motivated] by personal gain is the best way to advance public welfare." *Harper & Row, Publishers, Inc. v. Nation Enterprises*, 471 U.S. 539, 558 (1985), (quoting *Mazer v. Stein*, 347 U.S. 201, 219 (1954)).

[4] As amended, § 106 now provides: "Subject to sections 107 through 121, the owner of copyright under this title has the exclusive rights to do and to authorize any of the following:

"(1) to reproduce the copyrighted work in copies or phonorecords;

"(2) to prepare derivative works based upon the copyrighted work;

"(3) to distribute copies or phonorecords of the copyrighted work to the public by sale or other transfer of ownership, or by rental, lease, or lending;

"(4) in the case of literary, musical, dramatic, and choreographic works, pantomimes, and motion pictures and other audiovisual works, to perform the copyrighted work publicly;

"(5) in the case of literary, musical, dramatic, and choreographic works, pantomimes, and pictorial, graphic, or sculptural works, including the individual images of a motion picture or other audiovisual work, to display the copyrighted work publicly; and

"(6) in the case of sound recordings, to perform the copyrighted work publicly by means of a digital audio transmission."

separately," § 201(d)(2).[5] Congress also provided, in § 404(a), that "a single notice applicable to the collective work as a whole is sufficient" to protect the rights of freelance contributors. And in § 201(c), Congress codified the discrete domains of "copyright in each separate contribution to a collective work" and "copyright in the collective work as a whole." Together, § 404(a) and § 201(c) "preserve the author's copyright in a contribution even if the contribution does not bear a separate notice in the author's name, and without requiring any unqualified transfer of rights to the owner of the collective work." H. R. Rep. 122.

Section 201(c) both describes and circumscribes the "privilege" a publisher acquires regarding an author's contribution to a collective work:

> "In the absence of an express transfer of the copyright or of any rights under it, the owner of copyright in the collective work is presumed to have acquired *only* the privilege of reproducing and distributing the contribution as part of that particular collective work, any revision of that collective work, and any later collective work in the same series." (Emphasis added.)

A newspaper or magazine publisher is thus privileged to reproduce or distribute an article contributed by a freelance author, absent a contract otherwise providing, only "as part of" any (or all) of three categories of collective works: (a) "that collective work" to which the author contributed her work, (b) "any revision of that collective work," or (c) "any later collective work in the same series." In accord with Congress' prescription, a "publishing company could reprint a contribution from one issue in a later issue of its magazine, and could reprint an article from a 1980 edition of an encyclopedia in a 1990 revision of it; the publisher could not revise the contribution itself or include it in a new anthology or an entirely different magazine or other collective work." H. R. Rep. 122-123.

Essentially, § 201(c) adjusts a publisher's copyright in its collective work to accommodate a freelancer's copyright in her contribution. If there is demand for a freelance article standing alone or in a new collection, the Copyright Act allows the freelancer to benefit from that demand; after authorizing initial publication, the freelancer may also sell the article to others. Cf. *Stewart v. Abend*, 495 U.S. 207, 229 (1990) ("[w]hen an author produces a work which later commands a higher price in the market than the original bargain provided, the copyright statute [*i.e.*, the separate renewal term of former 17 U.S.C. § 24] is designed to provide the author the power to negotiate for the realized value of the work"); *id.* at 230 (noting author's "inalienable termination right" under current 17 U.S.C. §§ 203, 302). It would scarcely "preserve the author's copyright in a contribution" as contemplated by Congress, H. R. Rep. 122, if a newspaper or magazine publisher were permitted to reproduce or distribute copies of the author's contribution in isolation or within new collective works. See Gordon,

---

[5] It bears repetition here, see *supra*, at 7, that we neither decide nor express any view on whether the § 201(c) "privilege" may be transferred.

Fine-Tuning *Tasini*: Privileges of Electronic Distribution and Reproduction, 66 Brooklyn L. Rev. 473, 484 (2000).[6]

III

In the instant case, the Authors wrote several Articles and gave the Print Publishers permission to publish the Articles in certain newspapers and magazines. It is undisputed that the Authors hold copyrights and, therefore, exclusive rights in the Articles.[7] It is clear, moreover, that the Print and Electronic Publishers have exercised at least some rights that § 106 initially assigns exclusively to the Authors: LEXIS/NEXIS' central discs and UMI's CD-ROMs "reproduce . . . copies" of the Articles, § 106(1); UMI, by selling those CD-ROMs, and LEXIS/NEXIS, by selling copies of the Articles through the NEXIS Database, "distribute copies" of the Articles "to the public by sale," § 106(3); and the Print Publishers, through contracts licensing the production of copies in the Databases, "authorize" reproduction and distribution of the Articles, § 106.[8]

Against the Authors' charge of infringement, the Publishers do not here contend the Authors entered into an agreement authorizing reproduction

---

[6] The dissenting opinion suggests that a ruling for the Publishers today would maintain, even enhance, authors' "valuable copyright protection." *Post*, at 16-17 (opinion of STEVENS, J.). We are not so certain. When the reader of an article in a periodical wishes to obtain other works by the article's author, the Databases enable that reader simply to print out the author's articles, without buying a "new anthology . . . or other collective work," H. R. Rep. 122-123. In years past, books compiling stories by journalists such as Janet Flanner and Ernie Pyle might have sold less well had the individual articles been freely and permanently available on line. In the present, print collections of reviews, commentaries, and reportage may prove less popular because of the Databases. The Register of Copyrights reports that "freelance authors have experienced significant economic loss" due to a "digital revolution that has given publishers [new] opportunities to exploit authors' works." Peters Letter E182.

More to the point, even if the dissent is correct that some authors, in the long-run, are helped, not hurt, by Database reproductions, the fact remains that the Authors who brought the case now before us have asserted their rights under § 201(c). We may not invoke our conception of their interests to diminish those rights.

[7] The Publishers do not claim that the Articles are "work[s] made for hire." 17 U.S.C. § 201(b). As to such works, the employer or person for whom a work was prepared is treated as the author. *Ibid.* The Print Publishers, however, neither engaged the Authors to write the Articles as "employee[s]" nor "commissioned" the Articles through "a written instrument signed by [both parties]" indicating that the Articles shall be considered "work[s] made for hire." § 101 (1994 ed., Supp. V) (defining "work made for hire").

[8] Satisfied that the Publishers exercised rights § 106 initially assigns exclusively to the Author, we need resolve no more on that score. Thus, we do not reach an issue the Register of Copyrights has argued vigorously. The Register maintains that the Databases publicly "display" the Articles, § 106(5); because § 201(c) does not privilege "display," the Register urges, the § 201(c) privilege does not shield the Databases. See Peters Letter E182-E183.

of the Articles in the Databases. See *supra*, at 3, n. 1. Nor do they assert that the copies in the Databases represent "fair use" of the Authors' Articles. See 17 U.S.C. § 107 ("fair use of a copyrighted work . . . is not an infringement"; four factors identified among those relevant to fair use determination). Instead, the Publishers rest entirely on the privilege described in § 201(c). Each discrete edition of the periodicals in which the Articles appeared is a "collective work," the Publishers agree. They contend, however, that reproduction and distribution of each Article by the Databases lie within the "privilege of reproducing and distributing the [Articles] as part of . . . [a] revision of that collective work," § 201(c). The Publishers' encompassing construction of the § 201(c) privilege is unacceptable, we conclude, for it would diminish the Authors' exclusive rights in the Articles.

In determining whether the Articles have been reproduced and distributed "as part of" a "revision" of the collective works in issue, we focus on the Articles as presented to, and perceptible by, the user of the Databases. See § 102 (copyright protection subsists in original works fixed in any medium "from which they can be perceived, reproduced, or otherwise communicated"); see also § 101 (definitions of "copies" and "fixed"); Haemmerli, Commentary: *Tasini v. New York Times Co.*, 22 Colum.-VLA. J. L. & Arts 129, 142-143 (1998). In this case, the three Databases present articles to users clear of the context provided either by the original periodical editions or by any revision of those editions. The Databases first prompt users to search the universe of their contents: thousands or millions of files containing individual articles from thousands of collective works (*i.e.*, editions), either in one series (the Times, in NYTO) or in scores of series (the sundry titles in NEXIS and GPO). When the user conducts a search, each article appears as a separate item within the search result. In NEXIS and NYTO, an article appears to a user without the graphics, formatting, or other articles with which the article was initially published. In GPO, the article appears with the other materials published on the same page or pages, but without any material published on other pages of the original periodical. In either circumstance, we cannot see how the Database perceptibly reproduces and distributes the article "as part of "either the original edition or a "revision" of that edition.

One might view the articles as parts of a new compendium — namely, the entirety of works in the Database. In that compendium, each edition of each periodical represents only a minuscule fraction of the ever-expanding Database. The Database no more constitutes a "revision" of each constituent edition than a 400-page novel quoting a sonnet in passing would represent a "revision" of that poem. "Revision" denotes a new "version," and a version is, in this setting, a "distinct form of something regarded by its creators or others as one work." Webster's Third New International Dictionary 1944, 2545 (1976). The massive whole of the Database is not recognizable as a new version of its every small part.

Alternatively, one could view the Articles in the Databases "as part of" no larger work at all, but simply as individual articles presented individually. That each article bears marks of its origin in a particular periodical (less vivid marks in NEXIS and NYTO, more vivid marks in GPO) suggests the article was *previously* part of that periodical. But the markings do not mean the article is *currently* reproduced or distributed as part of the periodical. The Databases' reproduction and distribution of *individual* Articles — simply as individual Articles — would invade the core of the Authors' exclusive rights under § 106.[9]

The Publishers press an analogy between the Databases, on the one hand, and microfilm and microfiche, on the other. We find the analogy wanting. Microforms typically contain continuous photographic reproductions of a periodical in the medium of miniaturized film. Accordingly, articles appear on the microforms, writ very small, in precisely the position in which the articles appeared in the newspaper. The Times, for example, printed the beginning of Blakely's "Remembering Jane" Article on page 26 of the Magazine in the September 23, 1990, edition; the microfilm version of the Times reproduces that same Article on film in the very same position, within a film reproduction of the entire Magazine, in turn within a reproduction of the entire September 23, 1990, edition. True, the microfilm roll contains multiple editions, and the microfilm user can adjust the machine lens to focus only on the Article, to the exclusion of surrounding material. Nonetheless, the user first encounters the Article in context. In the Databases, by contrast, the Articles appear disconnected from their original context. In NEXIS and NYTO, the user sees the "Jane" Article apart even from the remainder of page 26. In GPO, the user sees the Article within the context of page 26, but clear of the context of page 25 or page 27, the rest of the Magazine, or the remainder of the day's newspaper. In short, unlike microforms, the Databases do not perceptibly reproduce articles as part of the collective work to which the author contributed or as part of any "revision" thereof.[10]

Invoking the concept of "media neutrality," the Publishers urge that the "transfer of a work between media" does not "alte[r] the character of" that work for copyright purposes. That is indeed true. See 17 U.S.C. § 102(a) (copyright protection subsists in original works "fixed in any tangible medium of expression"). But unlike the conversion of newsprint to micro-film, the transfer of articles to the Databases does not represent a mere

---

[9] The dissenting opinion takes as its starting point "what is sent from the New York Times to the Electronic Databases." See *post*, at 6-11. This case, however, is not ultimately about what is sent between Publishers in an intermediate step of Database production; it is about what is presented to the general public in the Databases. See *supra*, at 14. Those Databases simply cannot bear characterization as a "revision" of any one periodical edition. We would reach the same conclusion if the Times sent intact newspapers to the Electronic Publishers.

[10] The Court of Appeals concluded NEXIS was infringing partly because that Data-base did "almost nothing to preserve the copyrightable aspects of the [Print] Publishers' collective works," *i.e.*, their original "selection, coordination, and arrangement." 206 F.3d 161, 168 (CA2 1999). We do not pass on this issue. It suffices to hold that the Databases do not contain "revisions" of the Print Publishers' works "as part of" which the Articles are reproduced and distributed.

conversion of intact periodicals (or revisions of periodicals) from one medium to another. The Databases offer users individual articles, not intact periodicals. In this case, media neutrality should protect the Authors' rights in the individual Articles to the extent those Articles are now presented individually, outside the collective work context, within the Databases' new media.[11]

For the purpose at hand — determining whether the Authors' copyrights have been infringed — an analogy to an imaginary library may be instructive.[12] Rather than maintaining intact editions of periodicals, the library would contain separate copies of each article. Perhaps these copies would exactly reproduce the periodical pages from which the articles derive (if the model is GPO); perhaps the copies would contain only typescript characters, but still indicate the original periodical's name and date, as well as the article's headline and page number (if the model is NEXIS or NYTO). The library would store the folders containing the articles in a file room, indexed based on diverse criteria, and containing articles from vast numbers of editions. In response to patron requests, an inhumanly speedy librarian would search the room and provide copies of the articles matching patron-specified criteria.

Viewing this strange library, one could not, consistent with ordinary English usage, characterize the articles "as part of" a "revision" of the editions in which the articles first appeared. In substance, however, the Databases differ from the file room only to the extent they aggregate articles in electronic packages (the LEXIS/NEXIS central discs or UMI CD-ROMs), while the file room stores articles in spatially separate files. The crucial fact is that the Databases, like the hypothetical library, store and retrieve articles separately within a vast domain of diverse texts. Such a

---

[11] The dissenting opinion apparently concludes that, under the banner of "media-neutrality," a copy of a collective work, even when considerably changed, must constitute a "revision" of that collective work so long as the changes were "necessitated by . . . the medium." *Post*, at 9. We lack the dissent's confidence that the current form of the Databases is entirely attributable to the nature of the electronic media, rather than the nature of the economic market served by the Databases. In any case, we see no grounding in § 201(c) for a "medium-driven" necessity defense, *post*, at 9, n. 11, to the Authors' infringement claims. Furthermore, it bears reminder here and throughout that these Publishers and all others can protect their interests by private contractual arrangement.

[12] The Publishers have frequently referred to their products as "electronic libraries." We need not decide whether the Databases come within the legal coverage of the term "libraries" as used in the Copyright Act. For even if the Databases are "libraries," the Copyright Act's special authorizations for libraries do not cover the Databases' reproductions. See, *e.g.*, 17 U.S.C. § 108(a)(1) (reproduction authorized "without any purpose of direct or indirect commercial advantage"); § 108(b)(reproduction authorized "solely for purposes of preservation and security or for deposit for research use"); § 108(c) (1994 ed., Supp. V) (reproduction "solely for the purpose of replacement of a copy or phonorecord that is damaged, deteriorating, lost, or stolen, or if the existing format in which the work is stored has become obsolete").

storage and retrieval system effectively overrides the Authors' exclusive right to control the individual reproduction and distribution of each Article, 17 U.S.C. §§ 106(1), (3). Cf. *Ryan v. Carl Corp.*, 23 F. Supp. 2d 1146 (ND Cal. 1998) (holding copy shop in violation of § 201(c)).

The Publishers claim the protection of § 201(c) because users can manipulate the Databases to generate search results consisting entirely of articles from a particular periodical edition. By this logic, § 201(c) would cover the hypothetical library if, in response to a request, that library's expert staff assembled all of the articles from a particular periodical edition. However, the fact that a third party can manipulate a database to produce a noninfringing document does not mean the database is not infringing. Under § 201(c), the question is not whether a user can generate a revision of a collective work from a database, but whether the database itself perceptibly presents the author's contribution as part of a revision of the collective work. That result is not accomplished by these Databases.

The Publishers finally invoke *Sony Corp. of America v. Universal City Studios, Inc.*, 464 U.S. 417 (1984). That decision, however, does not genuinely aid their argument. *Sony* held that the "sale of copying equipment" does not constitute contributory infringement if the equipment is "capable of substantial noninfringing uses." *Id.* at 442. The Publishers suggest that their Databases could be liable only under a theory of contributory infringement, based on end-user conduct, which the Authors did not plead. The Electronic Publishers, however, are not merely selling "equipment"; they are selling copies of the Articles. And, as we have explained, it is the copies themselves, without any manipulation by users, that fall outside the scope of the § 201(c) privilege.

IV

The Publishers warn that a ruling for the Authors will have "devastating" consequences. The Databases, the Publishers note, provide easy access to complete newspaper texts going back decades. A ruling for the Authors, the Publishers suggest, will punch gaping holes in the electronic record of history. The Publishers' concerns are echoed by several historians, see Brief for Ken Burns et al. as *Amici Curiae*, but discounted by several other historians, see Brief for Ellen Schrecker et al. as *Amici Curiae;* Brief for Authors' Guild, Jacques Barzun et al. as *Amici Curiae.*

Notwithstanding the dire predictions from some quarters, see also *post,* at 16 (STEVENS, J., dissenting), it hardly follows from today's decision that an injunction against the inclusion of these Articles in the Databases (much less all freelance articles in any databases) must issue. See 17 U.S.C. § 502(a) (court "may" enjoin infringement); *Campbell v. Acuff-Rose Music, Inc.*, 510 U.S. 569, 578, n. 10 (1994) (goals of copyright law are "not always best served by automatically granting injunctive relief"). The parties (Authors and Publishers) may enter into an agreement allowing continued electronic reproduction of the Authors' works; they, and if necessary the courts and Congress, may draw on numerous models for distributing copyrighted works and remunerating authors for their distribution. See, *e.g.*, 17 U.S.C. § 118(b); *Broadcast Music, Inc. v. Columbia Broadcasting System, Inc.*, 441 U.S. 1, 4-6, 10-12 (1979) (recounting history of blanket music licensing regimes and consent decrees governing their operation).[13] In any event, speculation about future harms is no basis for this Court to shrink authorial rights Congress established in § 201(c). Agreeing with the Court of Appeals that the Publishers are liable for infringement, we leave remedial issues open for initial airing and decision in the District Court.

* * *

We conclude that the Electronic Publishers infringed the Authors' copyrights by reproducing and distributing the Articles in a manner not authorized by the Authors and not privileged by § 201(c). We further conclude that the Print Publishers infringed the Authors' copyrights by authorizing the Electronic Publishers to place the Articles in the Databases and by aiding the Electronic Publishers in that endeavor. We therefore affirm the judgment of the Court of Appeals.

It is so ordered.

JUSTICE STEVENS, with whom JUSTICE BREYER joins, dissenting.

This case raises an issue of first impression concerning the meaning of the word "revision" as used in § 201(c) of the 1976 revision of the Copyright Act of 1909 (1976 Act). Ironically, the Court today seems unwilling to acknowledge that changes in a collective work far less extensive than those made to prior copyright law by the 1976 "revision" do not merit the same characterization.

To explain my disagreement with the Court's holding, I shall first identify Congress' principal goals in passing the 1976 Act's changes in the prior law with respect to collective works. I will then discuss two analytically separate questions that are blended together in the Court's discussion of revisions. The first is whether the electronic versions of the collective works created

---

[13] Courts in other nations, applying their domestic copyright laws, have also concluded that Internet or CD-ROM reproduction and distribution of freelancers' works violate the copyrights of freelancers. See, *e.g., Union Syndicale des Journalistes Franais v. SDV Plurimdia* (T.G.I., Strasbourg, Fr., Feb. 3, 1998), in Lodging of International Federation of Journalists (IFJ) as *Amicus Curiae; S. C. R. L. Central Station v. Association Generale des Journalistes Professionnels de Belgique* (CA, Brussels, Belg., 9e ch., Oct. 28, 1997), transl. and ed. in 22 Colum.-VLA J. L. & Arts 195 (1998); *Heg v. De Volskrant B. V.* (Dist. Ct., Amsterdam, Neth., Sept. 24, 1997), transl. and ed. in 22 Colum.-VLA J. L. & Arts, at 181. After the French *Plurimdia* decision, the journalists' union and the newspaper-defendant entered into an agreement compensating authors for the continued electronic reproduction of their works. See *FR3 v. Syndicats de Journalistes* (CA, Colmar, Sept. 15, 1998), in Lodging of IFJ as *Amicus Curiae.* In Norway, it has been reported, a similar agreement was reached. See Brief for IFJ as *Amicus Curiae* 18.

by the owners of the copyright in those works (Print Publishers or publishers) are "revisions" of those works within the meaning of 17 U.S.C. § 201(c). In my judgment they definitely are. The second is whether the aggregation by LEXIS/NEXIS and UMI (Electronic Databases) of the revisions with other editions of the same periodical or with other periodicals within a single database changes the equation. I think it does not. Finally, I will consider the implications of broader copyright policy for the issues presented in this case.

I

As the majority correctly observes, prior to 1976, an author's decision to publish her individual article as part of a collective work was a perilous one. Although pre-1976 copyright law recognized the author's copyright in an individual article that was included within a collective work, those rights could be lost if the publisher refused to print the article with a copyright notice in the author's name. 3 M. Nimmer & D. Nimmer, Nimmer on Copyright § 10.01[C][2], p. 10-12 (2001).

This harsh rule was, from the author's point of view, exacerbated by the pre-1976 doctrine of copyright "indivisibility," which prevented an author from assigning only limited publication rights to the publisher of a collective work while holding back all other rights to herself.[1] *Ibid.* The indivisibility of copyright, in combination with the danger of losing copyright protection, put significant pressure on an author seeking to preserve her copyright in the contribution to transfer the entire copyright over to the publisher in trust. See Kaminstein, Divisibility of Copyrights, Study No. 11, in Copyright Law Revision Studies Nos. 11-13, prepared for the Senate Committee on the Judiciary, 86th Cong., 2d Sess., 18-22 (1960) (hereinafter Kaminstein).[2] Such authors were often at the mercy of publishers when they tried to reclaim their copyright. *Id.,* at 21.[3]

The 1976 Act's extensive revisions of the copyright law had two principal goals with respect to the rights of freelance authors whose writings

---

[1] Contractual attempts to assign such limited rights were deemed by courts to create mere licenses, such that the failure to accompany the article with an individual copyright in the author's name allowed the article to pass into the public domain. See 3 M. Nimmer & D. Nimmer, Nimmer on Copyright § 10.01[A], p. 10-5; § 10.01[C][2], p. 10-12 (2001).

[2] Cf. *Goodis v. United Artists Television, Inc.*,425 F.2d 397 (CA2 1970) (creating a legal fiction in which the publisher to whom an author gave first publication rights was considered the legal owner of the author's copyright, which the publisher was deemed to hold in trust for the "beneficial owner," the author).

[3] "Usually, publishers are perfectly willing to return copyright to the author, at least with respect to everything except enumerated serial or reprint rights. There have been allegations that smaller publishers sometimes believe that they are entitled to share in the subsidiary rights and refuse to reassign, or insist upon sharing part of the profits of [the] sales to motion picture, television or dramatic users. In these cases, the author must undertake the burden of proving his contract with the publisher and demonstrating his capacity to sue." Kaminstein 21.

appeared as part of larger collective works. First, as the legislative history of § 201(c) unambiguously reveals, one of its most significant aims was to "preserve the author's copyright in a contribution even if the contribution does not bear a separate notice in the author's name, and without requiring any unqualified transfer of rights to the owner of the collective work." H. R. Rep. No. 94-1476, p. 122 (1976) (hereinafter H. R. Rep.) (discussing the purpose of § 201(c)). Indeed, § 404(a) states that "a single notice applicable to the collective work as a whole is sufficient" to protect the author's rights.

The second significant change effected by the 1976 Act clarified the scope of the privilege granted to the publisher of a collective work. While pre-1976 law had the effect of encouraging an author to transfer her *entire* copyright to the publisher of a collective work, § 201(c) creates the opposite incentive, stating that, absent some agreement to the contrary, the publisher acquires from the author only "the privilege of reproducing and distributing the contribution as part of that particular collective work, any revision of that collective work, and any later collective work in the same series."[4] Congress intended this limitation on what the author is presumed to give away primarily to keep publishers from "revising the contribution itself or including it in a new anthology *or an entirely different magazine or other collective work.*" H. R. Rep. 122-123.[5]

---

[4] Respondents Garson and Robbins argue that the § 201(c) privilege is completely nontransferable. The District Court properly rejected this argument, see 972 F. Supp. 804, 815-816 (SDNY 1997), which, in my view, is supported by neither the text nor the legislative history of § 201(c). Publishers obviously cannot assign their publication privilege to another publisher such that the author's work appears in a wholly different collective work, but nothing in § 201(c) clearly prohibits a publisher from merely farming out the mundane task of printing or distributing its collective work or its revision of that collective work. Because neither the majority nor the Court of Appeals has reached this issue, however, see *ante,* at 7; 206 F.3d 161, 165, and n. 2 (CA2 2000), I will not address it further.

[5] As the District Court observed, representatives of authors had objected to an earlier draft of the 1976 Act that might have been read to give publishers the right to change the text of the contributions. That version gave publishers the privilege to print the individual article " 'as part of that particular collective work and any revisions of it.' " 972 F. Supp. at 819. Harriet Pilpel, "a prominent author representative," expressed the following concern:

"I have but one question with reference to the wording, and that is with respect to the wording at the end of subsection (c) '. . . and any revisions of it.' If that means 'any revision of the collective work' in terms of changing the contributions, or their order, or including different contributions, obviously the magazine writers and photographers would not object. But there is an implication, or at least an ambiguity, that somehow the owner of the collective work has a right to make revisions in the contributions to the collective work. This is not and should not be the law, and consequently I suggest that the wording at the end of subsection (c) be changed to make that absolutely clear." 1964 Revision Bill with Discussions and Comments, 89th Cong., 1st Sess., pt. 5, p. 9 (H. Comm. Print 1965), quoted in 972 F. Supp. at 819.

The majority is surely correct that the 1976 Act's new approach to collective works was an attempt to " 'clarify and improve the . . . confused and frequently unfair legal situation' " that existed under the prior regime. *Id.* at 122. It is also undoubtedly true that the drafters of the 1976 Act hoped to "enhance the author's position vis-a-vis the patron." *Ante*, at 9, n. 3. It does not follow, however, that Congress' efforts to "preserve the author's copyright in a contribution," H. R. Rep. 122, can *only* be honored by a finding in favor of the respondent authors.

Indeed, the conclusion that the petitioners' actions were lawful is fully consistent with both of Congress' principal goals for collective works in the 1976 Act. First, neither the publication of the collective works by the Print Publishers, nor their transfer to the Electronic Databases had any impact on the legal status of the copyrights of the respondents' individual contributions.[6]

By virtue of the 1976 Act, respondents remain the owners of the copyright in their individual works. Moreover, petitioners neither modified respondents' individual contributions nor, as I will show in Part II, published them in a "new anthology or an *entirely different magazine or other collective work.*" H. R. Rep. 122-123 (emphasis added). Because I do not think it is at all obvious that the decision the majority reaches today is a result clearly intended by the 1976 Congress, I disagree with the Court's conclusion that a ruling in petitioners' favor would "shrink authorial rights" that *"Congress* [has] established." *Ante*, at 21 (emphasis added).

II

Not only is petitioners' position consistent with Congress' general goals in the 1976 Act, it is also consistent with the text of § 201(c). That provision allows the publisher of a collective work to "reproduce and distribute the contribution as part of that particular collective work, any revision of that collective work, and any later collective work in the same series." The central question in this case, then, is whether petitioners are correct when they argue that publication of the respondents' articles in the various Electronic Databases at issue in this case is nothing more than "reproduction and distribution [of] the contribution as part of . . . revisions of [the original] collective works" in which respondents' articles appeared. I agree with petitioners that neither the conversion of the Print Publishers' collective works from printed to electronic form, nor the transmission of those electronic versions of the collective works to the Electronic Databases, nor even the actions of the Electronic Databases once they receive those

---

[6] Nor is the majority correct that, even if respondents retained copyright in their individual articles, the conclusion that petitioners could republish their collective works on the Electronic Databases would drain that copyright of value. See *infra*, at 17. Even on my view of this case, respondents retain substantial rights over their articles. Only the respondents, for example, could authorize the publication of their articles in different periodicals or in new topical anthologies wholly apart from the context of the original collective works in which their articles appeared.

electronic versions does anything to deprive those electronic versions of their status as mere "revisions" of the original collective works.

A proper analysis of this case benefits from an incremental approach. Accordingly, I begin by discussing an issue the majority largely ignores: whether a collection of articles from a single edition of the New York Times (*i.e.*, the batch of files the Print Publishers periodically send to the Electronic Databases) constitutes a "revision" of an individual edition of the paper. In other words, does a single article within such a collection exist as "part of" a "revision"? Like the majority, I believe that the crucial inquiry is whether the article appears within the "context" of the original collective work. *Ante*, at 16. But this question simply raises the further issue of precisely how much "context" is enough.

The record indicates that what is sent from the New York Times to the Electronic Databases (with the exception of General Periodicals on Disc (GPO)) is simply a collection of ASCII text files representing the editorial content of the New York Times for a particular day.[7] Each individual ASCII file contains the text of a single article as well as additional coding intended to help readers identify the context in which the article originally appeared and to facilitate database searches. Thus, for example, to the original text of an article, the New York Times adds information on the article's "headline, byline and title," "the section of the paper in which the article had originally appeared," and "the page in the paper or periodical on which the article had first appeared." *Id.* at 75a-76a.[8]

I see no compelling reason why a collection of files corresponding to a single edition of the New York Times, standing alone, cannot constitute a "revision" of that day's New York Times. It might be argued, as respondents appear to do, that the presentation of each article within its own electronic file makes it impossible to claim that the collection of files as a whole amounts to a "revision." But the conversion of the text of the overall collective work into separate electronic files should not, by itself, decide the question. After all, one of the hallmarks of copyright policy, as the majority recognizes, *ante*, at 17, is the principle of media neutrality. See H. R. Rep. 53.

No one doubts that the New York Times has the right to reprint its issues in Braille, in a foreign language, or in microform, even though such revisions might look and feel quite different from the original. Such differences, however, would largely result from the different medium being employed. Similarly, the decision to convert the single collective work newspaper into a collection of individual ASCII files can be explained as

---

[7] ASCII (American Standard Code for Information Interchange) is a standard means for storing textual data. It assigns a unique binary code for each letter of the alphabet, as well as for numbers, punctuation, and other characters. It cannot be used to convey graphical information. See C. MacKenzie, Coded Character Sets: History and Development 211-213 (1980).

[8] Substantially the same process was used by the other Print Publishers to prepare their files for electronic publication.

little more than a decision that reflects the different nature of the electronic medium. Just as the paper version of the New York Times is divided into "sections" and "pages" in order to facilitate the reader's navigation and manipulation of large batches of newsprint, so too the decision to subdivide the electronic version of that collective work into individual article files facilitates the reader's use of the electronic information. The bare-bones nature of ASCII text would make trying to wade through a single ASCII file containing the entire content of a single edition of the New York Times an exercise in frustration.[9]

Although the Court does not separately discuss the question whether the groups of files that the New York Times sends to the Electronic Databases constitute "revisions," its reasoning strongly suggests that it would not accept such a characterization. The majority, for example, places significant emphasis on the differences between the various Electronic Databases and microform, a medium that admittedly qualifies as a revision under § 201(c).[10] As with the conversion of individual editions into collections of separate article-files, however, many of the differences between the electronic versions and microform are necessitated by the electronic medium. The Court therefore appears to back away from principles of media neutrality when it implicitly criticizes ASCII-text files for their inability to reproduce "Remembering Jane" "in the very same position, within a film reproduction of the entire Magazine, in turn within a reproduction of the entire September 23, 1990, edition." *Ante*, at 16.[11]

In contrast, I think that a proper respect for media neutrality suggests that the New York Times, reproduced as a collection of individual ASCII files, should be treated as a "revision" of the original edition, as long as each article explicitly refers to the original collective work and as long as substantially the rest of the collective work is, at the same time, readily accessible to the reader of the individual file. In this case, no one disputes that the first pieces of information a user sees when looking at an individual ASCII article file are the name of the publication in which the article

---

[9] An ASCII version of the October 31, 2000, New York Times, which contains 287 articles, would fill over 500 printed pages. Conversely, in the case of graphical products like GPO, the demands that memory-intensive graphics files can place on underpowered computers make it appropriate for electronic publishers to divide the larger collective work into manageably sized subfiles. The individual article is the logical unit. The GPO version of the April 7, 1996, New York Times Magazine, for example, would demand in the neighborhood of 200 megabytes of memory if stored as a single file, whereas individual article files range from 4 to 22 megabytes, depending on the length of the article.

[10] See Brief for Respondent Garson et al. 4-5, n. 3.

[11] The majority's reliance on the fact that the GPO user cannot "flip" the page to see material published on other pages, *ante*, at 5, n. 2, and that the text database articles "appear disconnected from their original context," *ante*, at 16, appears to be nothing more than a criticism of Electronic Databases' medium-driven decision to break down the periodicals it contains into smaller, less unwieldy article-units. See n. 9, *supra*.

appeared, the edition of that publication, and the location of the article within that edition. I agree with the majority that such labeling alone is insufficient to establish that the individual file exists as "part of" a revision of the original collective work. See *ante*, at 15. But such labeling is not all there is in the group of files sent to the Electronic Databases.

In addition to the labels, the batch of electronic files contains the entire editorial content of the original edition of the New York Times for that day. That is, while I might agree that a single article, standing alone, even when coded with identifying information (e.g., publication, edition date, headline, etc.), should not be characterized as a "part of" a larger collective work, I would not say the same about an individual article existing as "part of" a collection of articles *containing all the editorial content of that day's New York Times.* This is all the more true because, as the District Court correctly noted, it is the Print Publishers' *selection* process, the editorial process by which the staff of the New York Times, for example, decides which articles will be included in "All the News That's Fit to Print," that is the most important creative element they contribute to the collective works they publish. 972 F. Supp. 804, 823 (SDNY 1997).[12] While such superficial features as page placement and column width are lost in ASCII format, the Print Publishers' all-important editorial selection is wholly preserved in the collection of individual article-files sent to the Electronic Databases.

To see why an electronic version of the New York Times made up of a group of individual ACSCII article-files, standing alone, may be considered a § 201(c) revision, suppose that, instead of transmitting to NEXIS the articles making up a particular day's edition, the New York Times saves all of the individual files on a single floppy disk, labels that disk "New York Times, October 31, 2000," and sells copies of the disk to users as the electronic version of that day's New York Times. The disk reproduces the creative, editorial selection of that edition of the New York Times. The reader, after all, has at his finger tips substantially all of the relevant content of the October 31 edition of the collective work. Moreover, each individual article makes explicit reference to that selection by including tags that remind the reader that it is a part of the New York Times for October 31, 2000. Such a disk might well constitute "that particular collective work"; it would surely qualify as a "revision" of the original collective work. Yet all the features identified as essential by the majority and by the respondents would still be lacking. An individual looking at one of the articles contained on the disk would still see none of the original formatting context and would still be unable to flip the page.

Once one accepts the premise that a disk containing all the files from the October 31, 2000, New York Times can constitute a "revision," there is no reason to treat any differently the same set of files, stored in a folder on the hard disk of a computer at the New York Times. Thus, at least before

---

[12] "*The New York Times* perhaps even represents the paradigm, the epitome of a publication in which selection alone reflects sufficient originality to merit copyright protection." 972 F. Supp. at 823.

it is republished by the Electronic Databases, the collection of files that the New York Times transmits to them constitutes a revision, in electronic form, of a particular edition of the New York Times.

III

The next question, then, is whether anything that the Electronic Databases do to the transmitted "revision" strips it of that status. The heart of the Court's reasoning in this respect, as I understand it, is that, once received and processed by Electronic Databases, the data transmitted by the New York Times cannot be viewed as "revisions" within the meaning of § 201(c) because of the way that data is stored and made available to the public by those Databases. First, the Court points to the fact that "the three Databases present articles to users clear of the context provided either by the original periodical editions or by any revision of those editions." *Ante*, at 14. I have already addressed these formatting concerns. Second, and not wholly unrelated to the first point, however, the Court appears to think that the commingling of my hypothetical collection of ASCII article-files from the October 31, 2000, New York Times with similar collections of files from other editions of the New York Times (or from other periodicals) within one database would deprive that collection of revision status. See *ibid.* Even if my imaginary floppy disk could, in isolation, be considered a revision, the majority might say, that status would be lost if the floppy disk were to contain, not only the files from the October 31, 2000, New York Times, but also from the New York Times for every other day in 2000 (and other years) and from hundreds of other periodicals. I disagree.

If my hypothetical October 31, 2000, floppy disk can be a revision, I do not see why the inclusion of other editions and other periodicals is any more significant than the placement of a single edition of the New York Times in a large public library or in a book store. Each individual file still reminds the reader that he is viewing "part of" a particular collective work. And the *entire* editorial content of that work still exists at the reader's fingertips.[13]

It is true that, once the revision of the October 31, 2000, New York Times is surrounded by the additional content, it can be conceptualized as existing as part of an even larger collective work (*e.g.*, the entire NEXIS database). See *ante*, at 14-15. The question then becomes whether this ability to conceive of a revision of a collective work as existing within a larger "collective work" changes the status of the original revision. Section 201(c)'s requirement that the article be published only as "part of . . . any revision of *that collective work*" does not compel any particular answer to that question. A microfilm of the New York Times for October 31, 2000, does not cease to be a revision of that individual collective work simply because it is stored on the same roll of film as other editions of the Times or on a library shelf containing hundreds of other microfilm periodicals. Nor does

---

[13] In NEXIS, for example, the reader can gather all the content of the October 31, 2000, New York Times by conducting the following simple search in the correct "library": "date(is 10/31/2000)."

§ 201(c) compel the counterintuitive conclusion that the microfilm version of the Times would cease to be a revision simply because its publishers might choose to sell it on rolls of film that contained a year's editions of both the New York Times *and* the Herald-Tribune. Similarly, the placement of our hypothetical electronic revision of the October 31, 2000, New York Times within a larger electronic database does nothing to alter either the nature of our original electronic revision or the relationship between that revision and the individual articles that exist as "part of" it.

Finally, the mere fact that an individual user may either view or print copies of individual articles stored on the Electronic Databases does not change the nature of the revisions contained within those databases. The same media-specific necessities that allow the publishers to store and make available the original collective work as a collection of individual digital files make it reasonable for the Electronic Databases to enable the user to download or print only those files in which the user has a particular interest. But this is no different from microfilm. Just as nothing intrinsic in the nature of microfilm dictates to a user how much or how little of a microform edition of the New York Times she must copy, nothing intrinsic in the Electronic Databases dictates to a user how much (or how little) of a particular edition of the New York Times to view or print. It is up to the user in each instance to decide whether to employ the publisher's product in a manner that infringes either the publisher's or the author's copyright. And to the extent that the user's decision to make a copy of a particular article violates the author's copyright in that article, such infringing third-party behavior should not be attributed to the database.[14] See *Sony Corp. of America v. Universal City Studios, Inc.*, 464 U.S. 417, 434 (1984).

IV

My reading of "revision," as encompassing products like the Electronic Databases, is not the only possible answer to the complex questions presented by this case. It is, nevertheless, one that is consistent with the statutory text and entirely faithful to the statute's purposes. Respect for the policies motivating its enactment, to which I now turn, makes it wrong for the Court to reject this reading of § 201(c).

It is likely that the Congress that enacted the 1976 revision of the law of copyright did not anticipate the developments that occurred in the 1980s which gave rise to the practices challenged in this litigation. See Miller, Copyright Protection for Computer Programs, Databases, and Computer Generated Works: Is Anything New Since CONTU?, 106 Harv. L. Rev. 977,

---

[14] The majority finds that NEXIS infringes by "cop[ying]" and "distribut[ing]" copies of respondents' articles to the public. Perhaps it would be more accurate to say that NEXIS makes it possible for *users* to make and distribute copies. In any event, the Court has wisely declined to reach the question whether the Electronic Databases publicly "display" the articles within the meaning of § 106. *Ante,* at 13, and n. 8.

979 (1993) (in 1976, "Congress . . . decided to avoid grappling with technological issues that obviously required more study than the legislative process was then willing to give them").[15] Thus, in resolving ambiguities in the relevant text of the statute, we should be mindful of the policies underlying copyright law.

Macaulay wrote that copyright is "a tax on readers for the purpose of giving a bounty to writers." T. Macaulay, Speeches on Copyright 11 (A. Thorndike ed. 1915) That tax restricts the dissemination of writings, but only insofar as necessary to encourage their production, the bounty's basic objective. See U.S. Const., Art. I, § 8, cl. 8. In other words, "the primary purpose of copyright is not to reward the author, but is rather to secure 'the general benefits derived by the public from the labors of authors.'" 1 M. Nimmer & D. Nimmer, Nimmer on Copyright § 1.03[A] (2001) (quoting *Fox Film Corp. v. Doyal*, 286 U.S. 123, 127 (1932)); see also Breyer, The Uneasy Case for Copyright: A Study of Copyright in Books, Photocopies, and Computer Programs, 84 Harv. L. Rev. 281, 282 (1970) (discussing the twin goals of copyright law — protecting the reader's desire for access to ideas and providing incentives for authors to produce them). The majority's decision today unnecessarily subverts this fundamental goal of copyright law in favor of a narrow focus on "authorial rights." *Ante*, at 21. Although the desire to protect such rights is certainly a laudable sentiment,[16] copyright law demands that "private motivation must ultimately serve the cause of promoting *broad public availability* of literature, music, and the other arts." *Twentieth Century Music Corp. v. Aiken,* 422 U.S. 151, 156 (1975) (emphasis added).

The majority discounts the effect its decision will have on the availability of comprehensive digital databases, *ante*, at 19-21, but I am not as confident. As petitioners' *amici* have persuasively argued, the difficulties of locating individual freelance authors and the potential of exposure to statutory damages may well have the effect of forcing electronic archives to purge freelance pieces from their databases.[17] "The omission of these materials from electronic collections, for any reason on a large scale or even an occasional basis, undermines the principal benefits that electronic

---

[15] See also H. R. Rep. 116. In the quarter century since the 1976 Act became law, "the databases [in existence] have grown by a factor of 39. . . . In 1975, the 301 databases in existence contained about 52 million records. The 11,681 databases in 1999 contained nearly 12.86 billion records for a growth by a factor of 242." Williams, Highlights of the Online Database Industry and the Internet: 2000, in Proceedings of the 21st Annual National Online Meeting 1 (Williams ed., 2000).

[16] But see Breyer, The Uneasy Case for Copyright: A Study of Copyright in Books, Photocopies, and Computer Programs, 84 Harv. L. Rev. 281, 286-290 (1970) (criticizing the use of copyright as a means of protecting authorial rights).

[17] Indeed, today's decision in favor of authors may have the perverse consequence of encouraging publishers to demand from freelancers a complete transfer of copyright. If that turns out to be the case, we will have come full circle back to the pre-1976 situation.

archives offer historians — efficiency, accuracy and comprehensiveness."[18] Brief for Ken Burns et al. as *Amici Curiae* 13.

Moreover, it is far from clear that my position even deprives authors of much of anything (with the exception of perhaps the retrospective statutory damages that may well result from their victory today).[19] Imagine, for example, that one of the contributions at issue in this case were a copyrighted version of John Keats' Ode on a Grecian Urn, published on page 29 of our hypothetical October 31, 2000, New York Times. Even under my reading of § 201(c), Keats retains valuable copyright protection. No matter how well received his ode might be, it is unlikely — although admittedly possible — that it could be marketed as a stand-alone work of art. The ode, however, would be an obvious candidate for inclusion in an anthology of works by romantic poets, in a collection of poems by the same author, or even in "a 400-page novel quoting a [poem] in passing," *ante*, at 15. The author's copyright would protect his right to compensation for any such use. Cf. *Stewart v. Abend*, 495 U.S. 207, 228 (1990) (discussing the value to authors of derivative works). Moreover, the value of the ode surely would be enhanced, not decreased, by the accessibility and readership of the October 31, 2000, edition of the New York Times. The ready availability of that edition, both at the time of its first publication and subsequently in libraries and electronic databases, would be a benefit, not an injury, to most authors. Keats would benefit from the poem's continued availability to database users, by his identification as the author of the piece, and by the database's indication of the fact that the poem first appeared in a prestigious periodical on a certain date. He would not care one whit whether the database indicated the formatting context of the page on which the poem appeared. What is overwhelmingly clear is that maximizing the readership of the ode would *enhance* the value of his remaining copyright uses.

Nor is it clear that Keats will gain any prospective benefits from a victory in this case. As counsel for petitioners represented at oral argument, since 1995, the New York Times has required freelance authors to grant the Times "electronic rights" to articles. And the inclusion of such a term has had *no effect* on the compensation authors receive. See *ibid.* This is understandable because, even if one accepts the majority's characterization of the Electronic Databases as collections of freestanding articles, demand for databases like NEXIS probably does not reflect a "demand for a freelance article standing alone," *ante*, at 11, to which the publishers are

---

[18] If the problem is as important as amici contend, congressional action may ultimately be necessary to preserve present databases in their entirety. At the least, Congress can determine the nature and scope of the problem and fashion on appropriate licensing remedy far more easily than can courts. Compare 17 U.S.C. § 108(d)(1).

[19] It is important to remember that the prospect of payment by the Print Publishers was sufficient to stimulate each petitioner to create his or her part of the collective works, presumably with full awareness of its intended inclusion in the Electronic Databases.

greedily helping themselves. Cf. *Ryan v. Carl Corp.*, 23 F. Supp. 2d 1146, 1150-1151 (ND Cal. 1998) ("[T]he value added by the publisher to a reproduced article is significant").

Instead, it seems far more likely that demand for the Electronic Databases reflects demand for a product that will provide a user with the means to quickly search through scores of complete periodicals. The comments of historian Douglas Brinkley are instructive in this respect:

> " 'As an historian, when I want to write a biography, if I'm going to write a biography of Bill Clinton, the first thing I would do would be to index *The New York Times*. I would work through [the] microfiche and get any time Bill Clinton's name ever appeared in *The New York Times*. I'd get a copy of that. So you'd have boxes of files. So for each month, here's Clinton this month. You then would fill that in with . . . other obvious books or articles from *Foreign Affairs* or *Foreign Policy* or *The New Yorker*, or the like and you'd start getting your first biography of Bill Clinton.' " Panel Discussion: The Observer's View (D. Brinkley, M. Frankel, H. Sidey), White House Historical Association (Nov. 16, 2000) (C-SPAN Archives No. 160577) (quoted in Brief for Ken Burns et al. as *Amici Curiae* 17).

Users like Douglas Brinkley do not go to NEXIS because it contains a score of individual articles by Jonathan Tasini.[20] Rather, they go to NEXIS

---

[20] Even assuming, as the majority does, see *ante*, at 12, n. 6, that the existence of databases like NEXIS may have some adverse effect on the market for stand-alone compilations of authors' contributions to collective works, I fail to see how, on that basis, electronic databases are any different from microform. With respect to effects on the market for stand-alone works, the only difference between the two products is the speed with which digital technology allows NEXIS users to retrieve the desired data. But the 1976 Act was not intended to bar the use of every conceivable innovation in technology that might " 'give[] publishers [new] opportunities to exploit authors' works.' " *Ibid.* Copyright law is not an insurance policy for authors, but a carefully struck balance between the need to create incentives for authorship and the interests of society in the broad accessibility of ideas. See U.S. Const., Art. I, § 8, cl. 8 (in order to promote production, Congress should allow authors and inventors to enjoy "exclusive Right[s]," but only "for *limited* Times" (emphasis added)); see also *supra*, at 15. The majority's focus on authorial incentive comes at the expense of the equally important (at least from the perspective of copyright policy) public interest.

Moreover, the majority's single-minded focus on "authorial rights" appears to lead it to believe that, because *some* authors may benefit from its decision, that decision must be the one intended by Congress. It cites the " 'economic philosophy behind the [Copyright Clause]' " as consistent with its view that Congress adjusted "the author/publisher balance" precisely to avoid the types of uses embodied in the Electronic Databases. See *ante*, at 9, n. 3. But, as I have already argued, see *supra*, at 14-15, there is no indication that Congress ever considered the issue presented in this case. It thus simply begs the question for the majority to argue that the right not to have a work included within the Electronic Databases is an "authorial right" that "*Congress* [has] established," *ante*, at 21 (emphasis added), or that — given Congress' failure clearly to address itself to the question — a decision allowing such

because it contains a comprehensive and easily searchable collection of (intact) periodicals. See *id.* at 8 ("The efficiency, accuracy, reliability, comprehensiveness and immediacy of access offered by searchable full-text digital archives are but a few of the benefits historians and other researches have reaped from the advancement in the technology of information").

Because it is likely that Congress did not consider the question raised by this case when drafting § 201(c), because I think the District Court's reading of that provision is reasonable and consistent with the statute's purposes, and because the principal goals of copyright policy are better served by that reading, I would reverse the judgment of the Court of Appeals. The majority is correct that we cannot know in advance the effects of today's decision on the comprehensiveness of electronic databases. We can be fairly certain, however, that it will provide little, if any, benefit to either authors or readers.

AFTER *TASINI*

At first blush, the Supreme Court's decision in *Tasini* may seem a nice victory for freelance journalists. But perhaps, on second glance, it was not so nice for anyone. The freelancers' victory celebrations notwithstanding, a party pooper might suggest that the freelancers won the battle but lost the war.

What happened is this. In the 1990s, with the *Tasini* case looming in the background, publishers (like the *New York Times*) became fully aware of the possible risk of liability and began insisting on "all rights" agreements designed to allow their reuse of freelancers' contributions. The contracts are standard now, but it is not clear whether freelancers were able to extract larger profits in negotiating the agreements. After all, media outlets for freelance articles have continued to consolidate, so that the publishers are in a virtual monopoly position. In other words, the market is now a buyer's market: "You want to write an article for us? Then sign over those rights." Thus, the freelancers may have earned a modest one-time windfall at best.

If the freelancers have earned an ambiguous victory, and the publishers have suffered an ambiguous loss, what about the public interest in access to information? Here is where the story gets depressing. The public appears to have lost unambiguously. Many newspapers and other print media, uncertain as to which articles in their archives were written by freelancers, have resort to overly inclusive purges to avoid liability. Thus, a researcher who wants access to a certain article may not be able to go on-line to obtain

---

inclusion would amount to "*diminish[ing]*" authorial "rights" on the basis of "our conception of their interests." *Ante*, at 12-13, n. 6 (emphasis added).

it, and is forced to find a library that keeps paper (or microfiche) copies of the publication.

For the future, can you think of a way to protect the rights of freelance writers and the public interest at the same time? Does the answer lie in state regulation of contract law that sets, for example, a limited term — e.g., seven years — for "all rights" contracts?

§ 4.02   Transfers of Rights

USAGE: On page 314, ADD the following text at the conclusion of § 4.02[B]:

Courts now have reconsidered the concept of divisibility in a series of cases under the 1976 Act.

For example, the Ninth Circuit has held that an exclusive licensee does *not* have the right to transfer its rights without the consent of the licensor. *Gardner v. Nike, Inc.,* 279 F.3d 774 (9th Cir. 2002). In 1992, Nike signed an agreement giving Sony the exclusive right to use a cartoon character in connection with sound recordings and associated promotional activity. After Sony assigned its rights to Gardner, Nike challenged Gardner's use of the material, and Gardner sued Nike for a declaration that Sony's transfer of rights was valid.

The Court of Appeals affirmed a District Court order finding that Gardner, as a licensee, lacked standing to sue. The court found that, under § 201(d) (2) of the 1976 Act, an exclusive licensee is entitled to the "protection and remedies" afforded by the Act, but not to rights of "owner-ship" (as specified under § 101) such as the right to transfer. The court noted that Congress was aware that, prior to the 1976 Act, licensees could not sublicense their right in an exclusive license. The fact that Congress chose not to address this issue explicitly, coupled with the limiting language of § 201(d) (2), indicated to the court that the state of the law remains unchanged. Moreover, placing the burden on the licensee to get the licen-sor's explicit consent was said to assure that the licensor will be able to monitor the use of copyright.

Are you convinced by the court's rationale? After all, Congress explicitly abolished the 1909 Act doctrine of indivisibility, and § 101 defines an exclusive licensee as an owner of copyright. Moreover, an exclusive licensee may now sue in his own name for an infringement of the assigned right. Shouldn't the right to sublicense follow from this? Or is it better, from a policy standpoint, that the parties should be made to negotiate explicitly the right to sublicense?

Other recent cases concerning divisibility have focused on registration requirements under § 411(a) of the 1976 Act. For discussion of those cases, see § 6.03 of this Supplement.

USAGE: On page 321, ADD the following text after note (7):

(7A) What law determines whether an implied nonexclusive license exists? As *Effects Associates* indicates, nonexclusive licenses need not be in writing and may be granted orally or by implication. The writing requirement of § 204(a) of the 1976 Act is inapplicable because that provision applies only to transfers of ownership (assignments and exclusive licenses), not to nonexclusive licenses. The court in *Effects Associates* did not explicitly decide, however, which law — state or federal — is to be applied in determining whether an implied nonexclusive license has been granted under the circumstances.

In *Foad Consulting Group, Inc. v. Musil Govan Azzalino,* 270 F. 3d 821 (9th Cir. 2001), the court held that an implied nonexclusive license may be based on federal law, but that state law determines the contract question of whether such a license was in fact granted. One might ask whether it makes much difference whether state or federal law applies. The answer is that it might, depending on the state law at issue. For example, as the court pointed out in *Foad,* California has a liberal parole evidence rule, permitting consideration of extrinsic evidence to explain the meaning of the terms of a contract even though the meaning appears unambiguous.

Judge Kozinski, in a concurring opinion, disagreed, arguing that that the implied license is an incident of federal law. Can you think of any good reason, from a copyright policy standpoint, why an implied nonexclusive license should be an incident of federal copyright law, rather than of state contract law?

USAGE: On page 328, SUBSTITUTE the following text for note (7):

(7) Do the "authors" of collective works have the right to exploit the collective work in new media without obtaining the permission of the owners of each of the individual copyrighted works? See the discussion of *Tasini v. The New York Times Co., Inc.,* 1121 S.Ct. 2381 (2001), in § 4.01.

(8) When a publishing contract from (say) the 1960s grants right to "print, publish and sell the work in book form," does that mean "e-books" as well as the old-fashioned codex variety? This was the question before the court in *Random House, Inc. v. Rosetta Books LLC,* 244 F.3d 1267 (2d Cir. 2001). The analysis is an interesting and persuasive one, marred only by its reliance on the now-questionable reasoning of *Greenberg v. National Geographic Society.* Note also that a similar issue is posed by a lawsuit brought by members of such musical groups as the Chambers Brothers, the Original Drifters and the Coasters against various music industry defendants, alleging, *inter alia,* that the contracts under which these artists worked from the 1950s through the mid-1990s did not effectively transfer rights in the digital versions of their sound recordings. *See Chambers v. Time Warner, Inc.,* 282 F.3d 147 (2d Cir. 2002) (vacating an order of dismissal).

Chapter 5

DURATION, RENEWAL, AND
TERMINATIONS OF TRANSFERS

§ 5.01   Duration and Renewal

[B]   Duration

USAGE: On page 347, ADD the following text after note (8):

(8A) Up to now, we have focused on the term of protection for works published before January 1, 1978. What term is applicable to a work created before 1978 *but never published*? For pre-1978 unpublished works, § 303(a) of the Copyright Act provides:

> Copyright in a work created before January 1, 1978, but not theretofore in the public domain or copyrighted, subsists from January 1, 1978, and endures for the term provided by section 302 [*i.e.,* life plus 70]. In no case, however, shall the term of copyright in such a work expire before December 31, 2002; and, if the work is published on or before December 31, 2002, the term of copyright shall not expire before December 31, 2047.

What this means is that an unpublished letter by Mark Twain will go into the pubic domain on January 1, 2003 but, if published before that date, will enjoy copyright protection through 2047. Note the difference between this regime and the regime applicable to *published* works after the Sonny Bono Copyright Term Extension Act. Surely, some owners of copyrights in *unpublished* works will neglect to publish these works by 2002, possibly making the year 2003 a banner year for the public domain (in that regard only). On the other hand, some vigilant owners who timely publish will enjoy rights well beyond life plus 70 years!

USAGE: Also on page 347, SUBSTITUTE the following text for note (9):

(9) How good are the chances that the Bono Act *itself* will be found to have exceeded the "limited Times" empowerment of Congress to enact intellectual property protection under Art. I, § 8, cl. 8? The legislation has been challenged in an action filed by Stanford Law Professor Lawrence Lessig (and others) on behalf of various plaintiffs claiming to have been harmed by the Act, including Eldritch Press. Eldritch is a nonprofit organization that posts literary works on the Internet once they fall into the public domain. The complaint alleged that Eldritch had been directly and adversely affected by Congress's extension of the copyright term because it had been prevented by the Act from posting on-line works which were created in 1923 and which could legally have been copied as of January

1, 1999, were it not for Congressional extension of the term of such works from 75 years to 95 years. Eldritch claimed that the extension was unconstitutional. The Act, as you will see immediately below, survived harm at least through the Court of Appeals, but will now be considered by the Supreme Court of the United States in its October 2002 Term. By the time you finish reading the materials that follow, you may well know "the rest of the story"!

ELDRED v. RENO, ATTORNEY GENERAL

United States Court of Appeals, District of Columbia Circuit
239 F.3d 372 (2001)

GINSBURG, *Circuit Judge:*

The plaintiffs in this case, corporations, associations, and individuals who rely for their vocations or avocations upon works in the public domain, challenge the constitutionality of the Copyright Term Extension Act of 1998 (CTEA), Pub. L. No. 105-298, 112 Stat. 2827. This marks the first occasion for an appellate court to address whether the First Amendment or the Copyright Clause of the Constitution of the United States constrains the Congress from extending for a period of years the duration of copyrights, both those already extant and those yet to come. We hold that neither does.

I. Background

The CTEA amends various provisions of the Copyright Act of 1976, *17 U.S.C. § 101 et seq.* The portions of the CTEA at issue here extend the terms of all copyrights for 20 years as follows: (1) For a work created in 1978 or later, to which an individual author holds the copyright, the Act extends the term to the life of the author plus 70 years. *See* Pub L. No. 105-298 § 102(b)(1), 112 Stat. 2827; *17 U.S.C. § 302* (a). (2) For a work created in 1978 or later that is anonymous, or pseudonymous, or is made for hire, the term is extended from 75 to 95 years from the year of publication or from 100 to 120 years from the year of creation, whichever occurs first. *See* Pub. L. No. 105-298 § 102(b)(3), 112 Stat. 2827; *17 U.S.C. § 302* (c). (3) For a work created before 1978, for which the initial term of copyright was 28 years, the renewal term is extended from 47 to 67 years, thereby creating a combined term of 95 years. *See* Pub. L. No. 105-298 § 102(d), 112 Stat. 2827; *17 U.S.C. § 304.* In all three situations, therefore, the CTEA applies retrospectively in the sense that it extends the terms of subsisting copyrights. As a result, the CTEA better aligns the terms of United States copyrights with those of copyrights governed by the European Union. *See* S. Rep. No. 104-315, at 7-8 (1996); Council Directive 93/98, art. 7, 1993 O.J. (L 290) 9.

The CTEA is but the latest in a series of congressional extensions of the copyright term, each of which has been made applicable both prospectively and retrospectively. In 1790 the First Congress provided, both for works "already printed" and for those that would be "thereafter made and composed," initial and renewal terms of 14 years, for a combined term of

28 years. Act of May 31, 1790 § 1, 1 Stat. 124, 124. In 1831 the Congress extended the initial term to 28 years, thereby creating a combined term of 42 years. *See* Act of Feb. 3, 1831 § 1, 4 Stat. 436, 436. So the term remained until 1909, when the Congress extended the renewal term as well to 28 years, making for a combined term of 56 years. *See* Act of March 4, 1909 § 23, 35 Stat. 1075, 1080.

Between 1962 and 1974 the Congress passed a series of laws that incrementally extended subsisting copyrights. *See* Pub. L. No. 87-668, 76 Stat. 555 (1962); Pub. L. No. 89-142, 79 Stat. 581 (1965); Pub. L. No. 90-141, 81 Stat. 464 (1967); Pub. L. No. 90-416, 82 Stat. 397 (1968); Pub. L. No. 91-147, 83 Stat. 360 (1969); Pub. L. No. 91-555, 84 Stat. 1441 (1970); Pub. L. No. 92-170, 85 Stat. 490 (1971); Pub. L. No. 92-566, 86 Stat. 1181 (1972); Pub. L. No. 93-573, title I, § 104, 88 Stat. 1873 (1974). In 1976 the Congress altered the way the term of a copyright is computed so as to conform with the Berne Convention and with international practice. *See* H.R. Rep. No. 94-1476, at 135 (1976). Thenceforth the term would be the life of the author plus 50 years or, where there was no identifiable author, the earlier of 75 years from the year of publication or 100 years from the year of creation. *See* Pub. L. No. 94-553 § § 302-05, 90 Stat. 2541, 2572-76 (1976). The CTEA amends this scheme by adding 20 years to the term of every copyright.

The plaintiffs filed this suit against the Attorney General of the United States to obtain a declaration that the CTEA is unconstitutional. Among the plaintiffs are a non-profit association that distributes over the internet free electronic versions of books in the public domain; a company that reprints rare, out-of-print books that have entered the public domain; a vendor of sheet music and a choir director, who respectively sell and purchase music that is relatively inexpensive because it is in the public domain; and a company that preserves and restores old films and insofar as such works are not in the public domain, needs permission from their copyright holders — who are often hard to find — in order to exploit them.

The district court entered judgment on the pleadings in favor of the Government and dismissed the plaintiffs' case in its entirety. On appeal, the plaintiffs renew their claims that the CTEA both violates the First Amendment to the Constitution and is in various ways inconsistent with the Copyright Clause of Article I, § 8 of the Constitution, which authorizes the Congress: "To promote the Progress of Science and useful Arts, by securing for limited Times to Authors and Inventors the exclusive Right to their respective Writings and Discoveries."

II. Analysis

The plaintiffs claim that the CTEA is beyond the power of the Congress and therefore unconstitutional for three reasons: first, the CTEA, in both its prospective and retrospective applications, fails the intermediate scrutiny appropriate under the First Amendment; second, in its application to preexisting works, the CTEA violates the originality requirement of the Copyright Clause; and third, in extending the term of subsisting copyrights, the CTEA violates the "limited Times" requirement of the Copyright Clause

— a requirement that they say is informed by the goal of "promoting the Progress of Science and useful Arts." Because each of these grounds presents a pure question of law, we consider them *de novo. See, e.g., United States v. Popa, 337 U.S. App. D.C. 411, 187 F.3d 672, 674 (D.C. Cir. 1999).*

A. First Amendment

The First Amendment aspect of the plaintiffs' complaint attacks the CTEA not only in its application to subsisting copyrights but also insofar as it extends the terms of copyrights for works yet to be created. The Government questions plaintiffs' standing to complain in the latter regard.

1. Standing

Consider first the plaintiffs' standing with respect to works that, though now subject to subsisting copyrights, will in due course enter the public domain: The plaintiffs benefit from using works in the public domain and, but for the CTEA, they would be able to exploit additional works the copyrights to which would have expired in the near future. As such, they suffer an injury in fact that is traceable to the CTEA and that we could redress by holding the Act invalid. *See Lujan v. Defenders of Wildlife, 504 U.S. 555, 560-61, 119 L. Ed. 2d 351, 112 S. Ct. 2130 (1992).* The Government concedes as much.

In view of the plaintiffs' standing to challenge the CTEA with respect to works already copyrighted, the Government's objection to the plaintiffs' standing with respect to works yet to be created seems very weak indeed. The plaintiffs benefit from works in the public domain and are deprived of that benefit so long as such works are under copyright. That is as true for works not yet created as for extant works on which the copyrights are about to expire; the Government does not draw any meaningful distinction between the two categories of works. We conclude therefore that the plaintiffs have standing to pursue their prospective claim under the First Amendment.

2. The merits

The decisions of the Supreme Court in *Harper & Row Publishers Inc. v. Nation Enters., 471 U.S. 539, 85 L. Ed. 2d 588, 105 S. Ct. 2218 (1985),* and of this court in *United Video, Inc. v. FCC, 281 U.S. App. D.C. 368, 890 F.2d 1173 (1989),* stand as insuperable bars to plaintiffs' first amendment theory. In *Harper & Row* the Court held that a magazine's advance publication of excerpts from the memoirs of former President Gerald Ford infringed the copyright thereon. *471 U.S. at 569.* In doing so the Court explained how the regime of copyright itself respects and adequately safeguards the freedom of speech protected by the First Amendment.

Copyright's idea/expression dichotomy "strikes a definitional balance between the First Amendment and the Copyright Act by permitting free communication of facts while still protecting an author's expression." No author may copyright his ideas or the facts he narrates. *17 U.S.C. § 102* (b). *See, e.g., New York Times Co. v. United States, 403 U.S. 713, 726, 29*

L. Ed. 2d 822, 91 S. Ct. 2140, n. (1971) (BRENNAN, J., concurring) (Copyright laws are not restrictions on freedom of speech as copyright protects only form of expression and not the ideas expressed).

471 U.S. at 556 (citation omitted). The first amendment objection of the magazine was misplaced "in view of the First Amendment protections already embodied in the Copyright Act's distinction between copyrightable expression and uncopyrightable facts and ideas, and the latitude for scholarship and comment traditionally afforded by fair use." *Id. at 560.*

In keeping with this approach, we held in *United Video* that copyrights are categorically immune from challenges under the First Amendment. There, certain cable companies petitioned for review of an FCC regulation providing that the supplier of a syndicated television program could agree to the program being broadcast exclusively by a single station in a local broadcast area. *890 F.2d at 1176-78.* We rejected the first amendment aspect of their challenge as follows:

> In the present case, the petitioners desire to make commercial use of the copyrighted works of others. There is no first amendment right to do so. Although there is some tension between the Constitution's copy-right clause and the first amendment, the familiar idea/expression dichotomy of copyright law, under which ideas are free but their particular expression can be copyrighted, has always been held to give adequate protection to free expression.

890 F.2d at 1191.

The plaintiffs argue that "these authorities are restricted solely to the narrow case where a litigant demands a right to use otherwise legitimately copyrighted material," which case is "plainly distinct from [this] First Amendment challenge[ ] to the constitutionality of the statute granting a copyright in the first instance." We think the plaintiffs' purported distinction is wholly illusory. The relevant question under the First Amendment — regardless whether it arises as a defense in a suit for copyright infringement or in an anticipatory challenge to a statute or regulation — is whether the party has a first amendment interest in a copyrighted work. The works to which the CTEA applies, and in which plaintiffs claim a first amendment interest, are by definition under copyright; that puts the works on the latter half of the "idea/expression dichotomy" and makes them subject to fair use. This obviates further inquiry under the First Amendment.

The plaintiffs cite no case to the contrary. In two of the cases they do cite, *Reno v. ACLU, 521 U.S. 844, 871-79, 138 L. Ed. 2d 874, 117 S. Ct. 2329 (1997),* and *Simon & Schuster, Inc. v. Members of NY State Crime Victims Bd., 502 U.S. 105, 115-23, 116 L. Ed. 2d 476, 112 S. Ct. 501 (1991),* the Supreme Court held statutes unconstitutional under the First Amendment because they were unjustifiably content based; the plaintiffs here do not claim that the CTEA is anything but content neutral. In *San Francisco Arts & Athletics, Inc. v. United States Olympic Committee,* also cited by the plaintiffs, the Court did indeed apply heightened scrutiny under the First

Amendment to a statute granting the United States Olympic Committee trademark-like protection for the word "Olympic." *483 U.S. 522, 535-41, 97 L. Ed. 2d 427, 107 S. Ct. 2971 (1987)*. Restricting the use of particular words "runs a substantial risk of suppressing ideas in the process," the Court explained. *Id. at 532*. As we have seen, however, copyright protection cannot embrace ideas; it therefore does not raise the same concern under the First Amendment. Finally, although the plaintiffs assert that the Second Circuit has reached the merits of a first amendment challenge to an aspect of the Copyright Act of 1976, in fact that court, after reviewing the case law, concluded that the plaintiffs categorically lacked "any right to distribute and receive material that bears protection of the Copyright Act." *Authors League of America v. Oman, 790 F.2d 220, 223 (1986)*.

As this is all the support plaintiffs muster for their proposition, we need not linger further in disposing of it. Suffice it to say we reject their first amendment objection to the CTEA because the plaintiffs lack any cognizable first amendment right to exploit the copyrighted works of others.

B. Requirement of Originality

The plaintiffs' second challenge ostensibly rests upon *Feist Publications, Inc. v. Rural Telephone Service Co.,* in which the Supreme Court held that telephone listings compiled in a white pages directory are uncopyrightable facts: "The *sine qua non* of copyright is originality." *499 U.S. 340, 345, 111 S. Ct. 1282, 113 L. Ed. 2d 358 (1991)*. "Originality is a constitutional requirement" for copyright because the terms "Authors" and "Writings," as they appear in the Copyright Clause, "presuppose a degree of originality." *Id. at 346*.

The plaintiffs reason from this that the CTEA cannot extend an extant copyright because the copyrighted work already exists and therefore lacks originality. Not so. Originality is what made the work copyrightable in the first place. A work with a subsisting copyright has already satisfied the requirement of originality and need not do so anew for its copyright to persist. If the Congress could not extend a subsisting copyright for want of originality, it is hard to see how it could provide for a copyright to be renewed at the expiration of its initial term — a practice dating back to 1790 and not questioned even by the plaintiffs today.

The plaintiffs' underlying point seems to be that there is something special about extending a copyright beyond the combined initial and renewal terms for which it was initially slated. Nothing in *Feist* or in the requirement of originality supports this, however: All they tell us is that facts, like ideas, are outside the ambit of copyright. Undaunted in trying to advance their novel notion of originality, the plaintiffs point to cases that do not address the requirement of originality for copyright *per se*. They point to no case or commentary, however, that calls into question the distinction between a new grant of copyright — as to which originality is an issue — and the extension of an existing grant. That distinction reflects, at bottom, the difference between the constitutionally delimited subject matter of copyright and the Congress's exercise of its copyright authority with respect to that subject matter.

The plaintiffs do point out that the Supreme Court has said the "Congress may not authorize the issuance of patents whose effects are to remove existent knowledge from the public domain, or to restrict free access to materials already available." *Graham v. John Deere Co., 383 U.S. 1, 6, 15 L. Ed. 2d 545, 86 S. Ct. 684 (1966)*. The Court similarly stated, over a century ago, that the issuance of a trademark could not be justified under the Copyright Clause because the subject matter of trademark is "the adoption of something already in existence." *Trade-Mark Cases, 100 U.S. 82, 94, 25 L. Ed. 550 (1879)*. Applied *mutatis mutandis* to the subject of copyright, these teachings would indeed preclude the Congress from authorizing under that Clause a copyright to a work already in the public domain.

The plaintiffs read the Court's guidance more broadly, in the light of *Feist,* to mean that a work in the public domain lacks the originality required to qualify for a copyright. That is certainly not inconsistent with the Court's opinion: A work in the public domain is, by definition, without a copyright; where the grant of a copyright is at issue, so too is the work's eligibility for copyright, and thus the requirement of originality comes into play. We need not adopt a particular view on that point, however, as it has nothing to do with this case. Here we ask not whether any work is copyrightable — indeed, the relevant works are already copyrighted — but only whether a copyright may by statute be continued in force beyond the renewal term specified by law when the copyright was first granted. For the plaintiffs to prevail, therefore, they will need something other than the requirement of originality upon which to make their stand.

C. The Limitation of "limited Times"

We come now to the plaintiffs' contention that the CTEA violates the constitutional requirement that copyrights endure only for "limited Times." This claim at last speaks to the duration rather than to the subject matter of a copyright: If the Congress were to make copyright protection permanent, then it surely would exceed the power conferred upon it by the Copyright Clause.

The present plaintiffs want a limit well short of the rule against perpetuities, of course. And they claim to have found it — or at least a bar to extending the life of a subsisting copyright — in the preamble of the Copyright Clause: "The Congress shall have power &hellip To promote the Progress of Science and useful Arts. . . ." Their idea is that the phrase "limited Times" should be interpreted not literally but rather as reaching only as far as is justified by the preambular statement of purpose: If 50 years are enough to "promote . . . Progress," then a grant of 70 years is unconstitutional. Here the plaintiffs run squarely up against our holding in *Schnapper v. Foley,* 215 U.S. App. D.C. 59, 667 F.2d 102, 112 (1981), in which we rejected the argument "that the introductory language of the Copyright Clause constitutes a limit on congressional power." The plaintiffs, however, disclaim any purpose to question the holding of *Schnapper*;

indeed, they expressly acknowledge "that the preamble of the Copyright Clause is not a substantive limit on Congress' legislative power." Their argument is simply that "the Supreme Court has interpreted the terms 'Authors' and 'Writings' in light of that preamble, and that this Court should do the same with 'limited Times.'"

The problems with this argument are manifest. First, one cannot concede that the preamble "is not a substantive limit" and yet maintain that it limits the permissible duration of a copyright more strictly than does the textual requirement that it be for a "limited Time." Second, although the plaintiffs claim that *Feist* supports using the preamble to interpret the rest of the Clause, the Court in *Feist* never suggests that the preamble informs its interpretation of the substantive grant of power to the Congress (which there turned upon the meaning of "Authors" and of "Writings," each standing alone). *499 U.S. at 345-47.* Similarly, the *Trade-Mark Cases* cited in *Feist* rest upon the originality implied by "invention [and] discovery" and by the "writings of authors," and make no reference at all to the preamble. 100 U.S. at 93-94.

III. The Dissent

The foregoing suffices to dispose of plaintiffs' arguments — as Judge Sentelle, dissenting, implicitly recognizes.— and hence to resolve this case. Our dissenting colleague nonetheless adopts the narrow view of *Schnapper* urged by an amicus, although that argument is rejected by the actual parties to this case and therefore is not properly before us. *See, e.g,* 16A CHARLES ALAN WRIGHT ET AL., FEDERAL PRACTICE AND PROCEDURE § 3975.1 & n.3 (3d ed. 1999); *Resident Council of Allen Parkway Vill. v. HUD, 980 F.2d 1043, 1049 (5th Cir. 1993)* (amicus constrained "by the rule that [it] generally cannot expand the scope of an appeal to implicate issues that have not been presented by the parties to the appeal"); *cf. Lamprecht v. FCC, 294 U.S. App. D.C. 164, 958 F.2d 382, 389 (D.C. Cir. 1992)* (intervenor as nonparty "cannot expand the proceedings" or "enlarge those issues presented"). This is particularly inappropriate because a court should avoid, not seek out, a constitutional issue the resolution of which is not essential to the disposition of the case before it. Moreover, because the plaintiffs conspicuously failed to adopt the argument of the amicus, the Government was not alerted to any need to argue this point and did not do so. *See Harmon v. Thornburgh, 278 U.S. App. D.C. 382, 878 F.2d 484, 494 (D.C. Cir. 1989)* (court must "avoid unnecessary or premature constitutional rulings" and this concern "is heightened by the absence of meaningful argument by the parties on [constitutional] question"); *Ashwander v. Tennessee Valley Authority, 297 U.S. 288, 346, 80 L. Ed. 688, 56 S. Ct. 466 (1936)* (Brandeis, J., concurring) ("Court will not 'anticipate a question of constitutional law in advance of the necessity of deciding it'").

Even were we to proceed as urged by the amicus and the dissent, however, we would only review the CTEA as we would any other exercise of a power enumerated in Article I. That is we would ask, following *McCulloch v. Maryland, 17 U.S. 316, 421, 4 L. Ed. 579 (1819),* whether the CTEA is a "necessary and proper" exercise of the power conferred upon the Congress by the Copyright Clause; assuming Judge Sentelle is correct and *Schnapper* is wrong about the relationship of the preamble to the rest of that Clause, this would require that the CTEA be an "appropriate" means, and "plainly adapted" to the end prescribed in the preamble, "promoting Progress of Science and useful Arts." The Congress found that extending the duration of copyrights on existing works would, among other things, give copyright holders an incentive to preserve older works, particularly motion pictures in need of restoration. *See* S. REP. NO. 104-315, at 12 (1996). If called upon to do so, therefore, we might well hold that the application of the CTEA to subsisting copyrights is "plainly adapted" and "appropriate" to "promoting progress." *See Ladd v. Law & Technology Press, 762 F.2d 809, 812 (9th Cir. 1985)* (upholding the deposit requirement of the Copyright Act of 1976 as "necessary and proper" because the purpose was "to enforce contributions of desirable books to the Library of Congress").

Judge Sentelle concludes otherwise only because he sees a categorical distinction between extending the term of a subsisting copyright and extending that of a prospective copyright. This distinction is not to be found in the Constitution itself, however. The dissent identifies nothing in text or in history that suggests that a term of years for a copyright is not a "limited Time" if it may later be extended for another "limited Time." Instead, the dissent suggests that the Congress — or rather, many successive Congresses — might in effect confer a perpetual copyright by stringing together an unlimited number of "limited Times," although that clearly is not the situation before us. The temporal thrust of the CTEA is a good deal more modest: The Act matches United States copyrights to the terms of copyrights granted by the European Union, *see* Council Directive 93/98, art. 7, 1993 O.J. (L 290) 9; in an era of multinational publishers and instantaneous electronic transmission, harmonization in this regard has obvious practical benefits for the exploitation of copyrights. This is a powerful indication that the CTEA is a "necessary and proper" measure to meet contemporary circumstances rather than a step on the way to making copyrights perpetual; the force of that evidence is hardly diminished because, as the dissent correctly points out, the EU is not bound by the Copyright Clause of our Constitution. As for the dissent's objection that extending a subsisting copyright does nothing to "promote Progress," we think that implies a rather crabbed view of progress: Preserving access to works that would otherwise disappear — not enter the public domain but disappear — "promotes Progress" as surely as does stimulating the creation of new works.

The position of our dissenting colleague is made all the more difficult because the First Congress made the Copyright Act of 1790 applicable to subsisting copyrights arising under the copyright laws of the several states. *See* Act of May 31, 1790, § § 1 and 3, 1 Stat. 124-25. * The construction

---

* Indeed, each of the four later Congresses that extended the terms of copyrights followed suit in doing so for subsisting as well as prospective copyrights. *See* Act

of the Constitution "by [those] contemporary with its formation, many of whom were members of the convention which framed it, is of itself entitled to very great weight, and when it is remembered that the rights thus established have not been disputed [for this long], it is almost conclusive." *Burrow-Giles Lithographic Co. v. Sarony, 111 U.S. 53, 57, 28 L. Ed. 349, 4 S. Ct. 279 (1884).* The plaintiffs, recognizing the import of this "almost conclusive" point for their own theory, try to avoid it with the suggestion that application of the Act of 1790 to subsisting copyrights "is fully understandable under a Supremacy Clause analysis" in that it "clarified which law (state or federal) would govern those copyrights." But that will not do: A federal law is not valid, let alone supreme, if it is not first an exercise of an enumerated power. And the First Congress was clearly secure in its power under the Copyright Clause to extend the terms of subsisting copyrights beyond those granted by the States.

Such guidance as the Supreme Court has given further confirms us in this view of the matter. The Court has made plain that the same Clause permits the Congress to amplify the terms of an existing patent. As early as 1843 it established that the status of a particular invention and its protections

> must depend on the law as it stood at the emanation of the patent, together with such changes as have been since made; for though they may be retrospective in their operation, that is not a sound objection to their validity; the powers of Congress to legislate upon the subject of patents is plenary by the terms of the Constitution, and as there are no restraints on its exercise, there can be no limitation of their right to modify them at their pleasure, so that they do not take away the rights of property in existing patents.

McClurg v. Kingsland, 42 U.S. 202, 206, 11 L. Ed. 102.

Within the realm of copyright, the Court has to the present era been similarly deferential to the judgment of the Congress. "As the text of the Constitution makes plain, it is Congress that has been assigned the task of defining the scope of the limited monopoly that should be granted to authors or to inventors in order to give the appropriate public access to their work product;" that "task involves a difficult balance between [competing interests]" as reflected in the frequent modifications of the relevant statutes. *Sony Corp. v. Universal City Studios, Inc., 464 U.S. 417, 429, 78 L. Ed. 2d 574, 104 S. Ct. 774 (1984).* And still more recently: "The evolution of the duration of copyright protection tellingly illustrates the difficulties Congress faces [in exercising its copyright power]. . .. It is not our role to alter the delicate balance Congress has labored to achieve." *Stewart v. Abend, 495 U.S. 207, 230, 109 L. Ed. 2d 184, 110 S. Ct. 1750 (1990).*

---

of Feb. 3, 1831 § 1, 4 Stat. 436-39; Act of March 4, 1909 § 23, 35 Stat. 1075-88; Pub. L. No. 94-553 § 301, 90 Stat. 2541-2602 (1976); Pub. L. No. 105-298, 112 Stat. 2827 (2000).

IV. Conclusion:

In sum, we hold that the CTEA is a proper exercise of the Congress's power under the Copyright Clause. The plaintiffs' first amendment objection fails because they have no cognizable first amendment interest in the copyrighted works of others. Their objection that extending the term of a subsisting copyright violates the requirement of originality misses the mark because originality is by its nature a threshold inquiry relevant to copyrightability, not a continuing concern relevant to the authority of the Congress to extend the term of a copyright.

Whatever wisdom or folly the plaintiffs may see in the particular "limited Times" for which the Congress has set the duration of copyrights, that decision is subject to judicial review only for rationality. This is no less true when the Congress modifies the term of an existing copyright than when it sets the term initially, and the plaintiffs — as opposed to one of the amici — do not dispute that the CTEA satisfies this standard of review. The question whether the preamble of the Copyright Clause bars the extension of subsisting copyrights — a question to which the analysis in *Schnapper* seems to require a negative answer — may be revisited only by the court sitting *en banc* in a future case in which a party to the litigation argues the point.

For the foregoing reasons, the decision of the district court is *Affirmed*.

SENTELLE, *Circuit Judge, dissenting in part*:

While I concur with much of the majority's opinion, insofar as it holds constitutional the twenty-year or more extension of copyright protection for existing works, I dissent. This issue calls upon us to consider the scope of one of the clauses granting enumerated powers to Congress, specifically, Art. I, § 8, cl. 8:

> Congress shall have power . . . to promote the progress of science and useful arts, by securing for limited times to authors and inventors the exclusive right to their respective writings and discoveries. . . .

In ascertaining the breadth of an enumerated power, I would follow the lead of the United States Supreme Court in *United States v. Lopez, 514 U.S. 549, 552, 131 L. Ed. 2d 626, 115 S. Ct. 1624 (1995)*, and "start with first principles." The governing first principle in *Lopez* and in the matter before us is that "the Constitution creates a Federal Government of enumerated powers." *514 U.S. at 552* (citing Art. I, § 8). The Framers of the Constitution adopted the system of limited central government "to ensure the protection of our fundamental liberties." *Gregory v. Ashcroft, 501 U.S. 452, 458, 115 L. Ed. 2d 410, 111 S. Ct. 2395 (1991)* (internal quotations and citations omitted). The *Lopez* decision, considering the validity of the so called Gun-Free School Zones Act, reminded us that "congressional power under the Commerce Clause . . . is subject to outer limits." *514 U.S. at 556-57; see also United States v. Morrison, 529 U.S. 598, 120 S. Ct. 1740, 1748-49, 146 L. Ed. 2d 658 (2000)*.

It would seem to me apparent that this concept of "outer limits" to enumerated powers applies not only to the Commerce Clause but to *all* the enumerated powers, including the Copyright Clause, which we consider today. In determining whether the legislation before it in such cases as *Lopez* exceeded the outer limit of the authority granted under the Commerce Clause, the *Lopez* Court laid out a precise outline concededly not applicable by its terms to the construction of other clauses, but I think most useful in conducting the same sort of examination of the outer limits of any enumerated power. As a part of that analysis, the Court examined the extension of congressional authority to areas beyond the core of the enumerated power with a goal of determining whether the rationale offered in support of such an extension has any stopping point or whether it would lead to the regulation of all human activity. *See 514 U.S. at 564* ("Thus, if we were to accept the Government's arguments, we are hard pressed to posit any activity by an individual that Congress is without power to regulate."). I fear that the rationale offered by the government for the copyright extension, as accepted by the district court and the majority, leads to such an unlimited view of the copyright power as the Supreme Court rejected with reference to the Commerce Clause in *Lopez*.

What then do I see as the appropriate standard for limiting that power? Again, the *Lopez* decision gives us guidance as to the application of first principles to the determination of the limits of an enumerated power. Citing *Gibbons v. Ogden, 22 U.S. (9 Wheat.) 1, 189-190, 6 L. Ed. 23 (1824),* the *Lopez* Court acknowledged "that limitations on the commerce power are inherent in the very language of the Commerce Clause." *514 U.S. at 553.* Just so with the Copyright Clause. What does the clause empower the Congress to do?

> To promote the progress of science and useful arts, by securing for limited times to authors and inventors the exclusive right to their respective writings and discoveries. . . .

That clause empowers the Congress to do one thing, and one thing only. That one thing is "to promote the progress of science and useful arts." How may Congress do that? "By securing for limited times to authors and inventors the exclusive right to their respective writings and discoveries." The clause is not an open grant of power to secure exclusive rights. It is a grant of a power to promote progress. The means by which that power is to be exercised is certainly the granting of exclusive rights—not an elastic and open-ended use of that means, but only a securing for limited times. *See Stewart v. Abend, 495 U.S. 207, 228, 109 L. Ed. 2d 184, 110 S. Ct. 1750 (1990)* ("The copyright term is limited so that the public will not be permanently deprived of the fruits of an artist's labors."). The majority acknowledges that "if the Congress were to make copyright protection permanent, then it surely would exceed the power conferred upon it by the Copyright Clause." Maj. Op. at 10. However, there is no apparent substantive distinction between permanent protection and permanently available authority to extend originally limited protection. The Congress that can extend the protection of an existing work from 100 years to 120 years; can extend that protection from 120 years to 140; and from 140 to 200; and from 200 to 300; and in effect can accomplish precisely what the majority admits it cannot do directly. This, in my view, exceeds the proper understanding of enumerated powers reflected in the *Lopez* principle of requiring some definable stopping point.

Returning to the language of the clause itself, it is impossible that the Framers of the Constitution contemplated permanent protection, either directly obtained or attained through the guise of progressive extension of existing copyrights. The power granted by the clause again is the power "to promote the progress of science and useful arts." As stated above, Congress is empowered to accomplish this by securing for limited times exclusive rights. Extending existing copyrights is not promoting useful arts, nor is it securing exclusivity for a limited time.

The government has offered no tenable theory as to how retrospective extension can promote the useful arts. As the Supreme Court noted in *Lopez* and again in *United States v. Morrison,* that Congress concluded a given piece of legislation serves a constitutional purpose "does not necessarily make it so." *Lopez, 514 U.S. at 557 n.2* (internal quotes omitted); *Morrison, 120 S. Ct. at 1752.* Pressed at oral argument, counsel for the government referred to keeping the promise made in the original grant of exclusivity for a limited time. The easy answer to this assertion is that Congress is not empowered to "make or keep promises" but only to do those things enumerated in Article I. The second problem with the government's assertion is that Congress made no promise to commit such an extension but only to secure the exclusive rights for the original limited period. Thirdly, the means employed by Congress here are not the securing of the exclusive rights for a limited period, but rather are a different animal altogether: the extension of exclusivity previously secured. This is not within the means authorized by the Copyright Clause, and it is not constitutional.

The majority responds to this problem of the statute's exceeding the constitutional grant by reliance on *Schnapper v. Foley, 215 U.S. App. D.C. 59, 667 F.2d 102 (D.C. Cir. 1981),* "in which we rejected the argument 'that the introductory language of the Copyright Clause constitutes a limit on congressional power.' " Maj. Op. at 10 (quoting *667 F.2d at 112*). I will concede that it does not matter if I disagree with the language of *Schnapper* (which in fact I do) as it is our Circuit precedent and we are bound by its holding unless and until that holding is changed by this court *en banc* or by the higher authority of the Supreme Court. *See, e.g., LaShawn A. v. Barry, 318 U.S. App. D.C. 380, 87 F.3d 1389, 1395 (D.C. Cir. 1996)* (en banc) ("One three-judge panel . . . does not have the authority to overrule another threejudge panel of the court. That power may be exercised only by the full court."(citations omitted)); *United States v. Kolter, 315 U.S. App. D.C. 166, 71 F.3d 425, 431 (D.C. Cir. 1995)* ("This panel would be bound by [a prior] decision even if we did not agree with it.").

Therefore, it is immaterial that the prior opinion is, in my view, erroneous in styling the granting clause of the sentence as merely introductory when in fact it is the definition of the power bestowed by that clause. Thus, unless and until this precedent is wiped away, if *Schnapper* has held that we may not look to the language of this phrase to determine the limitations of the clause then I must concede that we are bound by that holding and join the majority's result. However, it does not appear to me that this is the holding of *Schnapper*. The *Schnapper* Court dealt with limited questions related to the application of the copyright laws to works commissioned by the U.S. government. In answering those questions, the *Schnapper* Court held that "Congress need not 'require that each copyrighted work be shown to promote the useful arts.'" *667 F.2d at 112* (quoting *Mitchell Bros. Film Group v. Cinema Adult Theater,* 604 F.2d 852, 860 (5th Cir. 1979)). It was in that context that the *Schnapper* Court employed the wording relied upon by the majority concerning the "introductory language" of the Copyright Clause. Insofar as that wording is taken to be anything more than the determination concerning that limited analysis, it is not a holding but simply *dicta* (perhaps *obiter dicta)* and not binding on future panels.

Rather, the *Schnapper* analysis again takes us back to the *Lopez* approach to judicial interpretation of the enumerated powers clauses. In *Lopez,* one of the means employed to determine the constitutionality of extended application of the Commerce Clause is an elemental inquiry into whether in each case the purportedly regulated action "in question affects interstate commerce." *514 U.S. at 561.* However, the jurisdictional element is not necessary under *Lopez* analysis of Commerce Clause regulation where Congress is directly regulating "the use of the channels of interstate commerce" or "persons or things in interstate commerce." *Id. at 558.* Similarly, I suggest that in analyzing the extent of congressional power under the Copyright Clause, the *Schnapper* holding that each individual application of copyright protection need not promote the progress of science and the useful arts does not mean that Congress's power is otherwise unlimited, anymore than the lack of a necessity for case-by-case analysis of the effect on interstate commerce validates anything Congress may wish to do under the rubric of the Commerce Clause. Though, under *Schnapper,* we may not require that each use of a copyright protection promote science and the arts, we can require that the exercise of power under which those applications occur meet the language of the clause which grants the Congress the power to enact the statute in the first place. This the extension does not do. It is not within the enumerated power.

The majority suggests that my reading of *Schnapper* is somehow foreclosed by the fact that it accepts the argument of an amicus. *See* Maj. Op. at 11 (citing 16A CHARLES ALAN WRIGHT ET AL., FEDERAL PRACTICE AND PROCEDURE § 3975.1 & n.3 (3d ed. 1999); *Resident Council of Allen Parkway Vill. v. HUD, 980 F.2d 1043, 1049 (5th Cir. 1993)).* The disposition I suggest would offend nothing in either Professor Wright's treatise or the cases aligned with it. Neither I nor the amicus raise any issue not raised by the parties to the case, nor disposed of by a majority of the court. Appellants raise the issue "whether . . . the Copyright Clause of the Constitution of the United States constrains the Congress from extending for a period of years the duration of copyrights, both those *already extant* and those yet to come." Maj. Op. at 2 (emphasis added). The majority addresses that issue and holds against the appellant. Maj. Op. at 15 ("we hold that the CTEA is a proper exercise of the Congress's power under the Copyright Clause"). That the amicus argues more convincingly in appellants' favor on the issue raised by the appellants than they do themselves is no reason to reject the argument of the amicus. Indeed, our Circuit Rules provide that an amicus brief "must avoid repetition of facts or legal arguments made in the principal (appellant/petitioner or appellee/respondent) brief and focus on points not made or adequately elaborated upon in the principal brief, although relevant to the issues before this court." Circuit Rule 29. Obviously that is precisely what the amicus has done in this case.

Resident Council of Allen Parkway Village, relied on by the majority, highlights this difference between introducing issues not raised by the parties on the one hand and making new arguments for issues otherwise properly raised on the other. As the Fifth Circuit noted in that case, "we are constrained only by the rule that an amicus curiae generally cannot expand the scope of an appeal to implicate *issues* that have not been presented by the parties to the appeal." *980 F.2d at 1049* (emphasis added).

Our Circuit Rule and the Fifth Circuit are in good company in allowing amici to make additional arguments that address issues which the parties have raised but not argued in the same fashion. The Supreme Court has approved precisely that approach. In *Teague v. Lane, 489 U.S. 288, 103 L. Ed. 2d 334, 109 S. Ct. 1060 (1989),* that Court considered a question of retroactivity as to a fair crosssection jury venire in a case also raising a claim under *Batson v. Kentucky, 476 U.S. 79, 90 L. Ed. 2d 69, 106 S. Ct. 1712 (1986).* The Court noted that "the question of retroactivity with regard to petitioner's fair cross section claim has been raised only in an *amicus* brief." *489 U.S. at 300.* Noting that the "question is not foreign to the parties, who have addressed retroactivity with respect to petitioner's *Batson* claim," *id.,* the Court proceeded to address the merits of the argument.

Nor are we constrained by the parties' apparent agreement as to the state of the law under *Schnapper.* The Supreme Court has made it clear that we cannot be bound by stipulations of law between the parties, where there is "a real case and controversy extending to that issue." *United States Nat'l Bank of Or. v. Indep. Ins. Agents of Am., Inc., 508 U.S. 439, 446, 124 L. Ed. 2d 402, 113 S. Ct. 2173 (1993).* As the High Court put it, " 'when an issue or claim is properly before the court, the court is not limited to the particular legal theories advanced by the parties, but rather retains the independent power to identify and apply the proper construction of governing law.' " *Id.* (quoting *Kamen v. Kemper Fin. Servs., Inc., 500 U.S. 90, 99, 114 L. Ed. 2d 152, 111 S. Ct. 1711 (1991)).*

I find two other arguments the majority invokes against my dissent unpersuasive. The enactment by the first Congress in 1790 regularizing the state of copyright law with respect to works protected by state acts preexisting the Constitution appears to me to be *sui generis*. Necessarily, something had to be done to begin the operation of federal law under the new federal Constitution. The Act of May 31, 1790, 1 Stat. 124, created the first (and for many decades only) federal copyright protection; it did not *extend* subsisting *federal* copyrights enacted pursuant to the Constitution. *Cf. Wheaton v. Peters,* 33 U.S. (8 Pet.) 591, 661, 8 L. Ed. 1055 (1834) ("Congress, then, by this [copyright] act, instead of sanctioning an existing right, as contended for, created it."). The fact that the CTEA "matches United States copyrights to the terms of copyrights granted by the European Union," Maj. Op. at 13 (citing Council Directive 93/98, art. 7, 1993 O.J. (L 290) 9), is immaterial to the question. Neither the European Union nor its constituent nation states are bound by the Constitution of the United States. That Union may have all sorts of laws about copyrights or any other subject which are beyond the power of our constitutionally defined central government.

Therefore, I respectfully dissent.

ELDRED v. ASHCROFT, ATTORNEY GENERAL

No. 01-618
Certiorari granted, Feb. 19, 2001
Order amended, Feb. 25, 2002

. . . The petition for a writ of certiorari is granted limited to Questions 1 and 2 presented in the petition.

[From the petition:]

QUESTIONS PRESENTED

1. Did the D.C. Circuit err in holding that Congress has the power under the Copyright Clause to extend retroactively the term of existing copyrights?

2. Is a law that extends the term of existing and future copyrights "categorically immune from challenge[ ] under the First Amendment"?

BRIEF FOR PETITIONERS
in the
SUPREME COURT OF THE UNITED STATES

Filed May 20, 2002

. . .

OPINIONS BELOW

The opinion of the United States Court of Appeals for the District of Columbia Circuit is reported at 239 F.3d 372, and is reproduced in the appendix to the petition ("Pet. App.") at 1a. The order denying the petition for rehearing and for rehearing en banc (Pet. App. 24a) is reported at 255 F.3d 849 (2001). The memorandum opinion of the district court (Pet. App. 34a) is reported at 74 F. Supp. 2d 1 (1999).

JURISDICTION

The judgment of the Court of Appeals was issued on February 16, 2001. Petitioners filed a timely petition for rehearing or rehearing en banc, which the Court of Appeals denied on July 13, 2001. The petition for certiorari was filed on October 11, 2001. The Court granted the writ on February 19, 2002 and amended the grant on February 25, 2002. This Court has jurisdiction over this petition under 28 U.S.C. § 1254(1).

CONSTITUTIONAL AND STATUTORY PROVISIONS INVOLVED

The Copyright and Patent Clause confers upon Congress the power:

To promote the Progress of Science and useful Arts, by securing for limited Times to Authors and Inventors the exclusive Right to their respective Writings and Discoveries.

U.S. CONST. art. I, § 8, cl. 8.

The First Amendment provides, in pertinent part, that "Congress shall make no law . . . abridging the freedom of speech, or of the press. . . ." *Id.* amend. I.

The pertinent provisions of the Sonny Bono Copyright Term Extension Act, Pub. L. No. 105-298, Title I, 112 Stat. 2827 (1998) (amending 17 U.S.C. §§ 301-304), and the other copyright laws cited in this petition are reprinted in the appendix to the petition (Pet. App. 54a-67a) and the addendum to this brief.

STATEMENT OF THE CASE

This case is about the limits on Congress's Copyright Clause power, both internal to its enumeration in Article I, and under the constraints imposed by the Free Speech and Press Clause of the First Amendment.

1. The Constitution gives Congress the power to "promote the Progress of Science" by granting "exclusive Right[s]" to "Authors" for "limited Times." U.S. CONST. art. I, § 8, cl. 8. Congress now regularly escapes the restriction of "limited Times" by repeatedly extending the terms of existing copyrights —eleven times in the past forty years.[1] These blanket extensions were initially short (one or two years). In 1976, the extension was for nineteen years. Pub. L. No. 94-553, § 304(a), 90 Stat. 2573-74. In the statute at issue in this case, the Sonny Bono Copyright Term Extension Act (CTEA or Act), Pub. L. No. 105-298, Title I, 112 Stat. 2827, Congress has extended the term of existing and future copyrights by an additional twenty years. *Id.* § 102(b)&(d), 112 Stat. 2827-28 (amending 17 U.S.C. §§ 302, 304).

2. CTEA extends the duration of copyrights within the basic framework of the 1976 Act, which itself changed the system for calculating copyright duration. Before the 1976 Act, duration was a fixed term (28 years), renewable once. Act of March 4, 1909, ch. 320, § 23, 35 Stat. 1080. The 1976 Act replaced the 1909 system with a dual system for calculating terms. Under this new system, the basic term for authors was the life of the author plus 50 years, but for works made for hire, and anonymous or pseudonymous works, the term was 75 years. Pub. L. No. 94-553, §§ 302-304, 90 Stat. 2572-76 (1976).

CTEA extends both types of terms, retroactively as well as prospectively. For any work published before January 1, 1978, and still under copyright on October 27, 1998, CTEA extends the copyright term to 95 years. Pub. L. No. 105-298, § 102(b)(1), 112 Stat. 2827. For work created on or after January 1, 1978, the term depends upon the nature of the "author." If the "author" is a natural and known person, then the term is extended to the life of the author plus 70 years. *Id.* § 102(b)(1)&(2), 112 Stat. 2827. If the author is a corporation (under the work made for hire doctrine), or is anonymous or pseudonymous, then the term is the shorter of 95 years from the year of first publication, or 120 years from creation. *Id.* § 102(b)(3), 112 Stat. 2827. *See generally* 17 U.S.C. § 302(a).

Thus, because of CTEA, works authored from 1923 on, which would initially have begun to fall into the public domain in 1998, will now remain under copyright until the end of 2018 at the earliest —a term of 95 years,

---

[1] *See* Pub. L. No. 87-668, 76 Stat. 555 (1962); Pub. L. No. 89-142, 79 Stat. 581 (1965); Pub. L. No. 90-141, 81 Stat. 464 (1967); Pub. L. No. 90-416, 82 Stat. 397 (1968); Pub. L. No. 91-147, 83 Stat. 360 (1969); Pub. L. No. 91-555, 84 Stat. 1441 (1970); Pub. L. No. 92-170, 85 Stat. 490 (1971); Pub. L. No. 92-566, 86 Stat. 1181 (1972); Pub. L. No. 93-573, Title I, § 104, 88 Stat. 1873 (1974); Pub. L. No. 94-553, § 304, 90 Stat. 2572 (1976); Pub. L. No. 105-298, § 102, 112 Stat. 2827 (1998); *see also* Pet. App. 42a-58a (reprinting statutes). This pattern is substantially different from the history of copyright during the Republic's first 150 years. In the first hundred years of federal copyright regulation, Congress extended the terms of copyrights once. Act of February 3, 1831, ch. 16, §§ 1, 16, 4 Stat. 436, 439. In the next fifty years, Congress again extended the terms only once. Act of March 4, 1909, ch. 320, §§ 23-24, 35 Stat. 1080-81.

unless extended again. Because of CTEA, future copyrights will now extend for the life of the author plus 70 years, or for works made for hire, 95 years, unless extended again. These terms contrast with the Framers' initial term of 14 years, renewable once if the author survived. Act of May 31, 1790, ch. 15, § 1, 1 Stat. 124. As applied to an author who produced throughout a long lifetime in the pattern of Irving Berlin, the current rule would produce a term of 140 years.

3. Petitioners are various individuals and businesses that rely upon speech in the public domain for their creative work and livelihood. Most of the petitioners are commercial entities that build upon the public domain. Best known in this group is Dover Publications, a large-scale publisher of high-quality paperback books, including fiction and children's books. J.A. 18-19. Prior to CTEA, Dover had planned to republish a number of works from the 1920's and 1930's, including "The Prophet" by Kahlil Gibran and "The Harp-Weaver" by Edna St. Vincent Millay. J.A. 19. CTEA has delayed the entry of these works into the public domain by 20 years. *Id.* Other petitioners engaged in commercial ventures face a similar constraint. Petitioners Luck's Music Library, Inc. and Edwin F. Kalmus & Co., Inc. specialize in selling and renting classical orchestral sheet music. J.A. 16-17. Both sell to thousands of customers worldwide, including many community and scholastic orchestras. J.A. 16. Both had made preparations to release new sheet music for work that was to pass into the public domain in 1998. This included the work of Bela Bartok, Maurice J. Ravel, Richard Strauss. J.A. 16-17. Those plans have been blocked for 20 years.

Petitioners Higginson Book Company and Tri-Horn International publish historical works that draw upon the public domain. Higginson Book Company specializes in genealogy, historical maps, and local and county histories. J.A. 14. It reprints works that are in the public domain or with the permission of copyright holders. Because of the expense of tracing copyright ownership, Higginson must often wait until works pass into the public domain. *Id*; *see also* J.A. 14-15 (describing example). Tri-Horn sells products relating to the history and traditions of golf. J.A. 15. Because of the nature of this content, it is often difficult, if not impossible, to identify the copyright owner of this material. As a consequence, although prior to CTEA Tri-Horn expected to be able to release works based on golfers Bobby Jones and Walter Hagen, it has postponed its plans to do so. J.A. 15-16.

The American Film Heritage Association is a non-profit film preservation group. It represents documentary filmmakers and other commercial organizations who oppose copyright term extensions because of their significant adverse effects on film preservation. J.A. 17-18. Moviecraft, Inc. is a related commercial entity that depends upon old film for its business. J.A. 18. Much of this film is "orphaned" because current copyright holders cannot be identified, and all of it is now decaying because of the unstable properties of nitrate-based film and even so-called "safety" film. *Id.*; *see* Brief of *Amici* Hal Roach Studios & Michael Agee at 11-12 ["Agee Br."]. Moviecraft restores these old films when they pass into the public domain but under CTEA no films will pass into the public domain for 20 years. J.A. 18.

Petitioners also include noncommercial individuals and entities that depend upon the public domain. Jill Crandall was a choir director at St. Gregory the Great Episcopal Church, in Athens, Georgia. J.A. 15. The high cost of sheet music for copyrighted works forced her to select much of her music from work within the public domain. *Id.*; *see also* J.A. 16 (noting that Luck's Music sells some public domain works for half the amount charged for renting copyrighted pieces). Before CTEA, she had planned to perform work by Ralph Vaughan Williams and Edward Elgar. Under CTEA, these works will be unavailable for another generation. J.A. 15. Lead petitioner, Eric Eldred, is a noncommercial publisher of existing works and a creator of new derivative ones.[2] In 1995, Eldred founded an Internet-based press, Eldritch Press. J.A. 12. Eldritch Press creates free versions of public domain works for the World Wide Web, as well as works for which he has obtained permission. These works are coded in the hypertext markup language (HTML) that underlies the Web. Eldred's press specializes in collections of Hawthorne, Oliver Wendell Holmes, Sr., and Henry James, among others. J.A. 12-14.

Eldred's creations are both copies and derivative works. J.A. 12-13. By using the technology of the Internet, he is able to build texts that are available freely around the world. By integrating search technologies and links, his texts enable students and scholars to study these works in ways that would be impossible with printed books. *Id.* In this sense, Eldred is building a library of public domain works, but with a technological capacity far exceeding that of the ordinary library.

Unlike a library, however, every part of an online collection is potentially regulated by copyright law. Because each posting of a work is technically a "copy," each posting is within the reach of the Copyright Act. In contrast, a library benefits from the "first sale doctrine," which assures that once a book is sold, that copy can be retransferred and even redistributed free of continuing control by the copyright owners. 17 U.S.C. § 109(a). Libraries can therefore build their collections free of ongoing regulation by copyright law. If the Derry New Hampshire Public Library, for example, wanted to build a special collection of the works of by Robert Frost, including his 1923 book of poems "New Hampshire," it could simply purchase copies of those works and make them available to the public. For Eldred to compile the same collection, he would have to secure the permission of the Frost estate. Eldred's need for a rich public domain is therefore greater than the need of an ordinary library.

The impact on the Internet of the copyright extensions being challenged here is the concern of many of the *amici* in this case. *Amicus* Brewster

---

[2] Other noncommercial activities affected by CTEA are described in the briefs of *amici. See, e.g.,* Brief of *Amici* Internet Archive *et al.* at 1 (libraries and internet archives) ["Internet Archive Br."]; Brief of *Amici* American Ass'n of Law Libraries *et al.* § III.A (historical and cultural preservation projects and scholarly research) ["AALL Br."]; Brief of *Amici* College Art Ass'n *et al.* at 3-16 (educational programs and materials, scholarly works, paintings, novels, art books, dramatic performances, anthologies, and historical publications).

Kahle, for example, through his "Internet Archive," has stored copies of the entire Internet over the past 6 years. With Rick Prelinger, Kahle has also built an archive of public domain movies which will make film available in a digital form to viewers and filmmakers around the world. The technical capacity of this archive is limited only by the number of machines linked to the network. *See* Internet Archive Br. § II.C. But the regulatory constraints of copyright cannot be so easily overcome. The copyright owners of many of these films cannot even be identified. Their work thus cannot be made available on the Internet. Again, were Kahle and Prelinger to build the same archive off the Internet, their licensing costs would be much lower, but their ability to spread knowledge would be more restricted as well. A similar point is raised by *Amici* College Art Association *et al.* on pages 15-16 of their brief. The ability of educators, museum professionals, and librarians to educate depends upon the ability to use creative work. Extensions of copyright terms increase the cost of that education, and restrict the scope of knowledge these professionals can convey.

Petitioners have been harmed because of the delay that CTEA has inflicted on their ability to build upon and use content. Copyright law had, in effect, vested in these petitioners, as well as in the public, a remainderman interest in the works at stake. CTEA took that remainderman interest, and vested it in the current copyright holder. As a consequence, work that was promised to pass into the public domain at the end of 1998 has now been withheld until 2019, with no assurance that in 2019 it will not be withheld again.

Some numbers will put this change in context. Between 1923 and 1942, there were approximately 3,350,000 copyright registrations. Approximately 425,000 (13%) of these were renewed.[3] The Congressional Research Service ("CRS") estimated that of these, only 18%, or approximately 77,000 copyrights, would constitute "surviving works"—works that continue to earn a royalty. The annual royalties for one segment of those surviving works, books, music, and film (which total 49,001 in the CRS study) will be, CRS estimates, approximately $317,000,000 (in 1997 dollars). Edward Rappaport, *Copyright Term Extension: Estimating the Economic Values,* CONGRESSIONAL RESEARCH SERVICE REPORT FOR CONGRESS 8, 12, 15, 16 (May 11, 1998). This means that in order to give the holders of less than 50,000 copyrights $317,000,000 in annual royalties, CTEA has blocked for two decades the entry into the public domain of more than 375,000 other works. Or put differently, because of CTEA, the public will *both* have to pay an additional $317 million annually in royalties for the approximately 50,000 surviving works, and be denied the benefits of those and 375,000 other creative works passing into the public domain in the first 20 years

---

[3] U.S BUREAU OF THE CENSUS, STATISTICAL HISTORY OF THE UNITED STATES FROM COLONIAL TIMES TO THE PRESENT 606 (1965); THE LIBRARY OF CONGRESS, 65 ANN. REP. OF THE REG. OF COPYRIGHTS 16 (1963); THE LIBRARY OF CONGRESS, 70 ANN. REP. OF THE REG. OF COPYRIGHTS 26 (1968); THE LIBRARY OF CONGRESS, 73 ANN. REP. OF THE REG. OF COPYRIGHTS 20 (1971).

alone. (Today, the proportions would be far more significant, since there is no "renewal" requirement that moves over 85% of the works copyrighted into the public domain. Under current law, 3.35 million works would be blocked to protect 77,000.)

4. In January 1999, petitioners filed a facial challenge to CTEA, arguing that the retroactive aspect of CTEA exceeded Congress's power under the Copyright Clause, and that the retroactive and prospective aspects of CTEA violated the Free Speech and Press Clauses of the First Amendment. J.A. 1, 4-26. Standing was based on the harm petitioners have suffered, and the threat of prosecution under the No Electronic Theft Act of 1997, Pub. L. No. 105-147, 111 Stat. 2678. J.A. 7, 10. On a motion by the United States for judgment on the pleadings, the District Court dismissed the complaint. Pet. App. 34a-39a.

Petitioners appealed the Copyright Clause and First Amendment claims to the Court of Appeals for the D.C. Circuit. Over the dissent of Judge Sentelle, the court affirmed the District Court's judgment. Pet. App. 1a-23a.

The court rejected petitioners' First Amendment argument. While it held that petitioners had standing to raise a First Amendment challenge to both the prospective and retroactive aspects of CTEA, Pet. App. 4a-5a, the court held the substance of petitioners' claim barred by circuit precedent and this Court's decision in *Harper & Row Publishers, Inc. v. Nation Enterprises,* 471 U.S. 539 (1985). Pet. App. 5a-8a. According to the circuit court, this authority establishes that there is no "first amendment right to exploit the copyrighted works of others." Pet. App. 8a. By challenging a statute that extends the term of copyrights, the court concluded, petitioners were "by definition" asserting a First Amendment right to exploit the copyrighted works of others. Pet. App. 6a-8a. Indeed, according to the circuit court, "copyrights are categorically immune from challenges under the First Amendment." Pet. App. 6a.

The Court of Appeals also rejected petitioners' Copyright Clause claims. The court rejected petitioners' argument that the term "limited Times" should be read in light of the requirement that Congress "promote the Progress of Science." Pet. App. 10a-11a. The court held instead that this text does not restrict or even influence the scope of Congress's power at all. *Id.* Under the lower court's rule, an extension (or multiple extensions) of a "limited" term was permissible so long as each extension itself was limited. Pet. App. 10a-14a. The court also rejected petitioners' argument that CTEA violated the "originality" requirement of *Feist Publications v. Rural Telephone Service Co.,* 499 U.S. 340 (1991). Pet. App. 8a-10a.

Judge Sentelle dissented from the panel's decision with respect to the "limited Times" claim. Pet. App. 16a-23a. Following this Court's approach in *United States v. Lopez,* 514 U.S. 549 (1995), and *United States v. Morrison,* 529 U.S. 598 (2000), he reasoned that a court must be able to discover the "outer limits" to a power granted Congress. Pet. App. 17a. To do that, Judge Sentelle asked whether "the rationale offered in support of [the extension of power] has any stopping point." *Id.* The answer was "no." The government had argued that any individual extension, no matter how repeatedly conferred, would be constitutional so long as each was for a fixed length. Pet. App. 18a-19a. That "rationale," Judge Sentelle reasoned, led to an "unlimited view of the copyright power"—just the same sort of "unlimited view" this Court had "rejected with reference to the Commerce Clause in *Lopez*." Pet. App. 17a.

Instead, Judge Sentelle maintained, the proper limit to Congress's power is found by "[r]eturning to the language of the clause itself"—in particular, its "grant of a power." Pet. App. 18a. Interpreting that language, Judge Sentelle wrote:

> [I]t is impossible that the Framers of the Constitution contemplated permanent protection, either directly obtained or attained through the guise of progressive extension of existing copyrights. . . . Extending existing copyrights is not promoting useful arts, nor is it securing exclusivity for a limited time.

Pet. App. 18a-19a.

5. Petitioners filed for rehearing and rehearing en banc. J.A. 3. The panel declined rehearing, and the D.C. Circuit denied rehearing en banc. Pet. App. 24a-27a. Judge Sentelle, joined by Judge Tatel, dissented from the denial of rehearing en banc. Pet. App. 28a-29a.

SUMMARY OF ARGUMENT

"The powers of the legislature are defined and limited; and that those limits may not be mistaken or forgotten, the constitution is written." *Marbury v. Madison,* 5 U.S. (1 Cranch) 137, 176 (1803).

This case is about one important limit on the legislature's power that Congress has clearly "forgotten." The Copyright Clause gives Congress the power to "promote the Progress of Science," by granting "exclusive Right[s]" to "Authors" "for *limited Times.*" U.S. Const. art. I, § 8, cl. 8 (emphasis added).

There is no mystery about what the Framers had in mind for the duration of copyright—they expected it would be "short" so that after a "short interval," creative work would pass into the public domain "without restraint." JOSEPH STORY, COMMENTARIES ON THE CONSTITUTION OF THE UNITED STATES § 557, at 402-03 (reprinted with introduction by R. Rotunda & J. Nowak eds., 1987). Nor is there any doubting the Framers' fear about the power that they were creating: the resolution against monopolies was as strong in the framing generation as in any time since; they, more than we, were keenly sensitive to the dangers of state-backed monopolies.

But their hope was that the government might help spur learning and innovation. And to balance their hope against their fears, the Framers crafted the most carefully circumscribed power within Article I, § 8. The Copyright Clause is the only power in Article I that specifies both its ends—"to promote the Progress of Science"—and also its means—"by securing for limited times . . . exclusive Right[s]." Monopolies were to be allowed, but only to "promote [] Progress."

Congress has now found a way to evade this constitutional restraint. Rather than granting authors a fixed (i.e., "limited") term of copyright, Congress has repeatedly extended the terms of existing copyrights—eleven times in the past forty years. These extensions are for works that have already been created. They are not grants that require any new creation in return.

These repeated, blanket extensions of existing copyright terms exceed Congress's power under the Copyright Clause, both because they violate the "limited Times" requirement and because they violate this Court's "originality" requirement. They violate the "limited Times" requirement, first, because terms subject to repeated, blanket extensions are not "limited"; second, because a term granted to a work that already exists does not "promote the Progress of Science"; and third, because the grant of a longer term for already existing works violates the Copyright Clause's quid pro quo requirement—that monopoly rights be given *in exchange* for public benefit in return.

Retroactive extensions of the duration of existing copyrights also violate the Free Speech and Press Clauses of the First Amendment. The court below held that copyrights were "categorically immun[e]" from First Amendment scrutiny. That holding is erroneous. Copyright term extensions, like any content-neutral regulation of speech, must be subject to intermediate scrutiny. The government has offered, and could offer, no "important governmental interest" that could satisfy intermediate review. Moreover, even if the government could identify an important governmental interest, it has not (and could not) argue that CTEA was narrowly tailored to such an interest. This Court should therefore strike down the retroactive aspect of CTEA under the First Amendment as well. And because the retroactive aspect of CTEA is inseverable from its prospective aspect, CTEA's entire extension should be set aside.

This Court has never been called upon to interpret the meaning of "limited Times." It has assumed that this constitutional limit has been respected. As Justice Stevens wrote in *Sony Corp. v. Universal City Studios, Inc.,* because "copyright protection is not perpetual, the number of . . . works in the public domain *necessarily* increases each year." 464 U.S. 417, 443 n.23 (1984) (emphasis added). That "necessity" was certainly the Framers' design. It is not Congress's current practice.

ARGUMENT

I. THE COPYRIGHT TERM EXTENSION ACT'S BLANKET RETROACTIVE EXTENSION OF EXISTING COPYRIGHT TERMS EXCEEDS CONGRESS'S POWER UNDER THE COPYRIGHT CLAUSE

The opinion of the Court of Appeals suggests that alone among the enumerated powers, the Copyright Clause grants Congress effectively unbounded authority. Despite this Court's instruction in *United States v. Lopez,* 514 U.S. 549 (1995), *City of Boerne v. Flores,* 521 U.S. 507 (1997), *Kimel v. Florida Board of Regents,* 528 U.S. 62 (2000), and *United States v. Morrison,* 529 U.S. 598 (2000), that "[t]he powers of the legislature are defined and limited," and that these limits are "not solely a matter of legislative grace," *Morrison,* 529 U.S. at 616, the Court of Appeals ruled that the most distinctive feature of the Copyright Clause—its grant of power "[t]o promote the Progress of Science"— " 'constitutes [no] limit on congressional power.' " Pet.App. 10a (quotation omitted). Thus freed from the Constitution's actual text, the Court of Appeals adopted a reading of the term "limited Times" that permits Congress to evade the Framers' clear intent that copyright terms be fixed, and that after a "short interval," creative works pass into the public domain "without restraint." STORY, *supra,* at 402.

This failure to interpret and apply the limits of the Copyright Clause is error enough in light of this Court's longstanding practice interpreting that Clause. No other clause in Article I, § 8 has a longer history of substantive constraints on Congress's power recognized by this Court. *See Wheaton v. Peters,* 33 U.S. 591 (1834) (rejecting common law copyright); *Trade-Mark Cases,* 100 U.S. 82 (1879) (holding trademark law unsupported by Copyright Clause power); *Graham v. John Deere Co.,* 383 U.S. 1, 5 (1966) (clause "both a grant of power and a limitation"); *Bonito Boats, Inc. v. Thunder Craft Boats, Inc.,* 489 U.S. 141 (1989) (rejecting state law adding patent-like protection); *Feist Publ'ns v. Rural Tel. Ser. Co.,* 499 U.S. 499 U.S. 340, 346 (1991) ("originality" a constitutional requirement).

But especially in light of this Court's clear instruction that enumerated powers are "subject to outer limits," *Lopez,* 514 U.S. at 556-57, and that those limits must be judicially determined, *see Boerne,* 521 U.S. at 557, the refusal to give *any* meaning to the Constitution's plain text ("to promote the Progress of Science") is error. As the Court wrote in *Morrison,* citing *Marbury,* it is so "that . . . limits may not be mistaken or *forgotten* [that] the constitution is written." *Morrison,* 529 U.S. at 607 (citation omitted) (emphasis added). By ignoring the Constitution's text, the Court of Appeals has allowed the Framers' limits to be ignored.

The limits of the Copyright Clause, like the limits of the Commerce Clause, are both express and "inherent in [the] text and constitutional context." *Morrison,* 529 U.S. at 619. As Judge Sentelle argued in dissent below, to determine their scope, a court must identify a "stopping point" to the enumerated power. Pet. App. 17a (Sentelle, J., dissenting). If the government cannot articulate a practical stopping point to the expansion of Congress's power, then its understanding of that enumerated power is incomplete. *Id.*

In this case, the government could identify no such "stopping point." So long as each extension of copyright terms was itself fixed, the government argued that the constitutional requirement was met. That reading, Judge Sentelle rightly found, renders the constitutional restriction meaningless.

"[T]here is no apparent substantive distinction between permanent protection and permanently available authority to extend originally limited protection." Pet. App. 18a. Indeed, as is demonstrated below (*see infra* pp. 23-28), the government's interpretation creates precisely the destructive incentives that the Framers were trying to avoid. Thus under the principle of enumeration, a different interpretation of "limited Times" is required— one that forbids retroactive extensions of existing terms.

In *Lopez* and *Morrison,* the principle of enumeration supported values of federalism. But there could be no principled reason why federalist limits should be judicially enforced while copyright's limits should not. If anything, the reasons favoring the application of a principle of enumeration to the Copyright Clause are more compelling than its application in the context of federalism. The textual limits are more certain; copyright values intersect with First Amendment liberties; and the political interests are not subject to self-regulation through competition between sovereigns. These reasons explain this Court's long history enforcing the limits of the Copyright and Patent Clause. They reinforce Judge Sentelle's conclusion that the principle of enumeration applies to the Copyright Clause as it does to other limits on federal power.

Petitioners do not argue that there is no room for congressional discretion in setting authors' creative incentives through copyright law. *See, e.g., Pennock v. Dialogue,* 27 U.S. 1, 16-17 (1829) ("this exclusive right shall exist but for a limited period, and that the period shall be subject to the discretion of congress."). But it is *"within the limits* of the constitutional grant [that] Congress may . . . implement the stated purpose of the Framers by selecting the policy which in its judgment best effectuates the constitutional aim." *Graham,* 383 U.S. at 6 (emphasis added). There is no discretion over whether the grant has any limits at all.

Nor do petitioners argue, as the Court of Appeals implied, that "50 years are enough to 'promote . . . Progress,' . . . [but] a grant of 70 years is unconstitutional." Pet. App. 10a. Whether 50 years is enough, or 70 years too much, is not a judgment meet for this Court. But whether extensions for works already created prevent copyrights from being for "limited Times," and exceeds a power to "promote the Progress of Science," *is* a judgment that this Court can appropriately make. The line between *prospective* and *retroactive* extensions is a clear one. If "limited Times" is to have any meaningful content, it is a line this Court must draw.

A. Text and Structure of the Copyright Clause

Petitioners' argument depends fundamentally upon the text, structure and original meaning of the Copyright Clause. The Copyright Clause gives Congress the power:

[a] To promote the Progress of Science and useful Arts [b] by securing for limited Times to Authors and Inventors the exclusive Right to their respective Writings and Discoveries.

U.S. CONST. art. I, § 8, cl. 8. (brackets added). To help clarify its meaning, petitioners refer to [a] as the *progress* part of the Copyright Clause, and

[b] as the *rights* part. (As the "useful Arts" is understood to refer to the patent authority, EDWARD C. WALTERSCHEID, THE NATURE OF THE INTELLECTUAL PROPERTY CLAUSE: A STUDY IN HISTORICAL PERSPECTIVE 18 (2002), petitioners refer to the "Progress of Science" only.)

In the context of the framing, the aim of this clause was nothing new. Its structure, however, was distinct. England had passed the Statute of Anne 80 years before; its ideal to "promote learning" was familiar in state legislation of the time. Brief of *Amici* Tyler T. Ochoa *et al.* at 5-6, 11-13 ["Historians' Br."]. That the Constitution would grant Congress the power to "promote learning" was not surprising. The only genuine question was how.

The answer was a clause that is unique within Article I. The Copyright Clause is the only clause in Article I that "describes both the objective which Congress may seek and the means to achieve it." *Goldstein v. California*, 412 U.S. 546, 555 (1973). That "objective" is identified in the *progress* part of the clause— "to promote the Progress of Science." *Feist*, 499 U.S. at 349 ("primary objective"); *Pennock v. Dialogue*, 27 U.S. at 19 ("main object"). The "means" are enumerated in the *rights* part— "by securing for limited Times to Authors . . . the exclusive Right to their . . . Writings." The two parts together grant Congress the power *to* do X *by* means of Y—*to* promote the Progress of Science *by* exchanging time-limited copyrights to authors for their writings.

1. *"To promote . . . Progress"*: The words of the *progress* half of the Copyright Clause have been defined by this Court consistently with the Framers' understanding. "To promote," this Court has said, means "'to stimulate,' 'to encourage,' or 'to induce.'" *Goldstein*, 412 U.S. at 555. "[T]he Progress of Science" means "artistic creativity," *Twentieth Century Music Corp. v. Aiken*, 422 U.S. 151, 156 (1975), "the creative activity of authors," *Harper & Row, Publishers v. Nation Enters.*, 471 U.S. 539, 546 (1985) (citing *Sony*, 464 U.S. at 429), "the creative effort," *id.* at 450, "the creation of useful works," *id.* at 558, or simply "creation," *Feist*, 499 U.S. at 347.[4] The aim was to induce the production of something "new to the world," *Pennock*,

---

[4] At the time of the framing, the term "science" did not have our contemporary meaning. Instead, "science" meant "knowledge" or "learning." WALTERSCHEID, NATURE, *supra*, at 125. In contrast, "Progress" did have a sense that is still familiar today. As Samuel Johnson defined the term, "progress" meant "advancement; motion forward" as in this passage from Locke: "The bounds of all body we have no difficulty to arrive at; but when the mind is there, it finds nothing to hinder its progress into the endless expansion," or alternatively, "intellectual improvement; advancement in knowledge." SAMUEL JOHNSON, A DICTIONARY OF THE ENGLISH LANGUAGE (W. Strahan 1755). The latter definition is closest to the framing purpose. Webster's definition is not far from Johnson's: "[t]he action or progress of advancing or improving by marked stages or degrees; gradual betterment; as, assured of his progress; the history of educational progress; specifically progressive development or evolution of mankind, as a process or fact." WEBSTER'S NEW INT'L DICTIONARY 1977 (2d ed. 1950) (4th entry).

27 U.S. at 20, using a state-granted monopoly "to bring forth new knowledge." *Graham,* 383 U.S. at 8-9.

2. *"By securing for limited Times . . . exclusive Right[s]"*: The technique of the *rights* part of the Copyright Clause was also familiar to the Framers. In exchange for an "exclusive Right" limited in duration, the "Author[]" must produce a "Writing[]." U.S. Const. art. I., § 8, cl. 8. The mechanism is a quid pro quo. *Pennock,* 27 U.S. at 23 (rejecting patent for work released to the public because there "would be no quid pro quo"); *see also Brenner v. Manson,* 383 U.S. 519, 534 (1966) (describing the "basic quid pro quo"). Congress may give authors rights *in exchange for* writings. The clause gives Congress the power to secure a bargain—this for that.[5]

These two parts of the Copyright Clause were plainly meant to function together. The means specified in the *rights* part ("by securing for limited Times . . . exclusive Right") were set against the ends specified in the *progress* part ("to promote the Progress of Science"), so that the limited purpose for which monopolies could be granted would be clear, and not *"forgotten." Marbury v. Madison,* 5 U.S. at 176 (emphasis added). Just as the Necessary and Proper Clause is constrained by the enumerated powers, such that the only power granted by that clause is the power to promote "proper" legislative ends,[6] so too is the *rights* half of the Copyright Clause ("by securing for limited Times . . . exclusive Right") constrained by its enumerated end ("to promote the Progress of Science"). Indeed, the structure of Article I, § 8, cl. 8 mirrors the overall structure of Article I, § 8—the *rights* part of the Copyright Clause stands to the *progress* part as the Necessary and Proper Clause stands to the other enumerated powers.

3. *"Limited Times"*: The duration of the copyright grant was to be "limited." In the framing context, the meaning of "limited" was as plain as

---

[5] This language of "exchange" is uniform throughout the history of the Copyright Clause. The monopoly granted is "the equivalent given by the public for benefits bestowed," *Fox Film Corp. v. Doyal,* 286 U.S. 123, 127-28 (1932); it is to "repay[]" the author for what otherwise "would not . . . have existed." *Butcher's Union Slaughter-House & Live-Stock Landing Co. v. Crescent City Live-Stock Landing & Slaughter House Co.,* 111 U.S. 746, 763 (1884). As Judge Learned Hand described it, the "monopoly [is] in exchange for a dedication" to the public, *RCA Mfg. Co. v. Whiteman,* 114 F.2d 86, 89 (2d Cir. 1940), which this Court held the "States may not render fruitless" by adding new restrictions to the ones that Congress has set. *Bonito,* 489 U.S. at 152. The grant is made upon the "condition" that the work will pass into the public domain upon the copyright's "expiration." *Singer Mfg. Co. v. June Mfg. Co.,* 163 U.S. 169, 185 (1896). The author "impliedly agrees" to this "condition," *id.* at 191-92, as the grant is, as James Madison wrote, "a compensation for a benefit actually gained to the community as a purchase of property." James Madison, *Aspects of Monopoly One Hundred Years Ago,* 128 HARPER'S MONTHLY MAGAZINE 490 (1914). *See generally* Paul J. Heald & Suzanna Sherry, *Implied Limits on the Legislative Power: The Intellectual Property Clause as an Absolute Constraint on Congress,* 2000 U. ILL. L. REV. 1119, 1162-64.

[6] *See Printz v. United States,* 521 U.S. 898, 924 (1997) (citing Gary Lawson & Patricia Granger, *The "Proper" Scope of Federal Power: A Jurisdictional Interpretation of the Sweeping Clause,* 43 DUKE L.J. 267, 297-33 (1993)).

it is today. A term is limited if it is "appointed, fixed," "narrow," or "circumscribed." WEBSTER'S NEW INT'L DICTIONARY 1434 (2d ed. 1950); *see also* SAMUEL JOHNSON, A DICTIONARY OF THE ENGLISH LANGUAGE (W. Strahan 1755) (defining "to limit": "to confine within certain bounds; to restrain; to circumscribe; not to leave at large"). In the drafting of the Copyright Clause, Charles Pinckney of South Carolina first proposed the term "a certain time." "Certain" was struck, and "limited" was put in its place. *See* III DOCUMENTARY HISTORY OF THE CONSTITUTION OF THE UNITED STATES 556 (Dep't of State 1900) (Convention, Aug. 18, 1787). "Certain" suggests a fixed, knowable period; "limited" suggests not just that the period be fixed, but that it also be short in duration. STORY, *supra,* at 402 ("a short interval").

B. CTEA's Retroactive Aspect Violates the "Limited Times" Requirement of the Copyright Clause

This Court has never decided whether Congress has the power, consistent with the "limited Times" requirement, to extend the terms of existing copyrights. It is undisputed that, as the government concedes, and both the majority and dissent agreed below, Congress has no power under the Copyright Clause to grant permanent monopolies. Pet. App. 10a. Thus, the sole issue is whether Congress may achieve indirectly what it cannot achieve directly—a perpetual term "on the installment plan." *The Copyright Term Extension Act of 1995: Hearings on S. 483 before the Senate Judiciary Comm.,* 104th Cong. 73 (1995) (statement of Jaszi) [1995 Senate Hearings].

This Court should hold that it cannot. A blanket extension of existing copyright terms violates the "limited Times" requirement because it is (a) not a "limited Time[]," (b) not a "limited Time[]" that "promotes the Progress of Science," and (c) not compatible with the quid pro quo requirement of the Copyright Clause. These three requirements are all confirmed by the history of the framing context. CTEA fails all three.

1. Retroactively Extended Copyright Terms Are Not "Limited"

As described above, the Constitution requires that the duration of a copyright term be "limited." Under the recent practice of Congress—extending the terms of existing copyrights eleven times in the past forty years—copyright terms are no longer "limited." This practice shows that, rather than fixed, or certain, or "limited," terms are perpetually changeable and expandable. Under the reasoning of the Court of Appeals, so long as each extension is for a fixed length, Congress is free to extend copyright terms ad infinitum. Pet. App. 10a-14a.

The consequence is that no author or artist can rely upon work passing into the public domain. *See* Agee Br. at 10 (describing reliance interests). An author who wants to release a counter-story to a famous novel cannot know when (or whether) that novel will pass into the public domain. *See, e.g., Suntrust Bank v. Houghton Mifflin Co.,* 268 F.3d 1257 (11th Cir. 2001) (suit to enjoin publication of THE WIND DONE GONE). A director who wants to adapt a play in a manner inconsistent with the original author's wish can never know when the author's rights will end. *See* Dinitia Smith, *Immortal Words, Immortal Royalties?*, N.Y. TIMES, Mar. 28, 1998, at B7 (noting that Gershwin's "Porgy and Bess" is only licensed for a Black cast). It is by permitting retroactive extensions that this uncertainty is created, and this uncertainty defeats the Framers' purpose in protecting the public domain. It shows that terms are not "limited."

The government concedes that some limit is necessary. It argued below that "[i]t may well be that some term extensions are so long . . . that a court could conclude that Congress has in effect created an unlimited term." Appellee's Br. 17. But how long is too long? Is 75 years for software "in effect . . . an unlimited term"? As in *Morrison* and *Lopez,* the government promises a limit, but offers no way to find it. On the government's test, "[t]he Congress that can extend the protection of an existing work from 100 years to 120 years, can extend that protection from 120 years to 140; and from 140 to 200; and from 200 to 300." Pet. App. 18a. (Sentelle, J., dissenting).[7]

The uncertainty in this standardless test, and the uncertainty about whether copyright terms expire, means that by any reasonable standard copyright terms are not "limited." On this basis alone, this Court should conclude CTEA exceeds Congress's power, stating a clear and certain test that retroactive extensions are not permitted.

2. Retroactively Extended Copyright Terms Do Not "Promote the Progress of Science"

Because the "limited Times" requirement "stands connected" to the power "to promote the Progress of Science," *Wheaton,* 33 U.S. at 661, its meaning must be determined in light of that specified end. *Id.* The Court of Appeals declined to do this. It expressly "rejected the argument 'that the introductory language of the Copyright Clause constitutes a limit on congressional power.'" Pet. App. 10a.

The conclusion of the Court of Appeals is plainly erroneous.This Court has consistently interpreted the scope of Congress's Copyright Clause power in light of the requirement that Congress "promote the Progress of Science." Indeed, there is no way to make sense of this Court's most significant Copyright Clause cases, *except* in terms of the language and inherent restrictions of the *progress* part of the Copyright Clause.

In *Feist Publications v. Rural Telephone Service Co.,* 499 U.S. 340 (1991), for example, this Court unanimously confirmed that the copyright power

---

[7] There are, to be sure, always line-drawing problems. But it was in part in response to them that the Court in *Lopez* and *Morrison* emphasized also a categorical limit to Congress's power under the Commerce Clause: in *Lopez* the Court emphasized that the law had "nothing to do with the regulation of commercial activity," 514 U.S. at 577, and in *Morrison* that "our cases have upheld Commerce Clause regulation of intrastate activity only where that activity is economic in nature." 529 U.S. at 613. Similarly here, the retroactive extension in the Act violates the Constitution not only as a matter of degree, but also of kind. It crosses the line of any plausible limit.

may only be deployed to protect work that is "original." "Originality is a constitutional requirement," *id.* at 346, "the sine qua non of copyright." *Id.* at 345. Because of this requirement, Congress is not permitted to grant copyright protection to the mere statement of "facts," or to works within the "public domain." *Id.* at 350.

Yet the term "original" does not appear in the text of the Copyright Clause. Nor is this restriction explained by reference to the words "Authors" or "Writings" alone. *Cf. Trade-Mark Cases, supra* (explaining restriction). As this Court defined the term, "[o]riginal . . . means only that the work was independently created by the author (as opposed to copied from other works), *and that it possesses at least some minimal degree of creativity.*" *Feist,* 499 U.S. at 345 (emphasis added). While the requirement that the work be "independently created by the author" might derive from the requirement that copyright be granted to "Authors" for *"their* Writings" (emphasis added), the additional requirement that it "possess[] at least some minimal degree of creativity" necessarily depends upon the concept of "progress" set forth in the first half of the Copyright Clause. For example, abstracted from the clause as a whole (as the Court of Appeals read the term "limited Times"), there would be no violence done to the word "Author" by referring to the compiler of a book of discount and interest rate tables as an "author." Nor would there be error in calling that book a "writing." But a book of discount and interest rate tables is not an "original" work under *Feist,* because a report of "facts" is not the "creation" of the facts reported. Tyler T. Ochoa, *Patent and Copyright Term Extensions and the Constitution: A Historical Perspective,* 49 J. COPYR. SOC'Y USA 19, 47, 51 (2002) (describing example and *Feist*). *Feist's* requirement of "some minimal degree of creativity" can only be explained in light of the requirement that copyrights "promote the Progress of Science." *Accord* WALTERS-CHEID, NATURE, *supra,* at 396-97.

The same conclusion follows from this Court's repeated insistence that Congress may not use its power under the Copyright Clause to "remove existent knowledge from the public domain." *Bonito,* 489 U.S. at 146, citing *Graham,* 383 U.S. at 6 (patents); *Feist,* 499 U.S. at 350 (copyrights). There is no "public domain" clause in the Copyright Clause, and absent the requirement that patents "promote the Progress of . . . useful Arts," there is no textual reason why Congress today could not grant a patent to an "Inventor" for his "Discover[y]" just because that discovery has already passed into the public domain. There would be no misuse of the terms "Inventor" and "Discoveries," for example, if Congress today restored a patent to Thomas Edison (and hence his heirs) for his 1923 patent relating to disk phonograph record production (patent no. 1,546,573), which entered the public domain over half-acentury ago. Yet as this Court has held, in light of the "limitations" built into the clause, "monopolies" are not permitted under the Copyright Clause when there is no "concomitant *advance* in the 'Progress of Science and useful Arts.'" *Bonito,* 489 U.S. at 146 (emphasis added). Instead, as the Court has instructed, "*[t]his is the standard expressed in the Constitution," "and it may not be ignored." Graham,* 383 U.S. at 6 (emphasis added).

These restrictions on Congress's power make sense only in light of the requirement that Congress "promote the Progress of Science." They are consistent with a long line of authority that reads the power of Congress under the *rights* part of the Copyright Clause in light of the ends identified in the *progress* part.[8] They manifest a consistent method for interpreting Congress's power to grant monopoly *rights* under a power to promote *progress.* That same method should apply to the term "limited Times."

So interpreted, a term would be a "limited Time[]" if it "stimulate[s]," *Goldstein,* 412 U.S. at 555, "the creative activity of authors," *Sony,* 464 U.S. at 429. It follows that a blanket extension of existing copyrights cannot be a "limited Time[]" that "promote[s] the Progress of Science." It cannot, because the incentive is being given for work that has already been produced. Retroactive extensions cannot "promote" the past. No matter what we offer Hawthorne or Hemingway or Gershwin, they will not produce anything more. Retroactive extension might promote harmonization— CTEA does not (*see infra* pp. 43-44) but a hypothetical statute could. It might increase the reward to heirs of long-dead authors. It might even induce some to restore decaying films—though again, petitioners deny that CTEA does so, and deny that that alone is a sufficient interest. *See infra* pp. 44-45. These alternative ends might well be actual or legitimate. But they are *not* the ends specified in the *progress* half of the Copyright Clause. *Whatever else* a monopoly protection under that clause may do, it must promote "creative activity" to satisfy the limits of the Constitution. *Sony,* 464 U.S. at 429.

3. Retroactively Extended Copyright Terms Violate the Quid Pro Quo Requirement of the Copyright Clause

The text and structure of the *rights* part of the Copyright Clause ("by securing for limited Times to Authors . . . exclusive Right") imbeds a quid

---

[8] *See Pennock v. Dialogue,* 27 U.S. at 19 (Story, J.) (patent would "materially retard the progress of science and the useful arts"); *Kendall v. Winsor,* 62 U.S. 322, 328 (1858) (same); *Clayton v. Stone,* 5 F. Cas. 999, 1003 (C.C.S.D. N.Y. 1829) (No. 2,872) (Thompson, J.) ("object [of statute] was the promotion of science"); *Baker v. Selden,* 101 U.S. 99, 105 (1879) (relying on *Clayton*); *Higgins v. Keufel,* 140 U.S. 428, 430 (1891) (act read in light of purpose); *Sony Corp.,* 464 U.S. at 477 (rejecting copyrights "in which strict enforcement . . . would inhibit the very 'Progress of Science and Useful Arts' that copyright is intended to promote"); *Campbell v. Acuff-Rose Music, Inc.,* 510 U.S. 569, 575 (1994) ("From the infancy of copyright protection, some opportunity for fair use of copyrighted materials has been thought necessary to fulfill copyright's very purpose, 'to promote the Progress of Science and useful Arts . . .'"); *see also Frantz Mfg. Co. v. Phenix Mfg. Co.,* 457 F.2d 314, 327 n.48 (7th Cir. 1972) ("The congressional power . . . is likewise limited to that which accomplishes the stated purpose of promoting 'the Progress of Science and useful Arts'") (Stevens, J.); ARTHUR W. WEIL, AMERICAN COPYRIGHT LAW 31 (1917) ("Copyright acts must be passed for the promotion of the progress of science . . . [and] for this purpose only").

pro quo. Congress may make a trade—it may grant an "exclusive Right" for a "limited Time[]" *in exchange for* a "Writing" by an "Author." It may not handout a monopoly over speech in exchange for nothing —*quid pro nihilo.* This was the Framers' clear understanding, confirmed by this Court in its cases interpreting Congress's Copyright Clause power. *See supra* p. 16 & n.5.

The retroactive aspect of CTEA violates this requirement of exchange. Whatever material benefit might flow to the author or his heirs or publisher from the extension of this exclusive right, Congress has not conditioned that grant upon a gain by the public. The grant is thus a windfall, not an incentive. Rather than "a compensation for a benefit actually gained to the community as a purchase of property," Madison, *Aspects of Monopoly, supra,* at 490, CTEA is simply a boon to the heirs of copyright holders. It thus violates the core of the quid pro quo built into the Copyright Clause.

Congress certainly has the power to grant such windfalls through tax benefits, or outright gifts. But its Copyright Clause power is contingent upon an exchange. As nothing is received by the public in exchange for, or conditioned upon, the retroactive extension, CTEA is beyond Congress's power.

4. The Historical Context Confirms that a Blanket, Retroactive Extension Exceeds Congress's Power

The Framers had a purpose in crafting the Copyright Clause as carefully, and uniquely, as they did. Petitioners' interpretation of "limited Times" makes sense of that purpose. The Court of Appeals' interpretation does not. Indeed, the interpretation of the court below *exacerbates* the very problem that the Framers were trying to avoid.

The Framers drafted the Copyright Clause against the background of English experience with monopolies in general, and with publishing monopolies in particular. Their clear aim was to avoid the "corruption" experienced with both. Royal abuse of the Crown's prerogative to grant monopoly had been a major cause of the English Civil War. *See, e.g.,* CHRISTINE MACLEOD, INVENTING THE INDUSTRIAL REVOLUTION: THE ENGLISH PATENT SYSTEM, 1660-1800, at 16 (1988). By the time of the framing, England had restrained the excesses of the Crown's monopolistic practices generally, and weakened the monopolistic control the London publishers held on learning. Both experiences meant that the Framers "were not about to give the Congress any general power to create monopolies," WALTERSCHEID, NATURE, *supra,* at 95, nor any specific power to grant monopolies (such as the Copyright and Patent Clause) unless carefully limited.

Of particular concern was the Crown's practice of granting monopolies for objects or items of trade that were already in existence. As this Court has explained, the clause "was written against the backdrop of the practices—eventually curtailed by the Statute of Monopolies—of the Crown in granting monopolies to court favorites in goods or businesses which had long before been enjoyed by the public." *Graham,* 383 U.S. at 5; *see also* George Ramsey, *The Historical Background of Patents,* 18 J. PAT. OFF. SOC'Y 6, 7 (1936) ("during [Elizabeth's] Reign patents were granted that were monopolistic in character and covered most of the necessities of life"). King Henry VIII issued a printer's patent for the Bible. Roger Syn, *Copyright God: Enforcement of Copyright in the Bible and Religious Works,* 14 REGENT U. L. REV. 1, 4 (2001). King James I issued a patent for the "sole right of making certain writs in the Court of Common Pleas," as well as for clay pipes, printing ballads and playbills, gold and silver thread, and most famously, playing cards. Malla Pollack, *Purveyance and Power, or Over-Priced Free Lunch: The Intellectual Property Clause as an Ally of the Takings Clause in the Public's Control of Government,* 30 SW. U. L. REV. 1, 65-66 (2000). Such an unrestrained monopoly power in America, the Framers believed, would simply create the incentive for the same kind of corruption. Henry H. Permit, Jr., *Electronic Freedom of Information Act,* 50 ADMIN. L. REV. 391, 410 n.131 (1998) ("Some of the revolutionary fervor both for the English revolution and the American one more than a century later came from reaction to perceived corruption associated with the grant of [monopolies]").

The practice of granting monopolies to industries already in existence had an obvious, and deleterious, effect not only on consumer welfare, but on incentives to innovate. "The very possibility of securing exclusive privileges was an invitation to those at court to join in the race for favors." WILLIAM HYDE PRICE, THE ENGLISH PATENTS OF MONOPOLY 16 (1906). That race was not for "new inventions." *Id.* New inventions were "left for poor and often chimerical inventors." *Id.* Instead, the powerful competed for "monopolies in old industries." *Id.*; *see also* Paul S. Heald & Suzanna Sherry, *Implied Limits on the Legislative Power: The Intellectual Property Clause as an Absolute Constraint on Congress,* 2000 U. ILL. L. REV. 1119, 1143; DAVID DEAN, LAW-MAKING AND SOCIETY IN LATE ELIZABE-THAN ENGLAND: THE PARLIAMENT OF ENGLAND, 1584-1601, at 163-64 (1996). This in turn produced what the Framers referred to as "the spirit of monopoly"—the tendency to look to government for favors and protection in industry rather than to compete with new innovations and creativity.Hall & Sellers, THE PENNSYLVANIA GAZETTE, Feb. 16, 1785, Item No. 71221.

Today, the conduct that the Framers sought to prevent would be called "rent-seeking"—economically inefficient attempts by some private parties to gain advantage through invocations of the political process.[9] The

---

[9] James Buchanan explains the concept and its historical roots:

Suppose that, instead of discovering a new commodity or service or production process, an innovating entrepreneur discovers a way to convince the government that he "deserves" to be granted a monopoly right, and the government will enforce such a right by keeping out all potential entrants. No value is created in the process; indeed, the monopolization involves a net destruction of value. The rents secured reflect a diversion of value from consumers generally to the favored rent seeker, with a net loss of value in the process.

Framers employed a different vocabulary, but similarly recognized that governmental grants of exclusive rights for already existing creations served no social end, but merely induced private parties to dissipate "effort, time and other productive resources" in currying lawmakers' favor. TOWARD A THEORY OF THE RENT-SEEKING SOCIETY 8 (James Buchanan, Robert Tollson & Gordon Tullock, eds., 1980).

This danger was a particular concern for the Framers in the context of copyright. Until the Statute of Anne (1710), copyright in England had been perpetual. Historians' Br. at 5-6. After the Statute of Anne limited the copyright term, publishers continued to insist that their common law copyright remained perpetual, the Statute of Anne notwithstanding. Not until 1774 was this question finally resolved against the publishers. *Donaldson v. Beckett,* 4 Burr. 2408, 98 Eng. Rep. 257 (H.L. 1774). But by that time, publishers had achieved a strong control over the publication of new works, fueled by their monopolistic control over the publication of old works. The Framers feared that publishers in America would achieve the same power over learning that they held in England. Marci Hamilton, *Copyright Duration Extension and the Dark Heart of Copyright,* 14 CARDOZO ARTS & ENT. L.J. 655, 659 (1996). They therefore crafted the Copyright Clause so as to "prevent the formation of oppressive monopolies." *Aiken,* 422 U.S. at 164.

Their technique was familiar—a "mechanism[] [for] decentralizing and controlling power." Marci Hamilton, *The Historical and Philosophical Underpinnings of the Copyright Clause,* 5 OCCASIONAL PAPERS IN-TELL. PROP. FROM BENJAMIN N. CARDOZO SCH. L., YESHIVA U. 6 (1999). Just as the Framers had responded to fear about federal power (federalism), and to fear about the power of the church (the Establishment Clause), "[t]he Framers' solution [to the fear about concentrated power in publishers] was to divide power, to demarcate its limits, and to establish mechanisms that would guard against [its] aggrandizement." *Id.* Thus, unlike the Statute of Anne, the Copyright Clause gave Congress the power to vest copyrights in "Author[s]," not "booksellers." 8 Anne, ch. 19, § 1 (1710). The "English experience," Professor Patterson has written, "caused the framers . . . to exclude publishers from the copyright clause." L. Ray Patterson, *Free Speech, Copyright, and Fair Use,* 40 VAND. L. REV. 1, 32-33 (1987). The Copyright Clause is thus not so much "pro-author but rather anti-publisher."[10] Hamilton, *Historical and Philosophical Underpinnings, supra,* at 8. By securing copyrights to "Authors" who individually

---

TOWARD A THEORY OF THE RENT-SEEKING SOCIETY 7 (James Buchanan, Robert Tollson & Gordon Tullock, eds., 1980).

[10] Milton had a view of those publishers that was shared generally: "old patentees and monopolizers in the trade of bookselling, men who do not labour in an honest profession to learning is indetted." PHILIP WITTENBERG, THE PROTECTION OF LITERARY PROPERTY 31 (1968) (citing JOHN MILTON, AREOPAGITICA & OF EDUCATION 43 (Kathleen Lea ed., 1973)); *see also* L. RAY PATTERSON, COPYRIGHT IN HISTORICAL PERSPECTIVE 178-79 (1968).

would never control the market generally, and by securing those rights for just "limited Times," the Framers established a mechanism to staunch the concentration of power over speech in the hands of a historically suspect few. Against the background of these concerns over corruption, and over the concentration of power in the hands of publishers,[11] this Court should apply a meaning of "limited Times" that would achieve the Framers' purpose. The Copyright Clause would achieve that end if read to prohibit an indefinite and endless power to extend existing terms.

The interpretation by the court below does not achieve this end. Contrary to the Framers' intent, under the reading of the Court of Appeals, "publishers" retain a perpetual incentive to lobby Congress to extend existing terms. The incentives to decentralize control over speech intended by the Framers are thus erased.[12]

There is no reason that "limited Times" needs to be read to defeat the Framers' plain purpose. A plain meaning of the term, in light of the structure of the clause, and consistent with the history of its interpretation, yields a result that would achieve the Framers' ends. An interpretation of "limited Times" banning blanket retroactive extensions of the duration can eliminate (a) the incentive to lobby for extended terms, (b) the tendency to concentration, and (c) an excessive reliance by those publishers on works from the past to the exclusion of the new.

5. The Copyright Act of 1790 Gives No Support to Congress's Retroactive Extension of Copyright Terms

The Court of Appeals suggested that, because the First Congress in its first copyright act granted copyrights to works "already printed," it itself "extended the terms of existing copyrights," Pet. App. 13a-14a, and so must have considered permissible extensions such as the one challenged here. This argument is plainly mistaken.

The Copyright Act of 1790 did not extend the terms of existing copyrights. As this Court "has repeatedly said, [the 1790 Act] did not sanction an existing right, but created a new one." *Fox,* 286 U.S. at 127; *see also Mazer v. Stein,* 347 U.S. 201, 214-15 (1954); *Wheaton,* 33 U.S. at 661. The federal

---

[11] These concerns are not simply historical. As the Wall Street Journal wrote, the clear effect of "leaving [CTEA] intact will [be to] do nothing more than create an ever-growing cartel of ownership of intellectual property that will stifle the continuing growth and spread of ideas." *Unfair Use,* WALL ST. J., Feb. 21, 2002, at A16.

[12] Indeed, between the interpretation of "limited Times" proposed by the Court of Appeals and a perpetual term, a perpetual term would better avoid the incentives to corruption that were at least part of the Framers' concern. At least with a perpetual term, there would be no need repeatedly to direct resources towards Congress to secure a continuing monopoly right as there had been in England to secure monopoly favor. *See* ROBERT B. EKELUND & ROBERT D. TOLLISON, MERCANTILISM AS A RENT-SEEKING SOCIETY: ECONOMIC REGULATION IN HISTORICAL PERSPECTIVE 18 (1981).

copyright was the replacement for whatever rights—state statutory copyrights, or common law copyrights—might have existed prior to the 1790 statute.

The need for this replacement was obvious to the first Congress, in light of the general and continued confusion about whether there was a common law copyright, and in light of the states' decision (at the request of the Continental Congress) to create state law copyrights. U.S. COPYRIGHT OFFICE, COPYRIGHT ENACTMENTS: LAWS PASSED IN THE UNITED STATES SINCE 1783 RELATING TO COPYRIGHT, BULLETIN NO. 3, at 1-21 (rev. ed. 1963); L. RAY PATTERSON, COPYRIGHT IN HISTORICAL PERSPECTIVE 183 (1968). Although this Court in 1834 concluded in the *Wheaton* case that there was no common law copyright that protected an author after a work was published, *see supra* p. 12, it is clear from the mix of state statutes granting state law copyrights, as well as from the variously expressed views of different Framers and contemporaneous legal authority, that at the time the Constitution was enacted, the matter was at least uncertain. Edward C. Walterscheid, *Inherent or Created Rights: Early Views on the Intellectual Property Clause,* 19 HAMLINE L. REV. 81, 87 (1995); WALTERSCHEID, NATURE, *supra,* at 76; *see also* 1 WILLIAM W. CROSSKEY, POLITICS AND THE CONSTITUTION IN THE HISTORY OF THE UNITED STATES 477 (1953) ("the Common Law of the United States . . . was in a highly uncertain state on the subject of copyrights"). Rawle believed there were common law copyrights in the United States as late as 1825. WILLIAM RAWLE, A VIEW OF THE CONSTITUTION OF THE UNITED STATES OF AMERICA 102 (1825). And Congress in its first major revision of copyright law in 1831 treated copyright as a creature of natural law—mistakenly, as *Wheaton* would show. 7 GALES AND SEATON'S REGISTER OF DEBATES IN CONGRESS 424 (21st Cong., 2d Sess. 1831) ("merely the legal provision for a protection of a natural right").

In light of this uncertainty, the first Congress was fully justified in granting authors and proprietors of "already printed" works a federal copyright to replace any common law or state granted copyright the work might possess. The Framers' aim was to terminate any conflicting state or common law claims. CROSSKEY, *supra,* at 477. The federal grant can thus be understood as a *compensation* for the expected displacement of a state-protected right. *Accord* WALTERSCHEID, NATURE, *supra,* at 436-38.

It is therefore simply incorrect to infer from the 1790 Act that the Framers envisioned a general exception to the rule that "exclusive Rights" were to "promote [ ] progress." The statute of 1790 stands for nothing more than the need of the First Congress to address fundamental issues of transition from a state federation to a national government. *Cf. U.S. Term Limits, Inc. v. Thornton,* 514 U.S. 779, 793 (1995) (citing Justice tory's account of conceptual problems of a transition to a federal government). That they chose this relatively uncumbersome method (as opposed to the formal surrender of a right in the context of patents, *see* Act of February 21, 1793, ch. 11, § 7, 1 Stat. 322) does not demonstrate a general principle permitting the blanket extension of the term of existing copyrights.

To be sure, a rule against retroactive copyright extensions would cast into doubt the 1831 and 1909 Acts, and possibly the 1976 Act. All three can be distinguished from CTEA.[13] As petitioners have argued, the 1831 statute was the product of what this Court determined in 1834 to be a mistaken understanding of the nature of the copyright power. *See supra* p. 29. The 1909 and 1976 statutes simply followed the examples that preceded them. Never during this time was any court asked to rule on the constitutionality of the retroactive extensions under the "limited Times" clause. Neither can the extension in 1831 be attributed to the Framers (no Framer sat in Congress in 1831), nor can two extensions in 150 years be held to be a constitutionally ratified practice. *Cf. Burrow-Giles Lithographic Co. v. Sarony*, 111 U.S. 53, 57 (1884) (deference for "[t]he construction placed upon the constitution by the first act of *1790* and the act of *1802*, by the men *who were contemporary with its formation*") (emphasis added). Whether or not two extensions in 150 years are excusable, the eleventh in forty years must be held to have crossed the line.

6. If Retroactive Extensions Are Not Per Se Invalid, They Must at a Minimum Be Tested for "Congruence and Proportionality" to the Ends of the Copyright Clause

Petitioners advance a *per se* rule banning blanket retroactive extensions of copyright terms. Just as the "originality requirement" bans all grants of copyright to works that are not "original," this rule would ban blanket retroactive extensions of copyright terms as not being terms that are "limited." Such a rule would provide clarity and certainty for both copyright holders and those building upon the public domain.

Even if this Court does not adopt this rule, however, Congress must not be left to define on its own the limits the Constitution sets. At a minimum, this Court should adopt a rule of heightened review, requiring that any extensions be "congruent and proportional" to proper Copyright Clause ends. This Court recognized a similar standard in *City of Boerne* where it wrote that "[t]here must be a congruence and proportionality between the injury to be prevented or remedied and the means adopted to that end" for

---

[13] The 1831 Act extended, both prospectively and retrospectively, the initial term from 14 to 28 years (and left the renewal term at 14 years). Act of Feb. 3, 1831, § 2, 16. In order for a new work to receive a copyright, however, the Act imposed several requirements, including depositing a copy of the work with the federal government for recording and paying a fee. *Id.* § 4. Similar prerequisites were imposed under the predecessor statute, the Act of 1790, Act of May 31, 1790, § 3, as amended by Act of April 29, 1802, ch. 36, 2 Stat. 171, which would have applied to the copyrights whose terms the 1831 Act retroactively extended. Similarly, the 1909 Act extended the renewal term to 28 years for both existing and future copyrights. Act of March 4, 1909, ch. 320, §§ 23-24, 35 Stat. 1080-81. This extension did not automatically benefit every eligible author, however. In order to obtain a renewal term of 28 years, an author (or his heirs) had to properly file an application for renewal in the Copyright Office. *Id.* These requirements had the salutary effect of keeping registrations of existing and protected work. No comparable requirements exist under CTEA or current copyright law.

legislation passed pursuant to § 5 of the 14th Amendment to pass constitutional review. 521 U.S. at 508. The same structure can guide the Court in enforcing the limits of the Copyright Clause.

Like the power to enforce the 14th Amendment in § 5, the power to "secure for limited Times to Authors . . . exclusive Right[s]" is a *means* to a constitutionally specified *end* —to "promote the Progress of Science." Like § 5, the power to "secure for limited Times" also contains language in the "affirmative grant of congressional power [that] also serves to limit that power." *Kimel,* 528 U.S. at 81. Accordingly, as with § 5, this Court should ensure that Congress does not exceed its power to "secure for limited Times" by granting "exclusive Right[s]"where there is no proportional Copyright Clause benefit.

The need for some form of heightened review is particularly clear in this case. The Court of Appeals offered just one justification for the retroactive extension of existing copyrights—that it would create incentives to restore old films. Pet. App. 13a. Petitioners would contest the factual premise of the court's judgment. *See infra* pp. 44-45. As *Amicus* Agee argues, it is the extension of copyright terms that create the transaction costs making restoration impossible. Agee Br. at 10-17. But even if the court below were correct, the notion that the need to restore old films could justify an across-the-board extension to all existing copyrights in all media is simply astounding. Just to encourage the preservation of film, a full generation of creative work is denied to another generation of creators.

Therefore, in the alternative, this Court should reverse and remand for consideration by the court below whether the extension of the existing terms challenged here can be shown to be "congruent and proportional" to Congress's legitimate Copyright Clause ends. *See* AALL Br. § III. The government should bear the burden of such a showing, and the court below should reject it if the extension is significantly broader than is necessary to achieve the government's legitimate end. *Cf. Turner Broad. Sys. v. FCC,* 520 U.S. 180, 182 (1997) (speech burden must be "congruent to the benefits") (*Turner II*).

C. The Retroactive Aspect of CTEA Violates the "Originality" Requirement of *Feist*

Independent of CTEA's violation of the "limited Times" provision in the Copyright Clause, its retroactive extension of existing terms violates the "originality" requirement of *Feist. Feist* requires that copyrights be granted to works that are "original." While existing works with copyrights affected by CTEA were presumptively original when copyright protection first attached, this Court's precedent shows that the constitutional requirement of "originality" continues beyond that initial vesting. If "the sine qua non of copyright is originality," *Feist,* 449 U.S. at 345, then whenever Congress extends to an "Author" an "exclusive Right," that grant too must be tested for originality.

The authority for this claim is *Feist* itself. *Feist* characterized material "in the public domain" as "not original." *Id.* at 350; *see also Harper,* 471

U.S. at 548 ("copyright does not prevent subsequent users from copying from a prior author's work those constituent elements that are *not original* —for example . . . *materials in the public domain*") (emphasis added). But obviously, material in the public domain was, at one point, original. Nathaniel Hawthorne's *The Scarlet Letter* (1850) is in the public domain. If a new copyright could not be granted to it now because it is no longer "original," that is not because it failed to satisfy the requirements of "originality" when written. It must instead be because the requirements of "originality" restrict subsequent grants.

This Court expressed that same understanding in the *Trade-Mark Cases*. In concluding that trademark legislation could not be upheld under the Copyright Clause power, this Court reasoned that trademarks were often granted for expression "already in existence." *Trade-Mark Cases,* 100 U.S. at 94. That fact, the Court held, put trademarks beyond the scope of the "Authors" and "Writings" intended to be covered by the Copyright Clause. Even though some of these marks were plainly, at one point at least, "Writings" by some "Author," the Court found they were not sufficiently "original" to merit a new grant of statutory protection.

The same reasoning should apply to retroactive extensions of existing copyright terms. Such extensions are granted for works that are "already in existence." *Id.* at 94. Like works in the public domain, these works may once have been "original"; but like works in the public domain, they are "original" no longer. Thus, under the reasoning of *Feist* and the *Trade-Mark Cases,* the retroactive aspect of CTEA is beyond Congress's power for this reason as well.

II.   CTEA'S BLANKET RETROACTIVE AND PROSPECTIVE EXTENSIONS OF COPYRIGHT TERMS ARE NOT IMMUNE FROM FIRST AMENDMENT SCRUTINY

Even if Congress were found to have authority under the Copyright Clause to extend copyright terms without regard to their effect upon the "Progress of Science," CTEA violates the Free Speech and Press Clauses of the First Amendment. Under ordinary principles of First Amendment review, the restrictions on speech effected by both extensions greatly outweigh any plausible free speech benefit. The Court of Appeals held otherwise only by declining to apply any First Amendment scrutiny at all to the challenged extensions. Stating that Congress's mere decision to place works under copyright, regardless of the strength or weakness of its justification, "obviates further inquiry under the First Amendment," Pet. App. 7a, the court below announced the novel rule that "copyrights are categorically immune from challenges under the First Amendment." Pet. App. 6a. That ruling was in error.

A. *Harper & Row* Does Not Exempt Copyright Statutes from First Amendment Review

In categorically dismissing petitioners' free speech claims, the court below erroneously relied upon this Court's decision in *Harper & Row Publishers, Inc. v. Nation Enterprises,* 471 U.S. 539 (1985), treating *Harper & Row* as an "insuperable bar[]" to a First Amendment challenge to any copyright statute. Pet. App. 5a. *Harper & Row,* however, is no such thing.

In *Harper & Row,* this Court declined to craft "a public figure exception to copyright" that would have expanded beyond recognition the exception already recognized for fair use. 471 U.S. at 560. Harper & Row had an exclusive right to President Gerald Ford's autobiography. The Nation Magazine "scooped" part of that autobiography without Harper & Row's consent. In defending against an infringement action, The Nation argued that because President Ford was a "public figure," and his pardon of President Nixon was of significant public import, free speech values should trump Harper & Row's copyright interests, forcing an exception to the enforcement of an otherwise valid and pre-existing copyright.

The Nation Magazine did not argue that Harper & Row's copyright was invalid, that the law granting Harper & Row's copyright was unconstitutional, or that copyright law could not properly extend to works about public figures. Instead, it simply asserted that it had a First Amendment right to trespass on Harper & Row's exclusive right.

This Court properly rejected The Nation's argument. By creating an incentive to produce speech that otherwise would not be produced, the Court explained, copyright functions as an "engine of free expression." 471 U.S. at 558. If a work lost that protection simply because it became important, or because it was about a public figure, that would destroy much of the speech-inducing effect that copyright law produced. *Id.* This would defeat the purpose of copyright protection. Thus, so long as copyright law protects expression rather than "facts or ideas," and so long as it preserves space for "fair use," this Court found "no warrant for expanding the doctrine of fair use to create what amounts to a public figure exception to copyright." *Id.* at 560.

This Court's refusal to carve out a public figure exception to the scope of copyright in *Harper & Row,* however, plainly did not establish a general First Amendment immunity for all copyright statutes. At most, the case established a presumption against the need to engage in a First Amendment analysis every time a *copyright owner* seeks to enforce his copyright against an infringer. *Id.* But nothing in *Harper & Row* suggests that *Congress* could evade First Amendment review should it amend the copyright statute to eliminate the idea/expression distinction or to constrict the scope of fair use. Nor would *Harper & Row* immunize from First Amendment review a copyright act that was content-based simply because it reached expression only. (If France, for example, adopted a statute banning copyright for "hate speech," and Congress sought to "harmonize" with that rule, *Harper & Row* would not preclude First Amendment review.) *Harper*

& *Row* simply applied the First Amendment to the existing exceptions for ideas and fair use, and found them sufficient to satisfy the requirements of the Free Speech and Press Clauses on the merits. Nothing in *Harper & Row* obviated the need for First Amendment inquiry into whether a copyright law has permissibly struck the balance between copyright and free speech at the outset.

The First Amendment interests raised by copyright's duration are in any event distinct from the First Amendment interests raised by the scope of protection enjoyed during the term of a copyright. *Harper & Row* held that copyright law is justified by substantial content-neutral interests that make copyright "an engine of free expression," 471 U.S. at 558, *so long as* it creates a market in authors' expression and does not give an author a property right in his ideas, *see id.* at 560; *id.* at 582 (Brennan, J., dissenting), and *so long as* the "fair use" exception limits the scope of a copyright owner's control over his expression. *Id.* at 560.

The idea/expression and fair use limitations, however, are irrelevant to the First Amendment interests protected by limitations on the duration of copyright. The whole point of the Framers' directive that terms be "limited" was that copyrighted works would pass into a public domain where they would "admit the people at large . . . to the full possession and enjoyment of all writings and inventions without restraint." STORY, *supra,* at 402-03. The constitutional interest in the public domain is an interest in guaranteeing access not just to the author's ideas but also his expression. The idea/expression distinction cited in *Harper & Row* and relied on by the court below by definition cannot protect this interest.

Likewise with the limitations of "fair use." As this Court explained,

> [A] use that has no demonstrable effect upon the potential market for, or the value of, the copyrighted work need notbe prohibited in order to protect the author's incentive to create. The prohibition of such *noncommercial* uses would merely inhibit access to ideas without any countervailing benefit.

Sony, 464 U.S. at 450-51 (emphasis added). By contrast, a limitation of the duration of copyright enables both commercial and non-commercial actors to vindicate First Amendment interests in drawing upon the creator's work. The purpose of the public domain—the default state that copyright is temporarily permitted to alter—is to free material for any kind of use. As "fair use" does not extend the benefit of use to commercial and non-commercial actors alike, it is insufficient to vindicate the Framers' objective in limiting copyright terms.

In sum, *Harper & Row* does not bar First Amendment scrutiny of extensions of copyright terms. To the contrary, the injury to vital First Amendment interests caused by elongating copyrights should be reviewed under the very same standard that *Harper & Row* announced and applied: that copyright law may be upheld against First Amendment challenge insofar—but only insofar—as it protects an "engine of free expression,"

Harper & Row, 471 U.S. at 558, and it should be invalidated if its restrictions "merely inhibit access to ideas without any countervailing benefit." *Sony,* 464 U.S. at 450-51. The decision of the court below to bypass the First Amendment entirely was therefore plain error.

B. CTEA Is a Content-Neutral Regulation of Speech Subject to Intermediate Scrutiny under the Standard of *Turner*

By barring the unauthorized use or dissemination of copyrighted works, copyright law regulates speech. To be sure, copyright law is content-neutral speech regulation, for its sole purpose is to provide an economic incentive for authors to produce "original" work, without regard to the content of the material protected, the viewpoint of the author, or the subject matter of the speech. *See, e.g., CBS Broad., Inc. v. EchoStar Communications Corp.,* 265 F.3d 1193, 1211 (11th Cir. 2001) (copyright law is content-neutral speech regulation), *petition for cert. filed,* 70 U.S.L.W. 3626 (Mar. 28, 2002) (No. 01-1450); *Satellite Broad. & Communications Ass'n v. FCC,* 275 F.3d 337, 355 (4th Cir. 2001) (same), *petition for cert. filed,* 70 U.S.L.W. 3580 (Mar. 7, 2002) (No. 01-1332); *Universal City Studios, Inc. v. Corley,* 273 F.3d 429, 450-51 (2d Cir. 2001) (same); *see also* Neil Weinstock Netanel, *Locating Copyright Within the First Amendment Skein,* 54 STAN. L. REV. 1, 47-54 (2001). But there can be no dispute that copyright law prevents willing speakers who would adapt or distribute copyrighted works from reaching willing audiences. It is regulation "in derogation of common right," as Jefferson's attorney general, Levi Lincoln, said of patents. Levi Lincoln, *Patents for Inventions, 26 May 1802, reprinted in* 3 THE FOUNDERS' CONSTITUTION 41 (P. Kurland & R. Lerner eds., 1987). It is therefore speech regulation.

The significance of this speech regulation has only increased over time. The scope of the monopoly that the government confers under the copyright laws has expanded dramatically over the nation's history, and with it the severity of copyright's interference with freedom of speech. The "exclusive Right" of which the Framers spoke was little more than an unfair competition law, directed exclusively against publishers, reaching only the right to "publish, republish, and vend" a particular writing, and lasting for just 14 years, renewable once. Act of May 31, 1790, § 1, 1 Stat. 124. In the two centuries since, Congress has expanded this "exclusive Right" to cover "copying" as well as publishing, to regulate derivative as well as original works, and to last often for more than a century. The consequence is that authors now may bar translations, abridgments, dramatizations, performances, and other uses of copyrighted works that the Framers left unregulated. *See* 17 U.S.C. § 106; Netanel, *supra,* at 16-17. And now, because of the emergence of the Internet (and the technological fact that every interaction in the context of the Internet makes a "copy" of something), copyright law will increasingly control ordinary uses of creative content in activities that before the Internet were not even remotely within the reach of copyright. *See, e.g.,* L. Ray Patterson & Judge Stanley F. Birch, *Copyright and Free Speech Rights,* 4 J. INTELL. PROP. L. 1, 3 (1996) ("New technology provides new means [to] enable[] the copyright owner to control access"); L. Ray Patterson, *Free Speech, Copyright, and Fair Use, supra,* at 48 ("copyright owner's right to control access to the work far exceeds what could have been imagined in 1841").

These changes are not necessarily improper. But they must be tested against unchanging principles—that speech regulations go no further than is necessary to achieve important governmental interests. Accordingly, like any other form of content-neutral regulation that tries to balance free speech interests "on both sides of the equation," *Turner II,* 520 U.S. at 227 (Breyer, J., concurring), CTEA should be subject to intermediate scrutiny under the First Amendment. Like cable regulation (which restricts the free speech rights of cable operators in order to balance speech rights of viewers, *see Turner II, supra*), or privacy regulation (which "directly interfere[s] with free expression . . . [in order] to protect . . . an interest . . . 'in fostering private speech,'" *Bartnicki v. Vopper,* 532 U.S. 514, 536 (2001) (Breyer, J., concurring)), copyright regulation restrictsthe reach of the public domain in order to fuel an "engine of free expression" by authors. But like all regulation that allocates the right to speak among speakers, copyright regulation too must be justified under intermediate review. *Cf. Turner Broadcasting v. FCC,* 512 U.S. 622, 675-76 (1994) (describing speaker-based regulation subject to intermediate scrutiny) (Turner I).

C. CTEA's Retroactive Extension of Copyright Does Not Satisfy Intermediate Scrutiny

CTEA can withstand First Amendment review only "[1] if it advances important governmental interests unrelated to the suppression of free speech and [2] does not burden substantially more speech than necessary to further those interests." *Turner II,* 520 U.S. at 189; *see also United States v. O'Brien,* 391 U.S. 367, 377 (1968); *Ward v. Rock Against Racism,* 491 U.S. 781, 791 (1989) (applying intermediate scrutiny to time, place, and manner regulation of speech in the public forum); *San Francisco Arts & Athletics, Inc. v. U.S. Olympic Comm.,* 483 U.S. 522, 537 (1987) (applying *O'Brien* review to a law protecting the word "Olympic" under trademark law).

In *Turner,* this Court suggested that the "important governmental interests" advanced to sustain such regulation must have been Congress's at the time it legislated. As the Court wrote, a reviewing court must "assure that, in formulating its judgments, Congress has drawn reasonable inferences based on substantial evidence." *Turner I,* 512 U.S. at 666; *Turner II,* 520 U.S. at 195. But whether this Court limits itself to what Congress considered, or considers anew any interest the government could have advanced, CTEA cannot sustain the burden of intermediate review. The "mere assertion of dysfunction or failure in a speech market, without more, is not sufficient to shield a speech regulation" from First Amendment review, 512 U.S. at 640, and Congress engaged in little more than "assertion" in this case.

Indeed, as we now show, the legislative record falls so far short of *Turner*'s requirements that this Court may review CTEA under the *Turner* standard and deem it invalid on its face without remand.[14]

1. CTEA Fails to Advance an "Important Governmental Interest"

In the court below, the government did not advance any interest in retroactive copyright extension that it claimed would satisfy intermediate scrutiny. Nor could it, for the only contentneutral interest that this Court has recognized as sustaining copyright's speech restrictions—namely, providing incentives to authors to create original works, *Harper,* 471 U.S. at 558—is irrelevant once a work has been created. *See* Pet. App. 32a-33a; Brief of *Amici* Akerlof *et al.* at 3-9 ["Economists' Br."] The other reasons the government might advance for CTEA's retroactive extension of the duration of copyright are all either illegitimate, insignificant, or hypothesized after the fact in violation of *Turner*'s actual purpose requirement. None is substantial enough to outweigh the free speech burden upon those who have long relied on the expectation that the "limited Times" requirement would assure that works would enter the table domain.

a. *Income to heirs*: The government argued below that Congress's desire to secure a longer economic return to aged living authors and dead authors' heirs is a sufficient justification for the retroactive extension of terms under rational basis scrutiny. *See* Appellee's Br. at 22-28. But windfall benefits for the economic well-being of authors and their heirs *independent of any claimed incentive to create* cannot constitute a legitimate, much less an important or substantial, governmental interest sufficient to justify a restriction of speech. Whatever their permissibility elsewhere in the legislative lexicon, naked wealth transfers between speakers are forbidden by the First Amendment. *Buckley v. Valeo,* 424 U.S. 1, 48-49 (1976) ("[T]he concept that government may restrict the speech of some elements of our society in order to enhance the relative voice of others is wholly foreign to the First Amendment").

By retroactively extending copyright terms, Congress is directly reallocating the right to speak. It is choosing favored speakers (including rightly-beloved speakers, such as Disney, or the estate of Robert Frost) and

---

[14] Because the prospective extension of copyrights in CTEA is inseverable from the retroactive, *see infra* § III, the prospective extension stands or falls under the First Amendment with the strength of the justification for the retroactive extension. Alternatively, this Court should strike the retroactive extension and remand for an evidentiary hearing under the *Turner* standard on the prospective extension.

Because the court of appeals found CTEA immune from First Amendment scrutiny, it did not conduct the *Turner* balancing. Accordingly, our petition sought only a remand on the First Amendment claims. However, in its opposition, the Government broadened the second question to include the merits of the First Amendment claim, and therefore we believe that the Court may consider it. As Part III of this brief demonstrates, a remand is necessary to consider the non-severability of the prospective CTEA extension from the retroactive extension.

disfavoring other speakers who would, but for this regulation, be permitted to develop derivative works, or perform free of the restrictions of copyright. Such speech restrictions for the benefit of some speakers at the expense of other speakers and listeners, if unrelated to the incentive to create, are no more sanctioned by the First Amendment than a tax on CNN to benefit C-SPAN. *Cf. Turner I,* 512 U.S. at 676 (O'Connor, J., dissenting) (noting that a "preference for broadcasters over cable programmers" that was "justified with reference to content" rather than market incentives would be subject to strict scrutiny under the First Amendment).

b. *Speech promotion*: The only justification this Court has ever recognized for restricting speech in order to benefit authors has been the incentives that restriction produces to create more speech. *See* Rebecca Tushnet, *Copyright as a Model for Free Speech Law,* 42 B.C. L. REV. 1, 35-67 (2000); Netanel, *supra,* at 26-30. Such an incentive to create could qualify as an "important governmental interest" *if* Congress could reasonably have believed that the restriction it imposed through CTEA's retroactive copyright extensions actually advanced the incentive to create. But no such plausible inference is possible when the extension is granted long after the moment of creation or in many cases after the author's own death.

The government argued below that a windfall to the heirs of creators, and to companies that hold copyrights, might inspire them to produce new, creative work that they otherwise would not have created. *See* Appellee's Br. at 37. Were this true, it might well constitute an "important governmental interest." But Congress had before it no evidence whatever that creators' heirs or corporate holders of copyrights are more likely to make creative use of earlier work than those who, like petitioners, have eagerly awaited that work's entry into the public domain. Neither is there any such evidence. Nor is there any logical reason to conclude that such windfalls would increase creativity. When copyright is offered as a quid pro quo, the conferral provides an important incentive. But when an extension is granted without a quid pro quo, there is no change in incentives to produce. Economists' Br. at 8-10; ROBERT L. BARD & LEWIS KURLANTZICK, COPYRIGHT DURATION 59-63, 81-84 (1999). The extension is a windfall, pure and simple, not an "engine of free expression." There is no more reason to believe the heirs of Gershwin will use this windfall to produce new work than that they will use it to fund a longer vacation. As Congressman Hoke stated, in support of CTEA, "I think it's a sham to try to hang on the theory that we're creating incentives." *Copyright Term, Film Labeling, and Film Preservation Legislation: Hearings on H.R. 989, H.R. 1248, and H.R. 1734 Before the Subcomm. on Courts and Intell. Prop. of the House Comm. on the Judiciary,* 104th Cong., 420 (1995) (Statement of Rep. Hoke) [1995 House Hearings].

c. *Harmonization with international regimes*: The government has also argued that harmonization with European copyright terms provides a rational basis for the retroactive extension of terms. With respect to existing works, however, the only effects that harmonization might possibly have are (1) reducing the transaction costs for commercial use of copyrighted work, or (2) increasing income to authors and their heirs. The second interest is insufficient for the reasons already given. The first interest is not one that CTEA plausibly advances, and even if it did, it would be insufficiently substantial to satisfy intermediate review.

The government has yet to demonstrate any meaningful sense in which CTEA "harmonized" copyright terms. Nor could it, for CTEA in fact does no such thing. As the Register of Copyrights, Marybeth Peters testified, the bill "does not completely harmonize our law with the [EU directive]. In some cases, the U.S. term would be longer; in others the EU terms would be." 1995 House Hearings, *supra,* at 197. Scholars agreed that CTEA would achieve no harmonization between American and global property regimes. *Id.* 305 (statement of Professor Karjala); 349 (statement of Professor Patry); 382-87 (statement of Professor Reichman); *see also* Copyright Law Professors Br. at 16-20; BARD & KURLANTZICK, *supra,* 191-93, 198-200 nn. 276-77. Indeed, as many noted, CTEA actually *increases* the disharmony between American and EU law. *See, e.g.,* 1995 House Hearings, *supra,* at 372 (statement of Prof. Reichman) (noting that CTEA would "unilaterally worsen the existing disparities").

The fantasy of alleged "harmonization" is apparent from even a cursory review of the statute. The only categories of work that CTEA harmonized are works by non-corporate authors after 1978. Every other category of published copyrighted work has either not been harmonized, or has had its dissonance increased. *See* Dennis S. Karjala, *Harmonization Chart,* http://makeashorterlink.com/?R2FB432E (mapping out difference between U.S. and EU law) (reprinted in Addendum at 15a-19a). Six out of twenty categories of copyright are actually *less* harmonized now than they were prior to CTEA. *Id.* In no meaningful sense, then, can CTEA be said to harmonize terms.

Even with respect to the work of non-corporate authors after 1978, however, the government has yet to show how the change from life plus 50 to life plus 70 increased harmonization from a global perspective. There are 76 countries today with a life plus 50 regime but only 26 with life plus 70. *See* National Copyright Legislation, *http://www.unesco.org/culture/copy.* CTEA, thus, moved the United States from the dominant world standard to a minority one. The copyright term within the United States is therefore actually less harmonized with foreign copyright terms today than before CTEA and in important categories even less harmonized with EU policy.

But even assuming CTEA did actually harmonize terms, the only possible benefit from harmonization *itself* is a reduction in the transaction costs of copyright licensing. Congress made no showing—nor could it—that the transaction costs in calculating terms were interfering with the creation of copyrighted work. But even if it could, merely increasing administrative convenience has never been deemed a sufficiently substantial governmental interest to satisfy intermediate review. As this Court has held in parallel contexts, the reduction of administrative burdens is not an "important governmental interest" that could satisfy any standard more demanding than mere rationality review. *See, e.g., Frontiero v. Richardson,* 411 U.S. 677, 690 (1973) (holding "any statutory scheme which draws a sharp line between the sexes, solely for the purpose of achieving administrative convenience," violates equal protection). Nor should such an interest, even if found credible, be found substantial here.

d. *Preservation of existing works*: Finally, the government has argued, and the Court of Appeals found below, that CTEA's retroactive extension of copyright would provide an incentive "to preserve older works, particularly motion pictures in need of restoration." Pet. App. 12a.

Were there any substantial evidence in the legislative record to support the belief that longer terms would increase the incentives of holders of "older works" to restore them, this might well be an "important governmental interest." (It would not, however, constitute a Copyright Clause interest if the restored work were not "original." *Feist, supra.*). But as *Amici* College Art Association *et al.* demonstrate, there was absolutely no credible evidence presented to Congress upon which this Court could rely to conclude that CTEA would spur restoration. *See* College Art Ass'n Br. at 19-20. Indeed, as *Amici* Agee exhaustively demonstrates, extended terms *reduce* the likelihood that films will be restored. More often than not, the most significant barrier to restoring and distributing old films is the legal barrier caused by old and untraceable copyrights. *See* Agee Br. at 14-17. The large number of "orphaned" films described by the Librarian of Congress testifies to the costs of extended terms. Report of the Librarian of Congress, *Film Preservation 1993:A Study of the Current State of American Film Preservation* 5-10 (1993). These are films that cannot be restored and distributed by the copyright owners because the owners cannot be identified. Increased terms only increase this cost. *See* AALL Br. at 21-25; Agee Br. at 15-17; College Art Ass'n Br. at 5-10. There is no way, on the legislative record actually compiled, that this Court could conclude that Congress found to the contrary on the basis of substantial evidence.

2. CTEA Burdens Substantially More Speech than Necessary

Even if the government could demonstrate that CTEA advanced an important governmental interest in speech promotion or preservation, the law burdens far more speech than necessary to achieve such interests. While a content-neutral "regulation need not be the least speech-restrictive means of advancing the Government's interests," *Turner I,* 512 U.S. at 662, the requirement of intermediate scrutiny is not satisfied when a "substantial portion of the burden on speech does not serve to advance" the important governmental interest. *Id.* at 682 (O'Connor, dissenting). "That some speech within a broad category causes harm . . . does not justify restricting the whole category." *Id.*

The example relied upon by the Court of Appeals—the supposed incentive to film preservation—is the clearest case of such excessive overbreadth. Based on the figures provided by the Congressional Research Service, it can be estimated that approximately 19,000 films under copyright from 1923-42 have been affected by CTEA. Of these, 5,000 would continue to earn royalties and survive to expiration. Rappaport, *supra,* at 15. If the interest advanced by the government is that films that would not have been restored will now be restored because of CTEA, then it could only be a portion of the remaining 14,000 films.

Yet even if CTEA produced enough incentive to restore all of these films, there is no reason for CTEA to reach beyond these films to *all copyrighted material,* including books, magazine articles, works of art, music and musical recordings, plays, and other artistic creations bearing no relation whatever to the physical properties of decaying celluloid film. More than 400,000 works are affected by the extension of CTEA in its first 20 years. *See supra* p. 7. The preservation of even 15,000 films could not possibly justify the exclusion of willing speakers and listeners from use of more than 400,000 other creative works. Congress may not "burn the house to roast the pig." *Butler v. Michigan,* 352 U.S. 380, 383 (1957). A restriction of all existing copyrights just to save a relatively tiny number of films restricts "substantially more speech than is necessary to further the government's legitimate interests." *Ward,* 491 U.S. at 799.

In any event, Congress could easily have achieved the same alleged pro-speech benefit by conditioning the extension of copyright upon the copyright holder's restoration of the endangered work. By granting an extension that is unconditional, Congress not only provides a weak incentive for copyright holders to restore these old works, but also creates a legal thicket ensuring that no one else can restore these works either. As the Librarian of Congress testified, the vast majority of old, early films needing preservation have copyrights that are held by unknown entities. *Redefining Film Preservation: A National Plan; Recommendations of the Librarian of Congress in Consultation with the National Film Preservation Board* 25 (1994). These "orphaned works" cannot be released because the copyrights cannot be cleared. Here the law serves no function except to block access to creative works. A more narrowly tailored restriction could have avoided this harm.

The same problem with extreme overbreadth affects each of the other alleged governmental interests that might be asserted in CTEA's defense. If international harmonization is an important governmental interest, then it would only justify extensions that actually harmonized terms, or harmonization for foreign works only, or harmonized prospectively. CTEA's extensions do not. If the incentive to heirs of authors or holders of copyright were an important governmental interest, then Congress could have conditioned the grant upon new creativity. There was no need to grant a windfall rather than the traditional quid pro quo. And finally, if income to heirs of authors were a legitimate, much less an important, governmental interest, then Congress could have adopted the proposal of the Congressional Research Service to make any extension contingent upon the payment of a user fee. Then only owners of copyrights in works generating an estimated income exceeding the user fee would pay the fee. Rappaport, *supra,* at 17-20. The balance of the copyrighted works would have passed into the public domain.

On the legislative record actually compiled in Congress, it is impossible to conclude that Congress could rationally have found CTEA's blanket retroactive copyright term extension narrowly tailored to increasing speech or any other important governmental interest. This Court should therefore find the retroactive aspect of CTEA unconstitutional, and strike down its prospective aspect as inseverable (see Part III below).

3. At a Minimum, the First Amendment Requires Reversal and Remand for Development of an Evidentiary Record

If this Court cannot conclude on the record before it whether CTEA survives intermediate scrutiny under the First Amendment, then it should remand this case to the District Court to hold a *Turner* hearing to consider the evidence. While petitioners have requested intermediate scrutiny throughout this litigation, neither the District Court nor the Court of Appeals conducted any First Amendment review whatever. As a consequence, if this Court believes that CTEA might be justified by some argument not yet advanced or fully articulated by the government, it should reverse the judgment below and remand with instructions that any such proffered justifications be subjected to intermediate scrutiny as set forth in *Turner.*

III. CTEA'S PROSPECTIVE AND RETROACTIVE EXTENSIONS OF COPYRIGHT TERMS ARE INSEVERABLE

If this Court agrees with petitioners that CTEA is unconstitutional in its retroactive extension of existing copyrights, then it must decide how the court below should proceed on remand. While this question is not expressly within the scope of the questions presented, petitioners are bound to advise this Court that under its precedents, the retroactive aspect of CTEA cannot be severed from the prospective aspect. As petitioners argued below, *see* Pl. Summ. J. Mem. at 87-89, § 102 of CTEA must therefore be struck in its entirety.

As this Court has recognized, the standard for severability is "well established: 'Unless it is evident that the Legislature would not have enacted those provisions which are within its power, independently of that which is not, the invalid part may be dropped if what is left is fully operative as a law.'" *Alaska Airlines, Inc. v. Brock,* 480 U.S. 678, 684 (1987) (citing *Buckley v. Valeo,* 424 U.S. 1, 108 (1976) (per curiam), quoting *Champlin Ref. Co. v. Corp. Comm'n of Okla.,* 286 U.S. 210, 234 (1932)). Of course, "Congress could not have intended a constitutionally flawed provision to be severed from the remainder of the statute if the balance of the legislation is incapable of functioning independently." *Alaska Airlines,* 480 U.S. at 684. Moreover, it is impermissible for a court "to give to the words used by Congress a narrower meaning than they are manifestly intended to bear,"

Trade-Mark Cases, 100 U.S. at 98, or "to dissect an unconstitutional measure and reframe a valid one out of it *by inserting limitations it does not contain." Hill v. Wallace,* 259 U.S. 44, 70 (1922) (emphasis added).

Although CTEA is silent on the issue of severability, it is immediately apparent on the face of § 102 that it cannot be severed in a way to apply only prospectively to works created *after CTEA became effective.* Subsection (b) contains the relevant portion of § 102 that applies prospectively to works created after CTEA's effective date. Pub. L. No. 105-298, § 102(b). That subsection, however, applies retroactively as well, applying generally to "works created on or after January 1, 1978." *Id.* There is no distinction made in § 102(b) between retroactive or prospective application of CTEA— between works, in other words, that are produced on or after October 27, 1998, and works created before.

Likewise, 17 U.S.C. § 302, the relevant section of the Copyright Act which was amended by § 102(b) of CTEA, suffers from the same flaw: it applies generally to "a work created on or after January 1, 1978" and contains no language whatsoever that can limit CTEA's application *to works created on or after the date CTEA became effective.* Those words simply do not appear anywhere in the provision. To insert those limiting words now is "legislative work beyond the power and function of the court." *Hill,* 259 U.S. at 70. *Cf. Sloan v. Lemon,* 413 U.S. 825, 834 (1973) (statute that gave financial aid to students of nonpublic schools violated Establishment Clause and could not be severed to apply only to nonpublic, nonsectarian schools because "[t]he statute nowhere sets up this suggested dichotomy between sectarian and nonsectarian schools").[15] As this Court has long recognized, severability cannot be achieved "by inserting [words] that are not now there." *United States v. Reese,* 92 U.S. 214, 221 (1875); *see also Reno v. ACLU,* 521 U.S. 844, 884-85 (1997) ("This Court 'will not rewrite a . . . law to conform it to constitutional requirements.'") (quoting *Virginia v. Am. Booksellers Ass'n,* 484 U.S. 383, 397 (1988)). Accordingly, § 102 of CTEA must be struck in its entirety.

There is no reason in the text or history of CTEA to suppose that Congress would have enacted the prospective aspect absent its retroactive aspect. Where Congress fails to include a severability clause, and fails to craft the Act to permit severability, there is no warrant for this Court to engage in legislative drafting.

---

[15] Even were it permissible for a court to insert limiting words in a statute in place of the ones found there, this Court could not merely insert "works created on or after CTEA became effective" in place of "works created on or after January 1, 1978" in 17 U.S.C. § 302, since to do so would create a gap in the law. There would be no provision in the Copyright Act to set the term duration for works created on or after January 1, 1978 but before CTEA became effective. An entirely new provision would have to be drafted to cover those works—a task which is clearly Congress's.

CONCLUSION

For the foregoing reasons, this Court should reverse the decision of the Court of Appeals for the D.C. Circuit and remand to the District Court for further proceedings, holding (1a) that the retroactive aspect of CTEA is beyond Congress's Copyright Clause power, or (1b) that the retroactive aspect of CTEA must be found to be "congruent and proportional" to the relevant Copyright Clause ends; (2) that copyright is not "immune" from First Amendment review, and (2a) that the retroactive aspect of CTEA violates the First Amendment or (2b) that the prospective and retroactive aspects of CTEA must be tested under intermediate First Amendment review; and (3) if the retroactive aspect of CTEA is invalid, then the prospective aspect is invalid because not severable.

BRIEF FOR RESPONDENT
in the
SUPREME COURT OF THE UNITED STATES

[As the Supplement went to press, the Attorney General's brief had not yet been filed with the Court. To see the brief when it is filed, and for other materials in the case, see *http://eon.law.harvard.edu/openlaw/ eldredvashcroft/legaldocs.html. — Eds.*]

BRIEF *AMICUS CURIAE*
of
THE ORGANIZATION OF AMERICAN HISTORIANS
and
H-LAW: HUMANITIES AND SOCIAL SCIENCES ONLINE

by Tyler T. Ochoa, Mark Rose and Edward T. Walterscheid

SUMMARY OF ARGUMENT

The British experience with patents and copyrights prior to 1787 is instructive as to the context within which the Framers drafted the Patent and Copyright Clause. The 1624 Statute of Monopolies, intended to curb royal abuse of monopoly privileges, restricted patents for new inventions to a specified term of years. The Stationers' Company, a Crown-chartered guild of London booksellers, continued to hold a monopoly on publishing, and to enforce censorship laws, until 1695. During this time, individual titles were treated as perpetual properties held by booksellers. In 1710, however, the Statute of Anne broke up these monopolies by imposing strict term limits on copyright, and in the 1730s Parliament twice rejected booksellers' attempts to preserve their monopolies by extending the copyright term. Failing to achieve their ends through legislation, the booksellers sought to circumvent Parliament by arguing that the Statute of Anne was only supplementary to an underlying common-law right that was perpetual; but this effort, too, was rebuffed when the House of Lords determined in 1774 that the only basis for copyright was the Statute of Anne.

In America, too, anti-monopoly sentiment was strong; and when the Constitution was being drafted, the Framers, influenced by the British experience, specified that patents and copyrights could only be granted "for limited Times." The Patent and Copyright Acts of 1790 copied the limited terms of protection provided by the Statute of Monopolies and the Statute of Anne. As in England, advocates of perpetual copyright argued that statutory copyright merely supplemented an existing perpetual common-law right. But following the precedent set by the House of Lords, in 1834 the U.S. Supreme Court rejected the common-law argument and perpetual copyright, confirming the Framers' view that patents and copyrights should be strictly limited in duration in order to serve the public interest.

ARGUMENT

The Constitutional provision granting Congress the power "To promote the Progress of Science and useful Arts" by securing copyrights and patents "for limited Times,"[2] and the implementation of that power by the First Congress in 1790, both reflect the Framers' knowledge of and reliance on the earlier British experience with patents and copyrights.[3] Indeed, the 1790 Copyright Act is directly modeled on the British Statute of Anne,[4] both in its title ("An Act for the Encouragement of Learning") and in many of its provisions, notably its specification of the basic term of copyright as 14 years.[5] An understanding of the prior British experience with patents and copyrights -and specifically with the matter of the limited term -is thus essential to understanding the Framers' approach to copyright.

---

[2] U.S. Const., Art. I, § 8, cl. 8.

[3] See Graham v. Deere, 383 U.S. 1, 5 (1966) ("The clause . . . was written against the backdrop of the practices -eventually curtailed by the Statute of Monopolies -of the Crown in granting monopolies to court favorites in goods or business which had long before been enjoyed by the public.").

[4] An Act for the Encouragement of Learning, by Vesting the Copies of Printed Books in the Authors or Purchasers of such Copies, during the Times therein mentioned, 8 Anne, ch. 19. (1710) (Eng.).

[5] An Act for the encouragement of learning, by securing the copies of maps, charts, and books, to the authors and proprietors of such copies, during the times therein mentioned, § 1, ch. 15, 1 Stat. 124 (1790).

I. English Antecedents

A. The Statute of Monopolies

Around 1550, British monarchs began to grant monopoly privileges by means of "letters patent," in order to encourage foreign tradesmen and manufacturers to introduce their trades into England, and to train apprentices in their craft.[6] During the second half of Elizabeth's reign, however, the Queen began to dispense monopoly patents not for the introduction of new trades, but as rewards for political patronage.[7] Her 1598 grant of a monopoly over the manufacture of playing cards led to the landmark case of *Darcy v. Allen*[8] in which the judges of the King's Bench held that a patent granting a monopoly over an existing trade, as opposed to a new trade or invention, was invalid. Similar conditions were imposed on the Crown's use of monopoly patents in *The Clothworkers of Ipswich,*[9] in which it was held:

> [I]f a man hath brought in a new invention and a new trade within the kingdom, . . . or if a man hath made a new discovery of any thing, . . . [the King] may grant by charter unto him, that he only shall use such a trade or trafique for a certain time . . . . [B]ut when that patent is expired, the King cannot make a new grant thereof; for when the trade is become common, and others have been bound apprentices in the same trade, there is no reason that such should be forbidden to use it.[10]

Despite these rulings, King James I continued to abuse the royal privilege of granting monopolies.[11] This led to the enactment in 1624 of the Statute of Monopolies,[12] which declared broadly that all monopoly grants were invalid. The Statute had a number of exceptions, however, including one for new inventions "for the Term of fourteen Years or under."[13] The Statute also contained an exception for *existing* monopoly patents for inventors, "for the Term of one and twenty Years only, to be accounted from the Date of the first Letters Patents and Grants thereof made."[14] This was a transitional measure, in effect imposing a term limit on those patents which had been granted for longer terms or which had been unlimited in time.

---

[6] *See* Adam Mossoff, *Rethinking the Development of Patents: An Intellectual History, 1550-1800,* 52 Hast. L.J. 1255, 1259-64 (2001).

[7] *Id.* at 1264-67; Malla Pollack, *Purveyance and Power, or OverPriced Free Lunch: The Intellectual Property Clause as an Ally of the Takings Clause in the Public's Control of Government,* 30 Sw. U. L. Rev. 1, 40-54 (2000).

[8] 74 Eng. Rep. 1131 (K.B. 1603).

[9] 78 Eng. Rep. 147 (K.B. 1615).

[10] *Id.* at 148.

[11] Pollack, *supra* note 7, at 65-70.

[12] 21 Jac. I, ch. 3 (1624) (Eng.).

[13] *Id.* § 6.

[14] *Id.* § 5.

B. The Statute of Anne

The Statute of Anne was enacted in 1710 in response to petitions from the Stationers' Company, a Crownchartered guild of booksellers and printers which held a near monopoly on printing and publishing in England until 1695.

Prior to 1710, the Stationers maintained a system whereby guild members could register their "copies," as publishing rights were called, with the guild. Once secured by registration, the right to print a book continued forever, and might be bequeathed or sold to other stationers.[15] These rights were available only to guild members -booksellers and printers, not authors -and thus were not properties that might be freely exchanged in a public market. Under the terms of the Licensing Act of 1662 and its predecessors, no book could be printed in England unless it had first been registered with the Stationers.[16] In 1695, the Licensing Act of 1662 expired, throwing the book trade into disarray. The Stationers at first sought the revival of licensing,[17] but when that attempt failed,[18] they petitioned Parliament for an act that would reinstitute their traditional guild system by confirming the Stationers' Company copyrights.[19] As introduced, the proposed legislation did not limit the duration of the Stationers' copyrights.[20]

Parliament was sympathetic to the booksellers' claims about disorders in the trade, but it was not sympathetic to the monopolizing practices whereby the booksellers had turned the literary classics into perpetual private estates. Accordingly, the Statute of Anne acted in two ways to break the booksellers' monopolies. First, the Act established authors as the original proprietors of copyrights. Thus, for the first time, one no longer had to be a member of the Stationers' Company to own copyrights.[21] Second, the proposed legislation was amended to impose term limits modeled on those in the Statute of Monopolies.[22] The term of copyright in new works was limited to 14 years, with the possibility of renewal for a

---

[15] See LYMAN RAY PATTERSON, COPYRIGHT IN HISTORICAL PERSPECTIVE 47-49 (1968).

[16] 14 Car. 2, ch. 33 (1662) (Eng.). This requirement was used by the Crown as an instrument of censorship. See PATTERSON, *supra* note 15, at 114-142.

[17] See PATTERSON, *supra* note 15, at 138-42. One of the House of Commons' principal objections to renewing the Licensing Act was the monopoly enjoyed by the Stationers' Company. *Id.* at 139-40.

[18] It was during this period that party politics first emerged, and neither party trusted the other with the power of press censorship. See FREDRICK SEATON SIEBERT, FREEDOM OF THE PRESS IN ENGLAND 1476-1776: THE RISE AND DECLINE OF GOVERNMENT CONTROLS 260-63 (1952).

[19] See MARK ROSE, AUTHORS AND OWNERS: THE INVENTION OF COPYRIGHT 42-43 (1993).

[20] *Id.* at 43.

[21] PATTERSON, *supra* note 15, at 147; ROSE, *supra* note 19, at 47-48.

[22] PATTERSON, *supra* note 15, at 144, 147-150; ROSE, *supra* note 19, at 43-45.

second 14-year term if the author were still living at the end of the first.[23] For books that were already in print, including such valuable old literary properties as the works of Shakespeare and Milton, the act provided a single 21-year term.[24] Like the parallel provision in the Statute of Monopolies, this was a transitional provision. The stationers had always treated their guild publishing rights as perpetual; thus, the effect of the 21-year provision was to limit rights that previously had been regarded as unlimited.

The great London booksellers could accept some of the novel provisions of the Act, but not the limited terms of protection, which struck at the heart of the Stationers' Company system. For a time they simply ignored the term limit provision and continued to buy and sell copyrights as if they were still perpetual. Then in 1735, when they believed the political climate favored their cause, the booksellers asked Parliament to change the term of copyright for all books, old and new, to 21 years.[25] The booksellers argued that the proposed change would improve the author's position and foster learning and knowledge; but in fact the consequences for living authors would have been minimal. The most significant effect would have been to extend the statutory copyright on classics such as Shakespeare and Milton until 1756. The booksellers' purposes in requesting the new term did not go unremarked at the time. As one anonymous pamphleteer said:

> I see no Reason for granting a further Term now, which will not hold as well for granting it again and again, as often as the Old ones Expire; so that should this Bill pass, it will in Effect be establishing a perpetual Monopoly, a Thing deservedly odious in the Eye of the Law; it will be a great Cramp to Trade, a Discouragement to Learning, no Benefit to the Authors, but a general Tax on the Publick; and all this only to increase the private Gain of the Booksellers . . .[26]

Not surprisingly, the booksellers' bill failed in the House of Lords, which was particularly hostile to anything that smacked of monopoly.[27] Two years later in 1737, when the booksellers again sought a term extension, a second bill was also defeated by the House of Lords.[28]

---

[23] 8 Anne ch. 19 (1710) (Eng.).

[24] *Id.*

[25] ROSE, *supra* note 19, at 52-53. This bill actually reduced the copyright on new books from two fourteen-year terms, or a total of twenty-eight years, to a single twenty-one-year term. In effect, it traded a shorter term on new books for extended protection of valuable old books.

[26] A LETTER TO A MEMBER OF PARLIAMENT CONCERNING THE BILL NOW DEPENDING IN THE HOUSE OF COMMONS (1735). A transcript of this pamphlet is attached as Appendix A.

[27] ROSE, *supra* note 19, at 56. The bill died when the second reading was postponed. 24 H.L. Jour. 550 (1735).

[28] ROSE, *supra* note 19, at 56 n.3. Again, the Lords allowed the bill to die at the end of the term. 25 H.L. Jour. 91, 99, 106 & 111-12 (1737).

C. Donaldson v. Beckett

In the 1730s and 1740s, as titles began entering the public domain, a group of Scottish booksellers began printing their own editions of out-of-copyright titles. Despite the Statute of Anne, the great London booksellers regarded these reprints as piracies. They argued that copyright was fundamentally a matter of common law, not statutory law. Labor, they maintained, gave authors a natural right of property in their works, a right that lasted forever just like a right in a parcel of land or a house; and this right passed undiminished to the booksellers when they purchased literary works from authors.[29] The Statute of Anne merely provided supplemental remedies to an underlying common-law right that was perpetual; therefore all reprints of fairly purchased copyrights were illegal, no matter how old the work in question.

Starting in the 1740s, the booksellers pressed their common-law argument in a series of cases. No decision was reached, however, until 1769, when in *Millar v. Taylor*[30] the court of King's Bench ruled by a three-to-one vote that there was a common-law right and that literary property was perpetual. As an English court, however, the jurisdiction of King's Bench did not extend to Scotland, where the reprint industry continued to thrive. In 1773, in *Hinton v. Donaldson,*[31] the Scottish Court of Sessions reached the opposite decision, determining that in Scotland there was no such thing as a common-law right of literary property. Finally, in the landmark decision of *Donaldson v. Beckett,*[32] the House of Lords, acting as the Supreme Court of Great Britain, decisively rejected the claim of perpetual common-law copyright and established that the only basis for copyright was the Statute of Anne.

The historical record left the basis for the Lords' decision somewhat unclear. In 1774 the House of Lords still decided cases by a general vote of the peers, lawyers and laymen alike. In important cases such as *Donaldson,* the twelve common-law judges of the realm (the judges of King's Bench, Common Pleas, and the Exchequer) would be summoned to the House to give their advice on matters of law, after which the peers would debate the issue and vote. The judges were closely divided in their advisory opinions in *Donaldson,* and the most widely cited report of the case indicates that while seven of the eleven judges believed there was a common-law copyright that survived publication, a bare majority of six believed that the common-law right had been divested by the Statute of Anne.[33] Contemporary

---

[29] ROSE, *supra* note 19, at 4-8 & 67-91.

[30] 4 Burr. 2303, 98 Eng. Rep. 201 (K.B. 1769).

[31] *See* JAMES BOSWELL, THE DECISION OF THE COURT OF SESSION UPON THE QUESTION OF LITERARY PROPERTY IN THE CAUSE OF HINTON AGAINST DONALDSON (Edinburgh 1774), *reprinted in* THE LITERARY PROPERTY DEBATE: SIX TRACTS 1764-1774 (Stephen Parks, ed. 1975).

[32] 4 Burr. 2408, 98 Eng. Rep. 257 (H.L. 1774).

[33] *Id.* In fact, historians now believe that one vote was incorrectly recorded, and

accounts of the subsequent debate, however, indicate that the claim of common-law copyright was vigorously disputed, and that the peers rejected perpetual copyright by a strong majority.[34]

The great booksellers of London regarded *Donaldson* as a disaster, claiming with some justification that in an instant hundreds of thousands of pounds worth of literary properties had been annihilated.[35] But for the publishing trade as a whole and for the public at large, which was now able to buy cheap reprints of classic works, the decision had positive effects. It also had positive effects on authors. Prior to *Donaldson,* the most valuable properties were the old classics that the booksellers could count on as perennials. The *Donaldson* decision meant that now publishers had to pay greater attention to living authors in order to replenish their continually expiring stock of copyrights.[36] In several ways, then, *Donaldson* contributed to the statutory goal of "the encouragement of learning." As a result of the Lords' decision, classic books became more readily accessible, and living authors acquired new incentives to write.

II. The Patent and Copyright Clause of the Constitution

The history of copyright in the United States bears many similarities to the history of copyright in England prior to the Revolution. In America, as in England, proponents of the natural right view of copyright repeatedly sought a perpetual copyright; in America, as in England, the term of copyright was instead strictly limited in order to serve the public interest; and in America, as in England, it took an authoritative decision by the highest court in the land to firmly establish the utilitarian rationale as the dominant rationale for copyright.

A. State Copyright and Patent Laws under the Articles of Confederation

In March 1783, in response to several authors' petitions, the Continental Congress appointed a committee "to consider the most proper means of

---

that the judges had voted six-to-five that a common-law copyright had survived the Statute of Anne. *See* ROSE, *supra* note 19, at 98-99, 154-58; Howard B. Abrams, *The Historic Foundation of American Copyright Law: Exploding the Myth of Common-Law Copyright,* 29 Wayne L. Rev. 1119, 1164-71 (1983). This error allowed advocates of common-law copyright to claim that the peers had simply followed the vote of the judges, which was not the case. *Id.* at 1169-70; ROSE, *supra* note 19, at 107-10.

[34] *See* ROSE, *supra* note 19, at 97-103. Although it is unclear whether a formal division of the house occurred, *id.* at 102, an often cited account published in 1813 reports that the vote was 22-11 against perpetual copyright. Donaldson v. Beckett, 17 Parl. Hist. Eng. 953, 992-1003 (H.L. 1774). *See* Abrams, *supra* note 33, at 1159-64.

[35] *See* ROSE, *supra* note 19, at 97.

[36] On the impact of the *Donaldson* decision, *see* Terry Belanger, *Publishers and Writers in Eighteenth-Century England,* in BOOKS AND THEIR READERS IN EIGHTEENTH CENTURY ENGLAND 5-25 (Isabel Rivers ed. 1982).

cherishing genius and useful arts throughout the United States by securing to the authors or publishers of new books their property in such works."[37] The committee reported that it was "persuaded that nothing is more properly a man's own than the fruit of his study, and that the protection and security of literary property would greatly tend to encourage genius, to promote useful discoveries and to the general extension of arts and commerce."[38] Under the Articles of Confederation, the Continental Congress had no authority to issue copyrights; so on May 2, 1783, it passed a resolution encouraging the States

> to secure to the authors or publishers of any new books not hitherto printed . . . the copy right of such books for a certain time not less than fourteen years from the first publication; and to secure to the said authors, if they shall survive the term first mentioned, . . . the copy right of such books for another term of time not less than fourteen years.[39]

Three states had already enacted copyright statutes earlier that year; and within three years all of the remaining states except Delaware had followed suit.[40] As had the Continental Congress' resolution, the preambles of several of these statutes set forth both natural right and utilitarian justifications for copyright. Significantly, however, all of them were limited to a specified term of years. Seven of the States followed the Statute of Anne and the Continental Congress' resolution in providing two 14-year terms.[41] The five remaining States granted copyrights for single terms of 14,[42] 20,[43] and 21[44] years' duration, with no right of renewal.

South Carolina's copyright statute also included the only general state patent law enacted prior to the Constitution. It provided "that the inventors

---

[37] NATIONAL ARCHIVES, PAPERS OF THE CONTINENTAL CONGRESS, No.36, II, folios 113-114, *reprinted in* BRUCE W. BUGBEE, THE GENESIS OF AMERICAN PATENT AND COPYRIGHT LAW 112 (1967). The Committee consisted of Hugh Williamson of North Carolina, Ralph Izard of South Carolina, and James Madison of Virginia. *See* 24 JOURNALS OF THE CONTINENTAL CONGRESS 211n (March 24, 1783).

[38] 24 JOURNALS OF THE CONTINENTAL CONGRESS 326 (May 2, 1783). In so stating, this report set forth both natural right and utilitarian justifications for copyright.

[39] Resolution of May 2, 1783, *reprinted in* COPYRIGHT ENACTMENTS OF THE UNITED STATES 1783-1906 11 (2d ed. 1906).

[40] *See* COPYRIGHT ENACTMENTS, *supra* note 39, at 11-31.

[41] *See* Act of Jan. 29, 1783 (Conn.); Act of Apr. 21, 1783 (Md.); Act of May 27, 1783 (N.J.); Act of Mar. 15, 1784 (Pa.); Act of Mar. 26, 1784 (S.C.); Act of Feb. 3, 1786 (Ga.); Act of Apr. 29, 1786 (N.Y.), *in* COPYRIGHT ENACTMENTS at 11-13, 15-17, 20-24, 27-31.

[42] Act of Nov. 18, 1785 (N.C.), *in* COPYRIGHT ENACTMENTS at 25-27.

[43] Act of Nov. 7, 1783 (N.H.), *in* COPYRIGHT ENACTMENTS at 18.

[44] *See* Act of Mar. 17, 1783 (Mass.); Act of Dec. 1783 (R.I.); Act of Oct. 1785 (Va.), *in* COPYRIGHT ENACTMENTS at 14-15, 19, 24-25.

of useful machines shall have a like exclusive privilege of making or vending their machines for the like term of fourteen years, under the same privileges and restrictions hereby granted to, and imposed on, the authors of books."[45] Throughout this time period, however, the states continued to enact individual patents.[46] The terms of these patents were sometimes as short as five years; but the English fourteen-year term became "almost universal among state patents issued in 1786 and thereafter."[47]

B. The Constitutional Convention and Ratification Debates

At the Constitutional Convention of 1787, both James Madison of Virginia and Charles Pinckney of South Carolina submitted proposals to give Congress the power to grant copyrights. Madison's proposal read: "To secure to literary authors their copy rights for a limited time."[48] Pinckney's proposal read: "To secure to Authors exclusive rights for a certain time."[49] Pinckney also proposed that Congress be given the power "to grant patents for useful inventions."[50] These proposals were referred to the Committee on Detail. Later, provisions which had not been acted upon were referred to the Committee of Eleven (of which Madison was a member),[51] which drafted the Patent and Copyright Clause as it exists today, and recommended its adoption.[52] The clause was unanimously approved by the delegates with no debate.[53]

The language of the Clause is ambiguous when it speaks of "securing" exclusive rights. For the next years, the meaning of this term would be debated, with proponents of perpetual copyright arguing that "securing" meant the affirmation of pre-existing rights, and proponents of the utilitarian view arguing that "securing" meant nothing more than "to obtain" or "to provide." In *Wheaton v. Peters,*[54] this Court held the utilitarian view was correct, noting that the term "securing" applies to both "authors" and "inventors," and that in England, it had always been the case that inventors did not have a natural right in their inventions.[55]

---

[45] Act of Mar. 26, 1784 (S.C.), *in* COPYRIGHT ENACTMENTS, at 23.

[46] *See generally* BUGBEE, *supra* note 37, at 84-103.

[47] *Id.* at 101.

[48] JAMES MADISON, NOTES OF DEBATES IN THE FEDERAL CONVENTION OF 1787 (Ohio Univ. Press 1966) at 477 (Aug. 18, 1787).

[49] *Id.* at 478.

[50] *Id.*

[51] *Id.* at 569 (Aug. 31, 1787).

[52] *Id.* at 580 (Sept. 5, 1787).

[53] *Id.* at 581 (Sept. 5, 1787).

[54] 33 U.S. (8 Pet.) 591 (1834). *See* Section III.D., below.

[55] *Id.* at 661. *See also* CHRISTINE P. MACLEOD, INVENTING THE INDUSTRIAL REVOLUTION: THE ENGLISH PATENT SYSTEM 1660-1800 198 (1988) (in *Donaldson,* "the *lack* of a natural right in mechanical inventions provided a fixed

In the ratification debates, the Clause was rarely mentioned. The most significant reference came in the Federalist No. 43, authored by James Madison:

> The utility of this power will scarcely be questioned. The copy right of authors has been solemnly adjudged in Great Britain to be a right at Common Law. The right to useful inventions seems with equal reason to belong to the inventors. The public good coincides in both cases with the claims of individuals. The States cannot separately make effectual provision for either of the cases, and most of them have anticipated the decision of this point by laws passed at the instance of Congress.[56]

In light of the decision in *Donaldson v. Beckett,*[57] Madison's statement that copyright had been adjudged to be a common-law right is problematic. It has been suggested that Madison was relying on the first American edition of Blackstone's *Commentaries,* which reported the decision in *Millar v. Taylor,* but not its subsequent overruling in *Donaldson.*[58] It has also been suggested that Madison was relying on Burrow's report of the *Donaldson* case, in which it was reported that the advisory judges were of the opinion that copyright was a common-law right, but one that had been divested by the Statute of Anne.[59] It is also possible that Madison was referring only to the commonlaw right of first publication; or that he was simply trying to win the support of those who believed that copyright was a natural right.[60] In any case, Madison later took the position that the English common law was deliberately not made applicable in the United States by the new Constitution.[61] This seems to preclude any argument that Madison

---

pole of the debate.") (emphasis in original). In a letter to Isaac MacPherson, Thomas Jefferson set forth a famous critique of the natural rights view with regard to inventions. *See* Letter of Aug. 13, 1813, *in* THE COMPLETE JEFFERSON 1011, 1015-16 (Saul K. Padover ed. 1943).

[56] James Madison, The Federalist No. 43 at 279 (Modern Library ed. 1941).

[57] *See* Section I.C., above.

[58] *See* 2 SIR WILLIAM BLACKSTONE, COMMENTARIES ON THE LAWS OF ENGLAND 405-07 (Philadelphia 1771). Blackstone qualified his report of *Millar v. Taylor,* however, stating that "[n]either with us in England hath there been any final determination upon the right of authors at the common law." *Id.* at 406-07. It should be noted that Blackstone was a prominent advocate of common-law copyright, and that he argued the booksellers' cause in both *Tonson v. Collins* (1760) and *Millar v. Taylor.*

[59] *See* Section I.C., above. The fourth volume of Burrow's reports was published in 1776, and citations to it are found in early Pennsylvania cases. *See, e.g.,* Respublica v. Doan, 1 U.S. (1 Dall.) 86, 90-91 (Pa. 1784); Nathan v. Virginia, 1 U.S. (1 Dall.) 77, 78 (Pa. C.P. 1781).

[60] *See* Abrams, *supra* note 33, at 1177-78.

[61] *See* Letter from James Madison to George Washington (Oct. 18, 1787), *in* 3 MAX FARRAND, THE RECORDS OF THE FEDERAL CONVENTION OF 1787 129-30 (1911).

believed the Clause was "securing" a pre-existing right.[62]

What is clear from the Federalist is that Madison believed that the state copyright laws were ineffectual. This point was also made during the ratification debates by Thomas McKean of Pennsylvania,[63] and future Justice James Iredell of North Carolina.[64] Iredell also set forth the utilitarian justification for copyright, saying, "such encouragement may give birth to many excellent writings which would otherwise have never appeared."[65]

The stipulation that patent and copyright protection be granted only "for limited Times," only to "authors" and "inventors," and only "To promote the Progress of Science and useful Arts," appears to have been aimed at preventing the kinds of abuses that had prompted the Statute of Monopolies 150 years earlier. It is clear that many of the Framers were concerned with restraining monopolies of all kinds. This concern was most clearly expressed in correspondence between Thomas Jefferson and James Madison concerning the proposed Constitution.

After receiving a draft of the Constitution, Jefferson wrote to Madison, saying: "I will now add what I do not like. First, the omission of a bill of rights providing clearly and without the aid of sophisms for . . . restriction against monopolies."[66] Jefferson amplified his views in a letter to Madison dated July 31, 1788:

> [I]t is better to . . . abolish . . . Monopolies, in all cases, than not to do it in any . . . . The saying there shall be no monopolies lessens the incitements to ingenuity, which is spurred on by the hope of a monopoly for a limited time, as of 14 years; but the benefit even of limited monopolies is too doubtful to be opposed to that of their general suppression.[67]

Madison replied in a letter dated October 17, 1788:

> With regard to Monopolies they are justly classed among the greatest nuisances in Government. But is it clear that as encouragements to literary works and ingenious discoveries, they are not too valuable to be wholly renounced? Would it not suffice to reserve in all cases a right to the public to abolish the privilege at a price to be specified in the grant of it?[68]

---

[62] For a more extensive analysis, *see* EDWARD C. WALTERSCHEID, THE NATURE OF THE INTELLECTUAL PROPERTY CLAUSE: A STUDY IN HISTORICAL PERSPECTIVE 201-238 (2002).

[63] *See* 2 THE DOCUMENTARY HISTORY OF THE RATIFICATION OF THE CONSTITUTION 415 (Merrill Jensen, ed. 1976).

[64] *See* 16 DOCUMENTARY HISTORY, *supra* note 63, at 386 note (c).

[65] *Id.* at 382.

[66] Letter from Jefferson to Madison (Dec. 20, 1787), *in* 12 THE PAPERS OF THOMAS JEFFERSON 440 (Princeton 1955).

[67] Letter from Jefferson to Madison (July 31, 1788), *in* 13 THE PAPERS OF THOMAS JEFFERSON 442-43 (Princeton 1956).

[68] Letter from Madison to Jefferson (Oct. 17, 1788), *in* 14 THE PAPERS OF THOMAS JEFFERSON 21 (Princeton 1958).

Madison's explanation is revealing in several respects. First, it endorses the utilitarian justification for copyrights and patents. Second, in using the words "privilege" and "grant," it indicates that patents and copyrights are bestowed by the government, rather than merely confirming existing rights. Third, in recommending that the public reserve the right to buy out the author or inventor during the term of the grant, Madison suggests that even the 14-year terms with which he was familiar might work a hardship upon the public in certain circumstances.

Jefferson was apparently persuaded by Madison's argument; but he remained concerned that the power to grant exclusive rights could be abused. Upon receiving Madison's draft of the Bill of Rights, Jefferson wrote:

> I like it as far as it goes; but I should have been for going further. For instance, the following alterations and additions would have pleased me . . . . Art. 9. Monopolies may be allowed to persons for their own productions in literature and their own inventions in the arts for a term not exceeding ＿＿ years but for no longer term and for no other purpose. [69]

Jefferson's concerns were widely shared by others at the time. George Mason, a delegate to the Constitutional Convention from Virginia, refused to sign the proposed Constitution, in part because "[u]nder their own construction of the general clause at the end of the enumerated powers, the Congress may grant monopolies in trade and commerce." [70] Elbridge Gerry of Massachusetts refused to sign for similar reasons. [71] In New York, "A Son of Liberty" wrote that "Monopolies in trade [will be] granted to the favorites of government, by which the spirit of adventure will be destroyed, and the citizens subjected to the extortion of those companies who will have an exclusive right." [72] In addition, the ratifying conventions of four states requested an amendment expressly restricting Congress' power to grant "exclusive advantages of commerce." [73]

Proponents of the Constitution responded to these concerns not by denying that monopolies were generally harmful, but by emphasizing the utilitarian justification for copyrights and patents, and the limitations

---

[69] Letter from Jefferson to Madison (Aug. 28, 1789), *in* 15 THE PAPERS OF THOMAS JEFFERSON 367-68 (Princeton 1958).

[70] 8 DOCUMENTARY HISTORY, *supra* note 63, at 45.

[71] 4 DOCUMENTARY HISTORY, *supra* note 63, at 14.

[72] 13 DOCUMENTARY HISTORY, *supra* note 63, at 482. *See also* 4 DOCUMENTARY HISTORY, *supra* note 63, at 428 ("The unlimited right to regulate trade, includes the right of granting exclusive charters . . . . We hardly find a country in Europe which has not felt the ill effects of such a power . . . . [In England,] Individuals have been enriched, but the country at large has been hurt.") ("Agrippa").

[73] 2 THE DOCUMENTARY HISTORY OF THE CONSTITUTION OF THE UNITED STATES OF AMERICA 1786-1870 (State Dept. 1894) at 95 (Massachusetts), 142 (New Hampshire), 198 (New York) 274 (North Carolina).

placed on them by the Clause. [74] Expressions of anti-monopoly sentiment were sometimes qualified in this regard. [75] Many years later, in a manuscript published after his death, Madison summed up his views as follows:

> Monopolies though in certain cases useful ought to be granted with caution, and guarded with strictness against abuse. The Constitution of the U.S. has limited them to two cases, the authors of Books, and of useful inventions, in both which they are considered as a compensation for a benefit actually gained to the community as a purchase of property which the owner otherwise might withhold from public use. There can be no just objection to a temporary monopoly in these cases; but it ought to be temporary, because under that limitation a sufficient recompense and encouragement may be given . . . . [76]

Thus, the Clause appears to have been designed not so much to limit the means by which Congress could promote the progress of science and useful arts, but rather to limit he duration and purposes for which exclusive rights could be granted.

III. Statutory and Judicial Interpretation

A. The Copyright and Patent Acts of 1790

The Copyright Act of 1790 granted copyrights for a term of 14 years, with a right of renewal for another 14-year term if the author survived to the end of the first term. [77] The Act covered "any map, chart, book or books already printed within these United States," as well as "any map, chart, book or books already made and composed, but not printed or published, or that shall hereafter be made and composed." [78] Except for the addition of maps and charts, this language was copied almost verbatim from the Statute of Anne.

---

[74] *See* Remarks on the Amendments to the Federal Constitution by the Rev. Nicholas Cottin, *in* 6 THE AMERICAN MUSEUM 303 (1789), *reprinted in* Walterscheid, *supra* note 62, at 10.

[75] James Kent of New York wrote to Nathaniel Lawrence, a delegate to the New York ratifying convention: "I have just been reading Smith *on the Wealth of Nations* & he has taught me to look with an unfavorable eye on monopolies -But a monopoly of the mental kind I take to be laudable and an exception to the rule." 14 DOCUMENTARY HISTORY, *supra* note 63, at 76. And in Pennsylvania, "Centinel" wrote "that monopolies in trade or arts, other than to authors of books or inventors of useful arts, ought not to be suffered." 13 DOCUMENTARY HISTORY, *supra* note 63, at 466.

[76] JAMES MADISON, WRITINGS 756 (Jack N. Rakove ed. 1999). This essay was published posthumously in 1914. *See* James Madison, *Aspects of Monopoly One Hundred Years Ago,* 128 HARPER'S MAG. 489, 490 (1914).

[77] An Act for the encouragement of learning, § 1, ch. 15, 1 Stat. 124 (1790).

[78] *Id.*

Granting federal copyrights to previously published works was consistent with the Statute of Anne and with the utilitarian justification for copyright. Just as the Statute of Anne had provided a term of 21 years for previously published works, in order to limit previously unlimited guild rights and to ease the transition from a state-licensed monopoly to a free market,[79] the Copyright Act of 1790 likewise may have provided protection to previously published works in order to limit the term of any claims based on state or common law, and to ease the transition from uncertain and largely ineffective state copyright protection to a single federal copyright. The initial 14-year term was shorter than the term provided by four of the states;[80] but the availability of a renewal term ensured that no author would be deprived of the term that he or she had been promised under previous state legislation.

The Patent Act of 1790 permitted patents to be granted "for any term not exceeding fourteen years."[81] No provision was made for the extension or renewal of a patent.[82] Unlike the Copyright Act of 1790, the Patent Act of 1790 did not expressly address the issue of retroactivity; but the Patent Act of 1793 expressly required that an inventor relinquish any state patent rights as a condition of obtaining a federal patent.[83]

B. Private Patent and Copyright Laws

In 1808, Congress extended by private act the term of a patent owned by inventor Oliver Evans.[84] Evans' patent had been held invalid because the face of the document did not recite the allegations made in the patent application.[85] The form of the document, however, was drafted by the Secretary of State, not by Evans. James Madison, then Secretary of State, reported that "a compliance with [the decision] would admit the invalidity of all the patents issued in the same form since the commencement of the Government."[86] As a result, Congress agreed to extend the term of Evans'

---

[79] See Section I.B., above.

[80] See Section II.A., above.

[81] An Act to promote the progress of useful Arts, § 1, ch. 7, 1 Stat. 110 (1790).

[82] Because of this omission, many inventors petitioned Congress for extension or renewal of their individual patents. See Section III.B., below. In 1832, Congress enacted a statute specifying the conditions under which it would consider such petitions. Act of July 3, 1832, § 2, ch. 162, 4 Stat. 559. In 1836 this was replaced with an administrative procedure by which a single extension of seven years could be granted. Patent Act of 1836, § 18, ch. 357, 5 Stat. 124-25. This provision was repealed in 1861, when the basic patent term was increased from 14 years to 17 years. Act of March 2, 1861, ch. 88, § 16, 12 Stat. 249. See Tyler T. Ochoa, *Patent and Copyright Term Extension and the Constitution: A Historical Perspective,* 49 J. Copyr. Soc'y USA 19, 52-54 (2002).

[83] Patent Act of 1793, § 7, ch. 11, 1 Stat. 322.

[84] An Act for the relief of Oliver Evans, ch. 13, 6 Stat. 70 (1808).

[85] Evans v. Chambers, 8 F. Cas. 837 (C.C.D. Pa. 1807) (No. 4,555).

[86] See AMERICAN STATE PAPERS, No. 231, 1 Misc. 646 (1807).

patent to compensate him for the administrative error. While this action indicates that the Congress of 1808 believed it could extend the term of a patent for equitable reasons,[87] it is also consistent with the utilitarian rationale. Evans had relied on the benefit of a 14-year patent term, and he was deprived of a portion of that term not through any fault of his own, but as a result of an administrative error. Granting an extension restored to Evans the benefit of his patent bargain.[88] Similar equitable adjustments of individual patent terms have been granted in recent years for reasons beyond the inventor's control, such as war, judicial corruption, and delay in FDA approval.[89]

In 1828, Congress extended by private act the copyright in a book of tables of discount and interest compiled by James Rowlett.[90] Rowlett had invested a great deal of time and money in ensuring the accuracy of his tables, and he sought an extension to recover some of the money he had lost on the first edition.[91] At that time, the investment of time and money was at least arguably an acceptable basis for copyright protection; but now that this Court has firmly rejected the "sweat of the brow" doctrine as inconsistent with the Patent and Copyright Clause, the basis of Rowlett's claim to an extension has been eroded.[92] Since then, Congress has extended a copyright by private act only once, and that extension was held invalid.[93]

C. The Copyright Act of 1831

In 1826, Noah Webster wrote to Daniel Webster, seeking his assistance in securing a perpetual copyright, saying "an author has, by common law, or natural justice, the sole and *permanent* right to make profit by his own labor."[94] Daniel Webster replied that he would forward the letter to the House Judiciary Committee, but he added "I confess frankly that I see, or

---

[87] Congress also extended the terms of nine more patents between 1809 and 1836. *See* Bloomer v. McQuewan, 55 U.S. (14 How.) 539, 543 (1852) (listing extensions). It should be noted, however, that by 1808 only one delegate to the 1787 Constitutional Convention, Nicholas Gilman of New Hampshire, remained in Congress; and that of the nine additional extensions, only one was enacted prior to Gilman's leaving Congress in 1814.

[88] In fact, however, Congress was more generous than necessary, granting Evans a full 14-year extension. For a more extensive analysis, *see* Ochoa, *supra* note 82, at 58-72, 97-109.

[89] *See* Ochoa, *supra* note 82, at 72-82.

[90] An Act to continue a copy-right to John Rowlett, ch. 145, 6 Stat. 389 (1828).

[91] *See* Ochoa, *supra* note 82, at 46-48.

[92] Feist Publications, Inc. v. Rural Telephone Service Co., 499 U.S. 340 (1991); *see* Ochoa, *supra* note 82, at 50-51.

[93] Priv. L. No. 92-60, 85 Stat. 857 (1971); United Christian Scientists v. Christian Science Board of Directors, 829 F.2d 1152 (D.C. Cir. 1987).

[94] Noah Webster, *Origin of the Copy-Right Laws in the United States,* in A COLLECTION OF PAPERS ON POLITICAL, LITERARY AND MORAL SUBJECTS 176 (1843) (emphasis in original).

think I see, objections to make it perpetual. At the same time I am willing to extend it further than at present."[95]

Noah Webster's son-in-law, William W. Ellsworth, was elected to Congress in 1828 and was appointed to the Judiciary Committee. Webster "applied to him to make efforts to procure the enactment of a new copy-right law."[96] The Report prepared by Ellsworth for the Judiciary Committee shows the influence of Webster's views. It states: "[u]pon the first principles of proprietorship in property, an author has an exclusive and perpetual right, in preference to any other, to the fruits of his labor."[97] It also asserts (erroneously) that:

> In England, the right of an author to the exclusive and perpetual profits of his book was enjoyed, and never questioned, until it was decided in Parliament, by a small vote . . . that the statute of Ann had abridged the common law right, which, it was conceded, had existed, instead of merely guarding and securing it by forfeitures for a limited time, as was obviously intended."[98]

Despite this endorsement of perpetual copyright as a natural right, the bill provided only for an initial term of 28 years and a renewal term of 14 years,[99] the term of which was extended to all subsisting copyrights.[100]

When the bill was debated in Congress, Rep. Michael Hoffman of New York complained that it would "establish a monopoly of which authors alone would reap the advantage, to the public detriment."[101] He noted that patents were limited to 14 years, and argued:

> So it should be . . . with the author or publisher. There was an implied contract between them and the public. They, in virtue of their copyright, sold their books to the latter at an exorbitant rate; and the latter . . . had the right to avail themselves of the work, when the copyright expired.[102]

Ellsworth replied, arguing that the bill would "enhance the literary character of the country, by holding forth to men of learning and genius additional inducements to devote their time and talents to literature and the fine arts."[103] Ellsworth did not explain how this justified the retroactive extension; but Rep. Gulian C. Verplanck of New York maintained that "[t]here was no contract; the work of an author was the result of his own

---

[95] *Id.* at 176-77.

[96] *Id.* at 177.

[97] 7 GALES & SETON'S REGISTER OF DEBATES IN CONGRESS cxx (Dec. 17, 1830).

[98] *Id.* at cxix.

[99] Copyright Act of 1831, §§ 1-2, ch. 16, 4 Stat. 436.

[100] *Id.* § 16, 4 Stat. 439.

[101] 7 GALES & SETON'S REGISTER OF DEBATES at 423 (Jan. 6, 1831).

[102] *Id.*

[103] *Id.*

labor. It was a right of property existing before the law of copyrights had been made. That statute did not give the right, it only secured it."[104]

This record reveals that the 1831 term extension was based on the view that copyright was a natural right of the author.[105] Three years later, this view was rejected by the U.S. Supreme Court in *Wheaton v. Peters*.

D. Wheaton v. Peters

In 1827, Richard Peters succeeded Henry Wheaton as the reporter of decisions for the U.S. Supreme Court.[106] In 1829, Peters began to publish "Condensed Reports" of the cases that had been decided prior to his appointment.[107] Wheaton and his publisher sued, alleging that Peters had copied Wheaton's Reports. Peters answered that Wheaton had not complied with the requirements for obtaining a statutory copyright, and that no right to common-law copyright existed. Circuit Judge Joseph Hopkinson agreed, dismissing the complaint and dissolving the preliminary injunction on January 9, 1833.[108]

On appeal, Elijah Paine, arguing for Wheaton, contended that "An author was entitled, at common law, to a perpetual property in the copy of his works, and in the profits of their publication."[109] Representing Peters, Joseph Reed Ingersoll argued that Wheaton's view was inconsistent with the Patent and Copyright Clause, saying "[t]here would be no occasion to secure for a limited time, if the exclusive right already existed in perpetuity."[110]

Justice McLean delivered the majority opinion, which dealt a decisive blow to the notion of copyright as a perpetual common-law right:

> [T]he law appears to be well settled in England, that, since the statute of 8 Anne, the literary property of an author in his works can only be asserted under the statute. And that, notwithstanding the opinion of a majority of the judges in the great case of Millar v. Taylor was in favour of the common law right before the statute, it is still considered, in England, as a question by no means free from doubt.

---

[104] *Id.* at 424. Verplanck also stated erroneously that in "the great case of literary property . . . the judges were unanimously of opinion that an author had an inherent right of property in his works." *Id.*

[105] It should be noted that by 1831, not a single member of the Constitutional Convention or the First Congress remained in Congress.

[106] *See* Craig Joyce, *The Rise of the Supreme Court Reporter: An Institutional Perspective on Marshall Court Ascendancy,* 83 Mich. L. Rev. 1291, 1351-58 (1985).

[107] *Id.* at 1362-70.

[108] Wheaton v. Peters, 29 F. Cas. 862 (C.C.E.D. Pa. 1832) (No. 17,486), *rev'd,* 33 U.S. (8 Pet.) 591 (1834). Although the judgment was reversed and remanded for a determination whether Wheaton had complied with the requirements for a statutory copyright, the Supreme Court opinion made it clear that Wheaton could not claim a commonlaw copyright.

[109] 33 U.S. at 595-96, *citing* Millar v. Taylor, 4 Burr. 2303 (K.B.1769).

[110] 33 U.S. at 629.

> That an author, at common law, has a property in his manuscript, and may obtain redress against any one who deprives him of it, or by improperly obtaining a copy endeavours to realise a profit by its publication, cannot be doubted; but this is a very different right from that which asserts a perpetual and exclusive property in the future publication of the work, after the author shall have published it to the world . . . .[111]

In so holding, the Court expressly relied on the lack of a natural right in inventions.[112] It said:

> [T]he word secure, as used in the constitution, could not mean the protection of an acknowledged legal right. It refers to inventors, as well as authors, and it has never been pretended, by any one, either in this country or in England, that an inventor has a perpetual right, at common law, to sell the thing invented.[113]

The Court concluded that "Congress, then, by this act, instead of sanctioning an existing right, as contended for, created it . . . . [I]f the right of the complainants can be sustained, it must be sustained under the acts of congress."[114]

In rejecting Wheaton's claim of perpetual common-law copyright, the U.S. Supreme Court confirmed the utilitarian view embodied in the Constitution that patents and copyrights are exclusive rights of limited duration, granted in order to serve the public interest in promoting the creation and dissemination of new works. By placing these limits in the Constitution, the Framers hoped to avoid the kinds of abuse of monopoly power that had existed in England. In the words of Madison, "[t]here can be no just objection to a temporary monopoly in these cases; but it ought to be temporary, because under that limitation a sufficient recompense and encouragement may be given."[115]

CONCLUSION

When the U.S. Constitution granted Congress the power to secure copyrights "for limited Times," it did so in the context of the British struggles to restrain the booksellers' monopoly claims. The circumstances of the present case seem strikingly parallel to those of 18th-Century Britain. Once again the underlying struggle is between the great holders of old copyrights (movie studios, music publishers, and others) and those who would reprint or otherwise reproduce classic works and circulate them more widely. The Framers were wary about allowing perpetual monopolies,

---

[111] *Id.* at 657.

[112] *Id.* at 657-58.

[113] *Id.* at 661. *See also* note 55, above.

[114] *Id.* at 661-62. The court added that "[i]t may be proper to remark that the court are unanimously of the opinion, that no reporter has or can have any copyright in the written opinions delivered by this court; and that the judges thereof cannot confer on any reporter any such right." *Id.* at 668.

[115] JAMES MADISON, WRITINGS 756 (Jack N. Rakove ed. 1999).

and there is every reason to believe that they would have been as skeptical as the British pamphleteer of 1735 who remarked that allowing an endless series of term extensions would establish a de facto perpetual monopoly, "a Thing deservedly odious in the Eye of the Law." His warning seems as relevant today as they did then: If the CTEA is upheld, what is to prevent the great copyright holders from obtaining further extensions again and again, as often as the old ones expire? In the words of the pamphleteer, it will be "a great Cramp to Trade, a Discouragement to Learning, no Benefit to the Authors, but a general Tax on the Publick; and all this only to increase the private Gain of the Booksellers."

APPENDIX A

A Letter to a Member of Parliament concerning the Bill now depending in the House of Commons, for making more effectual an Act in the 8th Year of the Reign of Queen Anne, entitled, An Act for the Encouragement of Learning, by Vesting the Copies of Printed Books in the Authors or Purchasers of such Copies, during the Times therein mentioned (London, 1735)[1]

Sir,

The Bill now depending in your House for making more effectual, An Act for the Encouragement of Learning, etc. having the specious Shew of being calculated for the Furtherance of Learning, and the Securing of Property; two things for which you have always shewn a becoming Zeal; I wonder not, that you should at first be inclin'd to favour it, especially considering the many deceitful Arts, and false Insinuations which some have made use of, in order to make the World entertain that Opinion of it: But when, upon a serious Review, those Arts shall be exposed, and the Falsehoods detected, it will plainly appear to be so far from having any real Tendency to the promoting of Learning, that, on the contrary, it will greatly cramp it, and manifestly hinder its spreading in the World; so far from the securing of Property, that it will notoriously invade the natural Rights of Mankind, and subject the Publick to an exorbitant Tax, in order to increase the Profits of those, who have neither Colour of Title, nor Pretence of Merit; and when this shall appear to be the Case, I doubt not but the same laudable Motives which at first prompted you to encourage it, will prevail with you to oppose a Design so unjust in itself, and so detrimental to the Interest it is pretended to promote.

And whereas many have been artfully made to believe, that the aforesaid Act passed in the 8th Year of Queen Anne is now expired, and therefore have the more readily concurred in promoting a Bill which they look on only as the Continuance or Revival of an expiring Law, it will be proper to give you a true State of the Case in that Particular.

---

[1] This is a transcript of a broadside publication, from the copy in the Bodleian Library, Oxford (Ms. Carte 207 f. 31).

Before the Act of the 8th of Queen Anne, there was no Law which vested in any one the sole Copy-Right of any Books which were published to the World; but when once a Treatise was made publick, every one was at Liberty to make free with it. This, to be sure, was a great Discouragement to Authors, who were by this means in great measure deprived of the Profit of their Works; and this was the Grievance which gave Occasion to the making of that Act, in order to remedy which, by giving due Encouragement to Authors, and yet to prevent the contrary Extreme, by giving a Monopoly for too long a Time, that Act provides as follows.

1. As to such Books which were printed and published before the Date of the Act, viz. April 10. 1710, the Authors, or those who had purchased of the Authors, should have the sole Right and Liberty of Printing them for the Term of Twenty One Years from the Date of the Act.

2. As to such Books which should be afterwards printed and published, the Authors, or those who should purchase them of the Authors, should have the sole Right and Liberty of Printing them for the Term of Fourteen Years from the Time of their being first published; and if the Authors be living at the End of that Term, they should have another Term for Fourteen Years, in all Twenty eight Years; and all others are prohibited under certain Penalties from Re-printing or Importing the same.

As this was not a temporary Law, and stands unrepealed, it is as much in Force now as ever, only the Term of Twenty One Years, which was granted for Books printed and published before the Date of the Act is expired. But the Booksellers, it seems, do not think this Term sufficient, and are therefore desirous to have it renewed for another Twenty One Years. But what Reasons have they offer'd why such a Request should be granted? In all other Inventions, which yet are as much the natural Property of the Inventors, as Books are of the Authors, the Law deems Monopolies so destructive of the publick Good, that the Crown is restrained by 21 Jac. cap. 3. from granting a Patent for any Term exceeding Fourteen years. In this Instance therefore the Legislature has already been more than ordinary liberal; and tho' they very justly thought, that some certain Term should be secured to the Authors, yet, at the same time, they judg'd it reasonable that some Limitation should be set to that Term, that one time or other the Publick might have the common Benefit of a Work, after they had for several Years contributed to the Author's Profit. This Limitation they have fix'd to Twenty One Years; and therefore the Act provides that the sole Liberty of Printing etc. shall continue no longer. And why is not this Encouragement sufficient? Or, what has since happen'd, which should occasion the Legislature to alter their Judgment in this Point? Is there any room to think, that any useful or valuable Work has been supprest, for want of a longer Term to the Authors? No, the Authors, for what appears, are very well satisfied with the Encouragement the Law allows them; for it is not they, but the Booksellers who make this Application; and what Pretence can the Booksellers have to a larger Term? Will Learning be encourag'd by giving them a longer Interest in Books already published, even to the Exclusion of the Authors themselves? But it is said they have purchased the Copies of the Authors; but what have they purchased? Only an Interest for Twenty One Years. The Author by Law had no more, and therefore could grant no greater Interest to the Booksellers than what they themselves had. So that, if it were reasonable to enlarge the Term, surely it ought to be enlarged to the Authors, and not the Booksellers, who cannot be supposed to have paid a Consideration greater than what was adequate to the Interest assigned to them. To what Purpose then is any Argument fetch'd from Family Settlements? Can private Settlements overturn the Law? Or, can any one gain a greater Interest in an Estate, by taking upon him to make a Disposition of that which he has no Right to dispose of?

But it is pretended, that if the Authors could assign a larger Interest, the Booksellers could afford them a better Price for their Copy. This then is a Concession, that they have hitherto allowed the Authors only in Proportion to the Interest which the Laws now in Being would permit them to convey; how unreasonable then is it, that the additional Term sought for should be vested in the Booksellers, who have paid no Consideration for the same, consequently have no natural nor equitable Right thereto. And as to any Books hereafter to be published, what additional Advantage can it be expected an Author can have by a longer Term, over and above what he may now have for his Fourteen Years, and a Covenant for Fourteen Years longer, if he lives? The Booksellers will always take care, to extort from the Author the whole Interest he is able to convey; I would gladly know therefore, what these generous Booksellers would be willing to advance to an Author for a Reversion after Twenty eight Years, and by that some Judgment may be made what additional Benefit a longer Term will be to the Author. I believe most People will be ready to answer, little or nothing. Where then is the Advantage that will accrue thereby to the Author? On the contrary, if the Author should outlive the exclusive Property of the Bookseller, he may hope, by re-printing his own Work, to gain some new Profit, since an Edition published by the Author will always have the Preference to any other. Thus it is in respect to the Author; but, as to the Publick, should the Bill pass, it would be much worse; for many Tradesmen who can now employ themselves in their respective Callings, must then stand still for want of Work. Books will now be sold at much easier Rates, and consequently, by passing into more Hands, will render the Knowledge contained in them more diffusive; but should this Bill pass into a Law, by being the sole Property of one or a few, they will be sold at higher Prices, and consequently be confined to a small Number, in comparison of what they would otherwise be. Many Books that are now scarce will probably be re-printed, while they are left free and open to the Publick, which while they are private Property, may long continue out of Print; the particular Proprietors either thro' Indolence, or for some other Reason, being indisposed to venture a new Impression of them.

As to any Argument drawn from the Employment of Printers, Bookbinders, Women and Children, it is certain, while the Liberty of Printing and

Selling Books is left at large, they will be sold cheaper, and in larger Numbers, and therefore will increase the Business of these Trades, and of the Women and Children employed therein, much more than if they are restrained to be the Property of a few, as Experience abundantly shews.

As to the Pretence of furnishing foreign Markets, there can be no doubt but that End will be best attained by such Methods as may enable us to afford our Books at so low a Price, that Foreigners may not be able to undersell us; which can be done no way so well, as by leaving it open to the whole Trade: For, as to the Method of settling the Price of Books by the Archbishop of Canterbury, etc. The Booksellers very well know, that the Nature of their Trade is such, as renders the same impracticable; for which Reason, it has scarce ever been exercised, altho' the booksellers have not been wanting in furnishing just Cause of Complaint.

Here I cannot but observe one Artifice made use of by the Booksellers in Reprinting Mr. Addison's Tatler, No. 101. upon this Subject, at this Juncture, as if that Ingenious Author had thought the Term of Twenty-One Years not sufficient. But it is to be noted, that whatever is there said by him is said on behalf of Authors and not Booksellers, and was said before the Act of Q. Anne; so that whatever Ground of Complaint there might then be, the same was wholly taken away by that Statute, and Mr. Addison must be understood to complain only of the Law as it then stood, and not as it has been since alter'd by that Statute to which his Arguments are no Way applicable. Upon the whole, I see no Reason for granting a further Term now, which will not hold as well for granting it again and again, as often as the Old ones Expire; so that should this Bill pass, it will in Effect be establishing a perpetual Monopoly, a Thing deservedly odious in the Eye of the Law; it will be a great Cramp to Trade, a Discouragement to Learning, no Benefit to the Authors, but a general Tax on the Publick; and all this only to increase the private Gain of the Booksellers, who as they can have no natural Title to the Copy, so they can have no legal or equitable Title thereto, beyond the Interest assigned them by the Author, which could be for no more than the Term allowed by Law. For these Reasons I doubt not your Zeal for the Publick Good, which you have used to exert on other Occasions, will be exerted on this, to prevent a Law, which is likely to be productive of such mischievous Consequences to the Publick.

BRIEF *AMICUS CURIAE*
of
NATIONAL WRITERS UNION et al.

by Peter Jaszi

SUMMARY OF ARGUMENT

The United States Court of Appeals for the District of Columbia Circuit incorrectly held that the Copyright Term Extension Act[2] ("CTEA") as passed by Congress in 1998 is constitutional.[3] The CTEA violates the Constitution by failing to promote the progress of science and useful arts.[4] The Framers of the Constitution understood that the creation of new works and subsequent public access to those works were vital to society; thus, they limited the copyright monopoly's duration to assure the development of a healthy public domain. The public domain serves not only as the repository of accessible works for enjoyment and use, but also as a foundation for new creations. The CTEA's passage has already significantly diminished the public domain, which remains in jeopardy.

The Constitution imposes a duty upon Congress in enacting any intellectual property law to determine that its legislation promotes innovation. However, of the major justifications for term extension set forth before Congress, including European Union harmonization, benefits to authors' families and film preservation are peripheral to the stated purpose of copyright: to promote cultural progress. Nor does the CTEA provide meaningful incentives to that end. In enacting the CTEA, Congress failed to ensure the progress of science and the useful arts, as required in the exercise of its power to create copyright protection.

ARGUMENT

I. THE FRAMERS INTENDED THAT COPYRIGHT PROTECTION PROVIDE A BALANCE BETWEEN PROTECTION FOR CREATIONS AND PUBLIC ACCESS TO THEM

Following the model of the English Statute of Anne, the founders of the American system of government created a copyright law that would operate for public, not private, benefit.[5] So strong were their sentiments about the

---

[2] Pub. L. No. 105-298, 112 Stat. 2827 (1998). The CTEA grants an additional twenty years of protection to all works, except those created before Jan. 1, 1978 and not published prior to Jan. 1, 2003. Copyright Act, 17 U.S.C. §§ 302-303 (2000).

[3] *Eldred v. Reno,* 239 F.3d 372 (D.C. Cir. 2001).

[4] U.S. Const. art. I, § 8, cl. 8 ("Congress shall have the Power . . . To promote the Progress of Science and useful Arts, by securing for limited Times to Authors and Inventors the exclusive Right to their respective Writings and Discoveries.").

[5] *See generally* Paul J. Heald and Suzanna Sherry, *Implied Limits on the Legisla-*

appropriate goals of copyright legislation that the grant to Congress of only limited power to act with respect to copyright was set forth in the Constitution.[6] The author is at the center of United States ("U.S.") copyright doctrine, but not because creators are its intended beneficiaries. Rather, innovators and creators are the instruments through which the law's public purpose is carried out. Characterizing this constitutional approach, the Court stated in *Harper & Row Publishers, Inc. v. Nation Enterprises*:[7]

> By establishing a marketable right to the use of one's expression, copyright supplies the economic incentive to create and disseminate ideas. This Court stated in *Mazer v. Stein, 347 U.S. 201, 209 (1954)*: "The economic philosophy behind the clause empowering Congress to grant patents and copyrights is the conviction that encouragement of individual effort by personal gain is the best way to advance public welfare through the talents of authors and inventors in 'Science and useful Arts.'"

As recently as last term, this Court reiterated that incentives for "individual effort" by creators are an essential part of the scheme envisioned in the Constitution.[8]

For the public purpose of copyright to be fulfilled, however, more than just economic incentives to authors are required: A healthy and vibrant public domain is essential to assure the continued supply of source material for innovation and creation. This aspect of the architecture of U.S. copyright law is reflected in the constitutional restriction on the duration of intellectual property protection to "limited times."[9] Thus, copyright term extension has the potential to undermine the very purpose of copyright law, the promotion of cultural and scientific progress. Such legislation, of which the CTEA is the most recent example, should therefore be subject to careful constitutional scrutiny.[10]

Over the years the Court has repeatedly affirmed the Framers' vision of copyright. In *Steward v. Abend,* the Court stated, "the copyright term is limited so that the public will not be permanently deprived of the fruits of an artist's labor."[11] Similarly, in *Sony Corp. v. Universal City Studios, Inc.,* it stated that copyright "is intended to motivate the creative activity of authors and inventors by the provision of a special reward, and to allow

---

tive Power: The Intellectual Property Clause as an Absolute Constraint on Congress, 2000 U. Ill. L. Rev. 1119 (2000); Edward C. Walterscheid, *Defining the Patent and Copyright Term: Term Limits and the Intellectual Property Clause,* 7 J. Intell. Prop. L. 315 (2000).

[6] U.S. Const. art. I, § 8, cl. 8.

[7] 471 U.S. 539, 558 (1985).

[8] *New York Times Co. v. Tasini,* 533 U.S. 483, 496 n.3 (2001).

[9] U.S. Const. art. I, § 8, cl. 8.

[10] *See generally* Tyler T. Ochoa, *Patent and Copyright Term Extension and the Constitution: A Historical Perspective,* 49 J. Copyright Soc'y 19 (2001) (discussing the history of copyright term extension).

[11] 495 U.S. 207, 288 (1990).

the public access to the products of their genius after the limited period of exclusive control has expired."[12] Additionally, *Twentieth Century Music Corp. v. Aiken* acknowledged that:

> The limited scope of the copyright holder's statutory monopoly, like the limited copyright duration required by the Constitution, reflects a balance of competing claims upon the public interest: Creative work is to be encouraged and rewarded, but private motivation must ultimately serve the cause of promoting broad public availability of literature, music, and the other arts.[13]

Indeed, since 1834, when its decision in *Wheaton v. Peters*[14] categorically rejected natural or "common law" rights in literary property, the Court has repeatedly reaffirmed that the various copyright statutes enacted by Congress must represent a balance between providing protection to authors and assuring access to "the result of their labours [that] may be ... beneficial to society."[15]

If the goal of copyright law is to "stimulate artistic creativity,"[16] then the integrity of the public domain must not be compromised. The creation of new works is largely dependent upon access to the varied language, research, images, and other content of previous works. The concept that all, or even most, new works are wholly original is unfounded; rather, many great works have been the artful retelling of others' stories.[17] New creations and innovations require the interaction of inspiration with the availability of previous works in all genres, including books, music, software, the visual arts and film.

Many literary works are the interpretations of older stories. Mark Twain was a vocal advocate of broad copyright protection but freely admitted that his work was less than wholly original.[18] Twain once wrote that "substantially all ideas are second-hand, consciously or unconsciously drawn from millions of sources . . . ; whereas there is not a rag of originality about

---

[12] 464 U.S. 417, 429 (1984).

[13] 422 U.S. 151, 156 (1975).

[14] 33 U.S. (8 Pet.) 591 (1834).

[15] *Id.* at 657-8; *see also* L. Ray Patterson, *Eldred v. Reno: An Example of the Law of Unintended Consequences,* 8 J. Intell. Prop. L. 223, 231 (2001): "[T]he Constitution requires that the copyright statute Congress enacts shall be designed to do three things: to promote learning, because the clause so states; to protect the public domain, because copyright is available only to authors only for their original writings only for a limited time; and public access . . . ."

[16] *Aiken,* 422 U.S. at 156.

[17] *See* Jessica Litman, *The Public Domain,* 39 Emory L. J. 965, 966 (1990) ("The very act of authorship in *any* medium is more akin to translation and recombination than it is to creating Aphrodite from the foam of the sea.").

[18] *See generally* Siva Vaidhyanathan, *Copyrights and Copywrong: The Rise of Intellectual Property and How it Threatens Creativity* 56 (2001) (noting that Twain boasted of liberally borrowing from others' stories).

them. . . ."[19] The truth behind this colorful overstatement is seen in Twain's famous work, *The Adventures of Huckleberry Finn,* which was his retelling of Homer's *The Odyssey.* [20] Twain's reliance on the public domain, however, did not end there. Not only is Huck Finn an American version of Ulysses, but Huck's narrative voice draws on and improves the American oral storytelling tradition.

Judge Richard Posner, building upon Melville Nimmer's assertion that *West Side Story* would infringe *Romeo and Juliet* if *Romeo and Juliet* were copyrighted, concluded:

> Measure for Measure would infringe *Promos and Cassandra, Ragtime* would infringe *Michael Kohlhaas,* and *Romeo and Juliet* itself would have infringed Arthur Brooke's *The Tragicall Historye of Romeo and Juliet,* published in 1562, which in turn would have infringed several earlier *Romeo and Juliets,* all of which probably would have infringed Ovid's story of Pyramus and Thisbe -which in *A Midsummer Night's Dream* Shakespeare staged as a play within the play. If the Old Testament had been copyrighted, *Paradise Lost* would have infringed it, not to mention *Joseph and his Brothers.* [21]

Aggressive copyright laws, in particular the CTEA, impermissibly threaten this kind of cumulative creativity.[22] Similarly, many renowned musical works are based on previous creations. For example, "Good Night Sweetheart" (1931) is based on themes from Schubert's Symphony in C and Liszt's Preludes, "Love Me Tender" (1956) is based on "Aura Lee" by George Poulton, and "The Lion Sleeps Tonight" (or "Wimoweh") (1962) is based on a traditional African song.[23]

The American blues tradition also illustrates the reliance of creative innovators on the music of the past. The blues originally derived from West African music and rhythm and developed as musicians of each generation repeated and embellished the musical and lyrical contributions of their predecessors. This dynamic process not only carries forward cultural traditions but has generated new musical movements such as jazz and rock and roll.[24]

In other very different domains of innovation, such as computer software development, reliance on pre-existing material in the creation of new works

---

[19] *Mark Twain's Letters* 731 (Albert Bigelow Paine ed., 1917), *quoted in* Vaidhyanathan. *Id.* at 64.

[20] Vaidhyanathan, *supra* note 18, at 69

[21] Richard A. Posner, *Law and Literature* 399 (2d ed. 2000) (citation omitted).

[22] *Id.* at 403 ("The more extensive is copyright protection, the more inhibited is literary imagination. This is not a good reason for abolishing copyright, but it is a reason possibly for narrowing it, and more clearly for not broadening it.").

[23] Stephen Fishman, *The Public Domain, How to Find and Use Copyright* 4/38 (2001). *See also* Ochoa, *supra* note 10, at n.10, (discussing additional musical works based on existing works from the public domain).

[24] Vaidhyanathan, *supra* note 18, at 125.

also is ubiquitous. The rapid development of the U.S. software industry since the 1970's has been fueled by the fact that:

> Innovation in software development is typically incremental. Programmers commonly adopt software design elements .. . by looking around for examples or remembering what worked in other programs. These elements are sometimes adopted wholesale, but often they are adapted to a new context or set of tasks. In this way, programmers both contribute to and benefit from a cumulative innovation process.[25]

Software is a young field, and no software has yet entered the public domain via copyright expiration. Nevertheless, software engineers understand the importance of access so well that some programs have achieved near-public domain status. One is the so-called "Berkeley TCP/IP stack" that enables computers to be connected to the Internet. The University of California licenses it on terms that allow anyone to make any use of it, with proper attribution. This software was incorporated into several popular operating systems and played an important role in the growth of the Internet. Ultimately, however, such affirmatively designed substitutes for the public domain cannot be relied upon alone to sustain cumulative innovation.[26]

Corporate producers of intellectual property as well as individual creators repeatedly have reaped the benefits of using previously created works for inspiration. Most of the Walt Disney Company's widely acclaimed animated feature films are based upon preexisting stories. For example, *Snow White* and *Cinderella* are based upon the Grimm Brothers' *Children and Household Tales (Grimms' Fairy Tales)*; while *Pinocchio, The Little Mermaid, The Jungle Book,* and the *Hunchback of Notre Dame* are based upon modern literary works by Carlo Collodi, Hans Christian Anderson, Rudyard Kipling and Victor Hugo, respectively. Moreover, all these literary works were in the public domain when the films were released. Even the ubiquitous Mickey Mouse bears a striking resemblance to an earlier large-eared,

---

[25] *See* Pamela Samuelson, *et al., A Manifesto Concerning the Legal Protection of Computer Programs,* 94 Colum. L. Rev. 2308, 2330-31 (1994).

[26] Another attempt to approximate a public domain for software is the GNU Public License ("GPL"), which covers many popular copyrighted software programs including the Linux operating system. Software covered by the GPL may be examined and used freely byanyone, provided that any derivative works are also licensed under the GPL. A large and diverse community of programmers works on GPL-covered software and thus contributes to the GPL's pseudo-public domain. Opponents of the GPL's use, such as Microsoft, point out that the GPL prevents the software it covers from being incorporated into commercial products; and thus, they argue, the GPL's pseudopublic domain is an inferior substitute for a real public domain. *See, e.g.,* Prepared Text of Remarks by Craig Mundie, Senior Vice President, Microsoft, Inc., *"The Commercial Software Model,"* New York University Stern School of Business, May 3, 2001, http://www.microsoft.com/presspass/exec/craig/05-03sharedsource.asp (last visited May 13, 2002).

big-footed, button-nosed, wide-eyed, britches-wearing character called Oswald the Lucky Rabbit.[27]

Another example of the derivation of figures of popular culture from preexisting material is the Wile E. Coyote character. Created by cartoonist Chuck Jones for Warner Bros., Wile E. Coyote not only carries the mark of Jones' creativity, but also incorporates elements of multiple preexisting sources and traditions, including Mark Twain's tales of coyotes in *Roughing It* and the Trickster figure of Native American folklore.[28]

Ironically, companies and industries that have drawn freely on preexisting materials (including those in the public domain) to create their own copyrighted works were instrumental in advocating copyright term extension. The result was legislation, the CTEA, that created a 20-year moratorium on the addition of material to a vital public resource. The public domain enables creation or "artful retelling" by serving as "a device that permits the rest of the system to work by leaving the raw material of authorship available for authors to use."[29] In addition to academic commentators, the judiciary has recognized the importance of this resource:

> Overprotecting intellectual property is as harmful as underprotecting it. Creativity is impossible without a rich public domain. Nothing today, likely nothing since we tamed fire, is genuinely new: Culture, like science and technology, grows by accretion, each new creator building on the works of those who came before. Overprotection stifles the very creative forces it's supposed to nurture.[30]

The CTEA exemplifies the concern to which this passage points: freezing the public domain by limiting contemporary creators' access to many works that could generate new creation. This legislation does not nurture creative minds, but instead stifles the process of innovation through overprotection.

Amongst the most glaring omissions Congress made when considering the CTEA were its failures to assess the cost of the legislation to the public domain and the future of innovation and to balance that cost against whatever benefits the legislation might offer the public welfare.

---

[27] *See* Russell Merritt and J.B. Kaufman, *Walt in Wonderland* 86-119 (1993). The similarities between the two characters illustrate the extent to which new creations in the realm of popular culture often rely on preexisting materials. Walt Disney's early Oswald cartoons drew heavily on general cartooning motifs and specific prior copyrighted works. After losing the rights to the design of the Oswald character, Disney nonetheless reused many of its elements in creating Mickey Mouse. *Id.*

[28] *See* Shelly Fisher Fishkin, *Lighting Out for the Territory: Reflections on Mark Twain and American Culture* 147-9 (1997); *see also* Lewis Hyde, *Trickster Makes This World* 18-19 (1999) (describing the Native American Trickster character as a coyote that often fell prey to his own traps).

[29] Litman, *supra* note 17, at 968.

[30] Kozinski, J., dissenting from the denial of the petition for rehearing *en banc*, *White v. Samsung Electronics Inc.*, 971 F.2d 1395, *petition for reh'g en banc denied*, 989 F.2d 512, 513; *cert. denied*, 508 U.S. 951 (1993).

II. CONGRESS FAILED IN ITS OBLIGATION TO FULLY CONSIDER THE EFFECTS OF ENACTING THE CTEA

Every law enacted by Congress must be based on powers granted to it by the Constitution: "The powers of the legislature are defined and limited; and that those limits may not be mistaken or forgotten, the Constitution is written."[31] The ultimate question for this Court is whether Congress, in enacting the CTEA, violated its constitutional duty when it extended monopoly protection for copyrighted works without regard to the impact upon the accessibility of cultural products for new creation and the enrichment of the public. The Constitution grants Congress the power to legislate copyright protection for authors, but requires that Congress exercise this power in order to promote the public interest. Congress neglected this limiting principle when it enacted the CTEA, which blocks the entry of works into the public domain and thereby damages a mechanism that contributes substantially to cultural progress.

Any major adjustment in the scope of intellectual property protection must be directly linked to the promotion of creation and innovation. In *Graham v. John Deere Co.*, the Court stated that the grant of authority over patents in the intellectual property clause:

[I]s both a grant of power and a limitation. This qualified authority, unlike the power often exercised in the sixteenth and seventeenth centuries by the English Crown, is limited to the promotion of advances in the 'useful arts.'[32]

The Court further stated that "Congress in the .. . exercise of the patent power may not . . . enlarge the patent monopoly without regard to the innovation, advancement, or social benefit gained thereby."[33] While *Graham* specifically addressed constraints on the congressional patent power, Congress' power over copyrights is similarly limited.[34] But in enacting the CTEA, Congress failed to give due regard to the public purposes of copyright.

Before passing the CTEA, Congress appears to have paid insufficient attention to the Constitutional basis for its actions and to have given great credence to issues tangential to its constitutional duty. Had it thoroughly examined the implications of the extension, Congress would have found it constitutionally unwarranted. While the House and Senate Judiciary Committees issued reports after holding numerous hearings in successive Congresses, the Congress did not adequately address many issues that should have been considered, including the threat term extension poses to the public domain as a "creative commons."[35]

---

[31] *Marbury v. Madison,* 5 U.S. (1 Cranch) 137, 176 (1803).

[32] 383 U.S. 1, 5 (1966).

[33] *Id.* at 6.

[34] *See* Ochoa, *supra* note 10, at 103-6.

[35] *See generally* S. Rep. No. 104-315 (1996); H.R. Rep. No. 105-452 (1998).

Of course, Congress did suggest various affirmative justifications for the CTEA, but none of these furthered the constitutional purpose of copyright. Their presence in the record is insufficient to uphold legislation that violates the constitutional limitation on the exercise of its congressional power.

In *United States v. Lopez,* the Court held that Congress' exercise of regulatory authority under the commerce clause must be carefully scrutinized when it is in tension with an important limiting constitutional principle. [36] There this Court took a critical view of the congressional justifications for the exclusion of guns from school zones because Congress' power was constrained by constitutional limitations relating to federalism. Here, this Court should scrutinize the proffered congressional justifications for the CTEA with similar care, because the constitutional grant of power to create protections for authors is constrained by the intellectual property clause's requirement that such protection be solely for the promotion of cultural and scientific progress. In exercising this power, Congress "may not overreach the restraints imposed by the stated constitutional purpose." [37]

Among the asserted justifications for term extension were harmonization of U.S. copyright law with the law of the European Union ("E.U."), the provision of benefits to authors and their heirs, and even the promotion of motion picture preservation. The foregoing reasons, however, all fail to support an exercise of congressional power that disregards the constitutional mandate to balance exclusive rights with the promotion of progress. All of these justifications are irrelevant to the constitutional purpose of copyright and most are without factual foundation. In addition, the CTEA fails to provide meaningful incentives to creativity and innovation of the kind that the U.S. copyright system is designed to afford.

A. EUROPEAN UNION HARMONIZATION

The justification most widely offered to Congress in support of the CTEA was the importance of bringing U.S. copyright law into alignment with E.U. law. [38] For example, the Motion Picture Association of American ("MPAA") offered testimony stating that copyrighted works were America's most successful export, earning roughly $45 billion a year abroad, but that some additional potential revenue was diverted from U.S. copyright holders due to the disparity of protection between the U.S. and some European nations. [39] Accordingly, the industry concluded that this revenue could be

---

[36] 514 U.S. 549, 564 (1995) ("We rejected these [government] arguments because . . . if we were to accept the Government's arguments, we are hard pressed to posit any activity by an individual that Congress is without power to regulate."). In the Court of Appeals below, Judge Sentelle stated, "Congress concluded a given piece of legislation that serves a constitutional purpose 'does not necessarily make it so.'" *Eldred v. Reno* 253 F.3d at 854 (2001) (Sentelle, J., dissenting) (citing *Lopez,* 549 514 U.S. at 557 n.2, *United States v. Morrison,* 529 U.S. 598, 614 (2000).

[37] *Graham,* 383 U.S. at 5-6.

[38] *See generally* S. Rep. No.104-315 (1996); H.R. No. 105-452 (1998).

[39] *See The Copyright Term Extension Act of 1995: Hearing on S. 483 Before the*

preserved only by passing the CTEA and, thus, securing 20 years of additional protection for U.S. works in Europe. However, the maintenance of the U.S. position in the international information marketplace, whether desirable or undesirable, is an objective unrelated to the kind of "progress" envisioned in the constitutional clause regarding intellectual property.

The goal of copyright is not to create wealth, but to stimulate innovation. While E.U. harmonization might produce wealth for some, the costs to domestic "progress" are potentially steep. Americans, who are greater users of U.S. works than citizens of other countries, now must suffer from the discouraging effects of copyright extension upon domestic creativity.[40]

The inappropriateness of discouraging new domestic creativity in order to align U.S. law with that of Europe becomes even more apparent when one considers the different bases of European and U.S. intellectual property systems. The ultimate goal of European copyright law is to benefit authors and creators rather than to promote a larger public purpose; European law embodies a natural rights theory that treats copyright as a simple entitlement.[41] Conversely, the U.S. copyright system is based on the unequivocal constitutional directive that new innovation be promoted through limited economic incentives. This incentive-based scheme explicitly rejects any focus on natural rights.[42] Consequently, the U.S. cannot, consistent with the Constitution, fully align itself with the philosophically different E.U. system.[43]

Senate Judiciary Comm., 104th Cong. 40-41 (1995) ["1995 Senate Hearings"] (statement of Jack Valenti, President and Chief Executive Officer, Motion Picture Association of America (["Valenti statement"])).

[40] *See infra* notes 50-66 and accompanying text.

[41] *See* Sam Ricketson, *The Berne Convention for the Protection of Literary and Artistic Works: 1886-1986* 5-6 (1987) "([Eighteenth century French copyright laws placed authors' rights on a more elevated basis than the [British] Statute of Anne . . . . [T]he rights being protected [were treated] as being embodied in natural law . . . . This new conception of author's rights had a great effect on the law of France's neighbors . . . .").

[42] *See* 33 U.S. (8 Pet.) at 657-63, *see also* H.R. Rep. No. 2222, at 7 (1909):

The enactment of copyright legislation by Congress under the terms of the Constitution is not based on any natural right that the author has in his writings, for the Supreme Court has held that such rights as he has are purely statutory rights, but on the grounds that the welfare of the public will be served and the progress of science and useful arts will be promoted . . . .

By the same token, in the United States copyright is viewed as an "impingement on the public domain," a concept that would have no meaning in the European philosophical context. *See* L. Ray Patterson, *Free Speech, Copyright and Fair Use*, 40 Vand. L. Rev. 1,7 (1987).

[43] *See* Dennis S. Karjala *et al.*, *Statement of Copyright and Intellectual Law Professors in Opposition to H.R. 604, H.R. 2589, and S.505* (Jan. 28, 1998) http://www.law.asu.edu/HomePages/Karjala/OpposingCopyrightExtension/legmats/1998Statement.html (last visited, May 14, 2002): ("[W]e cannot allow discrimination in Europe to force us to change our entire intellectual property philosophy — based on the public interest — just to put a few dollars into the pockets of descendants and assignees of creative authors from the distant past.")

B. BENEFIT TO AUTHORS

In justifying the CTEA, Congress also relied on the fact that term extension would generate benefits to copyright owners, including individual authors and their families, in the form of possible additional revenue from their works. While such benefits may be welcome, they do not in themselves represent "progress" in the constitutional sense and therefore cannot be weighed against the costs to new creativity that flow from the harm the CTEA has wreaked on the public domain.

As demonstrated below,[44] neither the prospect of additional income from Europe, nor the increased domestic protection provided by the CTEA, functions as a meaningful incentive to new creativity or innovation, the only constitutional basis that would have enabled congressional action in enacting the CTEA. In the legislative history, however, it is suggested that Congress may have regarded the benefits of term extension to copyright owners, particularly the heirs of individual authors, as an independent justification for term extension.[45] If so, this rationale represents a fundamental congressional misunderstanding of the constitutional goals of the U.S. intellectual property system.

This is true, in particular, with respect to one provision of the CTEA that was specifically designed to benefit individual authors and their successors, which amends section 304 of the Copyright Act. The amendment grants an extra opportunity to reclaim rights that authors and their successors had assigned away. This provision was specifically designed to give "original authors or their dependents ... the opportunity to bargain for the rights provided by the 20-year copyright term extension," (if and only if they had not already exercised termination rights in the 19-year additional term provided by the 1976 Act.)[46] In other words, the CTEA gives some authors and heirs an additional chance to take a "second bite at the apple" in exploiting their works. Although this economic opportunity may represent a desirable reallocation of wealth among authors' families and authors' assignees, it is irrelevant to the constitutional purpose of copyright and fails to serve as a true incentive to new creation.

C. FILM PRESERVATION

Another rationale presented to and embraced by Congress was the purported effect of term extensions in promoting the preservation of historic American films.[47] However, this justification fails to support the enactment of the CTEA for several reasons. As important as maintaining old commercial motion pictures may be, this function is not the objective of the copyright system, which exists to promote *new* innovation and creativity.

---

[44] *See* discussion *infra* pp. 23-28.

[45] *See, e.g., 1995 Senate Hearings, supra* note 39, at 58-59 (statement of Mrs. Henry Mancini, widow of Henry Mancini).

[46] Copyright Act, 17 U.S.C. §§ 303-304 (2000).

[47] *See* Valenti statement, *supra* note 39, at 42, and S. Rep. No.104-315 at 13 (1996).

Moreover, Congress had before it no testimony from which it could conclude that the asserted connection between extended protection and film preservation was a genuine one.[48]

Because the physical instability of nitrate motion picture stock results in the certain eventual decomposition of the original negatives as well as surviving prints, this extension serves to make films that would have entered the public domain unavailable for preservation by independent enthusiasts and entrepreneurs while that preservation is still possible.[49] Thus, this extension, by making these films legally inaccessible, actually prevents many priceless motion pictures from ever being restored.

D. LACK OF ADDITIONAL INCENTIVES AND NEW DISINCENTIVES FOR INDIVIDUAL CREATORS

Although promoting creativity was a rationale for enacting the CTEA,[50] Congress did not seriously evaluate the CTEA's incentive effects, if any, on authors considering new creative efforts. In one respect, of course, the incentive rationale was utterly without merit: By definition, retrospective term extension for existing works cannot promote new creativity. There can be no incentives to create works that already exist.

Moreover, as the Register of Copyrights conceded in her Senate testimony, the positive incentive effects of the additional terms for new works are at best trivial.[51] The additional protection will only take effect far in the future, when the present discounted value of any additional revenue

---

[48] See Ochoa, *supra* note 10, at 123-4

"The CTEA is not narrowly tailored to serve this objective; it extends all existing copyrights, whether or not the work is in any danger of deterioration . . . reward[ing] those corporate copyright owners who allowed the films to deteriorate in the first place, without requiring any restoration efforts at all. If films were allowed to enter the public domain sooner rather than later, they would not disappear; instead they could be restored by [other] organizations."

[49] See John McDonough, *Motion Picture Films and Copyright Extension* (2002), http://www.public.asu.edu/~dkarjala/commentary/McDonough.html (last visited May 13, 2002).

[50] See, e.g., *1995 Senate Hearings, supra* note at 55-57 (statements of Don Henley, Bob Dylan and Carlos Santana) (asserting that support of the CTEA was based primarily on the potential exploitations of their grandchildren); *compare with* S. Rep. No. 104-315, at 32 (1996) (statement of Sen. Brown in dissent):

There is nothing in the hearing record that suggests extending the copyright term will result in more works or higher quality works. Indeed our success as a nation of creators suggests the opposite. The majority report observes that copyright term extension may provide an incentive to create for corporate creators: another 20 years of revenue from current works might, for example, subsidize new motion pictures. However, this is more a corporate subsidy than an incentive to create.

[51] See *infra* note 64.

is vanishingly small, to say nothing of highly uncertain. In contrast, through additional access costs and problems in obtaining copyright clearances, the CTEA imposes immediate and significant disincentives on contemporary authors seeking to create new works.

The CTEA added 20 years of protection to the end of an existing life-plus-50 year term. The possibility of income so far in the future can provide at best a negligible additional incentive for current productive effort, even given unrealistically generous assumptions. An example would be the case of a 35-year old author, who writes a book today that will generate an assured annual royalty of $5,000 throughout the term of protection under the CTEA -110 years if the author lives to be 75. If this individual's personal discount rate is 5 percent, the total economic value of the final 20 years of protection at the time of the work's creation would be only $771.80.[52] In fact, individuals' real discount rates are actually much higher, reducing further any present incentive value of copyright protection in the remote future.[53] Moreover, for many creative works the potential for future returns is highly uncertain, rather than assured, and likely to decrease over time. These factors would cause the contemporary author to further discount the present value of possible future income.[54] However, there is no indication that in enacting the CTEA Congress took the economic realities of incentives into account in assessing the benefits and costs to creativity.

The CTEA imposes substantial and immediate disincentives on authors seeking to create new works that far outweigh any trivial and uncertain economic incentives for current production. Because of the CTEA, authors will continue to need rights clearances to draw upon existing copyrighted

---

[52] By contrast the cumulative *present* value of economic returns from years 0 to 90 is $98,761.31. This can be measured by summing the present value of each year's return. The present value of a payment in the future is $[1/(1+r)t]A$, where r is the discount rate, t is the years in the future, and A is the payment amount. *Cf.* Stephen Breyer, *The Uneasy Case for Copyright,* 84 Harv. L. Rev. 281, 324 (1970) (increased present value of term extension is "hardly enough to effect [the author's] decision to write in the first place . . . .").

[53] The discount rate should reflect both the inflation rate and some additional amount, because people prefer money in the short term and could make alternative investments of money (or creative effort). *See, e.g.,* Richard L. Revesz, *Environmental Regulation, Cost-Benefit Analysis, and the Discounting of Human Lives,* 99 Colum. L. Rev. 941, 958-59 (1999).) Individuals may have personal economic discount rates that approach 50% per year, which are not limited to monetary decisions, but also affect other choices. *See, e.g.,* U. Benzion, *et al., Discount Rates Inferred from Decisions: An Experimental Study,* 35 Management Science 270 (1989); R.H. Thaler, *Some Empirical Evidence on Dynamic Inconsistency,* 8 Economic Letters 201 (1981); G.B. Chapman, *Temporal Discounting and Utility for Health and Money,* 22 J. Exper. Psych.: Learning, Memory, and Cognition 771 (1996).

[54] *See, e.g.,* Breyer, *supra* note 53, at 324, n.169; *see also* Paul Goldstein, *Copyright* § 4.7, at 4:138 (Supp. 2001) ("According to the 1961 Report of the Register of Copyrights, fewer than fifteen percent of all copyrights were renewed under the 1909 Act.").

material that would otherwise enter the public domain. As a result, they will encounter extra expense, hardship and uncertainty, all of which stifle the creative process.[55] For example, concerns over potential liability dictate that any copyrighted work used in a film, even incidentally, must be cleared.[56] This applies even to the use of a poster on a wall or a billboard in the background: "Almost every piece of artwork, any piece of furniture, or sculpture, has to be cleared before you can use it."[57] This clearance problem was highlighted by a successful director who, when asked what advice he would give to a young film maker, replied:

> I would say to an 18-year-old artist, you're totally free to do whatever you want. But -and then I would give him a long list of all the things that he couldn't include in his movie because they would not be cleared, legally cleared. That he would have to pay for them. [So freedom? Here's the freedom]: You're totally free to make a movie in an empty room, with your two friends.[58]

Another serious inhibition on the creative process resulting from copyright extension is the rigid control often wielded by heirs to works, long after the original authors' deaths. Such barriers, now wholly disassociated from the incentives that once inspired the works' creation, frustrate the creativity of new authors. For example, the Gershwin Family Trust retains complete control over the present stage uses of *Porgy and Bess* (1935),[59] demanding absolute compliance with their wishes by potential licensees. A notable condition is that the work be performed only by an all-black cast.[60] George Gershwin has been dead for 65 years; new and varied styles of performance and theatrical representation have emerged since his death.[61] His work could serve as an inspiration for creative interpretations of the powerful themes he introduced; however, his heirs remain inflexible.

---

[55] Lawrence Lessig, *The Future of Ideas* 3-4 (2001).

[56] *See, e.g., Woods v. Universal City Studios, Inc.*, 920 F. Supp. 62 (S.D.N.Y. 1996) (enjoining distribution of the film *Twelve Monkeys* because an artist claimed a chair shown briefly in the movie resembled a sketch of a piece of furniture he had designed).

[57] Lessig, *supra* note 56, at 3 (quoting Davis Guggenheim in a telephone interview conducted by Lawrence Lessig on Nov. 15, 2000).

[58] *Id.* at 5.

[59] *See* John Ardoin, *The Great "Porgy" Debate,* http://www.pbs.org/wnet/gperf/porgy/html/work.html (last visited May 8, 2002). *Porgy and Bess* is derived from Edwin DuBuse Heyward's book *Porgy* (1924). The book was based upon newspaper articles and real life memories of Heyward's life in Charleston: his access to the public domain enriched his story and Gershwin's subsequent opera. *Id.* ; *See also* Anthony Tommasini, *All-Black Casts for 'Porgy'? That Ain't Necessarily So,* N.Y. Times, Mar. 20, 2002, at E1.

[60] *See* Gail Russell Chaddock, *Public Interest v. Private Rights,* Chi. Sun-Times, June 2, 1998, at 31.

[61] *See, e.g., Patrick Stewart: The Veteran Shakespearean Actor Brings a "New Kind of Othello" to The Shakespeare Theatre,* http://www.shakespearedc.org/stewart1.html (last visited May 9, 2002) (discussing the novelty of the casting of Patrick Stewart as Othello while casting people of color in all other principal roles).

Similarly, Margaret Mitchell's estate maintains an iron grip on the classic novel *Gone With the Wind,* published in 1936. Although the copyright for *Gone With the Wind* was initially due to expire in 1992, successive term extensions culminating with the CTEA have restricted the free availability of the work for use and adaptation by artists and the public until 2031. The Mitchell estate is thus in a position to aggressively prosecute authors such as Alice Randall. Randall recently attempted to draw upon *Gone With the Wind* as a source for creating her own Afro-centric comment on this historically important work. Her creative effort resulted not only in a socially relevant work, *The Wind Done Gone,* but a lengthy lawsuit including, initially, an injunction against the book's publication.[62] Some determined authors, like Randall, ultimately may succeed in overcoming the chilling effect of copyright term extension. However, its discouraging effect on others, and the resultant costs to public culture, are incalculable.

E. ECONOMICS OF CORPORATE CULTURAL PRODUCTION

With respect to both prospective and retrospective copyright term extensions provided by the CTEA, Congress may also have been influenced by a rationale advanced by corporate copyright holders, most persuasively in the testimony of Jack Valenti, President of the MPAA: Valenti argued that corporations would respond to the economic benefit they received from term extension by engaging in new production of copyrightable works, stating that:

> One of the great secrets of the American dominance in the world is their ability to pour into a film enormous resources. The most talented people in the world cost money . . . . Unless we are able to protect what we own in our libraries, we will be unable in the future, in the year 2010 and thereabouts, when the new technology has avalanched through this whole landscape, not in this country, but around the world, then we are doing a terrible economic injustice to the Treasury of the United States.[63]

At least one government witness echoed this rationale:

> [I]t is difficult to see how moving from a term of life-plus-50 to life-plus-70 will encourage authors to write. It could, however, provide additional income that would finance the production and publication of new works.[64]

---

[62] *See Suntrust Bank v. Houghton Mifflin Co.,* 136 F. Supp.2d 1357 (N.D. Ga. 2001), *rev'd,* 268 F.3d 1257 (11th Cir 2001); *see also* David Kirkpatrick, *Mitchell Estate Settles ' Gone With the Wind' Suit,* N.Y. Times, May 10, 2002, at C6, Col. 1 (discussing the case's recent settlement). The issues raised by the case remain pertinent because "the settlement did not affect rights to film adaptations or any other versions of 'The Wind Done Gone.'" *Id.*

[63] Valenti statement, *supra* note 39, at 90.

[64] *1995 Senate Hearings, supra* note, at 6 (statement of Marybeth Peters, Register of Copyrights, U.S. Copyright Office).

However, Congress could not constitutionally employ the grant of intellectual property power to distribute economic windfalls that might (or might not) be used to finance hypothetical future production in general, as Valenti requested. As this Court has repeatedly noted, the Constitution contemplates incentives for the "encouragement of individual effort" by authors to create particular new works.[65] In arguing for the CTEA, corporate copyright owners sought and received an umbrella of additional copyright protection designed to increase their overall economic security and profitability, rather than to directly promote specific creative projects.

This justification for the CTEA may represent the vision of corporate copyright owners today, but it is in direct conflict with the vision, intent and practice of the Framers. U.S. copyright law was designed to promote the public good by giving direct incentives to creativity and innovation, not to enhance corporate balance sheets.

This Court recently expressed skepticism about arguments that cultural progress can best be achieved by interpreting copyright law to accommodate large scale information industry business models. In *Tasini,* which concerns the imbalance of power between large publishing companies and freelance writers who contributed to their publications, this Court concluded that the "public welfare" would suffer if the interests of individual writers were overshadowed by the welfare of corporate content aggregators.[66] As this Court has appropriately recognized, copyright law as envisioned by the Framers was designed to promote the public welfare by encouraging authors to create, not by subsidizing corporate scale.

CONCLUSION

Congress failed the American people by not performing its constitutional duty to balance the speculative and questionable benefits of copyright term extension against the certain harms to the public domain. This failure is reflected in the lack of any rationale for the legislation that is supported by a legitimate constitutional purpose. Congress enacted the CTEA based upon justifications that, although superficially attractive, were not relevant to, or lacked a demonstrated connection with, the Framers' mandate that copyright law promote cultural progress. Instead, the CTEA stifles creativity that draws upon existing works and denies society the benefits of a vibrant public domain. This Court must ensure that Congress, in exercising power over copyrights, fulfills its constitutional duty to consider with great care the effect of copyright protection on the progress of "Science and the useful Arts." Protections that do not promote this progress should be struck down.

---

[65] *Harper & Row,* 471 U.S. at 558.

[66] *Tasini,* 533 U.S. at 496 n. 3 (citing *Harper & Row,* 471 U.S. at 558 (quoting *Mazer,* 347 U.S. at 219)) (protecting the copyrights of freelance authors that had been preempted by print publishers and database corporations).

BRIEF *AMICUS CURIAE*
of
53 INTELLECTUAL PROPERTY LAW PROFESSORS

by Jessica Litman, Jonathan Weinberg and Dennis Karjala

SUMMARY OF ARGUMENT

The CTEA's extension of the terms of existing copyrights exceeds Congress's power under the Copyright and Patent Clause, for it advances no goal cognizable under that clause. The overriding goal of the CTEA was to extend the period in which copyright holders could control and collect royalties from their old copyrights; its constriction of the public domain carries with it none of the countervailing public benefits required by the Copyright and Patent Clause. In addition, both the CTEA's extension of existing copyright terms and its extension of copyright in works not yet created violate the First Amendment.

ARGUMENT

I. THE CTEA IS BEYOND CONGRESS'S POWER UNDER THE COPYRIGHT AND PATENT CLAUSE

A. CONGRESS HAS NO POWER TO ENACT LEGISLATION UNDER THE COPYRIGHT AND PATENT CLAUSE UNLESS THAT LEGISLATION PROMOTES "THE PROGRESS OF SCIENCE AND USEFUL ARTS," AND IT HAS NO POWER TO GRANT EXCLUSIVE RIGHTS THAT EXTEND BEYOND "LIMITED TIMES"

The Copyright Term Extension Act was enacted pursuant to Congress's power under the Copyright and Patent Clause. That clause vests Congress with power

> To promote the Progress of Science and useful Arts, by securing for limited Times to Authors and Inventors the exclusive Right to their respective Writings and Discoveries.

The Framers intended the Copyright and Patent Clause to give Congress the power to encourage the creation, broad dissemination, and widespread use of writings and inventions, by promising authors and inventors exclusive rights that would be limited in both scope and duration.[25] The promise of exclusive rights was designed to encourage authors to create and inventors to discover.[26]

---

[25] See *Twentieth Century Music v. Aiken,* 422 U.S. 151, 156 (1975); *Graham v. John Deere,* 383 U.S. 1, 5-6 (1966); *Mazer v. Stein,* 347 U.S. 201, 219 (1954); *Trade-Mark Cases,* 100 U.S. 82, 93-94 (1879).

[26] See *Feist Publications, Inc. v. Rural Telephone Service,* 499 U.S. 340 (1991); *Graham v. John Deere,* 383 U.S. 1, 9 (1966).

The restriction to limited times was designed to ensure that the public will have unrestricted access to and use of protected writings and inventions at the expiration of a short period of exclusivity.[27]

As the Court explained in *Sony Corp. of America v. Universal City Studios, Inc.,* 464 U.S. 417, 429 (1984):

> The monopoly privileges that Congress may authorize are neither unlimited nor primarily designed to provide a special private benefit. Rather, the limited grant is a means by which an important public purpose may be achieved. It is intended to motivate the creative activity of authors and inventors by the provision of a special reward, and to allow the public access to the products of their genius after the limited period of exclusive control has expired.[28]

The Framers' purpose in enacting the Copyright and Patent Clause is reflected in the specification of Congress's power as one "to promote the Progress of Science and useful Arts."[29] The D.C. Circuit, oddly, held that the clause's limitation of congressional power to enactments that "promote the Progress of Science and useful Arts" has no relevance to the scope of that power. *Eldred v. Reno,* 239 F.3d 372, 377-78 (D.C. Cir. 2001). That holding was fundamentally mistaken.

In *Graham v. John Deere,* 383 U.S. 1 (1966), a patent case, the Court described the bargain the Copyright and Patent Clause embodies. The Copyright and Patent Clause, the Court warned, grants only "qualified authority," because Congress's power under the clause "is limited to the promotion of advances in the 'useful arts.'" *Id.* at 5. In exercising the art. 1, sec. 8, cl. 8 power, Congress "may not overreach the restraints imposed by the stated constitutional purpose." *Id.* at 6. Because the patent system "by constitutional command must 'promote the Progress of . . . useful Arts,'" Congress may not "enlarge the patent monopoly without regard to

---

[27] See Michael H. Davis, *Extending Copyright and the Constitution: "Have I Stayed too Long?,"* 52 Fla. L. Rev. 989 (2000); Richard Graves, *Private Rights, Public Uses and the Future of the Copyright Clause,* 80 Neb. L. Rev. 64 (2001); Paul J. Heald & Suzanna Sherry, *Implied Limits on the Legislative Power: The Intellectual Property Clause as an Absolute Constraint on Congress,* 2000 U. Ill. L. Rev. 1119; Robert Patrick Merges & Glenn Harlan Reynolds, *The Proper Scope of the Copyright and Patent Power,* 37 Harv. J. on Legis 45 (2000); Edward C Walterscheid, *Defining the Patent and Copyright Term: Term Limits and the Intellectual Property Clause,* 7 J. Intell. Prop. L. 315 (2000).

[28] See also *Fogerty v. Fantasy, Inc.,* 510 U.S. 517, 527 (1994); *Feist Publications, Inc. v. Rural Telephone Service Co.,* 499 U.S. 340, 349-350 (1991); *Stewart v. Abend,* 495 U.S. 207, 228-29 (1990); *Twentieth Century Music Corp. v. Aiken,* 422 U.S. 151,156 (1975); *Fox Film Corp. v. Doyal,* 286 U.S. 123, 127-8 (1932).

[29] See Margaret Chon, *Postmodern Progress: Reconsidering the Copyright and Patent Power,* 43 DePaul L. Rev. 97 (1993); Malla Pollack, *What is Congress Supposed to Promote?: Defining "Progress" in Article I, Section 8, Clause 8 of the United States Constitution, or Introducing The Progress Clause,* 80 Neb. L. Rev. (forthcoming 2002).

the innovation, advancement or social benefit gained thereby." *Id.* It may not "authorize the issuance of patents whose effects are to remove existent knowledge from the public domain, or to restrict free access to materials already available." *Id.* It may enact no rule conferring a patent monopoly unless the rule advances "[i]nnovation, advancement, and things which add to the sum of useful knowledge." This, the Court explained, "is the *standard* expressed in the Constitution and it may not be ignored." *Id.* (emphasis in original).

Even without regard to *Graham v. John Deere,* the D.C. Circuit's position is contrary to the constitutional language. It is well-settled that the constitutional language conferring a power on Congress constrains the scope of that power. That, after all, is the very purpose of the constitutional text. The "powers of the legislature are defined, and limited; and that those limits may not be mistaken, or forgotten, the constitution is written." *United States v. Morrison,* 529 U.S. 598, 607-08 (2000) (quoting *Marbury v. Madison,* 5 U.S. (1 Cranch) 137, 176 (1803)); see also, e.g., *Railway Labor Executives' Assn v. Gibbons,* 455 U.S. 457, 468, 471 (1982) (finding in the "language of the Bankruptcy Clause itself" an "affirmative limitation or restriction upon Congress' power"). [30] In this case, the text of Art. I, sec. 8, cl. 8 empowers Congress to enact statutes that "promote the Progress of Science and useful Arts," much as other clauses of Art. 1, sec. 8 empower Congress to enact statutes that "regulate Commerce . . . among the several States," or that "establish Post Offices and Post Roads." The authority to enact statutes that "promote the Progress of Science and useful Arts" is the *power* the constitutional text confers. If a statute does not "promote the Progress of Science and useful Arts," it is outside the scope of the constitutional grant. [31]

The Copyright and Patent Clause's second phrase, restricting authors' and inventors' exclusive rights to "limited Times," is just as crucial to the constitutional bargain. The "limited times" restriction encourages early and broad distribution of protected writings and inventions, both by inducing authors and inventors to exploit their monopoly rights fully during their short term rather than hoard them, and by ensuring that after a brief period of exclusivity, the public will be able to use, consume, distribute, improve and build on those writings and inventions without limitation. See, e.g., *Stewart v. Abend,* 495 U.S. 207, 228-29 (1990). Authors and inventors build

---

[30] Similarly, the Court has made clear that "limitations on the commerce power are inherent in the very *language* of the Commerce Clause." *United States v. Lopez,* 514 U.S. 549, 553 (1995)(emphasis added); see also *South Dakota v. Dole,* 483 U.S. 203, 207 (1987) (Spending Cause); *City of Boerne v. Flores,* 521 U.S. 507, 519 (1997) (Fourteenth Amendment's Enforcement Clause).

[31] *Deep South Packing Co. v. Laitram Corp.,* 406 U.S. 518 (1972), is not to the contrary. That case stands for the unexceptional position that Congress, in exercising its authority to "promote the Progress of Science and useful Arts," may withhold some rights from copyright and patent holders. See *Sony Corp. of America v. Universal City Studios,* 464 U.S. 417, 433 (1984). It nowhere suggests that Congress may enact statutes that do *not* "promote the Progress of Science and useful Arts."

on the work of their predecessors. The public domain is the reservoir for the raw material that authors and inventors use to create new writings and discoveries.[32] The enrichment of the public domain is not a by-product of the "limited times" restriction but its purpose --it is the means that the Framers chose to ensure that our copyright and patent system would promote the progress of Science and useful Arts.[33]

The Framers' understanding of the need for limited terms had been shaped by the disastrous English experience with perpetual copyright. The Stationers' copyright, granted by the Tudor monarchs to the stationer's publishing cartel, functioned to suppress both dissent and competition.[34] The censorship and anticompetitive effects of the Stationers' copyright had led the English Parliament to abolish perpetual copyright and enact in its place a limited, fourteen year exclusive right to print and publish books, subject to a single fourteen year renewal if the author survived the expiration of the initial term.[35] The first U.S. copyright statute adopted the same duration provision.[36]

The "limited Times" restriction is even more important today than it was in 1790, when Congress enacted the first copyright statute. Until 1976, the vast majority of potentially copyrightable works entered the public domain upon publication, because the law required authors to affirmatively claim copyright protection by affixing copyright notice to publicly distributed copies.[37] Of the minority of potentially copyrightable works that gained copyright protection through publication with notice, most entered the public domain at the expiration of the 28-year initial term, because the

---

[32] See David Lange, *Recognizing the Public Domain,* 44 L. & Contemp. Probs. 147 (1981).

[33] See *Sony Corp. of America v. Universal City Studios, Inc.,* 464 U.S. 417, 428 (1984); L. Ray Patterson & Stanley Lindberg, *The Nature of Copyright: A Law of Users' Rights* 47-55 (1991).

[34] See Lyman Ray Patterson, *Copyright in Historical Perspective* 28-142 (1968).

[35] The influence of the English experience with the Stationers' copyright on the Framers' design of the Copyright and Patent Clause has been explored by a number of legal scholars. See Howard B. Abrams, *The Historic Foundation of American Copyright Law: Exploding the Myth of Common Law Copyright,* 29 Wayne. L. Rev. 1119 (1983); Paul J. Heald & Suzanna Sherry, *Implied Limits on The Legislative Power: The Intellectual Property Clause as an Absolute Constraint on Congress,* 2000 U. Ill. L. Rev. 1119, 1144-50; Lydia Pallas Loren, *Redefining the Market Failure Approach to Fair Use in an Era of Copyright Permission Systems,* 5 J. Intell. Prop. L. 1, 9-16 (1997); L. Ray Patterson, *Free Speech, Copyright, and Fair Use,* 40 Vand. L. Rev. 1, 19-36 (1987); Pamela Samuelson, *Copyright, Commodification, and Censorship: Past as Prologue -But to What Future?, in The Commodification of Information* 63 (Neil Netanel and Niva Elkin-Koren eds., forthcoming 2002).

[36] See An Act for the Encouragement of Learning, § 1, 1 Stat. 124 (1790); Tyler Ochoa, *Patent and Copyright Term Extension and the Constitution: A Historical Perspective,* 49 J. Copyr. Soc'y 19, 29-30 (2002).

[37] See Copyright Act of March 4, 1909, § 9, 35 Stat. 1075, *repealed by* Pub.L. No. 94-553, 90 Stat. 2541 (1976).

author failed to apply for copyright renewal. A 1960 Copyright Office study concluded that only 15% of registered works due to enter the public domain were renewed.[38]

In the years since 1976, Congress has amended the copyright law to remove most of the conditions and requirements that limited copyright protection.[39] Today, after several amendments, copyright is completely automatic, vesting in all eligible works at the moment of creation and continuing until 70 years after the author's death.[40] Neither publication nor notice of copyright is required. Works protected under the old system are still in theory subject to a renewal condition, but renewal vests automatically. The copyright owner need take no affirmative steps to renew.[41] Today, essentially everything that is eligible for copyright is protected by copyright. The limited term of copyright is the only remaining device for enriching the public domain.

The limited term, though, has been getting less limited. In 1976, after a series of interim extensions, Congress gave works with subsisting copyrights the benefit of a nineteen-year addition to their copyright term. In 1998, Congress enacted the CTEA, adding a 20-year term extension to all works, including the same works it had previously prevented — by prior term extension and automatic renewal —from entering the public domain. In the words of Professor Peter Jaszi, these repeated extensions resemble "perpetual copyright on the installment plan."[42]

The public domain, moreover, is under attack on another front. In the years since the first copyright statute, we have seen a remarkable expansion in both the works entitled to copyright and the breadth of the exclusive rights included in the grant.[43] In the early years of U.S. copyright law, copyright encompassed only a limited set of uses of copyrighted works. Copyright owners had no rights to prohibit or license translations, abridgements, performances or displays; those belonged to the public even during the copyright term.[44] Today, those uses are firmly at the core of the

---

[38] See Barbara Ringer, *Study Number 31: Renewal of Copyright* 187 (1960), *reprinted in* Subcomm. on Patents, Trademarks, and Copyrights of the Senate Comm. on the Judiciary, 86th Cong., 1st Sess., Copyright Law Revision (Comm. Print 1960).

[39] See 1976 Copyright Act § 302, Pub.L. No. 94-553, 90 Stat. 2541 (1976); Berne Convention Implementation Act § 7, 102 Stat. 2853 (1988); Copyright Renewal Act of 1992, Pub. L. No. 102-307, 106 Stat. 264 (codified as amended in 17 U.S.C. § 304).

[40] See 17 U.S.C. §§ 201, 302.

[41] See 17 U.S.C. § 304.

[42] *1995 Senate Hearing* at 72 (testimony of Peter A. Jaszi, Washington College of Law).

[43] See David Lange, *Recognizing the Public Domain,* 44 L. & Contemp. Probs. 147 (1981).

[44] See, e.g, *Stowe v. Thomas,* 23 F. Cas. 201 (C.C.E.D. Pa. 1853) (No. 13,514); L. Ray Patterson, *Free Speech, Copyright, and Fair Use,* 40 Vand. L. Rev. 1, 53-63 (1987).

copyright owners' exclusive rights. The recent expansion in the subject matter and scope of copyright has made the copyright grant more costly to the public, and has made the "limited Times" restriction even more important.[45]

B. THE EXTENSION OF THE TERMS OF EXISTING COPYRIGHTS EXCEEDS CONGRESS'S POWER UNDER THE COPYRIGHT AND PATENT CLAUSE

The CTEA's extension of existing copyrights oversteps Congress's power under the Copyright and Patent Clause. It does not plausibly promote "Progress of Science and useful Arts," and it violates the "limited Times" restriction.

1. The Extension Does Not Encourage The Creation Of New Works Of Authorship.

As the Court made clear in *Graham v. John Deere,* Congress may not enlarge the monopolies it creates under the Copyright and Patent Clause unless doing so will promote "[i]nnovation, advancement, and things which add to the sum of useful knowledge." But respondent has not claimed, as it could not, that Congress's purpose in extending extant copyrights was to encourage authorship retroactively.[46] The works covered by those copyrights were created long ago. One cannot reach back into the past and persuade their authors to have created them.[47]

2. The CTEA Does Not Harmonize U.S. Copyright Terms With Europe's And, In Fact, Heightens The Disparity Between Some Copyright Terms.

Respondent has characterized the Copyright Term Extension Act as a statute that matches U.S. copyright terms to the copyright terms prescribed by the European Union. See *Eldred v. Reno,* 239 F.3d 372, 379 (D.C. Cir. 2001). The benefits to copyright owners of a uniform term throughout the global marketplace are said to justify extending the copyright term. That assertion is difficult to defend: "The desire to cooperate with the international community may be a worthy goal, but it is not a blanket justification for passing otherwise unconstitutional legislation." Paul J. Heald & Suzanna Sherry, *Implied Limits on the Legislative Power: The Intellectual*

---

[45] See Melville B. Nimmer, *Does Copyright Abridge the First Amendment Guarantees of Free Speech and Press?,* 17 UCLA L. Rev. 1180, 1195-96 (1970); L. Ray Patterson, *Copyright in the New Millennium: Resolving the Conflict between Property Rights and Political Rights,* 62 Ohio St. L.J. 703 (2001).

[46] See Paul J. Heald & Suzanna Sherry, *Implied Limits on the Legislative Power: The Intellectual Property Clause as an Absolute Constraint on Congress,* 2000 U. Ill. L. Rev. 1119, 1169.

[47] See Dennis S. Karjala, *The Term of Copyright, in* Laura N. Gasaway, *Growing Pains: Adapting Copyright for Libraries, Education and Society* 33, 50 (1997).

Property Clause as an Absolute Constraint on Congress, 2000 U. Ill. L. Rev. 1119, 1171. This case does not, however, require decision of that question, since the Copyright Term Extension Act was not designed to, and does not, achieve harmonization of copyright terms with Europe.

United States copyright law measures copyright duration in two ways. Since 1978, works authored by identified natural persons receive a copyright term based on the life of the author. Until the enactment of the CTEA, that term was life of the author plus 50 years; today it is life of the author plus 70 years. 17 U.S.C. § 302(a). Works made for hire, and anonymous and pseudonymous works, receive a copyright term calculated from the date of the work's creation or first publication.[48] Before the enactment of the CTEA, that term was 100 years from creation or 75 years from publication. Today, it is 120 years from creation or 95 years from publication. 17 U.S.C. § 302(c).

The CTEA also extended the copyright term for works that were protected by federal copyright laws before the effective date of the 1976 Copyright Act. Before 1976, those works had received a 28-year copyright term that could be renewed for an additional 28 years. In 1976, Congress granted a 19-year extension, and in 1992, Congress made renewal of the copyright term automatic. Thus, before the CTEA, works published or registered before 1978 had a copyright term of 75 years. The CTEA lengthened their term further, to 95 years. 17 U.S.C. § 304.

In the European Union, works authored by identified natural persons receive a copyright term of life plus 70 years. *Council Directive 93/98/EEC* at Art. 1(1).[49] Few EU nations apply the work for hire doctrine (under which the employer of the natural person who creates a work of authorship is deemed to be the author of the work, see 17 U.S.C. § 201(b)), but the EU Directive does recognize works for which the copyright is owned by legal persons rather than authors. For those works, and for anonymous and pseudonymous works, the copyright term is set at 70 years after the work is first made available to the public. *Council Directive 93/98/EEC* at Art. 1(3), Art 1(4).[50]

Thus, before Congress enacted the CTEA, U.S. terms calculated on the basis of the life of the author were 20 years shorter than their European counterparts, while U.S. terms for works made for hire and anonymous and

---

[48] The Copyright Office does not keep current statistics on the percentage of registrations that are for works made for hire. As of 1955, works made for hire accounted for 40% of copyright registrations. See *Community for Creative Non-Violence v. Reid,* 490 U.S. 730, 737 n.4 (1989).

[49] See, e.g., Irish Copyright and Related Rights Act 2000, ch 3, § 24(1); Netherlands Copyright Act 1912 art. 37(1).

[50] The European concept of making a work available to the public is broader than publication under U.S. copyright. A work may be widely available but still remain unpublished under U.S. law. See, e.g., *Estate of Martin Luther King Jr., Inc. v. CBS, Inc.,* 194 F.3d 1211 (11th Cir. 1999); *Academy of Motion Picture Arts & Sciences v. Creative House Promotions Inc.,* 944 F.2d 1446 (9th Cir. 1991).

pseudonymous works were *already* at least five and as much as 30 years longer than their European counterparts. The CTEA *increased* the disparity between U.S. and EU terms, for the latter category of works, to at least 25 and as much as 50 years. Thus, while sections 102(b)(1) & (2) of the CTEA could be said to promote harmonization, sections 102(b)(3), (4) & (5) were antithetical to it.[51]

In some instances, the CTEA extended U.S. copyright terms that were simply incommensurable with their European counterparts. For works authored by identified natural persons before 1976, the U.S. measures the copyright by the age of the work, while Europe measures it by the life of the author. As the example of H.G. Wells's novels demonstrates, works created and published early in an author's life expired earlier under the U.S. system, while works published late in the author's life might enter the public domain later than in Europe. Instead of revising the fixed 75-year term to match the EU term of life plus 70 for works authored by natural persons and 70 years for works made for hire, Congress simply added an additional 20 years to all copyright terms.[52]

None of the supposed benefits of harmonizing copyright terms flow from those amendments: an author's works will still enter the public domain at different times in different jurisdictions. The only effect of these amendments is to give a windfall to current proprietors of works first published or registered during the 55 years between 1923 and 1978, and to put off for another 20 years the already-delayed entry of those works into the public domain.[53]

The failure of the CTEA to promote genuine harmonization of copyright terms should not be surprising. The primary purpose of the extension act was not harmonization, but to prevent works from entering the public domain. Congress amended copyright terms to match the terms prescribed by the European Union where doing so would increase the copyright term, and delay for 20 years the works' entry into the public domain. In cases in which the U.S. term already significantly exceeded the term granted in Europe, Congress extended the U.S. copyright terms further, in order to

---

[51] Sections 102(c) and (d) were antithetical to harmonization in the same way, insofar as they applied to works made for hire and anonymous and pseudonymous works; there as well, the CTEA extended copyrights that were already longer than in the EU.

[52] Similarly, under the EU Directive, sound recordings are protected for a term of 50 years. *Council Directive 93/98/EEC,* at Art. 3(2). The copyright term for motion pictures is based on the lives of its principal creative contributors. *Id.* at Art. 2(2); see, e.g., Netherlands Copyright Act 1912, at Art. 40. Before and after the CTEA, there is little relationship between U.S. and EU copyright terms for sound recordings, typically measured by the life of the author in the U.S. and by a flat term of years in the E.U. and for motion pictures, typically measured by a term of years in the U.S. and by the authors' lives in the EU.

[53] See William Patry, *The Failure of the American Copyright System: Protecting the Idle Rich,* 72 Notre Dame L. Rev. 907 (1997).

postpone the entry of those works into the public domain, despite the fact that doing so would *increase* the disparity between U.S. and European terms.

3.   The CTEA Is Not Justified By An Increase In The Commercial Life Of Copyrighted Works.

Witnesses and members of Congress suggested that the fact that works of authorship now enjoyed a longer commercial life obliged Congress to extend the copyright term to enable copyright owners to continue to earn money from the exploitation of their parents', grandparents', or employees' works for as long as such exploitation remained profitable.[54] This implies that the public domain is intended to be a repository for only those works that are no longer marketable. Under that rationale, the symphonies of Ludwig Van Beethoven (1770-1827) would be protected indefinitely. The basis for restricting copyright terms to "limited Times" is to enable broad public availability while the work is still valuable.

Moreover, the expiration of copyright does not prevent authors from continuing to develop and exploit their creations; it simply allows the public unrestricted access on an equal footing. Copyright owners who control works that remain profitable many years after they were created will, even after the works enter the public domain, continue to exercise control over and to earn revenue from any derivative works created after the initial work. See 17 U.S.C. § 103(b). When the copyright in the 1928 film *Steamboat Willie,* the first motion picture featuring Mickey Mouse, expires, the original black and white cartoon of Mickey Mouse will enter the public domain. Disney will continue to control and earn revenue from more recent renditions of Mickey, along with hundreds of works based on Mickey Mouse created in the years since *Steamboat Willie* appeared. Each of those works is copyrightable in its own right. Disney's revisions, adaptations, and elaborations of the character will continue to enjoy copyright protection until the copyrights in the derivative works expire,[55] just as Disney enjoys copyright protection for its many adaptations of other public domain works.[56]

---

[54] See *1995 Senate Hearing* at 18 (testimony of Marybeth Peters, Register of Copyrights); *id.* at 59-62 (statement of Ellen Donaldson, daughter of composer Walter Donaldson); *1995 House Hearing* at 272 (statement of Mary Ellin Barrett, daughter of composer Irving Berlin).

[55] In addition, courts have held that rights under the Lanham Trademark Protection Act, 15 U.S.C. §§ 1051-1127, survive the expiration of a copyright or patent. See, e.g., *Frederick Warne & Co. v. Book Sales, Inc.,* 481 F. Supp. 1191 (S.D.N.Y. 1979) (copyright); *In re Worlds Finest Chocolate, Inc.,* 474 F.2d 1012 (C.C.P.A. 1973) (design patent). See generally Jessica Litman, *Mickey Mouse Emeritus: Character Protection and the Public Domain,* 11 U. Miami Ent. & Sports L. Rev. 429 (1994).

[56] See, e.g., *Alice in Wonderland* (1951); *The Hunchback of Notre Dame* (1996); *Snow White and the Seven Dwarfs* (1937).

Even if the growth in the commercial life of copyrighted works were an adequate justification for a prospective extension, it would still fail to support a retrospective one. Congress's overriding purpose in enacting the CTEA was to prevent works from entering the public domain, extending the period in which copyright holders would collect royalties. But this wealth transfer to copyright holders from the public at large brought with it none of the countervailing benefits required by the Copyright and Patent Clause.[57] By attempting to ensure that authors' grandchildren could wring every last drop of commercial value remaining in a work before it enters the public domain, Congress violated the bargain implicit in Art 1, § 8, cl. 8.

II. THE COPYRIGHT TERM EXTENSION ACT VIOLATES THE FIRST AMENDMENT

In addition to overstepping Congress's power under the Copyright and Patent Clause, the CTEA is unconstitutional for a second, independent reason: It violates the First Amendment.

A. COPYRIGHT LAWS RESTRICT SPEECH

Copyright laws impose restrictions on speech, and thus implicate the First Amendment. The essence of a copyright statute, after all, is to make it actionable to publish certain speech. If a court finds that the language of a newspaper article infringes the language of some other literary work, then it can enjoin the author from further publication, or order her to pay statutory damages flowing from the publication. Copyright gives the government authority to seize books and newspapers and the machines used to publish them; if a jury finds by a preponderance of the evidence that books are infringing, the court can order them destroyed. It is difficult to imagine a more stark restraint on speech. "Whenever the law permits the sheriff to walk into people's offices and confiscate their publications, or levy against their belongings because of something they said or how they said it, the First Amendment is deeply implicated."[58]

This is not a new idea. It is the thesis of the foundational article on the relationship between copyright and the First Amendment: Melville B. Nimmer, *Does Copyright Abridge the First Amendment Guarantees of Free Speech and Press?*, 17 UCLA L. Rev. 1180 (1970).[59] Nimmer's article noted

---

[57] See Richard Epstein, *Congress's Copyright Giveaway,* Wall Street Journal, Dec. 21, 1998, at A19.

[58] Yochai Benkler, *Constitutional Bounds of Database Protection: The Role of Judicial Review in the Creation and Definition of Private Rights in Information,* 15 Berkeley Tech. L.J. 535, 553 (2000); see also, e.g., Neil Weinstock Netanel, *Locating Copyright within the First Amendment Skein,* 54 Stan. L. Rev. 1 (2001); Eugene Volokh & Brett McDonnell, *Freedom of Speech and Independent Judgment Review in Copyright Cases,* 107 Yale L.J. 2431 (1998).

[59] The Nimmer article provided the initial basis for the Court's case law on copy-

that the copyright statute, by punishing expression, "fl[ies] directly in the face" of the First Amendment. *Id.* at 1181. Nimmer urged, though, that a court could strike a balance between the government interests promoted by copyright, and the speech interests it impinged on, through "definitional balancing" such as that the Court used in the libel context in *New York Times Co. v. Sullivan,* 376 U.S. 254 (1964). See 17 UCLA L. Rev. at 1184. In general, he continued, a rule that copyright could extend to expression but not to ideas represented an acceptable definitional balance. "In some degree it encroaches upon freedom of speech . . . but this is justified by the greater public good in the copyright encouragement of creative works." *Id.* at 1192.

However, Nimmer explained, copyright even in expression will not necessarily have adequate First Amendment justification. In particular, he stressed, the First Amendment bars an inappropriately long copyright term - as the copyright term lengthens into perpetuity, the incremental incentive it provides vanishes, so there is nothing on the copyright side of the First Amendment balance. *Id.* at 1193. Similarly, should Congress seek to extend the copyright term for already existing works, the extension serves no interest that could be balanced against the speech interest it disserves. *Id.* at 1195.

A broad consensus of legal scholars, over the years, has adhered to the view that copyright law, as a restriction on speech, is subject to First Amendment constraints.[60] Nevertheless, the D.C. Circuit stated that copyright is

right and the First Amendment. *See* Neil Netanel, *Locating Copyright in the First Amendment Skein,* 54 Stan. L. Rev. 1, 10-11 (2001). The Court first cited it in *Zacchini v. Scripps-Howard Broadcasting Co.,* 433 U.S. 562, 577 n.13 (1977), and numerous courts followed suit. In *Harper & Row v. Nation Enterprises,* 471 U.S. 539 (1985), the Court approved the "definitional balance" approach the article originated, and cited Nimmer's treatise, which in turn cited and relied on his earlier article. See *id.* at 556; cf. *id.* at 548, 549, 551, 552, 554, 556, 560, 562, 563, 564, 566, 567, 568 (citing the treatise for various points).

[60] See, e.g., Floyd Abrams, *First Amendment and Copyright,* 35 J. Copr. Soc'y 1 (1987); C. Edwin Baker, *First Amendment Limits on Copyright,* 55 Vand. L. Rev. 891 (2002); Yochai Benkler, *Free as the Air to Common Use: First Amendment Constraints on Enclosure of the Public Domain,* 74 N.Y.U. L. Rev. 354 (1999); Julie E. Cohen, *A Right to Read Anonymously: A Closer Look at "Copyright Management" in Cyberspace,* 28 Conn. L. Rev. 981 (1996); Robert C. Denicola, *Copyright and Free Speech: Constitutional Limitations on the Protection of Expression,* 67 Calif. L. Rev. 283 (1979); Gary L. Francione, *Facing The Nation: The Standards for Copyright, Infringement, and Fair Use of Factual Works,* 134 U. Pa. L. Rev. 519 (1986); Stephen Fraser, *The Conflict Between the First Amendment and Copyright Law and Its Impact on The Internet,* 16 Cardozo Arts & Ent. L.J. 1 (1998); Charles C. Goetsch, *Parody as Free Speech—The Replacement of the Fair Use Doctrine by First Amendment Protection,* 3 W. New Eng. L. Rev. 39 (1980); Paul Goldstein, *Copyright and the First Amendment,* 70 Colum. L. Rev. 983 (1970); Mark A. Lemley & Eugene Volokh, *Freedom of Speech and Injunctions in Intellectual Property Cases,* 48 Duke L.J. 147 (1998); Michael J. Madison, *Complexity and Copyright in Contradiction,* 18 Cardozo Arts & Ent. L.J. 125, 159-73 (2000); Neil Weinstock Netanel, *Locating*

"categorically immune" from First Amendment scrutiny. None of the court's purported or possible justifications for that far-reaching statement hold up to analysis.

1. Harper & Row Did Not Hold That Copyright Laws Are Immune From First Amendment Scrutiny.

The D.C. Circuit insisted that this Court's decision in *Harper & Row v. Nation Enterprises,* 471 U.S. 539 (1985), forbade any First Amendment scrutiny of copyright law provisions. *Eldred v. Reno,* 239 F.3d at 375. But *Harper & Row* did not say that. The Court in *Harper & Row* noted that copyright serves important public goals that enrich the system of freedom of expression. It is "the engine of free expression": by enhancing the economic incentives for authorship, it stimulates the creation of useful works and thus serves the general public good. 471 U.S. at 558. The Court rejected a claim that the First Amendment forbade copyright liability for publishing a particular article of great public interest, finding that the First Amendment was implicated but not overthrown: Defendant's constitutional claim failed in light of "the First Amendment protections already embodied in the Copyright Act's distinction between copyrightable expression and uncopyrightable facts and ideas, and the latitude for scholarship and comment traditionally afforded by fair use." *Id.* at 560.

The Court's decision in *Harper & Row* sends a crucial message: The mere fact that copyright statutes *implicate* the First Amendment does not mean that they *violate* the First Amendment. As a general matter, a statute implicating free-speech rights will be upheld if it is sufficiently narrowly tailored to advance sufficiently important government interests. Most copyright legislation advances the important government interest in providing incentives for creation, and should be upheld where it is adequately narrowly tailored to those goals. Notwithstanding defendant's claim in *Harper & Row* that its infringement enabled its publication of material of

---

Copyright Within the First Amendment Skein, 54 Stan. L. Rev. 1 (2001); Hon. James L. Oakes, *Copyrights and Copyremedies: Unfair Use and Injunctions,* 18 Hofstra L. Rev. 983 (1990); L. Ray Patterson, *Free Speech, Copyright, and Fair Use,* 40 Vand. L. Rev. 1 (1987); David E. Shipley, *Conflicts Between Copyright and the First Amendment After* Harper & Row, Publishers v. Nation Enterprises, 1986 BYU L. Rev. 983 (1986); Hannibal Travis, *Pirates of the Information Infrastructure: Blackstonian Copyright and the First Amendment,* 15 Berkeley Tech. L.J. 777 (2000); Rebecca Tushnet, *Copyright as a Model for Free Speech Law: What Copyright Has in Common with Anti-Pornography Laws, Campaign Finance Reform, and Telecommunications Regulation,* 42 B.C. L. Rev. 1 (2000); Eugene Volokh & Brett McDonnell, *Freedom of Speech and Independent Judgment Review in Copyright Cases,* 107 Yale L.J. 2431 (1998); Alfred C. Yen, *A First Amendment Perspective on the Idea/Expression Dichotomy and Copyright in a Work's "Total Concept and Feel,"* 38 Emory L.J. 393 (1989); Geri J. Yonover, *The Precarious Balance: Moral Rights, Parody, and Fair Use,* 14 Cardozo Arts & Ent. L.J. 79 (1996); Diane Leenheer Zimmerman, *Information as Speech, Information as Goods: Some Thoughts on Marketplaces and the Bill of Rights,* 33 Wm. & Mary L. Rev. 665, 666 (1992).

great public interest, the Court deemed the copyright statute before it to be sufficiently closely tailored to withstand defendant's First Amendment attack.

The most important reason copyright law and the First Amendment have coexisted for two centuries with only infrequent clashes is that copyright rights are limited both in scope and in time. A significant increase in either the scope or duration of copyright necessarily implicates the First Amendment balance. For this reason, the Court's opinion in *Harper & Row* should be read cautiously. One of the most troubling aspects of copyright in recent years is that the limitations on copyright liability, including the idea-expression distinction and fair use, have been steadily shrinking via judicial construction; at the same time, copyright owners' exclusive rights have been growing.[61] Nothing in *Harper & Row* approves new copyright law that, by virtue of legislative amendment and judicial reinterpretation, is substantially less speech-protective than the copyright law before the Court in that case. The lasting lesson of *Harper & Row,* on the contrary, is that the First Amendment is relevant to copyright law.[62] When a court hears a First Amendment challenge to copyright legislation, it must satisfy itself that the statute is sufficiently narrowly tailored to withstand constitutional attack.

2. *The Idea/Expression Distinction Does Not Immunize Copyright From First Amendment Scrutiny.*

The D.C. Circuit urged that regulation of expression raises no First Amendment concerns so long as the law allows the free communication of *ideas:* the copyist can express his thoughts in a different, non-infringing form. This is a fundamental misconception. While the Court held in *Harper & Row* that the idea/expression distinction helps copyright statutes *survive* First Amendment scrutiny, it does not follow that copyright statutes are not *subject* to First Amendment scrutiny. On the contrary, under black-letter First Amendment law, even where a speech restriction leaves people free to convey their ideas in another manner, its restriction of expression must nonetheless be narrowly tailored to important government interests. See, e.g., *Ward v. Rock Against Racism,* 491 U.S. 781 (1989) (subjecting to First Amendment analysis a regulation limiting the loudness of music

---

[61] See Jessica Litman, *Digital Copyright* 77-88, 175-176 (2001); Neil Weinstock Netanel, *Locating Copyright within the First Amendment Skein,* 54 Stan. L. Rev. 1, 12-30 (2001; Hannibal Travis, *Pirates of the Information Infrastructure: Blackstonian Copyright and the First Amendment,* 15 Berkeley Tech. L.J. 777 (2000).

[62] The First Amendment has been held to limit government enforcement of a wide range of private rights, even where the laws creating those rights -like copyright -have internal limits that help protect First Amendment values. See, e.g., *Bartnicki v. Vopper,* 532 U.S. 514 (2000); *Hustler Magazine, Inc. v. Falwell,* 485 U.S. 46 (1988); *Time, Inc. v. Hill,* 385 U.S. 374 (1967); *New York Times v. Sullivan,* 376 U.S. 254 (1964). See generally Neil Weinstock Netanel, *Locating Copyright within the First Amendment Skein,* 54 Stan. L. Rev. 1, 4 (2001).

at public concerts). The Court has made clear that freedom of speech implicates the ability to choose one's words as well as one's ideas. See *Cohen v. California,* 403 U.S. 15 (1971) (rejecting the state's contention that it could forbid Cohen to wear a jacket emblazoned "Fuck the Draft" because he could convey the same idea using other words).[63]

3.   Characterizing Copyright As A Property-Rights Regime Does Not Immunize It From First Amendment Scrutiny.

Finally, one court has suggested that the First Amendment is irrelevant to copyright because copyright merely vindicates property rights.[64] This is incorrect as well. Enforcement of property rights *in land,* to be sure, does not raise substantial First Amendment concerns. A speaker does not have a legal right to commandeer the printing presses of the *Washington Post* for her own expression. The reason is that the laws of real and tangible personal property are neutral laws of general applicability, unrelated to speech and with only incidental effects on it. "[T]he First Amendment does not invalidate every incidental burdening of the press that may result from the enforcement of civil or criminal statutes of general applicability."[65] The Court has repeatedly so held in the context of laws that regulate a broad swath of activity and encompass speech only incidentally.

But that principle does not apply when a law — even one with goals unrelated to the suppression of speech — regulates speech in particular. The copyright statute is such a law. It regulates speech and speech alone. The rights it announces have no general applicability. They are property rights *in speech.* In *Turner Broadcasting System v. FCC,* 512 U.S. 622, 640 (1994), the government urged that rules requiring cable systems to carry broadcast channels should be seen as neutral laws with no special First Amendment applicability, mere "industry-specific antitrust legislation." The Court disagreed. Laws regulating speech and singling out particular

---

[63] See also *Hurley v. Irish-American Gay, Lesbian and Bisexual Group,* 515 U.S. 557, 570 (1995) ("Nor, under our precedent, does First Amendment protection require a speaker to generate, as an original matter, each item featured in the communication."). Copyright's bar, it is important to note, goes far beyond literal copying; it covers translations, fictionalizations, and "any other form in which a work may be recast, transformed, or adapted." See 17 U.S.C. §§ 101 (definition of derivative work), 106(2); see Hannibal Travis, *Pirates of the Information Infrastructure: Blackstonian Copyright and the First Amendment,* 15 Berkeley Tech. L.J. 777 (2000). One cannot seriously argue that such a bar to speech has no impact on FirstAmendment concerns.

[64] See *Dallas Cowboys Cheerleaders, Inc. v. Scoreboard Posters, Inc.,* 600 F.2d 1184, 1188 (5th Cir. 1979). But see *Rogers v. Grimaldi,* 875 F.2d 994, 999 (2d Cir. 1989); *L.L. Bean, Inc. v. Drake Publishers, Inc.,* 811 F.2d 26, 29 (1st Cir. 1987).

[65] *Branzburg v. Hayes,* 408 U.S. 665, 682 (1972); see also *University of Pennsylvania v. EEOC,* 493 U.S. 182, 201 (1990); *Associated Press v. NLRB,* 301 U.S. 103, 132 (1937) ("The publisher of a newspaper has no special immunity from the application of general laws.").

categories of speakers, it explained, cannot be seen as neutral; they always get heightened constitutional scrutiny.[66]

B. THE CTEA CANNOT SURVIVE FIRSTAMENDMENT SCRUTINY

Once subjected to First Amendment scrutiny, the CTEA cannot survive. Even a content-neutral restriction of speech must further an important and factually demonstrable government interest, and must advance that interest sufficiently to justify its abridgement of expressive activity. *Turner Broadcasting v. FCC,* 512 U.S. 622, 664-65 (1994). Neither the CTEA's extension of copyrights in existing works, nor its copyright extension for works not yet created, satisfies that test.

The CTEA's extension of copyrights in existing works advances no legitimate government interest. The government, to be sure, has an important stake in providing incentives for the creation of new works. But the CTEA's extension of existing copyrights does not advance that interest. Nor do its provisions harmonize our copyright law with Europe's. The CTEA is highly valued by the beneficiaries of the additional copyright monopoly it granted for old works. It extends, both in Europe and in the U.S., the period during which they will continue to control and profit from those works. But Congress's desire to provide those entities with a naked wealth transfer cannot justify its restriction of speech.

The CTEA's extension of future copyrights is invalid as well. Congress has great discretion to determine the appropriate length of a copyright term in order to stimulate authorship and wide distribution of new works, while ensuring that the public gains unrestricted access to those works after a period of limited duration. Where Congress determines that the existing copyright term is inadequate, extending the duration of copyright prospectively is an appropriate response. The Court should defer to such a "predictive judgment[]" so long as it is "based on substantial evidence." 512 U.S. at 666. But the Court cannot defer to a judgment Congress never made. There is nothing in the legislative record to suggest that Congress found the pre-CTEA terms inadequate. Witnesses and members of Congress described the U.S. copyright system as extraordinarily successful.[67] Indeed, the evidence presented to Congress on the extension's incentive value demonstrated that it would be insignificant, because the discounted present value of the extended term would be negligible.[68] And the prospective

---

[66] 512 U.S. at 640-41; see also *Simon & Schuster, Inc. v. Members of the N.Y. State Crime Victims Board,* 502 U.S. 105, 117 (1991); *San Francisco Arts & Athletics, Inc. v. United States Olympic Committee,* 483 U.S. 522, 534 (1987) (subjecting to First Amendment scrutiny a law granting a private entity "a limited property right in the word 'Olympic'").

[67] See *1995 Senate Hearing* at 26 (prepared statement of Bruce A. Lehman, Commissioner of Patents); testimony cited *supra* note 21.

[68] See *1995 House Hearing* at 300 (written testimony of Dennis Karjala); *id.* at

extension, like the retrospective one, does not harmonize U.S. and European copyright law.

CONCLUSION

The judgment of the court of appeals should be reversed.

USAGE: On page 351, ADD the following text immediately before subsection [C]:

Restored Works Update

Partial summary judgment for the plaintiff on the issue of copyright infringement recently was granted in the *Cordon Art* case, *see* 2002 U.S. Dist LEXIS 1611, based in part on the court's conclusion that the defendants were not "reliance parties" because they began to manufacture their Escher reproductions almost six months after December 8, 1994, the cut-off date to which the statute points.

The position of "reliance parties" is further addressed in *Hoepker v. Kruger,* 2002 U.S. Dist. LEXIS 7966 (S.D.N.Y. 2002), which involved a claim by a German photographer whose 1960 work had fallen into the U.S. public domain through nonrenewal against (among others) an American artist who had used the photo in a 1990 collage. Both the artist and a museum that had purchased her work (and a limited license to reproduce it) were found to be qualified reliance parties as to ongoing potentially infringing activities alleged in the complaint. The claim failed because the photographer neglected to give the required notice of intent to enforce his restored right, pursuant to subsection (d)(2) of § 104A. The case raises (but does not resolve) some interesting questions. What, if for example, the artist *had* given a proper notice in 1997: could the museum still have proceeded to make and sell gift items bearing the image of the collage, paying "reasonable compensation" for the use of the incorporated photograph? The answer would seem to turn on whether this use represented an "exploitation" of the collage within the meaning of subsection (d)(3). "Exploitation" is, of course, nowhere defined in § 104A.

Along the way, the German photographer also had raised (and the court dismissed) the contextually implausible argument that the challenged collage was not a "derivative work," and that the defendants therefore were not "reliance parties." A similar contention received closer scrutiny in *Dam Things from Denmark v. Russ Berrie & Co., Inc.,* 2002 U.S. App. LEXIS

---

420 (remarks of Rep. Hoke); Paul J. Heald & Suzanna Sherry, *Implied Limits on the Legislative Power: The Intellectual Property Clause as an Absolute Constraint on Congress,* 2000 U. Ill. L. Rev. 1119, 1173.

9448 (3rd Cir. 2002), which vacated a District Court preliminary injunction. At issue was the defendant's line of novelty "troll" figures (described by the court as "short, pudgy, plastic dolls with big grins and wild hair"). The defendant formerly had been a licensee of the Danish plaintiff; subsequently, in the late 1980s, it developed its own designs, which everyone involved appeared to concede would have been infringements had the plaintiff's original "troll doll" been protected in the U.S. At the time, however, it was not. Instead, the original design was in the public domain because the plaintiffs' dolls had been made and sold without sufficient copyright notice. The Court of Appeals remanded with instructions that the trial court reanalyze the evidence. In particular, it directed the court to focus on the subtle but important contrast between how works are compared in copyright infringement analysis and how their similarities and differences should be assessed when the question is whether a putative derivative work "author's creativity is enough to overcome a charge of triviality." The decision will repay reading, and as you peruse it you should be aware of a lurking issue that almost certainly will be raised in subsequent phases of the case: whether the § 104A restoration of copyright is constitutional.

In September 2001, a lawsuit directly raising that constitutional issue, *Golan v. Ashcroft,* No. 01-B-1854, was filed in the Federal District Court in Denver. The plaintiffs include a noted musical conductor, Laurence Golan, who was concerned about the effect of restoration on the availability of public domain scores for orchestral performance. The plaintiffs are represented by (among others) Professor Lawrence Lessig of Stanford Law School. The documents in the case can be found at */www.law.stanford.edu/ library/special/decisions.shtml,* and a good summary is David Horrigan, *Conductors Pose First Challenge to Copyright Law*, National Law Journal, Dec. 3, 2001, at A18. In addition to § 104A, the *Golan* plaintiffs also are challenging the 1998 Sonny Bono Copyright Term Extension Act, which, as we have just seen, is now before the Supreme Court in *Eldred v. Reno.* More generally, the fate of this lawsuit may turn on how the Court analyzes the constitutional issues in that case.

[C] Renewal

USAGE: On page 366, SUBSTITUTE the following text for the second full paragraph of § 5.01[C][1]:

A final incentive concerns the remedies available to those registering their renewals. Under previous acts, where an original registration was not made, statutory damages and attorneys' fees were unavailable. Under the 1992 Act, they are; and application may be made at any time during the renewal period. *See* Pub. L. No. 102-307, § 102(b), amending 17 U.S.C. § 101 (definition of "registration"); 138 Cong. Rec. H4134 (June 4, 1992 remarks of Mr. Hughes); and §§ 412, 504, and 505. Further remedy-related incentives to file before infringement have been considered but rejected by Congress.

§ 5.02   Terminations of Transfers*

[C]   Comparison of §§ 203 and 304(c)*

USAGE: On pages 392-393, SUBSTITUTE the following termination review questions:

(1) *A* publishes a work on July 1, 1930 and, on that same date, assigns the initial and renewal terms to *B*, with appropriate powers of attorney.

(a) What is the earliest date that *A*'s survivors could have effected termination of the grant, assuming that they wished to do so "during [the] period of five years beginning at the end of fifty-six years from the date copyright was originally secured," as permitted by 17 U.S.C. § 304(c)(3)?

(b) Suppose that *A*'s survivors properly terminate. On what date will their rights expire and the work enter the public domain?

(2) Same facts as above, except that *A*'s survivors failed to effect termination within the five-year window provided by § 304(c)(3).

(a) What is the earliest date on which they can effect termination under the "second bite at the apple" provisions of the Sonny Bono Copyright Term Extension Act as contained in 17 U.S.C. § 304(d)?

(b) Assume that the survivors fail to effect termination at the beginning of the relevant five-year window but still wish to do so before that window closes. What is the latest date on which they can file an effective notice of termination and still recapture rights in any of the remaining term of protection?

(c) Now assume that the survivors succeed in effecting the termination just considered. On what dates will their rights expire and the work enter the public domain?

(3) *A* publishes a work on July 1, 1960 and assigns, on the same date, the initial and renewal terms to *B*, again with appropriate powers of attorney. Assuming no further action by *A*, decide who can obtain what rights in the copyright, and in what years, if:

(a) *A* dies in 1980.

(b) *A* dies in 1990.

(c) *A* dies in 2025.

(4) *A* publishes a work on July 1, 1960 and assigns, on the same date, the initial term to *B*. In 1988, *A* renews the copyright and assigns the

---

* **Updating Note re 2001 Reprint:** On page 376, the third line from the top of the page should refer to works that were "in their *first or* renewal term" on January 1, 1978.

* Our thanks to Profs. Tyler Ochoa of Whittier Law School, Jay Dougherty of Loyola Law School-Los Angeles and Barry McDonald of Pepperdine University School of Law for their exceptionally helpful suggestions in updating these questions in the wake of the Sonny Bono Copyright Term Extension Act. — *Eds.*

renewal term to *B*. *A* dies in 1989. *A*'s statutory heirs inform you, their attorney, that they wish to recapture from *B* the final 39-year period added to the copyright by the 1976 Act (and the 1998 amendments). Advise them.

(5) In the preceding hypotheticals, can *A* or *A*'s survivors waive or assign in advance their power to terminate?

(6) *A* creates a work in 1980 and wills his copyright to *B* in 1981. *A* dies in 1985, leaving *W*, *i.e.*, his widow. The work is finally published in 1986. What is the first year in which *W* may terminate the transfer to *B*? (Watch out! This one is simpler than you may think.)

(7) *A* creates a work in 1980, and, on July 1 of the same year, transfers all publication rights to *B*, who first publishes the work on January 1, 1986. *A* dies in 1991, leaving *W* and four children.

(a) When may *A*'s survivors terminate the grant to *B*?

(b) What is the first year in which the survivors may give notice of termination to *B*?

(c) *W* and one child wish to terminate the grant to *B*, but the other three children do not. Can there be a termination?

(d) Suppose that the child who had planned to join with *W* in terminating the grant to *B* dies, leaving two children (*W*'s grandchildren). One of the grandchildren wishes to join *W* in terminating *B*'s grant, but the other does not. Can there be a termination?

(e) Assuming that there is a termination under one of the two immediately preceding scenarios, what share of the rights previously held by *B* may the terminating parties grant to *C*?

(8) *A* creates a work in 1980, and on July 1 of the same year, transfers the right to prepare derivative works to *D*. *D* produces a derivative work in 1990. *A* dies in 1991, leaving *W* and four children.

(a) When may *A*'s survivors terminate the grant to *D*?

(b) What is the last year in which they may give notice of termination to *D*?

(c) *A*'s survivors terminate *D*'s grant, but *D*'s derivative work remains popular. *A*'s survivors go to court to compel *D* to pay over future profits from the derivative work. Will they succeed?

(d) *A*'s survivors decide in the 35th year after the execution of *D*'s grant to terminate it at the earliest possible date and serve on *D* a notice appropriate to terminate the grant in its 37th year. In the grant's 36th year, *D* prepares a new derivative work. Can *A*'s survivors stop *D* from exploiting the new work?

Chapter 6

PUBLICATION AND FORMALITIES

§ 6.01   Publication

USAGE: On pages 409-410, SUBSTITUTE the following text for the carryover paragraph:

Finally, as of March 1, 1989, the effective date of the BCIA, the concept of publication acquired a *new* significance in American law. One situation in which a work may be considered the work of a "treaty party" under (post-URAA) § 101, and thus protected by § 104(b)(2), occurs where the work "is first published in the United States or in a foreign nation that, on the date of first publication, is a treaty party." The concluding paragraph of § 104(b) provides that, for purposes of the foregoing language, "a work that is published in the United States or a treaty party within 30 days after publication in a foreign nation that is not a treaty party shall be considered to be first published in the United States or such treaty party, as the case may be." Publication itself is defined in terms somewhat different from, and arguably more inclusive than, the definition referenced in Article 3(4) of Berne. Under § 101, publication is "the distribution of copies or phonorecords of a work to the public by sale or other transfer of ownership, or by rental, lease, or lending." Under Article 3(3) of Berne, by contrast, "[t]he expression 'published works' means works published with the consent of their authors, whatever may be the means of manufacture of the copies, provided that the availability of such copies has been such as to satisfy the reasonable requirements of the public, having regard to the nature of the work." The potential significance of the difference between these definitions will appear shortly.

[B]   Publication in the Courts

USAGE: On page 422, CONSIDER the following recent development in connection with note (5):

Publication of phonorecords. The 1997 amendment to Title 17, providing that the distribution of a phonorecord is not a publication of the underlying work, applies retroactively. *See ABKCO Music, Inc. v. Lavere*, 217 F.3d 684 (9th Cir 2000) (holding that retroactivity is appropriate because the act provided a clarification rather than a change in the law).

USAGE: On pages 423-424, SUBSTITUTE the following text for the last four paragraphs of note (8):

The definition of a "Berne Convention work" added to the 1976 Act by the BCIA reflected the foregoing rule regarding the *timing* of publication.

But the § 101 definition of "publication" was broader in this respect than the corresponding provision of the Berne Convention. Under Berne, publication does not occur unless enough copies of the work would have been made available to "satisfy the reasonable requirements of the public." Suppose that, within 30 days of a work's first appearance in his or her home country, an author who was a resident of a non-Berne country caused 15 copies of that work to be offered for sale at one bookstore in Los Angeles. Later, the author claimed protection in the United States on a "back door to Berne" basis. Which definition of publication — Berne Convention Article 3(3) or § 101 of the Copyright Act — would control the determination of that claim? Consider § 3 of the 1988 BCIA: "The provisions of the Berne Convention . . . shall not be enforceable in any action brought pursuant to the provisions of the Berne Convention itself." Does this provide a conclusive answer to the question?

Many American works published before March 1, 1989 are protected in other countries adhering to the Berne Convention by virtue of this "back door." In the pre-March 1, 1989 period, perhaps the simplest expedient for an American author wishing protection in a particular Berne Convention country was to arrange for timely publication there as a means of perfecting her rights.

In contrast to the situation under Berne, the "back door" to the Universal Copyright Convention is open only a crack: the U.C.C. has no provision for "simultaneous publication," and protection on the basis of place of publication is mandated in one U.C.C. country only if actual "first publication" occurred in some *other* country adhering to the treaty. As currently written, U.S. law observes this distinction, providing no protection for foreign works based on "simultaneous publication" in a U.C.C. country.

The Agreement on Trade-Related Aspects of Intellectual Property (TRIPs), which formed part of the 1994 World Trade Organization Agreement negotiations, called on members of the World Trade Organization to extend copyright protection to the works of nationals of WTO countries. Although it is not clear that this provision required that protection be extended, in addition, to works first published in the territory of such countries, legislative implementation of the TRIPs Agreement had this effect. *See generally* § 2.03 of the casebook. In addition, the legislation generalized the Berne-derived concept of "simultaneous" publication to apply to all works for which protection in the U.S. is claimed on the basis of publication in "treaty parties" (a new category including members of Berne and the U.C.C., as well as WTO countries).

USAGE: On page 425, ADD the following text immediately before subsection [C]:

(12) Does posting a work on a website from which it can be copied or downloaded constitute a "publication"? This issue arose in *Getaped.com, Inc. v. Cangemi,* 188 F. Supp. 2d (S.D.N.Y. 2002), and on it turned the availability of statutory damages to the plaintiff website designer. The court had little difficulty with what seems to have been, strictly speaking, a case

of the first impression, relying heavily on various cases that have found the § 106(3) distribution right infringed by unauthorized web posting, including the Ninth Circuit's *Napster* decision:

> The common theme running through these decisions is the ability of the Internet user to download a file containing a copyrighted work and thereby gain control of it, that is, gain a proprietary or possessory interest in the copyrighted work. As the foremost copyright treatise states, "a *sine qua non* of publication [is] the acquisition by members of the public of a possessory interest in tangible copies of the work in question." M. Nimmer and D. Nimmer, Nimmer on Copyright § 4.07 (2001). . . .

> By accessing a webpage, the user not only views the page but can also view — and copy — the code used to create it. In other words, merely by accessing a webpage, an Internet user acquires the ability to make a copy of that webpage, a copy that is, in fact, indistinguishable in every part from the original. Consequently, when a website goes live, the creator loses the ability to control either duplication or further distribution of his or her work. A webpage in this respect is indistinguishable from photographs, music files or software posted on the web — all can be freely copied. Thus, when a webpage goes live on the Internet, it is distributed and "published" in the same way the music files in Napster or the photographs in the various Playboy decisions were distributed and "published."

Id. at 401-402. Does this make sense? Should the answer turn on the purposes for which the concept of "publication" is being invoked? Are we comfortable, for example, concluding that anyone who posts a previously unpublished 19th Century work on a website prior to January 1, 2003 should automatically receive an additional 47 years of protection under § 303? Does it matter whether the material posted actually is copied or downloaded? Or whether the site is obscure or prominent?

[C] Publication, Derivative Works, and the Public Domain

USAGE: On page 427, ADD the following text at the end of § 6.01:

For an interesting application of the Shoptalk approach, see *Cordon Holding B.V. v. Northwest Publishing Corp.*, 2002 U.S. Dist. LEXIS 1611 (S.D.N.Y. 2002).

§ 6.03 Deposit and Registration

USAGE: On page 454, SUBSTITUTE the following text for the paragraph at the top of the page:

Under the scheme of the BCIA, the foregoing incentives to registration (and, perforce, deposit) were applied generally — that is, to all copyright proprietors and all works. But note how the BCIA treated the § 411(a) requirement that a copyright owner must register with the Copyright Office (or have a formally proper application for registration refused by it) before initiating an infringement action. The BCIA waived this requirement as of March 1, 1989 for one class of works: "Berne Convention works," which had as their "country of origin" Berne member countries other than the United States. Thus, unlike the across-the-board abolition of the mandatory notice requirement in the BCIA, Congress adopted a so-called "two-tier" approach as to registration. Congress justified this approach on the ground that the Berne Convention applies only to works for which protection is claimed under the Convention itself. Since the BCIA, Congress has further (and significantly) revised the Act, so that the § 411(a) pre-infringement registration requirement now applies *only* to "United States work[s]." The definition of "United States work[s]" contained in § 101 is not nearly so straightforward as the uninitiated might imagine. Accordingly, it will repay careful study.

USAGE: On page 476, ADD the following text after note (17):

(17A) *Registration formalities for owners of collective and derivative works.* Does registration of a *collective work* constitute registration of a component individual work sufficient for the owner of rights in the individual work to be able to bring suit for copyright infringement?

In *Morris v. Business Concepts, Inc.,* 283 F.3d 502(2d Cir. 2002), the Second Circuit (on rehearing, after *New York Times Co., Inc. v. Tasini,* 121 S.Ct. 2381 (2001), "to clarify part of the reasoning in our [earlier] decision") held that, regardless of whether there can or cannot be "more than a single copyright in a work," the registration of a collective work does not satisfy the registration requirement of § 411(a) regarding a component individual work.

In its earlier decision, *Morris v. Business Concepts, Inc.,* 259 F. 3d 65 (2d Cir. 2001), the court had ruled that a magazine, although owning an exclusive license to publish an individual article by the plaintiff author, could not be considered a copyright "owner" of the copyright in the licensed article, such that the magazine's registration of a copyright in the collective work satisfied the § 411(a) registration requirement applicable to the underlying work. The court had observed that copyright ownership is not divisible, even if rights under copyright are. Under § 201(d), the various rights such as publication, distribution and reproduction may be divided. But, according to the court's first opinion, that provision addresses the divisibility of "rights," not the divisibility of the copyright itself. In other words, there is "never" more that one copyright in a work, even though there can be multiple owners of exclusive rights (relying on the Nimmer treatise but pre-*Tasini*).

In so holding, the earlier opinion declined to embrace the reasoning of *Goodis v. United Artists Television, Inc.,* 425 F.2d 397 (2d Cir. 1970) (decided under the 1909 Act and discussed in § 4.02 of the casebook), that a magazine's copyright notice was sufficient for the author of an individual work contained in the magazine to obtain a valid copyright. The *Goodis* court noted that, otherwise, publication of the magazine would have thrust the author's work into the public domain — an "unnecessarily harsh result," given that it was apparent from the magazine's copyright notice that the author did not intend such a result.

In the rehearing, the *Morris* court, after suggesting that the law and secondary authorities are unclear on such matters under the 1976 Act, elected to rely on Copyright Office practice (Circular 62 for Copyright Registration for Serials on Form SE) for the proposition that a collective work registration does not apply to the separate contributed works unless all rights in those works have been transferred to the collective work owner.

No doubt these questions, including the divisibility issues, will be subject to further consideration by the courts.

On a (perhaps) related matter: can the owner of a *derivative work* rely on the registration of the underlying work for § 411(a) purposes? In *Murray Hill Publications, Inc. v. ABC Communications, Inc.,* 264 F.3d 622 (6th Cir 2001), the court held that subject matter jurisdiction for a copyright claim over an unregistered derivative work may not be satisfied by the registration of the underlying work. The court suggested, however, that registration of the derivative work would cover the original work.

The court in *Murray Hill* characterized the jurisdictional requirements of § 411(a) as adding clarity and certainty to the enforcement of copyrights. In your view, do the rules articulated in *Murray Hill* and *Morris* in fact foster the admirable qualities of certainty and clarity?

Chapter 7

EXCLUSIVE RIGHTS AND THEIR LIMITATIONS

§ 7.01 Overview

[D] Exclusive Rights in the Networked Information Environment

USAGE: On page 496, SUBSTITUTE the following text for the next-to-last paragraph in § 7.01[D]:

In the end, the Administration and Congress apparently thought better of the White Paper proposals, while concluding that U.S. copyright law measured up to the mandate of the new treaties in this respect. The Digital Millennium Copyright Act of 1998, enacted to "implement" the treaties, includes no modifications or clarifications of § 106. By contrast, the brand new European Community "Directive on the harmonisation of certain aspects of copyright and related rights in the information society," adopted April 9 (still unpublished in official form as of the date of this writing, but available in Part Two of this Supplement) prominently features an Article 3(1) that defines a new exclusive right tracking the language of the 1996 WIPO treaties.

§ 7.02 The Reproduction Right

[C] Reproduction on the Internet

USAGE: On pages 512-518, SUBSTITUTE the following text for the entire subsection:

The issues generally. The lure of the Internet can tempt entrepreneurs into undertaking large-scale infringements of copyright. Consider, for example, this passage from the recent decision in *UMG Recordings, Inc. v. MP3.com, Inc.*, 92 F. Supp. 2d 349 (S.D.N.Y. 2000):

> The technology known as "MP3" permits rapid and efficient conversion of compact disc recordings ("CDs") to computer files easily accessed over the Internet. . . . Utilizing this technology, defendant MP3.com, on or around January 12, 2000, launched its "My.MP3.com" service, which it advertised as permitting subscribers to store, customize, and listen to the recordings contained on their CDs from any place where they have an internet connection. To make good on this offer, defendant purchased tens of thousands of popular CDs in which plaintiffs held the copyrights,

and, without authorization, copied their recordings onto its computer servers so as to be able to replay the recordings for its subscribers. Specifically, in order to first access such a recording, a subscriber to MP3.com must either "prove" that he already owns the CD version of the recording by inserting his copy of the commercial CD into his computer CD-Rom drive for a few seconds (the "Beam-it Service") or must purchase the CD from one of defendant's cooperating online retailers (the "Instant Listening Service"). Thereafter, however, the subscriber can access via the Internet from a computer anywhere in the world the copy of plaintiffs' recording made by defendant. Thus, although defendant seeks to portray its service as the "functional equivalent" of storing its subscribers' CDs, in actuality defendant is re-playing for the subscribers converted versions of the recordings it copied, without authorization, from plaintiffs' copyrighted CDs.

92 F. Supp. 2d at 350.

As this statement of the facts suggests, MP3.com (and its attempt to assert a "fair use" defense) did not fare well in the *UMG* court; and the trial ended with the award of what may be largest sum of statutory damages ever. (More details on the remedial aspect of the case can be found in § 10.01[C][2] of this Part.) For the moment, though, the point is that even when copies are made in connection with an intended Internet use, the ordinary rules apply.

At first blush, digital network information technology seems to present no particular challenge to traditional concepts of the reproduction right. If an electronic message containing a copyrighted work is sent, via the Internet or an intranet, from one point to another, it is possible (and perhaps even likely) that the work will be reproduced upon the message's arrival — as, for example, would be the case if a stable, permanent copy were made on the hard drive of the recipient's personal computer. If this transmission were an unauthorized one, the recipient of the message might well have direct liability for infringement as the result of making such a copy, and the sender might be liable as well, for inducing or facilitating an infringing act.

Problems begin to appear, however, when one considers the ubiquity of temporary or ephemeral digital copies in the network environment. Thus, for example, an e-mail message may pass through dozens or even hundreds of separate "servers" on its way from origin to destination and, at each of these locations, a relatively short-lived reproduction of that message is created — only to be deleted when that particular machine's role in facilitating the transmission is complete. Does this mean that, where the message in question contains unauthorized copyrighted material, the owner or operator of each and every one of those servers has some potential exposure to liability for infringement, along with the original sender and ultimate recipient of the message?

Or consider the increasingly routine activity of "browsing" the World Wide Web. Suppose that, in your virtual wanderings, you encounter a site where copyrighted material has been posted without the permission of the owner. Obviously, you may be in trouble if you "download" content from that site. But what if you merely read it on the screen of your computer. Are you an infringer nonetheless? Before rushing to answer, consider the fact that words and images appear on your screen only because a digital version of the web site's content resides temporarily in the "random-access memory" (or "RAM") of your computer. And consider, further, that the performance of Internet "browser" programs (like Netscape and Microsoft's Internet Explorer) is enhanced by their capacity to create so-called "caches."

All the forms of reproduction referred to in the last two paragraphs are either absolutely essential, or at least highly desirable, for the operation of digital network technology. And all of them are temporary, in the sense that they are technologically destined to be expunged, although the actual duration of their existence may range from milliseconds to weeks. Nevertheless, if we follow the reasoning of the *MAI* decision (discussed earlier in these notes) and the narrative of the "White Paper," all of these examples implicate the exercise of the § 106(1) reproduction right. The result would be, of course, that potential liability for copyright infringement in connection with the net-based use of any given work could be extremely widely distributed.

Or consider the situation involved recently in *Ticketmaster Corp. v. Tickets.Com, Inc.,* 2000 U.S. Dist. LEXIS 12987 (C.D. Cal. 2000). There, the defendant company used robotic search agent programs (charmingly designated as "spiders") to search the World Wide Web for information about tickets for sale to sporting events, concerts, etc.:

> The T.Com computers enter the TM computers electronically through the home page and make note of the URL's (electronic addresses) of the interior web pages. They then methodically extract the electronic information from the event page [URL, price, time, date, place, etc.] and copy it temporarily (for 10-15 seconds) on its own computers. The T.Com programs then extract the purely factual information from the copied TM web pages and place the factual information in the T.Com format on its own web pages, using its own method of expression and format for its own web pages.

Ticketmaster, 2000 U.S. Dist. LEXIS 12987, at *8-9.

But what is the copyright significance of the 10-15 seconds of "temporary" copying? According to the court, "the copy is not used competitively. It is destroyed after its limited function is done. It is used only to facilitate obtaining non-protectable data—here the basic factual data." Therefore, the court concludes in denying preliminary injunctive relief, the copying is likely to be a "fair use."

Can there be — and, if so, should there be — a unified solution to this apparent general problem? The issue of "temporary reproduction" was widely discussed (as part of the "digital agenda") at the December 1996 WIPO Diplomatic Conference, but the results of that discussion were profoundly inconclusive. "Agreed Statements" (much like domestic legislative history) which accompany the two treaties concluded in Geneva say only that "the reproduction right . . . fully [applies] in the digital environment [and it] is understood that the storage of a protected work in digital form in an electronic medium constitutes a reproduction . . ." The ambiguity of this statement is self-evident, but it is worth noting that (given the context in which this language was negotiated) the term "storage" probably should be understood to refer to the making of permanent, stable copies (such as those on a computer's hard drive). In other words, the treaties do little, if anything, to resolve the question of how incidental reproduction in the network environment should be regarded by the law.

More recently, however, the European Union has taken a bold initiative in this area. Its recent "Directive on the harmonisation of certain aspects of copyright and related rights in the information society" (2001/29/EC), reproduced in Part Two of this Supplement, includes Article 5(1) providing: "Temporary acts of reproduction . . . which are transient or incidental, which are an integral and essential part of a technological process whose sole purpose is to enable (a) a transmission in a network between third parties by an intermediary or (b) a lawful use of a work . . . and which have no independent economic significance, shall be exempted from the reproduction right. . . ."

By contrast, the United States has yet to address the issue in a systematic fashion.

The DMCA as panacea? Perhaps surprisingly, perhaps not, the Digital Millennium Copyright Act, enacted in 1998 to (among other things) "implement" the WIPO treaties, like the treaties fails to address these issues generally. The DMCA does, however, include some important new rules addressing particular aspects of the topic. For example, Title III (the "Computer Maintenance Competition Act"), codified at § 117(c) of Title 17, specifically reverses the result in *MAI* by affirmatively permitting the owner of a computer which "lawfully contains an authorized copy of [a] computer program" to make or authorize the making of an automatically generated temporary copy of that program in connection with the repair or maintenance of the computer — and *only* for that purpose. But although the new provision undoes the specific mischief of *MAI*, it creates new uncertainties in the process: its apparent negative implication is that temporary copies *not* specifically authorized by statute may in fact infringe.

The other part of the DMCA dealing, in passing, with temporary reproduction is Title II, the "Online Copyright Infringement Liability Limitation Act" (discussed at greater length in § 7.07[C]). In the months and years preceding enactment of the DMCA, Internet service providers ranging from AOL to local public libraries expressed concern that, on one basis or another, they might be left holding the bag for the infringing on-line activities of those to whom they provided Internet connections. One — although only one — potential form of liability about which they were concerned was that associated with the temporary reproductions of digital works made, in the course of their transmission over the Internet, on various servers and routers maintained by service providers. Service providers took only cold comfort from the Administration's suggestion that no legislation was required on the point, because courts would be likely to regard incidental reproductions as "implicitly" licensed, or as "fair uses." The difficulty with this suggestion, of course, was that it can apply to incidental reproductions (for example, in the course of *authorized* network transmissions of protected works) more obviously than it does to those made in connection with *unauthorized* ones — and it is precisely in the latter circumstance that service providers' concerns about exposure to liability arise. Thus, service providers (and especially telecommunications companies) were active in promoting a solution to the problem of transitory reproduction as part of the 1996 WIPO treaties — an effort the outcome of which, as we have seen, can be counted as an at least partial success.

On the domestic legislative front, the service providers were even more successful. The provisions of Title II of the DMCA that are codified as new § 512(a) of 17 U.S.C. give service providers a "free ride" in connection with so-called "transitory digital network communications," such as e-mail service.

As long as someone other than the service provider initiated the transmission and chose its recipient, and the service provider does not interfere with its content, no liability can attach to the service provider in connection with that transmission. This includes liability in connection with transitory reproductions, so long as they are not "maintained on the system or network . . . for a longer period than is reasonably necessary for the transmission, routing, or provision of connections." As it turns out, the "intermediate or transient storage" exempted under § 512(a) can be relatively long-lived. In a challenge to America Online's invocation of this "safe harbor" from liability, a science fiction writer seeking to hold the company responsible for unauthorized exchanges of his works on the USENET pointed out that AOL may maintain USENET messages on its servers for as long as 14 days. Reviewing the legislative history of the provision, however, the court found that its provisions were satisfied. *See Ellison v. Robertson,* 189 F. Supp. 2d 1051, 1068-70 (C.D. Cal. 2002) (indicating that the statute was designed to codify and generalize the rule of *Religious Technology Center v. Netcom On-line Communications Services, Inc.,* 907 F. Supp. 1361 (N.D. Cal. 1995), where USENET messages had been maintained for 11 days).

In the DMCA, Congress also confronted another, potentially more serious problem relating to digital reproduction in the Internet environment: the liability of service providers who also provide "hosting" services by allocating server space to customers or clients who wish to make information available to others, typically by way of the World Wide Web. Pretty clearly, the individual who causes an unauthorized digital copy to be "posted" to a website, along with the individual or individuals "downloading" that material from the site, may have liability for (among other things) infringement of the § 106(1) reproduction right. But what of the company or non-profit institution that operates the server where the offending document resides? Part of the answer, such as it is, can now be found in 17 U.S.C. § 512(c), which codifies the provisions of Title II of the DMCA.

Web hosting activities pose a range of potential copyright concerns for service providers, including potential liability for direct infringement of the reproduction and distribution rights, and for indirect (contributory or vicarious) infringement by assisting or abetting the on-line activities of customers or patrons. The principle of strict liability applies to direct infringement but, as is detailed in § 8.04 of the casebook, liability for indirect infringement may depend on such factors as whether the person to be held responsible for the infringements of another had knowledge of them, was in a position to control them, or actively benefitted from them.

With respect to "web hosting" (and analogous) activities, the new provisions of § 512(c) cut across these various doctrines of infringement to provide a qualified defense against any and all financial liability (and some — though not all — forms of injunctive relief) for service providers who meet a series of statutory conditions: they must not know or have reason to know that particular material posted to websites they host is infringing; they must either be unable to control what their customers post to those sites or get no direct financial benefits from those postings (as they would, for example, if they charged a specified fee for each item posted); they must devise, publicize and implement a policy for terminating service to users who repeatedly infringe copyrights; they must operate their systems in ways that do not undercut the effectiveness of technological protection measures (such as encryption routines) which have emerged as industry "standards" agreed upon by copyright owners and service providers alike; and — crucially — they must participate in a "notice and take-down" scheme described in detail in § 512(c).

At the threshold, of course, are questions about who qualifies as a service provider who can potentially benefit from the "notice and take-down" provisions of the DMCA. Clearly, a wide range of different business models may fall within § 512(k)(1)(B). These include an on-line auction site, *see Hendrickson v. eBay Inc.,* 165 F. Supp. 2d 1082, 2001 U.S. Dist. LEXIS 14420 (C.D. Cal. 2001), and a service for real estate brokers that hosts descriptions and images of commercial real estate contributed by sellers, *see Costar Group, Inc. v. Loopnet, Inc.,* 164 F. Supp. 2d 688 (D. Md. 2001). But there may be limits. In *Perfect 10, Inc. v. Cybernet Ventures, Inc.,* 2002 U.S. Dist. LEXIS 7333 (C.D. Cal. 2002), the court expressed considerable skepticism about the statutory qualification of a company that operates an age verification service for adult websites and offers memberships giving members access to all the independent sites that subscribe to this service.

Of course, qualification as a service provider is just the beginning of a successful effort to limit liability. To achieve this goal, companies engaged in web-hosting also must have adopted and implemented, and informed subscribers of, a policy that provides for the termination in appropriate circumstances of subscribers who are repeat infringers. 17 U.S.C § 512(i)(1)(A). And they must respond appropriately to appropriate notices of specific claimed infringements by subscribers.

Briefly, compliance with the new rules on "notice and take-down" requires that every service provider designate an agent to receive notices of alleged infringement from copyright owners, by filing with the U.S. Copyright Office *and* by posting the agent's name and address (including an e-mail address) on a publicly accessible website. The function of this agent is to receive notices of claimed infringement from copyright owners, and the statute goes to some lengths to detail the elements that such a notice must contain, including requirements that (subject to various penalties for misrepresentation) it:

—   be sworn and physically or virtually signed;

—   be based on a good faith belief that the allegedly infringing material is being used without permission (although not, apparently, that the use is in fact an infringement, rather than, say, a "fair use");

—   identify the work allegedly infringed; and (perhaps most importantly)

—   identify the infringing material and provide "information reasonably sufficient to permit the service provider to locate the material."

One thing is clear: the statute, and only the statute, defines the nature of a qualifying notice. Courts have not smiled on the efforts of service providers to vary or modify that definition unilaterally. *See Perfect 10, Inc., v. Cybernet Ventures, Inc.,* 2002 U.S. Dist. LEXIS 7333, at *79-80 (C.D. Cal. 2002) (order granting preliminary injunction). That said, copyright owners have a strong motivation to provide notices that comply with the statutory requirements. A service provider is entitled to ignore any notice which is not in "substantial" compliance; and if it does, its receipt of the non-complying notice cannot be used against it in a subsequent effort to prove its "knowledge" of a customer's activities as an element of liability for contributory infringement.

Interesting questions also are beginning to arise about what constitutes "substantial" compliance with the very specifically-worded notice requirements. In fact, just such questions are now before the courts. In a case of the first impression, *ALS Scan, Inc. v. RemarQ Communities, Inc.,* 239 F.3d 619 (2001), the Fourth Circuit Court of Appeals dealt with a fact pattern in which the plaintiff company complained that its copyrighted "adult" photographs were being circulated on several Internet "newsgroups," to which the defendant service provider gave its subscribers access. The ISP persuaded the District Court that the plaintiff's § 512 notice was defective in that, among other things, it failed to identify with sufficient particularly the photographs alleged to have been infringed. The Court of Appeals disagreed, and stripped the "safe harbor" from the defendant:

> In this case, ALS Scan provided RemarQ with information that (1) identified two sites created for the sole purpose of publishing ALS Scan's copyrighted works, (2) asserted that virtually all the images at the two sites were its copyrighted material, and (3) referred RemarQ to two web

addresses where RemarQ could find pictures of ALS Scan's models and obtain ALS Sean's copyright information. In addition, it noted that material at the site could be identified as ALS Scan's material because the material included ALS Scan's "name and/or copyright symbol next to it." We believe that with this information, ALS Scan substantially complied with the notification requirement of providing a representative list of infringing material as well as information reasonably sufficient to enable RemarQ to locate the infringing material.

239 F.3d at 625. The decision has been subject to criticism on the grounds that flexible application of § 512 notice requirements may have the effect of undermining the congressional purpose of the DMCA's Title II: to allow the Internet to flourish in a litigious age. *See, e.g.,* Laura Rybka, *Als Scan, Inc. v. RemarQ Communities, Inc.: Notice and ISPs' Liability For Third Party Copyright Infringement,* 11 J. Art & Ent. L. 479 (2001).

Service providers are free to ignore even fully compliant notices, but in that case they do so at their peril. Not only do they lose the benefit of the "shield" from liability, which responding along the lines contemplated in § 512 provides, but their exposure to liability for contributory infringement may be considerably enhanced by the receipt of the notice. A service provider that strongly believes that a customer's or patron's on-line activities are lawful (perhaps because they constitute "fair use") may, however, choose to stand by the user and take its chances with ordinary legal process, rather than avail itself of the liability "shield" by "taking down" the offending content.

In order to secure to exemption, a service provider that does choose to respond to a notice must "respond[] expeditiously to remove, or disable access to, the material that is claimed to be infringing or to be the subject of infringing activity." Conveniently, § 512(g) immunizes service providers who act in good faith (either pursuant to a notice or otherwise) with a immunity from claims against them from the subscribers whose material is "taken down," if they take "reasonable" steps to notify those subscribers of the action.

The same section also describes a procedure by which a service provider may replace or restore access to material that has been taken down, without fear of incurring additional liability for copyright infringement. The procedure is triggered when and if the person whose material is at issue serves a "counter notification" including a sworn statement that he or she believes in good faith "that the material was removed or disabled as a result of mistake or misidentification of the material . . ." — language which raises a nice question about whether a statement asserting that the material is being used lawfully would suffice. In any event, the subscriber must then pass this counter-notification along to the copyright owner, which has 10 working days in which to seek judicial relief. If the owner does not do so, the service provider has four working days in which to restore the material or lose its exemption from claims by the subscriber relating to the "take-down."

Nor would a description of the "notice and take-down" provisions be complete without a reference to § 512(h), which basically allows any copyright owner who has served a compliant notice on a service provider to obtain an automatic *ex parte* court order requiring the service provider to identify the individual subscriber whose material or conduct was the subject of the original notice, and requiring the service provider to make this disclosure "expeditiously . . . notwithstanding any other provision of law . . ." Two points seem worth making here: first, that compliance with a court order would presumably shield a service provider from any liability for breach of the subscriber's privacy rights or breach of contract; and second, that this "subpoena" provision applies even to a service provider who has decided not to comply with a notice by "taking down" subscriber's material — thus putting it in the position of being required to supply the copyright owner with information that may be (among other things) part of a case against itself!

If all this seems complicated, it is. And there are still further nuances. Don't be surprised, for example, to see new materials on "copyright education" popping up on your university's computer system sometime soon. During deliberations over the DMCA, the higher education community was concerned that it might lose the benefits of the exemptions from liability provided in § 512 if faculty and teaching assistants were treated as general agents of their colleges and universities for all purposes, making these institutions automatically chargeable with participation in or knowledge of their instructors' own on-line activities. The resulting § 512(e) does not prevent schools from ultimately being held liable for the infringing activities of teachers on a theory of *respondeat superior*, but it does prevent them from being shut out of the § 512 service provider exemptions. In connection with some of the § 512 exemptions (like that for the provision of e-mail services), the "savings provisions" for institutions are absolute; with respect to others (like "web hosting"), they are qualified, subject to (among other things) a requirement that institutions provide all network users (faculty and non-faculty alike) with information that describes and "promote[s] compliance" with copyright law.

In addition to e-mail transmission and "web hosting" activities, § 512 also deals with two other potentially controversial activities of service providers in the Internet environment: performing "system caching" (storing local copies of the contents of frequently visited remote sites to speed or simplify user access), and making available information location tools such as search engines or links to material on remote servers. In the absence of an exemption, the former is clearly a matter of concern, in light of the general treatment of temporary digital reproduction in the DMCA. Potential liability in connection with the latter is still largely in the hypothetical realm, but seems almost certain to be litigated extensively in coming years. Section 512 gives qualified exemptions for both, subject to certain special limitations (such as the requirement that service providers cooperate with systems to assure accurate counting of "hits" on cached webpages), and are subject to versions of the "notice and take-down" scheme described above in connection with the exemption from liability for "web hosting."

In short — in case it is not already obvious — that § 512 in general, and its "notice and take-down" provisions in particular, raise a host of hard questions. Some are questions of law, and some questions of institutional practice.

For example, a penultimate subsection, labeled (somewhat ironically, in light of the automatic subpoena provisions described above) "Protection of Privacy," states that eligibility does not depend on a service provider monitoring its service or affirmatively seeking facts indicating infringing activity. Increasingly, however, copyright owners are "spamming" the registry of agents designated under § 512 with "notices" listing the names and descriptions of files of pirated material (such as illicit clips from popular new movies) that they believe may be widely distributed across the Internet in general. If such general bulletins are deemed to comply with § 512(c)(iii)(2), which requires that qualifying notices include

> [i]dentification of the material that is claimed to be infringing or to be the subject of infringing activity . . . and information reasonably sufficient to permit the service provider to locate the material

they would seem to impose on service providers something very much like an affirmative duty to police their networks — of the kind which § 512(m) denies.

In addition, there is ample room for argument about what constitutes a service provider's "expeditious" response to receipt of a qualifying notice. In particular, it will be interesting to discover whether the meaning of the term is "context-sensitive." May a university appropriately take longer in deciding whether to "take down" a posting by a senior member of the law school faculty than AOL should spend responding to a notice on the webpage of a computer-active 15 year old? Is making some preliminary inquiry of the subscriber or other system user ever an appropriate step, consistent with the duty of expeditious response? What about weekends?

And when should service providers just say "no," risking being found liable for infringement rather than denying system users access to their facilities? Is the topic one about which providers should develop internal policies? If so, are those policies likely to be different for commercial and noncommercial providers?

Finally, consider the following passage from the Ninth Circuit Court of Appeals' ruling in the *Napster* case:

> Napster also interposes a statutory limitation on liability by asserting the protections of the "safe harbor" from copyright infringement suits for "Internet service providers" contained in the Digital Millennium Copyright Act, 17 U.S.C. § 512. The district court did not give this statutory limitation any weight favoring a denial of temporary injunctive relief. The court concluded that Napster "has failed to persuade this court that subsection 512(d) shelters contributory infringers."

We need not accept a blanket conclusion that § 512 of the Digital Millennium Copyright Act will never protect secondary infringers. . . .

. . . We instead recognize that this issue will be more fully developed at trial. At this stage of the litigation, plaintiffs raise serious questions regarding Napster's ability to obtain shelter under § 512, and plaintiffs also demonstrate that the balance of hardships tips in their favor. . . .

Plaintiffs have raised and continue to raise significant questions under this statute, including: (1) whether Napster is an Internet service provider as defined by 17 U.S.C. § 512(d); (2) whether copyright owners must give a service provider "official" notice of infringing activity in order for it to have knowledge or awareness of infringing activity on its system; and (3) whether Napster complies with § 512(i), which requires a service provider to timely establish a detailed copyright compliance policy. . . .

239 F.3d 1004, 1025 (9th Cir. 2001).

The question of whether a "peer-to-peer" file sharing service like Napster is even definitionally eligible for a § 512 "safe harbor" is tougher than it first seems. Fairly obviously, this is not the sort of entity that Congress had in mind when enacting the DMCA. But the definition in § 512(k)(2), which applies to service providers supplying "information location tools" (among other things), is remarkably broad and non-specific: "a provider of online services or network access, or the operator of facilities therefor . . ." One might ask what practical difference it would have made at this stage of the proceedings to have found Napster to be potentially qualified for a § 512 "safe harbor." As we will see § 10.01[B][1] of this Supplement, the preliminary injunction in its final form apparently does require the recording companies to give Napster some form of notice concerning the identity of works allegedly being infringed by its subscribers.

As you can see, the fun is just beginning.

§ 7.03   The Adaptation Right *

§ 7.04   The Public Distribution Right

[B]   Domestic Distribution

USAGE: On page 542, ADD the following text after note (11):

(11A) *Software distribution: Sale or License?* The "second-hand" trade in genuine (as distinct from counterfeit) software products is a big little business, and it is coming under increasing legal fire from major software vendors. Typically, these enterprising resellers invoke "first sale," asserting that the firms and individuals from whom they bought their wares were themselves lawful purchasers. The manufacturers respond that the copies

---

* One of the co-authors' offspring has pointed out the obvious: the poster on page 521 is, of course, the "Nuke It" advertisement!

in question were never sold, merely "licensed." As evidence, they point to various terms in the "shrink-wrap" agreements that accompany these software products; when they are made available by or under the authority of their copyright owners — including the sorts of EULAs ("end user license agreements") with which you are (or should be) familiar. Different courts have taken dramatically different approaches to sorting out this conundrum. In *Adobe Systems, Inc. v. One Stop Micro, Inc.,* 84 F. Supp. 2d 1086 (N.D. Cal 2000), Judge Ware took what might be called a "formalistic" approach, giving much weight to the recitations of Adobe's standard agreements. By contrast, in *Softman Products Co., LLC v. Adobe Systems, Inc.,* 171 F. Supp. 2d 1075 (C.D. Cal 2001), Judge Pregerson looked beneath the surface of similar agreements and concluded that they amounted — in substance — to sales subject to § 109(a). *See also Novell v. CPU Distribution, Inc.,* 2000 U.S. Dist. LEXIS 9975 (S.D. Tex. 2000).

(11B) *"First Sale" Lives: A New Twist on an Old Problem.* Consider the following, from a story by David D. Kirpatrick, *Online Sales Of Used Books Draw Protest,* New York Times, Apr. 10, 2002, at C1, Col 5:

> Used books are also among Amazon's most profitable book sales. It directs customer orders to a network of consumers and bookstores that sell used copies, often for only a few dollars each or less, and makes a commission on each sale. Sometimes secondhand books are described on the site as "new" or never read but sold for less than half Amazon's retail price.

> Amazon began selling used books in November 2000, adding links that offer much cheaper used books to the same pages that showcased the more expensive new copies. The next month, the top executives of the Authors Guild and the Association of American Publishers protested in a conference call with Jeffrey P. Bezos, chief executive of Amazon. The executives were particularly upset that Amazon was offering used books for sale at the same time as the books' original publication.

> That suggested that free copies sent to potential reviewers were turning up for sale as used books at Amazon.com, usually for a small fraction of the retail price. (Selling review copies as used books was previously limited to stores in New York and other media centers.)

> "We asked could we at least talk about when something could become available as a used book? Could we maybe wait three months after the book was published?" said Patricia Schroeder, president of the Association of American Publishers. "The biggest problem is that it is legal, I think. I wring my hands, pound my desk and say, 'Aargh.'" (Most individual publishers are reluctant to criticize Amazon publicly for fear of alienating an important customer.)

Is Ms. Schroder correct?

[C] Public Distribution on the Internet

USAGE: On pages 543-545, SUBSTITUTE the following text for the entire subsection:

Suppose that you have paid for the privilege of downloading a copyrighted article on a recent antitrust case from a newspaper's website, and that, as a result, an authorized digital copy of that work now resides on the hard drive of your personal computer. What can you do with it without running afoul of the copyright law in general, and of the § 106(3) distribution right in particular? Can you send the article to your sister in California via e-mail? Or to 10 strangers whom you recently encountered on-line in a virtual "chat room" devoted to antitrust topics? Can you send it to all the other students in your antitrust class, via a dedicated "listserv" (*i.e.,* list-management software)? Can you post it at your homepage on the World Wide Web, where all comers can read and download it at will?

The 1995 "White Paper" on *Intellectual Property and the National Information Infrastructure* recommended (at p. 213) "that the Copyright Act be amended to expressly recognize that copies or phonorecords of works can be distributed to the public by transmission, and that such transmissions fall within the exclusive distribution right of the copyright owner," and proposed statutory language, included in an Administration-backed bill — the so-called NII Copyright Protection Act of 1995 — to bring about the desired result. The bill, however, failed to be enacted in the 104th Congress. Although the proposal was not particularly controversial in itself, some copyright users responded by demanding that any new legislation, besides updating the distribution right, should also include revisions to shore up provisions of the copyright law (*e.g.,* §§ 107 and 109) that protect user interests. The 1995 legislation failed, and later digital copyright bills, leading up to the Digital Millennium Copyright Act passed in 1998, sought to finesse these demands by simply omitting all reference to § 106(3) — apparently on the ground that the distribution right under existing law did (after all!) encompass transmissions with sufficient clarity. The legislative history of the DMCA is shot through with references making it clear that the shared assumption of all involved was that digital transmission to the public did constitute "distribution" within the meaning of 17 U.S.C. § 106. Indeed, had it been otherwise, further revisions to the Copyright Act would have been necessary, since the 1996 WIPO treaties clearly require that, in one way or another, party nations must prohibit the unauthorized making available to the public of copyright material by means of digital networks. Thus, for example, one reason that users of a peer-to-peer file-shared technology like Napster may be copyright infringers is that, when they make files resident on their own hard drives available to strangers, they are engaging in unauthorized acts of distribution — which would make them liable for violation of the copyright holder's § 106(3) right, unless, of course, those acts were privileged by way of (for example) the "fair use" doctrine.

Even so, not every on-line activity necessarily is a distribution. And this, of course, brings us back to where we started — and to our earlier questions relating to the scope of the distribution right in cyberspace. Where your sister in California is concerned, even the White Paper appears to concede that no distribution has occurred, because "transmission of a copyrighted work from one person to another in a private e-mail message would not constitute a distribution to the public" (p. 215). Once you leave your family circle, however, the matter becomes less clear. Conceivably, even sending a single piece of private e-mail to a stranger might represent a distribution of its contents. At least, this is the conclusion suggested by the *Ford Motor* case, discussed in the notes to *Hotaling* above.

And what is the definition of an individual's private "circle" in the age of the Internet? A recent development in the peer-to-peer file-sharing wars suggests that a court may soon have to grapple with this question. In early May 2001, the Aimster service (which enables file-sharing among members of "buddy lists" from services like AOL Instant Messenger), went on the legal offensive. Having received a letter from the Recording Industry of America demanding that it monitor uses of its utility for copyright compliance, along the lines of the surveillance imposed on the Napster service by the federal courts, Aimster responded by filing an action for a declaratory judgment to the effect that it was not liable (directly or indirectly) for copyright infringement. Among Aimster's claims is the assertion that exchanges of music files among friends do not constitute direct infringement — and that Aimster cannot, therefore, have secondary liability. As already noted in § 1.05[G] of this Supplement, this action has now been consolidated with a number of suits brought against the service by music industry companies.

Assuming, though, that you are dealing with strangers, does it matter to *how many* of them you send your message? If you post the story on your homepage, you don't send it to anyone in particular, of course. Yet, by making it available for downloading, you may well have done enough (once again) to constitute a distribution. *See Playboy Enterprises, Inc. v. Hardenburgh, Inc.*, 982 F. Supp. 503 (N.D. Ohio 1997), citing *Hotaling* in a discussion which concludes that making digital image files available to subscribers to a computer bulletin board constitutes infringing distribution by the BBS operator: "The phrase 'to the public,' in this sense, includes paying subscribers to an otherwise publicly available service." Can you see any basis for distinguishing the conduct analyzed in this holding from posting a file to a publicly accessible website? Does any distinction you can draw help or hurt where the website's proprietor is concerned?

Interesting as these questions may be in theoretical terms, do the answers really matter in practice? Remember that it is the nature of networked digital technology that, when a digital document is transmitted from one point to another, a whole series of reproductions, of varying degrees of permanence, will be made in the process. If the digital document in question is a copyrighted work which is being transmitted without authorization, don't these multiple acts of "copying" constitute a sufficient legal handle on the transaction, whether or not the distribution right is implicated? Fairly early on, there were indications that courts might well be inclined to find some basis for avoiding a finding of liability on this basis alone. *See, e.g., Religious Technology Center v. Netcom On-Line Communication Servs., Inc.,* 907 F. Supp. 1361 (N.D. Cal. 1995). As discussed above in § 7.02 of the casebook, however, the implication of the DMCA appears to be that, unless somehow specifically exempted by statute, even technologically incidental and necessary temporary reproduction in the digital environment may constitute infringement of the § 106(1) reproduction right.

Finally, where does the "first sale" doctrine figure in all this? According to the White Paper, the answer (at p. 92) is "nowhere":

> [T]he first sale doctrine limits only the copyright owner's distribution right; it in no way affects the reproduction right. Thus, the first sale doctrine does not allow the transmission of a copy of a work (through a computer network, for instance), because, under current technology the transmitter retains the original copy of the work while the recipient of the transmission obtains a reproduction of the original copy (*i.e.*, a *new* copy), rather than the copy owned by the transmitter.

Assuming, for the moment, that this analysis is technically correct, doesn't it beg the question of whether there *should* be a digital equivalent to analog "first sale"? A bill introduced in the 105th Congress in late 1996 included a provision amending § 109 to provide that:

> The authorization for use set forth in subsection (a) applies where the owner of a particular copy or phonorecord in a digital format lawfully made under this title, or any person authorized by such owner, performs, displays or distributes the work by means of transmission to a single recipient, if that person erases or destroys his or her copy or phonorecord at substantially the same time. The reproduction of a work, to the extent necessary for such performance, display, or distribution, is not an infringement.

H.R. 3048. Does this provision make good policy sense? How easy (or difficult) would it be to enforce? Could you draft a better "digital equivalent" to "first sale"?

The final version of the DMCA did not include any modifications to § 109(a), but it remains to be seen whether the issue is dead or only sleeping.

Section 104 of the DMCA did direct the Register of Copyrights and the Assistant Secretary of Commerce for Communications and Information to prepare a report for Congress examining the effects of the DMCA on the development of new technologies and electronic commerce and on the operation of § 109 and its "first sale" doctrine. A good account of the process undertaken by the Copyright Office and the National Telecommunications and Information Administration (NTIA), including comments filed and audio of public hearing held on November 29, 2000, can be found on the Copyright Office website: *www.loc.gov/copyright/reports/studies/dmca/dmca_study.html*. Perhaps even more interesting (and not available on the

Copyright Office site) is an objective summary of the comments and hearing prepared by NTIA, which can be found at *www.ntia.doc.gov/ntiahome/occ/ dmca2001/104gdmca.htm*. As the NTIA report notes, much of the controversy about "first sale" in the digital environment centers on so-called "forward and delete technology" and its ability to undergird any amendment to § 109 that would create a digital equivalent to the analog "first sale" doctrine. By this means, were it feasible, content providers might be able to enforce on end users (should they choose to do so) a technologically mandated election between maintaining a lawfully acquired copy of a work in digital format or transmitted a copy to a friend or other third party.

In August 2001, the Copyright Office finally issued a document entitled "A Report of the Register of Copyrights Pursuant to § 104 of the Digital Millennium Copyright." Because this document is of such general importance, the Executive Summary of the Report has been reproduced in full in Part Three of this Supplement. As you will see, the Report deals with "first sale" rather dismissively, and engages more completely with some of the other issues that were on the agenda.

On December 12 and 13, 2001, there were congressional hearings to consider the Report. *See Digital Millennium Copyright Act Section 104 Report*, Hearing Before the House Judiciary Subcomm. on Courts, the Internet, and Intellectual Property, 107th Cong., 1st Sess. (Ser. 52). So far, no legislation to implement the affirmative recommendations of the Study has been introduced, although some of its findings have become entangled with the dispute over compulsory license rates for the use of music on the Internet. A taste of some of the controversy to come may be had from the current dispute over whether and how the Copyright Office should respond to a tentative agreement among the RIAA, the National Music Publishers Assocation (NMPA) and the Harry Fox Agency, arrived at in October 2000, and designed to give the record labels' new digital music services, like Pressplay and MusicNet, access to all the musical compositions licensed by Harry Fox on behalf of composers and publishers. While the immediate parties have urged the Copyright Office to conduct a rulemaking that would make their agreement the basis for a general industry standard, others have resisted vigorously, noting that a premise of the agreement appears to be that, in addition to performance rights in copyrighted music, would-be providers of "streaming" audio on the Internet also must license "mechanical" rights (for temporary server reproduction, etc.) — and that this flies in the face of the Office's conclusions in the Section 104 Report. *See Draft Internet Streaming Deal Draws Attacks, Support,* Washington Internet Daily, Feb. 13, 2000, at 3 (and the comments collected at *http:// www.copyright.gov/carp/dpd/comments.html*); *see also The Rogers and Hammerstein Organization v. UMG Recordings, Inc.*, 2001 U.S. Dist. LEXIS 16111 (S.D.N.Y. 2001) (reflecting the unsettled state of the law on this subject).

Meanwhile, the report's treatment of the "first sale" doctrine as a incidental artifact of the law of property in chattels, rather than as an expression of affirmative cultural policy, as well as its reliance of market mechanisms to resolve this question of copyright policy, have attracted substantial criticism.

§ 7.05 The Public Performance Right

[A] Public Performances

USAGE: On page 566, SUBSTITUTE the following text for the last paragraph of note (10):

On March 7, 2001, Senators Orrin Hatch (R-Utah) and Patrick Leahy (D-Vt.) introduced S. 487, the "Technology, Education and Copyright Harmonization (TEACH) Act" (see Part One of this Supplement), which would implement some, although not all, of the Copyright Office's recommendations. Shortly, thereafter, the Senate Judiciary Committee held a hearing on the bill (see *http://www.senate.gov/~judiciary/hr031301.htm*), which would amend § 110(2) to expand the permitted uses currently available for instructional broadcasting to include the performance of any work (not produced primarily for instructional use) in "reasonable and limited" portions, while eliminating the requirement of a physical classroom and the limitation to students with disabilities and special circumstances. The bill would make clear that the instructional activities exempted in § 110(2) include digital as well as analogue transmissions — at the same time recognizing a limited right to reproduce and distribute transient copies created as part of the automated process of digital transmissions and providing safeguards to copyright owners by requiring that institutions taking advantage of the exemption promote compliance with copyright law and apply technological measures to prevent unauthorized access and uses. Further, the bill would amend § 112 to permit institutions to upload copyrighted works onto servers to be later transmitted to students in accordance with § 110, thus enabling asynchronous Internet-based distance education — while also providing safeguards against (a) retention or distribution of the copies other than as needed to accomplish the permitted instruction and (b) interference with technological measures used by the copyright owner. With amendments, the legislation cleared the Senate in June 2001, and moved quickly through the House Judiciary Subcommittee. There has been no action since July 11 of that year, and the prospects for passage in the 107th Congress are uncertain.

[B] Secondary Transmissions

USAGE: On pages 587-588, CONSIDER the following recent development in connection with note (11):

The Fairness in Music Licensing Act and TRIPs obligations. A World Trade Organization dispute resolution panel has affirmed that the United States violated global rules on intellectual property protection. In a proceeding initiated by the European Union on behalf of composers of European nationality, the three-member WTO dispute settlement panel concluded that § 110(5)(B) of the Copyright Act, enacted as part of the Fairness in Music Licensing Act, is inconsistent with the Agreement's Article 13, which confines limitations and exceptions on copyright under national law to "certain special cases which do not conflict with a normal exploitation of the work and do not unreasonably prejudice the legitimate interests of the right holder." In particular, the panel was concerned that the exemptions under § 110(5)(B) would allow 70 percent of restaurants and bars, and nearly half the retail stores in the United States, to avoid paying license fees for broadcast music played in their establishments. The panel also intimated strongly that the U.S. could not bring itself into compliance merely by reinstating the pre-FIMLA "home-type apparatus" provisions of § 110(5). Although the remnant of that provision now found in § 110(5)(A) of the Copyright Act was determined to be TRIPs-compatible, this was only because it no longer applied to non-dramatic musical works — for which there is the greatest demand, and which, hence, promise the greatest potential licensing revenue. The June 15, 2000 panel report (WT/DS/160/R) can be found in the dispute settlement area of the WTO's website: *http://www.wto.org/english/tratop_e/dispu_e/dispu_e.htm#disputes*

Although the United States had the option of appealing from the panel's action, it did not, with the result that the decision now stands as a final determination of the WTO Dispute Settlement Body. But what comes next? Representative James Sensenbrenner (R-Wis.), who was the principal sponsor of the FIMLA amendments, is now the chair of the House Judiciary Committee. At least for the moment, then, repeal seems unlikely. Theoretically, however, the United States could be subject to trade sanctions from other WTO members if it fails to bring its laws into compliance. The interim solution, suggested in a January 2002 "status report" filed by the U.S. Trade Representative with the WTO, appears to be a program of reparations — $1.1 million a year — to be paid to the EU over three years from the general revenues of the U.S. government. At this writing, the funds have not yet been appropriated. But even assuming they are, when the three years have passed, the underlying problem will remain!

§ 7.06   The Public Display Right

USAGE: On page 604, ADD the following text after note (15):

(16) The display right appears to be coming into its own in the Internet environment. For an important recent case in which it figured prominently, see *Kelly v. Arriba Soft Corp.*, 280 F.3d 934 (9th Cir. 2002), reproduced in § 9.06 of this Supplement.

§ 7.07 Miscellaneous Rights: In and Beyond Copyright

USAGE: On pages 604-625, SUBSTITUTE the following text for the entire section:

We have seen, in the preceding sections of this chapter, the basic architecture of rights and limitations in the 1976 Act as amended, and the content of the five fundamental rights contained in the Act. In addition, however, Congress has been busy in recent years considering, and in some instances enacting into law, what might be called "miscellaneous rights." What these miscellaneous rights have in common is that each is a nontraditional protection produced by the interaction of new technologies, modes of commerce, and "interest politics" by which much of contemporary copyright law and policy is shaped.

Once upon a time, who knows exactly how long ago, it might have made sense to speak of a "unified field" theory of copyright — one body of rules, that is, broadly applicable to all kinds of works and all kinds of uses. Indeed, the 1909 Copyright Act, as originally drafted, was a relatively straightforward document, with only a few embellishments (like the provisions for the mechanical right, the great granddaddy of today's rapidly proliferating statutory licenses). The 1971 Sound Recording Amendments, which brought in new subject matter while curtailing the exercise of rights with respect to it, marked a significant departure — the beginning of a tendency to incorporate various pieces of special purpose legislation within the law of copyright. By the time the smoke of the general revision process cleared in 1976, it was apparent that this tendency was in the ascendance. One needed to look no further than § 111 for a clear indication that, in the future, copyright law would increasingly be pressed into service as a vehicle for detailed regulation of new communications and information technologies. Even more recently, there has been a related trend toward the inclusion in Title 17 of new provisions which are specifically designed to interact with and affect the operation of copyright law, although they are technically not a part of it.

This section will explore these developments.

Before proceeding, however, we should note several matters which will *not* be covered here, but which are explored at other points in the casebook. The 1984 Semiconductor Chip Protection Act, which extends to non-copyrightable subject matter and is codified as a separate chapter of Title 17 independent of the Copyright Act itself, is treated in § 3.02. The rights granted in the 1994 Uruguay Round Agreements Act against bootleg sound recordings and music videos created by unauthorized taping of live music performances received consideration in § 2.01. Like the semiconductor chip provisions, they are codified in Title 17 but not as part of the Copyright Act — probably because they are perpetual in duration (a result not permissible under the "limited Times" language of Article I, § 8, cl. 8) and because they apply to unfixed performances (which lie beyond the constitutionally prescribed category of "Writings"). Finally, we do not address in the present section the recent efforts to provide protection outside of the Copyright Act (indeed, outside of Title 17) for factual compilations. For those developments, see § 3.03 above.

[A] The Digital Performance Right in Sound Recordings

[1] Introduction

The newest of the "miscellaneous" rights to be enacted into law — and the only one of these recently minted or proposed rights which actually forms part of the Copyright Act itself — is the right, "in the case of sound recordings, to perform the copyrighted work publicly by means of a digital audio transmission." 17 U.S.C. § 106(6). Enacted in 1995, the Digital Performance Right in Sound Recordings Act ("DPRSRA") both added to the Copyright Act the foregoing exclusive right and defined a variety of exemptions to that right, while imposing a complex regime of statutory licensing to effectuate it.

In one sense, the DPRSRA was a delayed legislative response to the dissatisfaction long expressed by the recording industry about the 1971 compromise which brought sound recordings within copyright. See § 3.02 of the casebook. In another sense, however, the DPRSRA was the result of recent technological developments — in particular, the transmission of digital audio by terrestrial means (such as cable and wireless relay), via direct broadcast satellites, or, ultimately, over the Internet. What all these technologies have in common is the potential to transmit large amounts of commercial-free audio to subscribers, and to do so on an interactive basis — that is, in a way that permits a subscriber to order precisely the music he or she wants to hear at any time, whether it is a single cut or an entire album.[1]

Thus, the Congressional decision to provide for the first time a performance right in sound recordings — albeit a limited one — reflects a determination that particular new technologies pose a special threat to the traditional market for pre-recorded music: if a consumer can order up a high-quality transmission of any piece of music at any time, why should he or she ever again pay for a tape or CD? Worse still, a digital service subscriber with consumer home audio equipment could easily download a digital transmission to a home recording format, to replay at leisure or even to resell.

Furthermore, Congressional action on the DPRSRA reflects an important political fact. Through the years, the over-the-air broadcasting industry has been the strongest and most effective opponent of performance rights in

---

[1] For a description of the technology and some of the ways in which it has been (or could be) deployed, see generally *Copyright Implications of Digital Audio Transmission Services: A Report of the Register of Copyrights* (GPO, Oct. 1991). For a far-reaching speculation on the significance of the technology, see P. Goldstein, COPYRIGHT'S HIGHWAY: FROM GUTENBERG TO THE CELESTIAL JUKEBOX 197–200 (1994).

sound recordings. That industry, however, had its own reason *not* to oppose the DPRSRA, because that legislation imposed licensing costs on digital audio subscription services — potentially the broadcasters' most significant future commercial competitors.

But there were still more players in the legislative drama that led to the enactment of the DPRSRA. Since 1971, musical copyright owners (and the organizations, like ASCAP, BMI and SESAC, which represent them) also have been skeptical about the desirability of performance rights in sound recordings. Those interests already receive performance royalties for the compositions incorporated in recordings, and they have reasoned that, if broadcasters and others have to pay an additional license fee to recording companies, this may mean a smaller share of the licensing dollar for composers. Thus, the 1995 Act had to be (and was) shaped to protect the interests of copyright owners and the performing rights organizations as well.

Nor was that all. In the end, the compromise which became the DPRSRA also embraced language intended to assure that the rights created by the Act would not be abused in ways that could stifle the development of the new business model represented by interactive subscription-based audio transmission services. And finally, the new Act attempted to anticipate and provide legal infrastructure for another potential new business model — the on-demand digital "delivery" of sound recordings by means of transmission — and to assure that the rights of all parties will be observed when and if it emerges. All in all, a tall order.

Perhaps, in fact, too tall! As it turned out, the original provisions of the DPRSRA would be revisited and (in some respects) extensively revised in the debates leading up to the enactment of the Digital Millennium Copyright Act — in part to take account of some emergent technologies that had not seemed significant, to the extent they were considered at all, in 1995. The resulting provisions — well illustrating the intersection of technology, commerce, and "interest politics" to which we referred at the outset of this section — are extremely complex. We sketch below only a few of the (alleged) highlights.

[2] Highlights of the DPRSRA

New § 106(6)

The new right. As noted, the DPRSRA adds a new subsection (6) — and a new exclusive right — to § 106 of the Copyright Act. From the language of new § 106(6), it follows as a general principle that unlicensed digital transmissions of sound recordings are prohibited. This principle, however, is subject to various special qualifications beyond those, like the applicability of fair use, which apply to all of the § 106 and 106A rights. These are detailed in a new subsection (d) of § 114 ("Scope of exclusive rights in sound recordings"), entitled "Limitations on exclusive right."

§ 114 Amendments

The role of exemptions. As originally enacted in 1995, the outright exemption to the new § 106(6) right provided in § 114(d)(1) applied potentially to various *non-interactive, non-subscription* services. Clearly, this exemption covered, and still covers, terrestrial broadcasters of "free" (or, more accurately, advertising-supported) radio and television programming. They will continue to be able to perform sound recordings without license just as they do today, even if they should choose to migrate their operations to digital technology. Various secondary transmissions of exempt primary transmissions (as well as program "feeds" directed to exempt broadcasters) are also made exempt. So are transmissions within business establishments and to those establishments (for use in the ordinary course of business) — so as to allow for commercial use of recordings as background music, and to permit background music services such as MUZAK to be carried on by digital means.

After the enactment of the original DPRSRA, however, there was some confusion about what other kinds of non-subscription consumer delivery, besides broadcasting, might be covered by the exemption. A particular area of concern was webcasting — a relatively new technique that uses so-called "streaming audio" technology to deliver sound recordings over the Internet. Under the original DPRSRA, "webcasting" was not clearly exempt, and — if non-exempt — it was apparently ineligible for compulsory licensing! The revisions to the DPRSRA included in the DMCA involve some narrowing of the original language of § 114(d)(1)(A), which clearly now applies to terrestrial broadcasts only. By the same token, however, revised § 114 makes it clear that so-called "eligible non-subscription transmissions" (*i.e.*, non-interactive services other than broadcasting, including but not limited to webcasting) are subject to compulsory licensing (if they comply with the various conditions discussed below).[2]

---

[2] The preceding paragraph states that § 114(d)(1)(A) "clearly" applies to terrestrial broadcasts only, but in the immediate aftermath of the enactment of the DMCA this conclusion was not so transparent to the traditional over-the-air broadcasters themselves. Instead, they took the position that they should be entitled, in addition, to webcast their programming under the coverage of this exemption, rather than having to comply with the various limiting conditions, and pay the compulsory licensing fees, to which other non-broadcaster webcasters are subject (about which more below.) As might be expected, the music industry (and the webcasters) strongly contested the broadcasters' reading of the statute. On December 11, 2000, over the objections of the National Association of Broadcasters, which would have preferred to take the issue directly to court, the Copyright Office dealt with the issue in a new regulation designed to (what else?) "clarify" the meaning of the contested provision. The rule, "Public Performance of Sound Recordings: Definition of a Service," which can be found at 65 F.R. 77292 (and, like other Federal Register entries referred to in these pages, on the Copyright Office's website at *http://www.loc.gov/copyright*) makes interesting reading, and includes a clearly written explanation of the legislative history of this portion of the DPRSRA (which, we note, the Office familiarly shortens to "DPRA"). The gist of the conclusion is that, in

The scheme of the DPRSRA obviously represents the outcome of political compromise, but it also expresses a considered Congressional choice to address only those aspects of digital broadcasting that promise (or threaten) to transform most dramatically the transmission environment as it affects sound recording owners — taking as a baseline the situation in 1971, when sound recordings first were recognized as copyrightable subject matter. The most "traditional" version of new digital technology applied to delivery of sound recordings — broadcasting — enjoys the benefit of the exemption. The versions that raised the greatest concerns among recording companies, so-called interactive services, can proceed only if they are expressly licensed by copyright owners, and those transmission services that pose intermediate threats to the economic well-being of the recording industry — such as webcasting — are made subject to compulsory licensing.

Compulsory licensing provisions. This familiar device represents the compromise struck under the DPRSRA with respect to digital transmission services that function as the digital audio equivalent of cable TV — subscription services that are non-interactive and generally (though not always) commercial-free. The mechanism for compromise adopted in the original DPRSRA is a familiar one: statutory licensing. Sections 114(d)(2),(e), and (f) describe a scheme in which so-called "voluntary negotiation proceedings" between representatives of various groups of copyright owners and transmitting entities are supposed to be convened at five-year intervals (with the first to occur within a month of the effective date of the Act) for the purpose of determining reasonable royalty rates. The DPRSRA, however, made the new statutory license potentially available to otherwise qualifying subscription services only under certain relatively stringent conditions, designed to minimize the impact of such services on other commercial distribution channels for recorded music.

To make things still more complicated, the DMCA added additional conditions, with the result that the current DPRSRA now incorporates two

---

enacting § 114(d)(A)(1), Congress was trying to create a space for new competitors, rather than to expand the privileges of existing ones. In response, on January 25, 2001, several broadcasting companies sued to overturn the Copyright Office's rule. This challenge was disposed of in *Bonneville Int'l Corp. v. Peters*, 153 F. Supp. 2d 763 (2001) (summary judgment in favor of rule's validity as an exercise of Copyright Office authority). Another consequence of the Office's decision was the reopening of the period during which interested parties were eligible to sign to participate in the next CARP to determine § 114 (f) and § 112(e) compulsory licensing rates — to allow the broadcasters to participate. *See* 65 F.R. 77393 (Dec. 11, 2000).

Also on that eventful day, the Copyright Office denied a petition for a Copyright Office rule-making to determine what degree of consumer influence amounts to "interactivity" within the meaning of the DPRSRA. This is a critical question, of course, because "interactive" services do not enjoy the benefit of a compulsory license. The Copyright Office declined to attempt to draw a bright line, but did indicate that merely because its consumers may express preferences for some kinds of content over others (for country music rather than classical, for example), a service is not necessarily rendered "interactive." So the courts have some work ahead of them.

sets of requirements for transmission services wishing to qualify for the license — one set for "grandfathered" services that were licensed or in operation before July 31, 1998, and another, more exacting set for other services.[3]

As amended, the DPRSRA also adopts a two-tiered approach to the determination of appropriate licensing rates where voluntary negotiations have failed to arrive at an agreement. With respect to "grandfathered" services that were qualified for the statutory license under the original version of the DPRSRA, its provisions continue to apply. Whereas the original provisions direct arbitration panels appointed in connection with this rate-setting exercise to consider what would constitute a "fair return" to the copyright owner, the new provisions direct them to set royalty rates considering "the rates and terms that would have been negotiated in the marketplace between a willing buyer and a willing seller" — subtly but significantly different standards.[4]

Miscellaneous protective provisions. Space limitations preclude further detailed discussion here of the various additional protective provisions built into the DPRSRA as the result of political compromise. You should, however, note the existence of such provisions in the statute. Section 114(g), for example, provides that, in limited circumstances, performers, both featured and non-featured, who render the words or music, will share in the royalties derived from licensing of the digital performance right. And § 114(h) provides means by which would-be entrants into the digital audio

---

[3] Thus, for example, a "grandfathered" transmission service may never play more than two consecutive selections, or more than three selections in a three-hour period, from a single album-length recording (with similar, though slightly more liberal, restrictions on selections from boxed sets). It also must forego giving listeners advance notice of selections to be performed, and must faithfully retransmit the identifying information digitally encoded in the recording (other than information relating to the copyright status of a work, which need not be retransmitted but must be reproduced accurately if it is). In addition, newly qualifying services also must (to cite some examples of the additional requirements) forego giving subscribers advance notice of the names of featured recording artists (except in general terms), observe strict limits on making available "archived programs," avoid abetting subscribers' efforts to make copies of transmissions, and take reasonable steps to design its own system to assure that technological protection measures (such as encryption) used by sound recording copyright owners will function effectively.

[4] License rate-setting is on-going. In addition to overseeing the statutory licenses provided in the original DPRSRA, the Copyright Office now also looks after several new ones introduced by the DMCA, including one for "nonexempt eligible nonsubscription transmissions" and another for "nonexempt transmissions by preexisting satellite digital audio radio services" (of which there are only two known examples in captivity). Proceedings to establish rates for this new licenses under §§ 112(e) and 114(f) were initiated on January 13, 2000, see 65 F.R. 2194 of that date, and led to a CARP report, Docket No. 2000-9, issued on February 20, 2002 and discussed at greater length below. Although the resolution of that proceeding still is pending, a new rate-setting cycle were initiated (as required by the statute) on January 30, 2002. See 67 F.R. 4472 of that date.

transmission marketplace can avoid being blocked by existing participants and arrangements.

In addition, § 114(i) of the DPRSRA makes clear that digital audio transmission services must license performing rights in the underlying music *as well as* in the sound recording itself (thereby attempting to assuage the historic concern of owners of copyrights in musical works that the payments of license fees to sound recording copyright owners will reduce the fees paid for performance rights in musical compositions as such). Indeed, § 114(i) goes so far as to insert into the Copyright Act a hortatory statement that "[i]t is the intent of Congress that royalties payable to copyright owners of music works for the public performance of their works shall not be diminished in any respect as a result of the rights granted by section 106(6)." All statements of Congressional intent aside, it remains to be seen what the real impact of the DPRSRA on the value of performance rights in music will be.

The webcasting dilemma. The future of webcasting may well be determined by the outcome of the rate-setting proceeding under the new § 114(f) compulsory license for digital performances of sound recordings by non-subscription services. As noted above, a CARP panel convened to consider this license issued its report on February 20, 2002. The document, and various comments in reponse to it, can be found at *http://www.copyright.gov/carp/webcasting_rates.html*. The panel followed the RIAA's suggestion that the statutory rates should be based on actual practice, and thus considered a number of negotiated license deals between recording companies and various webcasters. It discounted most of them, however, because it felt that the webcasters in question had lacked "resources, sophistication and market power" comparable to that of the recording industry. Instead, it settled on one deal — between webcasting pioneer Yahoo! and the RIAA — as a model, and on this basis concluded that websites should pay 0.14 cents for each song streamed on an Internet-only webcast and .07 cents for each song retransmitted as part of an AM or FM radio feed, with an additional 9 percent on top to cover ephemeral reproduction. The proposal also called for a $500 minimum annual license fee.

This recommendation, as can be imagined, has provoked considerable controversy. While recording companies have expressed disappointment that the rate was not pegged higher, the most serious doubts have been expressed by webcasters — especially small ones — who are concerned that they might not be able to survive in the envisioned licensing environment. *See* Dan Carnevale, *Proposed Fees for Broadcasting Songs Online Worry College Radio Official*, Chronicle of Higher Education, Mar. 8, 2002, at 32, col. 1. On May 15, 2002, the Senate Judiciary Committee held a hearing on the issue. The testimony and a webcast of the proceedings are available at *http://www.senate.gov/%7Ejudiciary/hearing.cfm?id=258*. Representatives of the webcasting industry castigated the proposed rate and proposed various changes in the legislation that they asserted would produce fairer results in the CARP process.

The controversy is all the more intense because some webcasters allege that, even if they could afford the proposed rates, they would be unable to satisfy the elaborate recording keeping requirements that are being proposed in connection with it. For additional details, see *http://www.copyright.gov/carp/114/comments.html* (from which page one can access, among other things, a webcast of a roundtable on the recordkeeping issue held on May 10, 2002).

As with any CARP recommendation, the final decision (at least insofar as the administrative process goes) lies with the Librarian of Congress, as advised by the Copyright Office — a process that produced an order rejecting the Panel's determination proposing rates and terms for these licenses. It can be found at *http://www.copyright.gov/carp/webcasting-rates-order.html*. The law provides that the Librarian shall issue his final determination within 30 days of his decision to reject the Panel's proposed rates and terms. The final determination is due on June 20, 2002. To what extent (and in what way) it will deviate from the CARP recommendations remains to be seen. In any event, we should know better then how the politics of this situation may play out.

§ 115 Amendments

The compulsory license for digital sound recording delivery. So far, we have examined only the new § 106(6) right and the various limitations upon it imposed by the DPRSRA in its amendments to § 114. We should not overlook the amendments made by the 1995 Act to § 115 (the compulsory license in musical works).

The § 115 amendments address yet another of the concerns of the owners of the copyrights underlying the transmissions which are the subject of the DPRSRA, namely, the possibility that interactive digital audio transmission technology will be used to "deliver" copies of sound recordings to consumers' orders. Pause for a moment to be sure that you understand a key distinction here between two types of commerce via the "celestial jukebox." The DPRSRA amendments to § 114 are addressed to issues concerning the transmission of sound recordings so that they can be heard in "real-time" by consumers — some of whom may also engage in simultaneous (and perhaps unlawful) home recording. The § 115 amendments address the quite different technological possibility that firms engaged in the digital "delivery" of sound recordings could make use of facilities such as the World Wide Web to provide customers with high-speed feeds of digital data intended to be downloaded for later playback. Although this business model has yet to emerge in the marketplace, it obviously has tremendous potential. Already, recording companies, emboldened by the new Secure Digital Music Initiative anti-piracy system (of which we will have more to say in § 7.07[B] and [C] below, are testing the waters. *See* Lieberman, *Bowie's Newet Disc to Hit Web Before Shelves*, N.Y. Post, Aug. 31, 1999, at p. 43, col. 1. Were they to lend their full support to the new marketing technology, it eventually could render traditional store-based systems for the distribution of sound recordings obsolete. The DPRSRA amendments to § 115 provide the legal infrastructure for such a transition.

Generally, we think of § 115 as a mechanism by which record producers can secure the rights to make new "cover" versions of compositions previously recorded under consensual license from the copyright owner, and to distribute them for (at least primarily) private use. In fact, the potential scope of the section is somewhat broader. In addition to making available to company C a compulsory license when it wishes to re-record a song by composer A which was previously recorded by company B, § 115 dictates what is due to A if C licenses from B the right to re-release (*i.e.*, distribute or "deliver") its original recording.

The DPRSRA amendments to § 115 make it clear that a digital delivery of a sound recording is an infringement unless it is authorized or licensed. § 115(c)(3)(H). Under amended § 115, however, services which offer their customers facilities to download digital versions of recorded music can avail themselves of a statutory license for the musical compositions in question. Here, from 2 NIMMER ON COPYRIGHT § 8.23 (1999), is a concrete example of how the process might work:

> [I]magine that Composer in 1980 authorizes Star to perform and sell copies to the public of her newly written Song. Thereafter in 1990, Upstart may invoke the compulsory license to assemble musicians to record his own version of Song; Upstart must pay compulsory license fees to Composer, with no obligation to Star. Now imagine that Techie wishes to avail itself of the newly added compulsory license to offer digital phonorecord delivery. Techie must remit the statutory fee to Composer for use of the music. Techie may use Star's or Upstart's sound recording only if it concludes a license agreement with either; absent successful licensing arrangements, Techie may wish to assemble its own musicians and singers (or cyberian facsimiles thereof) to record a new rendition of Song, which will then be the subject of digital phonorecord delivery. In that last instantiation, Techie will owe statutory license fees to Composer, and nothing to Star or Upstart.

If Techie makes an arrangement with Star or Upstart to deliver a preexisting recording to consumers by digital means, it will be entitled to take advantage of the statutory license only if all digitally encoded information about the work — other than information about copyright status — is transmitted along with the work. § 115(c)(3)(G).

The procedure for settling the practical aspects of such statutory licenses is specified by the DPRSRA. Section 115(c)(3)(B)-(F) provides that, under the umbrella of a limited antitrust exemption, affected parties may voluntarily negotiate terms and rates, subject to the impaneling of a CARP, if necessary, to resolve their differences.[5]

---

[5] As was true of Internet transmissions of music, so it is also the case that there is more to the regulation of digital musical delivery than rights in sound recordings. The underlying musical compositions must also be licensed, as the statute recog-

[3] Notes and Questions

(1) The statutory scheme just described is an exceptionally detailed one — designed not only to regulate known technologies but to anticipate emerging ones. As already noted, its terms are the result of a legislative process which blended far-sighted policymaking and mundane political compromise. Is legislation of this kind built to last? Or is it likely to be overtaken by technological development? Would Congress have been wiser to adopt more general legislative language and trust the courts to work out the details? Would there have been any other alternative?

(2) Read through the provisions that the DPRSRA added to §§ 114 and 115 of the Copyright Act, trying to put yourself in the position of a lay businessperson or a non-specialist lawyer. How much of this is comprehensible (let alone relatively transparent)? Does it matter? Is the Act, among other things, a guarantee of future full employment for copyright specialists?

(3) Can the decision to provide for a general digital performance right in sound recordings — while leaving analog performances unaddressed — be justified on any basis other than that of political expediency?

(4) The § 111 cable statutory licensing provisions have generated tremendous contention, with respect both to rate-setting and to the formula for sharing license fees among various kinds of copyright owners whose material is subject to cable retransmission. Will the § 114 provisions for statutory licensing prove any less productive of disputes?

(5) The savings provisions of § 114(g) are designed to assure that licensing revenues will reach performers as well as record companies. How effective would you expect those provisions to be in practice? How clear is it that

---

nizes. In 1999, the parties to a CARP on compulsory licensing fees for the reproduction of musical compositions in connection with so-called digital phonorecord downloads (DPDs) agreed on a basic rate, which is reflected at 64 F.R. 6221 (Feb. 9, 1999). But they failed to settle the question of rates for the special statutory category of "incidental" DPDs, in part because they could not agree what these were. In November 2000, the recording industry filed a petition requesting the Copyright Office to rule on the issue, and to convene a rate-setting CARP thereafter. The recording companies took the position that "incidental" DPDs include, for example, temporary copies of musical works made as part of the transmission process of streaming audio services (designed to deliver music that can be heard but not retained by end users). Needless to say, the decision about what "incidental" DPDs are (and what rates are set for them) is a matter of real economic consequence, on which various interested parties, including the Digital Interactive Media Association, have weighed in. On March 9, 2001, at 66 F.R. 14099, the Office published a "Notice of Inquiry" requesting public comments on how to proceed in traversing this minefield. Then came the RIAA/NMPA/HFA agreement described at the very beginning of this section, and (in response) a Copyright Office request for comments which was subsequently extended — with the effect that final reply comments were due on February 27, 2002. See 67 F.R. 4694, January 31, 2002. By the time you read this, the Office may have ruled on this difficult and important question.

they apply to situations where digital transmission services negotiate consensual licenses with sound recording copyright owners, rather than relying on the statutory licensing mechanism? *See* Watkins, *The Digital Performance Right in Sound Recordings Act of 1995: Delicate Negotiations, Inadequate Protection*, 20 Colum.-VLA J.L. & Arts 323 (1996).

(6) Are you surprised that — in the absence of a timely objection from an interested party — a privately negotiated agreement concerning statutory licensing rates for digital phonorecord "delivery" can become a final rule, binding on an entire industry, without further judicial or administrative scrutiny? Or is this sort of delegation of rule-making authority appropriate in the circumstances? Do the procedures described above provide any safeguards against abuse, other than the notice-and-comment procedure?

(7) Digital technology blurs traditional distinctions among the various § 106 rights — and, in particular, between the closely linked distribution rights, on the one hand, and the public performance right, on the other. All of these are rights which can be exercised (or infringed) by means of technologically indistinguishable digital "transmissions." Where sound recordings are concerned, the potential for confusion is particularly acute. In the analog environment, these two sets of rights correspond fairly neatly to the two distinct modes by which sound recordings generally are exploited. In the digital environment, a single use of a sound recording by means of transmission may entail reproduction, distribution, and public performance. How successful is the DPRSRA in dealing with this problem? Section 114(d)(4)(C) provides:

> Any limitations in this section on the exclusive right under section 106(6) apply only to the exclusive right under section 106(6) and not to any other exclusive rights under section 106. Nothing in this section shall be construed to annul, limit, impair or otherwise affect in any way the ability of the owner of a copyright in a sound recording to exercise the rights under sections 106(1), 106(2) and 106(3) . . .

Is that clear? Is it helpful? Does it mean that some providers of digital audio transmission services may have to pay twice: once for the right to distribute a work, and once for the right to perform it publicly?

(8) Another peculiar provision of the Act is § 115(c)(3)(L), which, as originally drafted, would have provided:

> The provisions of this section shall not apply to any exempt transmissions or retransmissions under section 114(d)(1).

This formulation gave rise to various questions. Did it mean that exempt transmissions cannot, by definition, violate the reproduction and distribution rights? Or that incidental reproductions and distributions occurring in connection with exempt transactions are not subject to compulsory licensing under § 115? The section now has been amended to add the following:

> The exemptions created in section 114(d)(1) do not expand or reduce the rights of copyright owners under section 106(1) through (5) with respect to such transmissions and retransmissions.

Is everything clear now? For more on the "convergence" of rights in the digital environment, see 2 M. Nimmer & D. Nimmer, NIMMER ON COPYRIGHT §§ 8.24[B]-[C] (2001).

(9) There are a number of points of contact and potential conflict between the DPRSRA and the Audio Home Recording Act of 1992, which is discussed immediately below. In some respects, the later Act conforms itself to the terms of the earlier. *See, e.g.,* §§ 114(d)(2)(E) and 115(c)(3)(G). In one important respect, however, the DPRSRA restricts the potential scope of the earlier legislation, by making it clear that the limitations on infringement actions provided in the Audio Home Recording Act operate in favor of equipment manufacturers and consumers, but do not apply to those involved in the making of digital audio transmissions to which the DPRSRA applies. In this connection, you should make a careful comparison of § 1008 (a part of the 1992 legislation) and new § 115(c)(3)(J).

[B] The Audio Home Recording Right

[1] Introduction

Congress enacted the DPRSRA, just discussed, in 1995. We have considered that legislation first, before turning our attention to the Audio Home Recording Act ("AHRA"), enacted in 1992, for one simple reason. Complex as it is, the DPRSRA is, for better or worse, part of the Copyright Act. By contrast, the AHRA (even though some of its provisions provided models for parts of the DPRSRA), is not. Violations of the AHRA's regulatory scheme, codified in a new Chapter 10 of Title 17 (along with the Chapter 9 provisions on protection of semiconductor chip products), do not give rise to actions for copyright infringement, although separate enforcement mechanisms and penalties are provided.

Nonetheless, the AHRA and the Copyright Act are joined at the hip. In effect, the AHRA represents a political bargain under which electronic equipment manufacturers accepted restrictions on new technologies in exchange for a general exemption from copyright infringement liability in connection with the manufacture, sale or use of their products. There is no way to understand the AHRA without understanding its history.

In the 1980s, the companies which make up the sound recording industry made the decision to shift their marketing emphasis emphatically. They moved away from conventional "analog" recording formats (like vinyl discs and magnetic tapes), and toward the new "digital format" of compact discs (or "CDs"). But just as consumers began to accept the new format and the technology which went along with it, an even newer format was being launched in Japan: the Digital Audio Tape (or "DAT"). Although less durable than CDs, DATs offered customers several apparent advantages. They (and the equipment on which they are played) are more portable, and (critically for what followed) they are easily programmed. Home users of DAT technology could record in the new format, as well as play back prerecorded DAT tapes.

From the standpoint of the American recording industry, home taping of prerecorded discs always has been problematic, but the near-perfect fidelity of multi-generational digital copies added new dimensions to that problem. While the risk to sales posed by home taping in "analog" format has been limited by the fact that sound quality degrades noticeably with each "generation" of copies, a key characteristic of digital media is that there is little appreciable, inter-generational difference between the sound quality of, say, a CD and that of a DAT recording copied from it. When and if DAT technology became widely available to American consumers, the recording companies feared, the resultant increase in home copying might pose a threat to the market in prerecorded CDs.[6]

The industry's response was to threaten (and, in at least one instance, to initiate suit against) manufacturers and importers considering the introduction of DAT recording and playback devices into the American market, based on their alleged potential contributory liability for private acts of copyright infringement which would be committed using the devices. Whether actions brought on this basis would have succeeded in the face of the precedent of *Sony Corp. of America v. Universal City Studios, Inc.* (the "Betamax" case introduced in § 7.01 above), which had involved a partially similar claim against manufacturers and importers of VCRs, is a moot question. In effect, the possibility of *Sony*-like litigation was enough to delay the introduction of the technology in this country until a legislative solution could be devised. When it came, in 1992, that legislation broke new ground for American intellectual property. Not only did it create a new compulsory license, but it created also a new cause of action, apart from copyright infringement — while also imposing legal limitations on technology itself, rather than solely on the uses to which that technology may be put.

The history of the legislation is of some interest in itself. Although the outlines of the solution finally embodied in the Audio Home Recording Act of 1992 were laid down in a compromise negotiated between recording companies and manufacturers and importers of electronic equipment, the legislation as finally enacted deviates from the terms of that compromise in some important ways. As introduced, the bill that became the AHRA followed the agreement by mandating use of a particular technology, the so-called Serial Copy Management System ("SCMS"), to prevent subsequent reproduction of digital copies made on covered machines. The final legislation, by contrast, authorizes the use of other, functionally equivalent technologies as well. In most of its substance, however, the Act closely tracks the negotiated arrangement.

[2] Highlights of the AHRA

The scope of the Act. The provisions of the AHRA avoid any use of the term "phonorecord" to describe the material objects to which the provisions

---

[6] *See* Kawamua, *Digital Audio Tape Technology: A Formidable Challenge to the American Copyright System*, 4 Am. U.J. Int'l L. & Pol'y 409 (1989).

apply. "Talking books" are excluded from coverage. Notably, however, coverage is *not* limited to DATs alone, even though DAT is the recording format which prompted the legislation.

Persons entitled to share in royalty distributions. The AHRA defines a class of persons who have stakes in the funds generated by the new statutory license, and who have standing to enter into negotiations and agreements — and, if necessary, to sue — with respect to the distribution of those funds. These "interested copyright parties" are not all "authors" or even copyright owners. They include: performing rights organizations such as ASCAP, BMI and SESAC, as well as so-called "featured recording artists" (who have a 40% share of the 66⅔% of overall royalties that flow into the so-called Sound Recording Fund, calculated after the deduction of 4% for nonfeatured artists); the owners of copyright in the sound recordings (who share the rest of the Sound Recording Fund); and the owners of the musical works copyrights (the music publishers and songwriters, who share the 33⅓% of overall royalties which go into the Musical Works Fund).

*Anti-serial copyright technology..*The AHRA requires the use of built-in devices or mechanisms to prevent "serial copying" on digital audio devices made, imported into, or sold in the United States, and bars the marketing of equipment designed to frustrate the devices. The Act also bars encoding inaccurate information about the copyright status of a sound recording or musical composition on a digital recording — although it does not affirmatively require that any information of this kind be encoded.

The royalty formula and the mechanics of royalty payments. The new Act creates an obligation on the part of importers and manufacturers of digital audio equipment to pay royalties, and to file periodic reports with the Copyright Office. The royalties are based on the "transfer price" of equipment distributed, with special provisions for audio systems which have digital and nondigital components. Royalties are also due on the "transfer price" of "digital audio recording media" (such as DAT tapes). "Transfer price" is the price charged by the domestic manufacturer of digital equipment or media, or the price entered for customs purposes (in the case of imported items). Significantly, no provision for adjustment of royalty rates had to be built into the AHRA, because the royalty formula is based on a percentage of transfer price.

Distribution of royalties and dispute resolution. The AHRA prescribes a scheme for the distribution of the royalties outlined above, and grants an anti-trust exemption allowing the "interested copyright parties" who belong to a group entitled to a percentage share of the royalties to appoint common agents to collect and distribute the funds — and to negotiate distribution of the funds within the group. As enacted, the legislation looks to the Copyright Royalty Tribunal to resolve intra-group disputes concerning distribution which cannot be negotiated successfully. Under the Copyright Royalty Tribunal Reform Act of 1993, this function has been reassigned to *ad hoc* Copyright Arbitration Royalty Panels.

Independent remedies for independent wrongs. The Act provides for civil actions to recover actual and statutory damages, as well as for injunctive relief, available in case of a failure to observe the serial copying regulation requirements or to pay the required royalties, with repeat offenders subject to enhanced penalties. The provisions also make clear that there can be no liability for copyright infringement in connection with noncommercial home taping by consumers using digital recording equipment and media — or for contributory infringement based on the manufacture, importation or distribution of such equipment or media. The meaning of this language has been clarified (if not narrowed) by new § 115(c)(3)(J), part of the DPRSRA.

[3] Notes and Questions

(1) The exemption from copyright infringement liability in certain circumstances introduced into Title 17 as § 1008 represents a central innovation of the amendments contained in the Audio Home Recording Act of 1992. Not only did these amendments define a new set of obligations and enforcement mechanisms, distinct from the Copyright Act of 1976, but, in turn, they limited the rights of copyright owners under § 106. Do you find it odd that *sui generis* legislation — legislation codified in Title 17, but not a part of the Copyright Act — limits rights under the Copyright Act? Is this the result of Congressional indifference to formal distinctions between copyright and legislation designed to regulate new technology? Or does the technique employed by Congress in crafting the AHRA reflect instead a concern for the integrity of the Copyright Act, and a judgment that carving out the subject matter of the AHRA for special treatment was preferable to tinkering more intrusively with the Copyright Act itself?

(2) Another innovation is the requirement imposed on manufacturers and importers to build safeguards against serial copying into digital recording equipment. Is this a wise approach? Suppose that, in the 1800s, it had been possible to impose a technical "fix" on printing presses to make it physically impossible to engage in the kind of wholesale book piracy to which the first copyright statute was a response. Would the results have been desirable?

Turning to the present day, should computer manufacturers be required to build "anti-copy" chips (which would shut down attempts to copy software carrying a digital indicator of copyright status) into the hardware systems they build and sell? Why or why not? Does your answer depend on the nature of any penalties imposed for circumvention of anti-copying devices? Should there be substantial fines or prison terms for the development of means to evade the better mouse-trap? Should it matter whether the circumvention device has legitimate, that is, non-infringing uses?

Should we be concerned that intellectual property legislation will degenerate into Congressional endorsement of private technological solutions, solutions which may be too broad and or outdated? Why should Congress be involved at all in enforcing such marketplace maneuverings?

(3) Under the terms of the AHRA, performers enjoy a statutorily prescribed share in the distribution of royalties. (In this connection, remember that many artists who participate in the making of sound recordings do so as "employees for hire," or assign away copyright in their employment agreements.) Moreover, the portion of the Sound Recording Fund allocated to these performers is to be paid out directly, rather than through the recording companies. Is this innovation good intellectual property policy? And how transferable is it to other rights or technologies?

The DPRSRA's provisions for the distribution of royalties in connection with the statutory licensing of performances are modeled, in some degree, on those of the AHRA, but they are considerably simpler. In contrast to the analogous AHRA provisions, they provide no role for the Copyright Office, nor do they rely so comprehensively on the creation of common funds and common agents. Moreover, under the DPRSRA, it is the responsibility of sound recording copyright owners to pass along the royalties that are due, as a statutory matter, to performers. What accounts for these differences?

(4) In its own right, the scheme for the distribution of royalties under the AHRA has proved problematic, in part because small individual claimants to disbursements from the various funds have the power to frustrate agreements among the agents who represent the overwhelming bulk of the individuals entitled to share in the funds deposited with the Copyright Office. Thus, it was not until February 1997 that the terms of the distribution of 1992–94 royalties were resolved by a Copyright Office decision (issued in the name of the Librarian of Congress). These terms revised the results arrived at by a CARP which had been appointed at the insistence of two songwriters who were the only holdouts from a settlement agreed to in early 1995 by organizations representing thousands of other claimants — from whose royalties were deducted the lion's share of the costs of the protracted determination. More recently, the Copyright Office announced the results of a CARP to distribute the 1995-1998 royalties at 66 F.R. 9360 (Feb. 7, 2001). The announcement is well worth reading as an illustration of how much trouble a few stubborn individualists can generate in such proceedings.[7] Is this process too cumbersome? Is the Government's role too large?

(5) To what extent did the general approach of the AHRA anticipate future developments in digital sound recording delivery? For several years, in an effort known as the Secure Digital Music Initiative (or "SDMI," described in greater detail at *www.sdmi.org*), recording companies have

---

[7] For the record, the Librarian sustained the CARP's award to one of the individual claimants, amounting to 0.000084% of the Writers Subfund for 1993 and 0.000082% of the Writers Subfund for 1994. He increased the other claimant's award from the Publisher's Subfund from 0.007096% to 0.014745% for 1992, from 0.001608% to 0.003802% for 1993, and from 0.003398 to 0.007066% for 1994. The decision can be found at 62 Fed. Reg. 6558. It contains some interesting observations on the standard of review to be applied to CARP panel decisions.

been huddling with high tech firms to come up with an industry standard for technological anti-copying protection. *See* Markoff, *New System for PC Music Stirs Concern Over Piracy*, N.Y. Times, May 3, 1998, at C1, col.6. On June 28, 1999, some 100 firms announced preliminary agreement on a new specification for digital music distribution. Copyright owners hoped that when it was fully implemented in a new generation of recordings and home electronics, they would be able to exercise control over what consumers can — and can't — do with recordings which they have downloaded from the Internet to their personal computers. Since then, however, the SDMI has faltered, in part because of disagreements between the electronics industries and content providers, and in part because of disagreements within the content community itself. Implementation has been postponed repeatedly, and it now seems entirely possible that the entire effort will collapse — leaving recording companies (and others) to roll out their own technological security measures, backed up (to at least a certain extent) by the anti-circumvention provisions of the DMCA. For a peek inside the SDMI negotiations, see Brad King, *Rethinking Music Security*, Wired News (May 22, 2001) at *http://www.wired.com/news/mp3/0,1285,43983,00.html*.

Recently, the SDMI gave itself a colorful shiner. After the organization invited computer scientists to attempt to "hack" its prototype security system, a lawyer for one of its members (the Recording Industry Association of America, or RIAA) threatened a team of researchers who had beaten the challenge with suit under the DMCA if they delivered an academic paper describing their strategy and thus exposing SDMI's shortcomings. *See* Lawrence Lessig, *Copyright Thugs*, The Industry Standard (May 4, 2000). An action for a declaratory judgment brought by the computer scientists (including Professor Edward Felten of Princeton) was dismissed in November 2001 by the New Jersey U.S. District Court, after the recording industry (and the U.S. government) offered assurances that the original threats had been misconceived and would not be repeated. For details, see the documents available at *http://www.eff.org/IP/DMCA/Felten_v_RIAA/*.

(6) Although the AHRA may have been the general inspiration for the SDMI, one specific impetus behind the new standard was the fact that the earlier legislation did not, in fact, apply to the MP3 technology that makes possible the authorized and unauthorized distribution of music over the Internet in the form of compressed digital files. In particular, the music industries failed in its efforts to challenge the sale of inexpensive portable MP3 players that can be loaded with music files previously downloaded from the Internet to a personal computer, thus allowing for their playback anywhere and anytime. Even before the first such device — the "Rio" — had come to market, several recording industry associations sued its manufacturer for (among other things) violation of the AHRA. In June 1999, the Ninth Circuit Court of Appeals concluded that, because computer drives do not constitute "digital audio recording devices" within the meaning of the statute and because players like the Rio merely allow consumers to "space-shift" digital music files for personal use, it is consistent with the spirit and letter of the statute of the AHRA to exempt them from its

coverage. *See Recording Industry Association of America v. Diamond Multimedia Systems, Inc.,* 180 F.3d 1072 (9th Cir. 1999).

An excellent law review note on the *Diamond Multimedia* decision, by Ines B. Gonzales, at 15 Berkeley Tech. L.J. 67 (2000), summarizes it thus (with apologies, the footnotes are omitted!):

The initial question on appeal was whether the Rio portable music player qualifies as a digital audio recording device subject to the restrictions of the AHRA. . . . [T]he Ninth Circuit determined that the Rio must be able to reproduce, either "directly" or "from a transmission," a "digital music recording" in order for it to be considered a digital audio recording device subject to the AHRA.

The Ninth Circuit first considered whether the Rio is able to reproduce directly a digital musical recording. According to the court's reasoning, the Rio cannot reproduce a "digital musical recording" because the input for the Rio comes from an MP3 file on a computer hard drive. The typical computer hard drive cannot serve as the source of a "digital musical recording" because it contains various software programs and databases that are not incidental to any "fixed sound" present in an MP3 file, as required by section1001(5)(A)(i). Because the latter section is not met, the court declared that the Rio cannot make a "digital audio copied recording" directly from another "digital musical recording."

Even though the Rio does not "directly" reproduce a "digital musical recording," the Ninth Circuit determined that the Rio could still qualify as a "digital recording device" if it could reproduce a digital music recording "from a transmission." The RIAA contended that section 1001(1) would cover direct reproductions from digital musical recordings and indirect reproductions from a transmission. Diamond, on the other hand, asserted that the adverb "indirectly" modifies the recording of the underlying "digital music recording," rather than the recording "from the transmission." The court concluded that Diamond's reading of AHRA was not only more logical, but that the RIAA's interpretation contradicted statutory language and common sense. Under the RIAA's reading, the AHRA would restrict the indirect recording of transmissions but would allow direct recording of transmissions, such as recording songs from the radio. The court also stated that the legislative history confirmed its reading of the statute that "indirectly' modifies . . . the making of the reproduction of the underlying digital music recording." The court concluded that a device falls within the AHRA's provisions if it can "indirectly copy a digital music recording by making a copy from a transmission of that recording." Because the Rio cannot make copies from transmissions, but instead, can only make copies from a computer hard drive, the court held that the Rio is not a digital audio recording device.

The Ninth Circuit also addressed the legislative history of the AHRA because it is consistent with the statute's plain meaning. The RIAA contended that "the legislative history reveals that the Rio does not fall

within the specific exemption from the digital musical recording definition of 'a material object in which one or more computer programs are
fixed.'" The RIAA asserted that the House Report describes the exemptions as "revisions reflecting exemptions for . . . computer programs."
The Ninth Circuit noted, however, that limiting the exemption to computer programs contradicts the plain meaning of the exemption because
a computer program is a "literary work" that "can be fixed in a variety
of material objects." The court stated that the exemption's plain language
excludes any copying from a computer hard drive from coverage under
the AHRA. Furthermore, the court concluded that the Rio is consistent
with the purpose of the AHRA because it facilitates personal use;
specifically, the AHRA exempts home taping of both digital and analog
music recordings. The court emphasized that the Rio "merely makes
copies in order to render portable, or 'space-shift,' those files that already
reside on a user's hard drive."

Is this perfectly clear? In any event, of course, this decision may have
implications well beyond its literal coverage — or, at least, litigants are
like to so claim. So, in the *Napster* litigation, for example, the Ninth Circuit
(whose opinion is reproduced in part in § 1.05 of this Part) confronted an
affirmative defense based on a claim of exemption from liability under the
AHRA. Here is the court's somewhat terse response:

> We agree with the district court that the Audio Home Recording Act
> does not cover the downloading of MP3 files to computer hard drives.
> First, "under the plain meaning of the Act's definition of digital audio
> recording devices, computers (and their hard drives) are not digital audio
> recording devices because their 'primary purpose' is not to make digital
> audio copied recordings." *Recording Indus. Ass'n of Am. v. Diamond
> Multimedia Sys., Inc.,* 180 F.3d 1072, 1078 (9th Cir. 1999). Second,
> notwithstanding Napster's claim that computers are "digital audio
> recording devices," computers do not make "digital music recordings" as
> defined by the Audio Home Recording Act. *Id.* at 1077 (citing S. Rep. 102-
> 294) ("There are simply no grounds in either the plain language of the
> definition or in the legislative history for interpreting the term 'digital
> musical recording' to include songs fixed on computer hard drives.")

239 F.3d at 1024.

Once again, is this perfectly clear? Is it consistent with *Diamond Rio*?
Is the Ninth Circuit simply reading the statute narrowly and precisely in
both cases?

The *Napster* defendants also took comfort from *Diamond Rio* in connection with their assertion that the "space-shifting" activities of Napster users
should be considered privileged fair use. For the fate of that contention,
see the discussion in § 9.04 of this Part.

(7) Some record companies have decided not to wait for the SDMI
standard to emerge. Instead, they have initiated their own measures to
copy-protecr CDs. *See* Chris Taylor, *Burn, Baby, Burn; Sales of music on*

CD are plummeting. Homemade discs are more popular than ever. What can the big record labels do?, Time, May 20, 2002, at B8. But what is the legal status of such self-help measures?

[C]   Technological Protections and Rights Management Systems

[1]   Copyright Management Information

The availability of a public record of information concerning the creation and ownership of copyrighted works — a function provided, historically, by the records of the Copyright Office — has proved of immeasurable benefit, both legally and culturally.[8] For one thing, those interested in using a copyrighted work may consult such records in order to determine whether a work is still under copyright, and if so, who owns the various rights in it. Copyright records, therefore, can serve an important role in clearing rights.

There are, of course, other vehicles for clearing rights, such as the performing rights societies like ASCAP, BMI and SESAC for musical works and the Copyright Clearance Center for certain literary works, not to mention direct contact with the copyright owner — when his or her identity is known.

Digital technology, with its ability to encode significant amounts of data, can greatly facilitate this last method of clearing rights. All pertinent information, such as name and address, telephone number, fax number, e-mail address, licensing rates, etc., can be encoded onto the work and displayed to a potential customer. For works available over digital networks, embedded links to the copyright owner can make electronic licensing even more convenient. As more and more works become available in electronic form, this sort of rights management information ("RMI") or — the synonym we will prefer here — copyright management information ("CMI") could significantly reduce the transaction costs associated with copyright licensing.

At the urging of many copyright owners, the 1996 WIPO treaties, which we introduced in § 1.04 above, went beyond encouraging the voluntary provision of CMI. In addition, they mandate that party states provide penalties for failing to transmit, or for deleting, such information.[9]

---

[8] For a discussion of some of the utilities of the copyright registration records, see the Appendices to the *Report of the Co-Chairs of the Advisory Committee on Copyright Registration and Deposit* (Library of Congress, Sept. 1993).

[9] As noted in the preceding subsections, both the Audio Home Recording Act and the Digital Performance Right in Sound Recordings Act have limiting provisions which address digitally encoded identifying information and require that it be preserved when digital works are reproduced or transmitted pursuant to the statutory licensing provisions of those statutory schemes. Significantly, however, both Acts carve out an exception to this requirement for information relating to the copyright status of works. Thus, the WIPO treaties can truly be said to break new ground.

The Digital Millennium Copyright Act of 1998, which implements the WIPO treaties, follows suit, adding a new § 1202 to Title 17. As originally proposed, the implementing legislation raised concerns that its prohibitions were overbroad, and might sweep in those who incidentally, unintentionally or innocently modified CMI distributed works with altered CMI (other than, of course, government investigators, who received a generous exemption.) There was also concern that, in the original legislation, CMI was defined as consisting of a list of specific categories of items (title, author, rights owner, terms and conditions, identifying symbols and number) and "such other information as the Register of Copyrights may provide."

This definition of CMI raised a red flag for advocates of electronic privacy, who feared that databanks of information about individuals' use of digital information (such as the embedded records of usage patterns on the World Wide Web sometimes referred to as "magic cookies") might be swept into the category of protected CMI, thus making it unlawful for consumers to correct or even delete their personal data.

As to the former concern about potential overbreadth, both the final text of the DMCA and its legislative history recognize the problem — but only insofar as broadcast stations (and similar entities) got complete relief. The DMCA excludes broadcasters from the requirement to reproduce CMI relating to the identities of various performers, writers, and directors (found in § 1202(c)(4) and (5)), and § 1202(e) further limits their liability in connection with innocent deletions of credit information which (in the case of analog transmissions) would not be "technically feasible" or would create an "undue financial hardship" to include — or (in the case of digital transmissions) where the CMI in question was not provided in the manner required by an voluntarily agreed-upon industry standard. The House Report on the DMCA goes further, indicating that:

> The prohibition of this subsection does not include ordinary and customary practices of broadcasters or inadvertent omission of credits from broadcasts of audiovisual works since, inter alia, such omissions are not made with knowledge that this will induce, enable, facilitate or conceal a copyright infringement.

H.R. Rep. 105-551 (Pt. 2), 105th Cong., 2d Sess. (1998), at 20-21.

As far as consumer privacy is concerned, the text of § 1202 included in the final version of the DMCA deals the issue by specifying that additional forms of CMI to be prescribed by regulation "may not require the provision of any information concerning the user of a copyright work." Despite the peculiarity of the wording, it appears to have been intended to prevent the Register of Copyrights from designating information about individual usage of copyright works as CMI, so as to prevent users from locating and altering or deleting such "tracking and usage" information on their systems. In addition, § 1202 is subject to a general provision of Title II, § 1205, which states:

> Nothing in this chapter abrogates, diminishes, or weakens the provisions of, nor provides any defense or element of mitigation in a criminal

prosecution or civil action under, any Federal or State law that prevents the violation of the privacy of an individual in connection with that individual's use of the Internet.

More generally, however, the final version of § 1202 raises more questions than it resolves. What, for example, is meant by "terms and conditions for the use of the work" in (b)(6)? Is a "condition" without any legal force ("This work may not be criticized in any way") still protected as CMI? And what are we to make of the discrepancies between the definition of protected CMI in the DMCA and the requirements of the 1992 AHRA, which mandates that permitted copies of digital recordings carry forward copyright status information about the work (whether it is protected or not) and generation status information (whether the copy being reproduced is an original, or, if not, what generation of reproduction it represents)? How, exactly, should the "intent" requirements incorporated in certain of § 1202's prohibitions be understood? Are they satisfied in every case where any identifying information is removed knowingly? Or do they imply a requirement of knowledge that the deleted items are or may be protected CMI? And what should we think of the exclusion from liability for deletions or alterations that are authorized by "the law?" What law? If one makes a "fair use" of a copyrighted work, is one thereby excused from the duty of maintaining the original CMI? And what about the requirement that liability for distributing works with modified CMI be done with knowledge not only that CMI has been removed or altered, but also with knowledge, or "with respect to civil remedies . . . having reasonable grounds to know, that it will induce, enable, facilitate, or conceal an infringement . . ."? How much protection does it afford to "innocent" parties?

Some preliminary insight into the last of these questions may be gleaned from the opinion in *Kelly v. Arriba Soft Corp.*, 77 F.Supp.2d 1116 (S.D.Cal. 1999) (the Court of Appeals decision in the case, which doesn't discuss the CMI issue, is reproduced in § 9.06 of this Supplement). Briefly, the defendant operated a "visual search engine" that located photographs posted on the World Wide Web and made "thumbnail" and full-sized images of them available to users — the latter along with links to the sites where the original images appeared. A professional photographer ("specializing in photographs of California gold rush country and related to the works of Laura Ingalls Wilder"), concerned that the Arriba Soft service competed with his own specialized photo websites, filed a complaint alleging, among other things, that, in the production of the "thumbnails," CMI had been stripped from the original images, in violation of new § 1202. But the court found the requisite knowledge was not present:

> To show a violation of that section, Plaintiff must show Defendant makes available to its users the thumbnails and full-size images, which were copies of Plaintiff's work separated from their copyright management information, even though it knows or should know this will lead to infringement of Plaintiff's copyrights. There is no dispute the [web] crawler removed Plaintiff's images from the context of Plaintiff's Web

sites where their copyright management information was located, and converted them to thumbnails in Defendant's index. There is also no dispute the search engine allowed full-size images to be viewed without their copyright management information.

Defendant's users could obtain a full-sized version of a thumbnailed image by clicking on the thumbnail. A user who did this was given the name of the Web site from which Defendant obtained the image, where any associated copyright management information would be available, and an opportunity to link there. Users were also informed on Defendant's Web site that use restrictions and copyright limitations may apply to images retrieved by Defendant's search engine.

77 F.Supp.2d. at 77.

Do these facts really negate a finding of the requisite "knowledge"? How important, practically, is such a disclaimer? Should it matter how easy (or difficult) it was to print or download images retrieved by the Arriba Soft service?

The court also addressed (albeit briefly and somewhat opaquely) the statutory prohibitions against intentional removal of CMI (and entailing a requirement as to knowledge of the consequences) was violated:

Section 1201(b)(1) does not apply to this case. Based on the language and structure of the statute . . . this provision applies only to the removal of copyright management information on a plaintiff's product or original work. Moreover, even if Sec. 1202(b)(1) applied, Plaintiff has not offered any evidence showing Defendant's actions were intentional, rather than merely an unintended side effect of the [web] crawler's operation.

Id.

The questions (or at least some of them) are not trivial, especially in light of the fact that § 1202 applies to analog as well as digital copies and transmissions. Future users and reusers of copyrighted works of all kinds could easily find themselves trammeled by these new provisions.[10]

Litigation about CMI issues has been fairly sparse to date, but it can be expected to accelerate as courts and litigants become more familiar with § 1202's provisions. *See, e.g., Learn2.com, Inc. v. Bell,* 2000 U.S. Dist. LEXIS 14283 (N.D. Tex. 2000), at *45-47 (exploring the application of the provision to information embedded in computer programs.) Note, however, that in at least one case, significant damages have been awarded for CMI tampering. *See Suze Randall Photography v. Reactor, Inc.,* 2000 U.S. Dist. LEXIS 6576 (N.D. Ill. 2000).

---

[10] For discussion of these issues, and other points relating to the emerging law of rights management, see Cohen, *Some Reflections on Copyright Management Systems and Laws Designed to Protect Them,* 12 Berkeley Tech. L.J. 161 (1997).

[2] Anti-Circumvention Measures

Legislation and Rule-Making

In the spectrum of current issues relating to copyright in the network environment, rights "beyond copyright" designed to promote and protect the use of digital CMI are not particularly controversial. The real controversy concerns so-called "copyright management systems" in which digital CMI is integrated with a variety of technological devices designed to frustrate unauthorized access to and use of works in digital format. Of course, technological safeguards (such as encryption and watermarking) are nothing new, and — at least as things stand today — there are no legal limits on the ability of copyright owners to employ such measures to protect works they wish to exploit in electronic commerce.[11]

What is new is the push for additional rights beyond copyright designed to discourage whenever possible, and penalize when necessary, the so-called "circumvention" of such technological protection systems. For all practical purposes, the debate over the desirability of "anti-circumvention" legislation dates from the August 1995 release of the "White Paper" on *Intellectual Property and the National Information Infrastructure*. (*See* § 7.01 of the casebook.) The "White Paper" proposed that "[t]he public will . . . have access to more copyright works via the NII if they are not vulnerable to the defeat of protection systems" and called for a ban on the importation, manufacture and sale of devices (and device components) "the primary purpose or effect of which" is to defeat such systems (p. 230).

The Administration carried an equivalent proposal to the WIPO Diplomatic Conference in December 1996, where, after heated debate, a compromise was struck, under which the new treaties called, in general, for national legislation to "provide adequate legal protection and effective legal remedies against the circumvention of effective technological measures that are used by authors in connection with the exercise of their rights . . ." Obviously, this formulation leaves a great deal to the discretion of national legislatures.

In the United States, the Digital Millennium Copyright Act of 1998 takes an approach to anti-circumvention that represents a compromise between the original Administration proposals for aggressive "implementing" legislation and alternative bills offered by members of Congress concerned about (among other things) the implications of anti-circumvention legislation for the continued vitality of the "fair use" doctrine. The Administration's proposals would have addressed the issue by categorically imposing a variety of civil and criminal penalties on the manufacture or sale of technologies capable of being used to overcome technological safeguards applied to copyrighted works, and on the use of such technologies to gain access —

---

[11] For a catalogue of such measures, see Schlachter, *The Intellectual Property Renaissance in Cyberspace: Why Copyright Law Could be Unimportant on the Internet*, 12 Berkeley Tech. L.J. 15 (1997).

for whatever purpose — to protected works. The alternative bills, such as H.R. 3048, called for no regulation of devices and components as such, nor would they have sanctioned the act of "circumvention" itself without reference to whether it was undertaken for a lawful or unlawful purpose. Instead, they would have provided that:

> No person, for the purpose of facilitating or engaging in an act of infringement, shall engage in conduct so as to knowingly remove, deactivate or otherwise circumvent the application of any effective technological measure used by a copyright owner to preclude or limit reproduction of a work or a portion thereof . . .

By linking the prohibition on circumvention to "infringement," supporters claimed that this formulation would carry into the scheme of this new right "beyond copyright" the full range of limitations and exceptions to exclusive rights which have been developed under the Copyright Act.

New § 1201 of Title 17, as provided in Title I of the DMCA, follows the general format of the original Administration proposals. But it shows the influence of the alternative bills — and of the critique which they embodied — in the various exceptions and qualifications it incorporates. Before attempting to summarize § 1201 below, we should make an overarching point: § 1201 (like the rest of new Chapter 12 of Title 17) is *not* copyright legislation — strictly, or even not so strictly, speaking. Rather, it represents a new and independent set of regulations on activities related to the use of copyrighted works, additional to and cumulative with those of copyright law itself. It is, in fact, what has been termed "paracopyright" legislation. In what follows, the distinction between copyright and "paracopyright" will be important. In parsing the provisions of § 1201, we cannot rely on our general understanding of copyright principles for guidance. For example, the exceptions and limitations on the traditional exclusive rights of copyright owners itemized in §§ 107-122 of the Copyright Act do not necessarily apply to the new "paracopyright" interests conferred by § 1201. Thus, we must pay special attention to those exceptions and limitations which are — and are not — built into the design of § 1201 itself.

At the threshold, there is the definitional question: Exactly what sorts of technological safeguards are the new provisions designed to protect against circumvention? To begin, the legislation applies only to "effective" safeguards. Usefully, the House Commerce Committee Report on the DMCA states that effective measures would include those "based on encryption, scrambling, authentication, or some other measure that requires the use of a 'key' provided by a copyright owner . . ." H.R. Rep. 105-551 (Pt. 2), 105th Cong., 2d Sess. (1998), at 39-40. Indeed, the requisite threshold of effectiveness is apparently quite low, so that even simple "password"-based systems — to say nothing about elaborate technological schemes like the Secure Digital Music Initiative, discussed above — are included. With this general qualification, § 1201 extends protection to two kinds of technological safeguards: those which control access to works, and those which control the exercise of rights with respect to works. The former are "gatekeeper" technologies which have been applied so that they must be bypassed (lawfully or otherwise) if a user is to read, see, hear, or otherwise perceive a work to which they have been applied; the latter are technologies (usually, in fact, the same technologies) which have been applied specifically to limit the further uses which can potentially be made of works to which access has been obtained, such as modification, reproduction, etc. In what follows, we will be referring to these safeguards, collectively, as "technological protection measures," or "TPMs."

Section 1201(a)(1), the provision of new Title 12 which deals with circumvention conduct as such (as distinct from circumvention technology), applies only to access-control TPMs. This limitation in scope has been described as an effort to assure that public will have continued ability to make fair use of copyrighted works, by providing that, while § 1201 prohibits circumventing technological measures that prevent unauthorized access, it does not apply to those that prevent copying. The reality is not so straightforward. The statute does not define "access," and there is nothing in law or technology to bar copyright owners from requiring that users wishing to make various uses of technologically protected works reaccess them for those purposes, or access them repeatedly while the use is being made. In other words, the "access/use" distinction tends to collapse under pressure.

In fact, the solicitude expressed in § 1201(a)(1) for the traditional use privileges of information is primarily a function of the various exceptions built into the statute itself, some narrowly specific, and at least one potentially (although not necessarily) quite broad.

The specific exceptions include a broadly worded "law enforcement" privilege (§ 1201(e)) and a "browsing privilege" in favor of libraries, archives and schools (§ 1201(d)), which are permitted to circumvent TPMs solely for the purpose of making a good faith determination as to whether they wish to copy the protected works or otherwise purchase authorized access to them. (The latter is a peculiar exception, in that no one in the affected communities either requested it or can imagine any real world circumstance in which it would come into play.) Other exceptions are more substantial, including one at § 1201(f) which applies to reverse engineering undertaken to achieve interoperability (although, at least literally, not for other currently lawful purposes). Another hard-fought battle was over encryption research, which received a carefully circumscribed exemption in § 1201(g). While this exemption did ultimately find its way into the DMCA, it is subject to a requirement that the Copyright Office and the Commerce Department report to Congress in a year on its impact. Computer security testing activities are covered in § 1201(j). Section 1201(i) provides a personal privacy exception, applicable when a TPM is capable of collecting or disseminating personally identifying information about the information use practices of an individual — which may or may not be an issue of real practical importance.

In contrast to these specific exceptions stands one that was most controversial in the forging of the final DMCA, and may yet prove either highly significant or largely trivial in its impact. The provisions of § 1201(a)(1)(B)-(E) suspend the operation of its prohibition against circumvention conduct for two years from the date of enactment (October 27, 1998), and decree that, during those two years, the Librarian of Congress is to conduct a formal rule-making proceeding to inquire into whether users are or are likely to be, in the ensuing three years, adversely affected in their ability to make otherwise lawful uses of particular "classes" of copyright works. If the inquiry determines this to be the case, the Librarian is authorized to make corresponding exceptions to the § 1201(a)(1) prohibitions on circumvention conduct, which will remain in effect for a three-year period, during which a similar rule-making will occur — and so on and so forth.

If all this seems a little vague and ungrounded, it is no wonder. There is no specific precedent for a rule-making of this kind, in intellectual property law or out of it, and no one is sure how it will proceed — let alone what the results will be. Who will be heard? What kind of evidence will be received? What threshold standard will apply to demonstrations of "likely" adverse effects? What, exactly, are "classes" of works? (We know from the legislative history that what is contemplated here are *not* the general categories of § 102(a), but, apparently, something more narrowly descriptive: "scientific journal articles," "general reference works," etc.)

The meaning of "class" was a key factor in shaping the Copyright Office's Recommendation in support of the rule, "Exemption to Prohibition on Circumvention of Copyright Protection Systems for Access Control Technologies," 65 F.R. 64555 (Oct. 27, 2000), issued by the Librarian of Congress after the initial § 1201(a)(1) rule-making. The Office rejected suggestions made in some public comments and hearing testimony (all of which is now conveniently collected at *http://www.loc.gov/copyright/1201/anticirc.html*) that, for example, the designation "works embodied in copies which have been lawfully acquired by users who subsequently seek to made non-infringing uses thereof" constituted an eligible "class," because it did not refer primarily to the qualities of the works themselves. The Copyright Office does note, however, that the Assistant Secretary of Commerce for Communications and Information, with whom the Librarian was required by statute to consult in reaching a decision, did endorse this proposal for an exemption (by a letter dated Sept. 29, 2000).

In this connection, a number of those submitting comments and testifying expressed concerns about so-called "persistent" access controls — those, that is, that would regulate not only consumer's initial access to purchased copies of works, but also effectively control their subsequent utilization by requiring a new permission for "acccess" each time the work was consulted. In the view of the Copyright Office, however, such concerns were too speculative to be taken into account under the statutory standard of actual or "likely" adverse affects on users' "ability to make noninfringing uses."[12]

---

[12] Such an implementation of access controls is not, however, a mere consumer's dark fantasy. Indeed, it was noted specifically during the rule-making proceeding, in the Joint Reply Comments of March 31, 2000 submitted by the American Market

Other proposals for exemptions with the potential to cut across the familiar statutory categories of copyright subject-matter — including one for "thin copyright works," for which the American Association of Universities advocated effectively, and another for "sole source works" — were rejected as failing for lack of "demonstrated" need. And a number of suggestions for more particular exemptions met the same fate.

Ultimately, the rule settled on two very narrowly defined classes to which § 1201(a)(1) was made inapplicable for a period of three years:

1. Compilations consisting of lists of websites blocked by filtering software applications; and

2. Literary works, including computer programs and databases, protected by access control mechanisms that fail to permit access because of malfunction, damage, or obsoleteness.

The first class was identified as necessary to promote research on the effectiveness of various web filters (including those used to screen indecent material); the latter (which addresses the problem of damaged "dongles," which we learn from the Copyright Office recommendation is a term of art for certain hardware locks) seems relatively self-explanatory.

Nowhere on the Copyright Office website does there seem to be any trace of the "Statement of James H. Billington, Librarian of Congress, on Section 1201(a)(1) Rulemaking" (Oct. 27, 2000), which appears to exist only in paper form and which expresses some dissatisfaction with the statutory criteria under which that rule was crafted by the Copyright Office. In pertinent part, Dr. Billington wrote:

The experience of the first rulemaking under the DMCA has raised several concerns. First of all, the rapidly changing technological world in which we live probably makes waiting three years to undertake a new rule-making too long. Potential damage to scholarship may well ensue in the course of a three-year period. Therefore, I intend to ask the Congress to take another look at the statutory time frame to see if it should be shortened.

Second, I will ask that Congress consider developing more appropriate criteria for assessing the harm that could be done to American creativity by the anti-circumvention provision of the statute. As presently crafted, the statute places considerable burdens on the scholarly, academic, and library communities to demonstrate and even to measure the required adverse impacts on users.

Association and 16 other organizations generally opposed to additional § 1201(a)(1) exemptions (item 112 at *http://www.loc.gov/copyright/1201/comments/reply/*). At page 21, the organizations state: "[T]he effects of access control measures are not simply initial binary permissions of denials of access; they can also allow the management of who can have access, when, how much, and from where." *See also* Thomas E. Weber, *Protecting Copyrights: How E-Books Will Be Like Parking Meters*, Wall Street J. (Sept. 22, 2000), at B1, col. 1.

Finally, the Register [of Copyrights], and the public at large, also need more precise guidance regarding the definition of a "class of works," as well as the standard of proof governing which classes can be eligible for the exemption.

These are among the topics that may be addressed in corrective legislation to be introduced by Rep. Rick Boucher (D-Va.). *See http://www.techjournal.com/intelpro/20010306/boucher.asp.* More generally, one might ask whether the delegation of what appears to be legislative power to the Librarian of Congress is even constitutional. *See* JeanAne Marie Jiles, *Copyright Protection in the New Millennium: Amending the Digital Millennium Copyright Act to Prevent Constitutional Challenges,* 52 Admin. L. Rev. 443 (2000). Having said all this, the provision is a remarkable one, and (if nothing else) will provide the forum for a robust, continuing public discussion of the fate of "fair use" under a regime of "paracopyright."

In any event, preparations for the next rulemaking, which should be completed by October 2003 if the process is to remain on schedule, already are beginning. On May 13, 2002, the news roundup in Audio Week magazine reported Register of Copyrights Marybeth Peters' statement that starting in June, "the Copyright Office will meet with high-tech companies to try to get a handle of what encryption technologies are in existence and what questions [the O]ffice should be asking about developments in the next 3 years. . . . Then sometime before the end of September, [the O]ffice will solicit public comments and set hearings. Every time this rulemaking happens 'it is going to get more and more difficult'. . . ." Does the Administrative Procedure Act have anything relevant to say about the appropriateness of such preliminary meetings with interested parties?

Of course, even if the scope of § 1201(a)(1) were someday to be significantly restricted as the result of the Librarian's rule-making, the practical ability of information consumers to exercise their circumvention privileges would be severely restricted by the non-availability of devices and services to assist them. Sections 1201(a)(2) and 1201(b) cover more than just "black boxes" designed specifically to facilitate electronic copyright piracy. Instead, they comprehensively prohibit trafficking in "any technology, product, service, device, component, or part thereof" that can be used to circumvent access to copyright works or limit the exercise of rights with respect to such works, if any of a series of conditions, stated in the disjunctive, is met. The prohibitions apply if the item or service is primarily designed or made for circumvention, if it has only "limited commercially significant purpose" other than circumvention, or if it is marketed for circumvention purposes — thorough coverage indeed! Obviously, the fact that a circumvention device or service might be made or sold to aid circumvention conduct that is found to be exempt in the course of the Librarian of Congress's rule-making does not — in itself — save the device or service from the sweep of these prohibitions.

Falling outside the sweep of §§ 1201(a)(2) and (b) are, to be sure, specialized means of circumvention designed to be used in connection with some (though not all) of the circumvention activities which are specifically exempt under the DMCA. Law enforcement personnel and software designers engaged in qualifying reverse engineering activities may develop circumvention hardware and software to counteract all kinds of TPMs, while encryption researchers, and computer security testers, may do so to circumvent TPMs which control access (but not those that control copying). Curiously, browsing libraries and computer users engaging in self-help to protect their personal privacy apparently have to do without the equipment and services they require to effectuate their circumvention privileges. Contrariwise, though § 1201 provides no exemption for circumvention conduct by parents seeking to protect their children from harmful on-line content, it does allow a court to excuse the maker of a hardware or software component designed exclusively for this purpose from liability.

Further, by their wording (and richly supported in the legislative history of the DMCA), §§ 1201(a)(2) and (b) do not reach general-purpose consumer electronics devices (such as VCRs and PCs) and telecommunications equipment that may incidentally perform some circumvention functions. Moreover, § 1201(c)(3) specifically states that such manufacturers are not required to design their products to respond affirmatively to (or facilitate the effectiveness of) any particular type of TPM — whether now in existence or to be developed in the future.[13]

This so-called "no mandate" provision represented a hard-won victory in the DMCA for the electronics and hardware industries, and it was won (in part) through compromise: § 1201(k) modifies the general "no mandate" provision by requiring that, within 18 months, all new analog VCRs should be built to conform with certain defined "copy-protection" technologies — generally referred to as "Macrovision" — that are commonly applied to videotapes offered for sale and rental.

Over the long haul, another portion of § 1201(k) actually may turn out to be among the most important features of the DMCA. In addition to the mandate relating to Macrovision just mentioned, the section also includes a bar on the application of Macrovision technology to prevent consumer copying of free over-the-air television broadcasts. In a world of "paracopyright," "encoding rules" barring the application of TPMs in certain circumstances may represent the most realistic legislative option for assuring the meaningful continuation of the traditional user privileges embedded in the

---

[13] Moreover, the legislative history of the DMCA strongly supports the conclusion that electronics manufacturers are free to modify the equipment in response to new or old TPMs in order to assure "playability." As the Commerce Committee report puts it:

> [N]othing would make it illegal for a manufacturer . . . to design or modify [its] product or device solely to the extent necessary to mitigate a frequently occurring and noticeable adverse effect on the authorized performance or display of a work that is caused by a technological protection measure in the ordinary course of its design or operation.

H.R. Rep. 105-551 (Pt. 2), 105th Cong., 2d Sess. (1998), at 40-41.

copyright law itself. Section 1201(k) strikes a small but notable blow for "fair use," and could serve as a model for other "encoding rules" to come.

Finally, we should note that the DMCA's new prohibitions against altering CMI and circumventing TPMs interact with the ongoing efforts to revise the general commercial law to assure, among many other things, the enforceability of "shrink-wrap" and "click-on" licenses (discussed in § 1.05 with reference to the digital challenge and in § 10.02 in connection with the preemption doctrine). Taken together, these developments could work to facilitate the emergence of a "pay per use" or "look but don't copy" business model for the commercial distribution of information over digital networks.

Under such a model, the Copyright Act's well-articulated balance of proprietary rights and use privileges would represent merely a default setting, subject to effective override by means of legally-protected technological safeguards and the terms of electronic contracts of adhesion. Large content providers suggest that curtailment of some or all of information consumers' traditional use privileges (under fair use, first sale, the § 110 exemptions, and so forth) is a reasonable price to pay for the greater availability of digital information that would result. They also point out that, in enacting the DMCA, the United States has seized an opportunity to influence the actions of other countries now considering WIPO treaty implementation by taking a strong position on anti-circumvention — an outcome which might assure even greater returns from the sale of our intellectual property products abroad. But is the game really worth the candle?

Let the Litigation Begin!

So much for Congress and the Copyright Office. The first lawsuits to allege violations of Chapter 12 have now begun.

On December 21, 1999, RealNetworks, Inc., whose products deliver "streamed" audio and video content over the Internet, brought suit against Redmond, Washington-based Steambox, Inc., for offering software usable for downloading RealNetworks' feeds in various data storage formats, including MP3, WAV and Windows Media. Since "streamed" audio and video technology is designed to safeguard content by preventing downloading, RealNetworks regarded Steambox's products as prohibited "circumvention" technologies and sued to bar their use — despite the fact that it was not the owner of copyright in the music and video content in question. In a opinion reported at 2000 U.S. Dist. LEXIS 1889 (W.D. Wash. 2000), a federal judge agreed that a number of RealNetwork's claims had enough merit to justify a preliminary injunction. Notably, he commented that Streambox's claim that it should escape liability under the rule of *Sony Corp. of America v. Universal City Studios, Inc.,* 464 U.S. 417 (1984), because its products had legitimate uses (including facilitating the making of "fair use copies" of RealMedia files) was unavailing: "[T]he 'Sony' decision did not involve interpretation of the DMCA. Under the DMCA, . . . Congress specifically prohibited the distribution of tools by which . . . circumvention could be accomplished." Indeed.

But that was only an early battle in the DMCA wars.

In August 2000, Judge Lewis A. Kaplan of the Southern District of New York weighed in -literally, if you have tried hefting his opinion! -with the first installment in a widely-watched dispute between the motion picture industry and the publishers of a "hacker's magazine" (in print and on-line). 111 F. Supp. 2d 294. Among other things, Judge Kaplan concluded that, by Congressional design, there is no "fair use" exception to the anti-circumvention provisions of the DMCA. He went on to assess whether the absence of such a provision (or any other characteristics of the statute) renders it constitutionally suspect. Bottom line: no. The decision was appealed. The outcome in the Second Circuit Court of Appeals follows.

UNIVERSAL CITY STUDIOS, INC. v. CORLEY

United States Court of Appeals, Second Circuit
273 F.3d 429 (2001)

JON O. NEWMAN, Circuit Judge.

When the Framers of the First Amendment prohibited Congress from making any law "abridging the freedom of speech," they were not thinking about computers, computer programs, or the Internet. But neither were they thinking about radio, television, or movies. Just as the inventions at the beginning and middle of the 20th century presented new First Amendment issues, so does the cyber revolution at the end of that century. This appeal raises significant First Amendment issues concerning one aspect of computer technology—encryption to protect materials in digital form from unauthorized access. The appeal challenges the constitutionality of the Digital Millennium Copyright Act ("DMCA"), *17 U.S.C. § 1201* et seq. (Supp. V 1999) and the validity of an injunction entered to enforce the DMCA.

Defendant-Appellant Eric C. Corley and his company, 2600 Enterprises, Inc., (collectively "Corley," "the Defendants," or "the Appellants") appeal from the amended final judgment of the United States District Court for the Southern District of New York (Lewis A. Kaplan, District Judge), entered August 23, 2000, enjoining them from various actions concerning a decryption program known as "DeCSS." *Universal City Studios, Inc. v. Reimerdes, 111 F. Supp. 2d 346 (S.D.N.Y. 2000)* ("Universal II"). The injunction primarily bars the Appellants from posting DeCSS on their web site and from knowingly linking their web site to any other web site on which DeCSS is posted. *Id. at 346-47*. We affirm.

Introduction

Understanding the pending appeal and the issues it raises requires some familiarity with technical aspects of computers and computer software, especially software called "digital versatile disks" or "DVDs," which are optical media storage devices currently designed to contain movies.[1] Those lacking such familiarity will be greatly aided by reading Judge Kaplan's extremely lucid opinion, *Universal City Studios, Inc. v. Reimerdes,* 111 F. Supp. 2d 294 (S.D.N.Y. 2000) ("Universal I"), beginning with his helpful section "The Vocabulary of this Case," *id. at 305-09.*

This appeal concerns the anti-trafficking provisions of the DMCA, which Congress enacted in 1998 to strengthen copyright protection in the digital age. Fearful that the ease with which pirates could copy and distribute a copyrightable work in digital form was overwhelming the capacity of conventional copyright enforcement to find and enjoin unlawfully copied material, Congress sought to combat copyright piracy in its earlier stages, before the work was even copied. The DMCA therefore backed with legal sanctions the efforts of copyright owners to protect their works from piracy behind digital walls such as encryption codes or password protections. In so doing, Congress targeted not only those pirates who would circumvent these digital walls (the "anti-circumvention provisions," contained in *17 U.S.C. § 1201* (a)(1)), but also anyone who would traffic in a technology primarily designed to circumvent a digital wall (the "anti-trafficking provisions," contained in *17 U.S.C. § 1201* (a)(2), (b)(1)).

Corley publishes a print magazine and maintains an affiliated web site geared towards "hackers," a digital-era term often applied to those interested in techniques for circumventing protections of computers and computer data from unauthorized access. The so-called hacker community includes serious computer-science scholars conducting research on protection techniques, computer buffs intrigued by the challenge of trying to circumvent access-limiting devices or perhaps hoping to promote security by exposing flaws in protection techniques, mischief-makers interested in disrupting computer operations, and thieves, including copyright infringers who want to acquire copyrighted material (for personal use or resale) without paying for it.

In November 1999, Corley posted a copy of the decryption computer program "DeCSS" on his web site, http://www.2600.com ("2600.com").[2] DeCSS

---

[1] DVDs are similar to compact disks (CDs), but differ, among other things, in that they hold far more data. For detailed information concerning DVDs and CDs, see "Fast Guide to CD/DVD" at http://searchWindowsManageability. techtarget.com/ sDefinition/0,,sid_ gci514667,00.html (last updated Aug. 3, 2001).

[2] "2600" has special significance to the hacker community. It is the hertz frequency ("a unit of frequency of a periodic process equal to one cycle per second," Webster's Third New International Dictionary 1061 (1993)) of a signal that some hackers formerly used to explore the entire telephone system from "operator mode," which was triggered by the transmission of a 2600 hertz tone across a telephone line, Trial Tr. at 786-87, or to place telephone calls without incurring long-distance toll charges, *United States v. Brady,* 820 F. Supp. 1346, 1355 & n.18 (D. Utah 1993). One such user reportedly discovered that the sound of a toy whistle from a box of Cap'n Crunch cereal matched the telephone company's 2600 hertz tone perfectly. *Id. at 1355 n.18.*

is designed to circumvent "CSS," the encryption technology that motion picture studios place on DVDs to prevent the unauthorized viewing and copying of motion pictures. Corley also posted on his web site links to other web sites where DeCSS could be found.

Plaintiffs-Appellees are eight motion picture studios that brought an action in the Southern District of New York seeking injunctive relief against Corley under the DMCA. Following a full non-jury trial, the District Court entered a permanent injunction barring Corley from posting DeCSS on his web site or from knowingly linking via a hyperlink to any other web site containing DeCSS. *Universal II, 111 F. Supp. 2d at 346-47*. The District Court rejected Corley's constitutional attacks on the statute and the injunction. *Universal I, 111 F. Supp. 2d at 325-45*.

Corley renews his constitutional challenges on appeal. Specifically, he argues primarily that: (1) the DMCA oversteps limits in the Copyright Clause on the duration of copyright protection; (2) the DMCA as applied to his dissemination of DeCSS violates the First Amendment because computer code is "speech" entitled to full First Amendment protection and the DMCA fails to survive the exacting scrutiny accorded statutes that regulate "speech"; and (3) the DMCA violates the First Amendment and the Copyright Clause by unduly obstructing the "fair use" of copyrighted materials. Corley also argues that the statute is susceptible to, and should therefore be given, a narrow interpretation that avoids alleged constitutional objections.

Background

For decades, motion picture studios have made movies available for viewing at home in what is called "analog" format. Movies in this format are placed on videotapes, which can be played on a video cassette recorder ("VCR"). In the early 1990s, the studios began to consider the possibility of distributing movies in digital form as well. Movies in digital form are placed on disks, known as DVDs, which can be played on a DVD player (either a stand-alone device or a component of a computer). DVDs offer advantages over analog tapes, such as improved visual and audio quality, larger data capacity, and greater durability. However, the improved quality of a movie in a digital format brings with it the risk that a virtually perfect copy, i.e., one that will not lose perceptible quality in the copying process, can be readily made at the click of a computer control and instantly distributed to countless recipients throughout the world over the Internet. This case arises out of the movie industry's efforts to respond to this risk by invoking the anti-trafficking provisions of the DMCA.

I. CSS

The movie studios were reluctant to release movies in digital form until they were confident they had in place adequate safeguards against piracy of their copyrighted movies. The studios took several steps to minimize the piracy threat. First, they settled on the DVD as the standard digital medium for home distribution of movies. The studios then sought an encryption scheme to protect movies on DVDs. They enlisted the help of members of the consumer electronics and computer industries, who in mid-1996 developed the Content Scramble System ("CSS"). CSS is an encryption scheme that employs an algorithm configured by a set of "keys" to encrypt a DVD's contents. The algorithm is a type of mathematical formula for transforming the contents of the movie file into gibberish; the "keys" are in actuality strings of 0's and 1's that serve as values for the mathematical formula. Decryption in the case of CSS requires a set of "player keys" contained in compliant DVD players, as well as an understanding of the CSS encryption algorithm. Without the player keys and the algorithm, a DVD player cannot access the contents of a DVD. With the player keys and the algorithm, a DVD player can display the movie on a television or a computer screen, but does not give a viewer the ability to use the copy function of the computer to copy the movie or to manipulate the digital content of the DVD.

The studios developed a licensing scheme for distributing the technology to manufacturers of DVD players. Player keys and other information necessary to the CSS scheme were given to manufacturers of DVD players for an administrative fee. In exchange for the licenses, manufacturers were obliged to keep the player keys confidential. Manufacturers were also required in the licensing agreement to prevent the transmission of "CSS data" (a term undefined in the licensing agreement) from a DVD drive to any "internal recording device," including, presumably, a computer hard drive.

With encryption technology and licensing agreements in hand, the studios began releasing movies on DVDs in 1997, and DVDs quickly gained in popularity, becoming a significant source of studio revenue.[3] In 1998, the studios secured added protection against DVD piracy when Congress passed the DMCA, which prohibits the development or use of technology designed to circumvent a technological protection measure, such as CSS. The pertinent provisions of the DMCA are examined in greater detail below.

II. DeCSS

In September 1999, Jon Johansen, a Norwegian teenager, collaborating with two unidentified individuals he met on the Internet, reverse-engineered a licensed DVD player designed to operate on the Microsoft operating system, and culled from it the player keys and other information necessary to decrypt CSS. The record suggests that Johansen was trying to develop a DVD player operable on Linux, an alternative operating system

---

[3] By the end of 1997, most if not all DVDs that were released were encrypted with CSS. Trial Tr. at 409; *Universal I, 111 F. Supp. 2d at 310.* Moreover, DVD players were projected to be in ten percent of United States homes by the end of 2000. Trial Tr. at 442; *Universal I, 111 F. Supp. 2d at 310.* In fact, as of 2000, about thirty-five percent of one studio's worldwide revenues from movie distribution was attributable to DVD sales and rentals. Trial Tr. at 403; *Universal I, 111 F. Supp. 2d at 310 n.69.*

that did not support any licensed DVD players at that time. In order to accomplish this task, Johansen wrote a decryption program executable on Microsoft's operating system. That program was called, appropriately enough, "DeCSS."

If a user runs the DeCSS program (for example, by clicking on the DeCSS icon on a Microsoft operating system platform) with a DVD in the computer's disk drive, DeCSS will decrypt the DVD's CSS protection, allowing the user to copy the DVD's files and place the copy on the user's hard drive. The result is a very large computer file that can be played on a non-CSS-compliant player and copied, manipulated, and transferred just like any other computer file.[5] DeCSS comes complete with a fairly user-friendly interface that helps the user select from among the DVD's files and assign the decrypted file a location on the user's hard drive. The quality of the resulting decrypted movie is "virtually identical" to that of the encrypted movie on the DVD. *Universal I, 111 F. Supp. 2d at 308, 313.* And the file produced by DeCSS, while large, can be compressed to a manageable size by a compression software called "DivX," available at no cost on the Internet. This compressed file can be copied onto a DVD, or transferred over the Internet (with some patience).[6]

Johansen posted the executable object code, but not the source code, for DeCSS on his web site. The distinction between source code and object code is relevant to this case, so a brief explanation is warranted. A computer

---

[5] An item of some controversy, both in this litigation and elsewhere, is the extent to which CSS-encrypted DVDs can be copied even without DeCSS. . . .

However, none of this detracts from these undisputed findings: some feature of either CSS itself, or another (unidentified) safeguard implemented by DVD manufacturers pursuant to their obligations under the CSS licensing scheme, makes it difficult to copy a CSS-encrypted DVD to a hard drive and then compress that DVD to the point where transmission over the Internet is practical. See *Universal I, 111 F. Supp. 2d at 338.* Conversely, a DVD movie file without CSS encryption is easily copied, manipulated, and transferred. See *id. at 313.* . . .

While there may be alternative means of extracting a non-encrypted, copyable movie from a DVD—for example, by copying the movie along with its encryption "bit-by-bit," or "ripping" a DVD by siphoning movie file data after CSS has already been decrypted by a licensed player—DeCSS is the superior means of acquiring easily copyable movies, see *id. at 342,* and in fact, is recommended by a DVD compression web site as the preferred tool for obtaining a decrypted DVD suitable for compression and transmission over the Internet, see id. We acknowledge the complexity and the rapidly changing nature of the technology involved in this case, but it is clear that the Defendants have presented no evidence to refute any of these carefully considered findings by the District Court.

[6] The District Court determined that even at high speeds, typical of university networks, transmission times ranged from three minutes to six hours. The Court noted, however, that "the availability of high speed network connections in many businesses and institutions, and their growing availability in homes, make Internet and other network traffic in pirated copies a growing threat." *Universal I, 111 F. Supp. 2d at 315.*

responds to electrical charges, the presence or absence of which is represented by strings of 1's and 0's. Strictly speaking, "object code" consists of those 1's and 0's. While some people can read and program in object code, "it would be inconvenient, inefficient and, for most people, probably impossible to do so." *Universal I, 111 F. Supp. 2d at 306.* Computer languages have been written to facilitate program writing and reading. A program in such a computer language—BASIC, C, and Java are examples—is said to be written in "source code." Source code has the benefit of being much easier to read (by people) than object code, but as a general matter, it must be translated back to object code before it can be read by a computer. . . . Within months of its appearance in executable form on Johansen's web site, DeCSS was widely available on the Internet, in both object code and various forms of source code. . . .

In November 1999, Corley wrote and placed on his web site, 2600.com, an article about the DeCSS phenomenon. His web site is an auxiliary to the print magazine, 2600: The Hacker Quarterly, which Corley has been publishing since 1984. As the name suggests, the magazine is designed for "hackers," as is the web site. While the magazine and the web site cover some issues of general interest to computer users—such as threats to online privacy—the focus of the publications is on the vulnerability of computer security systems, and more specifically, how to exploit that vulnerability in order to circumvent the security systems. Representative articles explain how to steal an Internet domain name and how to break into the computer systems at Federal Express. *Universal I, 111 F. Supp. 2d at 308-09.*

Corley's article about DeCSS detailed how CSS was cracked, and described the movie industry's efforts to shut down web sites posting DeCSS. It also explained that DeCSS could be used to copy DVDs. At the end of the article, the Defendants posted copies of the object and source code of DeCSS. In Corley's words, he added the code to the story because "in a journalistic world, . . . you have to show your evidence . . . and particularly in the magazine that I work for, people want to see specifically what it is that we are referring to," including "what evidence . . . we have" that there is in fact technology that circumvents CSS. Writing about DeCSS without including the DeCSS code would have been, to Corley, "analogous to printing a story about a picture and not printing the picture." Corley also added to the article links that he explained would take the reader to other web sites where DeCSS could be found.

2600.com was only one of hundreds of web sites that began posting DeCSS near the end of 1999. The movie industry tried to stem the tide by sending cease-and-desist letters to many of these sites. These efforts met with only partial success; a number of sites refused to remove DeCSS. In January 2000, the studios filed this lawsuit.

III. The DMCA

The DMCA was enacted in 1998 to implement the World Intellectual Property Organization Copyright Treaty ("WIPO Treaty"), which requires contracting parties to "provide adequate legal protection and effective legal remedies against the circumvention of effective technological measures that are used by authors in connection with the exercise of their rights under this Treaty or the Berne Convention and that restrict acts, in respect of their works, which are not authorized by the authors concerned or permitted by law." WIPO Treaty, art. 11, S. Treaty Doc. No. 105-17 (1997). Even before the treaty, Congress had been devoting attention to the problems faced by copyright enforcement in the digital age. Hearings on the topic have spanned several years. . . . This legislative effort resulted in the DMCA.

The Act contains three provisions targeted at the circumvention of technological protections. The first is subsection 1201(a)(1)(A), the anti-circumvention provision. This provision prohibits a person from "circumventing a technological measure that effectively controls access to a work protected under [Title 17, governing copyright]."

The second and third provisions are subsections 1201(a)(2) and 1201(b)(1), the "anti-trafficking provisions." Subsection 1201(a)(2), the provision at issue in this case, provides:

> No person shall manufacture, import, offer to the public, provide, or otherwise traffic in any technology, product, service, device, component, or part thereof, that—
>
> (A) is primarily designed or produced for the purpose of circumventing a technological measure that effectively controls access to a work protected under this title;
>
> (B) has only limited commercially significant purpose or use other than to circumvent a technological measure that effectively controls access to a work protected under this title; or
>
> (c) is marketed by that person or another acting in concert with that person with that person's knowledge for use in circumventing a technological measure that effectively controls access to a work protected under this title.

Id. § 1201(a)(2). To "circumvent a technological measure" is defined, in pertinent part, as "to descramble a scrambled work . . . or otherwise to . . . bypass . . . a technological measure, without the authority of the copyright owner." Id. § 1201(a)(3)(A).

Subsection 1201(b)(1) is similar to subsection 1201(a)(2), except that subsection 1201(a)(2) covers those who traffic in technology that can circumvent "a technological measure that effectively controls access to a work protected under" Title 17, whereas subsection 1201(b)(1) covers those who traffic in technology that can circumvent "protection afforded by a technological measure that effectively protects a right of a copyright owner under" Title 17. Id. § 1201(a)(2), (b)(1) (emphases added). In other words, although both subsections prohibit trafficking in a circumvention technology, the focus of subsection 1201(a)(2) is circumvention of technologies designed to prevent access to a work, and the focus of subsection 1201(b)(1) is circumvention of technologies designed to permit access to a work but prevent copying of the work or some other act that infringes a copyright. . . .

The DMCA contains exceptions for schools and libraries that want to use circumvention technologies to determine whether to purchase a copyrighted product, *17 U.S.C. § 1201* (d); individuals using circumvention technology "for the sole purpose" of trying to achieve "interoperability" of computer programs through reverse-engineering, id. § 1201(f); encryption research aimed at identifying flaws in encryption technology, if the research is conducted to advance the state of knowledge in the field, id. § 1201(g); and several other exceptions not relevant here.

The DMCA creates civil remedies, id. § 1203, and criminal sanctions, id. § 1204. It specifically authorizes a court to "grant temporary and permanent injunctions on such terms as it deems reasonable to prevent or restrain a violation." Id. § 1203(b)(1).

IV. Procedural History

Invoking subsection 1203(b)(1), the Plaintiffs sought an injunction against the Defendants, alleging that the Defendants violated the anti-trafficking provisions of the statute. On January 20, 2000, after a hearing, the District Court issued a preliminary injunction barring the Defendants from posting DeCSS. *Universal City Studios, Inc. v. Reimerdes, 82 F. Supp. 2d 211 (S.D.N.Y. 2000).*

The Defendants complied with the preliminary injunction, but continued to post links to other web sites carrying DeCSS, an action they termed "electronic civil disobedience." *Universal I, 111 F. Supp. 2d at 303, 312.* Under the heading "Stop the MPAA [(Motion Picture Association of America)]," Corley urged other web sites to post DeCSS lest "we . . . be forced into submission." *Id. at 313.*

The Plaintiffs then sought a permanent injunction barring the Defendants from both posting DeCSS and linking to sites containing DeCSS. After a trial on the merits, the Court issued a comprehensive opinion, Universal I, and granted a permanent injunction, Universal II.

The Court explained that the Defendants' posting of DeCSS on their web site clearly falls within section 1201(a)(2)(A) of the DMCA, rejecting as spurious their claim that CSS is not a technological measure that "effectively controls access to a work" because it was so easily penetrated by Johansen, *Universal I, 111 F. Supp. 2d at 318,* and as irrelevant their contention that DeCSS was designed to create a Linux-platform DVD player, *id. at 319.* The Court also held that the Defendants cannot avail themselves of any of the DMCA's exceptions, *id. at 319-22,* and that the alleged importance of DeCSS to certain fair uses of encrypted copyrighted material was immaterial to their statutory liability, *id. at 322-24.* The Court went on to hold that when the Defendants "proclaimed on their own site that DeCSS could be had by clicking on the hyperlinks" on their site, they were trafficking in DeCSS, and therefore liable for their linking as well as their posting. *Id. at 325.*

Turning to the Defendants' numerous constitutional arguments, the Court first held that computer code like DeCSS is "speech" that is "protected" (in the sense of "covered") by the First Amendment, *id. at 327,* but that because the DMCA is targeting the "functional" aspect of that speech, *id. at 328-29,* it is "content neutral," *id. at 329,* and the intermediate scrutiny of *United States v. O'Brien,* 391 U.S. 367 (1968), applies, *Universal I, 111 F. Supp. 2d at 329-30.* The Court concluded that the DMCA survives this scrutiny, *111 F. Supp. 2d at 330-33,* and also rejected prior restraint, overbreadth, and vagueness challenges, *id. at 333-39.*

The Court upheld the constitutionality of the DMCA's application to linking on similar grounds. . . . However, the Court concluded that a blanket proscription on linking would create a risk of chilling legitimate linking on the web. The Court therefore crafted a restrictive test for linking liability (discussed below) that it believed sufficiently mitigated that risk. The Court then found its test satisfied in this case. *111 F. Supp. 2d at 339-41.*

Finally, the Court concluded that an injunction was highly appropriate in this case. The Court observed that DeCSS was harming the Plaintiffs, [because among other things] the threat of piracy was very real, particularly as Internet transmission speeds continue to increase. *Id. at 314-15, 342.* Acknowledging that DeCSS was (and still is) widely available on the Internet, the Court expressed confidence in

> the likelihood . . . that this decision will serve notice on others that "the strong right arm of equity" may be brought to bear against them absent a change in their conduct and thus contribute to a climate of appropriate respect for intellectual property rights in an age in which the excitement of ready access to untold quantities of information has blurred in some minds the fact that taking what is not yours and not freely offered to you is stealing.

Id. at 345.

The Court's injunction barred the Defendants from: "posting on any Internet web site" DeCSS; "in any other way . . . offering to the public, providing, or otherwise trafficking in DeCSS"; violating the anti-trafficking provisions of the DMCA in any other manner, and finally "knowingly linking any Internet web site operated by them to any other web site containing DeCSS, or knowingly maintaining any such link, for the purpose of disseminating DeCSS." Universal II, at 346-47.

The Appellants have appealed from the permanent injunction. The United States has intervened in support of the constitutionality of the DMCA. We have also had the benefit of a number of amicus curiae briefs, supporting and opposing the District Court's judgment. After oral argument, we invited the parties to submit responses to a series of specific questions, and we have received helpful responses.

Discussion

I. Narrow Construction to Avoid Constitutional Doubt

The Appellants first argue that, because their constitutional arguments are at least substantial, we should interpret the statute narrowly so as to avoid constitutional problems. They identify three different instances of alleged ambiguity in the statute that they claim provide an opportunity for such a narrow interpretation.

First, they contend that subsection 1201(c)(1), which provides that "nothing in this section shall affect rights, remedies, limitations or defenses to copyright infringement, including fair use, under this title," can be read to allow the circumvention of encryption technology protecting copyrighted material when the material will be put to "fair uses" exempt from copyright liability. We disagree that subsection 1201(c)(1) permits such a reading. Instead, it simply clarifies that the DMCA targets the circumvention of digital walls guarding copyrighted material (and trafficking in circumvention tools), but does not concern itself with the use of those materials after circumvention has occurred. Subsection 1201(c)(1) ensures that the DMCA is not read to prohibit the "fair use" of information just because that information was obtained in a manner made illegal by the DMCA. The Appellants' much more expansive interpretation of subsection 1201(c)(1) is not only outside the range of plausible readings of the provision, but is also clearly refuted by the statute's legislative history.[13] . . .

Second, the Appellants urge a narrow construction of the DMCA because of subsection 1201(c)(4), which provides that "nothing in this section shall enlarge or diminish any rights of free speech or the press for activities using consumer electronics, telecommunications, or computing products." This language is clearly precatory: Congress could not "diminish" constitutional rights of free speech even if it wished to, and the fact that Congress also expressed a reluctance to "enlarge" those rights cuts against the Appellants' effort to infer a narrowing construction of the Act from this provision.

---

[13] The legislative history of the enacted bill makes quite clear that Congress intended to adopt a "balanced" approach to accommodating both piracy and fair use concerns, eschewing the quick fix of simply exempting from the statute all circumventions for fair use. H.R. Rep. No. 105-551, pt. 2, at 25 (1998). It sought to achieve this goal principally through the use of what it called a "fail-safe" provision in the statute, authorizing the Librarian of Congress to exempt certain users from the anticircumvention provision when it becomes evident that in practice, the statute is adversely affecting certain kinds of fair use. See *17 U.S.C. § 1201* (a)(1)(C). . . .

Congress also sought to implement a balanced approach through statutory provisions that leave limited areas of breathing space for fair use. A good example is subsection 1201(d), which allows a library or educational institution to circumvent a digital wall in order to determine whether it wishes legitimately to obtain the material behind the wall. See H.R. Rep. No. 105-551, pt. 2, at 41. It would be strange for Congress to open small, carefully limited windows for circumvention to permit fair use in subsection 1201(d) if it then meant to exempt in subsection 1201(c)(1) any circumvention necessary for fair use.

Third, the Appellants argue that an individual who buys a DVD has the "authority of the copyright owner" to view the DVD, and therefore is exempted from the DMCA pursuant to subsection 1201(a)(3)(A) when the buyer circumvents an encryption technology in order to view the DVD on a competing platform (such as Linux). The basic flaw in this argument is that it misreads subsection 1201(a)(3)(A). That provision exempts from liability those who would "decrypt" an encrypted DVD with the authority of a copyright owner, not those who would "view" a DVD with the authority of a copyright owner. In any event, the Defendants offered no evidence that the Plaintiffs have either explicitly or implicitly authorized DVD buyers to circumvent encryption technology to support use on multiple platforms.[16]

We conclude that the anti-trafficking and anti-circumvention provisions of the DMCA are not susceptible to the narrow interpretations urged by the Appellants. We therefore proceed to consider the Appellants' constitutional claims.

II. Constitutional Challenge Based on the Copyright Clause

In a footnote to their brief, the Appellants appear to contend that the DMCA, as construed by the District Court, exceeds the constitutional authority of Congress to grant authors copyrights for a "limited time," U.S. Const. art. I, § 8, cl. 8, because it "empowers copyright owners to effectively secure perpetual protection by mixing public domain works with copyrighted materials, then locking both up with technological protection measures." Brief for Appellants at 42 n.30. This argument is elaborated in the amici curiae brief filed by Prof. Julie E. Cohen on behalf of herself and 45 other intellectual property law professors. See also David Nimmer, A Riff on Fair Use in the Digital Millennium Copyright Act, *148 U. Pa. L. Rev. 673, 712 (2000)*. For two reasons, the argument provides no basis for disturbing the judgment of the District Court.

First, we have repeatedly ruled that arguments presented to us only in a footnote are not entitled to appellate consideration. *Concourse Rehabilitation & Nursing Center Inc. v. DeBuono, 179 F.3d 38, 47 (2d Cir. 1999); United States v. Mapp, 170 F.3d 328, 333 n.8 (2d Cir. 1999)* . . . Although an amicus brief can be helpful in elaborating issues properly presented by the parties, it is normally not a method for injecting new issues into an appeal, at least in cases where the parties are competently represented by counsel. . . .

---

[16] Even if the Defendants had been able to offer such evidence, and even if they could have demonstrated that DeCSS was "primarily designed . . . for the purpose of" playing DVDs on multiple platforms (and therefore not for the purpose of "circumventing a technological measure"), a proposition questioned by Judge Kaplan, see *Universal I, 111 F. Supp. 2d at 311 n.79,* the Defendants would defeat liability only under subsection 1201(a)(2)(A). They would still be vulnerable to liability under subsection 1201(a)(2)(C), because they "marketed" DeCSS for the copying of DVDs, not just for the playing of DVDs on multiple platforms.

Second, to whatever extent the argument might have merit at some future time in a case with a properly developed record, the argument is entirely premature and speculative at this time on this record. There is not even a claim, much less evidence, that any Plaintiff has sought to prevent copying of public domain works, or that the injunction prevents the Defendants from copying such works. . . .

III. Constitutional Challenges Based on the First Amendment

A. Applicable Principles

Last year, in one of our Court's first forays into First Amendment law in the digital age, we took an "evolutionary" approach to the task of tailoring familiar constitutional rules to novel technological circumstances, favoring "narrow" holdings that would permit the law to mature on a "case-by-case" basis. See *Name.Space, Inc. v. Network Solutions, Inc., 202 F.3d 573, 584 n.11 (2d Cir. 2000)*. In that spirit, we proceed, with appropriate caution, to consider the Appellants' First Amendment challenges by analyzing a series of preliminary issues the resolution of which provides a basis for adjudicating the specific objections to the DMCA and its application to DeCSS. . . . Based on our analysis of these issues, we then consider the Appellants' challenge to the injunction's provisions concerning posting and linking.

1. Code as Speech

Communication does not lose constitutional protection as "speech" simply because it is expressed in the language of computer code. Mathematical formulae and musical scores are written in "code," i.e., symbolic notations not comprehensible to the uninitiated, and yet both are covered by the First Amendment. If someone chose to write a novel entirely in computer object code by using strings of 1's and 0's for each letter of each word, the resulting work would be no different for constitutional purposes than if it had been written in English. The "object code" version would be incomprehensible to readers outside the programming community (and tedious to read even for most within the community), but it would be no more incomprehensible than a work written in Sanskrit for those unversed in that language. . . .

2. Computer Programs as Speech

. . . In general, programs may give instructions either to perform a task or series of tasks when initiated by a single (or double) click of a mouse or, once a program is operational ("launched"), to manipulate data that the user enters into the computer. Whether computer code that gives a computer instructions is "speech" within the meaning of the First Amendment requires consideration of the scope of the Constitution's protection of speech.

The First Amendment provides that "Congress shall make no law . . . abridging the freedom of speech . . . ." U.S. Const. amend. I. "Speech" is an elusive term, and judges and scholars have debated its bounds for two centuries. . . .

. . . Even dry information, devoid of advocacy, political relevance, or artistic expression, has been accorded First Amendment protection. [Citing cases including *Board of Trustees of Stanford University v. Sullivan, 773 F. Supp. 472, 474 (D.D.C. 1991)* ("It is . . . settled . . . that the First Amendment protects scientific expression and debate just as it protects political and artistic expression.")].

Thus, for example, courts have subjected to First Amendment scrutiny restrictions on the dissemination of technical scientific information, *United States v. Progressive, Inc., 467 F. Supp. 990 (W.D. Wis. 1979),* and scientific research, *Stanford University, 773 F. Supp. at 473,* and attempts to regulate the publication of instructions [citing cases regarding instructions for tax evasion, bomb-making, and engaging in dangerous sex acts].

Computer programs are not exempted from the category of First Amendment speech simply because their instructions require use of a computer. A recipe is no less "speech" because it calls for the use of an oven, and a musical score is no less "speech" because it specifies performance on an electric guitar. Arguably distinguishing computer programs from conventional language instructions is the fact that programs are executable on a computer. But the fact that a program has the capacity to direct the functioning of a computer does not mean that it lacks the additional capacity to convey information, and it is the conveying of information that renders instructions "speech" for purposes of the First Amendment.[20] The information conveyed by most "instructions" is how to perform a task.

Instructions such as computer code, which are intended to be executable by a computer, will often convey information capable of comprehension and assessment by a human being. . . . [P]rogrammers communicating ideas to one another almost inevitably communicate in code, much as musicians use notes.[22] Limiting First Amendment protection of programmers to descriptions of computer code (but not the code itself) would impede discourse among computer scholars, just as limiting protection for musicians to descriptions of musical scores (but not sequences of notes) would impede their exchange of ideas and expression. Instructions that communicate

---

[20] Of course, we do not mean to suggest that the communication of "information" is a prerequisite of protected "speech." Protected speech may communicate, among other things, ideas, emotions, or thoughts. We identify "information" only because this is what computer programs most often communicate, in addition to giving directions to a computer.

[22] Programmers use snippets of code to convey their ideas for new programs; economists and other creators of computer models publish the code of their models in order to demonstrate the models' vigor. . . . *Bernstein v. United States Department of Justice,* 176 F.3d 1132, 1141 (9th Cir.) (concluding that computer source code is speech because it is "the preferred means" of communication among computer programmers and cryptographers), reh'g in banc granted and opinion withdrawn, *192 F.3d 1308 (9th Cir. 1999).*

information comprehensible to a human qualify as speech whether the instructions are designed for execution by a computer or a human (or both).

Commodity Futures Trading Commission v. Vartuli, 228 F.3d 94 (2d Cir. 2000) is not to the contrary. The defendants in Vartuli marketed a software program called "Recurrence," which would tell computer users when to buy or sell currency futures contracts if their computers were fed currency market rates. The Commodity Futures Trading Commission charged the defendants with violating federal law for, among other things, failing to register as commodity trading advisors for their distribution of the Recurrence software. The defendants maintained that Recurrence's cues to users to buy or sell were protected speech . . . We rejected the defendants' constitutional claim, holding that Recurrence "in the form it was sold and marketed by the defendants" did not generate speech protected by the First Amendment. *Vartuli, 228 F.3d at 111.*

Essential to our ruling in Vartuli was the manner in which the defendants marketed the software and intended that it be used: the defendants told users of the software to follow the software's cues "with no second-guessing," id., and intended that users follow Recurrence's commands "mechanically" and "without the intercession of the mind or the will of the recipient," id. We held that the values served by the First Amendment were not advanced by these instructions, even though the instructions were expressed in words. . . .

For all of these reasons, we join the other courts that have concluded that computer code, and computer programs constructed from code, can merit First Amendment protection, see *Junger v. Daley, 209 F.3d 481, 484 (6th Cir. 2000); Bernstein v. United States Department of State, 922 F. Supp. 1426 (N.D. Cal. 1996), at 1434-36; see also Bernstein, 176 F.3d at 1140-41,* . . . although the scope of such protection remains to be determined.

3. The Scope of First Amendment Protection for Computer Code

. . . As the District Court recognized, *Universal I, 111 F. Supp. 2d at 327,* the scope of protection for speech generally depends on whether the restriction is imposed because of the content of the speech. Content-based restrictions are permissible only if they serve compelling state interests and do so by the least restrictive means available. . . . A content-neutral restriction is permissible if it serves a substantial governmental interest, the interest is unrelated to the suppression of free expression, and the regulation is narrowly tailored, which "in this context requires . . . that the means chosen do not 'burden substantially more speech than is necessary to further the government's legitimate interests.'" *Turner Broadcasting System, Inc. v. FCC, 512 U.S. 622, 662 (1994) (quoting Ward v. Rock Against Racism, 491 U.S. 781, 799 (1989)).*[26]

---

[26] The Supreme Court has used slightly different formulations to express the narrow tailoring requirement of a content-neutral regulation. Turner Broadcasting

[In determining whether government regulation of expressive activity is "content neutral,"] "[t]he government's purpose is the controlling consideration. A regulation that serves purposes unrelated to the content of expression is deemed neutral, even if it has an incidental effect on some speakers or messages but not others." *Ward, 491 U.S. at 791*. The Supreme Court's approach to determining content-neutrality appears to be applicable whether what is regulated is expression, see *id. at 791-93* (regulation of volume of music), conduct, see *O'Brien, 391 U.S. at 377,* or any "activity" that can be said to combine speech and non-speech elements, see *Spence v. Washington,* 418 U.S. 405, 410-11 (applying O'Brien to "activity" of displaying American flag hung upside down and decorated with a peace symbol). . . .

The Appellants vigorously reject the idea that computer code can be regulated according to any different standard than that applicable to pure speech, i.e., speech that lacks a nonspeech component. . . . We disagree. Unlike a blueprint or a recipe, which cannot yield any functional result without human comprehension of its content, human decision-making, and human action, computer code can instantly cause a computer to accomplish tasks and instantly render the results of those tasks available throughout the world via the Internet. The only human action required to achieve these results can be as limited and instantaneous as a single click of a mouse. These realities of what code is and what its normal functions are require a First Amendment analysis that treats code as combining nonspeech and speech elements, i.e., functional and expressive elements. . . .

. . . Judge Kaplan, in a passage that merits extensive quotation, cogently explained why this is especially so with respect to decryption code:

> The focus on functionality in order to determine the level of scrutiny is not an inevitable consequence of the speech-conduct distinction. Conduct has immediate effects on the environment. Computer code, on the other hand, no matter how functional, causes a computer to perform the intended operations only if someone uses the code to do so. Hence, one commentator, in a thoughtful article, has maintained that functionality is really "a proxy for effects or harm" and that its adoption as a determinant of the level of scrutiny slides over questions of causation that intervene between the dissemination of a computer program and any harm caused by its use.

> The characterization of functionality as a proxy for the consequences of use is accurate. But the assumption that the chain of causation is too attenuated to justify the use of functionality to determine the level of scrutiny, at least in this context, is not.

> Society increasingly depends upon technological means of controlling access to digital files and systems, whether they are military computers,

---

made clear that the narrow tailoring requirement is less demanding than the least restrictive means requirement of a content-specific regulation, id., and appears to have settled on the "substantially more" phrasing from Ward as the formulation that best expresses the requirement . . .

bank records, academic records, copyrighted works or something else entirely. There are far too many who, given any opportunity, will bypass security measures, some for the sheer joy of doing it, some for innocuous reasons, and others for more malevolent purposes. Given the virtually instantaneous and worldwide dissemination widely available via the Internet, the only rational assumption is that once a computer program capable of bypassing such an access control system is disseminated, it will be used. And that is not all.

There was a time when copyright infringement could be dealt with quite adequately by focusing on the infringing act. If someone wished to make and sell high quality but unauthorized copies of a copyrighted book, for example, the infringer needed a printing press. The copyright holder, once aware of the appearance of infringing copies, usually was able to trace the copies up the chain of distribution, find and prosecute the infringer, and shut off the infringement at the source.

In principle, the digital world is very different. Once a decryption program like DeCSS is written, it quickly can be sent all over the world. Every recipient is capable not only of decrypting and perfectly copying plaintiffs' copyrighted DVDs, but also of retransmitting perfect copies of DeCSS and thus enabling every recipient to do the same. They likewise are capable of transmitting perfect copies of the decrypted DVD. The process potentially is exponential rather than linear.

. . .

These considerations drastically alter consideration of the causal link between dissemination of computer programs such as this and their illicit use. Causation in the law ultimately involves practical policy judgments. Here, dissemination itself carries very substantial risk of imminent harm because the mechanism is so unusual by which dissemination of means of circumventing access controls to copyrighted works threatens to produce virtually unstoppable infringement of copyright. In consequence, the causal link between the dissemination of circumvention computer programs and their improper use is more than sufficiently close to warrant selection of a level of constitutional scrutiny based on the programs' functionality.

Universal I, 111 F. Supp. 2d at 331-32 (footnotes omitted). The functionality of computer code properly affects the scope of its First Amendment protection.

4. The Scope of First Amendment Protection for Decryption Code

In considering the scope of First Amendment protection for a decryption program like DeCSS, we must recognize that the essential purpose of encryption code is to prevent unauthorized access. Owners of all property rights are entitled to prohibit access to their property by unauthorized persons. Homeowners can install locks on the doors of their houses.

Custodians of valuables can place them in safes. Stores can attach to products security devices that will activate alarms if the products are taken away without purchase. These and similar security devices can be circumvented. Burglars can use skeleton keys to open door locks. Thieves can obtain the combinations to safes. Product security devices can be neutralized.

. . . CSS is like a lock on a homeowner's door, a combination of a safe, or a security device attached to a store's products.

DeCSS is computer code that can decrypt CSS. In its basic function, it is like a skeleton key that can open a locked door, a combination that can open a safe, or a device that can neutralize the security device attached to a store's products.[28] . . .

. . . DeCSS enables the initial user to copy the movie in digital form and transmit it instantly in virtually limitless quantity, thereby depriving the movie producer of sales. The advent of the Internet creates the potential for instantaneous worldwide distribution of the copied material.

At first glance, one might think that Congress has as much authority to regulate the distribution of computer code to decrypt DVD movies as it has to regulate distribution of skeleton keys, combinations to safes, or devices to neutralize store product security devices. However, despite the evident legitimacy of protection against unauthorized access to DVD movies, . . . [DeCSS] also is a form of communication, albeit written in a language not understood by the general public. . . . [Thus,] it has a claim to being protected by the First Amendment. But just as the realities of what any computer code can accomplish must inform the scope of its constitutional protection, so the capacity of a decryption program like DeCSS to accomplish unauthorized—indeed, unlawful—access to materials in which the Plaintiffs have intellectual property rights must inform and limit the scope of its First Amendment protection. . . .

B. First Amendment Challenge

The District Court's injunction applies the DMCA to the Defendants by imposing two types of prohibition, both grounded on the anti-trafficking provisions of the DMCA. The first prohibits posting DeCSS or any other technology for circumventing CSS on any Internet web site. *Universal II, 111 F. Supp. 2d at 346-47, P 1* (a), (b). The second prohibits knowingly linking any Internet web site to any other web site containing DeCSS. *Id. at 347, P 1* (c). The validity of the posting and linking prohibitions must be considered separately.

1. Posting

The initial issue is whether the posting prohibition is content-neutral, since, as we have explained, this classification determines the applicable

---

[28] More dramatically, the Government calls DeCSS "a digital crowbar." Brief for Intervenor United States at 19.

constitutional standard. The Appellants['] . . . argument fails to recognize that the target of the posting provisions of the injunction—DeCSS-has both a nonspeech and a speech component, and that the DMCA, as applied to the Appellants, and the posting prohibition of the injunction target only the nonspeech component. Neither the DMCA nor the posting prohibition is concerned with whatever capacity DeCSS might have for conveying information to a human being, and that capacity, as previously explained, is what arguably creates a speech component of the decryption code. The DMCA and the posting prohibition are applied to DeCSS solely because of its capacity to instruct a computer to decrypt CSS. . . .This type of regulation is therefore content-neutral, just as would be a restriction on trafficking in skeleton keys identified because of their capacity to unlock jail cells, even though some of the keys happened to bear a slogan or other legend that qualified as a speech component.

. . . The Government's interest in preventing unauthorized access to encrypted copyrighted material is unquestionably substantial, and the regulation of DeCSS by the posting prohibition plainly serves that interest. Moreover, that interest is unrelated to the suppression of free expression. The injunction regulates the posting of DeCSS, regardless of whether DeCSS code contains any information comprehensible by human beings that would qualify as speech. Whether the incidental regulation on speech burdens substantially more speech than is necessary to further the interest in preventing unauthorized access to copyrighted materials requires some elaboration.

Posting DeCSS on the Appellants' web site makes it instantly available at the click of a mouse to any person in the world with access to the Internet, and such person can then instantly transmit DeCSS to anyone else with Internet access. Although the prohibition on posting prevents the Appellants from conveying to others the speech component of DeCSS, the Appellants have not suggested, much less shown, any technique for barring them from making this instantaneous worldwide distribution of a decryption code that makes a lesser restriction on the code's speech component. n29[29] It is true that the Government has alternative means of prohibiting

---

[29] Briefs of some of the amici curiae discuss the possibility of adequate protection against copying of copyrighted materials by adopting the approach of the Audio Home Recording Act of 1992, *17 U.S.C. § 1002* (a), which requires digital audio tape recorders to include a technology that prevents serial copying, but permits making a single copy. . . . Even if the Government, in defending the DMCA, must sustain a burden of proof in order to satisfy the standards for content-neutral regulation, the Defendants must adduce enough evidence to create fact issues concerning the current availability of less intrusive technological solutions. They did not do so in the District Court. Moreover, we note that when Congress opted for the solution to serial copying of digital audio tapes, it imposed a special royalty on manufacturers of digital audio recording devices to be distributed to appropriate copyright holders. See *17 U.S.C. § § 1003* -1007. We doubt if the First Amendment required Congress to adopt a similar technology/royalty scheme for regulating the copying of DVDs. . . .

unauthorized access to copyrighted materials. For example, it can create criminal and civil liability for those who gain unauthorized access, and thus it can be argued that the restriction on posting DeCSS is not absolutely necessary to preventing unauthorized access to copyrighted materials. But a content-neutral regulation need not employ the least restrictive means of accomplishing the governmental objective. Id. It need only avoid burdening "substantially more speech than is necessary to further the government's legitimate interests." *Turner Broadcasting, 512 U.S. at 662* (internal quotation marks and citation omitted). The prohibition on the Defendants' posting of DeCSS satisfies that standard.[30]

2. Linking

. . . [I]t is evident from the District Court's opinion that it is concerned with "hyperlinks," *Universal I, 111 F. Supp. 2d at 307;* see *id. at 339.* A hyperlink is a cross-reference (in a distinctive font or color) appearing on one web page that, when activated by the point-and-click of a mouse, brings onto the computer screen another web page. . . . Or the hyperlink can appear as an image, for example, an icon depicting a person sitting at a computer watching a DVD movie and text stating "click here to access DeCSS and see DVD movies for free!" . . . With a hyperlink on a web page, the linked web site is just one click away.

In applying the DMCA to linking (via hyperlinks), Judge Kaplan recognized, as he had with DeCSS code, that a hyperlink has both a speech and a nonspeech component. It conveys information, the Internet address of the linked web page, and has the functional capacity to bring the content of the linked web page to the user's computer screen . . . As he had ruled with respect to DeCSS code, he ruled that application of the DMCA to the Defendants' linking to web sites containing DeCSS is content-neutral because it . . . applies whether or not the hyperlink contains any information, comprehensible to a human being, as to the Internet address of the web page being accessed. The linking prohibition is justified solely by the functional capability of the hyperlink.

. . . Judge Kaplan then ruled that the DMCA, as applied to the Defendants' linking, served substantial governmental interests and was unrelated to the suppression of free expression. Id. We agree. He then carefully considered the "closer call," id., as to whether a linking prohibition would satisfy the narrow tailoring requirement. In an especially carefully considered portion of his opinion, he observed that strict liability for linking to

---

[30] We have considered the opinion of a California intermediate appellate court in *DVD Copy Control Ass'n v. Bunner,* 93 Cal. App. 4th 648 (Cal. Ct. App. 2001), declining, on First Amendment grounds, to issue a preliminary injunction under state trade secrets law prohibiting a web site operator from posting DeCSS. To the extent that DVD Copy Control disagrees with our First Amendment analysis, we decline to follow it. [Since the Second Circuit's decision here, the *Bunner* opinion has been "depublished" as the result of a superceding grant of review by the California Supreme Court, 41 P.3d 2, 117 Cal. Rptr. 2d 167 (Cal. 2002); further proceedings are pending. -Eds.]

web sites containing DeCSS would risk two impairments of free expression. Web site operators would be inhibited from displaying links to various web pages for fear that a linked page might contain DeCSS, and a prohibition on linking to a web site containing DeCSS would curtail access to whatever other information was contained at the accessed site. *Id. at 340.*

To avoid applying the DMCA in a manner that would "burden substantially more speech than is necessary to further the government's legitimate interests," *Turner Broadcasting, 512 U.S. at 662* (internal quotation marks and citation omitted), Judge Kaplan adapted the standards of *New York Times Co. v. Sullivan, 376 U.S. 254, 283, 11 L. Ed. 2d 686, 84 S. Ct. 710 (1964),* to fashion a limited prohibition against linking to web sites containing DeCSS. He required clear and convincing evidence

> that those responsible for the link (a) know at the relevant time that the offending material is on the linked-to site, (b) know that it is circumvention technology that may not lawfully be offered, and (c) create or maintain the link for the purpose of disseminating that technology.

Universal I, 111 F. Supp. 2d at 341. He then found that the evidence satisfied his three-part test by his required standard of proof. Id.

In response to our post-argument request for the parties' views on various issues, including specifically Judge Kaplan's test for a linking prohibition, the Appellants replied that his test was deficient for not requiring proof of intent to cause, or aid or abet, harm, and that the only valid test for a linking prohibition would be one that could validly apply to the publication in a print medium of an address for obtaining prohibited material. Supplemental Brief for Appellants at 14. The Appellees and the Government accepted Judge Kaplan's criteria for purposes of asserting the validity of the injunction as applied to the Appellants, with the Government expressing reservations as to the standard of clear and convincing evidence. Supplemental Brief for Appellees at 22-23; Supplemental Brief for Government at 19-21.

Mindful of the cautious approach to First Amendment claims involving computer technology expressed in *Name.Space, 202 F.3d at 584 n.11,* we see no need on this appeal to determine whether a test as rigorous as Judge Kaplan's is required to respond to First Amendment objections to the linking provision of the injunction that he issued. It suffices to reject the Appellants' contention that an intent to cause harm is required and that linking can be enjoined only under circumstances applicable to a print medium. As they have throughout their arguments, the Appellants ignore the reality of the functional capacity of decryption computer code and hyperlinks to facilitate instantaneous unauthorized access to copyrighted materials by anyone anywhere in the world. Under the circumstances amply shown by the record, the injunction's linking prohibition validly regulates the Appellants' opportunity instantly to enable anyone anywhere to gain unauthorized access to copyrighted movies on DVDs.[33]

---

[33] We acknowledge that the prohibition on linking restricts more than Corley's ability to facilitate instant access to DeCSS on linked web sites; it also restricts his

At oral argument, we asked the Government whether its undoubted power to punish the distribution of obscene materials would permit an injunction prohibiting a newspaper from printing addresses of bookstore locations carrying such materials. . . .

. . . If a bookstore proprietor is knowingly selling obscene materials, the evil of distributing such materials can be prevented by injunctive relief against the unlawful distribution (and similar distribution by others can be deterred by punishment of the distributor). And if others publish the location of the bookstore, preventive relief against a distributor can be effective before any significant distribution of the prohibited materials has occurred. The digital world, however, creates a very different problem. If obscene materials are posted on one web site and other sites post hyperlinks to the first site, the materials are available for instantaneous worldwide distribution before any preventive measures can be effectively taken.

This reality obliges courts considering First Amendment claims in the context of the pending case to choose between two unattractive alternatives: either tolerate some impairment of communication in order to permit Congress to prohibit decryption that may lawfully be prevented, or tolerate some decryption in order to avoid some impairment of communication. . . . [T]he fundamental choice between impairing some communication and tolerating decryption cannot be entirely avoided.

In facing this choice, we are mindful that it is not for us to resolve the issues of public policy implicated by the choice we have identified. Those issues are for Congress. Our task is to determine whether the legislative solution adopted by Congress, as applied to the Appellants by the District Court's injunction, is consistent with the limitations of the First Amendment, and we are satisfied that it is.

IV. Constitutional Challenge Based on Claimed Restriction of Fair Use

Asserting that fair use "is rooted in and required by both the Copyright Clause and the First Amendment," the Appellants contend that the DMCA, as applied by the District Court, unconstitutionally "eliminates fair use" of copyrighted materials. We reject this extravagant claim.

Preliminarily, we note that the Supreme Court has never held that fair use is constitutionally required, although some isolated statements in its opinions might arguably be enlisted for such a requirement. In *Stewart v. Abend, 495 U.S. 207 (1990),* cited by the Appellants, the Court merely noted that fair use "'permits courts to avoid rigid application of the copyright statute when, on occasion, it would stifle the very creativity which that law

_____

ability to facilitate access to whatever protected speech is available on those sites. However, those who maintain the linked sites can instantly make their protected material available for linking by Corley by the simple expedient of deleting DeCSS from their web sites.

is designed to foster,'" id. (quoting *Iowa State University Research Foundation, Inc. v. American Broadcasting Cos., 621 F.2d 57, 60 (2d Cir. 1980)*); see also *Harper & Row, Publishers, Inc. v. Nation Enterprises, 471 U.S. 539, 560 (1985)* (noting "the First Amendment protections already embodied in the Copyright Act's distinction between copyrightable expression and uncopyrightable facts and ideas, and the latitude for scholarship and comment traditionally afforded by fair use"). In *Campbell v. Acuff-Rose Music, Inc., 510 U.S. 569 (1994)*, the Court observed, "From the infancy of copyright protection, some opportunity for fair use of copyrighted materials has been thought necessary to fulfill copyright's very purpose, 'to promote the Progress of Science and useful Arts . . . .'"[34] *Id. at 575* (citation omitted); see generally William F. Patry, The Fair Use Privilege in Copyright Law 573-82 (2d ed. 1995) (questioning First Amendment protection for fair use).

We need not explore the extent to which fair use might have constitutional protection, grounded on either the First Amendment or the Copyright Clause, because whatever validity a constitutional claim might have as to an application of the DMCA that impairs fair use of copyrighted materials, such matters are far beyond the scope of this lawsuit for several reasons. In the first place, the Appellants do not claim to be making fair use of any copyrighted materials, and nothing in the injunction prohibits them from making such fair use. They are barred from trafficking in a decryption code that enables unauthorized access to copyrighted materials.

Second, as the District Court properly noted, to whatever extent the anti-trafficking provisions of the DMCA might prevent others from copying portions of DVD movies in order to make fair use of them, "the evidence as to the impact of the anti-trafficking provisions of the DMCA on prospective fair users is scanty and fails adequately to address the issues." *Universal I, 111 F. Supp. 2d at 338 n.246.*

Third, the Appellants have provided no support for their premise that fair use of DVD movies is constitutionally required to be made by copying the original work in its original format.[35] Their examples of the fair uses that they believe others will be prevented from making all involve copying in a digital format those portions of a DVD movie amenable to fair use, a copying that would enable the fair user to manipulate the digitally copied

---

[34] Although we have recognized that the First Amendment provides no entitlement to use copyrighted materials beyond that accorded by the privilege of fair use, except in "an extraordinary case," *Twin Peaks Productions, Inc. v. Publications International, Ltd.,* 996 F.2d 1366, 1378 (2d Cir. 1993), we have not ruled that the Constitution guarantees any particular formulation or minimum availability of the fair use defense.

[35] As expressed in their supplemental papers, the position of the Appellants is that "fair use extends to works in whatever form they are offered to the public," Supplemental Brief for Appellants at 20, by which we understand the Appellants to contend not merely that fair use may be made of DVD movies but that the fair user must be permitted access to the digital version of the DVD in order to directly copy excerpts for fair use in a digital format.

portions. One example is that of a school child who wishes to copy images from a DVD movie to insert into the student's documentary film. We know of no authority for the proposition that fair use, as protected by the Copyright Act, much less the Constitution, guarantees copying by the optimum method or in the identical format of the original. Although the Appellants insisted at oral argument that they should not be relegated to a "horse and buggy" technique in making fair use of DVD movies,[36] the DMCA does not impose even an arguable limitation on the opportunity to make a variety of traditional fair uses of DVD movies, such as commenting on their content, quoting excerpts from their screenplays, and even recording portions of the video images and sounds on film or tape by pointing a camera, a camcorder, or a microphone at a monitor as it displays the DVD movie. The fact that the resulting copy will not be as perfect or as manipulable as a digital copy obtained by having direct access to the DVD movie in its digital form, provides no basis for a claim of unconstitutional limitation of fair use. A film critic making fair use of a movie by quoting selected lines of dialogue has no constitutionally valid claim that the review (in print or on television) would be technologically superior if the reviewer had not been prevented from using a movie camera in the theater, nor has an art student a valid constitutional claim to fair use of a painting by photographing it in a museum. Fair use has never been held to be a guarantee of access to copyrighted material in order to copy it by the fair user's preferred technique or in the format of the original.

Conclusion

We have considered all the other arguments of the Appellants and conclude that they provide no basis for disturbing the District Court's judgment. Accordingly, the judgment is affirmed.

NOTES AND QUESTIONS

(1) Obviously, lawyers usually must take the clients they are given. But if you were constructing a case to test the "device" provisions of the DMCA's prohibitions on circumvention, would you have chosen these defendants?

(2) Metaphors matter. One of the most prominent comparisons made by advocates of the DMCA's Chapter 12 was between devices (and services) that enable circumvention, on the one hand, and "burglar tools," on the other. Judge Newman, too, seems to find this metaphor compelling. Do you?

---

[36] In their supplemental papers, the Appellants contend, rather hyperbolically, that a prohibition on using copying machines to assist in making fair use of texts could not validly be upheld by the availability of "monks to scribe the relevant passages." Supplemental Brief for Appellants at 20.

(3) The Court of Appeals adopted Judge Kaplan's approach to the "linking" issues (which were, incidentally, a particular focus of many amicus briefs filed in the case, including one submitted by the American Civil Liberties Union). The DCMA creates a new kind of secondary liability (for circumvention "conduct") on top of that arising from copyright itself, and even a sort of tertiary liability (for supplying circumvention "devices") on top of that. How clear is it that the Act also was intended to penalize conduct — *i.e.,* linking — yet one step *further* removed from any actual harm to a protected intellectual property interest? How successful do you think the court's efforts to prevent chilling effects on legitimate "linkers" through a new, multi-part test based on *New York Times v. Sullivan*? How easy will it be for individuals to conform their conduct to this standard?

(4) The co-authors of the casebook are not First Amendment specialists — but you (or your teacher) may be. How representative of the mainstream jurisprudence of freedom of expression are the court's views as expressed in this opinion? How consistent are they with recent cases that consider the expressive content of computer code?

(5) The opinion notes that, after oral argument, the panel requested supplementary letter briefs focused on a series of questions related mainly to the First Amendment issues in the case. The questions, and the responsive briefs, are conveniently collected at *http://www.2600.com/news/display.shtml?id'474.*

(6) The campaign against DeCSS continues on various fronts. For documents relating to recent efforts to use state trade secret law to require that it be removed from various individuals websites, see *http://www.eff.org/IP/Video/DVDCCA_case/*. Where will this end? Or are we simply seeing happen what needs to happen if copyright holders' rights are to be properly protected?

(7) Another high-profile case involving criminal enforcement of the "device" provisions of § 1201 is ongoing. *See United States v. Elcom Ltd.,* 2002 U.S. Dist. LEXIS 9161 (N.D. Cal. 2002) (denying motion to dismiss indictment on constitutional grounds). The dispute began with the widely publicized arrest of a young Russian computer scientist, Dmitry Sklyarov, who had helped to devise a computer program that allows consumers to avoid restrictions on the use of e-book content (like limits on copying, printing and lending) enabled by the Adobe Acrobat eBook Reader software. The corporate defendant, on whom the prosecution subsequently focused, is a Russian company distributing the allegedly offending product. In many respects, the District Court's opinion tracks the analysis in *Corley*, although it takes some interesting turns of its own. Thus, for example, the court accepts the government's contention that the "device" provisions should be analyzed as an exercise of Congressional power under the Commerce Clause. But doesn't Art. I, § 8., cl. 8 still matter? The court concludes that it does, proceeding to apply the analysis developed in *United States v. Moghamdam,* 175 F.3d 1269 (11th Cir. 1999), for application to a constitutional challenge brought the "anti-bootlegging" provisions of 18 U.S.C.

§ 2319A. Under this test, why isn't the DMCA "fundamentally inconsistent" with the "limited Times" language of the Intellectual Property Clause? Doesn't it allow content to be "locked up" perpetually by technological means? Note that this is the issue that *Corley* declined to consider because it had been raised only in a footnote!

(8) The various constitutional issues in *Corley* and *Elcom* obviously are entangled with the issue of "fair use." One argument that falls flat for the defendants is that the DMCA's effective curtailment of fair use is unconstitutional because it interferes with third parties' First Amendment rights to receive information. Why does this position fail? Is it because the courts doubt that the First Amendment requires *any* "fair use" doctrine? Because the right to receive information is one of the less well-developed aspects of First Amendment jurisprudence? Or simply because the evidence on the point is scanty? Does it matter which reason predominates? How might this part of Judge Newman's discussion influence the way in which future challenges to the DMCA are designed? With those questions out of the way, we'll reserve some "fair use"-specific queries until § 9.06[B] below.

(9) Would it have been possible to design the DMCA to give greater scope to various kinds of consumer interests and traditional use privileges (including, but not limited to "fair use")? This issue is squarely posed by the EU "Directive on the harmonisation of certain aspects of copyright and related rights in the information society" (2001/29/EC), reproduced in Part Two of this Supplement. This is a document that was designed to serve multiple, and even seemingly contradictory, purposes. In effect, Article 5 invites each European legislature to go through the exercise of defining affirmatively the specific limitations and exceptions that will circumscribe copyright protection against unauthorized digital (as well as non-digital) uses of works; indeed, it even supplies a long list of possible, permissible derogations. But Article 6 then mandates that European countries implement the 1996 W.I.P.O. treaties by adopted DMCA-style prohibitions on circumvention conduct and devices. In an effort at reconciliation, Article 6(4) then commands (in part) that "Member states shall take appropriate measures to ensure that rightsholders make available to the beneficiar[ies of certain] limitation[s] and exception[s] provided for in national law . . . the means of benefitting from that exception or limitation. . . ." But how? An active debate is underway in Europe over the meaning of Article 6(4). *See, e.g.,* Michael Hart, *The Copyright in the Information Society Directive: An Overview,* 24 Eur. Intell. Prop. L. Rev. 58, 62-63 (2002). We may have more information by the end of 2002, by which time the EU countries are required to have completed their implementation of the Directive.

(10) Other countries also have faced the problem of how to reconcile consumer use privileges and anti-circumvention protection. For the controversial approach adopted in Australia's Copyright Amendment (Digital Agenda) Act 2000, see Tanya Aplin, *Contemplating Australia's Digital Future,* 23 Eur. Intell. Prop. L. Rev. 565 (2001).

(11) Meanwhile, back at home, there continue to be concerns that § 1201 did not go far enough — and, specifically, that consumers who lawfully

acquire digital content may still have the practical ability to retransmit it to others. Content owners are pursuing several different approaches to modified "digital rights management" (or DRM) technology to "plug the holes" in their security screen. On the one hand, many of them are in active discussions with major consumer electronics manufacturers to develop a voluntary standard that, when implemented in software and hardware, would work to provide additional security. In addition, some are actively supporting S. 2048, the "Consumer Broadband and Digital Television Promotion Act," which would mandate negotiations to develop such a standard and impose a government-crafted standard if those negotiations failed to produce one. Some of the parameters of this discussion were laid out at a March 14 Senate Judiciary Committee hearing, "Competition, Innovation, and Public Policy in the Digital Age: Is the Marketplace Working to Protect Digital Creative Works?" (at *http://judiciary.senate.gov/hearing.cfm?id=197*). One consequence of the hearing was that participants in the voluntary standard-setting process are now making regular reports to the committee, which can be found at *http://www.senate.gov/%7Ejudiciary/special/feature.cfm*. One of these, the MPAA's "Content Protection Status Report," of April 25, 2002, with its now-notorious reference to the importance of "plugging the 'analog hole'," has been a special target of criticism from consumer organizations — who, more generally, have expressed scepticism about the entire post-DMCA project and adamant opposition to the CBDTPA. *See, e.g.,* the materials collected by the Electronic Frontier Foundation at *http://www.eff.org/IP/SSSCA_CBDTPA/*.

(12) Finally, if that's not enough, there is another continuing technological standard-setting process that may have important implications, direct and indirect, for the future of copyright — and may even preempt many of the developments described in the previous note.

Here, a little background may be in order. The Federal Communications Commission has regulatory jurisdiction over the long-awaited roll-out of high-definition television in the U.S. market. Among other things, the Commission is considering rules on "navigation devices" (so-called set-top boxes) for the new market, and among the issues that have arisen is whether any form of technology should be mandated. On September 18, 2001, the FCC issued a "Further Notice of Proposed Rule Making And Declaratory Ruling" (CS Docket No. 97-80) that had the effect of kicking off a series of meetings of the so-called Broadcast Protection Discussion Group (BPDG) of the Copyright Protection Technical Working Group (CPTYWG), the latter being the industry organization that established the CSS standard for DVD encryption). Although the meetings were open, they proceeded without extensive involvement by non-industry participants (with the notable exception of the Electronic Frontier Foundation, whose engagement is chronicled, in part, at *http://www.eff.org/IP/Video/HDTV/*). Despite this, any standard that the BPDG recommended would likely have been highly influential — and the technological restrictions the suggested DRM regime imposed on consumer use of television programming (copying, space-shifting, retransmission, etc.) could well have been generalized. In late May 2002, a draft BPDG report stirred considerable controversy — and raised some doubts about whether the process could be successfully completed, see Mike Musgrove, *Digital TV Founders on Fear of Internet Piracy*, Washington Post, June 1, 2000, at E1, col. 2., which seemed to be confirmed when the final version was released in early June. *See* Amy Harmon, *Hollywood Has a Setback in Controls for Digital TV*, New York Times, June 5, 2002, at C4, col. 3. It will be interesting to see what comes next — more negotations, legislation, or something else again.

(13) BTW, an interesting new voice in the debate over the future of voluntary and mandatory DRMs is DigitalConsumer.org, founded by Excite.com founder Joe Kraus and other high-tech executives to advocate for (among other things) reasonable deployment of DRMs. Its "Consumer Technology Bill of Rights," along with supporting documentation, can be found at *http://www.digitalconsumer.org*.

§ 7.08 Moral Rights

USAGE: On page 646, ADD the following text after note (2):

(2A) The statutory standard of "recognized stature" continues to plague the courts, as does the tension between moral rights and the removal of big, invasive works of art in public places. *See Pollara v. Seymour,* 150 F.Supp.2d 393 (N.D.N.Y. 2001), holding that a prior public display of a work of art (a 10-foot by 30-foot mural) is not required for it to qualify as "a work of recognized stature" when the work was damaged by employees during removal from Albany's Empire State Plaza.

Chapter 8

INFRINGEMENT ACTIONS

§ 8.02 Framing the Lawsuit

[A] Jurisdictional Matters

USAGE: On pages 663-664, CONSIDER the following recent development in connection with notes (6)-(7):

Harms **revived.** In *Bassett v. Mashantucket Pequot Tribe*, 204 F.3d 343 (2d Cir. 2000), the Second Circuit decided that "arising under" analysis for determining subject matter jurisdiction for copyright cases should no longer be governed by the test in *Schoenberg*. Concluding that the *Schoenberg* test, in its references to the "essence" of the claim and to "claims incidental" to a contract, was vague and difficult to understand, the court reverted instead to the *Harms* test, with its focus on what is alleged on the face of the complaint and whether the claim is for a remedy appropriate under the Copyright Act. Elsewhere, however, things remain more uncertain. In the Ninth Circuit, the relevant questions seems to be whether the terms that have allegedly been breached are ones that "help define the scope of the license," *Sun Microsystems, Inc. v. Microsoft Corp.*, 188 F.3d 1115, 1121 (9th Cir. 1999), or are independent covenants. For an interesting recently application in the context of software licensing, see *Microberts Software, Inc. v. Media 1000, Inc.*, 2001 U.S. Dist. LEXIS 16794 (S.D. Ind. 2001).

USAGE: On page 667, ADD the following text at the end of the note concerning "Jurisdiction over the person of the defendant":

Recently, the rise of the Internet has given the law of personal jurisdiction some fascinating new twists — and, as you might expect, some of them have come in copyright cases. *See, e.g., The Winfield Collection, Ltd.*, 105 F.Supp. 2d 746 (E.D. Mich. 2000) (E-bay sales of Texas defendant's allegedly infringing craft items to Michigan residents insufficient for personal jurisdiction); *Mulcahy v. Cheetah Learning LLC*, 2002 U.S. Dist. LEXIS 8477 (D. Minn. 2002) (integrated campaign of self-promotion in Minnesota, including use of website, as sufficient basis for personal jurisdiction); *Bird v. Parsons*, 2002 U.S. App. LEXIS 9543 (6th Cir. 2002) (interactive national website through which thousands of Ohioans registered domain names sufficient basis for personal jurisdiction, leading to dismissal of copyright claims); *ALS Scan, Inc. v. Wilkins*, 142 F.Supp.2d 703 (D. Md. 2001) (no personal jurisdiction found in case of alleged Web-based infringement); and *The Winfield Collection v. McCauley*, 105 F. Supp.2d 746 (E.D. Mich. 2000) (no personal jurisdiction available based on sales of Texas defendant's craft items to several Michigan residents).

USAGE: On page 674, CONSIDER the following recent developments on connection with the text note on "Liability of State Governments for Copyright Infringement":

Sovereign immunity and copyright. Applying the Supreme Court's *Florida Prepaid* decision, the Fifth Circuit, in *Chavez v. Arte Publico Press*, 204 F.3d 601 (5th Cir. 2000), held that Congress lacked the power to abrogate the states' 11th Amendment immunity in copyright infringement cases.

Senator Leahy's bill to restore the right to bring infringement suits against the states made little headway in the 106th Congress, but his ascension to the chairmanship of the Judiciary Committee presumably cannot hurt the chances of its successor: S. 2031 (reproduced in Part One of this Supplement).

USAGE: On page 686, ADD the following text immediately preceding the note concerning "Jury trial":

Timely filing. In copyright cases, as in all federal litigation, parties must comply strictly with deadlines for submissions derived from the Federal Rules of Civil Procedure, local rules, case-specific scheduling orders, and other sections. But what should happen when a judge himself or herself misapplies the relevant standard — and then refuses to set matters straight? For one response, see *Picket v. Prince* ["the popular singer whose name at birth was Prince Rogers Nelson"], 297 F.3d 402 (7th Cir. 2000) (Posner, J.).

§ 8.03   Proving the Claim *

[B]   Copying

USAGE: On pages 697-698, CONSIDER the following recent development in connection with notes (4)-(5):

Subconscious copying. The doctrine of subconscious copying is alive and well. *See Three Boys Music Corp. v. Bolton*, 212 F.3d 477 (9th Cir 2000) (holding that a 1991 song infringed a 1964 song based on jury findings of widespread dissemination of the song and subconscious copying by the plaintiff). What role does the doctrine of subconscious copying play in the analysis of copyright infringement? By what means can one prove subconscious copying?

USAGE: On page 705, CONSIDER the following recent development in connection with note (1):

Access and striking similarity. The Fourth Circuit has followed *Ty* in *Bouchat v. Baltimore Ravens, Inc.*, 228 F.3d 489 (4th Cir. 2000) (holding

---

* **Updating Note re 2001 Reprint:** On page 747, in note (10), the reference should be to the "notes to *Nichols* and *Peter Pan* above" rather than to the *Laureyssens* notes.

that an inference of access is permitted where the works are so similar as to create a high probability of copying and negate a reasonable possibility of independent creation).

[C] Improper Appropriation

USAGE: On page 725, ADD the following text after note (11):

(12) Courts have applied the "total concept and feel" concept across the entire range of copyrightable subject matter, but perhaps more readily when dealing with works that contain visual elements. Is there a good reason why this should be the case? For an example of "total concept and feel" as applied to architectural works, see *Sturdza v. United Arab Emirates,* 281 F.3d 1287 (D.C. Cir. 2002). There, the court held that the defendant's design was sufficiently similar to the plaintiff's, in its individual elements and the overall look and feel, to preclude summary judgment. The Court of Appeals determined that the District Court had properly "filtered out" elements of the plaintiff's design that it viewed as unprotected ideas — as well as the design's unprotectible decorative "Islamic patterns," which were judged to be *scenes á faire* dictated by the plaintiff's desire to express the richness and variety of traditional Arab motifs. On the other hand, the defendant's selection and arrangement of the wind-towers, parapets, pointed domes, and other decorative patterns were quite similar to the plaintiff's expression in combining these elements. Accordingly, the appellate court reversed the trial court's non-infringement ruling and remanded the case for trial on the issue of substantial similarity — "a close question of fact for which summary judgment is frowned upon."

USAGE: On pages 733-734, CONSIDER the following recent development in connection with note (4):

Particularizing the intended audience. As the cases uniformly state, copyright infringement is to be measured through the eyes of the ordinary observer. Should this fictional person be a member of the intended audience for the plaintiff's work? Can the targeted audience be children? Yes, according to another Fourth Circuit decision. In *Lyons Partnership, L.P. v. Morris Costumes, Inc.*, 243 F.3d 789 (4th Cir. 2001), where the plaintiff was the owner of the copyright on the famous purple dinosaur character "Barney," the court held that the District Court's copyright infringement analysis should have considered the perspectives of the children to whom the works were targeted (*i.e.,* young children), not those of the adults who bought or rented the costumes.

USAGE: On page 747, ADD the following text after note (11):

(11A) The motion picture of the best-seller *Midnight in the Garden of Good and Evil* gave rise to a claim of infringement involving the image of a statue from a Savannah, Georgia, cemetery that appears on the book's dustjacket. A replica of the statute had been rephotographed for use in the film's advertising campaign, but the original photographer nevertheless alleged infringement by means of (among other things) a promotion website, a movie poster, a print advertisement, a soundtrack album cover, and an Internet icon(!). The opinion, declining to dismiss the claims just described (though disposing of others), includes a thoughtful discussion of "substantial similarity." *Leigh v. Warner Brothers, Inc.,* 212 F.3d 1210 (11th Cir. 2000).

What about the facts of *Andreas v. Volkswagen of America, Inc.,* 172 F. Supp. 2d 1168 (N.D. Iowa 2001)? There, the designer of angel poster bearing the printed phrase, "Some people don't know that there are angels whose only job is to make sure you don't get to comfortable & fall asleep and miss your life," alleged infringement by an Audi advertising campaign using the a voice-over recital that "I think I just had a wake-up call, and it was disguised as a car, and it was screaming at me not to get too comfortable and fall asleep and miss my life." Apparently, this claim succeeded. Should it have? For more on the damages phase of this litigation, see § 10.01[C] of this Supplement.

USAGE: On page 769, ADD the following text at the end of note 12:

In this connection, consider *O.P. Solutions, Inc. v. Intellectual Prop. Network, Ltd.,* 1999 U.S. Dist. LEXIS 979 (S.D.N.Y.), where the three-part test is applied in a case where the only substantial claims related to similarity in computer program interfaces.

USAGE: Also on page 769, to the same effect as *Adobe Systems,* is *Tradescape.com v. Shivaram,* 77 F. Supp. 2d 408 (S.D.N.Y.) (comparing code of programs for day-trading of stocks).

USAGE: On page 777, ADD the following text at the end of § 8.03:

So far, at least, "privileged" use hasn't caught on in the U.S. courts. But an interesting application of the panel's holding is found in *Torah Soft Ltd. v. Drosnin,* 136 F. Supp. 2d 276 (S.D.N.Y. 2001), involving a computer program design to analyze Hebrew bible text and a book that allegedly reproduced printouts generated by that program. In absolving the defendant publisher of liability, the court reasoned that, among other things, "the Software's ability to display multiple Bible code finds in a single matrix is a "process, system, [or] method of operation'" (citing *Lotus v. Borland* in the course of its *Altai*-based analysis).

§ 8.04   Contributory and Vicarious Infringement[*]

USAGE: On page 785, ADD the following text before the discussion of *Netcom*:

Napster (and *Sony*)

The question that concluded the last subsection leads us straight back into the heart of *Napster* country.

---

[*] **Updating Note re 2001 Reprint:** On page 783, in note (2), the parenthetical beginning six lines from the end should refer to "some employees of *defendant* company."

As you will remember from your reading of the Ninth Circuit's opinion, excerpted in § 1.05 of this Part, the court had little patience for Napster's *Sony*-based defense. Not only did it doubt the "fair use" qualifications of many Napster users (an aspect of the analysis to be addressed in § 9.04 below), but it found that — in any event — the providers of the peer-to-peer file sharing service could not avoid liability even if theirs was a true-multipurpose technology. On this point of indirect or derivative liability, the court's approach was two-fold. First, it asserted that where "contributory" infringement was concerned, the Supreme Court's *Sony* test (quoted in the immediately preceding note) should be understood as going only to whether a defendant could be deemed to have sufficient "knowledge" of likely direct infringements. This is obviously a limited reading of *Sony,* and arguably a fairly novel one. For authority, the court mentioned only some incidental language in the opinion of the *Sony* District Court opinion, a pre-DMCA case dealing with Internet service provider liability — *Religious Technology Center v. Netcom On-line Communication Services, Inc.,* 907 F. Supp. 1316 (N.D. Cal. 1995) (to be discussed shortly) — and, most notably, a recent article on the same topic: Fred Yen, *Internet Service Provider Liability for Subscriber Copyright Infringement, Enterprise Liability, and the First Amendment,* 88 Geo. L.J. 1833 (2000). *Netcom* doesn't actually discuss the *Sony* test, however, and perhaps for good reason: there are significant difference between the contributory infringement claims that might be brought against ISPs, based on the unauthorized transmission of particular infringing messages, and those that could lie (and do, in *Napster*) against providers of mixed-use technologies.

The court had another reason, as well, for finding that reliance on *Sony* cannot absolve Napster of liability, no matter how (or how many) of its users turn out to be paragons of copyright rectitude. The *Sony* test, it reasoned, applies to contributory infringement only, and the recording companies have alleged (and are likely to prove) the elements of vicarious infringement as well. Once more, the authority cited for this proposition is less than overwhelming: an article in a Practicing Law Institute coursebook, and (in an addition to the revised opinion not present in the version originally released by the court) a passage from NIMMER ON COPYRIGHT that associates the *Sony* test with contributory infringement analysis but does seem to exclude its broader application. Again, the correctness of the court's analysis must be assessed primarily on its own internal merits, and — of course — in terms of its consistency with *Sony.*

Interestingly, the *Napster* opinion does not reproduce or discuss the passages in the opinion of the *Sony* majority in which the rationale behind that Court's decision is described in terms of what might be called "technology policy." Specifically, as you are about to see, the Justices of the *Sony* majority apparently believed that, as courts expand doctrines of indirect or derivative copyright liability, they run a risk of depriving consumers of some of the benefits of technological progress.

Although, as we will see in Chapter 9, *Sony* has had to be clarified by the Court itself, on fair use issues, in the subsequent *Two Live Crew* decision, obviously the *Napster* court was bound to follow *Sony* on matters as to which it remains authoritative. That said, just how *far* the *Napster* court followed *Sony* is a subject open to discussion. So that you may be better able to debate the matter, we provide below a portion of the Supreme Court majority's opinion in *Sony* not reproduced elsewhere in the casebook. One warning: As you read, try to keep track of the Court's sometimes infuriatingly fluid vocabulary. Is "vicarious liability" the same as "vicarious infringement"? Did *Gershwin,* cited in note 18, actually involve a "contributory infringer"? Sometimes, the *Sony* Court seems to be using one umbrella term to describe all varieties of indirect or vicarious liability, sometimes another. And remember that patent law, from which the *Sony* test derives, doesn't recognize a category of "vicarious infringement" as such. All of this may be important in deciding how faithful to the letter and spirit of *Sony* the Ninth Circuit decision really is. Here, then, is the *Sony* Court on derivative liability in copyright:

III

The Copyright Act does not expressly render anyone liable for infringement committed by another. In contrast, the Patent Act expressly brands anyone who "actively induces infringement of a patent" as an infringer, *35 U. S. C. § 271* (b), and further imposes liability on certain individuals labeled "contributory" infringers, § 271(c). The absence of such express language in the copyright statute does not preclude the imposition of liability for copyright infringements on certain parties who have not themselves engaged in the infringing activity.[17] For vicarious liability is imposed in virtually all areas of the law, and the concept of contributory infringement is merely a species of the broader problem of identifying the circumstances in which it is just to hold one individual accountable for the actions of another.

Such circumstances were plainly present in *Kalem Co. v. Harper Brothers, 222 U.S. 55 (1911),* the copyright decision of this Court on which respondents place their principal reliance. In *Kalem,* the Court held that the producer of an unauthorized film dramatization of the copyrighted book *Ben Hur* was liable for his sale of the motion picture to jobbers, who in turn arranged for the commercial exhibition of the film. Justice Holmes, writing for the Court, explained:

---

[17] As the District Court correctly observed, however, "the lines between direct infringement, contributory infringement and vicarious liability are not clearly drawn. . . ." 480 F.Supp., at 457-458. The lack of clarity in this area may, in part, be attributable to the fact that an infringer is not merely one who uses a work without authorization by the copyright owner, but also one who authorizes the use of a copyrighted work without actual authority from the copyright owner.

. . . [R]easoned analysis of respondents' unprecedented contributory infringement claim necessarily entails consideration of arguments and case law which may also be forwarded under the other labels . . .

"The defendant not only expected but invoked by advertisement the use of its films for dramatic reproduction of the story. That was the most conspicuous purpose for which they could be used, and the one for which especially they were made. If the defendant did not contribute to the infringement it is impossible to do so except by taking part in the final act. It is liable on principles recognized in every part of the law." *Id., at 62-63.*

The use for which the item sold in *Kalem* had been "especially" made was, of course, to display the performance that had already been recorded upon it. The producer had personally appropriated the copyright owner's protected work and, as the owner of the tangible medium of expression upon which the protected work was recorded, authorized that use by his sale of the film to jobbers. . . .

Respondents argue that *Kalem* stands for the proposition that supplying the "means" to accomplish an infringing activity and encouraging that activity through advertisement are sufficient to establish liability for copyright infringement. This argument rests on a gross generalization that cannot withstand scrutiny. The producer in *Kalem* did not merely provide the "means" to accomplish an infringing activity; the producer supplied the work itself, albeit in a new medium of expression. Sony in the instant case does not supply Betamax consumers with respondents' works; respondents do. Sony supplies a piece of equipment that is generally capable of copying the entire range of programs that may be televised: those that are uncopyrighted, those that are copyrighted but may be copied without objection from the copyright holder, and those that the copyright holder would prefer not to have copied.

The Betamax can be used to make authorized or unauthorized uses of copyrighted works, but the range of its potential use is much broader than the particular infringing use of the film Ben Hur involved in *Kalem.* *Kalem* does not support respondents' novel theory of liability.

Justice Holmes stated that the producer had "contributed" to the infringement of the copyright, and the label "contributory infringement" has been applied in a number of lower court copyright cases involving an ongoing relationship between the direct infringer and the contributory infringer at the time the infringing conduct occurred. In such cases, as in other situations in which the imposition of vicarious liability is manifestly just, the "contributory" infringer was in a position to control the use of copyrighted works by others and had authorized the use without permission from the copyright owner.[18] This case, however,

---

[18] The so-called "dance hall cases," Famous Music Corp. v. Bay State Harness Horse Racing & Breeding Assn., Inc., 554 F.2d 1213 (CA1 1977) (racetrack retained infringer to supply music to paying customers); KECA Music, Inc. v. Dingus McGee's Co., 432 F.Supp. 72 (WD Mo. 1977) (cocktail lounge hired musicians to supply music to paying customers); Dreamland Ball Room, Inc. v. Shapiro, Bernstein & Co., 36 F.2d 354 (CA7 1929) (dance hall hired orchestra to supply music to paying customers), are often contrasted with the so-called landlord-tenant cases, in which

plainly does not fall in that category. The only contact between Sony and the users of the Betamax that is disclosed by this record occurred at the moment of sale. The District Court expressly found that "no employee of Sony, Sonam or DDBI had either direct involvement with the allegedly infringing activity or direct contact with purchasers of Betamax who recorded copyrighted works off-the-air." *480 F.Supp., at 460.* And it further found that "there was no evidence that any of the copies made by Griffiths or the other individual witnesses in this suit were influenced or encouraged by [Sony's] advertisements." *Ibid.*

If vicarious liability is to be imposed on Sony in this case, it must rest on the fact that it has sold equipment with constructive knowledge of the fact that its customers may use that equipment to make unauthorized

---

landlords who leased premises to a direct infringer for a fixed rental and did not participate directly in any infringing activity were found not to be liable for contributory infringement. *E.g.*, Deutsch v. Arnold, 98 F.2d 686 (CA2 1938). In Shapiro, Bernstein & Co. v. H. L. Green Co., 316 F.2d 304 (CA2 1963), the owner of 23 chainstores retained the direct infringer to run its record departments. The relationship was structured as a licensing arrangement, so that the defendant bore none of the business risk of running the department. Instead, it received 10% or 12% of the direct infringer's gross receipts. The Court of Appeals concluded:

> [The dance-hall cases] and this one lie closer on the spectrum to the employer-employee model, than to the landlord-tenant model. . . . [On] the particular facts before us, . . . Green's relationship to its infringing licensee, as well as its strong concern for the financial success of the phonograph record concession, renders it liable for the unauthorized sales of the 'bootleg' records.
>
> . . .
>
> . . . [The] imposition of *vicarious* liability in the case before us cannot be deemed unduly harsh or unfair. Green has the power to police carefully the conduct of its concessionaire . . . ; our judgment will simply encourage it to do so, thus placing responsibility where it can and should be effectively exercised." *Id., at 308 (emphasis in original).*

In Gershwin Publishing Corp. v. Columbia Artists Management, Inc.,443 F.2d 1159 (CA2 1971), the direct infringers retained the contributory infringer to manage their performances. The contributory infringer would contact each direct infringer, obtain the titles of the musical compositions to be performed, print the programs, and then sell the programs to its own local organizations for distribution at the time of the direct infringement. *Id., at 1161.* The Court of Appeals emphasized that the contributory infringer had actual knowledge that the artists it was managing were performing copyrighted works, was in a position to police the infringing conduct of the artists, and derived substantial benefit from the actions of the primary infringers. *Id., at 1163.*

In Screen Gems-Columbia Music, Inc. v. Mark-Fi Records, Inc., 256 F.Supp. 399 (SDNY 1966), the direct infringer manufactured and sold bootleg records. In denying a motion for summary judgment, the District Court held that the infringer's advertising agency, the radio stations that advertised the infringer's works, and the service agency that boxed and mailed the infringing goods could all be held liable, if at trial it could be demonstrated that they knew or should have known that they were dealing in illegal goods.

copies of copyrighted material. There is no precedent in the law of copyright for the imposition of vicarious liability on such a theory. The closest analogy is provided by the patent law cases to which it is appropriate to refer because of the historic kinship between patent law and copyright law.

In the Patent Act both the concept of infringement and the concept of contributory infringement are expressly defined by statute. The prohibition against contributory infringement is confined to the knowing sale of a component especially made for use in connection with a particular patent. There is no suggestion in the statute that one patentee may object to the sale of a product that might be used in connection with other patents. Moreover, the Act expressly provides that the sale of a "staple article or commodity of commerce suitable for substantial noninfringing use" is not contributory infringement. *35 U.S.C. § 271 (c)*.

When a charge of contributory infringement is predicated entirely on the sale of an article of commerce that is used by the purchaser to infringe a patent, the public interest in access to that article of commerce is necessarily implicated. A finding of contributory infringement does not, of course, remove the article from the market altogether; it does, however, give the patentee effective control over the sale of that item. Indeed, a finding of contributory infringement is normally the functional equivalent of holding that the disputed article is within the monopoly granted to the patentee.[21] For that reason, in contributory infringement cases arising under the patent laws the Court has always recognized the critical importance of not allowing the patentee to extend his monopoly beyond the limits of his specific grant. These cases deny the patentee any right to control the distribution of unpatented articles unless they are "unsuited for any commercial noninfringing use." *Dawson Chemical Co. v. Rohm & Hass Co., 448 U.S. 176, 198 (1980)*. Unless a commodity "has no use except through practice of the patented method," *id., at 199*, the patentee has no right to claim that its distribution constitutes contributory infringement. "To form the basis for contributory infringement the item must almost be uniquely suited as a component of the patented invention." P. Rosenberg, Patent Law Fundamentals § 17.02[2] (2d ed. 1982). "[A] sale of an article which though adapted to an infringing use is also adapted to other and lawful uses, is not enough to make the seller a contributory infringer. Such a rule would block the wheels of commerce." *Henry v. A. B. Dick Co., 224 U.S. 1, 48 (1912)*, overruled on other

---

[21] It seems extraordinary to suggest that the Copyright Act confers upon all copyright owners collectively, much less the two respondents in this case, the exclusive right to distribute VTR's simply because they may be used to infringe copyrights. That, however, is the logical implication of their claim. The request for an injunction below indicates that respondents seek, in effect, to declare VTR's contraband. Their suggestion in this Court that a continuing royalty pursuant to a judicially created compulsory license would be an acceptable remedy merely indicates that respondents, for their part, would be willing to license their claimed monopoly interest in VTR's to Sony in return for a royalty.

grounds, *Motion Picture Patents Co. v. Universal Film Mfg. Co., 243 U.S. 502, 517 (1917)*.

We recognize there are substantial differences between the patent and copyright laws. But in both areas the contributory infringement doctrine is grounded on the recognition that adequate protection of a monopoly may require the courts to look beyond actual duplication of a device or publication to the products or activities that make such duplication possible. The staple article of commerce doctrine must strike a balance between a copyright holder's legitimate demand for effective — not merely symbolic — protection of the statutory monopoly, and the rights of others freely to engage in substantially unrelated areas of commerce. Accordingly, the sale of copying equipment, like the sale of other articles of commerce, does not constitute contributory infringement if the product is widely used for legitimate, unobjectionable purposes. Indeed, it need merely be capable of substantial noninfringing uses.

IV

The question is thus whether the Betamax is capable of commercially significant noninfringing uses. In order to resolve that question, we need not explore *all* the different potential uses of the machine and determine whether or not they would constitute infringement. Rather, we need only consider whether on the basis of the facts as found by the District Court a significant number of them would be noninfringing. Moreover, in order to resolve this case we need not give precise content to the question of how much use is commercially significant. For one potential use of the Betamax plainly satisfies this standard, however it is understood: private, noncommercial time-shifting in the home. It does so both (A) because respondents have no right to prevent other copyright holders from authorizing it for their programs, and (B) because the District Court's factual findings reveal that even the unauthorized home time-shifting of respondents' programs is legitimate fair use . . . .

464 U.S. at 434-442.

USAGE: On page 790, ADD the following text prior to the last paragraph of § 8.04:

With that case behind it, Ticketmaster turned its attention to another competitor, Tickets.Com, Inc., which was up to similar tricks. That controversy has produced an interesting opinion denying the plaintiff a preliminary injunction: *Ticketmaster Corp. v. Tickets.Com, Inc.,* 2000 U.S. Dist. LEXIS 12987 (C.D. Cal. 2000). The court discusses whether the automated "data stripping" of the Ticketmaster website in which the defendant engaged while building its own site constituted infringement and, relying on *Sony Computer Entertainment v. Connectix Corp.,* 203 F.3d 596 (9th Cir. 2000), concludes that since the only material ultimately transferred to defendant's site was factual, there was no liability — even though more extensive intermediate copying of protected material had occurred along the way. (The court also dismisses the plaintiff's state law-based "trespass to chattels" theory, which sought to take advantage of the decision in *eBay, Inc. v. Bidder's Edge, Inc.,*100 F. Supp. 2d 1058 (C.D. Cal. 2000) (discussed in § 10.02 of this Part). But what is most interesting from the standpoint of the present discussion is that the possibility that Tickets.Com might have been liable for its hyperlinks back to the Ticketmaster site doesn't even come up!

§ 8.05 Extraterritoriality and Conflicts of Laws

USAGE: On page 806, ADD the following text at the end of note (4):

A notable recent decision exemplifying the openness of U.S. courts to claims based on foreign law is *Armstrong v. Virgin Records, Ltd.,* 91 F. Supp. 2d 628 (S.D.N.Y. 2000). Another is *Vapac Music Publishing, Inc. v. Tuff N' Rumble Management,* 2000 U.S. Dist. LEXIS 10027 (S.D.N.Y. 2000) (ordering a more definite statement of plaintiff's foreign law claims). Yet another is *Carell v. The Shubert Group,* 104 F. Supp. 2d 236 (S.D.N.Y. 2000) (involving a dispute over rights in the makeup designs for the musical "Cats"). *Carell* also reminds us that, although U.S. participation in international arrangements such as the Berne Convention and the TRIPs Agreement may provide the basis for foreign rights to be asserted in domestic fora, those agreements are not, in themselves, sources of enforceable rights. The point is reinforced in *Leutwyler v. Royal Hashemite Court of Jordan,* 184 F. Supp. 2d 303 (S.D.N.Y. 2001).

(5) An interesting application of *Itar-Tass,* demonstrating how difficult the tasks set by the Second Circuit may sometimes be to perform, can be found in *Films by Jove, Inc. v. Berov,* 154 F. Supp. 2d 432 (E.D.N.Y. 2001). There, the court was called upon to track the ownership of a group of Russian animated films as the studio that had produced them passed through various transformations as a result of the liberalizing trends in property ownership that accompanied Glasnost and Perestroika. In reaching its conclusions, the court dealt with battling U.S. academic experts on Russian law, and with a series of recent Russian court decisions. (The opinion also includes, by the way, an interesting discussion of the application of § 204(a), which will often be problematic in cases where the chain of title involves multiple transfers outside the U.S.)

Chapter 9

FAIR USE AND AFFIRMATIVE DEFENSES

§ 9.03 Fair Use, Free Speech, and Parody

USAGE: On page 836, ADD the following text after the first paragraph of note (8):

Sticking with the preamble for the moment: The fair use defense is alive in the Second Circuit, at least when the use involves scholarly and news reporting purposes. *See Video-Cinema Films, Inc. v. Cable News Network, Inc.*, 2001 Copr. L. Dec. (CCH) ¶ 28,327 (S.D.N.Y. 2001) (holding that the use of clips of the film "G.I. Joe" by television news networks to report actor Robert Mitchum's death was a fair use), and *Williamson v. Pearson Education, Inc.*, 2001 Copr. L. Dec. (CCH) ¶ 28, 337 (S.D.N.Y. 2001) (holding that a book whose chapter headings and commentary included quotations by and passages about George S. Patton from another book made fair use of that material).

USAGE: On page 838, CONSIDER the following recent development after note (11):

Fair use in comparative advertising. In *Sony Computer Entertainment America, Inc. v. Bleem*, LLC, 214 F.3d 1022 (9th Cir. 2000), the court held that, in enjoining the copying video game "screen shots" from a television display for comparative advertising purposes, the District Court abused its discretion (although the Court of Appeals could not determine whether the court below had employed a § 107 analysis in reaching its decision). Looking at the matter itself, the Ninth Circuit concluded that the market effect of the defendant's use favored a fair use finding because there is no market in video game screen shots, and that informing the public about a product, which was the effect of the comparative advertising, was a purpose of the defendant's use that also weighed in favor of fair use.

USAGE: On page 852, ADD the following text after note (3):

(3A) At least one significant jurist seems skeptical of the new vocabulary of transformativeness, though not necessarily of what lies behind it. As this Supplement went to press, the 7th Circuit handed down a decision on the interlocutory appeal in *Ty, Inc. v. Publications International Ltd.*, 2002 U.S. App. LEXIS 10191 (7th Cir. 2002). The case concerned an effort on the part of the plaintiff manufacturer of soft toys to shut down a company involved in, among other things, publishing a "Collectors' Guide" illustrated with photographs of the entire line of 150-odd "Beanie Babies" (some of them very odd indeed). The author of the opinion, Judge Richard Posner, as you may recall from Chapter 8, has met the Beanie Babies before. But this time the focus of the 7th Circuit's attention is fair use. Judge Posner begins his analysis by noting that Ty, Inc., has licensed its copyrights to collectors' publications both selectively and strategically, because (as the court puts it) "Ty doesn't like criticism" (an activity in which it might be said the unlicensed publisher it sued had shown the temerity to engage). In directing a remand for further consideration of the issue, the opinion makes a number of significant observations, a few of which we quote below (with most of the copious and interesting citations silently omitted):

Generalizing . . . in economic terminology that has become orthodox in fair-use case law, we may say that copying that is complementary to the copyrighted work (in the sense that nails are complements of hammers) is fair use, but copying that is a substitute for the copyrighted work (in the sense that nails are substitutes for pegs or screws), or for derivative works from the copyrighted work, is not fair use. If the price of nails fell, the demand for hammers would rise but the demand for pegs would fall. The hammer manufacturer wants there to be an abundant supply of cheap nails, and likewise publishers want their books reviewed and wouldn't want reviews inhibited and degraded by a rule requiring the reviewer to obtain a copyright license from the publisher if he wanted to quote from the book. So, in the absence of a fair-use doctrine, most publishers would disclaim control over the contents of reviews. The doctrine makes such disclaimers unnecessary. It thus economizes on transaction costs.

The distinction between complementary and substitutional copying (sometimes — though as it seems to us, confusingly — said to be between "transformative" and "superseding" copies, see, e.g., *Campbell v. Acuff-Rose Music, Inc., 510 U.S. 569, 579 (1994)*), is illustrated not only by the difference between quotations from a book in a book review and the book itself, but also by the difference between parody (fair use) and burlesque (often not fair use). A parody, which is a form of criticism (good-natured or otherwise), is not intended as a substitute for the work parodied. But it must quote enough of that work to make the parody recognizable as such, and that amount of quotation is deemed fair use. A burlesque, however, is often just a humorous substitute for the original and so cuts into the demand for it: one might choose to see Abbott and Costello Meet Frankenstein or Young Frankenstein rather than Frankenstein, or Love at First Bite rather than Dracula, or even Clueless rather than Emma. Burlesques of that character, catering to the humor-loving segment of the original's market, are not fair use. . . .

Book reviews and parodies are merely examples of types of work that quote or otherwise copy from copyrighted works yet constitute fair use because they are complements of (though sometimes negative complements, as in the case of a devastating book review) rather than substitutes for the copyrighted original. The commonest type is simply a quotation from a copyrighted work in a book or article on the same or a related subject. The complementary effect may be quite weak, but the quotation is unlikely to reduce the demand for the copyrighted work; nor could the copyright owner command a license fee commensurate with the costs of transacting with the copier. Such copying is therefore fair use.

. . . Indeed, a collectors' guide is very much like a book review, which is a guide to a book and which no one supposes is a derivative work. Both the book review and the collectors' guide are critical and evaluative as well as purely informational; and ownership of a copyright does not confer a legal right to control public evaluation of the copyrighted work.

Ty's concession that a Beanie Babies collectors' guide is not a derivative work narrows the issue presented by PIL's appeal nicely (at least as to those books that are plausibly regarded as collectors' guides) to whether PIL copied more than it had to in order to produce a marketable collectors' guide. . . . [T]o compete in the marketplace, [a collector's guide] has to be comprehensive. Given that Ty can license (in fact has licensed) the publication of collectors' guides that contain photos of all the Beanie Babies, how could a competitor forbidden to publish photos of the complete line compete? And if it couldn't compete, the result would be to deliver into Ty's hands a monopoly of Beanie Baby collectors' guides even though Ty acknowledges that such guides are not derivative works and do not become such by being licensed by it.

Does this discussion break new ground? Certainly, it takes a very different rhetorical tack from some of the Second Circuit cases.

USAGE: On page 855, ADD the following text after note (9):

(10) In France, an unauthorized continuation or recontextualization of a famous story might be analyzed in terms of "moral rights." Here at home, however, it usually will come down to a battle between the "adaptation right," on the one hand, and "fair use," on the other.

And so it has in the case of first-time African-American novelist Alice Randall's book, The Wind Done Gone ("TWDG"). TWDG utilizes certain plot elements, snatches of dialogue, and (without calling them by name) some characters from Margaret Mitchell's 1936 mega-bestseller, Gone With the Wind ("GWTW"). Randall's self-described purpose was to take on this cultural icon (and, in particular, its "racial stereotyping") by renarrating aspects of Mitchell's story from the point of view of a female slave, Cynara, who is probably the half-sister of Scarlett O'Hara — and definitely not a character devised by Mitchell (who preferred not to discuss master-slave sexual relationships and their human outcomes).

The announcement of publication plans for TWDG, not surprisingly, drew a lawsuit from the Mitchell estate. In *Suntrust Bank v. Houghton Mifflin Co.,* 136 F. Supp. 2d 1357 (2001), a judge of the U.S. District Court for the North District of Georgia, Atlanta Division(!), enjoined the publication, rejecting claims that the new novel qualified as a "parody" under "fair use." The court concluded that, while the new work was "partly transformative," it was more in the nature of a unauthorized "sequel," created for economic reasons, than a privileged "parody". The judge put it this way: "Parody has its place in copyright law, but the extent of the use of the copyrighted work and the purpose of the author's prose may limit the parodical effect and nullify the fair use doctrine." *Id.* at 1378.

The District Court opinion is now, however (how shall we say this?), "GWTW!"

SUNTRUST BANK v. HOUGHTON MIFFLIN CO.

United States Court of Appeals, Eleventh Circuit
268 F.3d 1257 (2001)

BIRCH, Circuit Judge:

In this opinion, we decide whether publication of The Wind Done Gone ("TWDG"), a fictional work admittedly based on Margaret Mitchell's Gone With the Wind ("GWTW"), should be enjoined from publication based on alleged copyright violations. The district court granted a preliminary injunction against publication of TWDG because it found that Plaintiff-Appellee SunTrust Bank ("SunTrust") met the four-part test governing preliminary injunctions. We VACATE the injunction and REMAND for consideration of the remaining claims.

I. BACKGROUND

A. Procedural History

SunTrust is the trustee of the Mitchell Trust, which holds the copyright in GWTW. Since its publication in 1936, GWTW has become one of the best-selling books in the world, second in sales only to the Bible. The Mitchell Trust has actively managed the copyright, authorizing derivative works and a variety of commercial items. It has entered into a contract authorizing, under specified conditions, a second sequel to GWTW to be published by St. Martin's Press. The Mitchell Trust maintains the copyright in all of the derivative works as well. See 17 U.S.C. § 103.[1]

Alice Randall, the author of TWDG, persuasively claims that her novel is a critique of GWTW's depiction of slavery and the Civil-War era American South. To this end, she appropriated the characters, plot and major scenes from GWTW into the first half of TWDG. According to SunTrust, TWDG "(1) explicitly refers to [GWTW] in its foreword; (2) copies core characters, character traits, and relationships from [GWTW]; (3) copies and summarizes famous scenes and other elements of the plot from [GWTW]; and (4) copies verbatim dialogues and descriptions from [GWTW]." SunTrust Bank v. Houghton Mifflin Co., 136 F. Supp. 2d 1357, 1364 (N.D.Ga. 2001), vacated, 252 F.3d 1165 (11th Cir. 2001). Defendant-Appellant Houghton Mifflin, the publisher of TWDG, does not contest the first three allegations,[2]

---

[1] Hereafter, the Copyright Act of 1976 shall be referred to by only the section number of the Act.

[2] Houghton Mifflin denies that there are passages from GWTW copied verbatim in TWDG.

but nonetheless argues that there is no substantial similarity between the two works or, in the alternative, that the doctrine of fair use protects TWDG because it is primarily a parody of GWTW.

After discovering the similarities between the books, SunTrust asked Houghton Mifflin to refrain from publication or distribution of TWDG, but Houghton Mifflin refused the request. Subsequently, SunTrust filed an action alleging copyright infringement, violation of the Lanham Act, and deceptive trade practices, and immediately filed a motion for a temporary restraining order and a preliminary injunction.

After a hearing, the district court granted the motion, preliminarily enjoining Houghton Mifflin from "further production, display, distribution, advertising, sale, or offer for sale of" TWDG. SunTrust Bank, 136 F. Supp. 2d at 1386. In a thorough opinion, the court found that "the defendant's publication and sale of [TWDG would] infringe the plaintiff's copyright interests as protected under the copyright laws." Id. Houghton Mifflin appealed. At oral argument, we issued an order vacating the injunction on the grounds that it was an unconstitutional prior restraint. SunTrust Bank v. Houghton Mifflin Co., 252 F.3d 1165 (11th Cir. 2001). We now vacate that order and issue this more comprehensive opinion.

B. Standard of Review

"We review the district court's grant of a preliminary injunction for abuse of discretion." Warren Pub., Inc. v. Microdos Data Corp., 115 F.3d 1509, 1516 (11th Cir. 1997) (en banc). We review decisions of law *de novo* and findings of fact for clear error. Mitek Holdings, Inc. v. Arce Eng'g Co., Inc., 89 F.3d 1548, 1554 (11th Cir. 1996).

II. DISCUSSION

Our primary focus at this stage of the case is on the appropriateness of the injunctive relief granted by the district court. In our analysis, we must evaluate the merits of SunTrust's copyright infringement claim, including Houghton Mifflin's affirmative defense of fair use.[3] As we assess the fair-use defense, we examine to what extent a critic may use a work to communicate her criticism of the work without infringing the copyright in that work. To approach these issues in the proper framework, we should

---

[3] I believe that fair use should be considered an affirmative *right* under the 1976 Act, rather than merely an affirmative defense, as it is defined in the Act as a use that is not a violation of copyright. See Bateman v. Mnemonics, Inc., 79 F.3d 1532, 1542 n.22 (11th Cir. 1996). However, fair use is commonly referred to an affirmative defense, see Campbell v. Acuff-Rose Music, Inc., 510 U.S. 569, 590, 114 S. Ct. 1164, 1177, 127 L. Ed. 2d 500 (1994), and, as we are bound by Supreme Court precedent, we will apply it as such. See also David Nimmer, A Riff on Fair Use in the Digital Millennium Copyright Act, 148 U. PA. L. REV. 673, 714 n. 227 (2000) (citing Bateman). Nevertheless, the fact that the fair use right must be procedurally asserted as an affirmative defense does not detract from its constitutional significance as a guarantor to access and use for First Amendment purposes.

initially review the history of the Constitution's Copyright Clause and understand its relationship to the First Amendment.

A. History and Development of the Copyright Clause

The Copyright Clause finds its roots in England, where, in 1710, the Statute of Anne "was designed to destroy the booksellers' monopoly of the booktrade and to prevent its recurrence." L. Ray Patterson, Understanding the Copyright Clause, 47 J. COPYRIGHT SOC'Y USA 365, 379 (2000). This Parliamentary statute assigned copyright in books to authors, added a requirement that only a new work could be copyrighted, and limited the duration, which had been perpetual, to two fourteen-year terms. 8 Anne, C.19 (1710), reprinted in 8 Melville B. Nimmer & David Nimmer, Nimmer on Copyright § 7-5 (2001). It is clear that the goal of the Statute of Anne was to encourage creativity and ensure that the public would have free access to information by putting an end to "the continued use of copyright as a device of censorship." Patterson at 379.[4] The Framers of the U.S. Constitution relied on this statute when drafting the Copyright Clause of our Constitution,[5] which reads,

> The Congress shall have Power . . . to promote the Progress of Science . . . by securing for limited Times to Authors . . . the exclusive Right to their respective Writings . . . .

U.S. CONST. art. 1, § 8, cl. 8. Congress directly transferred the principles from the Statute of Anne into the copyright law of the United States in 1783, first through a recommendation to the states to enact similar copyright laws,[6] and then in 1790, with the passage of the first American federal copyright statute.[7]

The Copyright Clause was intended "to be the engine of free expression." Harper & Row Publishers, Inc. v. Nation Enters., 471 U.S. 539, 558, 105 S. Ct. 2218, 2229, 85 L. Ed. 2d 588 (1985). To that end, copyright laws have been enacted achieve the three main goals: the promotion of learning, the

---

[4] The Statute of Anne providing for copyright is introduced as "an act for the encouragement of learning," and has a preamble that states one of the purposes as "the encouragement of learned men to compose and write useful books." 8 Anne, C.19 (1710), reprinted in 8 Nimmer § 7-5.

[5] See Edward C. Walterscheid, The Remarkable-and Irrational-Disparity Between the Patent Term and the Copyright Term, 83 J. PAT. & TRADEMARK OFF. SOC'Y 233, 235 (2001) ("The American Copyright Act of 1790 simply copied this same basic scheme [from the Statute of Anne] into the new American copyright law."); Pierre N. Leval, Nimmer Lecture: Fair Use Rescued, 44 UCLA L. REV. 1449, 1450 (1997) ("The law of copyright, [was] fashioned by the Statute of Anne in 1710 and recognized in our Constitution.").

[6] "Resolution of the Continental Congress Respecting Copyright" (1783), reprinted in 8 Nimmer § 7-11.

[7] 1 Stat. 124 (May 31, 1790), reprinted in 8 Nimmer § 7-41 ("AN ACT for the encouragement of learning . . .").

protection of the public domain, and the granting of an exclusive right to the author.

1. Promotion of Learning

In the United States, copyright has always been used to promote learning by guarding against censorship.[8] Throughout the nineteenth century, the copyright in literature was limited to the right "to publish and vend books." Patterson, at 383. The term "copy" was interpreted literally; an author had the right only to prevent others from copying and selling her particular literary work. See Stowe v. Thomas, 2 Wall. Jr. 547, 23 F. Cas. 201 (C.C.E.D. Pa. 1853) (holding that a translation of Uncle Tom's Cabin into German was not a copyright infringement because it was not a copy of the work as it was published).[9] This limited right ensured that a maximum number of new works would be created and published. It was not until the 1909 Act, which codified the concept of a derivative work, that an author's right to protect his original work against imitation was established. This change more closely represents current statutory copyright law and is consistent with copyright's constitutional mandate.

As a further protection of the public interest, until 1976, statutory copyright law required that a work be published before an author was entitled to a copyright in that work. Therefore, in order to have the sole right of publication for the statutory period, the author was first required to make the work available to the public. In 1976, copyright was extended to include any work "fixed in any tangible medium of expression" in order to adapt the law to technological advances. § 102(a). Thus, the publication requirement was removed, but the fair use right was codified to maintain the constitutionally mandated balance to ensure that the public has access to knowledge.

The Copyright Act promotes public access to knowledge because it provides an economic incentive for authors to publish books and disseminate ideas to the public. Harper & Row, 471 U.S. at 558, 105 S. Ct. at 2229 ("By establishing a marketable right to the use of one's expression, copyright supplies the economic incentive to create and disseminate ideas."). The Supreme Court has recognized that "the monopoly created by copyright thus rewards the individual author in order to benefit the public." Id. at 546, 105 S. Ct. at 2223 (quoting Sony Corp. of America v. Univ. City Studios,

---

[8] See Jane C. Ginsburg, Creation and Commercial Value: Copyright Protection in Works of Information, 90 COLUM. L. REV. 1865, 1873 (1990) ("The 1710 English Statute of Anne, the 1787 United States Constitution, and the 1790 United States federal copyright statute all characterized copyright as a device to promote the advancement of knowledge.").

[9] Under modern copyright, such a right to translate would enjoy protection as a "derivative work." § § 101 and 106. In Folsom v. Marsh, 9 F. Cas. 342 (C.C.Mass. 1841), Justice Story created the concept of "fair use," which actually expanded the copyright monopoly, since until that time a translation or abridgement was not considered an infringement.

Inc., 464 U.S. 417, 477, 104 S. Ct. 774, 807, 78 L. Ed. 2d 574 (1984) (Black-mun, J.,dissenting)). Without the limited monopoly, authors would have little economic incentive to create and publish their work. Therefore, by providing this incentive, the copyright law promotes the public access to new ideas and concepts.

2. Protection of the Public Domain

The second goal of the Copyright Clause is to ensure that works enter the public domain after an author's rights, exclusive, but limited, have expired. Parallel to the patent regime, the limited time period of the copyright serves the dual purpose of ensuring that the work will enter the public domain and ensuring that the author has received "a fair return for [her] labors." Harper & Row, 471 U.S. at 546, 105 S. Ct. at 2223. This limited grant "is intended to motivate the creative activity of authors . . . by the provision of a special reward, and to allow the public access to the products of their genius after the limited period of exclusive control has expired." Sony, 464 U.S. at 429, 104 S. Ct. at 782. The public is protected in two ways: the grant of a copyright encourages authors to create new works, as discussed in section II.A.1., and the limitation ensures that the works will eventually enter the public domain, which protects the public's right of access and use.[10]

3. Exclusive Rights of the Author

Finally, the Copyright Clause grants the author limited exclusive rights in order to encourage the creation of original works. Before our copyright jurisprudence developed, there were two separate theories of copyright in England — the natural law copyright, which was the right of first publica-tion, and the statutory copyright, which was the right of continued publica-tion. The natural law copyright, which is not a part of our system, implied an ownership in the work itself, and thus was preferred by the booksellers and publishers striving to maintain their monopoly over literature as well as by the Crown to silence "seditious" writings. Even after passage of the Statute of Anne, the publishers and booksellers resisted the loss of their monopoly in the courts for more than sixty years. Finally, in 1774, the House of Lords ruled that the natural law copyright, that is, the ownership of the work itself, expires upon publication of the book, when the statutory copyright attaches. Patterson at 382.

This bifurcated system was carried over into our copyright law. As of the 1909 Act, an author had "state common law protection [that] persisted until the moment of general publication." Estate of Martin Luther King, Jr. v. CBS, Inc., 194 F.3d 1211, 1214 (11th Cir. 1999). After the work was

---

[10] See Feist Publications, Inc. v. Rural Tel. Serv. Co., 499 U.S. 340, 349, 111 S. Ct. 1282, 1290, 113 L. Ed. 2d 358 (1991) ("The primary objective of copyright is not to reward the labor of authors, but 'to promote the Progress of Science and useful Arts.'").

published, the author was entitled to federal statutory copyright protection if she had complied with certain federal requirements (i.e. publication with notice). If not, the work was released into the public domain. Id. The system illustrates that the author's ownership is in the copyright, and not in the work itself, for if the author had an ownership interest in the work itself, she would not lose that right if she published the book without complying with federal statutory copyright requirements. Compliance with the copyright law results in the guarantee of copyright to the author for a limited time, but the author never owns the work itself. § 202 ("Ownership of a copyright, or of any of the exclusive rights under a copyright, is distinct from ownership of any material object in which the work is embodied.").

This has an important impact on modern interpretation of copyright, as it emphasizes the distinction between ownership of the work, which an author does not possess, and ownership of the copyright, which an author enjoys for a limited time. In a society oriented toward property ownership, it is not surprising to find many that erroneously equate the work with the copyright in the work and conclude that if one owns the copyright, they must also own the work. However, the fallacy of that understanding is exposed by the simple fact that the work continues to exist after the term of copyright associated with the work has expired. "The copyright is not a natural right inherent in authorship. If it were, the impact on market values would be irrelevant; any unauthorized taking would be obnoxious." Pierre Leval, Towards a Fair Use Standard, 105 Harv. L. Rev. 1105, 1124 (1990).

B. The Union of Copyright and the First Amendment

The Copyright Clause and the First Amendment,[11] while intuitively in conflict,[12] were drafted to work together to prevent censorship; copyright laws were enacted in part to prevent private censorship and the First Amendment was enacted to prevent public censorship.[13] There are "conflicting interests that must be accommodated in drawing a definitional balance" between the Copyright Clause and the First Amendment. 1 Nimmer § 1.10[B][1]. In establishing this balance "on the copyright side, economic encouragement for creators must be preserved and the privacy of unpublished works recognized. Freedom of speech[, on the other hand,] requires the preservation of a meaningful public or democratic dialogue,

---

[11] "Congress shall make no law . . . abridging the freedom of speech . . ." U.S. CONST. amend. I.

[12] While the First Amendment disallows laws that abridge the freedom of speech, the Copyright Clause calls specifically for such a law.

[13] See Rebecca Tushnet, Copyright as a Model for Free Speech Law: What Copyright Has in Common with Anti-Pornography Laws, Campaign Finance Reform, and Telecommunications Regulation, 42 B. C. L. REV. 1, 2 (2000) ("The First Amendment gets government off speakers' backs, while the Copyright Act enables speakers to make money from speaking and thus encourages them to enter the public marketplace of ideas.").

as well as the uses of speech as a safety valve against violent acts, and as an end in itself." Id.

In copyright law, the balance between the First Amendment and copyright is preserved, in part, by the idea/expression dichotomy and the doctrine of fair use. See Eldred v. Reno, 239 F.3d 372, 375 (D.C. Cir. 2001) ("The first amendment objection . . . was misplaced 'in view of the First Amendment protections already embodied in the Copyright Act's distinction between copyrightable expression and uncopyrightable facts and ideas, and the latitude for scholarship and comment traditionally afforded by fair use.'") (quoting Harper & Row, 471 U.S. at 560, 105 S. Ct. at 2218).

1. The Idea/ Expression Dichotomy

Copyright cannot protect an idea, only the expression of that idea. Baker v. Selden, 101 U.S. 99, 25 L. Ed. 841 (1879); Mitek, 89 F.3d at 1556 n.19; BellSouth Adver. & Publ'g Corp. v. Donnelley Info. Publ'g, Inc., 999 F.2d 1436, 1445 (1993); codified in § 102(b) ("In no case does copyright protection for an original work of authorship extend to any idea, procedure, process, system, method of operation, concept, principle, or discovery, regardless of the form in which it is described, explained, illustrated, or embodied in such work."). The result is that "copyright assures authors the right to their original expression, but encourages others to build freely upon the ideas and information conveyed by the work." Feist, 499 U.S. at 349-50, 111 S. Ct. at 1290. It is partly through this idea/expression dichotomy that copyright law embodies the First Amendment's underlying goal of encouraging open debate and the free exchange of ideas. See Harper & Row, 471 U.S. at 556, 105 S. Ct. at 2228 (citing as correct the Second Circuit's observation that "copyright's idea/expression dichotomy strikes a definitional balance between the First Amendment and the Copyright Act by permitting free communication of facts while still protecting an author's expression"); Worldwide Church of God v. Philadelphia Church of God, 227 F.3d 1110, 1115 (9th Cir. 2000), cert. denied, 532 U.S. 958, 149 L. Ed. 2d 373, 121 S. Ct. 1486 (2001) ("The public interest in the free flow of information is assured by the law's refusal to recognize a valid copyright in facts."); see also 1 Nimmer § 1-10[C][2] ("In general, the democratic dialogue — a self-governing people's participation in the marketplace of ideas — is adequately served if the public has access to an author's ideas, and such loss to the dialogue as results from inaccessibility to an author's 'expression' is counterbalanced by the greater public interest in the copyright system."). Holding an infringer liable in copyright for copying the expression of another author's ideas does not impede First Amendment goals because the public purpose has been served — the public already has access to the idea or the concepts.[14] A new author may use or discuss the idea, but must do so using her own original expression.

---

[14] See 1 Nimmer § 1.10[B][2] ("It is exposure to ideas, and not to their particular expression, that is vital if self-governing people are to make informed decisions.").

2. Fair Use

First Amendment privileges are also preserved through the doctrine of fair use.[15] Until codification of the fair-use doctrine in the 1976 Act, fair use was a judge-made right developed to preserve the constitutionality of copyright legislation by protecting First Amendment values. Had fair use not been recognized as a right under the 1976 Act, the statutory abandonment of publication as a condition of copyright that had existed for over 200 years would have jeopardized the constitutionality of the new Act because there would be no statutory guarantee that new ideas, or new expressions of old ideas, would be accessible to the public. Included in the definition of fair use are "purposes such as criticism, comment, news reporting, teaching . . ., scholarship, or research." § 107. The exceptions carved out for these purposes are at the heart of fair use's protection of the First Amendment, as they allow later authors to use a previous author's copyright to introduce new ideas or concepts to the public. Therefore, within the limits of the fair-use test, n16[16] any use of a copyright is permitted to fulfill one of the important purposes listed in the statute.

Because of the First Amendment principles built into copyright law through the idea/expression dichotomy and the doctrine of fair use, courts often need not entertain related First Amendment arguments in a copyright case. See, e.g., Eldred, 239 F.3d at 376 (where the works in question "are by definition under copyright; that puts the works on the latter half of the 'idea/expression dichotomy' and makes them subject to fair use. This obviates further inquiry under the First Amendment."); Nihon Keizai Shimbun, Inc. v. Comline Bus. Data, Inc., 166 F.3d 65, 74 (2d Cir. 1999) ("We have repeatedly rejected First Amendment challenges to injunctions from copyright infringement on the ground that First Amendment concerns are protected by and coextensive with the fair use doctrine."); Los Angeles News Serv. v. Tullo, 973 F.2d 791, 795 (9th Cir. 1992) ("First Amendment concerns are also addressed in the copyright field through the 'fair use' doctrine.").[17]

The case before us calls for an analysis of whether a preliminary injunction was properly granted against an alleged infringer who, relying largely on the doctrine of fair use, made use of another's copyright for comment and criticism. As discussed herein, *copyright does not immunize a work from comment and criticism.* Therefore, the narrower question in this case is to what extent a critic may use the protected elements of an original work of authorship to communicate her criticism without infringing the copyright in that work. As will be discussed below, this becomes essentially an analysis of the fair use factors. As we turn to the analysis required in this case, we must remain cognizant of the First Amendment protections interwoven into copyright law.

---

[15] § 107 ("Fair use of a copyrighted work . . . for purposes such as criticism [or] comment . . . is not an infringement of copyright.").

[16] See discussion, section II.C.1.b.

[17] For a more policy-based discussion, see 1 Nimmer § 1.10[D].

C. Appropriateness of Injunctive Relief

"The chief function of a preliminary injunction is to preserve the status quo until the merits of the controversy can be fully and fairly adjudicated." Northeastern Fl. Chapter of Ass'n of Gen. Contractors of Am. v. City of Jacksonville, Fl., 896 F.2d 1283, 1284 (11th Cir. 1990). The Copyright Act specifically vests the federal courts with power to grant injunctions "to prevent or restrain infringement of a copyright." § 502(a). While injunctive relief may be particularly appropriate in cases involving simple copying or "piracy" of a copyrighted work, the Supreme Court has cautioned that such relief may not be consistent with the goals of copyright law in cases in which the alleged infringer of the copyright has a colorable fair-use defense. Campbell v. Acuff-Rose Music, Inc., 510 U.S. 569, 578 n.10, 114 S. Ct. 1164, 1171 n.10, 127 L. Ed. 2d 500 (1994).[18]

The basic framework for our analysis remains, however, the standard test governing the issuance of preliminary injunctions. SunTrust is not entitled to relief in the form of a preliminary injunction unless it has proved each of the following four elements: "(1) a substantial likelihood of success on the merits, (2) a substantial threat of irreparable injury if the injunction were not granted, (3) that the threatened injury to the plaintiff outweighs the harm an injunction may cause the defendant, and (4) that granting the injunction would not disserve the public interest." Am. Red Cross v. Palm Beach Blood Bank, Inc., 143 F.3d 1407, 1410 (11th Cir. 1998).

1. Substantial Likelihood of Success on the Merits

a. Prima Facie Copyright Infringement

The first step in evaluating the likelihood that SunTrust will succeed on the merits is to determine whether it has established the prima facie elements of a copyright infringement claim: (1) that SunTrust owns a valid copyright in GWTW and (2) that Randall copied *original* elements of GWTW in TWDG. Feist, 499 U.S. at 361, 111 S. Ct. at 1296; Leigh v. Warner Bros., Inc., 212 F.3d 1210, 1214 (11th Cir. 2000). The district court found that SunTrust had carried its burden on both of these elements.

The first element, SunTrust's ownership of a valid copyright in GWTW, is not disputed. Houghton Mifflin does assert, however, that SunTrust did not establish the second element of infringement, that TWDG appropriates copyright-protected expression from GWTW. In order to prove copying, SunTrust was required to show a "substantial similarity" between the two works such that "an average lay observer would recognize the alleged copy as having been appropriated from the copyrighted work." Leigh, 212 F.3d at 1214 (quoting Original Appalachian Artworks, Inc. v. Toy Loft, Inc., 684 F.2d 821, 829 (11th Cir. 1982)). Not all copying of a work is actionable, however, for, as discussed in section II.B.1., "no author may copyright facts

---

[18] The Supreme Court reiterated this point in New York Times v. Tasini, 429 U.S. 298, ___, 150 L. Ed. 2d 500, 121 S. Ct. 2381, 2393 (2001).

or ideas. The copyright is limited to those aspects of the work-termed 'expression'-that display the stamp of the author's originality." Harper & Row, 471 U.S. at 547, 105 S. Ct. at 2224 (citation omitted). Thus, we are concerned with substantial similarities between TWDG and GWTW only to the extent that they involve the copying of original, protected expression. Leigh, 212 F.3d at 1214.[19]

There is no bright line that separates the protectable expression from the nonprotectable idea in a work of fiction. While often referred to as a test for distinguishing the idea from the expression, Judge Learned Hand's famous statement in Nichols v. Universal Pictures Corp., 45 F.2d 119 (2d Cir. 1930), is actually nothing more than a concise restatement of the problem facing the courts:

> Upon any work, and especially upon a play, a great number of patterns of increasing generality will fit equally well, as more and more of the incident is left out. The last may perhaps be no more than the most general statement of what the play is about, and at time might consist only of its title; but there is a point in this series of abstractions where they are no longer protected, since otherwise the playwright could prevent the use of his 'ideas,' to which, apart from their expression, his property is never extended.

Id. at 121. At one end of the spectrum, *scenes a faire* — the stock scenes and hackneyed character types that "naturally flow from a common theme" — are considered "ideas," and therefore are not copyrightable. Beal v. Paramount Pictures Corp., 20 F.3d 454, 459-60 (11th Cir. 1994). But as plots become more intricately detailed and characters become more idiosyncratic, they at some point cross the line into "expression" and are protected by copyright. See 1 Nimmer § 2.12 (2001).

After conducting a thorough comparison of the two works, the district court found that TWDG copied far more than unprotected scenes a faire from GWTW: "[TWDG] uses fifteen fictional characters from [GWTW], incorporating their physical attributes, mannerisms, and the distinct features that Ms. Mitchell used to describe them, as well as their complex relationships with each other. Moreover, the various [fictional] locales, . . . settings, characters, themes, and plot of [TWDG] closely mirror those contained in [GWTW]." SunTrust, 136 F. Supp. 2d at 1367.

Our own review of the two works reveals substantial use of GWTW. TWDG appropriates numerous characters, settings, and plot twists from GWTW. For example, Scarlett O'Hara, Rhett Butler, Bonnie Butler, Melanie Wilkes, Ashley Wilkes, Gerald O'Hara, Ellen O'Hara, Mammy, Pork,

---

[19] Originally the word "copie" was a noun, indicating the manuscript. Ownership of the "copie" thus meant ownership of the manuscript for the purposes of publishing it. Today, "copy" has become a verb, meaning the act of reproduction of a work. But in the development of copyright law it was intended to be a term of art, indicating a reproduction of a work for publication. Failure to understand and apply this distinction has confused many courts (assisted by overzealous advocates) into too expansive a view of the scope of the copyright monopoly.

Dilcey, Prissy, Belle Watling, Carreen O'Hara, Stuart and Brenton Tarleton, Jeems, Philippe, and Aunt Pittypat, all characters in GWTW, appear
in TWDG. Many of these characters are renamed in TWDG: Scarlett becomes "Other," Rhett Butler becomes "R.B.," Pork becomes "Garlic," Prissy
becomes "Miss Priss," Philippe becomes "Feleepe," Aunt Pittypat becomes
"Aunt Pattypit," etc. In several instances, Randall renamed characters
using Mitchell's descriptions of those characters in GWTW: Ashley becomes
"Dreamy Gentleman," Melanie becomes "Mealy Mouth," Gerald becomes
"Planter." The fictional settings from GWTW receive a similarly transparent renaming in TWDG: Tara becomes "Tata," Twelve Oaks Plantation
becomes "Twelve Slaves Strong as Trees." TWDG copies, often in wholesale
fashion, the descriptions and histories of these fictional characters and
places from GWTW, as well as their relationships and interactions with
one another. TWDG appropriates or otherwise explicitly references many
aspects of GWTW's plot as well, such as the scenes in which Scarlett kills
a Union soldier and the scene in which Rhett stays in the room with his
dead daughter Bonnie, burning candles. After carefully comparing the two
works, we agree with the district court that, particularly in its first half,
TWDG is largely "an encapsulation of [GWTW] [that] exploits its copyrighted characters, story lines, and settings as the palette for the new
story." SunTrust, 136 F. Supp. 2d at 1367.

Houghton Mifflin argues that there is no substantial similarity between
TWDG and GWTW because the retelling of the story is an inversion of
GWTW: the characters, places, and events lifted from GWTW are often cast
in a different light, strong characters from the original are depicted as weak
(and vice-versa) in the new work, the institutions and values romanticized
in GWTW are exposed as corrupt in TWDG. While we agree with Houghton
Mifflin that the characters, settings, and plot taken from GWTW are vested
with a new significance when viewed through the character of Cynara[20]
in TWDG, it does not change the fact that they are the very same copyrighted characters, settings, and plot.

b. Fair Use

Randall's appropriation of elements of GWTW in TWDG may nevertheless not constitute infringement of SunTrust's copyright if the taking is
protected as a "fair use." The codification of the fair-use doctrine in the
Copyright Act provides:

Notwithstanding the provisions of sections 106 and 106A, the fair use
of a copyrighted work . . . for purposes such as criticism, comment, news
reporting, teaching (including multiple copies for classroom use), scholarship, or research, is not an infringement of copyright. In determining
whether the use made of a work in any particular case is a fair use the
factors to be considered shall include—

---

[20] "Cynara" is the name of the poem by Ernest Dowson, from which GWTW's title
is derived ("I have forgot much, Cynara! gone with the wind, . . . ").

(1) the purpose and character of the use, including whether such use is of a commercial nature or is for nonprofit educational purposes;

(2) the nature of the copyrighted work;

(3) the amount and substantiality of the portion used in relation to the copyrighted work as a whole; and

(4) the effect of the use upon the potential market for or value of the copyrighted work.

§ 107.[21] In assessing whether a use of a copyright is a fair use under the statute, we bear in mind that the examples of possible fair uses given are illustrative rather than exclusive, and that "all [of the four factors] are to be explored, and the results weighed together in light of the purposes of copyright." Campbell, 510 U.S. at 577-78, 114 S. Ct. at 1170-71.[22] In light of the discussion in § § IIA and B, one of the most important purposes to consider is the free flow of ideas — particularly criticism and commentary.

Houghton Mifflin argues that TWDG is entitled to fair-use protection as a parody of GWTW. In Campbell, the Supreme Court held that parody, although not specifically listed in § 107, is a form of comment and criticism that may constitute a fair use of the copyrighted work being parodied. Id. at 579, 114 S. Ct. at 1171. Parody, which is directed toward a particular literary or artistic work, is distinguishable from satire, which more broadly addresses the institutions and mores of a slice of society. Id. at 580-81, 581 n.15, 114 S. Ct. at 1172, 1172 n.15. Thus, "parody needs to mimic an original to make its point, and so has some claim to use the creation of its victim's . . . imagination, whereas satire can stand on its own two feet and so requires justification for the very act of borrowing." Id. at 580-81, 114 S. Ct. at 1172.

The fact that parody by definition must borrow elements from an existing work, however, does not mean that every parody is shielded from a claim of copyright infringement as a fair use. "The [Copyright] Act has no hint of an evidentiary preference for parodists over their victims, and no workable presumption for parody could take account of the fact that parody often shades into satire when society is lampooned through its creative artifacts, or that a work may contain both parodic and nonparodic elements." Id. at 581, 114 S. Ct. at 1172. Therefore, Houghton Mifflin's fair-use defense of parody, like any other claim of fair use, must be evaluated in light of the factors set out in § 107 and the constitutional purposes of copyright law. Id., 114 S. Ct. at 1172.

Before considering a claimed fair-use defense based on parody, however, the Supreme Court has required that we ensure that "a parodic character may reasonably be perceived" in the allegedly infringing work. Id. at 582, 114 S. Ct. at 1173. The Supreme Court's definition of parody in Campbell,

---

[21] Interestingly, these elements harken back to Folsom v. Marsh, supra, where Justice Story first articulated the concept of "fair use."

[22] See section II.A. for a discussion of the purposes of copyright.

however, is somewhat vague. On the one hand, the Court suggests that the aim of parody is "comic effect or ridicule," but it then proceeds to discuss parody more expansively in terms of its "commentary" on the original. Id. at 580, 114 S. Ct. at 1172. In light of the admonition in Campbell that courts should not judge the quality of the work or the success of the attempted humor in discerning its parodic character, we choose to take the broader view. For purposes of our fair-use analysis, we will treat a work as a parody if its aim is to comment upon or criticize a prior work by appropriating elements of the original in creating a new artistic, as opposed to scholarly or journalistic, work.[23] Under this definition, the parodic character of TWDG is clear. TWDG is not a general commentary upon the Civil-War-era American South, but a specific criticism of and rejoinder to the depiction of slavery and the relationships between blacks and whites in GWTW. The fact that Randall chose to convey her criticisms of GWTW through a work of fiction, which she contends is a more powerful vehicle for her message than a scholarly article, does not, in and of itself, deprive TWDG of fair-use protection. We therefore proceed to an analysis of the four fair-use factors.

i. Purpose and Character of the Work

The first factor in the fair-use analysis, the purpose and character of the allegedly infringing work, has several facets. The first is whether TWDG serves a commercial purpose or nonprofit educational purpose. § 107(1). Despite whatever educational function TWDG may be able to lay claim to, it is undoubtedly a commercial product. n24[24] As the Supreme Court has stated, "the crux of the profit/nonprofit distinction is not whether the sole motive of the use is monetary gain but whether the user stands to profit from exploitation of the copyrighted material without paying the customary price." Harper & Row, 471 U.S. at 562, 105 S. Ct. at 2231. The fact that TWDG was published for profit is the first factor weighing against a finding of fair use. Id., 105 S. Ct. at 2231.

However, TWDG's for-profit status is strongly overshadowed and outweighed in view of its highly transformative use of GWTC's copyrighted elements. "The more transformative the new work, the less will be the significance of other factors, like commercialism, that may weigh against a finding of fair use." Campbell, 510 U.S. at 579, 114 S. Ct. at 1171. "The

---

[23] The benefit of our approach to "parody," which requires no assessment of whether or not a work is humorous, is apparent from the arguments made by the parties in this case. SunTrust quotes Michiko Kakutani's review of TWDG in the New York Times, in which she states that the work is "decidedly unfunny." Houghton Mifflin, on the other hand, claims that TWDG is an example of "African-American humor," which, Houghton Mifflin strongly implies, non-African-American judges are not permitted to evaluate without assistance from "experts." Under our approach, we may ignore Houghton Mifflin's questionable argument and simply bypass what would always be a wholly subjective inquiry.

[24] Randall did not choose to publish her work of fiction on the internet free to all the world to read; rather, she chose a method of publication designed to generate economic profit.

goal of copyright, to promote science and the arts, is generally furthered by the creation of transformative works." Id.. A work's transformative value is of special import in the realm of parody, since a parody's aim is, by nature, to transform an earlier work.

The second factor in the "purpose and character" analysis relevant to this case is to what extent TWDG's use of copyrighted elements of GWTW can be said to be "transformative." The inquiry is "whether the new work merely supersedes the objects of the original creation, or instead adds something new, with a further purpose or different character, altering the first with new expression, meaning, or message." Campbell, 510 U.S. at 579, 114 S. Ct. at 1171 (citations and internal punctuation omitted). The issue of transformation is a double-edged sword in this case. On the one hand, the story of Cynara and her perception of the events in TWDG certainly adds new "expression, meaning, [and] message" to GWTW. From another perspective, however, TWDG's success as a pure work of fiction depends heavily on copyrighted elements appropriated from GWTW to carry its own plot forward.

However, as noted above, TWDG is more than an abstract, pure fictional work. It is principally and purposefully a critical statement that seeks to rebut and destroy the perspective, judgments, and mythology of GWTW. Randall's literary goal is to explode the romantic, idealized portrait of the antebellum South during and after the Civil War. In the world of GWTW, the white characters comprise a noble aristocracy whose idyllic existence is upset only by the intrusion of Yankee soldiers, and, eventually, by the liberation of the black slaves. Through her characters as well as through direct narration, Mitchell describes how both blacks and whites were purportedly better off in the days of slavery: "The more I see of emancipation the more criminal I think it is. It's just ruined the darkies," says Scarlett O'Hara. GWTW at 639. Free blacks are described as "creatures of small intelligence . . . like monkeys or small children turned loose among treasured objects whose value is beyond their comprehension, they ran wild — either from perverse pleasure in destruction or simply because of their ignorance." Id. at 654. Blacks elected to the legislature are described as spending "most of their time eating goobers and easing their unaccustomed feet into and out of new shoes." Id. at 904.

As the district court noted: "The earlier work is a third-person epic, whereas the new work is told in the first-person as an intimate diary of the life of Cynara. Thematically, the new work provides a different viewpoint of the antebellum world." 136 F. Supp. 2d at 1367. While told from a different perspective, more critically, the story is transformed into a very different tale, albeit much more abbreviated. Cynara's very language is a departure from Mitchell's original prose; she acts as the voice of Randall's inversion of GWTW. She is the vehicle of parody; she is its means — not its end. It is clear within the first fifty pages of Cynara's fictional diary that Randall's work flips GWTW's traditional race roles, portrays powerful whites as stupid or feckless,[25] and generally sets out to demystify GWTW and strip the romanticism from Mitchell's specific account of this period of our history. Approximately the last half of TWDG tells a completely new story that, although involving characters based on GWTW characters, features plot elements found nowhere within the covers of GWTW.

Where Randall refers directly to Mitchell's plot and characters, she does so in service of her general attack on GWTW. In GWTW, Scarlett O'Hara often expresses disgust with and condescension towards blacks; in TWDG, Other, Scarlett's counterpart, is herself of mixed descent. In GWTW, Ashley Wilkes is the initial object of Scarlett's affection; in TWDG, he is homosexual.[26] In GWTW, Rhett Butler does not consort with black female characters and is portrayed as the captain of his own destiny. In TWDG, Cynara ends her affair with Rhett's counterpart, R., to begin a relationship with a black Congressman; R. ends up a washed out former cad. In TWDG, nearly every black character is given some redeeming quality — whether depth, wit, cunning, beauty, strength, or courage -that their GWTW analogues lacked.

In light of this, we find it difficult to conclude that Randall simply tried to "avoid the drudgery in working up something fresh." Campbell, 510 U.S. at 580, 114 S. Ct. at 1172. It is hard to imagine how Randall could have specifically criticized GWTW without depending heavily upon copyrighted elements of that book. A parody is a work that seeks to comment upon or criticize another work by appropriating elements of the original. "Parody needs to mimic an original to make its point, and so has some claim to use the creation of its victim's (or collective victims') imagination." Campbell, 510 U.S. at 580-81, 114 S. Ct. at 1172. Thus, Randall has fully employed those conscripted elements from GWTW to make war against it. Her work, TWDG, reflects transformative value because it "can provide social benefit, by shedding light on an earlier work, and, in the process, creating a new one." Campbell, 510 U.S. at 579, 114 S. Ct. at 1171.

---

[25] On pages 62-63 of TWDG, for example, Miss Priss explains that Mammy killed white male heirs to the plantation dynasty when they were babies in order to seal Garlic's and the other African-Americans' control over the drunken Planter. "What would we a done with a sober white man on this place?" Says Miss Priss. TWDG at 63.

[26] Randall's parodic intent vis-a-vis Ashley becomes manifest when the two works are read side-by-side. Mitchell has Gerald describe Ashley Wilkes: "The Wilkes are different from any of our neighbors-different from any family I ever knew. They are queer folk, and it's best that they marry their cousins and keep their queerness to themselves . . . And when I say queer, it's not crazy I'm meaning . . . there's no understanding him at all . . . . tell me true, do you understand his foderol about books and poetry and music and oil paintings and such foolishness?" GWTW at 34. Later, Mitchell describes how "Scarlett turned her prettiest smile on Ashley, but for some reason he was not looking at her. He was looking at Charles . . . " GWTW at 113. This particular element of Randall's parody takes on special relevance in the market-harm analysis of the case, because it is evident from the record evidence that SunTrust makes a practice of requiring authors of its licensed derivatives to make no references to homosexuality.

While "transformative use is not absolutely necessary for a finding of fair use, . . . the more transformative the new work, the less will be the significance of other factors." Id., 114 S. Ct. at 1171 (internal citations omitted). In the case of TWDG, consideration of this factor certainly militates in favor of a finding of fair use, and, informs our analysis of the other factors, particularly the fourth, as discussed below.

ii. Nature of the Copyrighted Work

The second factor, the nature of the copyrighted work, recognizes that there is a hierarchy of copyright protection in which original, creative works are afforded greater protection than derivative works or factual compilations. Id. at 586, 114 S. Ct. at 1175; Microdos, 115 F.3d at 1515 n.16. GWTW is undoubtedly entitled to the greatest degree of protection as an original work of fiction. This factor is given little weight in parody cases, however, "since parodies almost invariably copy publicly known, expressive works." Campbell, 510 U.S. at 586, 114 S. Ct. at 1175.

iii. Amount and Substantiality of the Portion Used

The third fair-use factor is "the amount and substantiality of the portion used in relation to the copyrighted work as a whole." § 107(3). It is at this point that parody presents uniquely difficult problems for courts in the fair-use context, for "parody's humor, or in any event its comment, necessarily springs from recognizable allusion to its object through distorted imitation . . . . When parody takes aim at a particular original work, the parody must be able to 'conjure up' at least enough of that original to make the object of its critical wit recognizable." Campbell, 510 U.S. at 588, 114 S. Ct. at 1176. Once enough has been taken to "conjure up" the original in the minds of the readership, any further taking must specifically serve the new work's parodic aims. Id., 114 S. Ct. at 1176.

GWTW is one of the most famous, popular, and enduring American novels ever written. Given the fame of the work and its primary characters, SunTrust argues that very little reference is required to conjure up GWTW. As we have already indicated in our discussion of substantial similarity, TWDG appropriates a substantial portion of the protected elements of GWTW. Houghton Mifflin argues that TWDG takes nothing from GWTW that does not serve a parodic purpose, the crux of the argument being that a large number of characters had to be taken from GWTW because each represents a different ideal or stereotype that requires commentary, and that the work as a whole could not be adequately commented upon without revisiting substantial portions of the plot, including its most famous scenes. Houghton Mifflin's argument is similar to that made by the defendants in Harper & Row, who argued for "expanding the doctrine of fair use to create what amounts to a public figure exception to copyright." 471 U.S. at 560, 105 S. Ct. at 2230. To the extent Houghton Mifflin argues for extra latitude in copying from GWTW because of its fame, the Supreme Court has squarely foreclosed any such privilege:

It is fundamentally at odds with the scheme of copyright to accord lesser rights in those works that are of greatest importance to the public . . . . To propose that fair use be imposed whenever the social value of dissemination outweighs any detriment to the artist, would be to propose depriving copyright owners of their right in the property precisely when they encounter those users who could afford to pay for it.

Id. at 559, 105 S. Ct. at 2229-30 (internal quotations and punctuation omitted). Notably, however, the Court did not go so far as to grant well-known works a special, higher copyright status either.

There are numerous instances in which TWDG appropriates elements of GWTW and then transforms them for the purpose of commentary. TWDG uses several of GWTW's most famous lines, but vests them with a completely new significance. For example, the final lines of GWTW, "Tomorrow, I'll think of some way to get him back. After all, tomorrow is another day," are transformed in TWDG into "For all those we love for whom tomorrow will not be another day, we send the sweet prayer of resting in peace." Another such recasting is Rhett's famous quip to Scarlett as he left her in GWTW, "My dear, I don't give a damn." In TWDG, the repetition of this line (which is paraphrased) changes the reader's perception of Rhett/R.B.- and of black-white relations—because he has left Scarlett/Other for Cynara, a former slave. Another clear instance in which a memorable scene from GWTW is taken primarily for the purpose of parody is Gerald/Planter's acquisition of Pork/Garlic. In GWTW, Gerald won Pork in a card game with a man from St. Simons Island. In TWDG, Planter wins Garlic in a card game with a man from St. Simons Island, but Garlic, far from being the passive "chattel" in GWTW, is portrayed as being smarter than either white character by orchestrating the outcome of the card game and determining his own fate. There are many more such transformative uses of elements of GWTW in TWDG.

On the other hand, however, we are told that not all of TWDG's takings from GWTW are clearly justified as commentary. We have already determined that TWDG is a parody, but not every parody is a fair use. SunTrust contends that TWDG, at least at the margins, takes more of the protected elements of GWTW than was necessary to serve a parodic function.

For example, in a sworn declaration to the district court, Randall stated that she needed to reference the scene from GWTW in which Jeems is given to the Tarleton twins as a birthday present because she considers it "perhaps the single most repellent paragraph in Margaret Mitchell's novel: a black child given to two white children as a birthday present . . . as if the buying and selling of children thus had no moral significance." Clearly, such a scene is fair game for criticism. However, in this instance, SunTrust argues that TWDG goes beyond commentary on the occurrence itself, appropriating such nonrelevant details as the fact that the twins had red hair and were killed at Gettysburg. There are several other scenes from GWTW, such as the incident in which Scarlett threw a vase at Ashley while Rhett was hidden on the couch, that are retold or alluded to without serving any apparent parodic purpose. Similar taking of the descriptions of charac-ters and the minor details of their histories and interactions that arguably are not essential to the parodic purpose of the work recur throughout: Melanie/Mealy Mouth is flat-chested, Mammy is described as being like an elephant and is proud of Scarlett/Other's small waist, Gerald/Planter had been run out of Ireland for committing murder and is an excellent horse-man, Bonnie/Precious wears a blue velvet riding habit and is afraid of the dark, Belle/Beauty has red hair and lives in Atlanta, Ellen/Lady likes lemon verbena, Carreen/Kareen ends up in a convent in Charleston. Clearly, TWDG uses these idiosyncratic characters. But we must determine whether the use is fair. In doing so, we are reminded that literary relevance is a highly subjective analysis ill-suited for judicial inquiry. Thus we are presented with conflicting and opposing arguments relative to the amount taken and whether it was too much or a necessary amount.

The Supreme Court in Campbell did not require that parodists take the bare minimum amount of copyright material necessary to conjure up the original work. Parody "must be able to conjure up *at least* enough of [the] original to make the object of its critical wit recognizable." Campbell, 510 U.S. at 588, 114 S. Ct. at 1176 (emphasis added; quotations omitted). "Parody frequently needs to be more than a fleeting evocation of an original in order to make its humorous point . . . . Even more extensive use [than necessary to conjure up the original] would still be fair use, provided the parody builds upon the original, using the original as a known element of modern culture and contributing something new for humorous effect or commentary." Elsmere Music, Inc. v. National Broad'g Co., 623 F.2d 252, 253 n. 1 (2d Cir. 1980).

A use does not necessarily become infringing the moment it does more than simply conjure up another work. Rather, "once enough has been taken to assure identification, how much more is reasonable will depend, say, [1] on the extent to which the [work's] *overriding purpose and character is to parody* the original or, in contrast, [2] the likelihood that the parody may serve as *a market substitute* for the original." Campbell, 510 U.S. at 588, 114 S. Ct. at 1176 (numeration and emphasis added). As to the first point, it is manifest that TWDG's *raison d'etre* is to parody GWTW.[27] The second

---

[27] SunTrust suggests that Houghton Mifflin decided-as a legalistic afterthought-to market TWDG as a "parody." We are mindful of Justice Kennedy's admonition that courts "ensure that no just any commercial takeoff is rationalized post hoc as a parody." Campbell, 510 U.S. at 600 (Kennedy, J., concurring). Justice Kennedy's concurrence simply underscores the danger of relying upon facile, formalistic labels, and encourages us to march this alleged infringement through fair use's four-pronged analysis as we would any other such work. Randall and Houghton-Mifflin may label their book a "parody," or a "novel," or whatever they like, and that fact would be largely irrelevant to our task. Defendants "need not label their [work] . . . a parody in order to claim fair use protection . . . Parody serves its goals whether labeled or not, and there is no reason to require parody to state the obvious . . . " Campbell, 510 U.S. at 583 n. 17. The only way in which Houghton Mifflin's marketing strategy might be relevant is if it diverted consumers from GWTW-related products to its own. In any case, such a practice, if it were found to exist, would likely fall under the market harm fair use factor.

point indicates that any material we suspect is "extraneous" to the parody is unlawful only if it negatively effects the potential market for or value of the original copyright. Based upon this record at this juncture, we cannot determine in any conclusive way whether "'the quantity and value of the materials used'" are reasonable in relation to the purpose of the copying.'" Id., 510 U.S. at 586, 114 S. Ct. at 1175 (quoting Folsom, 9 F. Cas. at 348).

iv. Effect on the Market Value of the Original

The final fair-use factor requires us to consider the effect that the publication of TWDG will have on the market for or value of SunTrust's copyright in GWTW, including the potential harm it may cause to the market for derivative works based on GWTW. Campbell, 510 U.S. at 590, 114 S. Ct. at 1177. In addressing this factor, we must "consider not only the extent of market harm caused by the particular actions of the alleged infringer, but also whether unrestricted and widespread conduct of the sort engaged in by the defendant [ ] would result in a substantially adverse impact on the potential market." Id., 114 S. Ct. at 1177 (quotations omitted). More specifically, the Campbell Court continued: "The only harm to derivatives that need concern us . . . is the harm of market substitution. The fact that a parody may impair the market for derivative uses by the very effectiveness of its critical commentary is no more relevant under copyright that the like threat to the original market." Id., 510 U.S. at 593, 114 S. Ct. at 1178.[28] See also Nimmer on Copyright, § 1305[A][4] at 181 (Vol. 4) (citing Consumers Union of U.S., Inc. v. General Signal Corp., 724 F.2d 1044 (2nd Cir. 1993)) ("The fourth factor looks to adverse impact only by reason of usurpation of the demand for plaintiff's work through defendant's copying of protectible expression from such work.").

As for the potential market, SunTrust proffered evidence in the district court of the value of its copyright in GWTW. Several derivative works of GWTW have been authorized, including the famous movie of the same name and a book titled Scarlett: The Sequel.[29] GWTW and the derivative works based upon it have generated millions of dollars for the copyright holders. SunTrust has negotiated an agreement with St. Martin's Press permitting it to produce another derivative work based on GWTW, a privilege for which St. Martin's paid "well into seven figures." Part of this agreement was that SunTrust would not authorize any other derivative works prior to the publication of St. Martin's book.

---

[28] "Whereas a work that merely supplants or supersedes another is likely to cause a substantially adverse impact on the potential market of the original, a transformative work is less likely to do so." Sony Computer Entertainment, Inc. v. Connectix Corp., 203 F.3d 596, 607 (9th Cir. 2000) (citing Campbell, 510 U.S. at 591, 114 S. Ct. at 1177, and Harper & Row Publishers, Inc. v. Nation Enters., Inc., 471 U.S. 539, 567-69, 85 L. Ed. 2d 588, 105 S. Ct. 2218 (1985)).

[29] See generally Trust Co. Bank v. MGM/UA Entertainment Co., 772 F.2d 740 (11th Cir. 1985).

An examination of the record, with its limited development as to relevant market harm due to the preliminary injunction status of the case, discloses that SunTrust focuses on the value of GWTW and its derivatives, but fails to address and offers little evidence or argument to demonstrate that TWDG would supplant demand for SunTrust's licensed derivatives. However, the Supreme Court and other appeals courts have made clear that, particularly in cases of parody, evidence of harm to the potential market for or value of the original copyright is crucial to a fair use determination. "Evidence about relevant markets" is also crucial to the fair use analysis. Campbell, 510 U.S. at 590, 114 S. Ct. at 1177. "Evidence of substantial harm to [a derivative market] would weigh against a finding of fair use." Id. at 593, 114 S. Ct. at 1178. "What is necessary is a showing by a preponderance of the evidence that *some* meaningful likelihood of future harm exits." Sony, 464 U.S. at 451, 104 S. Ct. at 793 (emphasis in original).[30] It should also be remembered that with a work as old as GWTW on which the original copyright may soon expire, creation of a derivative work only serves to protect that which is original to the latter work and does not somehow extend the copyright in the copyrightable elements of the *original* work. See § 103(b) ("The copyright in a . . . derivative work extends only to the material contributed by the author of such work, as distinguished from the preexisting material employed in the work, and does not imply any exclusive right in the preexisting material.").

In contrast, the evidence proffered in support of the fair use defense[31] specifically and correctly focused on market substitution and demonstrates

---

[30] See also Worldwide Church of God v. Philadelphia Church of God, Inc., 227 F.3d 1110, 1119 (9th Cir. 2000) (noting, in market harm analysis, that "undisputed evidence shows that individuals who received copies of [defendant's work] from [defendant] are present or could be potential adherents of [plaintiff's]"); Leibovitz v. Paramount Pictures Corp., 137 F.3d 109, 116 n. 6 (2nd Cir. 1998) (where plaintiff conceded lack of market harm for derivative works, "defendant had no obligation to present evidence to present evidence showing lack of harm"); Ringgold v. Black Entertainment Television, Inc., 126 F.3d 70, 81 (2nd Cir. 1997) ("In view of what Ringgold has averred is prepared to prove, the record on the fourth fair use factor is inadequate to permit summary judgment for the defendants."); Dr. Seuss Enter., L.P. v. Penguin Books USA, Inc., 109 F.3d 1394, 1403 (9th Cir. 1997)) (parties "must bring forward favorable evidence about relevant markets.").

[31] "Since fair use is an affirmative defense, its proponent would have difficulty carrying the burden of demonstrating fair use without favorable evidence about relevant markets." Campbell, 510 U.S. at 590, 114 S. Ct. at 1177. At the injunction stage, the burden remains in the party seeking restraint to demonstrate the likelihood of success on the merits. Thus, in a copyright infringement case, the copyright owner must demonstrate (after establishing copyright ownership and the taking of *original* elements), where a *prima facie* fair use defense is presented, that the fair use factors are insufficient to support such a defense. As a practical matter, the fair use proponent will anticipate its burden on the merits and counter with evidence to support its claim of fair use. That is often why district courts invoke Fed. R. Civ. P. 65(a)(2) to consolidate the trials of the action on the merits with the hearing on the application for preliminary injunction. The record in this case reflects that such a consolidation was not accomplished.

why Randall's book is unlikely to displace sales of GWTW.[32] Thus, we conclude, based on the current record, that SunTrust's evidence falls far short of establishing that TWDG or others like it will act as market substitutes for GWTW or will significantly harm its derivatives. Accordingly, the fourth fair use factor weighs in favor of TWDG.

c. Summary of the Merits

We reject the district court's conclusion that SunTrust has established its likelihood of success on the merits. To the contrary, based upon our analysis of the fair use factors we find, at this juncture, TWDG is entitled to a fair-use defense.

2. Irreparable Injury

The district court found that the second factor in the preliminary injunction analysis, irreparable injury to SunTrust, could be presumed following a showing of copyright infringement. SunTrust, 136 F. Supp. 2d at 1384 (citing Sony Corp., 464 U.S. at 451-52, 104 S. Ct. at 793). As we have previously indicated, however, the Supreme Court has made clear that there is no presumption of irreparable injury when the alleged infringer has a bona fide fair-use defense. Campbell, 510 U.S. at 578 n.10, 114 S. Ct. at 1171 n.10.

In evaluating irreparable injury we consider only the potential harm that the copyright holders of GWTW will suffer from the publication of TWDG itself. SunTrust argues that it has "incalculable millions of dollars riding on the appropriate cultivation of the [GWTW] franchise," but it has failed to show, at least at this early juncture in the case, how the publication of TWDG, a work that may have little to no appeal to the fans of GWTW who comprise the logical market for its authorized derivative works, will cause it irreparable injury. To the extent that SunTrust will suffer monetary harm from the infringement of its copyright, harms that may be remedied through the award of monetary damages are not considered "irreparable." Cunningham v. Adams, 808 F.2d 815, 821 (11th Cir. 1987).

Thus, a lack of irreparable injury to SunTrust, together with the First Amendment concerns regarding comment and criticism and the likelihood that a fair use defense will prevail, make injunctive relief improper and

---

[32] It is worth noting that in the several months since we lifted the injunction against publication of TWDG there have been sales of both GWTW and TWDG which may assist the district court in evaluating the economic harm fair use factor. The Court in Campbell did acknowledge that "even favorable evidence, without more, is no guarantee of fairness," and that the market harm factor, "no less than the other three, may be addressed only through a 'sensitive balancing of interests'" 510 U.S. at 590, n. 21, 114 S. Ct. at 1177, n. 21 (quoting Sony Corp., 464 U.S. at 455, n. 40, 104 S. Ct. 795, n. 40, 78 L. Ed. 2d 574). That the market harm factor may not always be a purely factual or evidentiary matter, however, does not mean that it is a purely legal matter. It is, like fair use generally, a mixed question of law and fact.

we need not address the remaining factors, except to stress that the public interest is always served in promoting First Amendment values and in preserving the public domain from encroachment. Siegel v. Lepore, 234 F.3d 1163, 1176 (11th Cir. 2000). Accordingly, we vacate the district court's injunction. We thereby substitute this opinion for our brief order issued on 25 May 2001, reported at 252 F.3d 1165 (11th Cir. 2001).

III. CONCLUSION

SunTrust initiated this action as one alleging copyright infringement and seeking monetary damages. SunTrust subsequently moved for a preliminary injunction to stay the publication of TWDG, which the district court granted. In granting the injunction, however, the district court incorrectly assessed the issues of "likelihood of success on the merits" and "irreparable harm" as discussed above. The Supreme Court has recognized that "the goals of copyright law, to stimulate the creation and publication of edifying matter, are not always best served by automatically granting injunctive relief when parodists are found to have gone beyond the bounds of fair use." Campbell, 510 U.S. at 578 n.10, 114 S. Ct. at 1171 n.10 (quotations omitted). The Court cited to an article by Judge Pierre Leval of the Second Circuit, in which he notes that injunctive relief is appropriate in "the vast majority of [copyright] cases" because "the infringements are simple piracy," but cautions that such cases are "worlds apart from many of those raising reasonable contentions of fair use where there may be a strong public interest in the publication of the secondary work and the copyright owner's interest may be adequately protected by an award of damages for whatever infringement is found." Id. (quoting Leval, Toward a Fair Use Standard, 103 HARV. L. REV. 1105, 1132 (1990)) (internal punctuation omitted).

In this case, we have found that to the extent SunTrust suffers injury from TWDG's putative infringement of its copyright in GWTW, such harm can adequately be remedied through an award of monetary damages. Moreover, under the present state of the record, it appears that a viable fair use defense is available. Thus, the issuance of the injunction was at odds with the shared principles of the First Amendment and the copyright law, acting as a prior restraint on speech because the public had not had access to Randall's ideas or viewpoint in the form of expression that she chose.

We **REVERSE** the judgment of the district court and **REMAND** the case for further proceedings consistent with this opinion.

MARCUS, Circuit Judge, specially concurring:

I concur in Judge Birch's thoughtful and thorough opinion but write separately to emphasize that, on this limited record, SunTrust has fallen well short of establishing a likelihood of success on its copyright infringement claim. I stress three points. First, the district court erred by finding that the critical or parodic element of The Wind Done Gone is anything but clear-cut. Far from amounting to "unabated piracy," 136 F. Supp. 2d

1357, 1369 (N.D. Ga. 2001), The Wind Done Gone is unequivocally parody, as both Judge Birch and the Supreme Court in Campbell v. Acuff-Rose Music, Inc., 510 U.S. 569, 127 L. Ed. 2d 500, 114 S. Ct. 1164 (1994), define that term. Indeed, the book is critical by constitution, its main aim being to shatter Gone With the Wind's window on life in the antebellum and Civil War South. Second, in service of this parodic design, Randall radically reshapes what she borrows from Mitchell. I would thus go even further than Judge Birch in underscoring the transformative nature of Randall's book; the "purpose and nature" prong of the fair use analysis is not a close call, in my view. Third, the preliminary record, if anything, suggests that The Wind Done Gone will not act as a substitute for Mitchell's original. What little evidence we have before us indicates that these two books aim at different readerships; to the extent that there is any overlap between these respective markets, further factfinding may well reveal that these two books will act as complements rather than substitutes. Moreover, the Mitchell estate seems to have made a specific practice of refusing to license just the sort of derivative use Randall has undertaken — a factor that further undermines SunTrust's copyright claim.

"'Parodies and caricatures . . . are the most penetrating of criticisms.'" Cardtoons, L.C. v. Major League Baseball Players Ass'n, 95 F.3d 959, 972 (10th Cir. 1996) (quoting Aldous Huxley, Point Counter Point, ch. 13 (1928)).[1] Parody has "long enjoyed a secure niche in the critical tradition, from Aristophanes' parodies of Aeschylus and Euripides to current lampoons of popular cartoon characters." II Paul Goldstein, Copyright § 10.2.1.2 (2001). As such, parody is "a vital commodity in the marketplace of ideas," Cardtoons, 95 F.3d at 972, that deserves "substantial freedom — both as entertainment and as a form of social and literary criticism," Berlin v. E. C. Pubs., Inc., 329 F.2d 541, 545 (2d Cir. 1964). When rendered in harmony with copyright law, parody enjoys "significant value as free speech under the First Amendment." Dr. Seuss Enterprises, L.P. v. Penguin Books USA, Inc., 109 F.3d 1394, 1400 (9th Cir. 1997).

The Wind Done Gone's critical nature is clearer than that of other works courts have found to be protected parodies. This case does not involve a pop song that simply "comments on the naivete of the original of an earlier day." Campbell, 510 U.S. at 583; see also Fisher v. Dees, 794 F.2d 432, 434 (9th Cir. 1986) (song entitled "When Sonny Sniffs Glue" was protected parody of "When Sunny Gets Blue"); Elsmere Music, Inc. v. National Broadcasting Co., Inc., 482 F. Supp. 741, 747 (S.D.N.Y.), aff'd, 623 F.2d 252 (2d Cir. 1980) (comedy sketch including song, "I Love Sodom," was protected parody of advertising jingle, "I Love New York"). It does not involve an

---

[1] Ernest Hemingway did not share Huxley's enthusiasm for the form: "The parody is the last refuge of the frustrated writer. Parodies are what you write when you are associate editor of the Harvard Lampoon. The greater the work of literature, the easier the parody. The step up from writing parodies is writing on the wall above the urinal." Paul Hirshson, "Names and Faces," The Boston Globe, July 22, 1989 at 7. Whatever parody's aesthetic value, copyright law has tended to agree with Huxley as to its social utility.

advertisement in which an actor apes a starlet's pose on a magazine cover. See Leibovitz v. Paramount Pictures Corp., 137 F.3d 109, 115 (2d Cir. 1998) ("'[A] ridiculous image of a smirking, foolish-looking pregnant'" Leslie Nielsen was a protected parody of a "'serious portrayal of a beautiful woman [Demi Moore] taking great pride in the majesty of her pregnant body.'").

Rather, we deal here with a book that seeks to rebut a classic novel's particular perspective on the Civil War and slavery.[2] This fact does not, of course, mean that we ought to grant Randall and Houghton Mifflin any special deference in making a fair use determination; the copyright laws apply equally to all expressive content, whether we might deem it of trifling import or utmost gravity. Cf. Bleistein v. Donaldson Lithographing Co., 188 U.S. 239, 251, 47 L. Ed. 460, 23 S. Ct. 298 (1903) (Holmes, J.) ("It would be a dangerous undertaking for persons trained only to the law to constitute themselves final judges of the worth of [a work], outside of the narrowest and most obvious limits. At the one extreme, some works of genius would be sure to miss appreciation. Their very novelty would make them repulsive until the public had learned the new language in which their author spoke."). The two books' shared subject matter simply helps demonstrate how The Wind Done Gone's critical character is more pronounced than many protected parodies. Our analysis might have been different had we faced a conflict between two literary worldviews of less perfect polarity, for example, or two works that differed over a matter of less sharp controversy. As Judge Birch explains in detail, though, The Wind Done Gone's plain object is to make war on Gone with the Wind's specific outlook — on a topic that itself tends to elicit no small comment and criticism.

In light of this, Appellee SunTrust's forecasts of a seismic shift in the publishing industry are premature and unfounded. First, our decision today does no more than explain our rationale for overturning the district court's grant of a preliminary injunction; while I am skeptical, for the reasons I explain here, that SunTrust will prevail below, I remind the parties that a full trial on the merits has yet to occur. Second, this opinion will not somehow compel courts to grant the fair use defense to every book that retells a copyrighted story from another character's point of view. Fair use adjudication requires case-by-case analysis and eschews bright-line rules. See Campbell, 510 U.S. at 577. After this case, as before it, only those works whose "parodic character may reasonably be perceived" and that survive the four-prong fair use analysis will be protected as parody. Id. at 582. Had Randall chosen to write The Wind Done Gone from the point of view of one of Mitchell's original characters, for example, and done no more than put a new gloss on the familiar tale without criticizing or commenting on its

---

[2] I need not expand upon Judge Birch's excellent explanation of the specific ways in which The Wind Done Gone criticizes or comments on aspects and characters of Gone With the Wind.

fundamental theme and spirit, Houghton Mifflin's case would have been much tougher.[3]

The Wind Done Gone's criticism of Gone With the Wind's substance is plain, but whether it parodies Mitchell's style is less clear. This does not weigh against Houghton Mifflin's parody defense, however, because a work need only exhibit "critical bearing on the substance or style of the original composition." Campbell, 510 U.S. at 580 (emphasis added). In any event, Randall's style is a marked departure from Mitchell's. The Wind Done Gone takes diary form; its chronology is disjunctive and its language often earthy. It is told from an introspective first-person point of view. Mitchell's story, by comparison, is a linear third-person narrative, epic in scope and staid in tone. Perhaps Randall based her story on the perceptions of a single character to underscore the inherent subjectivity of storytelling, in contrast to Mitchell's disembodied, "objective" narrator. To whatever extent it parodies Mitchell's authorial voice, Randall's narrative style furthers her overall parodic purpose by reinforcing the notion that The Wind Done Gone casts Gone With the Wind's story and characters in a new, and contrary, light.

The district court recognized that "the two works . . . present polar viewpoints," yet concluded that The Wind Done Gone recreates "the same fictional world, described in the same way and inhabited by the same people, who are doing the same things." 136 F. Supp. 2d at 1369. Of course, both works are set in the antebellum South, but The Wind Done Gone creates an alter universe described in a wholly different style, and inhabited by shrewd slaves who manipulate incompetent masters and free blacks who thrive independent of the white plantation system. Like a political, thematic, and stylistic negative, The Wind Done Gone inverts Gone With the Wind's portrait of race relations of the place and era.

Given this stark contrast, I would go further than Judge Birch in stressing the transformative nature of Randall's book. I agree with, and therefore will not echo, Judge Birch's analysis of the specific transformative uses Randall makes of elements of Gone With the Wind. I arrive, however,

---

[3] It is hazardous to speculate too much about the legality of various hypothetical parodies, given the many forms literary parody may take, and the levels of sophistication it may reach. See Margaret A. Rose, Parody: Ancient, Modern, and Post-Modern 36-38 (1993) (describing an array of parodic literary techniques and "signals"). The irony and self-awareness common in contemporary literature, in particular, may one day pose difficulties for the fair use doctrine. It is not hard to imagine a copyrighted story that parodies itself by design, or an author who makes a career out of parodying his own work in each subsequent one. (Vladimir Nabokov, among others, hinted at the potential for such practices. See, e.g., Vladimir Nabokov, Pale Fire (1962) (a novel consisting of a poem and substantial prose commentary on that poem).) Suppose that this hypothetical author in turn becomes the target of parody by another. Could the second author's work be said to usurp demand for the original author's self-parody? Here, we face a much simpler problem: Gone With the Wind lacks any apparent self-directed irony, and Randall's attack on it is just as straight-forward.

at a less qualified conclusion on the matter. Far from being "a double-edged sword" that only "militates in favor of a finding of fair use," the issue of transformation cuts decisively in Houghton Mifflin's favor, in my view. Even a cursory comparison of the two texts reveals that The Wind Done Gone profoundly alters what it borrows — indeed, at times beyond recognition. To catch some of Randall's allusions, even a reader familiar with Mitchell's work may need to refer to the original text. To create a successful parody, an author must keep certain elements constant while inverting or exaggerating other variables; "generally there is an incongruity between the borrowed and the new elements." Richard A. Posner, When Is Parody Fair Use? 21 J. Leg. Stud. 67, 68 (1992). In Randall's book, the ratio of the former to the latter is very low, and the incongruity between them wide.

Next, it is worth emphasizing that the limited record at this preliminary stage in no way supports the district court's finding that The Wind Done Gone might act as a market substitute for Gone with the Wind or its licensed derivatives. Turning to the affidavits submitted on behalf of Houghton Mifflin, one expert said that "The Wind Done Gone is unlikely to have any discernible effect on the market for sequels other than, possibly, through its criticism. . . . Audience members with a deep affection for Gone with the Wind are unlikely to be drawn to The Wind Done Gone, . . . [which] appeals to a distinctly contemporary sensibility for fresh, irreverent, realistic works of fiction that turn old ideas upside down." Another testified that The Wind Done Gone "will not appeal to any desire among readers for a sequel to Gone With the Wind . . . [because] the target audiences for the two books are . . . very different."

SunTrust's evidence for the contrary view is likewise incomplete. Experts submitted affidavits stating that The Wind Done Gone is a "parasitical work [that] has little merit [and] . . . exists solely to exploit Gone With the Wind," and that Randall's book would "seriously taint the original." One expert stressed "the need of the representatives of Margaret Mitchell's Gone With the Wind to protect the reputation" of their copyright. Another said that The Wind Done Gone will "capitalize on and thus benefit from the resulting notoriety that will accrue to it as the reading public makes the inevitable comparison to Gone With the Wind which has become and remains a popular classic since its publication." Still others reminded the district court that SunTrust has inked multi-million dollar deals for its licensed derivatives.

None of these statements provides any explanation or data regarding how Randall's book or others like it would act as substitutes for Gone With the Wind derivatives. "Capitalizing" on or "benefitting from . . . [a book's] notoriety" does not always amount to harmful substitution; if it did, no commercial parody, which by definition seeks to profit from another work's notoriety by mocking it, would be permitted. See Campbell, 510 U.S. at 584 (rejecting the notion that commercial uses are presumed unfair).

Furthermore, it is not copyright's job to "protect the reputation" of a work or guard it from "taint" in any sense except an economic one — specifically, where substitution occurs. See Campbell, 510 U.S. at 592 (describing the "distinction between potentially remediable displacement and unremediable disparagement"); Zacchini v. Scripps-Howard Broadcasting Co., 433 U.S. 562, 573, 53 L. Ed. 2d 965, 97 S. Ct. 2849 (1977) ("The goals of patent and copyright law . . . focus[] on the right of the individual to reap the reward of his endeavors and have little to do with protecting feelings or reputation."); Arnstein v. Porter, 154 F.2d 464, 473 (2d Cir. 1946) (stating that a copyright holder's "legally protected interest is not, as such, his reputation as a musician but his interest in the potential financial returns from his compositions which derive from the lay public's approbation of his efforts"); cf. Fisher, 794 F.2d at 440 (rejecting a copyright holder's claims of "defamation and disparagement" in the context of a parodic fair use). Since Randall's book seeks to upend Mitchell's view of the antebellum South, there is no great risk that readers will confuse it for part of Gone With the Wind's "ongoing saga." No one disputes that SunTrust's derivative rights are worth millions, but that fact tells nothing of how an anti-Gone With the Wind screed would act as a market substitute.

On remand, I believe the district court should remain mindful that "market harm" cannot be established simply by a showing that the original's sales have suffered or may do so. Rather, the market harm factor requires proof that The Wind Done Gone has usurped demand for Gone With the Wind, see Campbell, 510 U.S. at 592, or that widespread conduct of the sort engaged in by Randall[4] would harm SunTrust's derivative markets, see id. at 590. "If the secondary work harms the market for the original through criticism or parody, rather than by offering a market substitute for the original that supersedes it, 'it does not produce a harm cognizable under the Copyright Act.'" On Davis v. The Gap, Inc., 246 F.3d 152, 175 (2d Cir. 2001) (quoting Campbell, 510 U.S. at 592). "The role of the courts is to distinguish between biting criticism that merely suppresses demand and copyright infringement, which usurps [the market for the original]." Campbell, 510 U.S. at 592 (internal quotation marks omitted) (brackets omitted). In cases where it is "difficult to determine whence the harm flows . . . the other fair use factors may provide some indicia of the likely source of the harm. A work whose overriding purpose and character is parodic and whose borrowing is slight in relation to its parody will be far less likely to cause cognizable harm than a work with little parodic content and much copying." Id. at 593 n.24.

It is even possible that The Wind Done Gone will act as a complement to, rather than a substitute for, Gone With the Wind and its potential

---

[4] The fourth fair use factor "requires courts to consider not only the extent of market harm caused by the particular actions of the alleged infringer, but also 'whether unrestricted and widespread conduct of the sort engaged in by the defendant . . . would result in a substantially adverse impact on the potential market' for the original." Campbell, 510 U.S. at 590 (citation omitted). Here, "conduct of the sort engaged in by the defendant" would include only those parodies that make a similar frontal attack on Gone With the Wind and that, like Randall's book, radically transform elements borrowed from the original.

derivatives. Readers of Randall's book may want to refresh their recollections of the original.[5] It is not far-fetched to predict that sales of Gone With the Wind have grown since The Wind Done Gone's publication. A more fully developed record on the subject will no doubt aid the district court's analysis.

Finally, I wish to highlight a factor significant to the market harm inquiry: SunTrust's apparent practice of placing certain editorial restrictions on the authors of its licensed derivatives. Pat Conroy, the author of The Prince of Tides and Beach Music, among other novels, attested to the sorts of constraints the Mitchell estate sought to place on him as a potential author of a sequel to Gone With the Wind:

> I wrote an introduction to the sixtieth anniversary edition of [Gone With the Wind] . . . After the appearance of my introduction[,] which included my own deep appreciation for the artistry of GWTW, the estate of Margaret Mitchell contacted my agent, Julian Bach, in New York and asked if I would be interested in doing a sequel to GWTW . . . . When Julian Bach called me, he issued a strange decree from the estate that Julian said was non-negotiable . . . . He said, "You're not going to like this, but the estate will require you to sign a pledge that says you will under no circumstances write anything about miscegenation or homosexuality."[6]

In light of this, the The Wind Done Gone's transformation of Ashley Wilkes into a homosexual, its depiction of interracial sex, and its multiple mulatto characters take on additional relevance. The Supreme Court in Campbell explained how a copyright holder's reluctance to license certain kinds of derivatives affects the market harm analysis:

> The market for potential derivative uses includes only those that creators of original works would in general develop or license others to develop. Yet the unlikelihood that creators of imaginative works will license critical reviews or lampoons of their own productions removes such uses from the very notion of a potential licensing market.

510 U.S. at 592.

---

[5] As Jane Chelius attested: "It is easier to imagine a buyer of The Wind Done Gone wanting to read Gone With the Wind to find a reference point, than it is to imagine a reader who loved Gone With the Wind wanting to read a book such as The Wind Done Gone that parodies and puts it in a critical light."

[6] In a piece of documentary evidence submitted by SunTrust (Thomas Hal Clarke, attorney and member of the committee established by the trust instruments to direct the plaintiff SunTrust Bank), Conroy again indicates that the Mitchell Estate was loath to license a derivative work that contained such elements:

> All my resistance to your restrictions — all of them, and I include miscegenation, homosexuality, the rights of review and approval — I do because they begin inching toward the precincts of censorship.

Fax to Owen Laster from Pat Conroy, Nov. 10, 1998.

Other courts have echoed the principle that "'only traditional, reasonable, or likely to be developed markets'" ought to be considered when assessing the effect of a challenged use upon a potential market. Ringgold v. Black Entm't Television, Inc., 126 F.3d 70, 81 (2d Cir. 1997) (citation omitted); see also Nunez v. Caribbean Int'l News Corp., 235 F.3d 18, 25 (1st Cir. 2000); Infinity Broadcast Corp. v. Kirkwood, 150 F.3d 104, 111 (2d Cir. 1998). "In the cases where we have found the fourth factor to favor a defendant, the defendant's work filled a market niche that the plaintiff simply had no interest in occupying." Twin Peaks Prods., Inc. v. Publications Int'l, Ltd., 996 F.2d 1366, 1377 (2d Cir. 1993).

The preliminary record does not indicate why SunTrust sought to impose editorial restrictions on Conroy. To the extent that SunTrust may have done so to preserve Gone With the Wind's reputation, or protect its story from "taint," however, it may not now invoke copyright to further that goal. Of course, SunTrust can choose to license its derivatives however it wishes and insist that those derivatives remain free of content it deems disreputable. SunTrust may be vigilant of Gone With the Wind's public image — but it may not use copyright to shield Gone With the Wind from unwelcome comment, a policy that would extend intellectual property protection "into the precincts of censorship," in Pat Conroy's words. "Because the social good is served by increasing the supply of criticism — and thus, potentially, of truth — creators of original works cannot be given the power to block the dissemination of critical derivative works." Leibovitz, 137 F.3d at 115 n.3. "Copyright law is not designed to stifle critics. Destructive parodies play an important role in social and literary criticism and thus merit protection even though they may discourage or discredit an original author." Fisher, 794 F.2d at 438 (citation and internal quotation marks omitted).

The law grants copyright holders a powerful monopoly in their expressive works. It should not also afford them windfall damages for the publication of the sorts of works that they themselves would never publish, or worse, grant them a power of indirect censorship.

Finally, Appellee warns that our decision in this case will prompt an endless parade of litigants to test the boundaries of the rule we establish here. This is at least possible, but such a phenomenon is not exactly alien to our common law tradition. And to the extent authors and publishers will be encouraged to experiment with new and different forms of storytelling, copyright's fundamental purpose, "to promote the Progress of Science and useful Arts," will have been served. U.S. Const. Art. 1, § 8, cl. 8.

NOTES AND QUESTIONS

(1) How often does one see an opinion this concerned with copyright law's history and theory? Is the court's recitation of these materials helpful to your understanding of its ultimate holding in the case?

(2) In vacating the District Court's preliminary injunction as a prior restraint on the First Amendment, the Court of Appeals determined that

a viable fair use parody defense appeared to be available. In so holding, the court clearly took a broad view of parody fair use, one that avoids evaluating the quality of the work or the success of the attempted humor in discerning its parodic character. Thus, the work should be treated as a parody "if its aim is to comment upon or criticize a prior work by appropriating elements of the original in creating a new, artistic as opposed to scholarly or journalistic work." Moreover, a use does not necessarily become infringing the moment it does more than simply conjure up another work. Rather, a parody is unlawful only if it negatively affects the potential market for, or value of, the original copyrighted work.

In so holding, did the Eleventh Circuit enlarge the contours of "parody fair use"? The opinion suggests that proof of market harm is the key to the defense. How does one prove market harm in potential markets? What sort of evidence, ideally, would one proffer in showing potential market harm?

(3) Are there any limits to the holding in *Suntrust*? Would the Eleventh Circuit allow a fair use defense in a feminist retelling of a James Bond story through one of its female characters? After *SunTrust,* are all such sequels fair game for anyone showing a modicum of parodic intent?

(4) Suppose Alice Randall wishes to produce a "faithful" film version of *The Wind Done Gone.* Would she have, in effect, an automatic privilege to do so under the Eleventh Circuit's reasoning on parody fair use?

(5) Is *SunTrust* a clearer case parody fair use than *Campbell*? Harder?

§ 9.04 Fair Use and New Technologies[*]

USAGE: On page 867, ADD the following text after note (1):

(1A) Of course, as we saw in the discussion of the Ninth Circuit's *Napster* decision back in § 8.04 of this Part, *Sony*'s approach to defining the law/technology relationship recently has taken something of a beating. There, we concentrated on how the Court of Appeals construed the Supreme Court's conclusion that the provider of a technology with "substantial noninfringing uses" was insulated from indirect liability for copyright infringement. Here, we should focus for a moment on another issue: When are consumers employing technology to reproduce or distribute copyrighted works without authorization engaged in "fair" (and therefore noninfringing) uses?

Sony came out as it did, in part, because the Court identified even unauthorized "time-shifting" by VCR users (then, as now, the primary purpose to which the technology was being put) as "fair use." In reaching this conclusion the Court first embraced the District Court's reasoning and then added some observations of its own:

---

[*] **Updating Note re 2001 Reprint:** On page 867, in the second-to-last line of note (1), the reference should be to "contributory *infringement*" rather than contributory negligence.

. . . [T]he District Court restated its overall conclusion several times, in several different ways. "Harm from time-shifting is speculative and, at best, minimal." *480 F.Supp. at 467.* "The audience benefits from the time-shifting capability have already been discussed. It is not implausible that benefits could also accrue to plaintiffs, broadcasters, and advertisers, as the Betamax makes it possible for more persons to view their broadcasts." *Ibid.* "No likelihood of harm was shown at trial, and plaintiffs admitted that there had been no actual harm to date." *Id., at 468-469.* "Testimony at trial suggested that Betamax may require adjustments in marketing strategy, but it did not establish even a likelihood of harm." *Id., at 469.* "Television production by plaintiffs today is more profitable than it has ever been, and, in five weeks of trial, there was no concrete evidence to suggest that the Betamax will change the studios' financial picture." *Ibid.*

The District Court's conclusions are buttressed by the fact that to the extent time-shifting expands public access to freely broadcast television programs, it yields societal benefits. In *Community Television of Southern California v. Gottfried, 459 U.S. 498, 508, n. 12 (1983),* we acknowledged the public interest in making television broadcasting more available. Concededly, that interest is not unlimited. But it supports an interpretation of the concept of "fair use" that requires the copyright holder to demonstrate some likelihood of harm before he may condemn a private act of time-shifting as a violation of federal law. . . .

Congress has plainly instructed us that fair use analysis calls for a sensitive balancing of interests. The distinction between "productive" and "unproductive" uses may be helpful in calibrating the balance, but it cannot be wholly determinative. Although copying to promote a scholarly endeavor certainly has a stronger claim to fair use than copying to avoid interrupting a poker game, the question is not simply two-dimensional. For one thing, it is not true that all copyrights are fungible. Some copyrights govern material with broad potential secondary markets. Such material may well have a broader claim to protection because of the greater potential for commercial harm. Copying a news broadcast may have a stronger claim to fair use than copying a motion picture. And, of course, not all uses are fungible. Copying for commercial gain has a much weaker claim to fair use than copying for personal enrichment. But the notion of social "productivity" cannot be a complete answer to this analysis. A teacher who copies to prepare lecture notes is clearly productive. But so is a teacher who copies for the sake of broadening his personal understanding of his specialty. Or a legislator who copies for the sake of broadening her understanding of what her constituents are watching; or a constituent who copies a news program to help make a decision on how to vote.

464 U.S. at 454-55.

In other words (or so many commentators have suggested), "personal uses" of copyrighted materials deserve special solicitude in judicial "fair use" analysis.

If that is the proper reading of *Sony,* one might ask why the Ninth Circuit treated so unsympathetically Napster's assertions that its users were engaged in "fair use." Or can the so-called "personal use" doctrine be overstated?

(1B) From the perspective of 2002, the foregoing passages from *Sony* raise two general sets of issues. First, as we saw in *Napster,* there are questions about how the principles that *Sony* announced should be extended beyond the original context of that decision. Second, there are concerns about the continued vitality of the *Sony* approach even in that original context. In late 2001, 28 entertainment industry companies filed suit in Los Angeles Federal District Court against Sonicblue in connection with its ReplayTV 4000 digital video recorder, a model that gives consumers the capabilities to delete commercials from recorded programs automatically and to send recorded programs to other Replay4000 owners over the Internet. The lawsuit is still in its early procedural phases, although there have been some interesting developments: on May 15, for example, Judge Florence-Marie Cooper stayed a Magistrate Judge's earlier order directing Sonicblue to monitor and report on the use of the equipment by home users. *See* Richard Shim, *Sonicblue Granted Stay in "Spying" Order*, C/NET News.Com, May 15, 2002, at *http://news.com.com/2100-1040-914370.html?tag=fd_top*. As this supplement goes to press, it has just been reported that the order has been overturned on the basis that it would have imposed excessive burdens on the defendant, given that the same information could be provided by the use of a survey. *See* Joyzelle Davis, *Studios Lose Court Skirmish; TV-Recorder Maker Doesn't Have to Collect Data on Viewers*, Washington Post, June 1, 2002, at p. E2. Eventually, though, the case is almost certain to confront the meaning of *Sony*.

(1C) Back in § 7.04[C] of this Part, we made mention of *UMG Recordings, Inc. v. MP3.com, Inc.,* 92 F. Supp. 2d 349 (S.D.N.Y. 2000). There, the defendant company defended (in part) on the ground that it was merely facilitating 'space-shifting" by music consumers who had lawfully acquired copies of sound records — allowing them, for example, to listen to "their music" at the office while leaving their CD collections at home. This defense did not go far. Why? What real harm could the recording companies have alleged? Or is the problem one of "standing" to assert a "fair use" defense? Remember that the defendant company was alleged to have engaged in massive direct infringement, not contributory or vicarious infringement. You may want to revisit your answer to this question after you have considered the *Michigan Document* opinions in § 9.05 of the casebook.

USAGE: On page 868, CONSIDER the following recent development after note (7):

"Second generation" reverse engineering questions after Sega. Although *Sega* clearly established that reverse engineering of software would qualify as fair use under certain circumstances, the decision left several questions unanswered. *Sega* seemed to indicate that reverse engineering would be considered fair use only to the extent that it was necessary to identify and understand the unprotected elements of a copyrighted software program. The court, however, gave no guidance as to how literally this requirement was to be interpreted. The problem is that reverse engineering frequently is imprecise and may involve false starts and blind alleys. Would such acts be considered "strictly necessary" to the analysis of a competitor's software? In addition, what about the situation where alternative methods of analysis are available? Would the fair use defense apply only to the method which entailed the least amount of copying? And what if, during the reverse engineering process, some or all of the original program is used to test the validity of the information obtained to that point? Would such use still constitute fair use?

In *Sony Computer Entertainment, Inc. v. Connectix Corp.,* 203 F.3d 596 (9th Cir. 2000) (overruling the District Court opinion cited in the casebook at pages 769, 870 and 932), the Ninth Circuit read *Sega* expansively, permitting extensive intermediate copying in the reverse engineering context even where other, more limited methods existed for gaining access to plaintiff's unprotectible ideas. The court held that once the necessity of the defendant's method was established, the number of times that method was applied was not relevant. Because the defendant in *Connectix* had to make one copy of the Sony code to study it, it was permitted to make and use hundreds of subsequent copies to make the disassembly process more expedient. In addition, the court held that the new game platform was transformative because the defendant created its own new expression rather than just repackaging the plaintiff's code. It remains to be seen how all of this will "shake out" as more courts weigh in on how broadly to construe the privilege in the reverse engineering context.

USAGE: On page 871, ADD the following text after note (9):

(9A) A new kind of technological challenge to the "fair use" doctrine is posed by certain capabilities of the Internet (and, in particular, the World Wide Web). Back in § 7.07 of this Part, we introduced the facts of *Kelly v. Arriba Soft Corp.,* 280 F.3d 934 (9th Cir. 2002), involving a defendant who trawled the web for photographic images using a automated robotic program and then posted the results on its own websites. The images appeared on the site as "thumbnails," but also could be viewed in enlarged form by visitors to the site, along with links back to their originated websites. The case raised issues under the copyright management information provisions of § 1202, but on appeal it was decided primarily on other grounds, the court concluding that defendant's postings of the plaintiff's copyrighted images constituted "fair use." The Court of Appeals' opinion in excerpted in § 9.06.

§ 9.06   Fair Use and Copyright Policy

[A]   The Role of Guidelines

USAGE: On page 895, SUBSTITUTE the following text for footnote 4:

Examples include the new policy of Indiana University, available at *http://www.iupui.edu/%7Ecopyinfo/fupolicy.html*, and that adopted by the Regents of the University of Georgia, at *www.peachnet.edu/admin/legal/copyright/copy.html*.

USAGE: On page 902, SUBSTITUTE the following text for the three full paragraphs immediately preceding subsection [C]:

As we know from § 7.07 of this Part, however, the first round of rule-making produced few results that might benefit general information consumers — in part because some of the technologies of greatest concern have yet to be generally implemented. What resort, then, will there be for the individual user who finds himself or herself shut out by TPMs during the course of the next three years? Assuming that this individual has the technological know-how to break through the digital fence — a necessary assumption, given the effective bar on aiding and abetting circumvention imposed by §§ 1201(a)(2) and (b) — what defense will be available if he or she chooses to do so? Will it be possible to argue that, after all, old-fashioned § 107-type "fair use" *does* apply in the realm of "paracopyright"? For good or ill, the DMCA and its legislative history seem to close the door to this escape route all too firmly. The prospect remains, then, that courts will be called upon to invent a new exceptional doctrine (as, once upon a time, they invented "fair use"), rooted in constitutional values of free expression and specifically applicable to "paracopyright." *See* David Nimmer, *A Riff on Fair Use in the Digital Millennium Copyright Act*, 148 U. Pa. L. Rev. 673 (2000).

For ultimately the question is how best to achieve, in the face of the combined effect of technological safeguards, broad-brush legal sanctions against circumvention and network-based distribution of copyrighted works, a satisfactory successor regime to the carefully designed balance of owners' rights and users' privileges that historically was woven through the law of copyright itself.

KELLY v. ARRIBA SOFT CORP.

United States Court of Appeals, Ninth Circuit
280 F.3d 934 (2002)

T.G. NELSON, Circuit Judge:

This case involves the application of copyright law to the vast world of the internet and internet search engines. The plaintiff, Leslie Kelly, is a professional photographer who has copyrighted many of his images of the American West. Some of these images are located on Kelly's web site or other web sites with which Kelly has a license agreement. The defendant, Arriba Soft Corp., operates an internet search engine that displays its results in the form of small pictures rather than the more usual form of text. Arriba obtained its database of pictures by copying images from other web sites. By clicking on one of these small pictures, called "thumbnails," the user can then view a large version of that same picture within the context of the Arriba web page.

When Kelly discovered that his photographs were part of Arriba's search engine database, he brought a claim against Arriba for copyright infringement. The district court found that Kelly had established a prima facie case of copyright infringement based on Arriba's unauthorized reproduction and display of Kelly's works, but that this reproduction and display constituted a non-infringing "fair use "under Section 107 of the Copyright Act. Kelly appeals that decision, and we affirm in part and reverse in part. The creation and use of the thumbnails in the search engine is a fair use, but the display of the larger image is a violation of Kelly's exclusive right to publicly display his works. We remand with instructions to determine damages and the need for an injunction.

I.

The search engine at issue in this case is unconventional in that it displays the results of a user's query as" thumbnail" images. When a user wants to search the internet for information on a certain topic, he or she types a search term into a search engine, which then produces a list of web sites that have information relating to the search term. Normally, the list of results is in text format. The Arriba search engine, however, produces its list of results as small pictures.

To provide this functionality, Arriba developed a computer program that "crawls" the web looking for images to index. This crawler downloads full-sized copies of the images onto Arriba's server. The program then uses these copies to generate smaller, lower-resolution thumbnails of the images. Once the thumbnails are created, the program deletes the full-sized originals from the server. Although a user could copy these thumbnails to his computer or disk, he cannot increase the resolution of the thumbnail; any enlargement would result in a loss of clarity of the image.

The second component of the Arriba program occurs when the user double-clicks on the thumbnail. From January 1999 to June 1999, clicking on the thumbnail produced the" Images Attributes" page. This page contained the original full-sized image imported directly from the originating web site, along with text describing the size of the image, a link to the originating web site, the Arriba banner, and Arriba advertising. The process of importing an image from another web site is called inline linking. The image imported from another web site is displayed as though it is part of the current web page, surrounded by the current web page's text and advertising. As a result, although the image in Arriba's Image Attributes page was directly from the originating web site, and not copied onto Arriba's site, the user typically would not realize that the image actually resided on another web site.

From July 1999 until sometime after August 2000, the results page contained thumbnails accompanied by two links: "Source" and "Details." The "Details "link produced a screen similar to the Images Attributes page but with a thumbnail rather than the full-sized image. Alternatively, by clicking on the "Source" link or the thumbnail from the results page, the site produced two new windows on top of the Arriba page. The window in the forefront contained the full-sized image, imported directly from the originating web site. Underneath that was another window displaying the originating web page. This technique is known as framing. The image from a second web site is viewed within a frame that is pulled into the primary site's web page.[2]

In January 1999, Arriba's crawler visited web sites that contained Kelly's photographs. The crawler copied thirty-five of Kelly's images to the Arriba database. Kelly had never given permission to Arriba to copy his images and objected when he found out that Arriba was using them. Arriba deleted the thumbnails of images that came from Kelly's own web sites and placed those sites on a list of sites that it would not crawl in the future. Several months later, Arriba received Kelly's complaint of copyright infringement, which identified other images of his that came from third-party web sites. Arriba subsequently deleted those thumbnails and placed those third-party sites on a list of sites that it would not crawl in the future.

The district court granted summary judgment in favor of Arriba. Although the court found that Kelly had established a prima facie case of infringement based on Arriba's reproduction and display of Kelly's photographs, the court ruled that such actions by Arriba constituted fair use. The court determined that two of the fair use factors weighed heavily in Arriba's favor. Specifically, the court found that the character and purpose of Arriba's use was significantly transformative and the use did not harm the market for or value of Kelly's works. Kelly now appeals this decision.

II.

We review a grant of summary judgment de novo. We also review the court's finding of fair use, which is a mixed question of law and fact, by this same standard. "In doing so, we must balance the nonexclusive factors set out in *17 U.S.C. § 107*."[5]

This case involves two distinct actions by Arriba that warrant analysis. The first action consists of the reproduction of Kelly's images to create the thumbnails and the use of those thumbnails in Arriba's search engine. The second action involves the display of Kelly's images through the inline linking and framing processes when the user clicks on the thumbnails. Because these actions are distinct types of potential infringement, we will analyze them separately.

---

[2] Currently, when a user clicks on the thumbnail, a window of the home page of the image appears on top of the Arriba page. There is no window with just the image.

[5] *Los Angeles News Serv. v. Reuters Television Int'l. Ltd., 149 F.3d 987, 993 (9th Cir. 1998).*

A.

An owner of a copyright has the exclusive right to reproduce, distribute, and publicly display copies of the work. To establish a claim of copyright infringement by reproduction, the plaintiff must show ownership of the copyright and copying by the defendant. As to the thumbnails, there is no dispute that Kelly owned the copyright to the images and that Arriba copied those images. Therefore, Kelly established a prima facie case of copyright infringement.

A claim of copyright infringement is subject to certain statutory exceptions, including the fair use exception. This exception "permits courts to avoid rigid application of the copyright statute when, on occasion, it would stifle the very creativity which that law is designed to foster."[9] The statute sets out four factors to consider in determining whether the use in a particular case is a fair use. We must balance these factors, in light of the objectives of copyright law, rather than view them as definitive or determinative tests. We now turn to the four fair use factors.

1. Purpose and character of the use.

The Supreme Court has rejected the proposition that a commercial use of the copyrighted material ends the inquiry under this factor. Instead,

> the central purpose of this investigation is to see . . . whether the new work merely supersede[s]the objects of the original creation, or instead adds something new, with a further purpose or different character, altering the first with new expression, meaning, or message; it asks, in other words, whether and to what extent the new work is transformative.[13]

The more transformative the new work, the less important the other factors, including commercialism, become.

There is no dispute that Arriba operates its web site for commercial purposes and that Kelly's images were part of Arriba's search engine database. As the district court found, while such use of Kelly's images was commercial, it was more incidental and less exploitative in nature than more traditional types of commercial use.[15] Arriba was neither using Kelly's images to directly promote its web site nor trying to profit by selling Kelly's images. Instead, Kelly's images were among thousands of images in Arriba's search engine database. Because the use of Kelly's images was

---

[9] *Dr. Seuss Enters., L.P. v. Penguin Books USA, Inc., 109 F.3d 1394, 1399 (9th Cir. 1997)* (internal quotation marks and citation omitted).

[13] *Campbell v. Acuff-Rose Music, Inc., 510 U.S. 569, 579 (1994)* (internal quotation marks and citation omitted) (alteration in original).

[15] See, e.g., *A&M Records, Inc. v. Napster, Inc., 239 F.3d 1004, 1015 (9th Cir. 2001)* ("Commercial use is demonstrated by a showing that repeated and exploitative unauthorized copies of copyrighted works were made to save the expense of purchasing authorized copies.").

not highly exploitative, the commercial nature of the use only slightly weighs against a finding of fair use.

The second part of the inquiry as to this factor involves the transformative nature of the use. We must determine if Arriba's use of the images merely superseded the object of the originals or instead added a further purpose or different character. We find that Arriba's use of Kelly's images for its thumbnails was transformative.

Despite the fact that Arriba made exact replications of Kelly's images, the thumbnails were much smaller, lower-resolution images that served an entirely different function than Kelly's original images. Kelly's images are artistic works used for illustrative purposes. His images are used to portray scenes from the American West in an esthetic manner. Arriba's use of Kelly's images in the thumbnails is unrelated to any esthetic purpose. Arriba's search engine functions as a tool to help index and improve access to images on the internet and their related web sites. In fact, users are unlikely to enlarge the thumbnails and use them for artistic purposes because the thumbnails are of much lower resolution than the originals; any enlargement results in a significant loss of clarity of the image, making them inappropriate as display material.

Kelly asserts that because Arriba reproduced his exact images and added nothing to them, Arriba's use cannot be transformative. It is true that courts have been reluctant to find fair use when an original work is merely retransmitted in a different medium.[17] Those cases are inapposite, however, because the resulting use of the copyrighted work in those cases was the same as the original use. For instance, reproducing music CD's into computer MP3 format does not change the fact that both formats are used for entertainment purposes. Likewise, reproducing news footage into a different format does not change the ultimate purpose of informing the public about current affairs. . . .

This case involves more than merely a retransmission of Kelly's images in a different medium. . . . Because Arriba's use is not superseding Kelly's use but, rather, has created a different purpose for the images, Arriba's use is transformative.

Comparing this case to . . . recent cases in the Ninth and First Circuits reemphasizes the functionality distinction. . . .

. . . In Nunez v. Caribbean International News Corp., the First Circuit found that copying a photograph that was intended to be used in a modeling portfolio and using it instead in a news article was a transformative use. n23 By putting a copy of the photograph in the newspaper, the work was

---

[17] See *Infinity Broad. Corp. v. Kirkwood, 150 F.3d 104, 108 (2d Cir. 1998)* (concluding that retransmission of radio broadcast over telephone lines is not transformative); *UMG Recordings, Inc. v. MP3.com, Inc., 92 F. Supp. 2d 349, 351 (S.D.N.Y. 2000)* (finding that reproduction of audio CD into computer MP3 format does not transform the work); *Los Angeles News Serv., 149 F.3d at 993* (finding that reproducing news footage without editing the footage was not very transformative).

transformed into news, creating a new meaning or purpose for the work. The use of Kelly's images in Arriba's search engine is more analogous to the situation in Nunez because Arriba has created a new purpose for the images and is not simply superseding Kelly's purpose.

The Copyright Act was intended to promote creativity, thereby benefitting the artist and the public alike. To preserve the potential future use of artistic works for purposes of teaching, research, criticism, and news reporting, Congress made the fair use exception. Arriba's use of Kelly's images promotes the goals of the Copyright Act and the fair use exception. The thumbnails do not stifle artistic creativity because they are not used for illustrative or artistic purposes and therefore do not supplant the need for the originals. In addition, they benefit the public by enhancing information gathering techniques on the internet.

In Sony Computer Entertainment America, Inc. v. Bleem, we held that when Bleem copied "screen shots" from Sony computer games and used them in its own advertising, it was a fair use. In finding that the first factor weighed in favor of Bleem, we noted that "comparative advertising redounds greatly to the purchasing public's benefit with very little corresponding loss to the integrity of Sony's copyrighted material."[27] Similarly, this first factor weighs in favor of Arriba due to the public benefit of the search engine and the minimal loss of integrity to Kelly's images.

2. Nature of the copyrighted work.

"Works that are creative in nature are closer to the core of intended copyright protection than are more fact-based works."[28] Photographs used for illustrative purposes, such as Kelly's, are generally creative in nature. The fact that a work is published or unpublished also is a critical element of its nature. Published works are more likely to qualify as fair use because the first appearance of the artist's expression has already occurred.[30] Kelly's images appeared on the internet before Arriba used them in its search image. When considering both of these elements, we find that this factor only slightly weighs in favor of Kelly.

3. Amount and substantiality of portion used.

"While wholesale copying does not preclude fair use per se, copying an entire work militates against a finding of fair use."[31] However, the extent of permissible copying varies with the purpose and character of the use.

---

[27] Sony Computer Entertainment America, Inc. v. Bleem, 214 F.3d 1022, 1027 (9th Cir. 2000).

[28] A&M Records, 239 F.3d at 1016 (citing Campbell, 510 U.S. at 586) (internal quotation marks omitted).

[30] Harper & Row Publishers, Inc. v. Nation Enters., 471 U.S. 539, 564 (1985).

[31] Worldwide Church of God v. Philadelphia Church of God, 227 F.3d 1110, 1118 (9th Cir. 2000) (internal quotation marks and citation omitted).

If the secondary user only copies as much as is necessary for his or her intended use, then this factor will not weigh against him or her.

This factor will neither weigh for nor against either party because, although Arriba did copy each of Kelly's images as a whole, it was reasonable to do so in light of Arriba's use of the images. It was necessary for Arriba to copy the entire image to allow users to recognize the image and decide whether to pursue more information about the image or the originating web site. If Arriba only copied part of the image, it would be more difficult to identify it, thereby reducing the usefulness of the visual search engine.

4. Effect of the use upon the potential market for or value of the copyrighted work.

This last factor requires courts to consider "not only the extent of market harm caused by the particular actions of the alleged infringer, but also 'whether unrestricted and widespread conduct of the sort engaged in by the defendant . . . would result in a substantially adverse impact on the potential market for the original.'"[33] A transformative work is less likely to have an adverse impact on the market of the original than a work that merely supersedes the copyrighted work.

Kelly's images are related to several potential markets. One purpose of the photographs is to attract internet users to his web site, where he sells advertising space as well as books and travel packages. In addition, Kelly could sell or license his photographs to other web sites or to a stock photo database, which then could offer the images to its customers.

Arriba's use of Kelly's images in its thumbnails does not harm the market for Kelly's images or the value of his images. By showing the thumbnails on its results page when users entered terms related to Kelly's images, the search engine would guide users to Kelly's web site rather than away from it. Even if users were more interested in the image itself rather than the information on the web page, they would still have to go to Kelly's site to see the full-sized image. The thumbnails would not be a substitute for the full-sized images because when the thumbnails are enlarged, they lose their clarity. . . .[35] . . .

Arriba's use of Kelly's images also would not harm Kelly's ability to sell or license his full-sized images. Arriba does not sell or license its thumbnails

---

[33] *Campbell, 510 U.S. at 590* (quoting 3 M. Nimmer & D. Nimmer, Nimmer on Copyright § 13.05[A][4], at 13-102.61 (1993)) (ellipses in original).

[35] We do not suggest that the inferior display quality of a reproduction is in any way dispositive, or will always assist an alleged infringer in demonstrating fair use. In this case, however, it is extremely unlikely that users would download thumbnails for display purposes, as the quality full-size versions are easily accessible from Kelly's web sites.

In addition, we note that in the unique context of photographic images, the quality of the reproduction may matter more than in other fields of creative endeavor. The appearance of photographic images accounts for virtually their entire esthetic value.

to other parties. Anyone who downloaded the thumbnails would not be successful selling the full-sized images because of the low-resolution of the thumbnails. . . . Therefore, Arriba's creation and use of the thumbnails does not harm the market for or value of Kelly's images. This factor weighs in favor of Arriba.

Having considered the four fair use factors and found that two weigh in favor of Arriba, one is neutral, and one weighs slightly in favor of Kelly, we conclude that Arriba's use of Kelly's images as thumbnails in its search engine is a fair use.

B.

The second part of our analysis concerns Arriba's inline linking to and framing of Kelly's full-sized images. This use of Kelly's images does not entail copying them but, rather, importing them directly from Kelly's web site. Therefore, it cannot be copyright infringement based on the reproduction of copyrighted works as in the previous discussion. Instead, this use of Kelly's images infringes upon Kelly's exclusive right to "display the copyrighted work publicly."

1. Public display right.

In order for Kelly to prevail, Arriba must have displayed Kelly's work without his permission and made that display available to the public. . . . The legislative history of the Act makes clear that "since 'copies' are defined as including the material object 'in which the work is first fixed,' the right of public display applies to original works of art as well as to reproductions of them."[39] By inline linking and framing Kelly's images, Arriba is showing Kelly's original works without his permission.

The legislative history goes on to state that "'display' would include the projection of an image on a screen or other surface by any method, the transmission of an image by electronic or other means, and the showing of an image on a cathode ray tube, or similar viewing apparatus connected with any sort of information storage and retrieval system." This language indicates that showing Kelly's images on a computer screen would constitute a display.

The Act's definition of the term" publicly" encompasses a transmission of a display of a work to the public "by means of any device or process, whether the members of the public capable of receiving the performance or display receive it in the same place or in separate places and at the same time or at different times."[41] A display is public even if there is no proof that any of the potential recipients was operating his receiving apparatus at the time of the transmission.[42] By making Kelly's images available on

---

[39] H.R. Rep. No. 94-1476, at 64 (1976), reprinted in 1976 U.S.C.C.A.N. 5659, 5677.

[41] *17 U.S.C. § 101.*

[42] H.R. Rep. No. 94-1476, at 64-65 (1976), reprinted in 1976 U.S.C.C.A.N. 5659, 5678.

its web site, Arriba is allowing public access to those images. The ability to view those images is unrestricted to anyone with a computer and internet access.

. . . Looking strictly at the language of the Act and its legislative history, it appears that when Arriba imports Kelly's images into its own web page, Arriba is infringing upon Kelly's public display right. The limited case law in this area supports this conclusion.

No cases have addressed the issue of whether inline linking or framing violates a copyright owner's public display rights. However, in Playboy Enterprises, Inc. v. Webbworld, Inc., the court found that the owner of an internet site . . . violated Playboy's exclusive right to display its copyrighted works, noting that allowing subscribers to view copyrighted works on their computer monitors while online was a display.[47]

Although Arriba does not download Kelly's images to its own server but, rather, imports them directly from other web sites, the situation is analogous to Webbworld. By allowing the public to view Kelly's copyrighted works while visiting Arriba's web site, Arriba created a public display of Kelly'sworks. . . . Allowing this capability is enough to establish an infringement; the fact that no one saw the images goes to the issue of damages, not liability.

In a similar case, Playboy Enterprises, Inc. v. Russ Hardenburgh, Inc., the court held that the owner of an electronic bulletin board system infringed Playboy's copyrights by displaying copyrighted images on its system.[50] . . . Again, the court noted that adopting a policy that allowed the defendants to place images in files available to subscribers entailed a display.[53] This conclusion indicates that it was irrelevant whether anyone actually saw the images.

Both of these cases highlighted the fact that the defendants took an active role in creating the display of the copyrighted images. The reason for this emphasis is that several other cases held that operators of bulletin board systems and internet access providers were not liable for copyright infringement.[54] These cases distinguished direct infringement from contributory infringement and held that where the defendants did not take any affirmative action that resulted in copying copyrighted works, but only maintained a system that acted as a passive conduit for third parties' copies, they were not liable for direct infringement. . . .

---

[47] *Playboy Enterprises, Inc. v. Webbworld, Inc., 991 F. Supp. 543, 552 (N.D. Texas 1997).*

[50] *Playboy Enterprises, Inc. v. Russ Hardenburgh, Inc., 982 F. Supp. at 513 (N.D. Ohio 1997).*

[53] *Id.*

[54] See, e.g., *Religious Tech. Ctr. v. Netcom On-Line Communication Servs., Inc., 907 F. Supp. 1361, 1372-73 (N.D. Cal. 1995)* . . .; *Costar Group, Inc. v. Loopnet, Inc., 164 F. Supp. 2d 688, 695-96 (D. Md. 2001)* . . .

Like the defendants in Webbworld and Hardenburgh, Arriba is directly liable for infringement. Arriba actively participated in displaying Kelly's images by trolling the web, finding Kelly's images, and then having its program inline link and frame those images within its own web site. Without this program, users would not have been able to view Kelly's images within the context of Arriba's site. Arriba acted as more than a passive conduit of the images by establishing a direct link to the copyrighted images. Therefore, Arriba is liable for publicly displaying Kelly's copyrighted images without his permission.

2. Fair use of full-sized images.

The last issue we must address is whether Arriba's display of Kelly's full-sized images was a fair use. Although Arriba did not address the use of the full-sized images in its fair use argument, the district court considered such use in its analysis, and we will consider Arriba's fair use defense here.

Once again, to decide whom the first factor, the purpose and character of the use, favors, we must determine whether Arriba's use of Kelly's images was transformative.[58] Unlike the use of the images for the thumbnails, displaying Kelly's full-sized images does not enhance Arriba's search engine. The images do not act as a means to access other information on the internet but, rather, are likely the end product themselves. Although users of the search engine could link from the full-sized image to Kelly's web site, any user who is solely searching for images would not need to do so. Because the full-sized images on Arriba's site act primarily as illustrations or artistic expression and the search engine would function the same without them, they do not have a purpose different from Kelly's use of them.

Not only is the purpose the same, but Arriba did not add new expression to the images to make them transformative. Placing the images in a "frame" or locating them near text that specifies the size and originating web site is not enough to create new expression or meaning for the images. In sum, Arriba's full-sized images superseded the object of Kelly's images. Because Arriba has not changed the purpose or character of the use of the images, the first factor favors Kelly.

The analysis of the second factor, the nature of the copyrighted work, is the same as in the previous fair use discussion because Kelly's images are still the copyrighted images at issue. Therefore, as before, this factor slightly weighs in favor of Kelly.

The third fair use factor turns on the amount of the work displayed and the reasonableness of this amount in light of the purpose for the display. Arriba displayed the full images, which cuts against a finding of fair use. And while it was necessary to provide whole images to suit Arriba's purpose of giving users access to the full-sized images without having to go to another site, such a purpose is not legitimate, as we noted above. Therefore,

---

[58] See *Campbell*, 510 U.S. at 579.

it was not reasonable to copy the full-sized display. The third factor favors Kelly.

The fourth factor often depends upon how transformative the new use is compared to the original use. A work that is very transformative will often be in a different market from the original work and therefore is less likely to cause harm to the original work's market. Works that are not transformative, however, have the same purpose as the original work and will often have a negative effect on the original work's market.

As discussed in the previous fair use analysis, Kelly's markets for his images include using them to attract advertisers and buyers to his web site, and selling or licensing the images to other web sites or stock photo databases. By giving users access to Kelly's full-sized images on its own web site, Arriba harms all of Kelly's markets. Users will no longer have to go to Kelly's web site to see the full-sized images, thereby deterring people from visiting his web site. In addition, users would be able to download the full-sized images from Arriba's site and then sell or license those images themselves, reducing Kelly's opportunity to sell or license his own images. If the display of Kelly's images became widespread across other web sites, it would reduce the number of visitors to Kelly's web site even further and increase the chance of others exploiting his images. These actions would result in substantial adverse effects to the potential markets for Kelly's original works. For this reason, the fourth factor weighs heavily in favor of Kelly.

In conclusion, all of the fair use factors weigh in favor of Kelly. Therefore, the doctrine of fair use does not sanction Arriba's display of Kelly's images through the inline linking or framing processes that puts Kelly's original images within the context of Arriba's web site.

CONCLUSION

We hold that Arriba's reproduction of Kelly's images for use as thumbnails in Arriba's search engine is a fair use under the Copyright Act. We also hold that Arriba's display of Kelly's full-sized images is not a fair use and thus violates Kelly's exclusive right to publicly display his copyrighted works. The district court's opinion is affirmed as to the thumbnails and reversed as to the display of the full-sized images. We remand with instructions to determine damages for the copyright infringement and the necessity for an injunction. Each party shall bear its own costs and fees on appeal.

AFFIRMED in part, REVERSED in part, and REMANDED.

NOTES AND QUESTIONS

(1) What exclusive right or rights did Arriba Soft arguably violate? Were the violations direct or indirect? Do the answers of either of these questions matter, so far as the outcome is concerned?

(2) Is the portion of its reasoning that deals with the "fair use" and "thumbnails" as non-controversial as the Court of Appeals seems to think? How novel — and how compelling — is the vision of "transformativeness" that it adopts?

(3) How, exactly, does the court define the practice of "in-line" linking? Does it matter? Or is the reasoning of the second part of its opinion applicable to all hyperlinks?

(4) Footnote 2 in Judge Nelson's opinion reproduced above describes the linking practices of Arriba Soft at the time the case was decided. Obviously, those practices were not before the court. But suppose they had been? Would the analysis of linking as fair use have been the same?

(5) In denying Arriba Soft's "fair use" defense with regard to linking, the opinion notes with reference to the fourth factor that "Kelly's markets for his images include using them to attract advertisers and buyers to his web site, and selling or licensing the images to other web sites or stock photo databases." It is the former, "promotional" market that appears to be most seriously compromised (at least potentially) by the challenging hyperlinking. But is this really a "market" at all, in the sense that the term is used in § 107(4)? Or does that factor, properly understood, direct courts to inquire only whether the alleged infringements actually supercede sales or licenses for the works in question? Are you aware of any precedent for the Court of Appeals' broad understanding of the fourth factor? Is it bolstered by the statute's reference to "the potential market for *or value of* the copyrighted work." Or is the term "value" just verbiage, intended to clarify but not to modify the market focus? The legislative history of the provision might tell an interesting tale on this point.

(6) The question just suggested is raised poignantly in *Video Pipeline, Inc. v. Buena Vista Home Entertainment, Inc.,* 192 F.Supp. 2d 321 (E.D. Pa. 2002) (preliminary injunction granted). The defendant company is in the business of providing Internet sites that rent or sell videos and DVDs with short clips from its large cross-referenced database. When a customer requests a "preview" at one of these sites, the images (and accompanying sound) that he or she receives are actually being "streamed" from Video Pipeline's central servers. Most motion picture companies welcome this service, and cooperate to make it possible. Several, however, first refused to supply their own clips and then objected to Video Pipeline's practice of generating clips from purchased copies of their tapes and DVDs. These companies admit that there is no market in brief promotion video clips, as such, but they argue that, nevertheless, they should be entitled to funnel all consumers seeking previews of their films through their own proprietary websites — where other kinds of merchandising does occur. The defendants argue that their use is "transformational" in the core sense that they are providing a database for informational rather than entertainment purposes. How does *Kelly v. Arriba Soft* help or hurt Video Pipeline's fair use defense?

Kelly v. Arriba Soft refuses an invitation to immunize one of the most characteristic and (some would say) essential information practices associated with the World Wide Web under the "fair use" doctrine. Back in § 7.07[C] of this Supplement, we saw the Second Circuit in *Corley* taking a somewhat similar view of the relationship between fair use and evolving information technology, stating (we remind you) that:

> the DMCA does not impose even an arguable limitation on the opportunity to make a variety of traditional fair uses of DVD movies, such as commenting on their content . . . and even recording portions of the video images and sounds on film or tape by pointing a camera, a camcorder, or a microphone at a monitor as it displays the DVD movie. The fact that the resulting copy will not be as perfect or as manipulable as a digital copy . . . provides no basis for a claim of unconstitutional limitation of fair use.

Do these decisions unnecessarily circumscribe the evolutionary potential of the "fair use" doctrine? Will "fair use" remain an analog doctrine in an increasingly digital world?

(7) Before signing off the World Wide Web, turn your attention to a consideration of *Los Angeles Times v. Free Republic*, 2000 U.S. Dist. LEXIS 5669 (C.D.Cal. 2000). The defendants there operated a so-called "bulletin board" website, where they posted news stories from mainstream media (including the plaintiffs L.A. Times and Washington Post) and invited commentary from visitors to the site. Apparently, the defendant's site may have had a profit-making purpose, although there is no indication that they in fact made any money on the enterprise. Almost certainly, their motivation was at least partially ideological: although this isn't discussed in the court's opinion, the Free Republic site had a distinctly right-wing orientation. The defendants lost, on summary judgment, primarily because they could not persuade the court that their use of copyrighted news articles was significantly "transformative," and because the court credited the plaintiffs' claims that the Free Republic had the potential to reduce traffic to their own websites. How would you have gone about crafting counterarguments for this defendant with respect to the application of § 107(1) and (4)? In particular, consider whether (and if so when) the recontextualization of information can be considered transformative.

USAGE: On page 907, SUBSTITUTE the following text for the final paragraph (yes, that one sentence!) of § 9.06:

On the other hand, the outcome of the WTO Dispute Settlement Body panel on the TRIPs-compliance of § 110(5) of the U.S. Copyright Act (described in some detail in § 7.05 of this Part) seems to heighten the risk of future attacks on at least some aspects of "fair use." Suppose, for example, that the WTO were asked to consider whether the *Sony* approach to personal off-air videotaping for "time-shifting" purposes measures up to Article 13. What would be the likely result? In this connection, it is important to remember that, in most of the rest of the world, this issue has long been handled through schemes that authorize private taping while imposing fees on equipment and blank media, so as to assure some level of remuneration to copyright owners, *see* Reinhold Kreile, *Collection and Distribution of the*

Statutory Remuneration for Private Copying with Respect to Recorders and Blank Cassettes in Germany, 23 IIC 449 (1992), and that the European Union recently has imposed this approach as a sort of mandatory minimum for Europe as a whole in Article 5(2)(b) of the new "Directive on the harmonisation of certain aspects of copyright and neighboring rights in the information society" (2001/29/EC), reproduced in Part II of this Supplement.

But at least for now, fair use lives — sort of.

§ 9.07   Other Affirmative Copyright Defenses

[A]   Copyright Misuse

USAGE: On page 912, CONSIDER the following recent development after note (3):

Antitrust violations. In addition to copyright misuse, a full-blown antitrust violation could constitute a defense to copyright infringement on appropriate facts. For a recent and celebrated case involving the interplay of copyright and antitrust, see *U.S. v. Microsoft Corp.,* 87 F. Supp. 2d 30 (D.D.C. 2000) (holding that Title 17 does not confer on Microsoft a right to preserve the "integrity" of its computer operating system and Internet software by preventing licensees from shipping modified versions of its product without its permission, thereby avoiding the prohibitions of U.S. antitrust law).

[B]   Other Commonly Asserted Defenses

USAGE: On page 914, SUBSTITUTE the following text for the paragraph at the top of the page:

What happens if the plaintiff files the complaint in the action within three years after the infringement, but somehow fails to register the copyright in the work until the § 507(b) period has expired? The probable answer is that later attention to this jurisdictional prerequisite relates back, so that the complaint is not time-barred; and in principle this seems the appropriate outcome. *See Co-Opportunities, Inc. v. National Broadcasting Co.,* 510 F.Supp. 43 (N.D. Cal. 1981).

USAGE: Also on page 914, CONSIDER the following recent development after the discussion of "Abandonment or Forfeiture of Copyright":

Laches. In *Kling v. Hallmark Cards, Inc.,* 225 F.3d 1030 (9th Cir. 2000), the court held that the operative period of laches "runs only from the time that the plaintiff knew or should have known about an actual or impending infringement, not an adverse claim of ownership." The court reversed the District Court's summary judgment on laches, noting that there was nothing in the record to suggest that a reasonably diligent plaintiff would have known about the infringing video cassette distribution until the plaintiff's 1994 video store visit.

Chapter 10

REMEDIES, PREEMPTION, AND RELATED BODIES OF LAW

§ 10.01 Remedies Under Federal Law

[A] Introduction

USAGE: On page 922, SUBSTITUTE the following text for the first full paragraph at the top of the page, quoting from the House Report:

Section 507 . . . establishes a three-year statute of limitations for [civil actions and a five-year period for criminal proceedings, as discussed in Chapter 9 of the casebook].

USAGE: On page 932 (besides recalling our earlier warning that the District Court decision in *Connectix* was overruled by the Ninth Circuit, 203 F.3d 596, in 2000), ADD the following text after note (15):

(15A) The *Napster* saga continue, this time in the context of preliminary injunctive relief.

While finding squarely that the plaintiffs were likely to prevailing on the merits, the Ninth Circuit, in its *Napster* opinion (*see* § 1.05 of this Part for the principal excerpt), proceeded to set aside the preliminary injunction that had been granted by Judge Patel below, which it found to be:

> overbroad because it places on Napster the entire burden of ensuring that no "copying, downloading, uploading, transmitting, or distributing" of plaintiffs' works occur on the system. As stated, we place the burden on plaintiffs to provide notice to Napster of copyrighted works and files containing such works available on the Napster system has the duty to disable access to the offending content. Napster, however, also bears the burden of policing the system within the limits of the system. Here, we recognize that this is not an exact science in that the files are user named. In crafting the injunction on remand, the district court should recognize that Napster's system does not currently appear to allow Napster access to users' files.

239 F.3d at 1027.

Quite an order! Judge Patel's March 5, 2001 modification of the injunction can be found at 2001 U.S. Dist. LEXIS 2186. As we write, both sides in the litigation have filed notices of appeal contesting the order — while, at the same time, a motion for rehearing of the Circuit Court's panel decision is pending with the Ninth Circuit.

And how has this regime of "burden-sharing" worked out in practice? Of course, there has been considerable wrangling about exactly how and what the duties of the various parties are, but there is no doubt that the injunction has had an effect. Depending on who is talking, the number of songs available (and with it, the amount of traffic) on Napster is down by half, or 60 percent, or more. Where have all the users gone? At least some, it appears, have migrated to Gnutella, Bear Share, LimeWire, and various clones and competitors — second-generation peer-to-peer file-sharing programs that are, at least for now, less user-friendly that Napster (because they operate without a central index function) but also are much harder for copyright owners to control as a practical or legal matter (again, because they lack a central node). This, of course, hasn't stopped the entertainment industry from trying. *See* Lee Gomes, *Entertainment Firms Target Gnutella*, Wall St. J., May 4, 2001, at B6, col. 1.

Meanwhile, Napster has announced a business deal with RealNetworks and three major record label groups that would permit it to relaunch as a licensed subscription-based service — as early as the Summer of 2001. *See* Martin Peers, *Napster's Licensing Agreement With Musicnet Strains Relations*, Wall St. J., June 7, 2001, at B2, col. 3.

(15B) And are preliminary injunctions in copyright cases constitutionally permissible, in any case? See the provocative recent article by Mark Lemley and Eugene Volokh, *Freedom of Speech and Injunctions in Intellectual Property Cases*, 48 Duke L.J. 147 (1998) (questioning preliminary injunctions in copyright cases under the "prior restraint" doctrine). The article represents an interesting and important new trend in copyright scholarship, which for many years generally has assumed, without much rigorous inquiry, the general consistency of the scheme of copyright law, on the one hand, and the principles safeguarding free expression, on the other. But will courts be persuaded to take to the notion that the First Amendment limits their authority to fashion preliminary relief?

On May 25, 2001, after hearing the appeal from the grant of preliminary injunctive relief in *Suntrust Bank* (*a.k.a.* Gone with the Wind v. The Wind Done Gone) (mentioned earlier in § 9.03 of this Part), a panel of the Eleventh Circuit Court of Appeals ruled, from the bench, that "[i]t is manifest that the entry of a preliminary injunction in this copyright case was an abuse of discretion in that it represents an unlawful prior restraint in violation of the First Amendment." The balance of the brief order vacating the injunction suggests, however, that, had generally applicable standards for the grant of preliminary injunctive relief been satisfied, no constitutional violation would have been found. The court promised a "comprehensive opinion" to follow. So we will see.

USAGE: On page 934, ADD the following text after note (20):

(20A) In *Napster,* the Ninth Circuit also dismissed as an "easy out" the defendants' suggestion that it should impose a compulsory royalty payment schedule rather restricting the scope of its services — a suggestion based, in part, on its treatment of the remedial issues in *Abend*. Interestingly, a few weeks after the *Napster* decision, another federal appellate court took exactly this approach (although in a factually very different situation), concluding on remand:

> In assessing the appropriateness of any injunctive relief, we urge the [district] court to consider alternatives, such as mandatory license fees, in lieu of foreclosing the public's computer-aided access to this educational and entertaining work.

Greenberg v. National Geographic Society, 244 F.3d 1267, 1275 (11th Cir. 2001) (the decision construing § 201(c) of the Copyright Act as discussed above in § 4.01 of this Part).

Note that both *Abend* and *Greenberg* involved permanent, rather than preliminary, relief. Is a judicially imposed license less appropriate at the preliminary injunction phase of copyright litigation?

USAGE: On page 940, SUBSTITUTE the following text for the two full paragraphs (beginning with "For an interesting example . . .") immediately preceding note (6):

(5A) For an interesting example of the closely related issue of causation in the proof of actual damages, see *Par Microsystems, Inc. v. Pinnacle Development Corp.*, 995 F. Supp. 658 (N.D. Tex. 1998) (denying damages where "no reasonable jury" could have found that plaintiff's inability to sell its copyrighted software was caused by defendant's infringement, and declining to award "nominal damages" on the ground that "it is doubtful that Congress left room for such an award when it otherwise provided ample remedies for infringement").

(5B) What if the best a plaintiff can do is to claim that, by virtue of the defendant's infringements, it lost out on licensing fees that the defendant itself otherwise would have paid? Is the form of this argument too circular to withstand pressure? Or does it make some commercial sense? The answer may depend, in part, on the certainty with which the plaintiff can demonstrate the amount of the lost licensing revenues. *See Davis v. The Gap, Inc.*, 246 F.3d 152 (2d Cir. 2001) (extensive discussion noting that the Nimmer and Goldstein treatises are in conflict on the point but concluding that "the decisions in this and other courts support the view that the owner's actual damages may include in appropriate cases the reasonable license fee on which a willing buyer and a willing seller would have agreed for the use taken by the infringer").

Of course, actually calculating a "reasonable license fee" poses its own problems. Two examples follow.

Bruce v. Weekly World News, Inc., 150 F. Supp. 2d 313 (D. Mass. 2001), involved the defendant tabloid publisher's unauthorized manipulation of the plaintiff's freelance photograph of Bill Clinton to show the President shaking hands with an extraterrestrial, and the subsequent use of the photo in various publishing and merchandising contexts with captions such as "Alien Backs Clinton!" The court inquired in detail into industry usage and concluded, for example, that "an award of $1200 (or $75 per week) . . . is appropriate for the unauthorized use of the photo on WWN's website. (Both experts agreed that because the internet is a separate medium, industry practice requires a separate license for internet use." Perhaps more interesting still is the conclusion that "a multiple should be applied to fees charged where an infringer made unlicensed use of a photo . . . ," not as a penalty but as a matter of "standard industry practice." *Id.* at 321. The total award was $20,142.45 (with costs and attorneys' fees to follow).

Andreas v. Volkswagen of America, Inc., discussed at § 8.03[C][2], note (10A) of this Supplement, involved a claim by the designer of an angel poster against the automaker and its ad agency. At 2002 U.S. Dist. LEXIS 7561 (D. Iowa 2002), the court reduced a jury award of damages based on plaintiff's losses against VW from $570,000 to $115,000, but let stand an award of infringer's profits against the ad agency in the amount of $280,000.

(5C) For a further, thorough workout on the intricacies of undue speculation (not to mention the dangers of "double-counting" as described in the note below), see the Second Circuit's opinion in *Abeshouse v. Ultragraphics, Inc.*, 754 F.2d 467 (1985).

USAGE: On page 957, ADD the following text after note (7):

(7A) *How high can you go?* Sometimes, of course, the defendant's course of conduct may have involved systematic infringement of many individual works belonging to a copyright holder. And it is here where statutory damage awards can take on extraordinary proportions. Back in § 7.02[C] of this Part, we explained the underlying facts in the litigation between various recording companies and MP3.com arising out of its wholesale copying of thousands of CDS to launch a web-based "space-shifting" service, based on the flawed premise that it was doing no more than facilitating subscribers' storage and use of their own privately purchased CDS. Having found liability, Judge Rakoff then was required to turn his attention to damages. MP3.com had made no noticeable profits; and the plaintiffs might have been hard pressed to show measurable losses, given the model on which the service was based. They elected to pursue statutory damages instead, moving to have those damages calculated on a "per-song" rather than a "per-CD" basis. This motion was denied on August 23, 2000 (at 109 F. Supp. 2d 223), on grounds that the CDS were "compilations" of songs and that, under § 504(c)(1), only one award of damages was available for each such compilation. At a hearing on September 6 (a transcript of which appears at 2000 U.S. Dist. LEXIS 13293), the court first determined that the infringements had been willful, in that "the infringer either had actual knowledge that it was infringing the plaintiff's copyrights or else acted in reckless disregard of the high probability that it was . . . " That said, the court explored the question of where in the range of up to $150,000 per CD it should peg the damages. The decision: $25,000, taking into consideration the fact that the plaintiffs had made no attempt to show actual damages in connection with their request, as well as the importance of "general deterrence":

Some of the evidence in this case strongly suggests that some companies operating in the area of the Internet may have a misconception that, because their technology is somewhat novel, they are somehow immune from the ordinary application of the laws of the United States, including copyright laws. They need to understand that the law's domain knows no such limits.

Just how relevant a factor in setting statutory damages should such "general deterrence" be?

In any event, over the months that followed, MP3.com settled for various amounts with four of the five groups of recording companies that had spearheaded the action, perhaps in part because MP3.com had threatened a wholesale legal assault on the industry's copyright registration practices (valid registration prior to infringement being a precondition for statutory damages, as detailed later in this subsection). This left one plaintiff in the main action, Universal Music Group; and one issue to be determined, namely, how many of its copyrighted and registered CDS actually had been copied? Was it 10,000, as Universal claimed (which would have yielded damages of $25 million), or no more than 4,700, per MP3.com's count (for a mere $117.5 million)? In November 2000, MP3.com settled with Universal for "only" $53.4 million, with Universal also purchasing the rights to acquire a "significant amount" of MP3.com shares in the future. And on May 20, 2001, Universal (or, more accurately, Vivendi Universal, because in the meantime it had been acquired by the French media conglomerate) bought MP3.com for $372 million (presumably net of the prior damage award). *See* Andrew Ross Sorkin, *Vivendi in Deal for MP3.com to Life Online Distribution*, New York Times, May 21, 2001, at C1, col. 5.

The story has a comical footnote, suggesting the murky depths into which all of this might have taken the parties. On April 7, 2001, jurors in a relatively small related action, *Teevee Toons, Inc. v. MP3.com, Inc.*, 134 F. Supp. 2d 546 (S.D.N.Y. 2001), returned a verdict of nearly $300,000, which MP3.com hailed as a victory, given that 147 recordings had been involved. Over the weekend that followed, however, several of the jurors contacted the judge to say that they believed that they had made computational errors, and the following Monday the judge announced that "the total was supposed to be between two and three million. This matter is far from obvious in how it should be adjudicated." *See Jurors misstate payment in MP3.com suit*, C/Net News, April 9, 2001, at *http://cnet.com/news/0-1005-200-5547244.html*.

What lessons do you see in all this? Should there be outer limits on total awards of statutory damages?

(7B) And there is further evidence of judicial liberality in the award of statutory damages, at least in the context of Web-based infringement, and in particular where the adult entertainment industry (apparently a special topic of judicial solicitude) is concerned. *See Perfect 10, Inc. v. Talisman Communications Inc.*, 2000 U.S. Dist LEXIS 4564 ($300,000 award for the unauthorized reposting of six photographs covered by three copyrights, with the court noting that "a virtually unlimited number of copies can be made as a result of [defendant's] infringement); and *Suze Randall Photography v. Reactor, Inc.,* 2000 U.S. Dist. LEXIS 7676 (N.D. Ill. 2000) ($150,000 in statutory damages, and another $150,000 for tampering with copyright management information in violation of § 1202, plus damages on state law claims and attorneys' fees — all for the unauthorized use of 11 photographs).

USAGE: On page 961, ADD the following text immediately preceding the paragraph beginning "Note that, *Fogerty* notwithstanding . . .":

But here the symmetry for which *Fogerty* stands breaks down somewhat. Although awards of attorneys' fees to successful plaintiffs can be conditioned on timely registration, by their nature awards to successful defendants cannot. For a recent example of a determination that defendants should receive an award of fees where the plaintiff's claims were "objectively unreasonable and, at least in part, improperly motivated," having previously observed that a claim's "'novelty,' for purposes of a fee award turns on the uniqueness of the legal issues presented, not the eccentricity of the underlying subject matter," see *Torah Soft Ltd v. Drosnin,* 2001 U.S. Dist LEXIS 19217 (S.D.N.Y. 2001). *See also Earth Flag Ltd. v. Alamo Flag Co.,* 154 F. Supp. 2d 663 (S.D.N.Y. 2001) ($36,561.92 to the primary defendant, and $69,565 to eBay, through whose Internet-based auction site allegedly infringing merchandise had been sold).

§ 10.02 Preemption and State Law Remedies*

USAGE: On page 998, CONSIDER the following recent development in conjunction with note (12):

Clearly, the right of publicity has great potential to nullify the rights of the copyright owner, should courts decide not to immunize publicity rights from preemption under § 301. For example, suppose you photograph somebody on the street and wish to sell copies of your work. You certainly have a copyright in the photograph, but those rights may be worthless if the person in the photograph, by asserting her publicity right, is able to enjoin publication of the photograph. *See Downing v. Abercrombie & Fitch,* 265 F.3d 994 (9th Cir. 2001) (holding that a right of publicity claim not preempted because "a person's name or likeness is not a work of authorship within the meaning of 17 U.S.C. § 102" even when embodied in a copyrightable photograph, and that, because such names and likenesses are not copyrightable subject matter, "right of publicity claims . . . are not equivalent to the exclusive rights contained in § 106").

USAGE: On page 1011, SUBSTITUTE the following text for the last two pages on note (8):

NCCUSL then decided to repackage former draft UCC Article 2B as a free-standing model act — the "Uniform Computer Information

---

* On page 1009, the "not" at the end of the fifth line of note (2) should be deleted.

Transactions Act" (or "UCITA") — which would not require ALI approval. NCCUSL gave its own final approval to UCITA in July 1999. The language of § 105 quoted above was adopted with inconsequential semantic revisions. ALI critics were not amused — but the battleground has now shifted to the state legislatures, which must decide whether to enact or reject UCITA as approved.

Objections to UCITA from consumer organizations and others are by no means limited to its treatment of the copyright/contract connection. So far, two states—Maryland and Virginia—have done enacted UCITA, with some local modifications addressing non-intellectual property-related concerns. In others, the legislation has run into strong resistance. In Iowa, for example, the legislature actually has enacted a so-called "UCITA bomb shelter" provision to give Iowa consumers protection from the enforcement of other states' versions of UCITA. The relevant Iowa provision, part of the Iowa Uniform Electronic Transactions Act of 2000, is as follows:

> A choice of law provision, which is contained in a computer information agreement that governs a transaction subject to this chapter, that provides that the contract is to be interpreted pursuant to the laws of a state that has enacted the Uniform Computer Information Transactions Act, as proposed by the national conference of commissioners on uniform state laws, or any substantially similar law, is voidable and the agreement shall be interpreted pursuant to the laws of this state if the party against whom enforcement of the choice of law provision is sought is a resident of this state or has its principal place of business located in this state. For purposes of this subsection, a "computer information agreement" means an agreement that would be governed by the Uniform Computer Information Transactions Act or substantially similar law as enacted in the state specified in the choice of laws provision if that state's law were applied to the agreement.

Although originally designed to sunset in July, 2001, the legislation has been extended. Similar bills have been enacted in North Carolina and West Virginia, and one is under consideration in Ohio. The National Association of Attorneys General remains strongly opposed, as detailed in its letter of November 13, 2001 (available at *http://www.arl.org/info/letters/AGtoNCCUSL11.html*). More recently, an American Bar Association working group appointed to study and recommend a position on UCITA has issued a politely worded but far-reaching critique. The UCITA Standby Committee of NCCUSL, in turn, responded on May 29, 2002 with a series of proposed amendments. *See http://www.nccusl.org/nccusl/ucita/UCITA_Standby_Comm.htm.* Previously (in a move intended to address some of the concerns of UCITA's copyright critics), the committee had recommended adoption of a reverse engineering exception. *See* Jonathan Band, *Closing the Interoperability Gap,* 19 Computer & Internet Lawyer 1 (May 2002). None of these modifications, of course, were reflected in the versions of UCITA adopted in Maryland and Virginia. In the end, how "uniform" will this "uniform law be? The outcome, for UCITA proponents and foes alike, remains still far from clear. *See* Dan Gillmor, *Time to bury proposed software law*, May 12, 2001, at *http://www.siliconvalley.com/docs/opinion/dgillmor/dg051301a.htm*, and Ed Foster, *The Gripe Line: UCITA, the Undead,* InfoWorld, May 6, 2002, at 72.

For a comprehensive selection of views on Article 2B/UCITA, see the recent Symposium issues of the *Berkeley Technology Law Review* (Vol. 13, No. 3, Fall 1998) and the *California Law Review* (Vol. 87, No. 1, Jan. 1999). For a currently updated collection of anti-UCITA materials, reflecting viewpoints within the non-profit library and education communities, see *http://www.arl.org/info/frn/copy/ucitapg.html*. For a broader critique of UCITA, see the website of Americans for Fair Electronic Commerce Transactions (AFFECT) — *http://www 4cite.org/,*— which includes a link to state-by-state UCITA status updates maintained by the American Library Association (also accessible at *http://www.ala.org/washoff/ucita*)

USAGE: On page 1013, ADD the following text after note (10):

The foregoing trial court decision in *Wrench* now has been reversed by the Sixth Circuit. 256 F.3d 446 (2001). While refusing to make any blanket proclamations regarding nonpreemption and state contract law, the Court of Appeals held that the implied-in-fact contract in suit was not preempted because the plaintiff's expectation of payment made the claim qualitatively different from a copyright claim. The court declined to hold that *all* state law contract claims survive preemption simply because they involve the additional element of a promise:

> [A] contract which consisted only of a promise not to reproduce the copyrighted work would survive preemption even though it was limited to one of the exclusive rights enumerated in 17 U.S.C. § 106. If the promise amounts only to a promise to refrain from reproducing, performing, distributing or displaying the work, then the contract claim is preempted. The contrary result would clearly violate the rule that state law rights are preempted when they would be abridged by an act which in of itself would infringe one of the exclusive rights of § 106.

256 F.3d at 457-458.

(11) When we introduced the preceding note with the word "Finally" in the current edition of the casebook, we did not foresee the decision of the U.S. District Court for the Northern District of California in *eBay, Inc. v. Bidder's Edge, Inc.*, 100 F. Supp. 2d 1058 (2000). There, the plaintiff, an on-line auctioneer, objected to the activities of the defendant, an auction aggregator on whose website information about on-going sales at various primary auctions sites, with links to those sites, were to be found. This information was collected, in turn, by using software robots (or "web-crawlers") that patrolled the Internet in search of relevant data items. In granting preliminary injunctive relief, the court did not, for obvious reasons, rely on copyright. Instead, it resorted to a number of state law theories, including (notably) trespass to chattels. The theory was that the use of the defendant's webcrawlers deprived eBay of the use of some of the capacity

of a physical asset (its computer servers): while one aggregator robots may not interfere substantially with eBay's operations, the use of this data collection technique by multiple aggregators could have such an effect. Putting to one side the internal problems with this theory of recovery — which are admirably treated in Dan L. Burk, *The Trouble With Trespass,* 4 J. Small & Emerging Bus. L. 27 (2000) — what about preemption? The court concluded that "the right to exclude others from using physical personal property is not equivalent to any rights protected by copyright and therefore constitutes an extra element that makes trespass qualitatively different from a copyright infringement claim." 100 F. Supp. 2d at 1071. But it acknowledged that the court in *Ticketmaster Corp. v. Tickets.com,* 2000 U.S. Dist. LEXIS 12987 (C.D. Cal. 2000) (decided a few months earlier), had seen the issue differently and dismissed partly on grounds of preemption. Which side are you on?

§ 10.03   Related Bodies of State and Federal Law

[A]   Passing Off and the Protection of Trade Dress Under Federal Law

USAGE: On page 1021, SUBSTITUTE the following language for the discussion of *Samara Bros., Inc. v. Wal-Mart Stores, Inc.* in note (5) (last three sentences of first paragraph):

The U.S. Supreme Court has made the distinction between trade dress, *e.g.,* of the kind found in *Two Pesos,* and packaging, on the one hand, and product design, on the other hand. The former can obtain protection without a showing of secondary meaning if it is inherently distinctive, whereas the latter can be protected only if it has acquired distinctiveness. *See Wal-Mart Stores, Inc. v. Samara Brothers, Inc.,* 529 U.S. 205 (2000). Even more recently, the Court refused protection under federal unfair competition law for product features that had once enjoyed utility patent protection. *See TrafFix Devices, Inc., v. Marketing Displays, Inc.,* 121 S.Ct. 1255 (2001) (holding that existence of expired utility patents claiming protection for dual-spring design mechanism for keeping outdoor signs upright in adverse wind conditions created strong evidentiary inference of design's functionality, and that failure of manufacturer to overcome such inference by showing that design was merely ornamental, incidental or arbitrary precluded trade dress protection for design).

PART FIVE:

CUMULATIVE BIBLIOGRAPHY

CHAPTERS 1 and 11
THE LANDSCAPE OF COPYRIGHT
THE HORIZON OF COPYRIGHT

Reference Works

H. Abrams, THE LAW OF COPYRIGHT §§ 1.01 to 1.03, 18.01 to 18.03 (2002)

P. Goldstein, COPYRIGHT: PRINCIPLES, LAW AND PRACTICE §§ 1.0 to 1.16, 16.0 to 16.9 (2002)

M. Leaffer, UNDERSTANDING COPYRIGHT LAW §§ 1.1 to 1.14, 12.1 to 12.12 (3d ed. 1999)

M. Nimmer & D. Nimmer, NIMMER ON COPYRIGHT, OV-1 to OV-11, §§ 17.01 to 17.13, 18.01 to 18.08 (2002)

W. Patry, COPYRIGHT LAW AND PRACTICE, Chaps. 1, 17 (1994 & 2000 Supp.)

Copyright and Related Bodies of Law

M. Adelman, PATENT LAW PERSPECTIVES (2002)

R. Callmann, THE LAW OF UNFAIR COMPETITION, TRADEMARKS AND MONOPOLIES (L. Altman 4th ed. 1994 & Supp. 2002)

D. Chisum, PATENTS (2002)

J. Gilson & A.G. Lalonde, TRADEMARK PROTECTION AND PRACTICE (2001)

D. Farber, ENTERTAINMENT INDUSTRY CONTRACTS (1999)

R. Harmon, PATENTS AND THE FEDERAL CIRCUIT (4th ed. 2000 & 2001 Supp.)

M. Jager, TRADE SECRETS LAW (2001)

A. Lindey, LINDEY ON ENTERTAINMENT, PUBLISHING AND THE ARTS (2002)

E. Lipscomb, WALKER ON PATENTS (3d ed. 1991 & 2001 Supp.)

J.T. McCarthy, McCARTHY ON TRADEMARKS AND UNFAIR COMPETITION (2002)

C.R. McManis, INTELLECTUAL PROPERTY AND UNFAIR COMPETITION IN A NUTSHELL (2000)

R. Milgrim, MILGRIM ON TRADE SECRETS (2001)

R. Milgrim, MILGRIM ON LICENSING (2002)

M. Petry, TAXATION OF INTELLECTUAL PROPERTY (2001)

P. Rosenberg, PATENT LAW FUNDAMENTALS (2001)

T. Selz, M. Simensky, P.N. Acton & R. Lind, ENTERTAINMENT LAW (2d ed. 2001)

Copyright Law History

A. Birrell, SEVEN LECTURES ON THE LAW AND HISTORY OF COPYRIGHT IN BOOKS (1971)

B. Bugbee, GENESIS OF AMERICAN PATENT AND COPYRIGHT LAW (1967)

A. Clark, THE MOVEMENT FOR INTERNATIONAL COPYRIGHT IN NINETEENTH CENTURY AMERICA (1960)

G. Curtis, A TREATISE ON THE LAW OF COPYRIGHT (1847)

E. Drone, A TREATISE ON THE LAW OF PROPERTY IN INTELLECTUAL PRODUCTIONS (1879)

D. Eisenstein, THE PRINTING REVOLUTION IN EARLY MODERN EUROPE (1993)

P. Goldstein, COPYRIGHT'S HIGHWAY: FROM GUTENBERG TO THE CELESTIAL JUKEBOX (1995)

L.R. Patterson, COPYRIGHT IN HISTORICAL PERSPECTIVE (1968)

L.R. Patterson & S. Lindberg, THE NATURE OF COPYRIGHT: A LAW OF USERS' RIGHTS (1991)

F. Pierce, A UNIFIED FIELD THEORY OF COPYRIGHT (1870)

H. Ransom, THE FIRST COPYRIGHT STATUTE (1956)

M. Rose, AUTHORS AND OWNERS: THE INVENTION OF COPYRIGHT (1993)

E. Samuels, THE ILLUSTRATED HISTORY OF COPYRIGHT (2000)

C. Seville, LITERARY COPYRIGHT REFORM IN EARLY VICTORIAN ENGLAND: THE FRAMING OF THE 1842 COPYRIGHT ACT (1999)

T. Solberg, COPYRIGHT IN CONGRESS, 1789–1904: A BIBLIOGRAPHY, AND CHRONOLOGICAL RECORD OF ALL PROCEEDINGS (1905)

Abrams, *The Historic Foundation of American Copyright Law: Exploding the Myth of Common Law Copyright*, 29 Wayne L. Rev. 1119 (1983)

Aoki, *Authors, Inventors and Trademark Owners: Private Intellectual Property and the Public Domain (Parts I & II)*, 18 Colum.-VLA J.L. & the Arts, 1 & 191 (1994–1995)

Aoki, *Neocolonialism, Anticommons Property, and Biopiracy in the (Not-So-Brave) New World Order of International Intellectual Property*, 6 Ind. J. Global L. Stud. 11 (1998)

Benkler, *Free as the Air to Common Use: First Amendment Constraints on Enclosure of the Public Domain*, 74 N.Y.U. L. Rev. 354 (1999)

Birnhack, *The Idea of Progress in Copyright Law*, 1 Buff. Intell. Prop. L.J. 3 (2001)

Burr, *The Piracy Gap: Protecting Intellectual Property in an Era of Artistic Creativity and Technological Change*, 33 Willamette L. Rev. 245 (1997)

Crawford, *Pre-Constitutional Copyright Statutes*, 23 Bull. Copyright Soc'y 11 (1975)

Eilenberg, *Mortal Pages: Wordsworth and the Reform of Copyright*, 56 Eng. Lit. Hist. 351 (1989)

Feather, *The Book Trade in Politics: The Making of the Copyright Act of 1710*, 8 Pub. Hist. 19 (1980)

Geller, *Copyright History and the Future: What's Culture Got to Do With It?*, 40 J. Copyright Soc'y 209 (2000)

Ginsburg, *A Tale of Two Copyrights: Literary Property in Revolutionary France and America*, 64 Tul. L. Rev. 991 (1990)

Goldman, *The History of U.S.A. Copyright Law Revision from 1901 to 1954, Copyright Law Revision Study No. 1* (1960)

Grossman, *Cycles in Copyright*, 22 N.Y.L. Sch. L. Rev. 653 (1977)

Hamilton, *Copyright at the Supreme Court: A Jurisprudence of Deference*, 40 J. Copyright Soc'y 317 (2000)

Hesse, *Enlightenment Epistemology and the Laws of Authorship in Revolutionary France, 1777–1793*, 30 Representations 109 (1990)

Jaszi, *Towards a Theory of Copyright: The Metamorphoses of Authorship*, 1991 Duke L.J. 455

Joyce, *The Rise of the Supreme Court Reporter: An Institutional Perspective on Marshall Court Ascendancy*, 83 Mich. L. Rev. 1291 (1985)

Kastenmeier, *Copyright in an Era of Technological Change: A Political Perspective*, 14 Colum.–VLA J.L. & the Arts 1 (1989)

Kidwell, *Congressman Robert Kastenmeier and Professor John Stedman: A Thirty-Five Year Relationship*, 55 Law & Contemp. Probs. 129 (1992)

Kitch, *Property Rights in Inventions, Writings, and Marks*, 13 Harv. J. L. & Pub. Pol'y 119 (1990)

Lessig, *Copyright's First Amendment,* 48 UCLA L. Rev. 1057 (2001)

Litman, *Copyright as Myth,* 53 U. of Pitts. L. Rev. 235 (1991)

Litman, *Copyright, Compromise and Legislative History,* 72 Cornell L. Rev. 857 (1987)

Merges, *Symposium on Law in the Twentieth Century: One Hundred Years of Solicitude: Intellectual Property Law, 1900-2000,* 88 Calif. L. Rev. 2187 (2000)

Olson, *The Iron Law of Consensus: Congressional Responses to Proposed Copyright Reforms Since the 1909 Act,* 36 J. Copyright Soc'y 109 (1989)

Oman, *Bob Kastenmeier and the Legislative Process:* Sui Generis *and Proud of It,* 55 Law & Contemp. Probs. 241 (1992)

Oman, *The Copyright Clause: "A Charter For A Living People,"* 17 U. Balt. L. Rev. 99 (1987)

O'Rourke, *Evaluating Mistakes in Intellectual Property Law: Configuring the System to Account for Imperfection,* 4 J. Small & Emerging Bus. L. 167 (2000)

Patterson, *Copyright and "the exclusive Right" of Authors,* 1 J. Intell. Prop. L. 1 (1993)

Patterson & Joyce, *Monopolizing the Law: The Scope of Copyright Protection for Law Reports and Statutory Compilations,* 36 UCLA L. Rev. 719 (1989)

Patterson, *The Statute of Anne: Copyright Misconstrued,* 3 Harv. J. on Legis. 223 (1966)

Patterson, *Understanding the Copyright Clause,* 40 J. Copyright Soc'y 365 (2000)

Raskind, *Grading the Performance of a Legislator,* 55 Law & Contemp. Probs. 267 (1992)

Remington, *Robert W. Kastenmeier: Copyright Legislator Par Excellence,* 55 Law & Contemp. Probs. 297 (1992)

Rose, *The Author as Proprietor:* Donaldson v. Beckett *and the Genealogy of Modern Authorship,* 23 Representations 51 (1988)

Suchman, *Invention and Ritual: Notes on the Interrelation of Magic and Intellectual Property in Preliterate Societies,* 89 Colum. L. Rev. 1264 (1989)

Symposium, *Fundamentals of International Copyright: The Impact of Berne,* 8 Cardozo Arts & Ent. L.J. 1 (1989)

Temple, Johnson & Macpherson, *Cultural Authority and the Construction of Literary Property,* 5 Yale J. of L. & Human. 355 (1993)

VerSteeg, *The Roman Law Roots of Copyright*, 59 Md. L. Rev. 522 (2000)

Wicher, *The Ghost of* Donaldson v. Beckett: *An Inquiry into the Constitutional Distribution of Powers over the Law of Literary Property in the United States (Parts I and II),* 9 Bull. Copyright Soc'y 102 & 194 (1961–62)

Copyright in a Changing World

R. Barker, COPYRIGHT: THE NEW INTERNATIONAL CONVENTIONS (1971)

A. Bogsch, THE LAW OF COPYRIGHT UNDER THE UNIVERSAL COPYRIGHT CONVENTION (3d rev. ed. 1968)

P.E. Geller, INTERNATIONAL COPYRIGHT LAW AND PRACTICE (2001)

T. Kupferman & M. Foner, eds., UNIVERSAL COPYRIGHT CONVENTION ANALYZED (1955)

S. Ladas, THE INTERNATIONAL PROTECTION OF LITERARY AND ARTISTIC PROPERTY (1938)

M. Leaffer, INTERNATIONAL TREATIES ON INTELLECTUAL PROPERTY (2d ed. 1997)

C. Masouye, GUIDE TO THE BERNE CONVENTION (WIPO 1978)

C. Masouye, GUIDE TO THE ROME CONVENTION AND TO THE PHONOGRAMS CONVENTION (WIPO 1981)

P.E. Geller, INTERNATIONAL COPYRIGHT LAW AND PRACTICE (2001)

J. Reinbothe, THE WIPO TREATIES, 1996: THE WIPO COPYRIGHT TREATY AND THE WIPO PERFORMANCE AND PHONOGRAMS TREATY: COMMENTARY AND LEGAL ANALYSIS (2002)

S. Ricketson, THE BERNE CONVENTION FOR THE PROTECTION OF LITERARY AND ARTISTIC WORKS 1886–1986 (1987)

E. Schwartz, INTERNATIONAL COPYRIGHT INSTITUTE SYMPOSIUM: REPORTS ON COPYRIGHT DEVELOPMENT IN EASTERN EUROPE AND THE SOVIET UNION (1991)

T. Solberg, THE PRESENT INTERNATIONAL COPYRIGHT SITUATION: THREATS OF REPRISAL (1934)

T. Solberg, THE UNITED STATES AND INTERNATIONAL COPYRIGHT (1929)

S. Stewart & H. Sandison, INTERNATIONAL COPYRIGHT AND NEIGHBOURING RIGHTS (1989)

E. Yambrusic, TRADE-BASED APPROACHES TO THE PROTECTION OF INTELLECTUAL PROPERTY (1992)

Boytha, *Some Private International Law Aspects of the Protection of Authors' Rights,* 24 Copyright 399 (Oct. 1988)

Bradley, *Intellectual Property Rights, Investment, and Trade in Services in the Uruguay Round: Laying the Foundations,* 23 Stan. J. Int'l L. 57 (1987)

Brenner-Beck, *Do As I Say, Not As I Did (Economic Development of Less Developed Countries and the Protection of Intellectual Property),* 11 UCLA Pac. Basin L.J. 84 (1992)

Cate, *The First Amendment and the National Information Infrastructure,* 30 Wake Forest L. Rev 1 (1995)

Cate, *Global Information Policymaking and Domestic Law,* 1 Ind. J. Global Leg. Stud. 467 (1994)

Chinni, *Droit D'Auteur Versus the Economics of Copyright: Implications for American Law of Accession to the Berne Convention,* 14 W. New Eng. L. Rev. 145 (1992)

Cornish, *The International Relations of Intellectual Property,* 52 Cambridge L.J. 16 (1993)

Das, *Intellectual Property Dispute, GATT, WIPO: Of Playing by the Game Rules and Rules of the Game,* 35 Idea 149 (1994)

Dietz, *The Harmonization of Copyright in the European Community,* 16 IIC 379 (1985)

Dinwoodie, *A New Copyright Order: Why National Courts Should Create Global Norms,* 149 U. Pa. L. Rev. 469 (2000)

Dinwoodie, *The Development and Incorporation of International Norms in the Formation of Copyright Law,* 62 Ohio St. L.J. 733 (2001)

Dinwoodie, *International Intellectual Property Litigation: A Vehicle for Resurgent Comparativist Thought?,* 49 Am. J. Comp. L. 429 (2001)

Dittrich, *The Practical Application of the Rome Convention,* 26 Bull. Copyright Soc'y 287 (1979)

Doherty & Griffiths, *The Harmonization of European Union Copyright Law for the Digital Age,* 22 EIPR 17 (2000)

Dreier & von Lewinski, *The European Community's Activities in the Field of Copyright,* 39 J. Copyright Soc'y 96 (1991)

Dreyfuss & Lowenfeld, *Two Achievements of the Uruguay Round: Putting TRIPS and Dispute Settlement Together,* 27 Va. J. Int'l L. 275 (1997)

Dox, *Trade, Competition and Intellectual Property — TRIPS and its Antitrust Counterparts*, 29 Vand. J. Transnat'l L. 481 (1996)

Final Report of the Ad Hoc Working Group on U.S. Adherence to the Berne Convention, reprinted in 10 Colum.-VLA J.L. & the Arts 513 (1986)

Fitzpatrick, *Copyright Imbalance: U.S. and Australian Responses to the WIPO Digital Copyright Treaty*, 22 EIPR 214 (2000)

Garilov, *The Legal Protection of Folklore*, 20 Copyright 76 (1984)

Garon, *Media and Monopoly in the Information Age: Slowing the Convergence at the Marketplace of Ideas*, 17 Cardozo Arts & Ent L.J. 491 (1999)

Geller, *Conflicts of Law in Cyberspace: Rethinking International Copyright*, J. Copyright Soc'y 103 (1996)

Geller, *Copyright Protection in the Berne Union: Analyzing the Issues*, 5 Intell. Prop. J. 1 (1989)

Geller, *Harmonizing Copyright–Contract Conflicts Analyses*, 25 Copyright 49 (1989)

Geller, *Legal Transplants in International Copyright: Some Problems of Method*, 13 UCLA Pac. Basin L.J. 199 (1994)

Ginsburg, *Colors in Conflicts: Moral Rights and the Foreign Exploitation of Colorized U.S. Motion Pictures*, 36 J. Copyright Soc'y 81 (1988)

Ginsburg, *International Copyright: From a "Bundle" of National Copyright Laws to a Supranational Code?*, 40 J. Copyright Soc'y 265 (2000)

Ginsburg & Kernochan, *One Hundred and Two Years Later: The United States Adheres to the Berne Convention*, 13 Colum.-VLA J.L. & the Arts 1 (1988)

Ginsburg & Sirinelli, *Author, Creation and Adaptation in Private International Law and French Domestic Law: Reflections Based on the* Huston Case *(i)*, 150 Revue Internationale de Droit D'Auteur [R.I.D.A.] 2 (1991)

Hamilton, *The TRIPS Agreement: Imperialistic, Outdated, and Overprotective*, 29 Vand. J. Transnat'l L. 613 (1996)

Helfer, *Adjudicating Copyright Claims Under the TRIPs Agreement: The Case for a European Human Rights Analogy*, 39 Harv. Int'l L.J. 357 (1998)

Huet & Ginsburg, *Computer Programs in Europe: A Comparative Analysis of the 1991 EC Software Directive*, 30 Colum. J. Transnat'l L. 327 (1992)

Jacobs, *Work-for-Hire and the Moral Right Dilemma in the European Community: A U.S. Perspective,* 16 B.C. Int'l & Comp. L. Rev. 29 (1993)

Jaszi, *GATT or WIPO? New Ways in the International Protection of Intellectual Property (Symposium at Ringberg Castle, July 13–16, 1989)* (F.–K. Beier & G. Schricker, eds., IIC Studies 1989)

Jaszi & Woodmansee, *The Ethical Reaches of Authorship,* 95 S. Atlantic 947 (1996)

Jehoram, *The Nature of Neighboring Rights of Performing Artists, Phonogram Producers and Broadcasting Organizations,* 15 Colum.-VLA J. L. & the Arts 75 (1990)

Jones, *An Introduction to the European Economic Community and Intellectual Property,* 18 Brooklyn J. Int'l L. 665 (1992)

Lafuze & Stanford, *An Overview of Section 337 of the Tariff Act of 1983: A Primer for Practice Before the International Trade Commission,* 25 J. Marshall L. Rev. 159 (1992)

Leaffer, *International Copyright from an American Perspective,* 43 Ark. L. Rev. 373 (1990)

Leaffer, *Protecting American Intellectual Property Abroad: Toward a New Multilateralism,* 76 Iowa L. Rev. 273 (1991)

Lin, *The U.S.-Taiwan Copyright Agreement: Cooperation or Coercion?,* 11 UCLA Pac. Basin L.J. 155 (1992)

Lindner, *Revival of Rights v. Protection of Acquired Rights: The Interpretation of Article 10(3) of the Duration Directive by the European Court of Justice in the Butterfly Case,* 22 EIPR 133 (2000)

Lipton, *Copyright in the Digital Age: A Comparative Survey,* 27 Rutgers Computer & Tech. L.J. 333 (2001)

Long, *Copyright and the Uruguay Round Agreements: A New Era of Protection or an Illusory Promise?,* 22 AIPLA Q.J. 531 (1994)

Long, *"Globalization": A Future Trend or a Satisfying Mirage?,* 49 J. Copyright Soc'y 357 (2001)

Lupo, *International Trade Commission Section 337 Proceedings and Their Applicability to Copyright Ownership,* 32 J. Copyright Soc'y 193 (1985)

McKnight & Müggenburg, *Mexico's New Intellectual Property Regime: Improvements in the Protection of Industrial Property, Copyright, License, and Franchise Rights in Mexico,* 27 Int'l L. 27 (1993)

McManis, *Taking TRIPS on the Information Superhighway: International Intellectual Property Protection and Emerging Computer Technology,* 41 Vill. L. Rev. 207 (1996)

Mouchet, *Problems of the "Domaine Public Payant,"* 8 Colum.-VLA J. L. & the Arts 137 (1983)

Netanel, *Asserting Copyright's Democratic Principles in the Global Arena,* 51 Vand. L. Rev. 217 (1998)

Netanel, *The Next Round: The Impact of the WIPO Copyright Treaty on TRIPS Dispute Settlement,* 37 Va. J. Int'l L. 441 (1997)

D. Nimmer, *The Death of Copyright,* 48 Vand. L. Rev. 1385 (1996)

D. Nimmer, *GATT's Entertainment: Before and NAFTA,* 15 Loy. L.A. Ent. L.J. 133 (1995)

D. Nimmer, *A Tale of Two Treaties,* 22 Colum.-VLA J.L. & Arts 1 (1997)

D. Nimmer, *Nation, Duration, Violation, Harmonization: An International Copyright Proposal for the United States,* 55 Law & Contemp. Probs. 211 (1992)

Note, *The Search for a Solution to the U.S.-Caribbean Copyright Enforcement Controversy,* 16 Fordham Int'l L.J. 721 (1992–93)

Okediji, *Copyright and Public Welfare in Global Perspective,* 7 Ind. J. Global Leg. Stud. 117 (1999)

Perlmutter, *Future Directions in International Copyright,* 16 Cardozo Arts & Ent. L.J. 369 (1998)

Raskind, *Protecting Computer Software in the European Economic Community: The Innovative New Directive,* 18 Brooklyn J. Int'l L. 729 (1992)

Reichman, *Enforcing the Enforcement Procedures of the TRIPS Agreement,* 37 Va. J. Int'l L. 335 (1997)

Reichman, *Intellectual Property in International Trade: Opportunities and Risks of a GATT Connection,* 22 Vand. J. Transnat'l L. 747 (1989)

Rinaldo, *The Scope of Copyright Protection in the United States Under Existing Inter–American Relations: Abrogation of the Need for U.S. Protection Under the Buenos Aires Convention by Reliance Upon the U.C.C.,* 22 Bull. Copyright Soc'y 417 (1975)

Ringer, *The Role of the United States in International Copyright — Past, Present and Future,* 65 Geo. L.J. 1065 (1968)

Samuelson, *The U.S. Digital Agenda at WIPO,* 37 Va. J. Int'l L. 369 (1997)

Schwartz, *Recent Developments in the Copyright Regimes of the Soviet Union and Eastern Europe,* 38 J. Copyright Soc'y 123 (1991)

Simone, *Copyright in the People's Republic of China: A Foreigner's Guide,* 7 Cardozo Arts & Ent. L.J. 1 (1988)

Simone, *Protection of American Copyrights in Books on Taiwan,* 35 J. Copyright Soc'y 115 (1988)

Sobel, *The Framework of International Copyright,* 8 Cardozo Arts & Ent. L.J. 1 (1989)

Solberg, *The International Copyright Union,* 36 Yale L.J. 68 (1926)

Symposium, *Trade-Related Aspects of Intellectual Property,* 22 Vand. J. Transnat'l L. 689 (1989)

Turkewitz, *Authors' Rights Are Dead,* 38 J. Copyright Soc'y 41 (1990)

von Lewinski, *Copyright in the European Communities: The Proposed Harmonization Measures,* 28 Brooklyn J. Int'l L. 703 (1992)

U.S. Copyright Office, *Circular 38a: International Copyright Relations of the United States* (continually updated)

Zheng & Pendleton, *A Response to United States Government Criticisms of the Chinese Copyright Law,* 7 E.I.P.R. 257 (1991)

Copyright and the Digital Challenge

G.P. Albert, INTELLECTUAL PROPERTY LAW IN CYBERSPACE (1999)

J. Dratler, Jr., CYBERLAW: INTELLECTUAL PROPERTY IN THE DIGITAL MILLENNIUM (2002)

D. Katsh, LAW IN A DIGITAL WORLD (1995)

J. Litman, DIGITAL COPYRIGHT: PROTECTING INTELLECTUAL PROPERTY ON THE INTERNET (2001)

H. Perritt, LAW AND THE INFORMATION SUPERHIGHWAY (2000)

M. Remington, *NAPSTER* AND THE DIGITAL AGE: THE FUTURE OF COPYRIGHT LAW (2001)

Bartow, *Libraries in a Digital and Aggressively Copyrighted World: Retaining Patron Access through Changing Technologies,* 62 Ohio St. L.J. 821 (2001)

Bartow, *Our Data, Ourselves: Privacy, Propertization, and Gender,* 34 U.S.F. L. Rev. 633 (2000)

Beard, *Clones, Bones and Twilight Zones: Protecting the Digital Persona of the Quick, the Dead and the Imaginary,* 16 Berkeley Tech. L.J. 1165 (2001)

Boyle, *Intellectual Property Policy Online: A Young Person's Guide*, 10 Harv. J. L. & Tech. 47 (1996)

Burk, *Muddy Rules for Cyberspace*, 21 Cardozo L. Rev. 121 (1999)

Burk, *The Trouble with Trespass*, 4 J. Small & Emerging Bus. L. 27 (2000)

Cate, *The Technological Transformation of Copyright Law*, 81 Iowa L. Rev. 1395 (1996)

J. Cohen, *A Right to Read Anonymously: A Closer Look at "Copyright Management" in Cyberspace*, 28 Conn. L. Rev. 981 (1996)

Craig, *The Development of Internet Education and the Role of Copyright Law*, 40 J. Copyright Soc'y 75 (2000)

Elkin-Koren, *Cyberlaw and Social Change: A Democratic Approach to Copyright Law in Cyberspace*, 14 Cardozo Arts & Ent L.J. 215 (1996)

Gailey, *Who Owns Digital Rights? Examining the Scope of Copyright Protection for Electronically Distributed Works*, 18 Comm. & the Law 3 (1996)

Gasaway, *Distance Learning and Copyright*, 62 Ohio St. L.J. 783 (2001)

Ginsburg, *Putting Cars on the "Information Superhighway": Authors, Exploiters & Copyright in Cyberspace*, 95 Colum. L. Rev. 1466 (1995)

Glynn, *Cyber Copyrights: Internet Provider Liability*, 60 Tex. Bar J. 634 (1997)

Halpern, *Copyright Law in the Digital Age: Malum in Se and Malum Prohibitum*, 4 Marq. Intell. Prop. L. Rev. 1 (2000)

Halpern, *The Digital Threat to the Normative Role of Copyright Law*, 62 Ohio St. L.J. 569 (2001)

Hardy, *The Internet and the Law: Copyright and "New-Use" Technologies*, 23 Nova L. Rev. 657 (1999)

Hardy, *Not So Different: Tangible, Intangible, Digital, and Analog Works and Their Comparison for Copyright Purposes*, 26 U. Dayton L. Rev. 211 (2001)

Hardy, *The Proper Legal Regime for "Cyberspace"*, 55 U. Pitt. L. Rev. 993 (1994)

Hardy, *Property (and Copyright) in Cyberspace*, 1996 U. Chi. Legal F. 217

Johnson & Post, *Law and Borders: The Rise of the Law in Cyberspace*, 48 Stan. L. Rev. 1367 (1996)

Kaplan, *Copyright in the Digital Age,* 49 J. Copyright Soc'y 1 (2001)

Karjala, *Federal Preemption of Shrinkwrap and On-Line Licenses,* 22 U. Dayton L. Rev. 511 (1997)

Ku, *Creative Destruction of Copyright:* Napster *and the New Economics of Digital Technology,* 69 U. Chi. L. Rev. 263 (2002)

Kurtz, *Symposium: Copyright and the Internet — World Without Borders,* 43 Wayne L. Rev. 117 (1996)

Leaffer, *Protecting Authors' Rights in a Digital Age,* 27 U. Tol. L. Rev. 1 (1996)

Lee, *Culturally-Based Copyright Systems?: The U.S. and Korea in Conflict,* 79 Wash. U.L.Q. 1103 (2001)

Lemley, *Dealing with Overlapping Copyrights on the Internet,* 22 U. Dayton L. Rev. 547 (1997)

Litman, *Reforming Information Law in Copyright's Image,* 22 Dayton L. Rev. 587 (1997)

Litman, *Revising Copyright Law for the Information Age,* 75 Or. L. Rev. 19 (1996)

Liu, *Owning Digital Copies: Copyright Law and the Incidents of Copy Ownership,* 42 Wm. & Mary L. Rev. 1245 (2001)

Loundy, *Revising the Copyright Law for Electronic Publishing,* 14 J. Marshall J. Computer & Info. L. 1 (1995)

McCoy, *Cybertheft: Will Copyright Law Prevent Digital Tyranny on the Superhighway?,* 30 Wake Forest L. Rev. 169 (1995)

Menell, *The Challenges of Reforming Intellectual Property Protection for Computer Software,* 94 Colum. L. Rev. 2644 (1994)

Meurer, *Price Discrimination, Personal Use and Piracy: Copyright Protection for Digital Works,* 45 Buff. L. Rev. 845 (1997)

Mills, *Entertainment on the Internet: First Amendment and Copyright Issues,* 79 J. Pat. & Trademark Off. Soc'y 461 (1997)

Nachbar, *Paradox and Structure: Relying on Government Regulation to Preserve the Internet's Unregulated Character,* 85 Minn. L. Rev. 215 (2000)

R. Nimmer & P. Krauthaus, *Copyright on the Information Superhighway: Requiem for a Middleweight,* 6 Stan. L. & Pol'y Rev. 25 (1994)

Perlmutter, *Convergence and the Future of Copyright,* 24 Colum.-VLA J.L. & Arts 163 (2001)

Post, *Symposium:* Napster *& Beyond: Protecting Copyright in the Digital Millennium — His Napster's Voice,* 20 Temp. Envtl. L. & Tech. J. 35 (2001)

Radin, *Property Evolving in Cyberspace,* 15 J. L. & Com. 509 (1996)

Reichman, *Electronic Information Tools: The Outer Edge of World Intellectual Property Law,* 17 U. Dayton L. Rev. 853 (1992)

Rice, *Digital Information as Property and Product: U.C.C. Article 2B,* 22 U. Dayton L. Rev. 621 (1997)

Samuelson, *Digital Media and the Changing Face of Intellectual Property Law,* 16 Rutgers Computer & Tech. L.J. 323 (1990)

Samuelson, *Privacy As Intellectual Property?,* 52 Stan. L. Rev. 1125 (2000)

Shipley, *Liability Issues Facing Online Businesses,* 36-WTR Ark. Law 20 (2001)

Tomlinson, *Journalism and Entertainment as Intellectual Property on the Information Superhighway: The Challenge of the Digital Domain,* 6 Stan. L. & Pol'y Rev. 61 (1994)

Zimmerman, *Copyright in Cyberspace: Don't Throw Out the Public Interest with the Bathwater,* 1994 Annual Survey of American Law 403.

Thinking and Talking About Copyright Law

J. Boyle, SHAMANS, SOFTWARE & SPLEENS: LAW AND THE CONSTRUCTION OF THE INFORMATION SOCIETY (1996)

A. Friedman, THE LAW OF HIGH TECHNOLOGY INNOVATION (1992)

M. Jussawalla, THE ECONOMICS OF INTELLECTUAL PROPERTY IN A WORLD WITHOUT FRONTIERS: A STUDY OF COMPUTER SOFTWARE (1992)

B. Kaplan, AN UNHURRIED VIEW OF COPYRIGHT (1967)

L. Lessig, THE FUTURE OF IDEAS: THE FATE OF THE COMMONS IN A CONNECTED WORLD (2001)

C.B. MacPherson, THE POLITICAL THEORY OF POSSESSIVE INDIVIDUALISM (1962)

A. Moore, INTELLECTUAL PROPERTY: MORAL, LEGAL & INTERNATIONAL DILEMMAS (1997)

D. Nimmer, COPYRIGHT: SACRED TEXT, TECHNOLOGY, AND THE DMCA (2002)

A. Plant, THE NEW COMMERCE IN IDEAS AND INTELLECTUAL PROPERTY (1953)

S. Stewart, CRIMES OF WRITING: PROBLEMS IN THE CONTAINMENT OF REPRESENTATION (1991)

R. Towse, CREATIVITY, INCENTIVE AND REWARD: AN ECONOMIC ANALYSIS OF COPYRIGHT AND CULTURE IN THE INFORMATION AGE (2001)

M. Woodmansee, THE AUTHOR, THE ARTS, AND THE MARKET: RE-READING THE HISTORY OF AESTHETICS (1993)

M. Woodmansee and P. Jaszi (eds.), THE CONSTRUCTION OF AUTHORSHIP: TEXTUAL APPROPRIATION IN LAW AND LITERATURE (1994)

Barlow, *The Economy of Ideas*, 2.03 Wired 84 (Mar. 1994)

Benkler, *Free as the Air to Common Use: First Amendment Constraints on Enclosure of the Public Domain*, 74 N.Y.U. L. Rev. 354 (1999)

Benkler, *Siren Songs and Amish Children: Autonomy, Information, and Law,* 76 N.Y.U.L. Rev. 23 (2001)

Besen & Kirby, *Private Copying, Appropriability and Optimal Copying Royalties,* 32 J. Law & Econ. 255 (1989)

Besen & Raskind, *An Introduction to the Law and Economics of Intellectual Property,* 5 J. Econ. Persp. 3 (1991)

Boyle, *Cruel, Mean, or Lavish? Economic Analysis, Price Discrimination and Digital Intellectual Property*, 53 Vand. L. Rev. 2007 (2000)

Boyle, *A Theory of Law and Information: Copyright, Spleens, Blackmail, and Insider Trading,* 80 Cal. L. Rev. 1413 (1992)

Boytha, *The Justification of the Protection of Authors' Rights as Reflected in Their Historical Development,* 151 Revue Internationale de Droit D'Auteur [R.I.D.A.] 53 (1992)

Boytha, *Whose Right is Copyright?,* 6/7 GRUR Int'l 379 (1983)

Breyer, *The Uneasy Case for Copyright: A Study in Copyright of Books, Photocopies and Computer Programs,* 84 Harv. L. Rev. 281 (1970); Tyerman, *The Economic Rationale for Copyright Protection for Published Books: A Reply to Professor Breyer,* 18 UCLA L. Rev. 1100 (1971); Breyer, *Copyright: A Rejoinder,* 20 UCLA L. Rev. 75 (1972)

Chafee, *Reflections on the Law of Copyright,* 45 Colum. L. Rev. 503, 719 (1945)

Cohen, *The Law and Economics of Intellectual Property Rights: Copyright and the Perfect Curve,* 53 Vand. L. Rev. 1799 (2000)

Coombe, *The Properties and the Politics of Possessing Identity: Native Claims in the Cultural Appropriation Controversy*, 6 Can. J. L. & Juris. 249 (1993)

Dayan, *The Scope of Copyright in Information: An Alternative to Classic Theory*, 42 Fed. Comm. L.J. 239 (1990)

Dietz, *Copyright in the Modern Technological World: A Mere Industrial Property Right?*, 39 J. Copyright Soc'y 83 (1991)

Dursht, *Judicial Plagiariams: It May be Fair Use But is it Ethical?*, 18 Cardozo L. Rev. 1253 (1996)

Driedman, *Standards as Intellectual Property: An Economic Approach*, 19 U. Dayton L. Rev. 1109 (1994)

Ginsburg, *Authors and Users in Copyright*, 45 J. Copyright Soc'y 1 (1997)

Ginsburg, *Copyright and Control Over New Technologies of Dissemination*, 101 Colum L. Rev. 1613 (2001)

Ginsburg, *Copyright Without Borders? Choice of Forum and Choice of Law for Copyright Infringement in Cyberspace*, 15 Cardozo Arts & Ent. L.J. 153 (1997)

Ginsburg, *Creation and Commercial Value: Copyright Protection for Works of Information*, 90 Colum. L. Rev. 1865 (1990)

Goldstein, *Copyright*, 38 J. Copyright Soc'y (1991)

Goldstein, *Copyright and Its Substitutes*, 1997 Wis. L. Rev. 865 (1997)

Gordon, *A Property Right in Self-Expression: Equality and Individualism in the Natural Law of Intellectual Property*, 102 Yale L.J. 1533 (1993)

Gordon, *An Inquiry into the Merits of Copyright: The Challenges of Consistency, Consent, and Encouragement Theory*, 41 Stan. L. Rev. 1343 (1989)

Gordon, *Assertive Modesty: An Economics of Intangibles*, 94 Colum. L. Rev. 2579 (1994)

Gordon, *Asymetric Market Failure and Prisoner's Dilemna in Intellectual Property*, 17 U. Dayton L. Rev. 853 (1992)

Gordon, *On Owning Information: Intellectual Property Law and the Restitutionary Impulse*, 78 Va. L. Rev. 149 (1992)

Graves, *Private Rights, Public Uses, and the Future of the Copyright Clause*, 80 Neb. L. Rev. 64 (2001)

Greene, *Copyright, Culture & Black Music: A Legacy of Unequal Protection*, 21 Hastings Comm. & Ent. L.J. 339 (1999)

Hamilton, *Appropriation Art & the Imminent Decline in Authorial Control Over Copyrighted Works,* 42 J. Copyright Soc'y 93 (1994)

Hamilton, *Art and the Marketplace of Expression,* 17 Cardozo Arts & Ent. L.J. 167 (1999)

Hansen, *International Copyright: An Unorthodox Approach,* 29 Vand. J. Transnat'l L. 579 (1996)

Hardy, *The Ancient Doctrine of Trespass to Web Sites,* 1996 J. Online L., Art. 7

Harmon, *Law, Art, and the Killing Jar,* 79 Iowa L. Rev. 367 (1994)

Heald, *Reviving the Rhetoric of the Public Interest: Choir Directors, Copy Machines, and New Arrangements of Public Domain Music,* 46 Duke L.J. 241 (1996)

Hettinger, *Justifying Intellectual Property,* 18 Phil. & Pub. Aff. 31 (1989)

Hughes, *The Philosophy of Intellectual Property,* 77 Geo. L.J. 287 (1988)

Hughes, *"Recoding" Intellectual Property and Overlooked Audience Interests,* 77 Tex. L. Rev. 923 (1999)

Hurt & Schuchman, *The Economic Rationale of Copyright,* 56 Am. Econ. Rev. 42 (1966)

Jaszi, *A Garland of Reflections on Three Copyright Topics,* 8 Cardozo Arts & Ent. L.J. 47 (1989)

Jaszi, *Goodbye to All That — A Reluctant (and Perhaps Premature) Adieu to a Constitutionally-Grounded Discourse of Public Interest in Copyright Law,* 29 Vand. J. Transnat'l L. 595 (1996)

Jaszi, *On the Author Effect: Contemporary Copyright and Collective Creativity,* 10 Cardozo Arts & Ent. L.J. 293 (1992)

Johnson, *The Economics of Copying,* 93 J. Pol. Econ. 158 (1985)

Kauffman, *Exposing the Suspicious Foundations of Society's Primacy in Copyright Law: Five Accidents,* 10 Colum.–VLA J.L. & the Arts 381 (1986)

Kerever, *Copyright: The Achievements and Future Development of European Legal Culture,* 26 Copyright 130 (Apr. 1990)

Kreiss, *Accessability and Commercialization in Copyright Theory,* 43 U.C.L.A. L. Rev. 1 (1995)

Ladd, *The Harm of the Concept of Harm in Copyright,* 30 J. Copyright Soc'y 421 (1983)

Landes & Posner, *An Economic Analysis of Copyright Law,* 18 J. Leg. Stud. 325 (1989)

Lange, *At Play in the Fields of the Word: Copyright and the Construction of Authorship in the Post–Literate Millenium,* 55 Law & Contemp. Probs. 139 (1992)

Lange, *Recognizing the Public Domain,* 44 Law & Contemp. Probs. 147 (1981)

Lemley, *The Economics of Improvement in Intellectual Property Law,* 75 Tex. L. Rev. 989 (1997)

Litman, *Copyright and Information Policy,* 55 Law & Contemp. Probs. 185 (1992)

Litman, *Copyright, Compromise and Legislative History,* 72 Cornell L. Rev. 857 (1987)

Litman, *Copyright Legislation and Technological Change,* 68 Or. L. Rev. 275 (1989)

Litman, *Reforming Information Law in Copyright's Image,* 22 U. Dayton L. Rev. 587 (1997)

Litman, *The Exclusive Right to Read,* 75 Oreg. L. Rev. 299 (1996)

Litman, *The Public Domain,* 39 Emory L.J. 965 (1990)

Long, *First, "Let's Kill All the Intellectual Property Lawyers!": Musings on the Decline and Fall of the Intellectual Property Empire,* 34 J. Marshall L. Rev. 851 (2001)

Lovern, *Evaluating Resale Royalties for Used CD's,* 4 Kan. J.L. & Pub. Pol'y 113 (1994)

Lunney, *Reexamining Copyright's Incentives-Access Paradigm,* 49 Vand. L. Rev. 483 (1996)

Madison, *Complexity and Copyright in Contradiction,* 18 Cardozo Arts & Ent. L.J. 125 (2000)

Mathias, *Some Unhurried Reflections on Copyright,* 6 Cardozo Arts & Ent. L.J. 101 (1987)

Merges, *Of Property Rules, Coase, and Intellectual Property,* 94 Colum. L. Rev. 2655 (1994)

Merges & Reynolds, *The Proper Scope of the Copyright and Patent Power,* 37 Harv. J. on Legis. 45 (2000)

Netanel, *Copyright Alienability Restrictions and the Enhancement of Author Autonomy: A Normative Evaluation,* 24 Rutgers L.J. 347 (1993)

Netanel, *Copyright and a Democratic Civil Society,* 108 Yale L.J. 283 (1996)

Netanel, *Cyberspace Self-Governance: A Skeptical View from Liberal Democratic Theory,* 88 Calif. L. Rev. 395 (2000)

Netanel, *Locating Copyright Within The First Amendment Skein,* 54 Stan. L. Rev. 1 (2001)

Netanel, *Market Hierarchy and Copyright in Our System of Free Expression,* 53 Vand. L. Rev. 1879 (2000)

D. Nimmer, *The End of Copyright,* 48 Vand. L. Rev. 1385 (1995)

O'Rourke, *Essay: Evaluating Mistakes in Intellectual Property Law: Configuring the System to Account for Imperfection,* 4 J. Small & Emerging Bus. L. 167 (2000)

Palmer, *Intellectual Property: A Non-Posnerian Law and Economics Approach,* 12 Hamline L. Rev. 261 (1989)

Patry, *Copyright and the Legislative Process: A Personal Perspective,* 14 Cardozo Arts & Ent. L.J. 139 (1996)

Patterson, *Copyright in the New Millennium: Resolving the Conflict between Property Rights and Political Rights,* 62 Ohio St. L.J. 703 (2001)

Plant, *The Economic Aspects of Copyright in Books,* 1 Economica 167 (1934)

Radin, *Property and Personhood,* 34 Stan. L. Rev. 957 (1982); Schnably, *Property and Pragmatism: A Critique of Radin's Theory of Property and Personhood,* 45 Stan. L. Rev. 347 (1993)

Raskind, *The Continuing Process of Refining and Adapting Copyright Principles,* 14 Colum.–VLA J.L. & the Arts 125 (1990)

Reichman, *Legal Hybrids Between the Patent and Copyright Paradigms,* 94 Colum. L. Rev. 2432 (1994)

Reyes, *Can the Common Law Adequately Justify a Home Taping Royalty Using Economic Efficiency Alone?,* 16 N.Y.L. Sch. J. Int'l & Comp. L. 235 (1996)

Samuelson, *Digital Media and the Changing Face of Intellectual Property Law,* 16 Rutgers Computer & Tech. L.J. 323 (1990)

Schaumann, *Closely Held Business: Problems & Solutions: Small Business and Copyright Ownership,* 22 Wm. Mitchell L. Rev. 1469 (1996)

Sterk, *Rhetoric and Reality in Copyright Law,* 94 Mich. L. Rev. 1197 (1996)

Suchman, *Invention and Ritual: Notes on the Interrelation of Magic and Intellectual Property in Preliterate Societies,* 89 Colum. L. Rev. 1264 (1989)

Swanson, *The Role of Disclosure in Modern Copyright Law,* 70 J. Pat. & Trademark Off. Soc'y 217 (1988)

Symposium, *The Law and Economics of Intellectual Property*, 78 Va. L. Rev. 1 (1992)

Vaver, *Intellectual Property Today: Of Myths and Paradoxes*, 69 Can. Bar Rev. 98 (1990)

Waldron, *From Authors to Copiers: Individual Rights and Social Values in Intellectual Property*, 68 Chi.-Kent L. Rev. 847 (1993)

Wilde, *Replacing the Idea/Expression Metaphor with a Market-Based Analysis in Copyright Infringement Actions*, 16 Whittier L. Rev. 793 (1995)

Winslow, *Rapping on a Revolving Door: An Economic Analysis of Parody & Campbell v. Acuff-Rose Music, Inc.*, 69 S. Cal. L. Rev. 767 (1996)

Woodmansee, *The Genius and the Copyright*, 17 Eighteenth Century Studies 425 (1984)

Yen, *Copyright Opinions and Aesthetic Theory*, 71 S. Cal. L. Rev. 247 (1998)

Yen, *The Interdisciplinary Future of Copyright Theory*, 10 Cardozo Arts & Ent. L.J. 423 (1992)

Yen, *A Preliminary Economic Analysis of* Napster: *Internet Technology, Copyright Liability, and The Possibility of Coasean Bargaining*, 26 U. Dayton L. Rev. 247 (2001)

Yen, *Restoring the Natural Law: Copyright as Labor and Possession*, 51 Ohio St. L.J. 517 (1990)

CHAPTER 2
PREREQUISITES FOR COPYRIGHT PROTECTION

Reference Works

H. Abrams, THE LAW OF COPYRIGHT §§ 2.01 to 2.05, 8.01 to 8.02 (2002)

P. Goldstein, COPYRIGHT: PRINCIPLES, LAW AND PRACTICE §§ 2.0 to 2.5 (2002)

M. Leaffer, UNDERSTANDING COPYRIGHT LAW §§ 2.1 to 2.7, 2.13 to 2.14 (3d ed. 1999)

M. Nimmer & D. Nimmer, NIMMER ON COPYRIGHT §§ 1.01 to 1.11, 2.01 to 2.02, 5.05 to 5.06 (2002)

W. Patry, COPYRIGHT LAW AND PRACTICE, Chap. 2 (1994 & 2000 Supp.)

Fixation

Brandriss, *Writing in Frost on a Window Pane: E-mail and Chatting on RAM and Copyright Fixation,* 43 J. Copyright Soc'y 237 (1996)

Damman, *Copyright of Computer Display Screens: Summary and Suggestions,* 9 Computer L.J. 417 (1989)

Note, *Fixing Fixation: A Copyright With Teeth for Improvisational Performers,* 97 Colum. L. Rev. 1363 (1997)

Staines, *Idee or Idee Fixe?,* 50 Mod. L. Rev. 368 (1987)

Originality and Authorship Generally

D. Saunders, AUTHORSHIP AND COPYRIGHT (1992)

J. Gaines, CONTESTED CULTURE: THE IMAGE, THE VOICE, AND THE LAW (1991)

B. Sherman & A. Strowel, OF AUTHORS AND ORIGINS: ESSAYS ON COPYRIGHT LAW (1994)

Abrams, *Originality and Creativity in Copyright Law,* 55 Law & Contemp. Probs. 3 (1992)

Aoki, *(Intellectual) Property and Sovereignity: Notes Toward a Cultural Georgraphy of Authorship,* 48 Stan. L. Rev. 1293 (1996)

Baade, *Photographer's Rights: Case for Sufficient Originality Test in Copyright,* 30 J. Marshall L. Rev. 149 (1996)

Booth & Yera, *Judicial Review, Copyrightability and the Register's Discretion: A New Direction?*, 7 U. Miami Ent. & Sports L. Rev. 255 (1990)

Brown, *Eligibility for Copyright Protection: A Search for Principled Standards*, 70 Minn. L. Rev. 579 (1985)

Clifford, *Intellectual Property in the Era of Creative Computer Programs: Will the True Creator Please Stand Up?*, 71 Tul. L. Rev. 1675 (1997)

Comment, *How Much is Enough? The Search for a Standard of Creativity in Works of Authorship Under Section 102(a) of the Copyright Act of 1976*, 68 Neb. L. Rev. 835 (1989)

Durham, *Speaking of the World: Fact, Opinion and the Originality Standard of Copyright*, 33 Ariz. St. L.J. 791 (2001)

Dreier & Karnell, *Originality of the Copyrighted Work: A European Perspective*, 39 J. Copyright Soc'y 289 (1992)

Elkin-Koren, *Of Scientific Claims and Proprietary Rights: Lessons from the* Dead Sea Scrolls *Case*, 38 Hous. L. Rev. 445 (2001)

Gana, *Has Creativity Died in the Third World? Some Implications of the Internationalization of Intellectual Property*, 24 Denv. J. Int'l L. & Pol'y 109 (1995)

Hughes, *The Philosophy of Intellectual Property*, 77 Geo. L.J. 287 (1989)

Jaszi, *Toward a Theory of Copyright: The Metamorphosis of "Authorship,"* 41 Duke L.J. 455 (1991)

Karjala, *Copyright and Misappropriation*, 17 U. Dayton L. Rev. 885 (1992)

Lange, *At Play in the Fields of the Word: Copyright and the Construction of Authorship in the Post-Literate Millenium*, 55 Law & Contemp. Probs. 139 (1992)

Lanham, *Barbie and the Teacher of Righteousness: Two Lessons in the Economics of Attention*, 38 Hous. L. Rev. 499 (2001)

Litman, *The Public Domain*, 39 Emory L.J. 965 (1990)

D. Nimmer, *Copyright in the Dead Sea Scrolls: Authorship and Originality*, 38 Hous. L. Rev. 1 (2001)

Oakes, *The Dead Sea Scrolls: A Live Copyright Controversy*, 38 Hous. L. Rev. 219 (2001)

Olson, *Copyright Originality*, 48 Mo. L. Rev. 29 (1983)

Oppenheimer, *Originality in Art Reproductions: "Variations" in Search of a Theme*, 26 Bull. Copyright Soc'y 1 (1978)

Patterson, *Nimmer's Copyright in the Dead Sea Scrolls: A Comment*, 38 Hous. L. Rev. 431 (2001)

Ricketson, *The Concept of Originality in Anglo-Australian Copyright Law,* 39 J. Copyright Soc'y 265 (1992)

Samuels, *The Public Domain in Copyright Law,* 41 J. Copyright Soc'y 137 (1993)

Samuelson, *The Originality Standard for Literary Works Under U.S. Copyright Law,* 42 Am. J. Comp. L. 393 (1994)

Sookman, *Computer-Assisted Creation of Works Protected by Copyright,* 5 Intell. Prop. J. 165 (1990)

Symposium, *Intellectual Property and the Construction of Authorship,* 10 Cardozo Arts & Ent. L.J. 277–720 (1992)

VerSteeg, *Defining "Author" for Purposes of Copyright,* 45 Am. U. L. Rev. 1323 (1996)

VerSteeg, *Rethinking Originality (in Copyright),* 34 Wm. & Mary L. Rev. 801 (1993)

VerSteeg, *Sparks in the Tinderbox:* Feist, *Creativity and the Legislative History of the 1976 Copyright Act,* 57 U. Pitt. L. Rev. 549 (1995)

Weinstein, *Ancient Works, Modern Dilemmas: The Dead Sea Scrolls Copyright Case,* 43 Am. U. L. Rev. 1637 (1994)

Wilkof, *Copyright, Moral Rights and the Choice of Law: Where Did the* Dead Sea Scrolls *Court Go Wrong?,* 38 Hous. L. Rev. 463 (2001)

Woodmansee, *Response to David Nimmer,* 38 Hous. L. Rev. 231 (2001)

The Idea/Expression Dichotomy

A. Cohen, *Copyright Law and the Myth of Objectivity: The Idea-Expression Dichotomy and the Inevitability of Artistic Value Judgments,* 66 Ind. L.J. 175 (1990)

Comment, *Seen One, Seen Them All? Making Sense of the Copyright Merger Doctrine,* 45 UCLA L. Rev. 1125 (1998)

Detterman, *The Scope of Copyright Protection for Computer Programs: Exploring the Idea-Expression Dichotomy,* 20 Intell. Prop. L. Rev. 399 (1988)

Gambrell, Hamilton & Hood, Whelan & Altai: *Protecting Software by Abusing Idea and Expression,* 11 Computer Law. 9 (1994)

Katz, *Expanded Notions of Copyright Protection: Idea Protection Within the Copyright Act*, 77 B.U. L. Rev. 873 (1997)

Kravetz, *Idea/Expression Dichotomy and Method of Operation: Determining Copyright Protection for Computer Programs*, 8 DePaul Bus. L.J. 75 (1995)

Kurtz, *Speaking to the Ghost: Idea and Expression in Copyright*, 47 U. Miami L. Rev. 1221 (1993)

Libott, *Round the Prickly Pear: The Idea-Expression Fallacy in a Mass Communications World*, 14 UCLA L. Rev. 735 (1967)

Olson, *The Legal Protection for Printed Systems*, 81 W. Va. L. Rev. 45 (1979)

Olson, *The Uneasy Legacy of Baker v. Selden*, 43 S.D. L. Rev. 604 (1998)

Patry, *The Enumerated Powers Doctrine and Intellectual Property: An Imminent Constitutional Collision*, 67 Geo. Wash. L. Rev. 359 (1999)

Petraske, *Non–Protectible Elements of Software: The Idea–Expression Distinction Is Not Enough*, 29 Idea 35 (1988)

Reichman, *Computer Programs as Applied Scientific Know–How: Implication of Copyright Protection for Commercialized University Research*, 42 Vand. L. Rev. 639 (1989)

Samuels, *The Idea–Expression Dichotomy in Copyright Law*, 56 Tenn. L. Rev. 321 (1989)

Spivack, *Does Form Follow Function? The Idea–Expression Dichotomy in Copyright Protection of Computer Software*, 35 UCLA L. Rev. 723 (1988)

Wilde, *Replacing the Idea/Expression Metaphor with a Market-Based Analysis in Copyright Infringement Actions*, 16 Whittier L. Rev. 793 (1995).

Yen, *A First Amendment Perspective on the Idea/Expression Dichotomy and Copyright in a Work's "Total Concept and Feel,"* 38 Emory L.J. 393 (1989)

National Origin and Government Works

Nadiff, *Copyrightability of Works of the Federal and State Governments Under the 1976 Act*, 29 St. Louis U. L.J. 91 (1984)

Note, *A Constitutional Analysis of Copyrighting Government–Commissioned Work*, 84 Colum. L. Rev. 425 (1984)

CHAPTER 3
WORKS OF AUTHORSHIP

Reference Works

H. Abrams, THE LAW OF COPYRIGHT §§ 3.01 to 3.04, 5.10, 19.01 to 19.10 (2002)

P. Goldstein, COPYRIGHT: PRINCIPLES, LAW AND PRACTICE §§ 2.6 to 2.16, 15.26 to 15.34 (2002)

M. Leaffer, UNDERSTANDING COPYRIGHT LAW §§ 2.8 to 2.12, 3.1 to 3.22 (3d ed. 1999)

M. Nimmer & D. Nimmer, NIMMER ON COPYRIGHT §§ 2.03 to 2.20, 3.01 to 3.07, 8A.13 to 8A.21 (2002)

W. Patry, COPYRIGHT LAW AND PRACTICE, Chaps. 2 and 3 (1994 & 2000 Supp.)

Literary Works Generally

E.G. Perle & J.T. Williams, THE PUBLISHING LAW HANDBOOK (2d ed. 1992 & 1997 Supp.)

R. Wincor, *The Art of Character Licensing* (1996)

Aoki, *Contradiction and Context in American Copyright Law,* 9 Cardozo Arts & Ent. L.J. 303 (1991)

Bartholomew, *Protecting the Performers: Setting a New Standard for Character Copyrightability,* 41 Santa Clara L. Rev. 341 (2001)

Beall, *Can Anyone Own a Piece of the Clock? The Troublesome Application of Copyright Law to Works of Historical Fiction, Interpretation, and Theory,* 42 Emory L.J. 253 (1993)

Bilder, *The Shrinking Back: The Law of Biography,* 43 Stan. L. Rev. 299 (1991)

Burcart, *No Title to Titles: An Analysis of the Lack of Copyright Protection for Literary Titles,* 32 Copyright L. Symp. (ASCAP) 75 (1986)

Clark, *Of Mice and Men, and Superman: The Copyrightability of Graphic and Literary Characters,* 28 St. Louis U. L.J. 959 (1984)

Ginsburg, *Sabotaging and Reconstructing History: A Comment on the Scope of Copyright Protection in Works of History After Hoehling v. Universal City Studios,* 29 J. Copyright Soc'y 647 (1982)

Gorman, *Fact or Fancy? The Implications for Copyright*, 29 J. Copyright Soc'y 560 (1982)

Hill, *Copyright Protection for Historical Research: A Defense of the Minority View*, 31 Copyright L. Symp. (ASCAP) 45 (1984)

Kidwell, *Open Records Laws and Copyright*, 1989 Wis. L. Rev. 1021

Kurtz, *Protection for Title of Literary Works in the Public Domain*, 37 Rutgers L. Rev. 53 (1984)

Kurtz, *The Methuselah Factor: When Characters Outlive Their Copyrights*, 11 U. Miami Ent. & Sports L. Rev. 437 (1994)

Kurtz, *The Independent Legal Lives of Fictional Characters*, 1986 Wis. L. Rev. 429

Kurtz, *Copyright: The Scenes a Faire Doctrine*, 41 Fla. L. Rev. 79 (1989)

Lalor, *Copyrightability of Cartoon Characters*, 35 IDEA: J.L. & Tech. 497 (1995)

Nevins, *Copyright + Character = Catastrophe*, 39 J. Copyright Soc'y 303 (1992)

Niro, *Protecting Characters Through Copyright Law: Paving a New Road Upon Which Literary, Graphic, and Motion Picture Characters Can All Travel*, 41 DePaul L. Rev. 359 (1992)

Note, *When Mickey Mouse Is as Strong as Superman: The Convergence of Intellectual Property Laws to Protect Fictional Literary and Pictorial Characters*, 44 Stan. L. Rev. 623 (1992)

Page, *Licensing and Merchandising of Characters*, 11 U. Miami Ent. & Sports L. Rev. 421 (1994)

Pollack, *Intellectual Property Protection for the Creative Chef, or How to Copyright a Cake: A Modest Proposal*, 12 Cardozo L. Rev. 1477 (1991)

Shipley & Hay, *Protecting Research: Copyright, Common Law Alternatives, and Federal Preemption*, 63 N.C.L. Rev. 125 (1984)

Stim, *E.T. Phone Home: The Protection of Literary Phrases*, 7 U. Miami Ent. & Sports L. Rev. 65 (1989)

Tannenbaum, *Uses of Titles for Copyright and Public Domain Works*, 6 Bull. Copyright Soc'y 64 (1958)

Tushnet, *Legal Fictions: Copyright, Fan Fiction & a New Common Law*, 17 Loy. L.A. Ent. L.J. 651 (1997)

Zissu, *Whither Character Rights: Some Observations*, 29 J. Copyright Soc'y 121 (1981)

Software-Related Issues

D. Bender, COMPUTER LAW (1998)

S. Fishman, WEB AND SOFTWARE DEVELOPMENT: A LEGAL GUIDE (3d ed. 2001)

E.J. Louwers & C. Prins, INTERNATIONAL COPYRIGHT LAW (2002)

R. Nimmer, THE LAW OF COMPUTER TECHNOLOGY (Rev. ed. 2001)

Office of Tech. Assessment, COMPUTER SOFTWARE: COPYRIGHT, PATENTS AND THE CHALLENGE OF TECHNOLOGICAL CHANGE (1993)

B. Sookman, COMPUTER, INTERNET AND ELECTRONIC COMMERCE LAW (2002)

Amin, *The Lack of Protection Afforded Software Under the Current Intellectual Property Laws,* 43 Clev. St. L. Rev. 19 (1995)

Bender, *Protection for Computer Programs: The Copyright/Trade Secret Interface,* 47 U. Pitt. L. Rev. 907 (1986)

Bobko, *Open-Source Software and the Demise of Copyright,* 27 Rutgers Computer & Tech. L.J. 51 (2001)

Brown, Bryan & Conley, *Database Protection in a Digital World,* 6 Rich. J. L. & Tech. 2 (1999)

Butler, *Pragmatism in Software Copyright:* Computer Associates v. Altai, 6 Harv. J.L. & Tech. 183 (1992)

Capes, *The Software Copyright "Super Patent,"* 12 Computer Law. 8 (1995)

Cass, *Copyright, Licensing, and the "First Screen,"* 5 Mich. Telecomm. Tech. L. Rev. 35 (1999)

Clapes, Lynch & Steinberg, *Silicon Epics and Binary Bards: Determining the Proper Scope of Copyright Protection for Computer Programs,* 34 UCLA L. Rev. 1493 (1987)

J. Cohen, *Reverse Engineering and the Rise of Electronic Vigilantism: Intellectual Property Implications of "Lock-out" Programs,* 68 S. Cal. L. Rev. 1091 (1995)

Comment, *The Copyrightability of Nonliteral Elements of Computer Programs,* 94 Colum. L. Rev. 242 (1994)

Derwin, *It Is Time to Put "Look and Feel" Out to Pasture,* 15 Hastings Comm. & Ent. L.J. 605 (1993)

Englund, *Idea, Process, or Protected Expression? Determining the Scope of Copyright Protection of the Structure of Computer Programs,* 88 Mich. L. Rev. 866 (1990)

Ginsburg, *Copyright, Common Law, and Sui Generis Protection of Databases in the United States and Abroad,* 66 U. Cin. L. Rev. 151 (1997)

Ginsburg, *Four Reasons and a Paradox: The Manifest Superiority of Copyright Over* Sui Generis *Protection of Computer Software,* 94 Colum. L. Rev. 2559 (1994)

Goldberg & Carson, *Copyright Protection for Artificial Intelligence Systems,* 39 J. Copyright Soc'y 57 (1991)

Gordon, *Assertive Modesty: An Economics of Intangibles,* 94 Colum. L. Rev. 2579 (1994)

Gorman, *Comments on a Manifesto Concerning the Legal Protection of Computer Programs,* 5 Alb. L.J. Sci. & Tech. 277 (1996)

Graham & Zerbe, *Economically Efficient Treatment of Computer Software: Reverse Engineering, Protection & Disclosure,* 22 Rutgers Computer & Tech. L.J. 61 (1996)

Gross, *Researching Software Copyrightability: A Practical Guide,* 10 Santa Clara Computer & High Tech. L.J. 69 (1994)

Hamilton & Sabety, *Computer Science Concepts in Copyright Cases: The Path to a Coherent Law,* 10 Harv. J.L. & Tech. 239 (1997)

Hardy, *The Copyrightability of New Works of Authorship: "Xml Schemas" as an Example,* 38 Hous. L. Rev. 855 (2001)

Hardy, *Six Copyright Theories for the Protection of Computer Object Programs,* 26 Ariz. L. Rev. 845 (1984)

Hardy, *The Policy, Law, and Facts of Copyrighting Computer Screen Displays: An Essay,* 11 Computer L.J. 371 (1992)

Hazen, *Contract Principles as a Guide for Protecting Intellectual Property Rights in Computer Software: The Limits of Copyright Protection, the Evolving Concept of Derivative Works, and the Proper Limits of Licensing Arrangements,* 20 U.C. Davis L. Rev. 105 (1986)

Hornik, *Combating Software Piracy: The Softlifting Problem,* 7 Harv. J.L. & Tech. 377 (1994)

Karjala, *A Coherent Theory for the Copyright Protection of Computer Software and Recent Judicial Interpretations,* 66 U. Cin. L. Rev. 53 (1997)

Karjala, *Copyright Law: Copyright Protection of Computer Program Structure,* 64 Brooklyn L. Rev. 519 (1998)

Karjala, *Copyright Protection of Computer Documents, Reverse Engineering, and Professor Miller,* 19 Dayton L. Rev. 975 (1994)

Karjala, *Lessons from the Computer Software Protection Debate in Japan,* 1984 Ariz. St. L.J. 53

Karjala, *Policy Considerations: Theoretical Foundations for the Protection of Computer Programs in Developing Countries,* 13 UCLA Pac. Basin L.J. 179 (1994)

Karjala, *The Relative Roles of Patent and Copyright in the Protection of Computer Programs,* 17 J. Marshall J. Computer & Info. L. 41 (1998)

Karjala, *Theoretical Foundations for the Protection of Computer Programs in Developing Countries,* 13 UCLA Pac. Basin L.J. 179 (1994)

Kasch, *The Semiconductor Chip Protection Act: Past, Present, and Future,* 7 High Tech. L.J. 71 (1992)

Kravetz, *"Idea/Expression Dichotomy" and "Method of Operation": Determining Copyright Protection for Computer Programs,* 8 DePaul Bus. L.J. 75 (1995)

Kreiss, *Copyright Protection and Reverse Engineering of Software,* 19 U. Dayton L. Rev. 837 (1994)

Kreiss, *Section 117 of the Copyright Act (Computer Programs),* 1991 B.Y.U. L. Rev. 1497 (1991)

Last Frontier Conference Report, *Computer Software and Copyright Protection,* 30 Jurimetrics J. 15 (1989)

Lemley & O'Brien, *Encouraging Software Reuse,* 49 Stan. L. Rev. 255 (1997)

Levine, *Comment on* Bonito Boats *Follow-Up: The Supreme Court's Likely Rejection of Non-Literal Software Copyright Protection,* 6 Computer Law. 29 (1989)

Loren, *The Changing Nature of Derivative Works in the Face of New Technologies,* 4 J. Small & Emerging Bus. L. 57 (2000)

Luettgen, *Functional Usefulness vs. Communicative Usefulness: Thin Copyright Protection for the Nonliteral Elements of Computer Programs,* 4 Tex. Intell. Prop. L.J. 233 (1996)

Lunney, Lotus v. Borland: *Copyright and Computer Programs,* 70 Tul. L. Rev. 2397 (1996)

Menell, *The Challenges of Reforming Intellectual Property Protection for Computer Software,* 94 Colum. L. Rev. 2644 (1994)

Menell, *Tailoring Legal Protection for Computer Software,* 39 Stan. L. Rev. 1329 (1987)

Miller, *Copyright Protection for Computer Programs, Databases, and Computer-Generated Works: Is Anything New Since CONTU?,* 106 Harv. L. Rev. 977 (1993)

R. Nimmer & P. Krauthaus, *Classification of Computer Software for Legal Protection: International Perspectives,* 21 Int'l Law. 733 (1987)

R. Nimmer & P. Krauthaus, *Copyright and Software Technology Infringement: Defining Third Party Development Rights,* 62 Ind. L.J. 13 (1986)

R. Nimmer & P. Krauthaus, *Software Copyright: Sliding Scales and Abstracted Expression,* 32 Hous. L. Rev. 317 (1995)

Oddi, *An Uneasier Case for Copyright Than for Patent Protection of Computer Programs,* 72 Neb. L. Rev. 351 (1993)

Patry, *Copyright and Computer Programs: It's All in the Definition,* 14 Cardozo Arts & Ent. L.J. 1 (1996)

Patry, *The Enumerated Powers Doctrine and Intellectual Property: An Imminent Constitutional Collision,* 67 Geo. Wash. L. Rev. 359 (1999)

Pollack, *The Right to Know?: Delimiting Database Protection at the Juncture of the Commerce Clause, the Intellectual Property Clause and the First Amendment,* 17 Cardozo Arts & Ent. L.J. 47 (1999)

Raskind, *The Uncertain Case for Special Legislation Protecting Computer Software,* 47 U. Pitt. L. Rev. 1131 (1986)

Rauch, *The Realities of Our Times: The Semiconductor Chip Protection Act of 1984 and the Evolution of the Semiconductor Industry,* 75 J. Pat. & Trademark Off. Soc'y 93 (1993)

Saadi, *Sound Recordings Need Sound Protection,* 5 Tex. Intell. Prop. L.J. 333 (1997)

Samuelson, *Allocating Ownership Rights in Computer-Generated Works,* 47 U. Pitt. L. Rev. 1185 (1986)

Samuelson, Benson *Revisited: The Case Against Patent Protection for Algorithms and Other Computer Program-Related Works,* 39 Emory L.J. 1025 (1990)

Samuelson, *Comparing U.S. and EC Copyright Protection for Computer Programs: Are They More Different Than They Seem?,* 13 J.L. & Com. 279 (1994)

Samuelson, *Computer Programs, User Interfaces, and Section 102(b) of the Copyright Act of 1976: A Critique of Lotus v. Paperback,* 55 Law & Contemp. Probs. 311 (1992)

Samuelson, *CONTU Revisited: The Case Against Copyright Protection for Computer Programs in Machine-Readable Form,* 1984 Duke L.J. 663

Samuelson, *Creating a New Kind of Intellectual Property: Applying the Lessons of the Chip Law to Computer Programs,* 70 Minn. L. Rev. 471 (1985)

Samuelson, *How to Interpret the* Lotus *Decision (And How Not To),* 33 Comm. of the ACM 27 (1990)

Samuelson, *Modifying Copyrighted Software: Adjusting Copyright Doctrine to Accommodate a Technology,* 28 Jurimetrics J. 179 (1988)

Samuelson, *Reflections on the State of American Software Copyright Law and the Perils of Teaching It,* 13 Colum.-VLA J.L. & the Arts 61 (1988)

Samuelson, *Some New Kinds of Authorship Made Possible by Computer and Some Intellectual Property Problems They Raise,* 53 U. Pitt. L. Rev. 685 (1992)

Samuelson, Davis, Kapor & Reichman, *A Manifesto Concerning the Legal Protection of Computer Programs,* 94 Colum. L. Rev. 2308 (1994)

Stern, *Copyright in Computer Programming Languages,* 17 Rutgers Computer & Tech. L.J. 321 (1991)

Stern, *Legal Protection for Screen Displays and Other User Interfaces for Computers: A Problem in Balancing Incentives for Creation Against Need for Free Access to the Utilitarian,* 14 Colum.-VLA J.L. & the Arts 283 (1990)

Szepes, *Maximizing Protection for Computer Software,* 12 Santa Clara Comp. & High Tech. L.J. 173 (1996)

Tache, *Copyrightability of Computer Languages: Natural Expansion of Copyright Law or Destruction of the Copytight / Patent Distinction?,* 72 J. Pat. & Trademark Off. Soc'y 564 (1990)

Teter, *Merger and the Machines: An Analysis of the Pro-Compatibility Trend in Computer Software Copyright Cases,* 45 Stan. L. Rev. 1061 (1993)

Velasco, *The Copyrightability of Nonliteral Elements of Computer Programs,* 94 Colum. L. Rev. 242 (1994)

Walker, *Protectable "Nuggets": Drawing the Line Between Idea and Expression in Computer Program Copyright Protection,* 44 J. Copyright Soc'y 79 (1996)

Walter, *Defining the Scope of Software Copyright Protection for Maximum Public Benefit,* 14 Rutgers Computer & Tech. L.J. 1 (1988)

Weinreb, *Copyright for Functional Expression,* 111 Harv. L. Rev. 1149 (1998)

Wilkins, *Protecting Computer Programs as Compilations Under Computer Associates v. Altai,* 104 Yale L.J. 435 (1994)

Musical Works and Sound Recordings

Brylawski, *Motion Picture Soundtrack Music: A Gap or Gaff in Copyright Protection?,* 40 J. Copyright Soc'y 333 (1993)

Calamita, *Coming to Terms with the Celestial Juke Box: Keeping the Sound Recording Copyright Viable in the Digital Age,* 74 B.U. L. Rev. 505 (1994)

Hall, *Blues and the Public Domain — No More Dues to Pay,* 42 J. Copyright Soc'y 215 (1995)

Heald, *Reviving the Rhetoric of the Public Interest: Choir Directors, Copy Machines, and New Arrangements of Public Domain Music,* 46 Duke L.J. 241 (1996)

Kravis, *Does a Song by any Other Name Still Sound As Sweet?: Digital Sampling and its Copyright Implications,* 43 Am. U. L. Rev. 231 (1993)

Nagarajan, *Public Performance Rights in Sound Recordings and the Threat of Digitalization,* 77 J. Pat. & Trademark Off. Soc'y 721 (1995)

Dramatic Works, and Pantomimes & Choreographic Works

Cramer, *Copyright Protection for Choreography: Can it Ever be "En Pointe"?,* 1 Syracuse J. Legis. & Pol'y 145 (1995)

Fisher, *The Copyright in Choreographic Works: A Technical Analysis of the Copyright Act of 1976,* 31 Copyright L. Symp. (ASCAP) 145 (1984)

Hilgard, *Can Choreography & Copyright Waltz Together in the Wake of Horgan v. MacMillan?,* 27 U.C. Davis L. Rev. 757 (1994)

Traylor, *Choreography, Pantomime and the Copyright Revision Act of 1976,* 16 New Eng. L. Rev. 227 (1981)

Varmer, *Copyright in Choreographic Works, Copyright Office Study No. 28* (1960)

Yellin, *New Directions for Copyright: The Property Rights of Stage Directors,* 24 Colum.-VLA J.L. & Arts 317 (2001)

Pictorial, Graphic & Sculptural Works

Brown, *Copyright-like Protection for Designs,* 19 U. Balt. L. Rev. 308 (1989)

Brown, *Design Protection: An Overview,* 34 UCLA L. Rev. 1341 (1987)

Burgunder, *Product Design Protection After* Bonito Boats: *Where It Belongs and How It Should Get There,* 28 Am. Bus. L.J. 1 (1990)

Comment, *Copyright Problems in Post-Modern Art,* 5 J. Art. & Ent. L. 115 (1994)

Denicola, *Applied Art and Industrial Design: A Suggested Approach to Copyright in Useful Articles,* 67 Minn. L. Rev. 707 (1983)

Fryer, *Industrial Design Protection in the United States of America—Present Situation and Plans for Revision,* 70 J. Pat. & Trademark Off. Soc'y 820 (1988)

Goldenberg, *The Long and Winding Road: A History of the Fight Over Industrial Design Protection in the United States,* 45 J. Copyright Soc'y 21 (1997)

Hamilton, *Art Speech,* 49 Vand. L. Rev. 73 (1996)

Hamilton, *Four Questions About Art,* 13 Cardozo Arts & Ent. L.J. 119 (1994)

LoBello, *The Dichotomy Between Artistic Expression and Industrial Design: To Protect or Not to Protect,* 13 Whittier L. Rev. 107 (1992)

Lynch, *Copyright in Utilitarian Objects: Beneath Metaphysics,* 16 U. Dayton L. Rev. 647 (1991)

Milch, *Protection for Utilitarian Works of Art: The Design Patent/ Copyright Conundrum.* 10 Colum.-VLA J.L. & the Arts 211 (1986)

Note, *Copyright Protection for Short-Lived Works of Art,* 51 Fordham L. Rev. 90 (1982)

Oberman & Lloyd, *Copyright Protection for Photographs in the Age of New Technologies,* 2 B.U. J. Sci. & Tech. 10 (1996)

Perlmutter, *Conceptual Separability and Copyright in the Design of Useful Articles,* 37 J. Copyright Soc'y 339 (1990)

Polakovic, *Should the Bauhaus Be in the Copyright Doghouse? Rethinking Conceptual Separability,* 64 U. Colo. L. Rev. 871 (1993)

Reichman, *Design Protection After the Copyright Act of 1976: A Comparative View of the Emerging Interim Models,* 31 J. Copyright Soc'y 267 (1984)

Reichman, *Design Protection and the Legislative Agenda,* 55 Law & Contemp. Probs. 281 (1992)

Reichman, *Design Protection and the New Technologies: The United States Experience in a Transnational Perspective,* 19 U. Balt. L. Rev. 6 (1990)

Reichman, *Design Protection in Domestic and Foreign Copyright Law: From the Berne Revision of 1948 to the Copyright Act of 1976,* 1983 Duke L.J. 1143

Silver, *A Bad Dream: In Search of a Legal Framework for Copyright Infringement Claims Involving Digital Imagery in Motion Pictures,* 35 IDEA: J.L. & Tech. 407 (1995)

Sullivan, *Copyright for Visual Art in the Digital Age: A Modern Adventure in Wonderland,* 14 Cardozo Arts & Ent. L.J. 563 (1996)

VerSteeg, *Jurimetric Copyright: Future Shock for the Visual Arts,* 13 Cardozo Arts & Ent. L.J. 125 (1994)

Ward, *Copyrighting Context: Law for Plumbing's Sake,* 17 Colum.-VLA J.L. & the Arts 159 (1993)

Whicher, *Originality, Cartography and Copyright,* 38 N.Y.U. L. Rev. 280 (1963)

Wolf, *Is There Any Copyright Protection for Maps after* Feist?, 39 J. Copyright Soc'y 224 (1992)

Wolf, *New Landscape in the Copyright Protection for Maps:* Mason v. Montgomery Data, Inc., 40 J. Copyright Soc'y 401 (1993)

Architectural Works

Dremann, *Copyright Protection for Architectural Works,* 23 AIPLA Q.J. 325 (1995)

Ginsburg, *Copyright in the 101st Congress: Commentary on the Visual Artists' Rights Act and the Architectural Works Copyright Protection Act of 1990,* 14 Colum.-VLA J.L. & the Arts 477 (1990)

Hancks, *Copyright Protection for Architectural Design: A Conceptual and Practical Criticism,* 71 Wash. L. Rev. 177 (1996)

Larsen, *The Effect of the Berne Implementation Act of 1988 on Copyright Protection for Architectural Structures,* 1990 U. Ill. L. Rev. 151 (1990)

Newsam, *Architecture & Copyright — Separating the Poetic from the Prosaic,* 71 Tul. L. Rev. 1073 (1997)

Note, *Copyright Protection for Architecture After the Architectural Works Copyright Protection Act of 1990,* 40 Duke L.J. 1598 (1992)

Pollock, *The Architectural Works Copyright Protection Act: Analysis of Probable Ramifications and Arising Issues,* 70 Neb. L. Rev. 873 (1991)

Roberts, *There Goes My Baby: Buildings as Intellectual Property Under the Architectural Works Copyright Protection Act,* 21 Construction Law. 22 (Spr. 2001)

Scaglione, *Building upon the Architectural Works Protection Copyright Act of 1990,* 61 Fordham L. Rev. 193 (1992)

Shipley, *Copyright Protection for Architectural Works,* 37 S.C. L. Rev. 393 (1986)

Thiel, *The Architectural Works Copyright Protection Gesture of 1990, or, "Hey, That Looks Like My Building,"* 7 DePaul-LCA J. Art & Ent. L. 1 (1996)

Derivative Works

Boyd, *Deriving Originality in Derivative Works: Considering the Quantum of Originality Needed to Attain Copyright Protection in a Derivative Work,* 40 Santa Clara L. Rev. 325 (1999)

Brandstetter, *The Lone Ranger: Have the Courts Unfairly Singled Out Musical Arrangements by Denying Them Protection as Derivative Works?,* 15 SPG Ent. & Sports Law. 1 (1997)

Comment, *A Proposal to Recognize Component Works: How a Teddy Bear's on the Competing Ends of Copyright Law,* 78 Cal. L. Rev. 1633 (1990)

Comment, *Copyright and the Musical Arrangement: An Analysis of the Law and Problems Pertaining to This Specialized Form of Derivative Work,* 7 Pepperdine L. Rev. 125 (1979)

Goldstein, *Derivative Rights and Derivative Works in Copyright,* 30 J. Copyright Soc'y 209 (1982)

Loren, *The Changing Nature of Derivative Works in the Face of New Technologies,* 4 J. Small & Emerging Bus. L. 57 (2000)

Note, *A Film of a Different Color: Copyright and the Colorization of Black and White Films,* 5 Cardozo Arts & Ent. L.J. 497 (1986)

Note, *Arrangements and Editions of Public Domain Music: Originality in a Finite System,* 34 Case W. Res. L. Rev. 104 (1983)

Ostertag, *The Use of Derivative Works After Copyright Termination — Does* Woods v. Bourne *Expose a Quagmire?,* 43 J. Copyright Soc'y 28 (1995)

Page, *The Works: Distinguishing Derivative Creations Under Copyright,* 5 Cardozo Arts & Ent. L.J. 415 (1986)

Prater, *When Museums Act Like Gift Shops: The Discordant Derivative Works Exception to the Termination Clause,* 17 Loy. L.A. Ent. L.J. 97 (1996)

Compilations

J. Baumgarten, Fact and Data Protection after *Feist* (1991)

R. Nimmer, The Law of Computer Technology (Rev. ed. 2001)

Register of Copyrights, Report on Legal Protection for Databases (1997)

Abrams, *Originality and Creativity in Copyright Law,* 55 Law & Contemp. Probs. 3 (Spr. 1992)

Arden, *The Conflicting Treatments of Compilations of Facts under the United States and British Copyright Laws,* 19 AIPLA Q.J. 267 (1991)

Baran, *Back to the Future: Learning from the Past in the Database Debate,* 62 Ohio St. L.J. 879 (2001)

Benkler, *The Role of Judicial Review in the Creation and Definition of Private Rights in Information,* 15 Berkeley Tech. L.J. 535 (2000)

Copyright Symposium: Copyright Protection for Computer Databases, CD-Roms and Factual Compilations, 17 U. Dayton L. Rev. 323–629, 731–1018 (1992)

Cate, *The EU Data Protection Directive, Information Privacy, and the Public Interest,* 80 Iowa L. Rev. 431 (1995)

Culber, *Copyright and Compilations: Protecting the Data in Computer Databases,* 6 No. 2 Intell. Prop. L. Bull. 15 (2001)

Denicola, *Copyright in Collections of Facts: A Theory for the Protection of Nonfiction Literary Works,* 81 Colum. L. Rev. 516 (1981)

Dreyfuss, *A Wiseguy's Approach to Information Products: Muscling Copyright and Patent into a Unitary Theory of Intellectual Property,* 1992 Sup. Ct. Rev. 195

Ginsburg, *Creation and Commercial Value: Copyright Protection of Works of Information,* 90 Colum. L. Rev. 1865 (1990)

Ginsburg, *Domestic and International Copyright Issues Implicated in the Compilation of a Multimedia Product,* 25 Seton Hall L. Rev. 1397 (1995)

Ginsburg, *No "Sweat"? Copyright and Other Protection of Works of Information after* Feist v. Rural Telephone, 92 Colum. L. Rev. 338 (1992)

Gordon, *On Owning Information: Intellectual Property and the Restitutionary Impulse,* 78 Va. L. Rev. 149 (1992)

Gordon, *Reality as Artifact: From* Feist *to Fair Use,* 55 Law & Contemp. Probs. 93 (1992)

Gorman, *Copyright Protection for the Collection and Representation of Facts,* 76 Harv. L. Rev. 1569 (1963)

Gorman, *The* Feist *Case: Reflections on a Pathbreaking Copyright Decision,* 18 Rutgers Computer & Tech. L.J. 731 (1992)

Hamilton, *Justice O'Connor's Opinion in* Feist Pub., Inc. v. Rural Telephone Service Co.: *An Uncommon Though Characteristic Approach,* 38 J. Copyright Soc'y 83 (1990)

Heald, *The Extraction/Duplication Dichotomy: Constitutional Line-Drawing in the Database Debate,* 62 Ohio St. L.J. 933 (2001)

Heald, *The Vices of Originality,* 1991 Sup. Ct. Rev. 143

Karjala, *Copyright in Electronic Maps,* 35 Jurimetrics J. 395 (1995)

Litman, *After* Feist, 17 U. Dayton L. Rev. 607 (1992)

McManis, *Comparative Perspectives: Database Protection in the Digital Information Age,* 7 Roger Williams U.L. Rev. 7 (2001)

Note, *Just the Facts, Ma'am: A Case for Uniform Federal Regulation of Information Databases in the New Information Age,* 48 Syracuse L. Rev. 1263 (1998)

Patterson & Joyce, *Monopolizing the Law: The Scope of Copyright Protection for Law Reports and Statutory Compilations,* 36 UCLA L. Rev. 719 (1989)

Patry, *Copyright and the Legislative Process: A Personal Perspective,* 14 Cardozo Arts & Ent. L.J. 139 (1996)

Patry, *Copyright in Collections of Facts: A Reply,* 6 Comm. & the Law 11 (1984)

Patry, *The Enumerated Powers Doctrine and Intellectual Property: An Imminent Constitutional Collision,* 67 Geo. Wash. L. Rev. 359 (1999)

Perlmutter, *The Scope of Copyright in Telephone Directories: Keeping Listing Information in the Public Domain,* 38 J. Copyright Soc'y 1 (1990)

Pollack, *The Right to Know?: Delimiting Database Protection at the Juncture of the Commerce Clause, the Intellectual Property Clause and the First Amendment,* 17 Cardozo Arts & Ent. L.J. 47 (1999)

Raskind, *Assessing the Impact of* Feist, 17 U. Dayton L. Rev. 331 (1992)

Raskind, *The Continuing Process of Refining and Adapting Copyright Principles,* 14 Colum.-VLA J. L. & the Arts 125 (1990)

Reichman, *Electronic Information Tools — The Outer Edge of World Intellectual Property Law,* 17 U. Dayton L. Rev. 797 (1992)

Reichman & Samuelson, *Intellectual Property Rights in Data?,* 50 Vand. L. Rev. 49 (1997)

Reichman & Uhlir, *Database Protection at the Crossroads: Recent Developments and Their Impact on Science and Technology,* 14 Berkeley Tech. L.J. 793 (1999)

Silverstein, *The Copyrightability of Factual Compilations: An Interpretation of* Feist *Through Cases of Maps and Numbers,* 1996 Ann. Survey Am. L. 147

Symposium, *Copyright Protection for Computer Databases, CD-ROMs and Factual Compilations,* 17 U. Dayton L. Rev. 323, 731 (1992)

VerSteeg, *Sparks in the Tinderbox:* Feist, *"Creativity," and the Legislative History of the 1976 Copyright Act,* 56 U. of Pitt. L. Rev. 549 (1995)

Wood, *Copyrighting the Yellow Pages: Finding Originality in Factual Compilations,* 78 Minn. L. Rev. 1319 (1994)

Wilkins, *Protecting Computer Programs as Compilations Under* Computer Associates v. Altai, 104 Yale L.J. 435 (1994)

Yen, *The Danger of Bootstrap Formalism in Copyright,* 5 J. Intell. Prop. L. 453 (1998)

Yen, *The Legacy of* Feist: *Consequences of the Weak Connection Between Copyright and the Economics of Public Goods,* 52 Ohio St. L.J. 1343 (1991)

Miscellaneous

Litman, *Copyright and Information Policy,* 55 Law & Contemp. Probs. 185 (1992)

Litman, *Copyright, Compromise and Legislative History,* 72 Cornell L. Rev. 857 (1987)

Litman, *Copyright Legislation and Technological Change,* 68 Or. L. Rev. 275 (1989)

Olson, *The Iron Law of Consensus: Congressional Responses to Proposed Copyright Reforms Since the 1909 Act,* 36 J. Copyright Soc'y 109 (1989)

CHAPTER 4
OWNERSHIP AND TRANSFERS

Reference Works

H. Abrams, THE LAW OF COPYRIGHT §§ 4.01 to 4.05 (2002)

P. Goldstein, COPYRIGHT: PRINCIPLES, LAW AND PRACTICE §§ 4.1 to 4.6 (2002)

M. Leaffer, UNDERSTANDING COPYRIGHT LAW §§ 5.1 to 5.15 (3d ed. 1999)

M. Nimmer & D. Nimmer, NIMMER ON COPYRIGHT §§ 5.01 to 5.04, 6.01 to 6.12, 6A.01 to 6A.05, 7.25, 10.01 to 10.15 (2002)

W. Patry, COPYRIGHT LAW AND PRACTICE, Chap. 4 (1994 & 2000 Supp.)

Initial Ownership

C. McSherry, WHO OWNS ACADEMIC WORK?: BATTLING FOR CON-TROL OF INTELLECTUAL PROPERTY (2001)

Angel & Tannenbaum, *Works for Hire Under S. 22,* N.Y.L. Sch. L. Rev. 209 (1976)

Beckett, *The Copyright Act of 1976: When Is It Effective?,* 24 Bull. Copyright Soc'y 391 (1977)

Brophy, *Joint Authorship Under the Copyright Law,* 16 Hastings Comm. & Ent. L.J. 451 (1994)

Cary, *Joint Ownership of Copyright, Copyright Law Revision Study No. 12* (1958)

Chon, *New Wine Bursting from Old Bottles: Collaborative Internet Art, Joint Works, and Entrepreneurship,* 75 Or. L. Rev. 257 (1996)

Ciolino, *How Copyrights Became Community Property (Sort Of): Through the* Rodrigue v. Rodrigue *Looking Glass,* 47 Loy. L. Rev. 631 (2001)

Ciolino, *Why Copyrights Are Not Community Property,* 60 La. L. Rev. 127 (1999)

Comment, *Collaboration in Theater: Problems and Copyright Solutions,* 33 UCLA L. Rev. 891 (1986)

Dreyfuss, *Collaborative Research: Conflicts on Authorship, Owner-ship, and Accountability,* 53 Vand. L. Rev. 1162 (2000)

Dreyfuss, *The Creative Employee and the Copyright Act of 1976,* 54 U. Chi. L. Rev. 590 (1987)

Fielkow, *Clashing Rights Under United States Copyright Law: Harmonizing an Employer's Economic Right with the Artist-Employee's Moral Rights in a Work Made for Hire*, 7 J. Art & Ent. L. 218 (1997)

Gordon, *Essay: Fine-Tuning* Tasini: *Privileges of Electronic Distribution and Reproduction*, 66 Brooklyn L. Rev. 473 (2000)

Hamilton, *Commissioned Works as Works Made for Hire Under the 1976 Copyright Act: Misinterpretation and Injustice*, 135 U. Pa. L. Rev. 1281 (1987)

Hardy, *Copyright Law's Concept of Employment & What Congress Really Intended*, 35 J. Copyright Soc'y 210 (1988)

Hudis, *Software "Made for Hire": Make Sure It's Really Yours*, 44 J. Copyright Soc'y 8 (1996)

Hyde & Hager, *Promoting the Copyright Act's Creator-Favoring Presumption: "Works Made For Hire" Under* Aymes v. Bonelli *& Avtec Systems, Inc. v. Pfeiffer*, 71 Denv. U.L. Rev. 693 (1994)

Jarett, *Joint Onwership of Computer Software Copyright: A Solution to the Work for Hire Dilemma*, 137 U. Pa. L. Rev. 1251 (1989)

Karlan, *Joint Ownership of Moral Rights*, 38 J. Copyright Soc'y 242 (1991)

Karp, ed., *Work Made for Hire — Practical Perspectives: A Roundtable Discussion*, 14 Colum.-VLA J.L. & Arts 507 (1990)

Kernochan, *Ownership and Control of Intellectual Property Rights in Audiovisual Works: Contracts and Practice*, 20 Colum.-VLA J. L. & Arts 359 (1996)

Kreiss, *Scope of Employment and Being an Employee Under the Work-Made-For-Hire Provision of the Copyright Law: Applying the Common-Law Agency Tests*, 40 Kan. L. Rev. 119 (1991)

Kwall, *"Author-Stories": Narrative's Implications for Moral Rights and Copyright's Joint Authorship Doctrine*, 75 S. Cal. L. Rev. 1 (2001)

Kwall, *Copyright Issues in Online Courses: Ownership, Authorship and Conflict*, 18 Computer & High Tech. L.J. 1 (2001)

Landau, *"Works Made for Hire" After* Community for Creative Non-Violence v. Reid: *The Need for Statutory Reform and the Importance of Contract*, 9 Cardozo Arts & Ent. L.J. 107 (1990)

Lape, *A Narrow View of Creative Cooperation: The Current State of the Joint Work Doctrine*, 61 Alb. L. Rev. 43 (1997)

Lape, *Ownership of Copyrightable Works of University Professors: The Interplay Between the Copyright Act and University Copyright Policies,* 37 Vill. L. Rev. 223 (1992)

Miller, *Photography and the Work For Hire Doctrine,* 1 Tex. Wesleyan L. Rev. 81 (1994)

Nelson, *Practical Impact of Supreme Court Ruling on Author/ Publisher Digital Use Concerns,* 17 No. 4 Ent. L. & Fin. 1 (2001)

Note, *Copyright, Computer Software, and Work Made for Hire,* 89 Mich. L. Rev. 661 (1990)

Note, *Does a Copyright Co-owner's Duty to Account Arise Under Copyright Law?,* 90 Mich. L. Rev. 1998 (1992)

Note, *Externally Sponsored Faculty Research Under the "Work for Hire" Doctrine: Who's the Boss?,* 39 Syracuse L. Rev. 1351 (1988)

Note, *Manifest Intent and Copyrightability: The Destiny of Joint Authorship,* 17 Fordham Urban L.J. 257 (1989)

Perwin, *Drafting "Work for Hire" Agreements After* Community for Creative Non-Violence v. Reid, 14 Nova L. Rev. 459 (1990)

Reichman, *Overlapping Proprietary Rights in University-Generated Research Products: The Case of Computer Programs,* 1992 Colum.-VLA J.L. & the Arts 51 (1992)

Roussel, *The Copyright of Salaried and Employed Authors: A Comparative Study of National Laws,* 26 Copyright 221 (1990)

Samuelson, *Allocating Ownership Rights in Computer-Generated Works,* 47 U. Pitt. L. Rev. 1185 (1986)

Samuelson, *Some New Kinds of Authorship Made Possible by Computers and Some Intellectual Property Questions They Raise,* 53 U. Pitt. L. Rev. 685 (1993)

Simon, *Faculty Writings: Are They "Works Made for Hire" Under the 1976 Copyright Act?,* 9 J. Coll. & Univ. L. 485 (1982–83)

Spyke, *The Joint Works Dilemma: The Copyrightable Contribution Requirement and Co-Ownership Principles,* 40 J. Copyright Soc'y 463 (1993)

Sterk, *Rhetoric and Reality in Copyright Law,* 94 Mich. L. Rev. 1197 (1996)

Varmer, *Works Made for Hire and On Commission, Copyright Law Revision Study No. 13* (1960)

VerSteeg, *Copyright and the Educational Process: The Right of Teacher Inception,* 75 Iowa L. Rev. 381 (1990)

VerSteeg, *Defining "Author" for the Purposes of Copyright*, 45 Am. U. L. Rev. 1323 (1996)

Wadley & Brown, *Working Between the Lines of Reid: Teachers, Copyrights, Work-For-Hire and a New Washburn University Policy*, 38 Washburn L.J. 385 (1999)

Wernick, *The Work Made for Hire and Joint Work Copyright Doctrines After CCNV v. Reid: "What! You Mean I Don't Own It Even Though I Paid in Full for It?"*, 13 Hamline L. Rev. 287 (1990)

Transfer and Recordation

Bramson, *Intellectual Property as Collateral: Patent, Trade Secrets, Trademarks and Copyrights*, 36 Bus. Law. 1567 (1981)

Brylawski, *The Role of Copyright in Acquisitions and Security Transactions*, 22 Beverly Hills B.A.J. 88 (1988)

Curtis, *Protecting Authors in Copyright Transfers: Revision Bill and the Alternatives*, 72 Colum. L. Rev. 799 (1972)

Ginsburg, *Putting Cars on the "Information Superhighway": Authors, Exploiters, and Copyright in Cyberspace*, 95 Colum. L. Rev. 1466 (1995)

Goldstein, *Preempted State Doctrines, Involuntary Transfers and Compulsory Licenses: Testing the Limits of Copyright*, 24 UCLA L. Rev. 1107 (1977)

Haemmerli, *Insecurity Interests: Where Intellectual Property and Commercial Law Collide*, 96 Colum. L. Rev. 1645 (1996)

Hamilton, *The Top Ten Intellectual Property Law Questions That Should Be Asked About Any Merger or Acquisition*, 66 U. Cin. L. Rev. 1315 (1998)

Jaszi, Tasini *and Beyond*, 23 Eur. Intell. Prop. L. Rev. 595 (2001)

Kaminstein, *Divisibility of Copyrights, Copyright Law Revision Study No. 11* (1960)

Kreiss, *The "In Writing" Requirement for Copyright and Patent Transfers: Are the Circuits in Conflict?*, 26 Dayton L. Rev. 43 (2000)

Latman, *Recordation of Copyright Assignments and Licenses, Copyright Law Revision Study No. 19* (1958)

Nayo, *Revisiting Worth: The Copyright as Community Property Problems*, 30 U.S.F.L. Rev. 153 (1995)

Nevine, *When an Author's Marriage Dies: The Copyright-Divorce Connection*, 37 J. Copyright Soc'y 382 (1990)

D. Nimmer, *Adams and Bits: Of Jewish Kings and Copyrights*, 71 S. Cal. L. Rev. 219 (1998)

R. Nimmer, *An Update on Financing with Intellectual Property as Collateral: Parts I and II*, 10 J. Proprietary Rts. 2 (1997) and 11 J. Proprietary Rts. 10 (1997)

Note, *Transfers of Copyright for Security Under the New Copyright Act*, 88 Yale L.J. 125 (1978)

Polacheck, *The "UN-Worthy" Decision: The Characterization of a Copyright as Community Property*, 17 Hastings Comm. & Ent. L.J. 601 (1995)

VerSteeg, *Copyright and the Educational Process: The Right of Teacher Inception*, 75 Iowa L. Rev. 381 (1990)

Victoroff, *The Other Curse of the Werewolf: Interpreting Copyright Transfers Under U.S. and English Law*, 17 Whittier L. Rev. 215 (1995)

Weiss & Benjamin, *Feature Film Secured Financing: A Transactional Approach*, 15 UCC L.J. 195 (1983)

Wong, *Asserting the Spouse's Community Property Rights in Copyright*, 31 Idaho L. Rev. 1087 (1995)

CHAPTER 5
DURATION, RENEWAL, AND TERMINATIONS OF TRANSFERS

Reference Works

H. Abrams, THE LAW OF COPYRIGHT §§ 7.01 to 7.05, 11.01 to 11.07, 12.01 to 12.06 (2002)

P. Goldstein, COPYRIGHT: PRINCIPLES, LAW AND PRACTICE §§ 4.7 to 4.11 (2002)

M. Leaffer, UNDERSTANDING COPYRIGHT LAW §§ 6.1 to 6.19 (3d ed. 1999)

M. Nimmer & D. Nimmer, NIMMER ON COPYRIGHT §§ 9.01 to 9.12, 9A.01 to 9A.06, 11.01 to 11.09 (2002)

W. Patry, COPYRIGHT LAW AND PRACTICE, Chap. 6 (1994 & 2000 Supp.)

Duration and Renewal

Allen & Swift, *Shattering Copyright Law: Will James Stewart's Rear Window Become a Pain in the Glass?*, 22 Pac. L.J. 1 (1990)

Bard & Kurlantzick, *Copyright Duration at the Millennium*, 40 J. Copyright Soc'y 13 (2000)

Bricker, *Renewal and Extension of Copyright,* 29 S. Cal. L. Rev. 23 (1955)

H. Brown & D. Miller, *Copyright Term Extension: Sapping American Creativity*, 44 J. Copyright Soc'y 94 (1996)

R. Brown, *The Widening Gyre: Are Derivative Works Getting Out of Hand?*, 3 Cardozo Arts & Ent. L. Rev. 1 (1984)

Brownlee, *Recent Changes in the Duration of Copyright in the United States and European Union: Procedures and Policy,* 6 Fordham I.P., Media & Ent. L. J. 579 (1996)

Chafee, *Reflections on the Law of Copyright,* 45 Colum. L. Rev. 503, 719 (1945)

Colby, *Helen Sousa Albert, Mary Baker Eddy, and Otto Harbach — The Road to a Copyright Term of Life Plus 50 Years,* 6 Comm. & the Law 3 (1984)

Hamilton, *Copyright Duration Extension and the Dark Heart of Copyright,* 14 Cardozo Arts & Ent. L.J. 655 (1996)

Hart & Kaufman, *An Overview of the Copyright Renewal Amendment and its Impact on Renewal Practices Under U.S. Law,* 17 Colum.-VLA J.L. & the Arts 311 (1994)

Heald & Sherry, *Implied Limits on the Legislative Power: The Intellectual Property Clause as an Absolute Constraint on Congress*, 2000 U. Ill. L. Rev. 1119 (2000)

Hughes, *Jurisprudential Vertigo: The Supreme Court's View of "Rear Window" Is for the Birds,* 60 Miss. L.J. 239 (1990)

Jaszi, *When Works Collide: Derivative Motion Pictures, Underlying Rights, and the Public Interest,* 28 UCLA L. Rev. 715 (1981)

Karjala, *Comment of U.S. Law Professors on the Copyright Office Term of Protection Study,* 12 Eur. Intell. Prop. Rev. 531 (1994)

Kreiss, *Abandoning Copyrights to Try to Cut Off Termination Rights,* 58 Mo. L. Rev. 85 (1993)

Kupferman, *Renewal of Copyright: Section 23 of the Copyright Act of 1909,* 44 Colum. L. Rev. 712 (1944)

Kurtz, *The Methuselah Factor: When Characters Outlive Their Copyrights*, 11 U. Miami Ent. & Sports L. Rev. 437 (1994)

Leval & Liman, *Are Copyrights for Authors or Their Children?,* 39 J. Copyright Soc'y 1 (1991)

Litman, *Mickey Mouse Emeritus: Character Protection and the Public Domain,* 11 U. Miami Ent. & Sports L. Rev. 429 (1994)

Merges & Reynolds, *The Proper Scope of the Copyright and Patent Power*, 37 Harv. J. on Legis. 45 (2000)

Miller, *Copyright Term Extension: Boon for American Creators and the American Economy,* 45 J. Copyright Soc'y 319 (1998)

Mimms, *Reversion and Derivative Works Under the Copyright Acts of 1909 and 1976,* 25 N.Y.L. Sch. L. Rev. 595 (1980)

Mota, Eldred v. Reno — *Is the Copyright Term Extension Act Constitutional?*, 12 Alb. L.J. Sci. & Tech. 167 (2001)

Nevins, *Little Copyright Dispute on the Prairie: Unbumping the Will of Laura Ingalls Wilder*, 44 St. Louis L.J. 919 (2000)

Nevins, *The Magic Kingdom of Will Bumping: Where Estates Law and Copyright Law Collide,* J. Copyright Soc'y 77 (1988)

D. Nimmer, Corcovado: *Renewal's Second Coming or False Messiah?,* 1 UCLA Ent. L. Rev. 127 (1994)

D. Nimmer, *Nation, Duration, Violation, Harmonization: An International Copyright Proposal for the United States,* 55 Law & Contemp. Probs. 211 (1992)

D. Nimmer, *Refracting the Window's Light:* Stewart v. Abend *in Myth and in Fact*, 39 J. Copyright Soc'y 18 (1991)

Note, *Reflections on the Intellectual Commons: Two Perspectives on Copyright Duration and Reversion*, 47 Stan. L. Rev. 707 (1995)

Ochoa, *Patent and Copyright Term Extension and the Constitution: A Historical Perspective,* 49 J. Copyright Soc'y 19 (2001)

Patry, *The Copyright Term Extension Act of 1995: Or How Publishers Managed to Steal the Bread from Authors,* 14 Cardozo Arts & Ent. L.J. 661 (1996)

Patry, *The Failure of the American Copyright System: Protecting the Idle Rich,* 72 Notre Dame L. Rev. 907 (1997)

Reichman, *An Evaluation of the Copyright Extension Act of 1995: The Duration of the Limits of Cultural Policy,* 14 Cardozo Arts & Ent. L.J. 625 (1996)

Ricketson, *The Copyright Term,* 23 IIC 753 (1992)

Ringer, *Renewal of Copyright, Copyright Law Revision Study No. 31* (1960)

Rosenbloum, *Give Me Liberty & Give Me Death: The Conflict Between Copyright Law and Estates Law,* 4 J. Intell. Prop. L. 163 (1996)

Walterscheid, *The Remarkable—and Irrational—Disparity Between the Patent Term and the Copyright Term,* 83 J. Pat & Trademark Off. Soc'y 233 (2001)

Terminations of Transfers

Abrams, *Who's Sorry Now? Termination Rights and the Derivative Works Exception,* 62 U. Det. L. Rev. 181 (1985)

Curtis, *Caveat Emptor in Copyright: A Practical Guide to the Termination Provisions of the New Copyright Code,* 25 Bull. Copyright Soc'y 19 (1977)

Curtis, *Protecting Authors in Copyright Transfers: Revision Bill § 203 and the Alternatives,* 72 Colum. L. Rev. 799 (1972)

Davis, *The Screenwriter's Indestructible Right to Terminate Her Assignment of Copyright: Once a Story Is "Pitched," A Studio Can Never Obtain All Copyrights in the Story,* 18 Cardozo Arts & Ent. L.J. 93 (2000)

Drisch & Fortnow, *Termination of Copyrights in Sound Recordings: Is There a Leak in the Record Company Vaults?,* 17 Colum.-VLA J.L. & the Arts 211 (1993)

Kreiss, *Abandoning Copyright to Try to Cut Off Termination Rights,* 58 Mo. L. Rev. 85 (1993)

M. Nimmer, *Termination of Transfers Under the Copyright Act of 1976*, 125 U. Pa. L. Rev. 947 (1977)

Note, *Bleak House Revisited: An Appraisal of the Termination Provisions of the 1976 Copyright Act—Sections 203 and 304(c)*, 65 Or. L. Rev. 829 (1986)

Note, *The Errant Evolution of Termination of Transfer Rights and the Derivative Works Exception*, 48 Ohio St. L.J. 897 (1987)

Ward, *The Perfection and Priority Rules For Security Interests In Copyrights, Patents, and Trademarks: The Current Structural Dissonance and Proposed Legislative Cures*, 53 Me. L. Rev. 391 (2001)

CHAPTER 6
PUBLICATION AND FORMALITIES

Reference Works

H. Abrams, THE LAW OF COPYRIGHT §§ 8.03 to 8.06, 9.01 to 9.11, 10.01 to 10.05 (2002)

P. Goldstein, COPYRIGHT: PRINCIPLES, LAW AND PRACTICE §§ 3.0 to 3.19 (2002)

M. Leaffer, UNDERSTANDING COPYRIGHT LAW §§ 4.1 to 4.17, 7.1 to 7.15 (3d ed. 1999)

M. Nimmer & D. Nimmer, NIMMER ON COPYRIGHT §§ 4.01 to 4.13, 7.01 to 7.24, 7.26 (2002)

W. Patry, COPYRIGHT LAW AND PRACTICE, Chap. 5 (1994 & 2000 Supp.)

Publication

Baumgarten & Meyer, *Effects of U.S. Adherence to the Berne Convention,* 3 World Intell. Prop. Rep. 73 (1989)

Brown, *Publication and Preemption in Copyright Law: Elegiac Reflections on* Goldstein v. California, 22 UCLA L. Rev. 1022 (1975)

Brylawski, *Publication: Its Role in Copyright Matters, Both Past and Present,* 31 J. Copyright Soc'y 507 (1984)

Landau, *Music: "Publication," Musical Compositions, and the Copyright Act of 1909: Still Crazy After All These Years,* 2 Vand. J. Ent. L. & Prac. 29 (2000)

M. Nimmer, *Preface—The Old Copyright Act as a Part of the New Act,* 22 N.Y.L. Sch. L. Rev. 471 (1977)

Segal, *Zombie Copyrights: Copyright Restoration Under the New Section 104A of the Copyright Act,* 13 Santa Clara Computer & High Tech. L.J. 71 (1997)

Formalities

Abromats, *Nondisclosure of Preexisting Works in Software Copyright Registrations: Inequitable Conduct in Need of a Remedy,* 32 Jurimetrics J. 571 (1992)

Arden, *The Questionable Utility of Copyright Notice: Statutory and Non Legal Incentives in the Post-Berne Era,* 24 Loy. U. Chi. L.J. 259 (1993)

Cole, *Of Copyright, Men, and a National Library,* 28 Q.J. Libr. Cong. 114 (1971)

Crews, *Legal Deposit in Four Countries: Laws and Library Services,* 80 Law Libr. J. 551 (1988)

Doyle, Cary, McCannon & Ringer, *Notice of Copyright, Copyright Law Revision Study No. 7* (1960)

Fisher, *Reserving All Rights Beyond Copyright: Non-statutory Restrictive Notices,* 37 J. Copyright Soc'y 249 (1987)

Geller, *Copyright Protection in the Berne Union: Analyzing the Issues,* 5 Intell. Prop. J. 1 (1989)

Ginsburg & Kernochan, *One Hundred and Two Years Later: The U.S. Joins the Berne Convention,* 13 Colum.-VLA J.L. & Arts 1 (1988)

Grubb, *Status of Works Published in Violation of the Manufacturing Requirements of the 1909 Copyright Act After the Effective Date of the 1976 Copyright Law,* 27 J. Copyright Soc'y (1980)

Haynie, *So the Copyright Office Has Refused to Register Your Claim to Copyright—What Does It Mean and What Can You Do About It?,* 21 AIPLA Q.J. 70 (1993)

Horwitz, *Proposed Changes in the Regulations Governing Deposits of Computer Programs with the Copyright Office,* 26 Jurimetrics J. 305 (1986)

Hurwitz, *Omission of Copyright Notice Under Section 405(a): What Kind of Oxymoron Makes a Deliberate Error?,* 60 N.Y.U. L. Rev. 956 (1985)

Jelaso, *APA Abuse of Discretion Review as Applied to the Copyright Office: Is the Standard Meaningless?,* 5 Am. U. Admin. L.J. 485 (1991)

Kaplan, *The Registration of Copyright, Copyright Law Revision Study No. 17* (1960)

Karp, *A Future Without Formalities,* 13 Cardozo Arts & Ent. L.J. 521 (1995)

Levine, *The End of Formalities: No More Second-Class Copyright Owners,* 13 Cardozo Arts & Ent. L.J. 553 (1995)

Lovitz, *Copyright Protection in the United States: It's All Berned Up,* 3 Temp. Int'l & Comp. L.J. 25 (1989)

Lyons, *The Manufacturing Clause: A Legislative History,* 29 J. Copyright Soc'y 8 (1981)

McLain, *The Copyright Notice Requirement in the United States: A Proposed Amendment Concerning Deliberate Omissions of Notice,* 18 Loy. L. A. L. Rev. 689 (1985)

Metalitz, *Copyright Registration after* Feist: *New Rules and New Roles?,* 17 U. Dayton L. Rev. 763 (1992)

Perlmutter, *Freeing Copyright From Formalities*, 13 Cardozo Arts & Ent. L.J. 565 (1995)

Peters, *The Copyright Office and the Formal Requirements of Registration of Claims to Copyright,* 17 U. Dayton L. Rev. 737 (1992)

Selkowitz, *A Well-Kept Secret: Informal Adjudication in the Copyright Office—A Freedom of Information Act Violation?,* 35 Admin. L. Rev. 133 (1983)

Sorkin, *The Futility of a Future Without Formalities,* 13 Cardozo Arts & Ent. L.J. 589 (1995)

Stim, *The Reform of Notice Omission:* Crumb v. A.A. Sales, Inc., 11 Colum.-VLA J.L. & the Arts 635 (1987)

Y'Barbo, *On Section 411 of the Copyright Code and Determining the Proper Scope of a Copyright Registration,* 34 San Diego L. Rev. 343 (1997)

The Copyright Office

Abrams, *The Role of the Copyright Office: An Introduction*, 13 Cardozo Arts & Ent. L.J. 27 (1994)

Samuelson, *Will the Copyright Office Be Obsolete in the Twenty-First Century?*, 13 Cardozo Arts & Ent. L.J. 55 (1994)

Schwartz, *The Role of the Copyright Office in the Age of Information*, 13 Cardozo Arts & Ent. L.J. 69 (1994)

CHAPTER 7
EXCLUSIVE RIGHTS AND THEIR LIMITATIONS

Reference Works

H. Abrams, THE LAW OF COPYRIGHT §§ 5.01 to 5.10 (2002)

P. Goldstein, COPYRIGHT: PRINCIPLES, LAW AND PRACTICE §§ 5.0 to 5.15, 12.4, 15.23 to 15.25 (2002)

M. Leaffer, UNDERSTANDING COPYRIGHT LAW §§ 8.1 to 8.31 (3d ed. 1999)

M. Nimmer & D. Nimmer, NIMMER ON COPYRIGHT §§ 7.27, 8.1 to 8.24, 8A.01 to 8A.12, 8B.01 to 8B.08, 8D.01 to 8D.10, 8E.01 to 8E.04, 12A.01 to 12A.19, 12B.01 to 12B.11 (2002)

W. Patry, COPYRIGHT LAW AND PRACTICE, Chaps. 7–14, and 16 (1994 & 2000 Supp.)

Overview

Cassler, *Copyright Compulsory Licenses: Are They Coming or Going?*, 37 J. Copyright Soc'y 231 (1990)

Francon, *The Future of Copyright*, 132 R.I.D.A. 2 (1987)

Goldstein, *Preempted State Doctrines, Involuntary Transfers and Compulsory Licenses: Testing the Limits of Copyright*, 24 UCLA L. Rev. 1107 (1977)

Kabat, *Proposal for a Worldwide Internet Collecting Society: Mark Twain and Samuel Johnson Licenses*, J. Copyright Soc'y (1998)

Kernochan, *Practical Limitations on Authors' Rights*, 24 Colum.-VLA J.L. & Arts 263 (2001)

Patterson & Birch, *Copyright and Free Speech*, 4 J. Intell. Prop. L. 1 (1996); Y'Barbo, *On Legal Protection for Electronic Texts: A Reply to Professor Patterson and Judge Birch*, 5 J. Intell. Prop. L. 195 (1997); Patterson, *A Response to Mr. Y'Barbo's Reply*, 5 J. Intell. Prop. L. 235 (1997)

Ringer, *Copyright and the Future of Authorship*, 101 Lib. L.J. 229 (1976)

Y'Barbo, *The Heart of the Matter: The Property Right Conferred by Copyright*, 49 Mercer L. Rev. 643 (1998)

Exclusive Rights and Limitations in the Digital Age

J. Delaney & A. Lichstein, THE LAW OF THE INTERNET: A SUMMARY OF U.S. CASELAW AND LEGAL DEVELOPMENTS (1998)

Benkler, *Free as the Air to Common Use: First Amendment Constraints on Enclosure of the Public Domain*, 74 N.Y.U. L. Rev. 354 (1999)

Bomser, *A Lawyer's Ramble Down the Information Superhighway,* 64 Fordham L. Rev. 697 (1995)

Cate, *The Technological Transformation of Copyright Law*, 81 Iowa L. Rev. 1395 (1996)

J. Cohen, *A Right to Read Anonymously: A Closer Look at "Copyright Management" in Cyberspace,* 28 Conn. L. Rev. 981 (1996)

Ginsburg, *Domestic and International Copyright Issues Implicated in the Compilation of a Multimedia Product,* 25 Seton Hall L. Rev. 1397 (1995)

Ginsburg, *Putting Cars on the "Information Superhighway": Authors, Exploiters, and Copyright in Cyberspace,* 95 Colum. L. Rev. 1466 (1995)

Glisson, *A Practioner's Defense of the White Paper,* 75 Or. L. Rev. 277 (1996)

Grogan, *Implied Licencing Issues in the Online World,* 14 Computer Law. 1 (No. 8) (1997)

Harrison, *Rules of the Road for the Information Superhighway: Electronic Communication and the Law,* 35 Hous. Law. 58 (1997)

Jaszi, *Caught in the Net of Copyright,* 75 Or. L. Rev. 299 (1996)

Lemley, *Dealing With Overlapping Copyrights on the Internet,* 22 U. Dayton L. Rev. 547 (1997)

Litman, *Reforming Information Law in Copyright's Image,* 22 Dayton L. Rev. 587 (1997)

Melton, *International Cyberspace Licensing Perils,* 496 PLI/Pat. 95 (1997)

D. Nimmer, *Time and Space,* 38 IDEA 501 (1998)

Tannenbaum, *Lost in Cyberia: Electronic Transmissions Under the Law of Copyright,* 490 PLI/Pat. 109 (1997)

The Reproduction Right

S. Bessen, COMPENSATING CREATORS OF INTELLECTUAL PROPERTY (1989)

Bloom, *Protecting Copyright Owners of Digital Music—No More Free Access to Cyber Tunes,* 45 J. Copyright Soc'y 179 (1997)

Geller, *Reprography and Other Processes of Mass Use,* 38 J. Copyright Soc'y 21 (1990)

Ginsburg, *Reproduction of Protected Works for University Research or Teaching*, 39 J. Copyright Soc'y 181 (1992)

Hardy, *Computer "RAM" Copies: A Hit or a Myth? Historical Perspectives on Caching as a Microcosm of Current Copyright Concerns*, 22 Dayton L. Rev. 423 (1997)

Note, *Digital Sound Sampling, Copyright and Publicity: Protecting Against the Electronic Appropriation of Sounds*, 87 Colum. L. Rev. 1723 (1987)

Reese, *Copyright and Internet Music Transmissions: Existing Law, Major Controversies, Possible Solutions*, 55 U. Miami L. Rev 237 (2001)

Rosenlund, *Compulsory Licensing of Musical Compositions for Phonorecords Under the Copyright Act of 1976*, 30 Hastings L.J. 683 (1979)

Yen, *Entrepreneurship, Copyright, and Personal Home Pages*, 75 Or. L. Rev. 331 (1996)

The Adaptation Right

Black & Page, *Add-On Infringements: When Computer Add-Ons and Peripherals Should (and Should Not) Be Considered Infringing Derivative Works Under* Lewis Galoob Toys Inc. v. Nintendo of America Inc. *and Other Recent Decisions*, 15 Hastings Comm. & Ent. L.J. 615 (1993)

A. Cohen, *When Does a Work Infringe the Derivative Works Right of a Copyright Owner?*, 17 Cardozo Arts & Ent L.J. 623 (1999)

Goldstein, *Derivative Rights and Derivative Works in Copyright*, 30 J. Copyright Soc'y 209 (1983)

Kreiss, *Section 117 of the Copyright Act*, [1991] BYU L. Rev. 1496

Lemley, *The Economics of Improvement in Intellectual Property Law*, 75 Tex. L. Rev. 989 (1997)

Lisby, *Web Site Framing: Copyright Infringement Through the Creation of an Unauthorized Derivative Work*, 6 Comm. L. & Pol'y 541 (2001)

Loren, *The Changing Nature of Derivative Works in the Face of New Technologies*, 4 J. Small & Emerging Bus. L. 57 (2000)

R. Nimmer & P. Krauthaus, *Copyright and Software Technology Infringement: Defining Third Party Development Rights*, 62 Ind. L.J. 13 (1986)

Note, *Unauthorized Photographs of Theatrical Works: Do They Infringe the Copyright?*, 87 Colum. L. Rev. 1032 (1987)

Samuelson, *Modifying Copyrighted Software: Adjusting Copyright Doctrine to Accommodate a Technology,* 28 Jurimetrics J. 179 (1988)

Sanjek, *"Don't Have to DJ No More": Sampling and the "Autonomous" Creator,* 10 Cardozo Arts & Ent. L.J. 607 (1992)

Wurzer, *Infringement of the Exclusive Right to Prepare Derivative Works: Reducing Uncertainty,* 73 Minn. L. Rev. 1521 (1989)

Voegtli, *Rethinking Derivative Rights,* 63 Brooklyn L. Rev. 1213 (1997)

The Public Distribution Right

L. Pierredon–Fawcett & J. Kernochan, THE DROIT DE SUITE IN LITERARY AND ARTISTIC PROPERTY: A COMPARATIVE LAW STUDY (1991)

Alderman, *Resale Royalties in the United States for Fine Visual Artists: An Alien Concept,* 40 J. Copyright Soc'y 265 (1992)

Colby, *The First Sale Doctrine: The Defense That Never Was?,* 32 J. Copyright Soc'y 77 (1984)

Comment, *The Parallel Importation of Unauthorized Genuine Goods: Analysis and Observations of the Gray Market,* 14 U. Pa. J. Int'l Bus. Law. 409 (1993)

Comment, *Third Party Intentional Interference With International Exclusive Dealing Contracts: An Alternative Solution to the Obstacles in Parallel Import Litigation,* 1 Tulsa J. Comp. & Int'l L. 359 (1994)

Determann & Fellmeth, *Don't Judge a Sale by Its License: Software Transfers Under the First Sale Doctrine in the United States and the European Community,* 36 U.S.F.L. Rev. 1 (2001)

Gervais, *Transmissions of Music on the Internet: An Analysis of the Copyright Laws of Canada, France, Germany, Japan, the United Kingdom, and the United States,* 34 Vand. J. Transnat'l L. 1363 (2001)

Getzels, *Importation of Out-Of-Print Works Under the Copyright Act of 1976,* 10 Fordham Int'l L.J. 782 (1987)

Ginsburg, *Copyright and Control Over New Technologies of Dissemination,* 101 Colum L. Rev. 1613 (2001)

Gordon, *Essay: Fine-Tuning* Tasini: *Privileges of Electronic Distribution and Reproduction,* 66 Brooklyn L. Rev. 473 (2000)

Hansen, *Gray Market Goods: A Lighter Shade of Black,* 13 Brooklyn J. Int'l L. 2459 (1987)

Horowitz, *The Record Rental Amendment of 1984: A Case Study in the Effort to Adapt Copyright Law to New Technology,* 12 Law & Arts 31 (1987)

Kernochan, *The Distribution Right in the United States of America: Review and Reflections,* 42 Vand. L. Rev. 107 (1989)

Kim, *In Pursuit of Profit Maximization By Restricting Parallel Imports: The U.S. Copyright Owner and Taiwan Copyright Law,* 5 Pac. Rim L. & Pol'y J. 205 (1995)

Leaffer, *Parallel Importation and the Gray Market in the United States,* in 1 International Intellectual Property Law and Policy, Chap. 37 (Hansen, ed., 1996)

Neumann, *The Berne Convention and* Droit de Suite *Legislation in the United States: Domestic and International Consequences of Federal Incorporation of State Law for Treaty Implementation,* 16 Colum.–VLA J.L. & the Arts 157 (1992)

Note, *Closing the Book on the Public Lending Right,* 63 N.Y.U. L. Rev. 878 (1989)

Note, *Decompilation of Collective Works: When the First Sale Doctrine Is a Mirage,* 76 Tex. L. Rev. 869 (1997)

Perlmutter, *Resale Royalties for Artists: An Analysis of the Register of Copyrights' Report,* 40 J. Copyright Soc'y 284 (1992)

Price, *Government Policy and Economic Security for the Artist: The Case of the* Droit de Suite, 77 Yale L.J. 1333 (1968)

Rice, *Licensing the Use of Computer Program Copies and the Copyright Act First Sale Doctrine,* 30 Jurimetrics J. 157 (1990)

Rubin, *Destined to Remain Grey: The Eternal Recurrence of Parallel Imports,* 26 Int'l Law. 579 (1992)

Seemann, *A Look at the Public Lending Right,* 30 Copyright L. Symp. (ASCAP) 71 (1983)

Weil, *Resale Royalties: Nobody Benefits,* ARTNews at 58 (Mar. 1978)

The Public Performance Right

A. Kohn & B. Kohn, Kohn on Music Licensing (2002)

W. Krasilovsky, S. Shemel & J. Gross, This Business of Music: The Definitive Guide to the Music Industry (8th ed. 2000)

Avery, *The Struggle over Performing Rights in Music:* BMI and ASCAP vs. Cable Television, 14 Hastings Comm. & Ent. L.J. 47 (1991)

Bard & Kurlantzick, *A Public Performance Right in Recordings: How to Alter the Copyright System Without Improving It,* 43 Geo. Wash. L. Rev. 152 (1974)

Bertrand, *Performing Rights Societies: The Price Is Right "French-Style," or the SACEM Cases,* 3 Ent. L. Rev. 146 (1992)

Cochran, *Why Can't I Watch This Video Here?: Copyright Confusion and Performances of Videocassettes and Videodiscs in Libraries,* 15 Hastings Comm. & Ent. L.J. 837 (1993)

Deutsch, *Politics and Poker—Music Faces the Odds: A Ten-Year Retrospective,* 34 J. Copyright Soc'y 38 (1986)

Disch, *Compulsory Licensing of Blacked Out Professional Team Sporting Event Telecasts (PTSETS): Using Copyright Law to Mitigate Monopolistic Behavior,* 32 Harv. J. on Legis. 403 (1995)

D'Onofrio, *In Support of Performance Rights in Sound Recordings,* 29 UCLA L. Rev. 168 (1981)

Finkelstein, *The Composer and the Public Interest—Regulation of Performing Right Societies,* 19 Law & Contemp. Probs. 275 (1954)

Garner, United States v. ASCAP: *The Licensing Provisions of the Amended Final Judgment of 1950,* 23 Bull. Copyright Soc'y 119 (1976)

Gasaway, *Distance Learning and Copyright,* 49 J. Copyright Soc'y 195 (2001)

Gasaway, *Impasse: Distance Learning and Copyright,* 62 Ohio St. L.J. 783 (2001)

Gorman, *The Recording Musician and Union Power: A Case Study of the American Federation of Musicians,* 37 Sw. L.J. 697 (1983)

Hartnick, *The Network Blanket License Triumphant—The Fourth Round of the ASCAP-BMI/CBS Litigation,* 2 Comm. & the Law 49 (1980)

Helfer, *World Music on a U.S. Stage: A Berne/TRIPs and Economic Analysis of the Fairness in Music Licensing Act,* 80 B.U. L. Rev. 93 (2000)

Jensen, *Is the Library Without Walls on a Collision Course with the 1976 Copyright Act?* 85 Law Libr. J. 619 (1993)

Kernochan, *Music Performing Rights Organizations in the United States of America: Special Characteristics, Restraints, and Public Attitudes,* 10 Colum.-VLA J.L. & the Arts 333 (1986)

Kheit, *Public Performance Copyrights: A Guide to Public Place Analysis,* 26 Rutgers Computer & Tech. L.J. 1 (1999)

Kim, *The Performers' Plight in Sound Recordings—Unique to the U.S.: A Comparative Study of the Development of Performers' Rights in the United States, England and France,* 10 Colum.-VLA J.L. & the Arts 453 (1986)

Korman, *Performance Rights in Music Under Sections 110 and 118 of the 1976 Copyright Act,* 22 N.Y.L. Sch. L. Rev. 521 (1977)

Korman & Koenigsberg, *Performing Rights in Music and Performing Rights Societies,* 33 J. Copyright Soc'y 332 (1987)

Loren, *Paying the Piper,* 3 J. Small & Emerging Bus. L. 231 (1999)

Martin, *Compulsory License for Jukeboxes: Why the Song Could Not Remain the Same,* 37 J. Copyright Soc'y 262 (1990)

Martin, *The WIPO Performances and Phonograms Treaty: Will the U.S. Whistle a New Tune?,* 45 J. Copyright Soc'y 157 (1997)

Nagarajan, *Public Performance Rights in Sound Recordings and the Threat of Digitalization,* 77 J. Pat. & Trademark Off. Soc'y 721 (1995)

Nevins, *Antenna Dilemma: The Exemption from Copyright Liability for Public Performances Using Technology Common in the Home,* 11 Colum.-VLA J.L. & the Arts 403 (1987)

Oman, *Source Licensing: The Latest Skirmish in an Old Battle,* 11 Colum.-VLA J.L. & the Arts 251 (1987)

Perrone, *Small and Grand Performing Rights (Who Cared Before "Jesus Christ Superstar"?),* 20 Bull. Copyright Soc'y 19 (1972)

Scorese, *Performing Broadway Music: The Demon Grand Rights Traps,* 14 Colum.-VLA J.L. & the Arts 123 (1989)

Shipley, *Copyright Law and Your Neighborhood Bar and Grill: Recent Developments in Performances and the Section 110(5) Exemption,* 29 Ariz. L. Rev. 475 (1987)

Sobel, *The Legal and Business Aspects of Motion Picture and Television Soundtrack Music,* 8 Loy. Ent. L.J. 231 (1988)

Timberg, *The Antitrust Aspects of Merchandising Modern Music: The ASCAP Consent Judgment of 1950,* 19 Law & Contemp. Probs. 294 (1954)

Tomlinson & Nielander, *Unchained Melody: Music Licensing in the Digital Age,* 6 Tex. Intell. Prop. L.J. 277 (1998)

The Public Display Right

Goetzl & Sutton, *Copyright and the Visual Artist's Display Right: A New Doctrinal Analysis,* 9 Art & L. 15 (1984)

Reese, *The Public Display Right: The Copyright Act's Neglected Solution to the Controversy over Ram "Copies"*, 2001 U. Ill. L. Rev. 83 (2001)

Miscellaneous Rights: In and Beyond Copyright

D. Sinacore-Guinn, COLLECTIVE ADMINISTRATION OF COPYRIGHTS AND NEIGHBORING RIGHTS: INTERNATIONAL PRACTICES, PROCEDURES, AND ORGANIZATIONS (1993)

Aplin, *Contemplating Australia's Digital Future*, 23 Eur. Intell. Prop. L. Rev. 565 (2001)

Bartow, *Arresting Technology: An Essay,* 1 Buff. Intell. Prop. L.J. 95 (2001)

Burk & J. Cohen, *Fair Use Infrastructure for Rights Management Systems,* 15 Harv. J.L. & Tech. 41 (2001)

Carlisle, *The Audio Home Recording Act of 1992,* 1 J. Intell. Prop. L. 335 (1994)

J. Cohen, Lochner *in Cyberspace: The New Economic Orthodoxy of "Rights Management"*, 97 Mich. L. Rev. 462 (1998)

Field, *Copyright Co-Ownership in Cyberspace: The Digital Merger of Content and Technology in Digital Rights Management and E-Commerce,* 19 Ent. & Sports Law. 3 (Fall 2001)

Ginsburg, *Copyright and Control Over New Technologies of Dissemination,* 101 Colum L. Rev. 1613 (2001)

Hart, *The Copyright in the Information Society Directive: An Overview*, 24 Eur. Intell. Prop. L. Rev. 58 (2001)

Hartman, *Don't Worry, Be Happy! Music Performance and Distribution on the Internet Is Protected After the Digital Performance Rights in Sound Recordings Act of 1995,* 7 DePaul LCA J. Art. & Ent. L. 37 (1996)

Kawamua, *Digital Audio Tape Technology: A Formidable Challenge to the American Copyright System,* 4 Am. U. J. Int'l L. & Pol'y 409 (1989)

Kurtlantzick & Pennino, *The Audio Home Recording Act of 1992 and the Formation of Copyright Policy,* 45 J. Copyright Soc'y 497 (1998)

Landau, *Has the Digital Millennium Copyright Act Really Created a New Exclusive Right of Access?: Attempting to Reach a Balance Between Users' and Content Providers' Rights,* 49 J. Copyright Soc'y 277 (2001)

Lastowka, *Free Access and the Future of Copyright*, 27 Rutgers Computer & Tech. L.J. 293 (2001)

Lunney, *The Death of Copyright: Digital Technology, Private Copying, and the Digital Millennium Copyright Act*, 87 Va. L. Rev. 813 (2001)

Martin, *The WIPO Performances and Phonograms Treaty: Will the U.S. Whistle a New Tune?*, 45 J. Copyright Soc'y 157 (1997)

McKuin, *Home Audio Taping of Copyrighted Works and the Audio Home Recording Act of 1992: A Critical Analysis*, 16 Hastings Comm. & Ent. L.J. 311 (1994)

Menard, *And The Shirt Off Your Back:* Universal City Studios, DECSS, *and the Digital Millennium Copyright Act*, 27 Rutgers Computer & Tech. L.J. 371 (2001)

D. Nimmer, *Aus der Neuen Welt*, 93 Nw. U. L. Rev. 195 (1998)

D. Nimmer, *Back from the Future: A Proleptic Review of the Digital Millennium Copyright Act*, 16 Berkeley Tech. L.J. 855 (2001)

D. Nimmer, *Ignoring the Public, Part I: On the Absurd Complexity of the Digital Audio Transmission Right*, 7 UCLA Ent. L. Rev. 189 (2000)

Note, *DAT's All Folks:* Cahn v. Sony *and the Audio Home Recording Act of 1991 — Merrie Melodies or Looney Tunes?*, 11 Cardozo Arts & Ent. L.J. 145 (1992)

Note, *Strange Fixation: Bootleg Sound Recordings Enjoy the Benefits of Improving Technology*, 47 Fed. Com. L.J. 611 (1995)

Patterson, *Copyright in the New Millennium: Resolving the Conflict Between Property Rights and Political Rights*, 62 Ohio St. L.J. 703 (2001)

Zimmerman, *Adrift in the Digital Millennium Copyright Act: The Sequel*, 26 U. Dayton L. Rev. 279 (2001)

Moral Rights

C. Lury, CULTURAL RIGHTS: TECHNOLOGY, LEGALITY, AND PERSONALITY (1993)

J.H. Merryman, LAW, ETHICS AND THE VISUAL ARTS (2d ed. 1987)

Register of Copyrights, WAIVER OF MORAL RIGHTS IN VISUAL ARTWORKS (1996)

Aide, *A More Comprehensive Soul: Romantic Conceptions of Authorship and the Copyright Doctrine of Moral Rights*, 48 U. Toronto L. Rev. 211 (1990)

Barnett, *From New Technology to Moral Rights: Passive Carriers, Teletext, and Deletion as Copyright Infringement—The WGN Case,* 31 J. Copyright Soc'y 427 (1984)

Beyer, *Intentionalism, Art, and the Suppression of Innovation: Film Colorization and the Philosophy of Moral Rights,* 82 Nw. U. L. Rev. 1011 (1988)

Burton, *Artists' Moral Rights: Controversy and the Visual Artists' Rights Act,* 48 SMU L. Rev. 639 (1995)

Ciolino, *Moral Rights and Real Obligations: A Property-Law Framework For the Protection of Authors' Moral Rights,* 69 Tul. L. Rev. 935 (1995)

Ciolino, *Rethinking the Compatibility of Moral Rights and Fair Use,* Wash. & Lee L. Rev. 33 (1997)

Comment, *Authors' Moral Rights in Non-European Nations: International Agreements, Economics, Mannu Bhandari, and the Dead Sea Scrolls,* 16 Mich. J. Int'l L. 545 (1995)

Comment, *On Moral Rights, Artist-Centered Legislation, and the Role of the State in Art Worlds: Notes on Building Sociology of Copyright Law,* 70 Tul. L. Rev. 313 (1995)

Cotter, *Pragmatism, Economics, and the Droit Moral,* 76 N.C. L. Rev. 1 (1997)

Damich, *A Critique of the Visual Artists Rights Act of 1989,* 14 Nova L. Rev. 407 (1990)

Damich, *State "Moral Rights" Statutes: An Analysis and Critique,* 13 Colum.–VLA J.L. & the Arts 291 (1989)

Damich, *The New York Artists' Authorship Rights Act: A Comparative Critique,* 84 Colum. L. Rev. 1733 (1984)

Damich, *The Right of Personality: A Common-Law Basis for the Protection of the Moral Rights of Authors,* 23 Ga. L. Rev. 1 (1988)

Damich, *The Visual Artists Rights Act of 1990: Toward a Federal System of Moral Rights Protection for Visual Art,* 39 Cath. U. L. Rev. 945 (1990)

DaSilva, Droit Moral *and the Amoral Copyright: A Comparison of Artists' Rights in France and the U.S.,* 28 Bull. Copyright Soc'y 1 (1980)

Davis, *State Moral Rights Law and the Federal Copyright System,* 4 Cardozo Arts & Ent. L.J. 233 (1986)

Dielkow, *Clashing the Rights Under United States Copyright Law: Harmonizing an Employer's Economic Right with the*

Artist-Employee's Moral Rights in a Work Made for Hire, 7 DePaul-LCA J. Art & Ent. L. 218 (1997)

Dietz, *The Moral Right of the Author: Moral Rights and the Civil Law Countries,* 19 Colum.-VLA J.L. & the Arts 199 (1995)

Dworkin, *The Moral Right of the Author: Moral Rights and the Common Law Countries,* 19 Colum.-VLA J.L. & Arts 229 (1995)

Francon & Ginsburg, *Authors' Rights in France: The Moral Right of the Creator of a Commissioned Work to Compel the Commissioning Party to Complete the Work,* 9 Colum.-VLA J.L. & the Arts 381 (1981)

Ginsburg, *Suppression and Liberty: Have Moral Rights Come of (Digital) Age in the United States?,* 19 Cardozo Arts & Ent. L.J. 9 (2001)

Ginsburg, *Colors in Conflicts: Moral Rights and the Foreign Exploitation of Colorized U.S. Motion Pictures,* 36 J. Copyright Soc'y 81 (1988)

Ginsburg, *Copyright in the 101st Congress: Commentary on the Visual Artists' Rights Act and the Architectural Works Copyright Protection Act of 1990,* 14 Colum.-VLA J.L. & the Arts 477 (1990)

Ginsburg, *Reforms and Innovations Regarding Authors' and Performers' Rights in France,* 10 Colum.-VLA J.L. & Arts 83 (1985)

Ginsburg & Sirinelli, *Authors and Exploitations in International Private Law: The French Supreme Court and the Huston Film Colorization Controversy,* 15 Colum.-VLA J.L. & the Arts 135 (1991)

Gorman, *Federal Moral Rights Legislation: The Need for Caution,* 14 Nova L. Rev. 421 (1990)

Gorman, *Visual Artists Rights Act of 1990,* 38 J. Copyright Soc'y 233 (1991)

Gunlicks, *A Balance of Interests: The Concordance of Copyright Law and Moral Rights in the Worldwide Economy,* 11 Fordham Intell. Prop. Media. & Ent. L.J. 601 (2001)

Hanson & Santilli, *Authors' and Artists' Moral Rights: A Comparative Legal and Economic Analysis,* 26 J. Legal Stud. 95 (1997)

Karlen, *Joint Ownership of Moral Rights,* 38 J. Copyright Soc'y 242 (1991)

Karlen, *Moral Rights and Real Life Artists,* 15 Hastings Comm. & Ent. L.J. 929 (1993)

Kelly, *Moral Right and the First Amendment: Putting Honor Before Free Speech?,* 11 U. Miami Ent. & Sports L. Rev. 211 (1995)

King, *The "Moral Rights" of Creators of Intellectual Property,* 9 Cardozo Arts & Ent. L.J. 267 (1991)

Kwall, *Copyright and the Moral Right: Is an American Marriage Possible?,* 38 Vand. L. Rev. 1 (1985)

Kwall, *How Fine Art Fares Post VARA,* 1 Marq. Intell. Prop. L. Rev. 1 (1997)

Kwall, *Preserving Personality and Reputational Interests of Constructed Personas Through Moral Rights: A Blueprint for the Twenty-First Century,* 2001 U. Ill. L. Rev. 151 (2001)

Leaffer, *Of Moral Rights and Resale Royalties: The Kennedy Bill,* 7 Cardozo Arts & Ent. L.J. 234 (1989)

Lee, *Toward an American Moral Rights in Copyright,* 58 Wash. & Lee L. Rev. 795 (2001)

Lemley, *Rights of Attribution and Integrity in Online Communications,* 1995 J. Online L., Art 2

Merryman, *The Refrigerator of Bernard Buffet,* 27 Hastings L.J. 1023 (1976)

Merryman, *The Wrath of Robert Rauschenberg,* 40 J. Copyright Soc'y 241 (1992)

Netanel, *Alienability Restrictions and the Enhancement of Author Autonomy in United States and Continental Copyright Law,* 12 Cardozo Arts & Ent. L.J. 1 (1994)

Note, *Safeguarding Style: What Protection is Afforded to Visual Artists by the Copyright and Trademark Laws?,* 93 Colo. L. Rev. 1157 (1993)

Note, *The Visual Artists' Rights Act of 1990: Why Moral Rights Cannot Be Protected Under the United States Constitution,* 24 Hofstra L. Rev. 1127 (1996)

Pitta, *Economic and Moral Rights Under U.S. Copyright Law: Protecting Authors and Producers in the Motion Picture Industry,* 12 WTR Ent. & Sports L. 3 (1995)

Roeder, *The Doctrine of Moral Right: A Study in the Law of Artists, Authors and Creators,* 53 Harv. L. Rev. 554 (1940)

Rudoff, *The Dancer and the Dance: An Essay on Composers, Performers, and Integrity Rights,* 29 Alberta L. Rev. 884 (1991)

Santilli, *United States' Moral Rights Developments in European Perpective,* 1 Marq. Intell. Prop. L. Rev. 89 (1997)

Sergent, *Building Reputational Capital: The Right of Attribution Under Section 43 of the Lanham Act,* 19 Colum.-VLA J. L. & Arts 45 (1995)

Serra, *"Tilted Arc" Destroyed,* 14 Nova L. Rev. 385 (1990)

Strauss, *The Moral Right of the Author, Copyright Law Revision Study No. 4* (1960)

Traphagen, *Stretching the Canvas: Protection of Visual Artistic Styles in Works of Fine Art Under Section 43(a) of the Lanham Act,* 10 Ent. & Sports Law. 3 (1992)

Treece, *American Law Analogues of the Author's "Moral Right,"* 16 Am. J. Comp. L. 487 (1968)

VerSteeg, *Federal Moral Rights for Visual Artists: Contract Theory and Analysis,* 67 Wash. L. Rev. 827 (1992)

Wang, *(Re)productive Rights: Copyright and Postmodern Art,* 14 Colum.-VLA J.L. & the Arts 261 (1990)

Wilkof, *Copyright, Moral Rights and the Choice of Law: Where Did the* Dead Sea Scrolls *Court Go Wrong?,* 38 Hous. L. Rev. 463 (2001)

Yonover, *The "Dissing" of Da Vinci: The Imaginary Case of* Leonardo v. Duchamp: *Moral Rights, Parody, and Fair Use,* 29 Val. U. L. Rev. 935 (1995)

Yonover, *The Precarious Balance: Moral Rights, Parody, and Fair Use,* 14 Cardozo Art & Ent. L.J. 79 (1996)

CHAPTER 8
INFRINGEMENT ACTIONS

Reference Works

H. Abrams, THE LAW OF COPYRIGHT §§ 13.01 to 13.12, 14.01 to 14.06, 18.04 to 18.05 (2002)

P. Goldstein, COPYRIGHT: PRINCIPLES, LAW AND PRACTICE §§ 6.0 to 6.3, 7.1 to 7.4, 8.0 to 8.6, 13.1 to 13.6, 14.1 to 14.6 (2002)

M. Leaffer, UNDERSTANDING COPYRIGHT LAW §§ 9.1 to 9.8, 9.17 to 9.21 (3d ed. 1999)

M. Nimmer & D. Nimmer, NIMMER ON COPYRIGHT §§ 12.01 to 12.12, 13.01 to 13.03 (2002)

W. Patry, COPYRIGHT LAW AND PRACTICE, Chaps. 8 and 15 (1994 & 2000 Supp.)

Procedural Aspects

Berman, Reese & Young, *State Accountability for Violations of Intellectual Property Rights: How to "Fix" Florida Prepaid (And How Not To)*, 79 Tex. L. Rev. 1037 (2001)

Blair & Cotter, *The Elusive Logic of Standing Doctrine in Intellectual Property Law*, 74 Tul. L. Rev. 1323 (2000)

Bohannon & Cotter, *When the State Steals Ideas: Is the Abrogation of State Sovereign Immunity from Federal Infringement Claims Constitutional in Light of Seminole Tribe?*, 4 Fordham L. Rev. (1999)

Burmeister, *Jurisdiction, Choice of Law, Copyright, and the Internet: Protection against Framing in an International Setting*, 9 Fordham I. P., Media & Ent. L.J. 625 (1999)

A. Cohen, *"Arising Under" Jurisdiction and the Copyright Laws*, 44 Hastings L. Rev. 337 (1993)

Berman, Reese & Young, *State Accountability for Violations of Intellectual Property Rights: How to "Fix" Florida Prepaid (And How Not To)*, 79 Tex. L. Rev. 1037 (2001)

Comment, *The Jurisdiction of Trademark and Copyright Infringement on the Internet*, 48 Mercer L. Rev. 1331 (1997)

Cross, *Suing the States for Copyright Infringement*, 39 Brandeis L.J. 337 (2000-01)

Feldman, *An Examination of the Right to Jury Trial Where Copyright Statutory Damages Are Elected*, 21 Hofstra L. Rev. 261 (1992)

Ghosh, *Toward a Theory of Regulatory Takings for Intellectual Property: The Path Left Open After* College Savings v. Florida Prepaid, 37 San Diego L. Rev. 637 (2000)

Glauberman, *Citizen Suits Against States: The Exclusive Jurisdiction Dilemma*, 45 J. Copyright Soc'y 63 (1997)

Heald & Sherry, *Implied Limits on the Legislative Power: The Intellectual Property Clause as an Absolute Constraint on Congress*, 2000 U. Ill. L. Rev. 1119 (2000)

Heald & Wells, *Remedies for the Misappropriation of Intellectual Property by State and Municipal Governments Before and After* Seminole Tribe: *The Eleventh Amendment and Other Immunity Doctrines*, 55 Wash. & Lee L. Rev. 849 (1998)

Kwall, *Governmental Use of Copyrighted Property: The Sovereign's Prerogative*, 67 Tex. L. Rev. 685 (1989)

Landau & Biederman, *The Case for a Specialized Copyright Court: Eliminating the Jurisdictional Advantage*, 21 Hastings Comm. & Ent. L.J. 717 (1999)

Latman & Tager, *Liability of Innocent Infringers of Copyright, Copyright Law Revision Study No. 25* (1960)

Kim, *Expert Testimony and Substantial Similarity: Facing the Music in (Music) Copyright Infringement Cases,* 19 Colum.-VLA J.L. & the Arts 109 (1995)

Meltzer, *Overcoming Immunity: The Case of Federal Regulation of Intellectual Property,* 53 Stan. L. Rev. 1331 (2001)

Menell, *Economic Implications of State Sovereign Immunity from Infringement of Federal Intellectual Property Rights*, 33 Loy. L.A. L. Rev. 1399 (2000)

Note, *After* College Savings v. Florida Prepaid: *Are States Subject to Suit for Copyright Infringement? The Copyright Remedy Clarification Act and* Chavez v. Arte Publico Press, 36 Hous. L. Rev. 1531 (1999)

Note, *The Right to Trial by Jury in Copyright Infringement Suits Seeking Statutory Damages*, 17 S. Ill. U. L.J. 135 (1992)

Note, Seminole Tribe: *Are States Free to Pirate Copyrights with Impunity?*, 22 Colum.-VLA J. L. & Arts 91 (1997)

Patry, *The Right to a Jury in Copyright Cases*, 29 J. Copyright Soc'y 139 (1981)

Shoiket, Creative Technology Ltd. v. Aztech System PTE, Ltd.: *Using Forum Non Conveniens to Dismiss a Copyright*

Infringement Action Brought by a Foreign Owner of U.S. Copyrights, 31 U.S.F. L. Rev. 505 (1997)

Swire, *Of Elephants, Mice, and Privacy: International Choice of Law and the Internet*, 32 Intl. Lawyer 991 (1998)

Volokh, *Sovereign Immunity and Intellectual Property*, 73 S. Cal. L. Rev. 1161 (2000)

Volokh & McDonnell, *Freedom of Speech and Independent Judgment Review in Copyright Cases*, 107 Yale L.J. 2431 (1998)

Wanat, *Copyright and Contracts: The Subject Matter Jurisdiction of Federal Courts Under 28 U.S.C. § 1338(a)*, 11 DePaul-LCA J. Art & Ent. L. 361 (2001)

Substantive Aspects Generally

Aoki, *Adrift in the Intertext: Authorship and Audience "Recoding" Rights*, 68 Chicago-Kent L. Rev. 805 (1993)

Bisceglia, *Summary Judgment on Substantial Similarity in Copyright Actions*, 16 Hastings Comm. & Ent. L.J. 51 (1993)

Broaddus, *Eliminating the Confusion: A Restatement of the Test for Copyright Infringement*, 5 J. Art & Ent. L. 43 (1994)

Brown, *The Corporate Receipt Conundrum: Establishing Access in Copyright Infringement Actions*, 77 Minn. L. Rev. 1409 (1993)

A. Cohen, *Masking Copyright Decisionmaking: The Meaninglessness of Substantial Similarity*, 20 U.C. Davis L. Rev. 719 (1987)

Druehwald, *Copyright Infringement of Musical Compositions: A Systematic Approach*, 26 Akron L. Rev. 15 (1992)

Francione, *Facing the Nation: The Standards for Copyright Infringement and Fair Use of Factual Works*, 134 U. Pa. L. Rev. 519 (1986)

Hartnick, *Summary Judgment in Copyright: From Cole Porter to Superman*, 3 Cardozo Arts & Ent. L.J. 53 (1984)

Jones, *Music Copyright in Theory and Practice: An Improved Approach for Determining Substantial Similarity*, 31 Duq. L. Rev. 277 (1993)

Katsh & Rifkin, *The New Media and a New Model of Conflict Resolution: Copying, Copyright, and Creating*, 6 Notre Dame J. L., Ethics & Pub. Pol'y 49 (1992)

Kegan, *Survey Evidence in Copyright Litigation*, 32 J. Copyright Soc'y 283 (1985)

Knowles & Palmieri, *Dissecting* Krofft: *An Expression of New Ideas in Copyright?*, 8 San Fern. V. L. Rev. 109 (1980)

Lape, *The Metaphysics of the Law: Bringing Substantial Similarity Down to Earth,* 98 Dick. L. Rev. 181 (1993)

Latman, *"Probative Similarity" as Proof of Copying: Towards Dispelling Some Myths in Copyright Infringement*, 90 Colum. L. Rev. 1187 (1990)

Lindenberg–Woods, *The Smoking Revolver: Criminal Copyright Infringement*, 27 Bull. Copyright Soc'y 63 (1979)

Malkan, *Stolen Photographs: Personality, Publicity, and Privacy,* 75 Tex. L. Rev. 779 (1997)

Myers, *Speaking Frankly About Copyright Infringement on Computer Bulletin Boards: Lessons to be Learned from* Frank Music, Netcom, *and the White Paper,* 49 Vand. L. Rev. 439 (1996)

Note, *Digital Sound Sampling, Copyright and Publicity: Protecting Against the Electronic Appropriation of Sounds*, 87 Colum. L. Rev. 1723 (1987)

Note, *The Role of the Expert Witness in Music Copyright Infringement Cases*, 57 Fordham L. Rev. 127 (1988)

Radin, *The Significance of Intent to Copy in a Civil Action for Copyright Infringement*, 54 Temp. L.Q. 1 (1981)

Sher, *The Search for a Suitable Standard of Substantial Similarity: The Ninth Circuit's Application of the* Krofft *Test,* 25 U.C. Davis L. Rev. 229 (1991)

Sorensen & Sorensen, *Re–Examining the Traditional Legal Test of Literary Similarity: A Proposal for Content Analysis*, 37 Cornell L.Q. 638 (1952)

Taylor, *Common Errors as Evidence of Copying*, 22 Bull. Copyright Soc'y 444 (1975)

Y'Barbo, *Aesthetic Ambition Versus Commercial Appeal: Adapting Novels to Film and the Copyright Law*, 10 St. Thomas L. Rev. 299 (1998)

Y'Barbo, *The Heart of the Matter: The Property Right Conferred by Copyright,* 49 Mercer L. Rev. 643 (1998)

Software Infringement

M. Lehmann & C. Tapper, eds., HANDBOOK OF EUROPEAN SOFTWARE LAW (1993)

R. Nimmer, THE LAW OF COMPUTER TECHNOLOGY (Rev. ed. 2001)

Brown, *"Analytical Dissection" of Copyrighted Computer Software — Complicating the Simple and Confounding the Complex*, 25 Ariz. St. L.J. 801 (1993)

Clapes, Lynch & Steinberg, *Silicon Epics and Binary Bards: Determining the Proper Scope of Copyright Protection for Computer Programs*, 34 UCLA L. Rev. 1493 (1987)

J. Cohen, *Reverse Engineering and the Rise of Electronic Vigilantism: Intellectual Property Implications of "Lock-Out" Programs*, 68 S. Cal. L. Rev. 1091 (1995)

Comment, *Let the Hackers Hack: Allowing the Revenue Engineering of Copyrighted Computer Programs to Achieve Compatibility*, 140 U. Pa. L. Rev. 1999 (1992)

Comment, *Privileged Use: Has Judge Boudin Suggested a Viable Means of Copyright Protection for the Non-Literal Aspects of Computer Software in* Lotus Development Corp. v. Borland International?, 46 Am. U. L. Rev. 149 (1996)

Dam, *Some Economic Considerations in the Intellectual Property Protection of Software*, 24 J. Legal Stud. 321 (1995)

Effross, *Assaying* Computer Associates v. Altai: *Will the "Golden Nuggett" Test Pan Out?*, 19 Rutgers Computer & Tech. L.J. 1 (1993)

Goldstein, *Infringement of Copyright in Computer Programs*, 47 U. Pitt. L. Rev. 1119 (1986)

Gordon, *Copying to Compete: The Tension Between Copyright Protection and Antitrust Policy in Recent Non-Literal Computer Program Copyright Infringement Cases*, 15 J. Marshall J. Computer & Info. L. 171 (1996)

Hamilton & Sabety, *Computer Science Concepts in Copyright Cases: The Path to a Coherent Law*, 10 Harv. J.L. & Tech. 239 (1997)

Karjala, *Copyright Computer Software and the New Protectionism*, 28 Jurimetrics J. 33 (1987)

Karjala, *Copyright Protection of Computer Software, Reverse Engineering, and Professor Miller*, 19 U. Dayton L. Rev. 975 (1994)

Litman, *Revising Copyright Law for the Information Age*, 75 Ore. L. Rev. 19 (1996)

Lowe, *A Square Peg in a Round Hole: The Proper Substantial Similarity Test for Nonliteral Aspects of Computer Programs*, 68 Wash. L. Rev. 351 (1993)

Lunney, Lotus v. Borland: *Copyright and Computer Programs,* 70 Tul. L. Rev. 2397 (1996)

Menell, *An Analysis of the Scope of Copyright Protection for Application Programs,* 41 Stan. L. Rev. 1045 (1989)

Menell, *Tailoring Legal Protection for Computer Software,* 41 Stan. L. Rev. 1329 (1987)

Miller, *Copyright Protection for Computer Programs, Databases, and Computer-Generated Works: Is Anything New Since CONTU?,* 106 Harv. L. Rev. 977 (1993)

D. Nimmer, *Brains and Other Paraphernalia of the Digital Age,* 10 Harv. J.L. & Tech. 1 (1996)

D. Nimmer, Bernacchi & Frischling, *A Structured Approach to Analyzing the Substantial Similarity of Computer Software in Copyright Infringement Cases,* 20 Ariz. St. L.J. 625 (1988)

R. Nimmer & Krauthaus, *Copyright and Software Technology Infringement: Defining Third Party Development Rights,* 62 Ind. L.J. 13 (1986)

Ogilvie, *Defining Computer Program Parts Under Learned Hand's Abstractions Test in Software Copyright Infringement Cases,* 91 Mich. L. Rev. 526 (1992)

Palmer & Vinje, *The E.C. Directive on the Legal Protection of Computer Software: New Law Governing Software Development,* 2 Duke J. Comp. & Int'l L. 65 (1992)

Patry, *Copyright and Computer Programs: It's All in the Definition,* 14 Cardozo Arts & Ent. L.J. 1 (1996)

Pinheiro & Lacroix, *Protecting the "Look and Feel" of Computer Software,* 1 High Tech. L.J. 411 (1986)

Risch, *How Can* Whelan v. Jaslow *and* Lotus v. Borland *Both Be Right? Reexamining the Economics of Computer Software Reuse,* 17 J. Marshall J. Computer & Info. L. 511 (1999)

Rosen, *Virtual Reality: Copyrightable Subject Matter and the Scope of Judicial Protection,* 33 Jurimetrics J. 35 (1992)

Samuelson, *Computer Programs, User Interfaces, and Section 102(b) of the Copyright Act of 1976: A Critique of Lotus v. Paperback,* 6 High Tech. L.J. 209 (1991)

Samuelson, *The Nature of Copyright Analysis for Computer Programs: Copyright Law Professors' Brief Amicus Curiae in "Lotus v. Borland",* 16 Hastings Comm. & Ent. L.J. 657 (1994)

Samuelson & Glushko, *Comparing the Views of Lawyers and User Interface Designers on the Software "Look and Feel" Law Suits*, 30 Jurimetrics J. 121 (1988)

Stevens, *Copyright Infringement of Computer Programs Stored on ROM Computer Chips*, 78 J. Patent & Trademark Off. Soc'y 640 (1996)

Symposium: A Manifesto Concerning the Legal Protection of Computer Programs, 94 Colum. L. Rev. 2308 (1994)

Symposium: Copyright Protection and Reverse Engineering of Software, 19 U. Dayton L. Rev. 837 (1994)

Symposium: Copyright Protection: Has Look & Feel Crashed?, 11 Cardozo Arts & Ent. LJ. 721 (1993)

Teter, *Merger and the Machines: An Analysis of the Pro-Compatibility Trend in Computer Software Copyright Cases*, 45 Stan. L. Rev. 1061 (1993)

Wright, *Litigation as a Mechanism for Inefficiency in Software Copyright Law*, 39 UCLA L. Rev. 397 (1991)

Contributory and Vicarious Infringement

Carmichael, *In Support of the White Paper: Why Online Service Providers Should Not Receive Immunity from Traditional Notions of Vicarious and Contributory Liability for Copyright Infringement*, 16 Loy. L.A. Ent. J.L. 759 (1996)

Cavasos & Miles, *Copyright on the WWW: Linking and Liability*, 4 Rich. J.L. & Tech. 3 (1997)

Comment, *Protecting Copyrights in Cyberspace: Holding Anonymous Remailer Services Contributorily Liable for Infringement*, 14 T.M. Cooley L. Rev. 317 (1997)

Comment, *When Should Computer Owners Be Liable for Copyright Infringement By Users*, 64 U. Chi. L. Rev. 709 (1997)

Dean, *Expanding the Doctrines of Vicarious and Contributory Copyright Infringement:* Fonovisa, Inc. v. Cherry Auction, Inc. *Targets the Primary Distribution Channels for Counterfeit Merchandise*, 4 Vill. Sports & Ent. L.J. 119 (1997)

Denster, *Fault-Based Libel and Copyright Infringement Liability for On-Line Content Providers and Bulletin Board Operators as "Information Distributors,"* 11 St. John's J. Legal Comment. 653 (1996)

Dogan, *Infringement Once Removed: The Perils of Hyperlinking to Infringing Content*, 87 Iowa L. Rev. 829 (2002)

Gilbert & Katz, *When Good Value Chains Go Bad: The Economics of Indirect Liability for Copyright Infringement,* 52 Hastings L.J. 961 (2001)

Ginsburg, *Putting Cars on the "Information Superhighway": Authors, Exploiters, and Copyright in Cyberspace*, 95 Colum. L. Rev. 1466 (1995)

Glynn, *Cyber Copyrights: Internet Provider Liability*, 60 Tex. B.J. 634 (1997)

Hamdani, *Who's Liable for Cyberwrongs?*, 87 Cornell L. Rev. 901 (2002)

Lewis, *The Yellow Submarine Steers Clear of U.S. Copyright Law: The Ninth Circuit Reexamines the Doctrine of Contributory Infringement*, 18 Loy. L.A. Int'l & Comp. L.J. 371 (1996)

Malone, *Contributory Liability for Access Providers: Solving the Conundrum Digitization Has Placed on Copyright Laws*, 49 Fed. Comm. L.J. 491 (1997)

Mota, *Napster: Facilitation of Sharing, Or Contributory and Vicarious Copyright Infringement?*, 2 Minn. Intell. Prop. Rev. 61 (2001)

D. Nimmer, *An Odyssey Through Copyright's Vicarious Defenses*, 73 N.Y.U. L. Rev. 162 (1998)

Note, *National and International Copyright Liability for Electronic System Operators*, 2 Ind. J. Global Legal Stud. 497 (1995)

Oddi, *Contributory Copyright Infringement: The Tort and Technology Tensions*, 64 Notre Dame L. Rev. 47 (1989)

Pomeroy, *Promoting the Progress of Science and the Useful Art in the Digital Domain: Copyright, Computer Bulletin Boards, and Liability for Infringement by Others*, 45 Emory L.J. 1035 (1996)

Schulman, *Internet Copyright Infringement Liability: Is an Online Access Provider More Like a Landlord or a Dancehall Operator?*, 27 Golden Gate U. L. Rev. 555 (1997)

Self, *The Vicarious Liability of Trade Show Organizers for the Copyright Infringement of Exhibitors*, 5 Tex. Intell. Prop. L.J. 81 (1996)

Stephens & Summer, *Catch 22: Internet Service Providers' Liability for Copyright Infringement Over the Internet*, 14 Computer Law. 1 (1997)

Yen, *Internet Service Provider Liability for Subscriber Copyright Infringement, Enterprise Liability, and the First Amendment*, 88 Geo. L.J. 1833 (2000)

Yen, *A Personal Injury Law Perspective on Copyright in an Internet Age,* 52 Hastings L.J. 929 (2001)

Yen, *A Preliminary Economic Analysis of* Napster: *Internet Technology, Copyright Liability, and The Possibility of Coasean Bargaining,* 26 U. Dayton L. Rev. 247 (2001)

Extraterritoriality and Conflicts of Laws

Austin, *Social Policy Choices and Choice of Law for Copyright Infringement in Cyberspace,* 79 Or. L. Rev. 575 (2000)

Bradley, *Territorial Intellectual Property Law in an Age of Globalism,* 37 Va. J. Int'l L. 505 (1997)

Chien-Hale, *Asserting U.S. Intellectual Property Rights in China: Expansion of Extraterritorial Jurisdiction,* 45 J. Copyright Soc'y 198 (1997)

Geller, *Conflicts of Laws in Cyberspace: Rethinking International Copyright,* 44 J. Copyright Soc'y 103 (1996)

Geller, *Harmonizing Copyright–Contract Conflicts Analyses,* 25 Copyright 49 (1989)

Ginsburg, *Colors in Conflicts: Moral Rights and the Foreign Exploitation of Colorized U.S. Motion Pictures,* 36 J. Copyright Soc'y 81 (1988)

Ginsburg, *Copyright Without Borders? Choice of Forum and Choice of Law for Copyright Infringement in Cyberspace,* 15 Cardozo Arts & Ent. L.J. 153 (1997)

Ginsburg, *Extraterritoriality and Multiterritoriality in Copyright Infringement,* 37 Va. J. Int'l L. 587 (1997)

Kirios, *Territoriality and International Copyright Actions,* 22 Copyright L. Symp. (ASCAP) 53 (1977)

Kloss, *Copyrights and the Conflict of Laws,* 1 Euro. Intell. Prop. Rev. [E.I.P.R.] 15 (1985)

Koneru, *The Right to Authorize in U.S. Copyright Law: Questions of Contributory Infringement and Extraterritoriality,* 37 IDEA: J.L. & Tech. 87 (1996)

M. Nimmer, *Who Is the Copyright Owner When the Laws Conflict?,* 5 IIC 62 (1974)

Patchel, *Software as a Commodity: International Licensing of Intellectual Property: Choice of Law and Software Licenses: A Framework for Discussion,* 26 Brooklyn J. Int'l L. 117 (2000)

Patry, *Choice of Law and International Copyright,* 48 Am. J. Comp. L. 383 (2000)

Schechter, *The Case for Limited Extraterritorial Reach of the Lanham Act,* 37 Va. J. Int'l L. 619 (1997)

Wilkof, *Copyright, Moral Rights and the Choice of Law: Where Did the* Dead Sea Scrolls *Court Go Wrong?,* 38 Hous. L. Rev. 463 (2001)

Wollman, *Maneuvering Through the Landmines of Multiterritorial Copyright Litigation: How to Avoid the Presumption Against Extraterritoriality When Attempting to Recover for the Foreign Exploitation of U.S. Copyrighted Works,* 104 W. Va. L. Rev. 343 (2002)

CHAPTER 9
FAIR USE AND AFFIRMATIVE DEFENSES

Reference Works

H. Abrams, THE LAW OF COPYRIGHT §§ 14.07, 15.01 to 15.07, 15A.01 to 15A.06 (2002)

P. Goldstein, COPYRIGHT: PRINCIPLES, LAW AND PRACTICE §§ 5.16 to 5.18, 9.1 to 9.6, 10.1 to 10.3 (2002)

M. Leaffer, UNDERSTANDING COPYRIGHT LAW §§ 10.1 to 10.21 (3d ed. 1999)

M. Nimmer & D. Nimmer, NIMMER ON COPYRIGHT §§ 13.04 to 13.09 (2002)

W. Patry, COPYRIGHT LAW AND PRACTICE, Chap. 9 (1994 & 2000 Supp.)

W. Patry, THE FAIR USE PRIVILEGE IN COPYRIGHT LAW (1995)

Development of the Fair Use Privilege

K. Crews, COPYRIGHT, FAIR USE, & THE CHALLENGE FOR UNIVERSITIES: PROMOTING THE PROGRESS OF HIGHER EDUCATION (1993)

L.R. Patterson & S.W. Lindberg, THE NATURE OF COPYRIGHT: A LAW OF USERS' RIGHTS (1991)

Anderson & Brown, *The Economics Behind Copyright Fair Use: A Principled and Predictable Body of Law,* 24 Loy. U. Chi. L.J. 143 (1993)

Ciolino, *Rethinking the Compatibility of Moral Rights and Fair Use,* 54 Wash. & Lee L. Rev. 33 (1997)

Cohen, *Fair Use in Copyright Law,* 6 Copyright L. Symp. (ASCAP) 42 (1955)

Conley, *Author, User, Scholar, Thief: Fair Use and Unpublished Works,* 9 Cardozo Arts & Ent. L.J. 15 (1990)

Dratler, *Distilling the Witches' Brew of Fair Use in Copyright Law,* 43 Miami L. Rev. 233 (1988)

Fisher, *Reconstructing the Fair Use Doctrine,* 101 Harv. L. Rev. 1659 (1988)

Francione, *Facing* The Nation: *The Infringement and Fair Use of Factual Works,* 134 U. Pa. L. Rev. 519 (1986)

Gordon, *Fair Use as Market Failure: A Structural and Economic Analysis of the* Betamax *Case and Its Predecessors,* 82 Colum. L. Rev. (1982)

Gordon, *Reality As Artifact: From* Feist *to Fair Use,* 55 Law & Contemp. Probs. 93 (1992)

Landes, *Copyright Protection of Letters, Diaries, and Other Unpublished Works: An Economic Approach,* 21 J. Legal Stud. 79 (1992)

Lape, *Transforming Fair Use: The Productive Use Factor in Fair Use Doctrine,* 58 Alb. L. Rev. 677 (1995)

Latman, *Fair Use of Copyrighted Works, Copyright Law Revision Study No. 14* (1960)

Lemley, *The Economics of Improvement in Intellectual Property Law,* 75 Tex. L. Rev. 989 (1997)

Leval, Campbell v. Acuff-Rose: *Justice Souter's Rescue of Fair Use,* 13 Cardozo Arts & Ent. L.J. 19 (1994)

Leval, *Fair Use or Foul?,* 36 J. Copyright Soc'y 167 (1989)

Leval, *Fair Use Rescued,* 44 UCLA L. Rev. 1449 (1997)

Leval, *Toward a Fair Use Standard,* 103 Harv. L. Rev. 1105 (1990)

Litman, *Copyright Law as Communications Policy: Convergence of Paradigms and Cultures War Stories,* 20 Cardozo Arts & Ent. L.J. 337 (2002)

Loren, *Redefining the Market Failure Approach to Fair Use in an Era of Copyright Permissions Systems,* 5 J. Intell. Prop. L. 1 (1997)

McJohn, *Fair Use and Privatization in Copyright,* 35 San Diego L. Rev. 61 (1998)

Miller, *Fair Use, Biographers, and Unpublished Works: Life After H.R. 4412,* 40 J. Copyright Soc'y 349 (1993)

Miner, *Exploiting Stolen Text: Fair Use or Foul Play?,* 37 J. Copyright Soc'y 1 (1989)

Morris, *Use of Copyrighted Images in Academic Scholarship and Creative Work: The Problems of New Technologies and Proposed Scholarly License,* 33 Idea 123 (1993)

Nelson, *The Fine Art of Reproduction: The Doctrine of Fair Use and Auction House Catalogues,* 18 Colum.-VLA J.L. & the Arts 291 (1994)

Newman, *Copyright Law and the Protection of Privacy,* 12 Colum.-VLA J.L. & the Arts 459 (1988)

Newman, *Not the End of History: The Second Circuit Struggles With Fair Use,* 37 J. Copyright Soc'y 12 (1989)

Note, *Copyright Protection, Privacy Rights, and the Fair Use Doctrine: The Post-Salinger Decade Reconsidered*, 72 N.Y.U. L. Rev. 1376 (1997)

Oakes, *Copyrights and Copyremedies: Unfair Use and Injunctions*, 18 Hofstra L. Rev. 983 (1990)

Patterson, *Folsom v. Marsh and Its Legacy*, 5 J. Intell. Prop. L. 431 (1998)

Patterson, *Understanding Fair Use*, 55 Law & Contemp. Probs. 249 (1992)

Patry, *Fair Use After* Sony *and* Harper & Row, 8 Comm. & the Law 21 (1986)

Raskind, *A Functional Interpretation of Fair Use*, 31 J. Copyright Soc'y 601 (1984)

Seltzer, *Exemptions and Fair Use in Copyright: The "Exclusive Rights" Tensions in the New Copyright Act*, 24 Bull. Copyright Soc'y 215 (1977)

Sobel, *Copyright and the First Amendment: A Gathering Storm?*, 19 Copyright L. Symp. (ASCAP) 43 (1971)

Weinreb, *Fair's Fair: A Comment on the Fair Use Doctrine*, 103 Harv. L. Rev. 1137 (1990)

Weinreb, *Fair Use and How It Got That Way*, 45 J. Copyright Soc. 634 (1998)

Zissu, *Fair Use: From* Harper & Row *to* Acuff Rose, 42 J. Copyright Soc'y 7 (1994)

Fair Use, Free Speech, and Parody

Bates, *Copyright Law: Parody and the "Heart" of the Fair Use Privilege*, 7 U. Fla. J.L. & Pub. Pol'y 365 (1994)

Comment, *The Right of Publicity & the First Amendment: A Comment on Why Celebrity Parodies are Fair Game for Fair Use*, 64 U. Cin. L. Rev. 179 (1995)

Farrell, *Fair Use of Copyrighted Material in Advertisement Parodies*, 92 Colum. L. Rev. 1550 (1992)

Goldstein, *Copyright and the First Amendment*, 70 Colum. L. Rev. 983 (1970)

Harmon, *Law, Art, and the Killing Jar*, 79 Iowa L. Rev. 367 (1994)

Kaplan, *Parody and the Fair Use Defense to Copyright Infringement: Appropriate Purpose and Object of Humor*, 26 Ariz. St. L.J. 857 (1994)

Leval, Campbell v. Acuff-Rose: *Justice Souter's Rescue of Fair Use*, 13 Cardozo Arts & Ent. L.J. 19 (1994)

Light, *Parody, Burlesque and the Economic Rationale for Copyright,* 11 Conn. L. Rev. 615 (1979)

McLean, *All's Not Fair in Art and War: A Look at the Fair Use Defense After* Rogers v. Koons, 59 Brooklyn L. Rev. 373 (1993)

Merges, *Are You Making Fun of Me? Notes on Market Failure and the Parody Defense in Copyright,* 21 AIPLA Q.J. 305 (1993)

M. Nimmer, *Does Copyright Abridge the First Amendment Guarantees of Free Speech and Press?,* 17 UCLA L. Rev. 1180 (1970)

Note, *The Cat in the Hat's Latest Bad Trick: The Ninth Circuit's Narrowing of the Parody Defense to Copyright Infringement in* Dr. Suess Enterprises v. Penguin Books USA, Inc., 20 Cardozo L. Rev. 287 (1998)

Note, *Deciphering the Fair Use Doctrine:* Campbell v. Acuff-Rose Music, Inc., 28 Creighton L. Rev. 505 (1995)

Note, *The "Fair Use" Doctrine and* Campbell v. Acuff-Rose: *Copyright Waters Remain Muddy*, 2 Vill. Sports & Ent. L.J. 311 (1995)

Note, *Toon Town: Do Cartoon Crossovers Merit Fair Use Protection?,* 38 B.C. L. Rev. 145 (1996)

Ochoa, *Dr. Seuss, the Juice and Fair Use: How the Grinch Silenced a Parody,* 45 J. Copyright Soc'y 546 (1998)

Patterson, *Free Speech, Copyright, and Fair Use,* 40 Vand. L. Rev. 1 (1987)

Patry & Perlmutter, *Fair Use Misconstrued: Profit, Presumptions, and Parody,* 11 Cardozo Arts & Ent. L.J. 667 (1993)

Posner, *When Is Parody Fair Use?,* 21 J. Legal Stud. 67 (1992)

Samuels, Campbell v. Acuff-Rose: *Bringing Fair Use Into Focus?,* 3 SPG Media L. & Pol'y 4 (1994)

Samuelson, *Reviving* Zacchini: *Analyzing First Amendment Defenses in Right of Publicity and Copyright Cases,* 57 Tul. L. Rev. 836 (1983)

Yen, *When Authors Won't Sell: Parody, Fair Use, and Efficiency in Copyright Law,* 62 U. Colo. L. Rev. 79 (1991)

Yonover, *The Precarious Balance: Moral Rights, Parody & Fair Use,* 14 Cardozo Arts & Ent. L.J. 79 (1996)

Fair Use and New Technologies

J. Cohen, *Reverse Engineering and the Rise of Electronic Vigilantism: Intellectual Property Implications of "Lock-Out" Programs,* 68 S. Cal. L. Rev. 1091 (1995)

Comment, *Bytes and Pieces: Fragmented Copies, Licensing, and Fair Use in a Digital World,* 86 Calif. L. Rev. 843 (1998)

Comment, *Now That the Future Has Arrived, Maybe the Law Should Take a Look: Multimedia Technology and Its Interaction with the Fair Use Doctrine,* 44 Am. U. L. Rev. 919 (1995)

Durdik, *Reverse Engineering as a Fair Use Defense to Software Copyright Infringement,* 34 Jurimetrics J. 451 (1994)

Fraser, *The Conflict Between the First Amendment and Copyright Law and Its Impact on the Internet,* 16 Cardozo Arts & Ent. L.J. 1 (1998)

Goldberg, *Now that the Future Has Arrived, Maybe the Law Should Take a Look: Multimedia Technology and its Interaction with the Fair Use Doctrine,* 44 Am. U.L. Rev. 919 (1995)

Ignatin, *Let the Hackers Hack: Allowing the Reverse Engineering of Copyrighted Computer Programs to Achieve Compatibility,* 140 U. Pa. L. Rev. 1999 (1992)

McJohn, *Fair Use of Copyrighted Software,* 28 Rutgers L.J. 593 (1997)

McManis, *Intellectual Property Protection and Reverse Engineering of Computer Programs in the United States and the European Community,* 8 High Tech. L.J. 25 (1993)

Note, *Is Turn About Fair Play? Copyright Law and the Fair Use of Computer Software Loaded into RAM,* 95 Mich. L. Rev. 654 (1996)

Note, *Will Fair Use Function on the Internet?,* 98 Colum. L. Rev. 169 (1998)

Owen, *Interfaces and Interoperablity in* Lotus v. Borland: *A Market Oriented Approach to the Fair Use Doctrine,* 64 Fordham L. Rev. 2381 (1996)

Samuelson, *Fair Use for Computer Programs and Other Copyrightable Works in Digital Form: The Implications of* Sony, Galoob *and* Sega, 1 J. Intell. Prop. L. 49 (1993)

Samuelson & Scotchmer, *The Law and Economics of Reverse Engineering,* 111 Yale L.J. 1575 (2002)

Soma, Winfield & Friesen, *Software Interoperability and Reverse Engineering,* 20 Rutgers Computer & Tech. L.J. 189 (1994)

Szymanski, *Audio Pastiche: Digital Sampling, Intermeditate Copying, Fair Use,* 3 UCLA Ent. L. Rev. 271 (1996)

Toedt, *Oh, Pretty Woman: Muddying Software Copyright Even Further with "Transformative Fair Use",* 11 Computer L. 15 (1994)

Varmer, *Photoduplication of Copyrighted Materials by Libraries, Copyright Law Revision Study No. 15* (1960)

Williams, *Can Reverse Engineering of Software Ever Be Fair Use? Application of* Campbell's *"Transformative Use" Concept,* 71 Wash. L. Rev. 255 (1996)

Fair Use in Corporations and Classrooms

K. Crews, COPYRIGHT, FAIR USE, AND THE CHALLENGE FOR UNIVERSITIES: PROMOTING THE PROGRESS OF HIGHER EDUCATION (1993)

Bartow, *Educational Fair Use in Copyright: Reclaiming the Right to Copy Freely,* 60 U. Pitt. L. Rev. 149 (1998)

Comment, *Photocopying for Research: A Fair Use Exception Favoring the Progress of Science & the Useful Arts,* 42 Wayne L. Rev. 1999 (1996)

Crews, *Copyright at a Turning Point: Corporate Responses to the Changing Environment,* 3 J. Intell. Prop. L. 2177 (1996)

Dratler, *To Copy or Not to Copy: The Educator's Dilemma,* 19 J.L. & Educ. 1 (1990)

Ginsburg, *Reproduction of Protected Works for University Research or Teaching,* 39 J. Copyright Soc'y 181 (1992)

Gorman, *Copyright Conflicts on the University Campus,* 40 J. Copyright Soc'y 291 (2000)

Kasunic, *Fair Use and the Educator's Right To Photocopy Copyrighted Material For Classroom Use,* 19 J.C. & U.L. 271 (1993)

Kreiss, *Copyright Fair Use of Standardized Tests,* 48 Rutgers L. Rev. 1043 (1996)

Miller, *Coursepacks & Copyright: Fair Use in* Princeton University Press v. Michigan Document Services, 23 J. C. & U. L. 525 (1997)

Miller, *Corporate Copyright Infringers Beware: Systematic Unauthorized Photocopying By For-Profit Corporations Does Not Constitute Fair Use:* American Geophysical Union v. Texaco, Inc., 30 Creighton L. Rev. 1521 (1997)

Patry, *American Geophysical Union v. Texaco, Inc.: Copyright and Corporate Photocopying,* 61 Brooklyn L. Rev. 429 (1995)

Patterson, *Regents Guide to Understanding Copyright and Educational Fair Use,* 5 J. Intell. Prop. L. 243 (1997)

Ster, *Photocopying & Fair Use: Exploring the Market for Scientific Journal Articles,* 30 Ind. L. Rev. 33 (1997)

Thau, *Copyright, Privacy, and Fair Use,* 24 Hofstra L. Rev. 179 (1995)

Weinberg, *The Photocopying Revolution and the Copyright Crisis,* 38 Pub. Interest 99 (1975)

Fair Use and Copyright Policy

Bartow, *Libraries in a Digital and Aggressively Copyrighted World: Retaining Patron Access through Changing Technologies,* 62 Ohio St. L.J. 821 (2001)

Bell, *Fair Use vs. Fared Use: The Impact of Automated Rights Management on Copyright's Fair Use Doctrine,* 76 N.C. L. Rev. 557 (1998)

J. Cohen, *Intellectual Privacy and Censorship of the Internet,* 8 Seton Hall Const. L.J. 693 (1998)

J. Cohen, *WIPO Copyright Treaty Implementation in the United States: Will Fair Use Survive?,* 21 Eur. Intell. Prop. Rev. 236 (1999)

Comment, *Copyright Protection in the New Millennium: Amending the Digital Millennium Copyright Act to Prevent Constitutional Challenges,* 52 Admin. L. Rev. 443 (2000)

Craig, *The Development of Internet Education and the Role of Copyright Law,* 40 J. Copyright Soc'y 75 (2000)

Crews, *The Law of Fair Use and the Illusion of Fair-Use Guidelines,* 62 Ohio St. L.J. 599 (2001)

Dam, *Self-Help in the Digital Jungle,* 28 J. Legal Stud. 393 (1999)

Denicola, *Mostly Dead? Copyright Law in the New Millennium,* 40 J. Copyright Soc'y 193 (2000)

Elliot, *Copyright Fair Use and Private Ordering: Are Copyright Holders and the Copyright Law Fanatical for Fansites?,* 11 DePaul-LCA J. Art & Ent. L. 329 (2001)

Gasaway, *Distance Learning and Copyright,* 62 Ohio St. L.J. 783 (2001)

Gorman, *Copyright Conflicts on the University Campus*, 40 J. Copyright Soc'y 291 (2000)

Green, *Reconciling* Napster *with the* Sony *Decision and Recent Amendments to Copyright Law*, 39 Am. Bus. L.J. 57 (2001)

Heide, *Copyright in the EU and U.S.: What "Access-Right"?*, 48 J. Copyright Soc'y 363 (2001)

Leaffer, *The Uncertain Future of Fair Use in a Global Information Marketplace*, 62 Ohio St. L.J. 849 (2001)

Madison, *Legal-Ware: Contract and Copyright in the Digital Age*, 67 Fordham L. Rev. 1025 (1998)

Merges, *Contracting into Liability Rules: Institutions Supporting Transactions in Intellectual Property Rights*, 84 Cal. L. Rev. 1293 (1997)

D. Nimmer, *A Riff on Fair Use in the Digital Millennium Copyright Act*, 148 U. Pa. L. Rev. 673 (2000)

Note, *What's Fair Here Is Not Fair Everywhere: Does the American Fair Use Doctrine Violate International Copyright Law?*, 51 Stan. L. Rev. 1633 (1999)

Okediji, *Givers, Takers, and Other Kinds of Users: A Fair Use Doctrine for Cyberspace*, 53 Fla. L. Rev. 107 (2001)

Okediji, *Toward an International Fair Use Doctrine*, 39 Colum. J. Transnat'l L. 75 (2000)

Other Affirmative Copyright Defenses

Aylward, *Copyright Law: The Fourth Circuit's Extension of the Misuse Doctrine to the Area of Copyright: A Misuse of the Misuse Doctrine?*—Lasercomb America, Inc. v. Reynolds, 17 U. Dayton L. Rev. 661 (1992)

Band & Levine, *You Say Misuse, I Say Fair Use . . .*, 13 Computer L. 10 (1996)

Bilicki, *Standard Antitrust and the Doctrine of Patent Misuse: A Unification Under the Rule of Reason*, 46 U. Pitt. L. Rev. 209 (1984)

Comment, *Copyright Misuse and Anticompetitive Software Licensing Restrictions:* Lasercomb America, Inc. v. Reynolds, 52 U. Pitt. L. Rev. 629 (1991)

Davidson & Engisch, *Copyright Misuse and Fraud on the Copyright Office: An Escape for Infringers?*, 13 Computer Law. 14 (1996)

Fine, *Misuse and Antitrust Defenses to Copyright Infringement Actions,* 17 Hastings L.J. 315 (1965)

Frischmann & Moylan, *The Evolving Common Law Doctrine of Copyright Misuse: A Unified Theory and Its Application to Software,* 15 Berkeley Tech. L.J. 865 (2000)

Geraldi, *Misuse: An Equitable Defense to Intellectual Property Infringement Actions,* 14 Hastings Comm. & Ent. L.J. 235 (1992)

Hanna, *Misusing Antitrust: The Search for Functional Copyright Misuse Standards,* 46 Stan. L. Rev. 401 (1994)

Heald, *Payment Demands for Spurious Copyrights: Four Causes of Action,* 1 J. Intell. Prop. L. 259 (1994)

Leaffer, *Engineering Competitive Policy and Copyright Misuse,* 19 Dayton L. Rev. 1087 (1994)

Lemley, *Antitrust Counterclaims in Patent and Copyright Infringement Cases,* 3 Tex. Intell. Prop. L.J. 1 (1994)

Note, *Clarifying the Copyright Misuse Defense: The Role of Antitrust Standards & First Amendment Values,* 104 Harv. L. Rev. 1289 (1991)

Note, *Redefining Copyright Misuse,* 81 Colum. L. Rev. 1291 (1981)

Paredes, *Copyright Misuse and Tying, Will Courts Stop Misusing Misuse?,* 9 High Tech. L.J. 271 (1994).

Susman, *Typing, Refusals to License, and Copyright Misuse: The Patent Misuse Model,* 36 J. Copyright Soc'y 300 (1989)

Webb & Locke, *Intellectual Property Misuses: Developments in the Misuse Doctrine,* 4 Harv. J.L. & Tech. 257 (1991)

CHAPTER 10
REMEDIES, PREEMPTION, AND RELATED BODIES OF LAW

Reference Works

H. Abrams, THE LAW OF COPYRIGHT §§ 6.01 to 6.06, 16.01 to 16.10, 17.01 to 17.04 (2002)

P. Goldstein, COPYRIGHT: PRINCIPLES, LAW AND PRACTICE §§ 11.0 to 11.4, 12.0 to 12.3, 15.0 to 15.22 (2002)

M. Leaffer, UNDERSTANDING COPYRIGHT LAW §§ 9.9 to 9.16, 11.1 to 11.11 (3d ed. 1999)

M. Nimmer & D. Nimmer, NIMMER ON COPYRIGHT §§ 8C.01 to 8C.05, 14.01 to 14.10, 15.01 to 15.04, 16.01 to 16.08 (2002)

W. Patry, COPYRIGHT LAW AND PRACTICE, Chap. 15 (1994 & 2000 Supp.)

Remedies Under Federal Law

Alexander, *Discretionary Power to Impound and Destroy Infringing Articles: An Historical Perspective,* 29 J. Copyright Soc'y 479 (1982)

Amend, *The Geographical Scope of Injunctions in Intellectual Property Cases,* 77 Trademark Rep. 49 (1987)

Blair & Cotter, *An Economic Analysis of Damages Rules in Intellectual Property Law*, 39 Wm. & Mary L. Rev. 1585 (1998)

Brown, *Civil Remedies for Intellectual Property Invasions,* 55 Law & Contemp. Probs. 45 (1992)

Brown, *The Operation of the Damages Provisions of the Copyright Law: An Exploratory Study, Copyright Law Revision Study No. 23* (1958)

Burgoyne, *The Copyright Remedy Clarification Act of 1990: State Educational Institutions Now Face Significant Monetary Exposure for Copyright Infringement,* 18 J.C. & U.L. 367 (1992)

Ciolino, *Reconsidering Restitution in Copyright*, 48 Emory L.J. 1 (1999)

Coblenz, *Intellectual Property Crimes*, 9 Alb. L.J. Sci. & Tech. 235 (1999)

Greene, *Motion Picture Copyright Infringement and the Presumption of Irreparable Harm: Toward a Reevaluation of the*

Standard for Preliminary Injunctive Relief, 31 Rutgers L. J. 173 (1999)

Jaszi, *505 and All That—The Defendant's Dilemma*, 55 Law & Contemp. Probs. 107 (1993)

Latman, *Preliminary Injunctions in Patent, Trademark and Copyright Cases*, 60 Trademark Rep. 506 (1970)

Lemley & Volokh, *Freedom of Speech and Injunctions in Intellectual Property Cases*, 48 Duke L.J. 147 (1998)

Lindenberg-Woods, *Smoking Revolver: Criminal Copyright Infringement*, 27 Bull. Copyright Soc'y 63 (1979)

Loren, *Digitization, Commodification, Criminalization: The Evolution of Criminal Copyright Infringement and the Importance of the Willfulness Requirement*, 77 Wash. U. L. Q. 835 (1999)

Marcus & D. Nimmer, *Forum on Attorney's Fees in Copyright Cases: Are We Running Through the Jungle Now or Is the Old Man Still Stuck Down the Road?*, 39 Wm. & Mary L. Rev. 65 (1997)

Noonan & Raskin, *Intellectual Property Crimes*, 38 Am. Crim. L. Rev. 971 (2001)

Note, *Denial of the Preliminary Injunction in Copyright Infringement Cases: An Emerging Judicially Crafted Compulsory License*, 10 Colum.-VLA J.L. & the Arts 277 (1986)

Note, *Pretrial Remedies in Infringement Actions: The Copyright Holder's Impound of Flesh?*, 17 Santa Clara L. Rev. 885 (1977)

Note, *Statutory Damages for the Multiple Infringement of a Copyrighted Work: A Doctrine Whose Time Has Come, Again*, 6 Cardozo Arts & Ent. L.J. 463 (1988)

Oakes, *Copyrights and Copyremedies: Unfair Use and Injunctions*, 38 J. Copyright Soc'y 63 (1990)

Ossola, *Registration and Remedies: Recovery of Attorney's Fees and Statutory Damages Under the Copyright Reform Act*, 13 Cardozo Arts & Ent. L.J. 559 (1995)

Owens, *Impoundment Proceedings Under the Copyright Act: The Constitutional Infirmities*, 14 Hofstra L. Rev. 211 (1985)

Saunders, *Criminal Copyright Infringement and the Copyright Felony Act*, 71 Denv. U. L. Rev. 671 (1994)

Thomas, *Willful Copyright Infringement: In Search of a Standard*, 65 Wash. L. Rev. 903 (1990)

Trunko, *Remedies for Copyright Infringement: Respecting the First Amendment*, 89 Colum. L. Rev. 1940 (1989)

Woodin, *Copyrights and State Liability,* 76 Iowa L. Rev. 701 (1991)

Y'Barbo, *On Fee-Shifting and the Protection of Copyright,* 44 J. Copyright Soc'y 23 (1996)

Preemption

Abrams, *Copyright, Misappropriation, and Preemption: Constitutional and Statutory Limits of State Protection,* 1983 Sup. Ct. Rev. 509

Baird, *Common Law Intellectual Property and the Legacy of* International News Service v. Associated Press, 50 U. Chi. L. Rev. 411 (1983)

Bell, *Escape from Copyright: Market Success vs. Statutory Failure in the Protection of Expressive Works,* 69 U. Cin. L. Rev. 741 (2001)

Bonser, *Preemption of "Shrink-Wrap" Legislation by the Copyright Act,* 37 Copyright L. Symp. (ASCAP) 127 (1990)

Brown, *Publication and Preemption in Copyright Law: Elegiac Reflections on* Goldstein v. California, 22 UCLA L. Rev. 1022 (1975)

Brown, *Unification: A Cheerful Requiem for Common Law Copyright,* 24 UCLA L. Rev. 1070 (1977)

J. Cohen, *Copyright and the Jurisprudence of Self-Help*, 13 Berkeley Tech. L.J. 1089 (1998)

Comment, *Federal Copyright and State Trade Secret Protection: The Case for Partial Preemption,* 33 Am. U. L. Rev. 667 (1984)

Dabney, *State Law Protection of Intellectual Creations: Privacy and Preemption,* 38 Syracuse L. Rev. 653 (1987)

Denicola, *Mostly Dead? Copyright Law in the New Millennium*, 40 J. Copyright Soc'y 193 (2000)

Diamond, *Preemption of State Law,* 25 Bull. Copyright Soc'y 204 (1978)

Douma, *The Uniform Computer Information Transactions Act and the Issue of Preemption of Contractual Provisions Prohibiting Reverse Engineering, Disassembly, or Decompilation,* 11 Alb. L.J. Sci. & Tech. 249 (2001)

Dreyfuss, *Do You Want to Know a Trade Secret? How Article 2B Will Make Licensing Trade Secrets Easier (But Innovation More Difficult),* 87 Calif. L. Rev. 191 (1999)

Elkin-Koren, *Copyrights in Cyberspace — Rights Without Laws?*, 73 Chi.-Kent. L. Rev. 1155 (1998)

Fellmeth, *Control Without Interest: State Law Of Assignment, Federal Preemption, and the Intellectual Property License,* 6 Va. J.L. & Tech. 8 (2001)

Fetter, *Copyright Revision and the Preemption of State "Misappropriation" Law: A Study in Judicial and Congressional Interaction,* 27 Copyright L. Symp. (ASCAP) 1 (1982)

Fisher, *Property and Contract on the Internet*, 73 Chi.-Kent. L. Rev. 1203 (1998)

Francione, *The California Art Preservation Act and Federal Preemption by the 1976 Act—Equivalence and Actual Conflict,* 31 Copyright L. Symp. (ASCAP) 105 (1984)

Froomkin, *Article 2B as Legal Software for Electronic Contracting Operating System or Trojan Horse?*, 13 Berkeley Tech. L.J. 1023 (1998)

Ginsburg, *Authors as "Licensors" of "Informational Rights" Under U.C.C. Article 2B*, 13 Berkeley Tech. L.J. 945 (1998)

Ginsburg, *No "Sweat"? Copyright and Other Protection of Works of Information After* Feist v. Rural Telephone, 92 Colum. L. Rev. 338 (1992)

Goldstein, *Federal System Ordering of the Copyright Interest,* 69 Colum. L. Rev. 49 (1969)

Goldstein, *Copyright and Its Substitutes*, 1997 Wis. L. Rev. 865 (1997)

Goldstein, *Preempted State Doctrines, Involuntary Transfers and Compulsory Licenses: Testing the Limits of Copyright,* 24 UCLA L. Rev. 1107 (1977)

Gordon, *Intellectual Property as Price Discrimination: Implications for Contract,* 73 Chi.-Kent. L. Rev. 1367 (1998)

Hardy, *The Ancient Doctrine of Trespass to Web Sites,* 1996 J. Online L., Art. 7

Hardy, *Contracts, Copyright and Preemption in a Digital World,* 1 Rich. J. L. & Tech. 2 (1995)

Heald, *Federal Intellectual Property Law and the Economics of Preemption,* 76 Iowa L. Rev. 959 (1991)

Jaccard, *Securing Copyright in Transnational Cyberspace: The Case for Contracting with Potential Infringers,* 35 Colum. J. Transnat'l L. 619 (1997)

Jorgensen & McIntyre-Cecil, *The Evolution of the Preemption Doctrine and Its Effect on Common Law Remedies,* 19 Idaho L. Rev. 85 (1983)

Karjala, *Federal Preemption of Shrinkwrap and On-Line Licenses,* 22 U. Dayton L. Rev. 511 (1997)

Kemp, *Preemption of State Law by Copyright Law,* 9 Computer L.J. 374 (1989)

Kobayashi & Ribstein, *Uniformity, Choice of Law and Software Sales,* 8 Geo. Mason L. Rev. 261 (1999)

Lee & Livingston, *The Road Less Traveled: State Court Resolution of Patent, Trademark or Copyright Disputes,* 19 St. Mary's L.J. 703 (1988)

Lemley, *Beyond Preemption: The Law and Policy of Intellectual Property Licensing,* 87 Calif. L. Rev. 111 (1999)

Lemley, *Intellectual Property and Shrinkwrap Licenses,* 68 S. Cal. L. Rev. 1239 (1995)

Litman, *Copyright Noncompliance (or Why We Can't "Just Say Yes" to Licensing),* 29 N.Y.U. J. Int'l L. & Pol. 237 (1997)

Litman, *The Tales that Article 2B Tells,* 13 Berkeley Tech. L.J. 931 (1998)

Maher, *The Shrink-Wrap License: Old Problems in a New Wrapper,* 34 J. Copyright Soc'y 292 (1987)

McGowan, *Free Contracting, Fair Competition, and Article 2B: Some Reflections on Federal Competition Policy, Information Transactions, and "Aggressive Neutrality",* 13 Berkeley Tech. L.J. 1173 (1998)

McNamara, *Copyright Preemption: Effecting the Analysis Prescribed by Section 301,* 24 B.C. L. Rev. 963 (1983)

Myers, *The Restatement's Rejection of the Misappropriation Tort: A Victory for the Public Domain,* 47 S.C. L. Rev. 673 (1996)

D. Nimmer, E. Brown & G. Frischling, *The Metamorphosis of Contract into Expand,* 87 Calif. L. Rev. 17 (1999)

R. Nimmer, *Article 2B: An Introduction,* 16 J. Marshall J. Computer & Info. L. 211 (1997)

R. Nimmer, *Breaking Barriers: The Relation Between Contract and Intellectual Property Law,* 13 Berkeley Tech. L.J. 827 (1998)

R. Nimmer, *Electronic Commerce: New Paradigms in Information Law,* 31 Idaho L. Rev. 937 (1995)

R. Nimmer, *Electronic Contracting: Legal Issues*, 14 J. Marshall J. Computer & Info. L. 211 (1996)

R. Nimmer, *Images and Contract Law — What Law Applies to Transactions in Information?*, 36 Hous. L. Rev. 1 (1999)

R. Nimmer, *Intangible Contracts: Thought of Hubs, Spokes, and Reinvigorating Article 2*, 35 Wm. & Mary L. Rev. 1337 (1994)

R. Nimmer, D. Cohn & E. Kirsch, *Licensing Contracts Under Article 2 of the Uniform Commercial Code: A Proposal*, 19 Rutgers Computer & Tech. L.J. 281 (1993)

R. Nimmer, *Licensing on the Global Information Infrastructure: Disharmony in Cyberspace*, 16 Nw. J. Int'l L. & Bus. 224 (1995)

R. Nimmer, *International Information Transactions: An Essay on Law in an Information Society*, 26 Brooklyn J. Int'l L. 5 (2000)

R. Nimmer, *Through the Looking Glass: What Courts and UCITA Say About the Scope of Contract Law in the Information Age*, 38 Duq. L. Rev. 255 (2000)

Note, *Consumer Shrink-Wrap Licenses and Public Domain Materials: Copyright Preemption and Uniform Commercial Code Validity in* ProCD v. Zeidenberg, 30 Creighton L. Rev. 1287 (1997)

Note, *The California Resale Royalties Act as a Test Case for Preemption Under the 1976 Copyright Law,* 81 Colum. L. Rev. 1315 (1981)

Ochoa, ETW Corp. v. Jireh Publishing, Inc.: *Introduction: Tiger Woods and the First Amendment,* 22 Whittier L. Rev. 381 (2000)

Olson, *Common Law Misappropriation in the Digital Era*, 64 Mo. L. Rev. 837 (1999)

O'Rourke, *Copyright Preemption After the* ProCD *Case: A Market-Based Approach,* 12 Berkeley Tech. L.J. 53 (1997)

O'Rourke, *Rethinking Remedies at the Intersection of Intellectual Property and Contract: Toward a Unified Body of Law*, 82 Iowa L. Rev. 1137 (1997)

O'Rourke, *Drawing the Boundary Between Copyright and Contract: Copyright Preemption of Software License Terms,* 45 Duke L.J. 479 (1995)

Phelan, *Digital Dissemination of Cultural Information: Copyright, Publicity, and Licensing Issues in Cyberspace,* 8 Sw. J.L. & Trade Am. 177 (2001-02)

Rabinowitz & Godin, *Copyright Preemption: New York's Erroneous Interpretation,* 39 J. Copyright Soc'y 243 (1992)

Raskind, *Licensing Under Antitrust Laws*, 20 Brooklyn J. Int'l L. 49 (1993)

Reichman & Franklin, *Privately Legislated Intellectual Property Rights: Reconciling Freedom of Contract with Public Good Uses of Information*, 147 U. Pa. L. Rev. 875 (1999)

Rice, *Public Goods, Private Contract and Public Policy: Federal Preemption of Software License Prohibitions Against Reverse Engineering*, 53 U. Pitt. L. Rev. 543 (1992)

Romm, *The Fine Art of Preemption: Section 301 and the Copyright Act of 1976*, 60 Or. L. Rev. 287 (1981)

Shipley, *Refusing to Rock the Boat, The* Sears/Compco *Preemption Doctrine Applied to* Bonito Boats v. Thundercraft, 25 Wake Forest L. Rev. 385 (1990)

Shipley, *Three Strikes and They're Out at the Old Ball Game: Preemption of Performers' Rights of Publicity Under the Copyright Act of 1976*, 20 Ariz. St. L.J. 369 (1988)

Shipley & Hay, *Protecting Research: Copyright, Common-Law Alternatives and Federal Pre-emption*, 63 N.C. L. Rev. 125 (1984)

Symposium, *Intellectual Property and Contract Law for the Information Age: The Impact of Article 2B of the Uniform Commercial Code on the Future of Information and Commerce*, 87 Calif. L. Rev. 1 (1999)

Warlick, *A Wolf in Sheep's Clothing? Information Licensing and De Facto Copyright Legislation in UCC 2B*, 45 J. Copyright Soc'y 158 (1997)

Wiley, Bonito Boats: *Uninformed But Mandatory Innovation Policy,* 1989 Sup. Ct. Rev. 283

Related Bodies of State and Federal Law

R. Callmann, THE LAW OF UNFAIR COMPETITION, TRADEMARKS AND MONOPOLIES (L. Altman 4th ed. 1994 & 2002 Supp.)

F. Cate, PRIVACY IN THE INFORMATION AGE (2001)

F. Cate, PRIVACY IN THE PERSPECTIVE AGE (2001)

J. Gilson & A.G. Lalonde, TRADEMARK PROTECTION AND PRACTICE (2001)

J.T. McCarthy, THE RIGHTS OF PUBLICITY AND PRIVACY (2d ed. 2000)

J.T. McCarthy, McCARTHY ON TRADEMARKS AND UNFAIR COMPETITION (2002)

C.R. McManis, INTELLECTUAL PROPERTY AND UNFAIR COMPETITION IN A NUTSHELL (2000)

Barnett, *First Amendment Limits on the Right of Publicity,* 30 Tort & Ins. L.J. 635 (1995)

Bartholomew, *Protecting the Performers: Setting a New Standard for Character Copyrightability,* 41 Santa Clara L. Rev. 341 (2001)

Barrett, *The "Law of Ideas" Reconsidered,* 71 J. Pat. & Trademark Off. Soc'y 691 (1989)

Beard, *Digital Replicas of Celebrities: Copyright, Trademark, and Right of Publicity Issues,* 23 U. Ark. Little Rock L. Rev. 197 (2000)

Bloom, *Preventing the Misappropriation of Identity: Beyond the Right of Publicity,* 13 Hastings Comm. & Ent. L.J. 489 (1991)

Brown, *Copyright and Its Upstart Cousins: Privacy, Publicity, Unfair Competition,* 33 J. Copyright Soc'y 301 (1986)

Dougherty, *Foreword: The Right of Publicity Towards a Comparative and International Perspective,* 18 Loy. L.A. Ent. L.J. 421 (1998)

Felcher & Rubin, *Privacy, Publicity, and the Portrayal of Real People by the Media,* 88 Yale L.J. 1577 (1979)

Gordon, *Of Harms and Benefits: Torts, Restitution and Intellectual Property,* 21 J. Legal Stud. 449 (1992)

Gordon, *On Owning Information: Intellectual Property and the Restitutionary Impulse,* 78 Va. L. Rev. 149 (1992)

Grady, *A Positive Economic Theory of the Right of Publicity,* 1 UCLA Ent. L. Rev. 97 (1994)

Haemmerli, *Whose Who? The Case for a Kantian Right of Publicity,* 49 Duke L.J. 383 (1999)

Hricik, *Remedies of the Infringer: The Use By the Infringer of Implied and Common Law Federal Rights, State Law Claims, and Contract to Shift Liability for Infringement of Patents, Copyrights, and Trademarks,* 28 Tex. Tech. L. Rev. 1027 (1997)

Kaplan, *Performer's Right and Copyright: The Capitol Records Case,* 69 Harv. L. Rev. 409 (1956)

Karjala, *Copyright and Misappropriation,* 17 U. Dayton L. Rev. 885 (1992)

Karjala, *Misappropriation as a Third Intellectual Property Paradigm,* 94 Colum. L. Rev. 2594 (1994)

Kwall, *Fame*, 73 Ind. L.J. 1 (1997)

Kwall, *The Right of Publicity v. the First Amendment: A Property and Liability Rule Analysis*, 70 Ind. L.J. 47 (1994)

Malkan, *Stolen Photographs: Personality, Publicity, and Privacy*, 75 Tex. L. Rev. 779 (1997)

Marks, *An Assessment of the Copyright Model in the Right of Publicity Cases*, 32 Copyright L. Symp. (ASCAP) 1 (1986)

McCarthy, *The Human Persona as Commercial Property: The Right of Publicity*, 19 Colum.-VLA J.L. & the Arts 129 (1995)

Note, *Human Cannonballs and the First Amendment: Zacchini v. Scripps-Howard Broadcasting Co.*, 30 Stan. L. Rev. 1185 (1978)

Patterson, *Copyright Overextended: A Preliminary Inquiry into the Need for a Federal Statute of Unfair Competition*, 17 U. Dayton L. Rev. 385 (1992)

Raskind, *The Misappropriation Doctrine as a Competitive Norm of Intellectual Property Law*, 75 Minn. L. Rev. 875 (1991)

Sease, *Misappropriation is Seventy-Five Years Old: Should We Bury It or Revive It?*, 70 N.D. L. Rev. 781 (1994)

Shapiro, *The Validity of Registered Trademarks for Titles and Characters after the Expiration of Copyright on the Underlying Work*, 31 Copyright L. Symp. (ASCAP) 69 (1984)

Singer, *The Right of Publicity: Star Vehicle or Shooting Star?*, 10 Cardozo Arts & Ent. L.J. 1 (1991)